Hugh of Poitiers

The Vézelay Chronicle

and other documents from MS. Auxerre 227 and elsewhere,
translated into English with notes,
introduction, and accompanying material

PEGASUS PAPERBOOKS

Hugh of Poitiers

The Vézelay Chronicle

and other documents from MS. Auxerre 227 and elsewhere,
translated into English with notes,
introduction, and accompanying material

by

JOHN SCOTT *and* JOHN O. WARD

with supplementary essays and notes by EUGENE L. COX

mediᴇval & Renaissance texts & studies
Binghamton, New York
1992

Library of Congress Cataloging-in-Publication Data

Hugh, of Poitiers, d. 1167.
    The Vézelay chronicle and other documents from MS. Auxerre 227 and elsewhere / Hugh of Poitiers ; translated into English with notes, introduction, and accompanying material by John Scott and John O. Ward; with supplementary essays and notes by Eugene L. Cox.
        p. cm.
    Includes bibliographical references (p.   ) and index.
    ISBN 0-86698-095-4
    1. Vézelay (Abbey)—History—Early works to 1800. 2. Vézelay Region (France)—Church history—Early works to 1800. I. Scott, John, 1947- . II. Ward, John O., 1940- . III. Cox, Eugene L. IV. Title.
BX2615.V49H84 1992
282'.4441'09021—dc20   92-10724
                                                                           CIP

Printed in the United States of America

Table of Contents

List of Figures

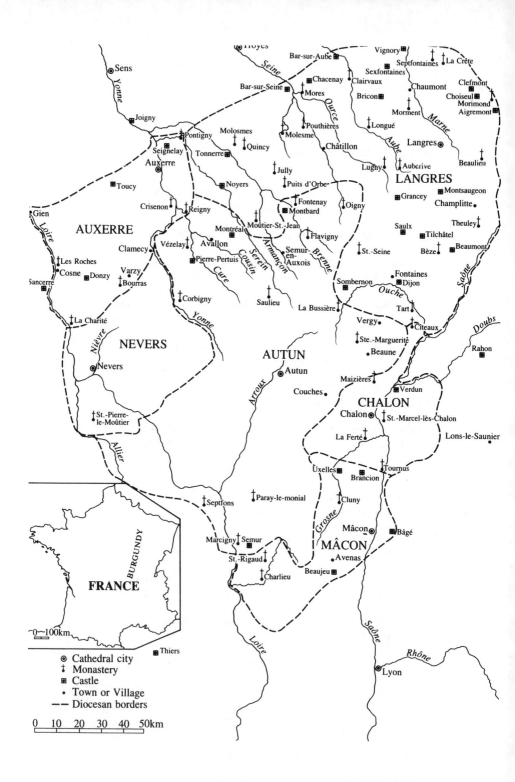

Fig. 1. Medieval Burgundy (from Bouchard [1987: 30],
by permission of the publisher, Cornell University Press).

Preface

The present project has been long in gestation. The original idea to prepare an English translation of the *Vézelay Chronicle* was conceived many years ago by Rodney Thomson, who had happened to purchase secondhand a copy of Rose Graham *An Abbot of Vézelay*, and John Ward, to whom he showed the volume and with whom, at that time, he was teaching in Sydney. Both were struck by the value of the *Chronicle*—as it appeared from Rose Graham's summary—for an understanding of twelfth-century European social, ecclesiastical, and legal history, and likened it in that regard to the "Memoirs" of Guibert of Nogent and the chronicle of Galbert of Bruges, both of which are valuable aids to the teaching of medieval European history.[1] A provisional translation was duly completed from the *PL* text, using the edition of the Guizot translation prepared by François Vogade; Rodney Thomson prepared a version of what was presented in the *PL* text as Book 4 of the *Chronicle*, and John Ward a version of *PL* Books 2-3 (Book 1 in the *PL* text being the "cartulary").

The project then lapsed, with other preoccupations taking precedence, though help and agreement had in the meantime been secured from Professors R. B. C. Huygens and R. K. Berlow, the latter's dissertation on Vézelay having been completed in 1971, and the former's edition of MS. Auxerre being expected in the future. This latter duly appeared and at once revolutionized Vézelay studies. Its excellence required a complete re-working of the Vézelay project. Professors Huygens and Berlow have answered many letters, given an *imprimatur* to the project, and, in the case of the latter, supplied much valuable and freely given advice and information. Rodney Thomson had by that time withdrawn from the project owing to his removal first to Melbourne and then Tasmania, and his many commitments elsewhere. Mr. John Scott, a pupil of both John Ward and Rodney Thomson, and well known for his edition/translation of William of Malmesbury's *De antiquitate Glastonie Ecclesie*[2] very kindly undertook at this stage to assume Rodney Thomson's share of the project. He revised the translation of Book 4 of the *Chronicle*, added notes to it, wrote sections of the introduction, calendared the cartulary (sharing the labor of translating selected documents from it), and devoted a great deal of time and expertise to reading through and correcting the whole, and seeing it through various stages of preparation. The final stage of preparation of the manuscript of the whole volume was undertaken by J. O. Ward.

Late in our combined labors we learned of a translation of the Vézelay *Chronicle* that had been prepared by Professor Eugene L. Cox of Wellesley College in Massachusetts, who had also completed a "History of the Abbey of

---

[1] See Ross (1960), Benton (1970). The Vézelay material was also used in another project begun jointly by J. O. Ward and R. M. Thomson, but in the end carried through only by the former: see Ward (1977c). The original "announcement" of the present Vézelay translation was in *Studium* 8 (Sydney, 1977): 4, and the envisaged cost was stated as two to three dollars!

[2] Published as *The Early History of Glastonbury* (Woodbridge: Boydell Press, 1981).

Vézelay 858–1312 AD." Professor Cox very kindly made both his translation and his history available to us, and we have been able to incorporate many improvements to our translation and annotation as a consequence. He has also very kindly allowed us to incorporate some of his "History" as separate essays under his own name[1] and we have done so as far as possible without burdening the reader with overmuch overlapping material. For his generosity in this regard, and for his interest in our project as a whole, we are much indebted to him.

To Katie Ward we owe thanks for her translation of Appendix E below. Professor Baudouin very kindly answered some queries for us in connection with the Vézelay monastic complex. For permission to reproduce information and illustrations from his many and valuable publications about Vézelay, we are greatly indebted to François Vogade, who was kind enough to correspond with us on the subject. Cornell University Press, and the Mediaeval Academy of America also kindly permitted us to reproduce illustrative material from their publications. Brepols, the publishers of Huygens's edition of the Vézelay material, graciously permitted us to make our translation from their edition. We are much indebted to those to whom the various 'publications' of our ever-expanding text have been entrusted, first Ms. Joan Hitchen of the History Department, Sydney University, who did most of the original computer entering/formatting, and, second, the highly skilled and ever-patient staff at MRTS, whose enthusiasm, and hospitality to one of the editors on the occasion of two visits made to Binghamton, would have aroused the envy even of the counts of Nevers! We would also like to thank the University of Sydney for a small grant to assist publication, and the Universities of Sydney and Chicago together with the National Endowment for the Humanities (USA) for making certain visits to North America possible.

Our project has in mind not only students and scholars who lack the time, skill, or opportunity to make extensive direct use of the work of Professors Berlow and Huygens and of the Auxerre manuscript text itself, but also the modern tourist visiting Vézelay, and perhaps also the general reader interested in the long past of class struggles, lordly power, oppression, liberty, and ecclesiastical autonomy as they are presented to us in vivid moments of crisis.

John Scott, John O. Ward
History Department
University of Sydney
July 1990

---

[1] See Table of Contents above.

Introduction

The Abbey of Vézelay and Its History

The modern abbatial town of Vézelay in Burgundy, 222 kilometers southeast of Paris, is today an attractive, small[1] and out-of-the way venue for tourists, hardly suggestive of its importance in earlier times. During the twelfth century AD, at its apogee, it was a major center of pilgrimage, to which the most important as well as the humblest figures of the day resorted for important festivals. The Second Crusade was launched there, Thomas à Becket fulminated there against Henry II in 1166, Richard the Lionheart and Philip Augustus held a rendezvous there en route to the Third Crusade, and even the heretical Cathars paid the town a visit.[2] According to one scholar, the population of Vézelay at its height would have been between 8,000 and 10,000 souls, "without counting the floating mass of pilgrims, foreign merchants and visitors of all kinds,"[3] a population larger than that of contemporary London. Some relics of its medieval importance have survived to our own day: "the most marvellous Romanesque doorway in France,"[4] depicting on its tympanum "the serene, majestic vision of the Ascension combined with the Mission to the Apostles,"[5] the basilica itself—"its interior is one of the most lovely and uplifting sights in the world"[6]—and, perhaps most importantly, the unique twelfth-century manuscript 227 of the Bibliothèque Municipale of Auxerre, which is here for the first time translated or summarized in English.

The contents of MS. Auxerre 227, though long known, printed a number of times, translated into modern French, and summarized in the remarkably readable and still valuable study of Rose Graham,[7] have not earned for Véze-

---

[1] Modern population 500–600 people. Vézelay is situated on the edge of the mountainous area known as the Morvan: Michelin, *Bourgogne-Morvan* (1988: 157–61) and regional map 65 (Auxerre/Dijon). Bibliographical references throughout the present volume are given, for the most part, by author and date of publication: for full details see General Bibliography below, where items are listed alphabetically by author and—usually—date of publication.

[2] See *Major Chronicle* Book 4 below §27 and 78; Barlow (1986: plates 22, 23 and pp. 146ff.); Berlow (1971: 2ff.); Borst (1953: 103); Guizot (1969: 257–58); Saxer (1975: 205ff.); Wakefield and Evans (1969: 247–49). Graham (1918: 10–19) gives an attractive account of the modern environment of Vézelay and the significant events and persons associated with it in the twelfth century. A fifteenth-century Italian history of the crusades preserves a legend that Pope Urban II convened the council of Clermont in 1095 *first* at Vézelay! (RHC 5: 663).

[3] Chérest (1863: 1:87), Huygens (1976: 45); Graham (1918: 34); Berlow (1971: 248ff. and 1980: 136). On the number of monks at Vézelay in Pons's time see Berlow (1971: 210ff.); perhaps 60 monks and 60 monastic servants in residence.

[4] Graham (1918: 36).

[5] Beckwith (1974: 214–18, 252); see below Aspects [C].

[6] Berlow (1981: 327ff.); Calmette and David; Delautre (1981: 24–26). See also Aspects [C] and Graham (1918: 34–46) on both the basilica and its sculpture.

[7] Graham (1918). The text was first printed—with the omission of many sections that were considered offensive to contemporary taste—in 1659 (see General Bibliography

lay any very secure place in the monographs and textbooks of modern scholars of the Middle Ages. Ignored in major monographs on revolutionary medieval peasant movements,[1] on medieval pilgrimage, or on episcopal politics in the middle ages;[2] scarcely mentioned in all the works of Georges Duby; occasionally cited in Marc Bloch's great *Feudal Society*,[3] Vézelay is only now securing a page or two in monographs on medieval Burgundy[4] and Auxerre[5] and has recently been dignified with a three-page entry in a general book on medieval popular religion.[6] Nevertheless, in view of the clarity and detail of *The Vézelay Chronicle*, the failure of modern writers of general texts on medieval social, political, and economic history to make fuller reference to it is surprising. This neglect is all the more puzzling in view of the exact and prolific scholarship devoted since the time of Augustin Thierry and François Guizot to the events recounted in MS. Auxerre 227.[7] It is unlikely, in fact, that research in the future will discover anything new about Vézelay. The problem is more one of popularization, particularly in English-speaking schools and universities. It is hoped that the present volume will help to bring to wider attention the startling and dramatic experiences of the monks of Vézelay as recorded in the

---

below, "D'Achery"), partially reprinted in Bouquet's *Recueil des Historiens des Gaules et de la France* 12:317–45 (Paris, 1781 [the volume also prints some of the short annals]—vols. 9 [1757], 15 [1808], and 16 [1813] reprint some of the charters and letters), in the *Monumenta Germaniae Historica, Scriptores* ([1882] 1964: 26:144–50 [fragment only]), and also in J. P. Migne's *Patrologia Latina* 189:1559 *et seq.* It has been completely re-edited by R. B. C. Huygens (see Huygens [1976] in General Bibliography below). The French translation by François Guizot (see Guizot [1969] in General Bibliography below) was first published in 1825. On all these see General Bibliography below, Berlow (1971: 24) and Huygens (1976: xxxvf.).

[1] For example Hilton (1973). Vézelay rates only two tiny mentions in Petit-Dutaillis's work on the French communes (1947, 1970) and the most important of these is a footnote: 104 and 305 n. 215. It is ignored in Reynolds (1984), as also in Geary's article (1986) on mechanisms for conflict resolution c. 1050–1200 AD.

[2] See Sumption (1975, though note the reference in Cohen 1980: 329), Kaiser (1981—note the single and totally incidental reference to Vézelay at 351n.1277) and Aspects [C] below 43n.2, etc.

[3] Bloch (1961: 95, 264–65).

[4] Bouchard (1987).

[5] Bouchard (1979).

[6] Brooke (1984: 91–94, 163). The value of the *Major Chronicle* of Hugh of Poitiers has long been known to historians of medieval Germany, if only for a minor episode in Book 4 (see Heinemeyer [1964]). For a reference to terracing along the river Cure by the abbots of Vézelay, see *Cambridge Economic History of Europe* (ed. M. M. Postan [Cambridge, 1966]), 126. Perhaps the most unexpected claim to fame that Vézelay can put forward is the fact that the figure of St. Eugenia on one of the abbey church capitals presents "an extremely rare image in Christian art of a woman's vagina" (Marina Warner, *Monuments and Maidens: The Allegory of the Female Form* [London, 1985], 303, plate 86). When the final draft of the present volume had been prepared there came to hand the annotated typescript translation of the *Major Chronicle* and "History of the Abbey of Vézelay 858–1312 AD" by Professor Eugene Cox: English language attention to Vézelay is certainly making up for lost ground! See Preface above.

[7] See Thierry, Berlow (1971), Chérest, Huygens (1976), Guizot (1969), Bourquelot, Bastard, etc. in General Bibliography below. Charles V. Langlois in his *Textes relatifs à l'histoire du Parlement depuis les origines jusqu'en 1314* (Paris, 1888), 25–29 (#XV) prints the portion of the *Major Chronicle* about Andrew of Marais (see below at 5n.2).

extraordinarily vivid and meticulous narrative of their historian, the notary Hugh of Poitiers, a devoted servant of the Magdalene and the mystical notion of untainted liberty associated with her cult at Vézelay.

The *potestas* of Vézelay appears to have been the scene of at least four serious social crises during the twelfth century. The first culminated in the murder of the abbot of the day (Abbot Artald or Artaud, d. 1106)[1] and the second produced the "accord" which is translated as Appendix B below (AD 1137).[2] The third (AD 1150–1155) was characterized by the formation of a commune amidst outbursts of violence, stirring episodes of comital demagoguery and rapine, and the intervention of both the king and the pope.[3] The fourth (1166) was preceded by a long period of scheming and violent manoeuvering on the part of the count of Nevers and his henchmen, both inside the town and beyond its walls. It reached a climax with the "exile" of the monks from their church, described in moving and emotional terms by the chronicler himself.[4] The intervention of the king was ultimately successful, as far as the monastery was concerned, in 1155; but between 1155 and 1167 the royal authority was often abused.

Between and surrounding these four crises, a spirit of unrest seems to have prevailed at Vézelay. This unrest was due principally to the peculiarly autonomous position of the original monastic foundation at Vézelay. When Count Gerard of Roussillon—a leading Carolingian nobleman celebrated in later *chansons de geste* as Girard(-t) de Roussillon (Vienne)—and his wife Bertha founded a monastery at Pothières on the Seine and a nunnery at St. Père-sous-Vézelay—the possible site of a Gallo-Roman villa of the later imperial period—around 860 AD, they ruled that no authority other than the church of Rome should have any power at all in those foundations or their appurtenances. This "immunity" was subsequently confirmed by both popes and French monarchs, although, in origin, it should be considered as much "a form of insurance, excluding other, more threatening claimants who might limit his (Gerard's) control over this property" as an act of piety.[5]

---

[1] Cf. *Major Chronicle* 2:162n.7, 181n.5, 4 §22; Graham (1918: 54); Berlow (1971: 122f.); Bastard (1851: 343ff.).

[2] Berlow (1971: 184ff.); Graham (1918: 55ff.).

[3] See below Aspects [B], the *History* or *Major Chronicle*, Books 2 and 3; Graham (1918: chaps. 3 and 5); Bastard (1851: 352ff.); and Bourquelot.

[4] *History* or *Major Chronicle*, below Book 4 §55. Hugh of Poitiers was not the only twelfth-century historian to notice these events: another Vézelay monk who later moved to St. Germain-des-Prés inserts his own account in a biography of Louis VII, written c. 1171–1173 AD: see Molinier (1887: xxv–vi, 174–76), Chérest 1:212–15, Huygens (1976: 112ff.), and below Aspects [B].

[5] See below Cartulary charters 1–3 and Appendix G, Berlow (1971: 58 and 52ff. generally and 1976), Cowdrey (1970: 13–14), Goffart (1966, index, s.v. "Vézelay"), Graham (1918: 19ff.) and also Aspects [A] below. According to Skinner (1984: 90) "Vézelay, the most famous [of women's monasteries in the period], was built in 867 for benedictine nuns in honor of St. Mary Magdalene by the Count and Countess of Vienne." The original size of the Vézelay endowment might have been some 75 square kilometers (Berlow 1971: 70). On the transition to a regular (male) monastery see Berlow (1971: 78ff.). Louis VI's confirmation of the Vézelay immunity (1112 AD) is printed in Quantin 1, no. 121, 226–28. For a similar foundation see St. Odo of Cluny's *Life of Gerald of Aurillac* (trans. G. Sitwell

The nunnery was subsequently destroyed by Norman raids and refounded in the 870s or 880s as a monastery on top of the hill where it now stands. During the eleventh century the abbey became the center of the worship of St. Mary Magdalene and attracted many pilgrims. Its revenues and rights were coveted by neighboring secular lords (chief among whom was the count of Nevers, a vassal of the duke of Burgundy) and neighboring bishops (especially the bishop of Autun) or abbots (in particular the abbot of Cluny).

The monastery possessed lands and churches in the dioceses of Autun, Auxerre, Nevers, Mâcon, Clermont, Bourges, Poitiers, Saintes, Sens, Noyon, and Beauvais. "By the mid-twelfth century the abbey of Vézelay was at the head of an organization with daughter houses scattered in northern France, even in Italy"; "The country for some miles around Vézelay was the abbot's sovereign state, and the bounds of the '*poté*' (=*potestas* or 'power,' 'territory over which power was exercised') *de Vézelay* were market by great crosses" on the main roads.[1] These widespread possessions and the seigneurial control exercised by the abbot and monks over the banlieu or country-dwellers (*rustici*), and the *cives* or burghers—the town-dwellers at Vézelay—were a continual source of friction which neighboring powers (principally the count of Nevers) sought to exploit. The issue of serfdom and freedom was a controversial one in the twelfth century and provoked disturbances, riots, and structural changes on a wide front.[2] The pressures which bore upon serfs, town dwellers, and tenants on manorial estates are seldom so clearly visible as at Vézelay, where—as has been noted already—a revolutionary commune under the patronage of the count of Nevers was formed against the seigneurial control of the abbot,[3] and where the focal role played by servile administrators anxious to advance their own power and prominence by playing one lord off against another is strikingly clear.[4] The *Chronicle of Vézelay*, in fact, takes us into the heart of that process dear to Marxist historians whereby the power and dominance of the feudal mode of production were gradually repealed in favor of the capitalist spirit and the autonomous bourgeoisie and proletariat in a free market situation.[5]

[N.Y., 1985], 136). On Girart de Roussillon and the twelfth-century revolt cycle of *chansons de geste* see Louis (1946), Calin (1962: 1, 127ff.), and below *Major Chronicle* 4:294n.2. Some examples of the "revolt" cycle of *chanson* will be found translated in Glanville Price, ed., *William Count of Orange: Four Old French Epics* (London, 1975). For incursions by Count William II of Nevers into the abbey of Vézelay see below charter 57, curiously out of place in the *Cartulary*, but full of valuable proof texts for the abbey.

[1] Berlow (1971: 119, 222), Graham (1918: 50–51). Property acquisitions in the time of Abbot Pons: Berlow (1971: 213ff., and cf. 222–23). Berlow (1971: appendix A, 383ff.) lists the properties of the monastery. See also Chérest (1863: 1:27ff.) (Huygens [1976: 13ff.]).

[2] See Graham (1918: 54–55). On the "communal revolution" of the twelfth century whereby serfs, burgesses, and *cives* sought to evade, regularize, or restrict the arbitrary power of the *potentes, optimates, milites* over their persons, property, and movements, see below Aspects [B].

[3] See below *Major Chronicle* 2 §19 and Aspects [B]. The fullest account of the townsmen and their revolution is Berlow (1971: chap. 4, 248ff., especially 317–41; see also 375–82).

[4] See below *Major Chronicle* 2 §9, 4 §54 and Aspects [B]; Chérest 1:78ff. (Huygens [1976: 41ff.]).

[5] Mackrell (1973: 9); Dobb ([1946] 1963: chaps. 2–3); Marx, *Pre-Capitalist Economic*

Equally clear from the events set out in this volume is the conservative social attitude of the abbey and its leaders. Like the ecclesiastical leaders at Laon some decade or so into the twelfth century,[1] the monastic hierarchy at Vézelay had nothing but contempt (mixed with fear) for the idea of a communal association designed to further the interests of the *cives*; and their attitude toward serfdom was uncompromising. At one point, Abbot William (Pons's successor) was accused of holding one of the count's men in captivity (1166 AD). He replied: "Andrew of Marais does not in any way belong to you [the count]: he is mine from the sole of his foot to the crown of his head, for he is legally a serf of the monastery of Vézelay."[2]

The seigneurial grievances between the abbot and the townsmen of Vézelay were not, as has been indicated already, the only contentious issues in the town: the bishop of Autun claimed that he should exercise spiritual jurisdiction over the monastery, and the ensuing struggle occupied much of the reign of Abbot Pons of Vézelay (1138–1161 AD), brother of the famous Abbot Peter of Cluny (Peter the Venerable, abbot of Cluny 1122–1156).[3] The spiritual jurisdiction of a bishop involved such matters as the consecration of churches and chapels, the ordination of priests and monks, and the administration of abbey revenues and operations during a vacancy. We are fortunate in having a recent study that enables us to appreciate more fully than is possible from the *Vézelay Chronicle* the position of the bishops of the region.[4]

The major opponents of the abbey at Vézelay and the chief aristocratic rivals of the bishops were the counts of Nevers, a powerful local family whose origins in the late ninth and early tenth centuries can be barely glimpsed today from the sources available.[5] Ranking somewhat below the dukes of Burgundy, who play a surprisingly small part in the events surrounding the monastery of Vézelay,[6] the counts of Nevers appear from the *Vézelay Chronicle* to have been a typically roistering, rowdy, and flamboyant line of local leaders. Count William II (d. 1149 AD)[7] and his son William III (d. 1161) are

---

Formations; Bober (1965); Leach (1985: 46–47, 124ff.); etc.

[1] Guibert of Nogent *De vita sua (Memoirs)* Book 3 chapters 7 and 10, trans. Benton (1970: 167 and 183), ed. Labande (320 and 360). Cited also Graham (1918: 59). See also: Reynolds (1984: 177); Bastard (1848: 532ff.); Bourquelot; Appendix F below.

[2] Bloch (1961: 264–65); Berlow (1971: chap. 4; 1980: 140) and *Major Chronicle* 4 §70 below.

[3] Graham (1918: 62 and chap. 4). *Major Chronicle* or *History* below, Book 1.

[4] Bouchard (1979); see also Bouchard (1977), Arnold (1991: chap. 4). The interrelationship between episcopal and comital power in dioceses adjacent to Vézelay is discussed—without reference to Vézelay—in Kaiser (1981: 365–73 [Auxerre], 383–84 [Autun]).

[5] Graham (1918: 52–53 and chap. 3). Bouchard (1987: 340ff., 33–34) and below, the *Brief History*. See too Mirot (1945: 7–15).

[6] Bouchard (1987: 429, 275ff.). According to Petit-Dutaillis ([1947], 1970: 86) the dukes of Burgundy in the twelfth century were poor and powerless.

[7] Brooke (1984) discusses other sources for the life and character of this William II, who "was a man of great prestige and ability, held in the highest respect by King Louis VII of France, who tried to make him regent, with Abbot Suger, when he set off on the second crusade" (93). Elizabeth Siberry writes to us in a letter, "I agree that the counts were not shining examples of medieval nobility or chivalry." See also her article (1990), Graham (1918: chap. 2) and Berlow (1971: 32).

the anti-heroes of Books 2–3 of the *Vézelay Chronicle*. This latter William married Ida, sister of the countess of Champagne, and she, having been her husband's regent during his time as a crusader, appears in Book 4 of the *Vézelay Chronicle* as the capable and energetic mother/associate of her young and fiery son William IV (d. 1168), one of five children she bore to William III. There is more than a hint of these counts' extravagance and debt in the *Vézelay Chronicle*, and their desire to dominate the abbatial *seigneurie* and immunity—by way of advocacy and the right to hospitality—and thus to regularly milk its considerable agricultural, commercial, and pilgrimage revenues was the one consistent feature of their history. In this regard the counts of Nevers are typical of the nobility in twelfth-century Europe, for whom declining domainial revenues and increasing expenses associated with the new politics introduced by the more ambitious territorial lords of the day (some of whom, such as the lords of Anjou, later rulers of England and half of France, became rulers of high rank and extensive holdings) had to be compensated for by new ventures in commerce and the market, investments in urban property, crusading, aggression against local ecclesiastical land-owners, and similar activities.[1]

The counts of Nevers, citing practice elsewhere, based their right to exploit the abbey's revenues upon an act of one of Pons's abbatial ancestors, whereby the count was recognized as the secular *avoué* or advocate (= "protector") of the monastery in charge of its "justice," defense, roads, markets, and toll-points, and entitled, with his men, to hospitality from the abbot in the town, along with other perquisites. Deriving, it seems, from the ninth-century Carolingian views of the duties of monarchs and their delegates, the office of advocate was probably seen originally as a kind of compromise: "on the one hand, monks insisted that a reformed (monastic) house be free of outside meddling, and, on the other, the monks needed some kind of agent who was powerful enough to be respected outside the cloister walls. Hence the nobles who helped reform houses, in the eleventh century especially, and who promised to allow the monks to carry out their liturgical round without interference, frequently became the advocates of their foundations. Adopting the title *advocatus, custos,* or *adjutator*, secular nobles would take responsibility for collecting a house's revenues in distant areas, represent the house in legal cases, and take steps to protect the house from other laymen who had made attacks on its property."[2] "Most monasteries had advocates in the tenth and eleventh centuries"; "the churches of the eleventh century were so dependent on their

---

[1] See below, 8nn.3–6 and Aspects [B]. The demand for "procuration" was, in many respects, one of the most respectable that a lord could make in regard to a dependency: see Appendix F §22 below.

[2] Carl Stephenson ([1954] 1967: 44–45); Bouchard (1987: 125 and cf. generally chap. 5). Also below Aspects [A], *Major Chronicle* 2, 158n.3, 173n.6, and Chérest 1:53ff. (Huygens [1976: 27ff.]). In *Major Chronicle* 4 §68 below Count William IV of Nevers claims that an ancestor of King Louis VII gave Vézelay as a fief to an ancestor of his own. There is no record of such a grant: Louis VII himself is ignorant of it and the abbot of Vézelay counters it. That this claim emerges so late in the piece suggests that the count of Nevers was prepared to try any expedient and took his cue from the king's own references to his *feodum* (4 §56 and see §57:294n.2; also Arnold [1991: index s.v. "advocacy"]).

advocates that, if the advocate turned on them, they were almost helpless."[1] One of the major themes of the *Vézelay Chronicle* is the resistance mounted by the Vézelay abbots Pons[2] and William of Mello (abbot 1161–1171)—both from families of the regional nobility—against the claims of the counts of Nevers to the advocacy of their abbey. This resistance, which produced the absolutely extraordinary tale of litigation, rapine, and power-play recorded in the pages of this volume, must be ascribed not only to the Vézelay abbots' understandable zeal to evade the constant forced taxation of their abbey by the counts under the pretext of *procuratio*, but also to the heightened sense of clerical autonomy encouraged in the twelfth century by the pivotal Investiture Controversy of the late eleventh century.[3] The sense of clerical or ecclesiastical liberty which sustained the resistance of the Vézelay monks stressed the dependence of the church not on members of the secular hierarchy but on God alone, via the apostles St. Peter and St. Paul and their earthly custodians, the Roman pontiffs. If we ask why this sentiment of liberty should have been so pronounced at Vézelay the reply must be that the spiritual and economic wealth of the abbey in the twelfth century (due in large part to the flourishing of the Magdalene cult)[4] encouraged a rich literary, artistic, and liturgical life, one product of which was an interest in the abbey's past and its muniments. The cultural revival also produced persons endowed with literary training and skills sufficient to facilitate research into the abbey's literary and archival treasures. The result—and to some extent also the cause—of these circumstances, was the realization that, preserved in the muniments was, so to speak, a cast iron archival guarantee of the abbey's right to untrammelled enjoyment of the autonomy envisioned by the Gregorian reformers of earlier decades: Vézelay was a particular jewel in the new ecclesiological[5] armature of the contemporary papacy, demonstrating the proper, pristine, untrammelled, unspotted, and uncompromised liberty of the spiritual, the ecclesiastical, the clerical, and the religious, in, and above, a secular world which was itself very

---

[1] Bouchard (1987: 126–27); see also Howe (1988: 335), Haverkamp (1988: 154, 277).

[2] Bouchard (1987: 411, 431). Berlow (1971: 154 [and see page 160]) says "it is likely that Renald [see below *Major Chronicle* 2: 162n.1] acknowledged his [the count of Nevers's] role as advocate and guardian of the territory of Vézelay as well as the right to receive the hospitality of the monastery." On contested rights in Vézelay see Berlow (1971: 158ff.).

[3] Bouchard (1987: 128); Tellenbach (1966); Morrison (1969: part 2). The coincidence between communal revolution and investiture controversy, or ecclesiastical reform movement in general, is interesting and relevant to the Vézelay experience recorded in Book 1 below. To some extent the secular authority of a Bishop Gaudry in Laon would have been compromised because he was a flagrantly old style churchman, and at Milan, the effect of the reform movement was to create some sort of a power vacuum in the Milanese state by discrediting the bishop. Into this power vacuum stepped the pseudo-communal authority of Erlembald (J. P. Whitney's assertion [*Hildebrandine Essays* (Cambridge, 1932), 151] that Erlembald was "the first founder of an Italian commune" is only technically incorrect; on the Milanese background see the review of G. Dilcher, *Die Enstehung der lombardischen Stadtcommune* by Keller (1970: 34–64). At Vézelay the abbots wanted it both ways: old style secular power *and* clerical autonomy. For old style episcopal power see Southern (1953: 118ff.).

[4] Below Aspects [D] and Appendix D.

[5] Cf. Ullmann (1969: 43–44) for the term "ecclesiological."

much on the move. So, at any rate, thought the abbey intelligentsia and leading hierarchs, but the subtlety of it all was somewhat lost on the local episcopacy and comital families, as events were to demonstrate. At times even the pope, particularly the harassed schismatic pope Alexander III,[1] must have wished that the abbey of Vézelay with its pristine liberty and endless documentary justifications would just go away.

Three further circumstances must be noted to help explain the Vézelay phenomenon. One was the very novelty and precocity of papal power in the middle of the twelfth century. Although it was in the end the nascent French monarchy which took the rebellious count and his mother in hand, the chief support of the abbey throughout the tribulations recorded in the *Vézelay Chronicle* was the papacy, a circumstance inconceivable a century earlier. Indeed, one of the major features of the Vézelay material is the deep circumstantial insight it provides into the nature of royal and papal power at a time when the age of monarchical and papal bureaucratic might was just beginning to take shape, and the age of abbots and other charismatic holy men was passing away.[2]

A second necessary circumstance in the production of the Vézelay phenomenon—already touched upon—was the particular zeal with which the twelfth-century counts of Nevers sought to turn "protection" of the Vézelay abbey into "exploitation" of it. This zeal—which may have sprung from need or extravagance associated with the general economic crisis of the nobility in the period,[3] or else from the arrogant, swashbuckling sense of adventure which produced many an episode of knightly prowess in the period, from the foundation of the power of the house of Anjou[4] to the crusades[5]—coincided with the particular needs and situation of the burghers at the time.[6]

The count's tactics, in fact, concentrated especially on the encouragement of divisions between the abbot and the townsmen. In the 1152–1155 crisis he had as allies certain malcontents within the city who were aiming at control of urban justice, and in the years after the death of Pons, he had as an ally,

> a certain vile man, Hugh, surnamed Letard, a tenant-in-chief of the monastery, whose mother was cousin-german to Simon Fitzodo, provost of Vézelay, also the Church's serf, and the very man who betrayed and smote his lord, abbot Artald [Artauld] of Vézelay [1106]. The count made this Hugh his provost at his castle of Censoire, and he persecuted the Church more than all the rest of the count's followers.[7]

---

[1] AD 1159–1181; see Kelly (1986: 176–77).

[2] Hallam (1983: chap. 4); Barraclough (1968: chap. 3); Ullmann (1972: chaps. 8–9). The death of Bernard of Clairvaux in 1153 AD marks, perhaps, the end of the "age of the abbots and holy men."

[3] Duby (1974: pt.3). Cf. *Major Chronicle* 4 §35 below (Huygens [1976: 546.1322]): *ipse autem comes, ere graviter alieno pressus*. Also Calin (1962: 128).

[4] Southern (1953: chap. 2[i]).

[5] Mayer (1972: chaps. 1–3).

[6] See Aspects [B] below.

[7] See below *Major Chronicle* 4 §22, and, for Artaud, above 3n.1.

During the later intrigues the count was also able to rely on a party of monks within the monastery itself who wished to see the powers of the abbot reduced. In 1165 he invaded the monastery in force, but, with the intervention of the king, the monks were able to regain the place. The pacifist monarch, however, was not able effectively to rein in the anti-monastic energies of the youthful count until, in 1167, the latter took up the cross for a pilgrimage to Jerusalem.

Whatever we make of these circumstances, it would seem clear that without this particular conjunction of needs, energies, and motives on the part of count, burghers, and, eventually, a faction within the monastery of Vézelay itself, the old equilibrium between advocate and abbey might not have been so readily upset.

The third circumstance that has to be reckoned with in accounting for the Vézelay phenomenon recorded in the pages that follow is the personality of the chronicler to whom we owe the *Major History* or *Chronicle* of twelfth-century Vézelay. Hugh, a Poitevin by birth, is mentioned briefly in the manuscript of his *History*,[1] as a *notarius* and close associate of Abbot William of Mello and, apparently, as the literary pride of the abbey. At any rate, the poem added to the *History* between Books 1 and 2 praises his excellence as a chronicler, his wisdom, and his sense of correct order.[2] Hugh, described by Huygens as Abbot William's "secretary," received an adequate, if somewhat conventional literary training which left him more than capable of performing his notarial tasks, able to weave frequent biblical allusions and phrases into his *History*, and even up to making allusions to tags and snippets of classical wisdom here and there. His training and talent also included a remarkable ability to recreate vividly historical situations which he cannot in all cases have witnessed himself, and an ability to dramatize events with appropriate speeches which places him among the major rhetorical historians of the time rather than the mere chroniclers.[3]

He sits uneasily in this company, however. His *History* is marked by a narrowness of focus and a meticulous and dominating sense of detail lacking in the histories of many of his contemporaries, which reflect his notarial training and predilections, the isolated nature of Vézelay cultural life, and the litigant's passion for the letter of the law and the archival phrase. His mentality was stiffened by the same sense of tradition and privilege that animated his masters. Like Guibert of Nogent, Hugh speaks ill of the communal revolutionaries:[4] He calls the year 1166 "the 286th after the reception of the sacred body of the blessed handmaid of God, Mary Magdalene, the 11th after the destruction of the odious commune of the burghers." He speaks fervently and passionately of the liberties of the monastery of Vézelay, and of the illustrious inheritance of its abbots. It cannot be doubted, in fact, that he received his early training and apprenticeship in the abbey school under Abbot Pons, the

---

[1] Huygens (1976: xxivff.); Graham (1918: 65–66); Berlow (1971: 30ff.); Potthast, s.v. "Hugh of Poitiers" (627). See *Major Chronicle* 4 §§44, 55.

[2] Below, beginning of *Major Chronicle* Book 2.

[3] Below *Major Chronicle* 2 §§12 and 17. See Ward (1985).

[4] Guibert of Nogent, ed. Labande, 320; quoted in Benton (1970: 167) (Guibert of Nogent *De vita sua [Memoirs]* 3.7, trans. Benton [1970: 167 and 183], ed. Labande).

hero whom he idolized and whose character deficiencies he seems either oblivious to or anxious to cover up.[1]

The elements and forces just surveyed made of the Vézelay phenomenon a kaleidoscope of conflicting pressures both old and new. Vézelay, in fact, raised the lineaments of the new world in the cadre of the old. For, in one sense, traditional monasticism was a fading spiritual ideal in the twelfth century; or so, at any rate, it seemed to some of the most acute and best educated men of the day.[2] So too, it seemed to those who were driven to ever new refinements of the monastic ideal, in keeping with an ever more intense actualization of the ascetic impulse;[3] and so too it seems to most modern students of the subject.[4] At the same time there was much that was novel about the position Vézelay adopted. It represented a plea for the primacy of text and document over custom and precedent, and, as such, it attracted the interest of powers that were basing new pretensions on new modes (text, document, literacy, bureaucracy)[5]: specifically, the papacy and the "new" monarchy of Louis VII. Though the abbot of Vézelay's case depended in the short term upon customary (oral) witness to precedent, Hugh of Poitiers designed at least Books 1 and 2 of his *Major Chronicle* as an affirmation of the primacy of law, text, document: a recital of the privileges inherent in the foundation charter of Vézelay and its confirmations is in both cases followed by the intrusion, in Hugh's day, of the wart of spotty servitude, or the viperous vomit of a tyrant, in the form of an episcopal or comital affront to the pristine plant of *libertas*.[6]

In fact, contrary to the impression conveyed by Hugh of Poitiers, time and new custom must have long buried at Vézelay any particularly acute memory

---

[1] For the abbey school, cf. below *Major Chronicle* Book 1 at 139n.6, where an earlier (?) Hugh "of the School of Vézelay" gives evidence.

[2] Knowles ([1949] 1962: chap. 39). There is an interesting "controversy" between a monk and a cleric translated in Miller, Prosser, and Benson (1973: 188–96). It is by Rupert of Deutz (c. 1075–1135, abbot of the Benedictine monastery of St. Heribert in Deutz, Germany) and is entitled "A dispute between a monk and a cleric about whether a monk should be allowed to preach." On the little tract, see Van Engen (1983: 306–12).

[3] Leyser (1984).

[4] Baker (1979); Bethel (1969); Brooke (1984: 109–29) and (1985); Cantor (1960–61); Constable (1975) and (1976); Cowdrey (1973: 285–311); Duby (1982a: especially part 1); Flint (1975) and (1976); Ecclesiastical History Society (London) "Monks, Hermits and the Ascetic Tradition," *Studies in Church History* 22 (1985): 65ff., 109ff.; Fuhrmann (1986: 111); Knowles (1963: especially chaps. 3–4); Lackner (1972); Leclercq (1971: chap. 11 [cf. also chap. 2]); Leyser (1984); Little (1978: part 2, chaps. 4 and 6); Lynch (1975) and (1976); Rosenwein (1971) and (1982); Rosenwein and Little (1974); Southern (1953: chap. 3, sec. iii, "The Monasteries"); Van Engen (1986). For general works on medieval monasticism see: Brooke (1984: chaps. 1–4) and (1970); Knowles ([1949], 1962) and (1969); Southern (1970: chap. 6.1–2); Zarnecki (1972). Vézelay was by no means unique in its scenes of violence: Demm (1972: 49); Dimier (1972: 38–57); the reader may also recall Abelard's monastery at St. Gildas de Rhuys or the Irish Cistercian monasteries visited by Stephen of Lexington in the thirteenth century. On monasticism and the French medieval social structure in general see École Pratique des Hautes Études, Centre de Recherche, *Sous la Règle de St. Benoit.*

[5] See Stock (1983) and Clanchy (1979).

[6] Compare charters 1–3 below with *Major Chronicle* 1 §2 and 2 §§2–4.

of the conditions embodied in the ninth-century documents assembled by Hugh and his confrères in their cartulary. Hence, inspired by new winds of change, by rivalry with Cluny, by the new image of papal authority gaining ground in the twelfth-century world, or by sheer perversity, Pons arrived at the difficult decision to challenge, to confront, to wear down, the comfort of established custom, with the brittle dagger of document, the *testudo* of text, the shallow shield of law, literacy, and learned immunity.

For their part, the citizens of Vézelay also felt the winds of change. Whether Susan Reynolds is right or not in her fine distinction between the winning of "new liberties ... because of the new movements of association or new ideas about politics," and "new economic and political conditions in which values and habits of association which were already established in both rural and urban life were translated into a new range of institutions,"[1] the townsmen of Vézelay between 1137 and 1155 responded to new ideas and customs of communal association that had been established or attempted elsewhere over the preceding half century. In 1137 their seigneurial grievances had been aired before an aristocratic tribunal of their lords' choosing. Whether the terms of the 1137 *Accord* had been adhered to in the interval or not, they, after some prompting (and, Hugh of Poitiers would have us believe, no little rhetoric) responded to the new modes (as, apparently, put to them by the count and his minion, their own Hugh of St. Peter), and entered into a new form of corporate organization with the aim of commuting, reducing, or abolishing the trappings of their quasi-servile condition.[2] There was much that was new here, even though the count stood for the somewhat dubious past of customary precedent and intimidation, and even though the abbot's counterarguments seemed to draw much from the fresh conceptual winds of the age ushered in by the investiture controversy of the late eleventh century.

It is difficult, in fact, to draw up a balance sheet of conservative and innovative elements in the Vézelay events. A king who should have supported his secular delegate, the count, or at least the bishops whose sees, in Pacaut's phrase, were "effectivement royaux," throws his weight behind the autonomous pretensions of an abbey which seeks to blend the contradictory elements of spiritual liberty and seigneurial tyranny; a count who should have stood for precedent and intimidation woos the townsmen with the latest refined doctrines and practices of corporation theory; a pope, who should have supported the bishops as his proper delegates in the complex task of building up a comprehensive world-wide papal bureaucracy, puts his weight behind an abbot who claims no overlord other than St. Peter and St. Paul—an abbot whose pretensions and values seem to bespeak an age that is passing away.[3]

The later history of the abbey and town at Vézelay may not concern the reader of the present volume, but a résumé should serve to emphasize how

---

[1] Reynolds (1984: 155).

[2] See below Aspects [B].

[3] Fuhrmann (1986: 132–33) and 8n.2 above. See charter 68 below for the pope's appeal to the French monarch to resolve the Vézelay deadlock. For the bishoprics "effectivement royaux" (*all* the bishoprics with any claim to rights in Vézelay, except that of Nevers) see Pacaut (1957: map opposite 72 and 63ff.).

significant the twelfth-century developments really are.[1] As with Athens after the fifth century BC, or Florence in the fifteenth century AD, Vézelay after the events recorded in the *Major Chronicle* translated in the present volume fades from the historian's attention. This is, perhaps, an unfair circumstance, for the town and its abbey remained prominent for some time thereafter and under Abbot Girard d'Arcy (1171–1198) enjoyed considerable prosperity. Richard the Lionheart and Philip Augustus held a rendezvous there in 1190 for the third crusade; pilgrims continued to flood in; and the abbey choir was rebuilt on an extended scale. The burghers, following the disturbances of the 1160s, amply recorded in the fourth book of the *Major Chronicle* of Hugh of Poitiers, exacted from the abbots of Vézelay a written charter which assured them communal liberties that were the envy of their day and would certainly have been the envy of their forebears in the first half of the twelfth century. The interest of the French monarch in the area was also maintained. In 1181, following the death of Count William V, the comital properties descending from the celebrated Count Landric[2] passed to a child, William V's sister Agnès. Philip Augustus eventually took control of both Nevers and Auxerre, and from the château of Pierre-Perthuis (where his jurisdiction might not conflict with that of the abbot of Vézelay) proclaimed himself the protector of the church against the local feudality. He subsequently gave Agnès de Nevers in marriage to a member of the royal family. No less a person than Francis of Assisi also showed an interest in the district: in 1217 he founded the first French Franciscan mission on the spot from which St. Bernard preached the second crusade. The Franciscan chapel, La Cordelle, which later passed into the hands of the monks, and which is, in fact, the very chapel built by Abbot Pons to commemorate that event (Chapelle Sainte-Croix),[3] survives to the present day.

Decline set in with the abbacy of the dissolute Hugh (1198–1207) and the abbey's finances decayed with the general decline of Benedictine monasticism in France. The local nobility renewed their attacks on the weakened monastery,[4] and neither royal nor papal guarantees proved able to stem the tide of confusion or to prevent pilgrims and merchants from avoiding the troubled town. The burghers rose up against their abbot in 1250 and threatened at one point to leave for the French royal domain. The authenticity of the relics of

---

[1] The history of the abbey from 1161 to the French Revolution is dealt with in Appendix H below, and: Chérest vol. 2, chaps. 3 *et seq.*, Saxer (1975: 207ff.), and Vogade (1987: 11ff.), a reprint of the *Descriptions des villes et campagnes du départment de l'Yonne* 2, published at Auxerre in 1870 and written by Aimé Chérest [1826–1885, an Auxerre advocate whose pioneering history of Vézelay is selectively reprinted in Huygens (1976)] and Victor Petit; the portions consulted here were written by Chérest]. The charter referred to in the next paragraph is dated by Berlow (1987: 149) to "around the year 1200."

[2] See the *Brief History*, translated below from MS. Auxerre 227.

[3] Vogade (1987: 45–47). See *Major Chronicle* below 4 §42 (273n.3) and 374.

[4] Cf. the entry for 1230 AD in the *Minor* or *Little Chronicle* contained in MS. Auxerre 227 (Huygens [1976: 230]): "at the same time there arose a war on the part of Guido count of Nevers and Matilda his countess against the church of Vézelay and the burghers of the same town." See Cox's perceptive remarks on the decline of monasteries generally in thirteenth-century Europe in Appendix H below.

Mary Magdalene came under question in view of their apparent inability to protect Vézelay from decay. Pope Clement IV ordered a legatine enquiry into the affairs of the abbey. A solemn verification of the relics of the Magdalene was resolved upon, with King Louis IX, who had visited the abbey a number of times on pilgrimage, presiding over the ceremonies on 24 April 1267;[1] this date came to be more important in the town's festival calendar than the date of the Magdalene's feast.

The Magdalene's demise as a special protectress of Vézelay was, in fact, delayed only a few years by the above tactics. In 1279 St. Maximin in Provence[2] put forward a claim to possess the *real* body of the Magdalene, and the pope eventually approved this claim, thus abolishing one of the major sources of Vézelay's prosperity. Between this date and a royal ordinance of 1312 the domains of the abbey of Vézelay and of the count of Nevers were incorporated into the French royal domain and, at the price of their independence, the abbey and town secured a measure of peace and tranquillity. As a consequence of their new status within the royal domain, the abbots of Vézelay were constrained to establish in their *poté* a seigneurial bailiwick exclusively staffed by lay magistrates, a secular court with the right of appeal to the royal bailiwick of Sens. A period of burgher self-government brought on by the conditions of the Hundred Years War and the temporary captivity of the abbot of Vézelay after the battle of Poitiers did not solve the problem the townsmen had in maintaining their liberties against the abbot, but it certainly helped. In some respects, then, by the end of the fourteenth century, the burghers were better off than their twelfth century predecessors in terms of their autonomy vis-à-vis abbatial power.

The later abbots earned various kinds of notoriety. Artaud Flotte struts briefly and suspiciously on the main stage of history,[3] and Hugues de Maison-Comte (1353–1383) became a loyal counsellor of Charles V and helped his town to weather the storms of the Hundred Years War. A later abbot (Alexander) led Vézelay to join the anti-monarchist Burgundian faction under John the Fearless and Philip the Good, but by the late 1430s the town was safely back within the royal domain. Between 1430 and 1435 it was in fact the chief seat of the (Anglo-Burgundian) "royal" bailiwick of Sens in rivalry with the bailiwick of Charles VII at Sens itself! From 1477 to 1789 the town lay within the royal bailiwick of Auxerre.

The abbey was secularized in 1537 and a chapter of canons replaced the Benedictine monks. An unsuccessful attempt was made to turn the town into a bishopric. For a time in the sixteenth century Vézelay became a center of Huguenot protestantism; in fact, Theodore Beza (de Bèze), a theologian who assisted and later succeeded the Reformation leader Calvin, was born there in 1519. The protestant presence, together with the violent return of catholic power saw considerable damage done to the fabric of the abbey of Vézelay (especially during the catholic siege and protestant pillaging of 1569–1570). In the seventeenth century the ordinary jurisdiction of the bishop of Autun

---

[1] See Appendix D below.

[2] From whence the Magdalene came to Vézelay in the first place: Geary (1978: 92).

[3] See Favier (1963: 83 and 93).

swept away the last vestiges of abbatial autonomy, and Abbot Berthier (1752–1769) undertook the demolition of the gloomy, "out-of-fashion" abbatial palace. On 6 December 1790 the collegiate chapter of canons of the Magdalene at Vézelay ceased their ministry in accordance with Revolutionary Decrees emanating from Paris. "Thus disappeared (writes Chérest) the religious establishment founded by Gérard de Roussillon and to which Vézelay had owed the great part of its celebrity ... right down to the time of the Revolution the inhabitants of Vézelay, stripped of the municipal privileges they had enjoyed for more than two centuries, less free than their ancestors, floundered in sterile struggles. Their number continued to shrink. Their complaints were finally snuffed out. When the Estates-General that inaugurated the French Revolution finally met, Vézelay was no more than a humble rural market-town where the great memories of the past served only to reinforce the decadence and misery of the present."[1]

The fabric of the abbey of the Magdalene at Vézelay suffered damage during the Revolution, but between 1840 and 1861, in response to initiatives by Prosper Merimée,[2] Viollet-le-Duc carried out extensive renovations. In 1946, 40,000 pilgrims commemorated the eighth centenary of the second crusade, and the tide of modern tourists to the town has revived once again the memory of the medieval pilgrims in search of the Magdalene.

Aspects of the Vézelay History and Its Context

[A] Immunity, Advocacy, and Procuration at Vézelay

In a powerful and eloquent appeal, replete with Old Testament symbolism and delivered before the pope in 1165, William, abbot of Vézelay, lamented the destruction of the liberty of his church by the abbot of Cluny, the bishop of Autun, and the count of Nevers. In the words put into his mouth by Hugh of Poitiers, Abbot William portrays these enemies of Vézelay who were conniving to ruin his monastery as being similar to Jerusalem's foes of old who united to try to crush it. He imagines the bishop of Autun speaking thus: "You, Cluny, will obtain the citadel, their chapter; I, Autun, claim for myself their altar; and Assur (the count) will pillage the town."[3] It is against this dubious triumvirate that Hugh shows his heroes, abbots Pons and William, struggling.

The origins of these struggles lay in the ninth-century charter of foundation

---

[1] Cf. above 11n.4.

[2] Some of whose papers have been reprinted in recent years, for example *Études sur les arts du Moyen Age* (Paris, 1967)—which makes no mention of Vézelay.

[3] See *Major Chronicle* 4 §29. On the subject of the present chapter see also Cox in Appendices D and G below.

of Vézelay and the papal confirmation of it; the passions they aroused in Hugh of Poitiers can be explained by events that occurred subsequently. The liberty, under papal protection, with which its founder, Gerard, count of Roussillon and former count of Paris, had endowed Vézelay was, as mentioned in the Introduction above, as much a political gambit as a gesture of piety. Allied to Charles's brother Lothar by marriage, Gerard had abandoned his allegiance to Charles the Bald, king of west France after the Treaty of Verdun in 843, as well as his countship of Paris, to settle in Provence. This move, however, undermined Gerard's control of his estates in Burgundy, around Vézelay and Pothières, because they lay in Charles's territory.[1] Taking advantage of a lull in hostilities in 858, Gerard donated those estates to the church in the form of two monasteries founded and endowed by him. By retaining the usufruct during his lifetime he hoped to benefit from them himself, keep them out of the king's hands, and gain credit in heaven. In at least the first two of these aims he was successful, so much so that in 868 Charles the Bald issued a privilege of his own confirming Vézelay's immunity from secular authorities and acknowledging its dedication to the apostolic see of Rome.[2]

This special relationship with Rome was the key to Vézelay's later claims to ecclesiastical exemption, as the immunity of Charles the Bald was the basis for its claim to immunity from comital interference. The context of this dedication to Rome is not entirely clear, but it seems to have been a reaction to the increasing authority being claimed by Frankish bishops, especially after the compilation of the so-called Pseudo-Isidorean false decretals, an elaborate set of mid-ninth-century forgeries.[3] Soon after the appearance of these forgeries a number of papal privileges was issued, most by pope Nicholas I, which attempted to secure the independence of monasteries from episcopal control. Of these the most famous was the Vézelay privilege, our *charter* 3.[4] The crucial conditions of this privilege were the pope's acceptance of Gerard's assertion that the bishop of the diocese "has not been granted the right of ordination nor any right to rule over that place"[5] and his pronouncement forbidding anyone to accept an offering from the monastery on the occasion of any spiritual or temporal service (ordination, the giving of the chrism, and consecration are specifically mentioned).[6] The diocesan bishop was also specifically forbidden to perform public masses there,unless invited to do so by the abbess, to set up any liturgical stations there, or to demand any food or lodging. The monastery's right of free election of its head was also confirmed.[7]

It was these privileges, together with the founder's own wishes expressed in

---

[1] On the complex affairs of Gerard of Roussillon, see Chaume (1977: 1.176–79, 196–256).

[2] Ibid., 218; see also the discussion in Berlow (1971: 63–64).

[3] On the Frankish background see Goffart (1966: 6–21); and on Pseudo-Isidore see ibid., 66–69, and Stock (1983: 60–61).

[4] Goffart (1966: 20–21); Berlow (1976); and Cowdrey (1970: 85–87).

[5] See charter 2.

[6] Ibid.

[7] Charter 3.

charters 1 and 2, which the abbot and brothers of Vézelay invoked when their
monastery's immunity and liberty were in later years being disputed. They
were not, however, an issue for a long time. The monastery's early years were
concerned merely with survival, as monks replaced the original nuns and then
relocated themselves to the top of the hill of Vézelay to counter threats from
pagans and disloyal Christians.[1] What little is known about the monastery in
the tenth century indicates, in fact, that it fell under the influence of its
diocesan bishop at Autun. There is no evidence of the monks' later antipathy
toward him; indeed they gratefully accepted lands from him in 973.[2] Nonetheless the monks were careful to continue to seek confirmation of the original papal privilege from later popes.[3]

The first evidence of strife at Vézelay is found in a letter from William of
Volpiano, abbot of Dijon, to Odilo, abbot of Cluny in 1026–1027.[4] Count
Landric of Nevers, he tells Odilo, had expelled the abbot of Vézelay and all
the monks; in their place had been installed Cluniac monks, apparently at the
instigation of William himself. But this had been done without the approval
of the bishop of Autun, who, in retaliation, had withdrawn a gift earlier given
to Cluny, had placed an interdict on those churches in his diocese belonging
to Dijon, and had excommunicated the monks now at Vézelay. These, relying
on their papal privileges, had spurned his action and trampled his letter
underfoot. This arrogance had further angered the bishop and had turned
everyone who heard about it, both lay and clerical, against William and the
Cluniacs. William himself could suggest nothing but retreat and, although the
precise outcome of this wrangle is not known, a compromise must have been
reached since the expelled abbot, Herman, returned to continue his rule until
his death in 1037.

The protagonists in this quarrel would continue to fight about Vézelay for
the next century and a half. The bishop of Autun continued to claim, at least
until the papal hearing of 1151, that he had the right to exercise regular
diocesan supervision of Vézelay; the abbot of Cluny interfered more or less
successfully in the affairs of the monastery of Vézelay until the papal bull of
1159 removed it from his influence; and the count of Nevers never ceased
trying to exercise influence over what happened in Vézelay itself. Sometimes
the enemies of Vézelay joined together against it, as did Cluny and the count
in 1153;[5] more commonly each pursued his own interests; and, on occasion,

---

[1] Charters 4 and 5, and the confirmation of Charles the Bald's grant by Odo printed
at the end of this chapter.

[2] Charter 9; see also Chérest 1:48.

[3] Charters 6, 7, 8, 10, and 11 are all tenth-century papal confirmations of the original
privileges.

[4] The letter can be found in PL 141.869–872 and is translated in Appendix A below.
There is a brief (but slightly misleading) discussion in Cowdrey (1970: 86). The account in
Berlow (1971: 87) is vitiated by a radical mistranslation of the letter. Its significance has
been discussed most recently in Sassier (1986). For Cluny see Chagny (1938), and Cox in
Appendix D below.

[5] See Major Chronicle 2 §27 and 3 (Huygens [1976] lines 313–54). See also Saulnier-
Stratford (1), citing N. Bulst, Untersuchungen zu den Klosterreformen Wilhelms von Dijon (962–
1031), Bd. 11 (Bonn: Pariser Historische Studien, 1973), 190–92.

the monks of Vézelay were able to use one of its enemies against another, as when the bishop of Autun consecrated abbots Gerard and Baldwin in apparent defiance of the wishes of the abbot of Cluny.[1] For the purpose of explaining the background to and the main issues at stake in Vézelay's struggles against each of these opponents, they will be discussed separately.

Hugh of Poitier's harshest scorn is reserved for Cluny, the course of whose relations with Vézelay cannot even be clearly traced in the latter's records because of selective editing of the sources. This attempt to obfuscate the records confirms what Hugh's violent language suggests, namely that Vézelay especially feared the power and influence of Cluny. Such fear was amply justified. Despite the setback for Cluny in 1026–1027 when its attempt to depose the abbot and monks and replace them with personnel from its own monastery was defeated, it had acquired control of Vézelay by 1058. This is apparent from Stephen IX's confirmation of Cluniac liberties in that year, which includes Vézelay among the possessions of Cluny. A twelfth-century account, possibly based on an earlier document, asserts that when Geoffrey became abbot he found discipline in the monastery to be most unsatisfactory. This might be the context in which Cluny was able to obtain control over it.[2] Later charters of Gregory VII (1076) and Urban II (1095)[3] confirmed Cluny's influence over the affairs of Vézelay. Equally indicative of Cluniac influence are the origins of the early twelfth-century abbots of Vézelay: Renaud (1106–1128), successor to the murdered Artaud, was a monk of Cluny and a nephew of its abbot St. Hugh; Alberic (1131–1138) had been sub-prior of Cluny, and Pons (1138–1161) was the brother of Peter the Venerable, abbot of Cluny (1122–1156). It is no wonder that Hugh of Poitiers imagines the abbot of Cluny as wanting to control the chapter at Vézelay. Further evidence of Cluniac control of Vézelay is found in the biographies of Hugh, abbot of Cluny, who is said to have intervened in the internal affairs of Vézelay, probably in about 1096, on the grounds that the monastery was in need of reform.[4] It is not quite clear, however, what the relationship between Vézelay and Cluny was; certainly not that of more regular Cluniac houses whose heads were referred to as priors not abbots. Moreover, at the same time as the popes were confirming Cluny's possession of Vézelay, they were continuing to confirm the original privilege of Pope Nicholas I.[5] The best explana-

---

[1] A number of the abbot's witnesses in the papal hearing of 1151 refer to the consecration of Baldwin by the bishop of Autun; Cluny's hostility to the monks' choices emerges in *Major Chronicle* 4 §6.

[2] On the reported decline in monastic discipline see Saxer (1956: 238–39) and Saxer (1975: 188–89). On Stephen's role see Cherést (1863: 1:21); the pope's confirmation is in *PL* 143.879–84; see col. 883 for the reference to Vézelay. Sassier (1986) argues persuasively that it was in exactly 1058 that Cluny's authority over Vézelay was realized. For Cox's discussion see Appendix D below.

[3] See Berlow (1971: 105–7).

[4] Cowdrey (1970: 86) gives a reference to the anonymous *Life* and also suggests the date 1096. The allusion in the *Life* by Renaud, abbot of Vézelay, to Hugh's involvement is in *PL* 159.899C.

[5] Gregory VII's confirmation of the privileges of Vézelay (charter 14) was issued in the same year in which he included the monastery in a list of the possessions of Cluny.

tion of this apparent anomaly is that the popes were handing over to Cluny only the rights that had been granted to them by Count Gerard's original charter. This explanation accords with Urban II's words in his 1095 charter to Cluny stating that its rights over Vézelay "concerned supervision of ordination and regulation of the monastery."[1]

Whatever the precise relationship between Vézelay and Cluny was, the twelfth-century monks of Vézelay did not wish it to be known. Gregory VII's letter of 1076 is incomplete in the Vézelay manuscript[2] and a later bull of Paschal II, alluded to deprecatingly by Hugh as purporting to hand to Cluny the care and ordering of the church of Vézelay, is missing altogether from the cartulary. This letter, written to Abbot Artaud in 1102, confirmed the monastery's rights to seek the consecration of its churches and the ordination of its monks and clerks from any bishop, subject to the advice of the abbot of Cluny. The latter's right to oversee the election of the abbot of Vézelay was confirmed in the same letter.[3] Such a settlement must have been seen as too prejudicial to the interests of the diocesan bishop because in the following year Paschal sent his legate, Cardinal Milo of Palestrina, to mediate between Abbot Hugh and Norgaud, bishop of Autun 1096–1105, who resented Cluniac influence and had placed an interdict to prevent pilgrims going to Vézelay.[4] The parties met at Mazille, a dependent priory of Cluny, and reached an agreement only slightly less unfavorable to the bishop of Autun, from whom the monks were to receive holy orders, as long as he was canonically elected. If he were not, they might choose any canonically elected bishop; the agreement confirmed that the bishop could not exact a profession of obedience from the abbot of Vézelay.[5]

The outcome of this conflict was satisfactory to no one but the abbot of Cluny. The bishop of Autun had to accept defeat, for a time, but neither he nor his fellow bishops could easily tolerate loss of control over a monastery in their diocese. Their hostility toward Vézelay was such that those responsible for the murder of Abbot Artaud in 1106 were able to find shelter in neighboring bishoprics despite numerous papal letters of complaint.[6] Nor were the monks of Vézelay themselves pleased about the victory of Abbot Hugh and the confirmation of Cluniac control of their monastery. Their hostility toward Cluny must have been exacerbated by the rule of Artaud's successor, Renaud, who was a loyal son of Cluny throughout his life. This hostility built up during the 1120s and culminated in the enforced exile of most of the monks of Vézelay in chains in 1131.[7]

---

[1] This charter is number 3687 in Bruel (1974).

[2] See charter 14 and the appended note. Sassier (1986) argues that this was a deliberate act of sabotage, an opinion towards which Huygens also inclines, Huygens (1976: xxix–xxx).

[3] The letter is in *PL*, 163.102–4.

[4] See charter 15 and Cherést (1863: 1:49).

[5] There is an account of the meeting at Mazille in *PL* 159.978–79; see also Bruel (1974: no. 3819).

[6] See charter 25 and Chérest (1863: 1:51–52).

[7] On Renaud, see Aspects [C]; the chaining and exile of the monks are described in *Major Chronicle* 4 §6.

The events of these years cannot be recovered in detail; but it is quite clear that there was a reaction at Vézelay itself to the dominance of Cluny and that the monks attempted to assert their right to elect their abbot freely. The known facts are as follows: Abbot Renaud was not promoted to the archbishopric of Lyons until 1128. The *Annals*, however, record the election of Baldwin as abbot in 1124, and a witness at the 1151 papal hearing recalled having seen Bishop Stephen of Autun bless Abbot Baldwin. There is no other reference to Abbot Baldwin. An 1130 charter of agreement between Vézelay and Prémontré refers to an Abbot Gerard of Vézelay, who likewise is known from no other source. Pope Innocent II's letter of 1131 to Bishop Stephen of Autun (charter 20) announces the appointment of Alberic as abbot of Vézelay because of "the great temporal and spiritual detriment that the monastery has suffered due to the absence of a shepherd." Finally, there is Hugh's account in the *Major Chronicle*: "Vézelay had suffered a terrible outrage in the reign of Innocent II for demanding back its original liberty: by the violence of Innocent and the count of Nevers a certain Alberic was forced on it by the Cluniacs, and nearly all the brothers of the house were bound in chains and ignobly dispersed...."[1]

Although the dates of the most crucial events (the elections of Baldwin and Gerard) will always remain uncertain, the sources make it clear that an anti-Cluniac faction had become so strong at Vézelay that it was able to ensure the election of two abbots not approved of by Cluny—perhaps the timing was associated with the turmoil in Cluny itself in the early years of the abbacy of Peter the Venerable.[2] In taking this action the monks had the support, not surprisingly, of the bishop of Autun, who must have welcomed the opportunity to trump Cluny.[3] But at this time the influence of Cluny in Christendom was still so strong that once its internal affairs had been regularized, it was able to persuade the pope to support its claims and impose Alberic, sub-prior of Cluny, on the Vézelay monks as their abbot. But this aroused such intense feelings that the intrusion could be carried out only by manacling and exiling the majority of the monks of Vézelay.

The intruded monks did not retain their loyalty to Cluny for long. By 1153 when Vézelay was engaged in resisting the attempt by the local burghers to establish a commune, the monks had become suspicious of the intentions of Cluny. They feared that Peter the Venerable, abbot of Cluny and brother of Pons, abbot of Vézelay, was trying to strike a secret deal with the count of Nevers. Their fears were probably justified; neither Cluny nor the count could contemplate with equanimity the possibility of too much royal or papal authority over Vézelay, since in either case their own influence would decline. Despite this, Peter the Venerable became very angry over the reaction at Vézelay and stormed out of negotiations in a huff; relations between the

---

[1] *Major Chronicle* 4 §6. The whole episode has been discussed fully by Berlow (1981). She gives references to all the relevant primary sources. See too Cox in Aspects [F] below.

[2] Berlow (1981) canvasses the possibilities.

[3] The bishop's support reveals that the multitude of competitors for influence over Vézelay provided the monks of that place with an unexpected survival strategy: they could play their various enemies off against each other.

brothers were embittered after this, although a reconciliation seems to have been effected.[1] This long history of Cluniac influence over the affairs of Vézelay explains the eagerness with which the monks took advantage of Cluny's failure to support Alexander III in the papal schism that followed his election. William, abbot of Vézelay, was one of Alexander's strongest supporters and was rewarded for his loyalty by a papal bull which removed Vézelay completely from the authority of Cluny and confirmed its original liberty.[2] Thus a century of Cluniac control of Vézelay came to an end and the papal supervision envisaged by its founder was reinstated. Relations between the abbots of Cluny and Vézelay remained delicate, as evidenced by the tricky negotiations concerning what honor the latter should show the former when he visited Vézelay in 1166.[3]

Although Hugh of Poitiers pictured the abbot of Cluny and the bishop of Autun as collaborators in the destruction of Vézelay, their interests in fact were more often opposed than similar. The bishop's objection to Cluny's interference at Vézelay in 1026–1027 initiated more than a century of endeavour by the bishops of Autun to make good a claim of episcopal authority over Vézelay. The next recorded involvement of the bishop of Autun is Norgaud's demand mentioned above that the abbot of Vézelay make a profession of obedience to him. Upon the abbot's refusal, Norgaud issued an interdict to prevent pilgrims from going to Vézelay and making offerings there. This serious threat to the revenues of the monks led to a papal intervention, in the form of a letter from Paschal II to all the clergy, laity, and knights of France castigating Norgaud and removing his interdict. The end result was a decisive denial of the rights of the bishop of Autun because Paschal forbad the bishop to celebrate masses at Vézelay unless invited by the abbot, to demand any tribute, or to insist on the abbot's subjection.[4]

The struggle was taken up next by Humbert, bishop of Autun 1140–1148, who objected to Pons's request that Elias, bishop of Orleans, perform ordinations at Vézelay. He placed an interdict on the newly ordained clergy and appealed to the pope for support. Pope Innocent II, however, supported Vézelay, cancelled the interdict, and ordered Humbert to cease bothering the monks. But Humbert was not so easily deterred and it was only the intervention of Peter the Venerable which brought about a compromise, at Moulins in 1145, by which Humbert withdrew his objection to the ordination and Pons rescinded the prohibition against his clergy attending synods at Autun.[5]

The struggle by Norgaud and Humbert against Vézelay's attempt—supported by Cluny—to escape from diocesan control was one with which the whole

---

[1] Unfortunately, but perhaps not coincidentally, the account of these events cannot be fully recovered because it is at this point that the manuscript has been torn. See *Major Chronicle* 2 §27 and 3 (Huygens [1976: lines 313–59]).

[2] The papal bull is in *Major Chronicle* 4 §7.

[3] The visit and the negotiations are described in *Major Chronicle* 4 §75.

[4] See charter 15. The letter of Paschal II is printed in Quantin 2:41.

[5] The agreement at Moulins is known only from the reference in the account of the evidence presented before the papal court in 1151 described in 1 §5 (cf. 138n.11) of the *Major Chronicle*.

episcopate was familiar. Bishops and archbishops everywhere strove to resist the papacy's inclination to grant to more and more monasteries, and to whole orders, exemption from interference by their diocesan bishop. Episcopal resentment of Cluniac independence in particular is found as early as the beginning of the eleventh century. In fact, at about the same time as William of Volpiano was recording the Cluniacs' failure to take over Vézelay, Adalbero, bishop of Laon was satirizing the authoritarian pretensions of Odilo, abbot of Cluny, in his *Carmen ad Rotbertum Regem*.[1] Hostility to Cluny's exemption from episcopal control continued for at least the next century, as is made clear by Peter the Venerable's fierce defense of it in his famous letter 28 to St. Bernard.[2] Not that hostility to monastic exemption was confined to disputes involving Cluny. This was a burning issue in England too[3] and the passions it aroused may be indicated by the following remarks of Peter of Blois writing in about 1180 to pope Alexander III on behalf of Richard, archbishop of Canterbury: "... that mischief (exemption) is spreading widely. Abbots puff themselves up against primates and bishops and do not show reverence and honor to their elders.... Abbots detest having someone who corrects their excesses, they embrace their doubtful license with impunity, and they free the cloistered army from its yoke to pursue freely all its desires.... To take abbots from the jurisdiction of bishops is contumacious, an incitement to rebellion and an arming of sons against their parents."[4] The controversy and uncertainty surrounding the issue are brought out in one of the letters of Ivo, bishop of Chartres. Ivo advises the bishop of Orleans to take vengeance on a priory which has defied his interdict on the grounds of exemption if the bishop has the favor of the archbishop; otherwise he should just put up with the flouting of his authority.[5]

One of the fullest accounts of what was at stake in these fierce debates over monastic immunity is found in Book 1 of the *Major Chronicle*. Crucial issues in the early part of the twelfth century included the right of the diocesan bishop to carry out ordinations in the monasteries of his diocese and his right to demand a profession of obedience from the abbots of his diocese. It was the abbot of Vézelay's denial of the latter right that had provoked the promulgation of an interdict by Norgaud, bishop of Autun, in 1102; his later successor Humbert, bishop of Autun 1140-1148, had responded to Pons's invitation to the bishop of Orleans to perform ordinations by declaring such ordinations invalid. The pope intervened against Humbert who was forced eventually, in 1145, to agree to a reconciliation with Pons, after diplomatic representations were made by the abbot of Cluny, among others.[6] But with the election of Humbert's successor the conflict began again because Henry, bishop of Autun 1148-1170 and brother of the duke of Burgundy, renewed the attempt

---

[1] See the edition by Carozzi (1979: 8-12) and the discussion in Duby (1982a: especially 54-55).

[2] Constable (1967).

[3] See the references in Scott (1981: 31-32).

[4] Peter of Blois, letter 68 in Giles (1847: 1:201-5).

[5] The letter is in Leclercq (1949: 256-57).

[6] *Major Chronicle* 1 §2.

to exert Autun's authority over Vézelay. Hugh of Poitiers summed up his ambitions thus: "... (he) sought to win Vézelay into his own jurisdiction, to reduce it to the status of a subordinate parish within his diocese ... and to make it obedient to his synods."[1]

What this amounted to in practice is made clear by the evidence of the witnesses called by both sides at the papal hearing of 1151. As diocesan bishop, Autun claimed the right to bless the abbot, to consecrate altars, to ordain the monks, to celebrate masses on feast days, and to bless the chrism used at Vézelay. Moreover, he demanded that the monks of Vézelay attend his synod when summoned, as other religious in his diocese did.[2] The abbot and monks considered such claims to be an affront to the liberty of their church and a threat to its independence. They cherished this freedom, which they believed was guaranteed by their foundation charter and by subsequent papal letters, and resented particularly attempts to limit their right to order as they wished those crucial spiritual functions that centered on the altar (consecration, ordination, and benediction). Hence the abbot retorted to the bishop that he had the right to invite any bishop he chose to perform these spiritual services. In addition, to strengthen the abbot's claims to spiritual independence, his witnesses adverted to his judgment on marital disputes between citizens of Vézelay, matters that normally lay within the competence of a bishop or were delegated to his archdeacon.[3]

Such, in brief, were the main issues at stake between Autun and Vézelay. Each party argued its case before the pope and then called witnesses to prove its assertions. The abbot had initially been unwilling to participate at all, arguing that Vézelay's independence was guaranteed by the pope and proved by papal letters, but he was persuaded by the pope that the outcome would be favorable to him. The abbot's argument depended on the claim that Vézelay possessed its liberty "by proprietary right and ancient investiture of perpetual possession." The bishop, for his part, relied heavily on "established custom" (*ex longe temporis prescriptione*), but his case was weak because, although his witnesses could testify that he had indeed exercised such rights as he claimed, it was clear that other bishops had also performed the duties which he regarded as his.[4] Autun understood that his case was weak and eventually withdrew from the lawsuit, agreeing to a composition of peace arranged by his brother the duke.[5] Pons's triumph is symbolized for Hugh of Poitiers by the unchallenged invitation to Alan, bishop of Auxerre, to perform ordinations at Vézelay in 1155 in the presence of a Roman cardinal while his "adversary was

---

[1] *Major Chronicle* 1 §3.

[2] The general issues in dispute are discussed in Saxer (1956: 226–27). See Scott (1981: 31–32) and Brett (1975: 133–35) for similar disputed issues in the English church in the twelfth century.

[3] The evidence of the witnesses is recorded in *Major Chronicle* 1 §4 and §5. On jurisdiction over marriage disputes see Lot and Fawtier (1962: 264), and on increasing clerical involvement in the institution of marriage in the twelfth century, see Duby (1985).

[4] The quotations are from *Major Chronicle* 1 §4, which summarizes the arguments of the two sides.

[5] *Major Chronicle* 1 §7.

silent, his throat choked with envy, cast down by the authority of justice."[1]

By 1160, therefore, the abbot of Vézelay had consolidated his spiritual immunity. A century of control by Cluny had been brought to an end and Vézelay's right of exemption from interference by its diocesan bishop had been confirmed. But the third opponent of the liberty of Vézelay, the count of Nevers, proved to be a much more formidable adversary, one who could employ brute force to bolster his claims, not just legal argument. The tortuous history of the relations between Vézelay and three generations of counts of Nevers can be followed in the *Major Chronicle* and need not be rehearsed here, where it will be necessary only to explain some of the background and to highlight the main issues in dispute. In essence the question was whether Vézelay was within the advocacy of the count of Nevers. The count made it clear on a number of occasions that he believed himself to be the advocate (*advocatus*) of the church of Vézelay, but the most that the abbot or monks would admit was that he was the protector or defender (*defensor*) of the monastery.[2] It was as advocate that the count claimed the right to interfere in the election of the abbot, to summon the abbot and his men to appear before his court, and to be entertained at the monastery's expense when he visited it, especially during important feasts.

Advocacy was an ancient institution that had been regularized by Charlemagne, who made it a public office of particular importance in areas of ecclesiastical immunity. The advocate's main role then was to represent his church in legal matters. However, this role began to change as the order that was maintained by the Carolingians broke down, and increasingly the task of the advocate became one of defending the abbey he represented. Taking advantage of the weakness of central authority and their churchs' dependence on them, advocates began to demand greater rewards for their services, especially lodging and hospitality for themselves and their retinues. During the eleventh century abuses by advocates of their office—now becoming hereditary and not the free choice of the monastery—became more widespread as they tried to extend their judicial powers over the affairs of their advocacy, began to demand extra payments, and even intervened in the spiritual business of the monastery, especially the election of abbot.[3] Despite such oppression most monasteries were helpless, and needed to have an advocate; they had still to depend on him, even if he turned against them. Even the monks of Vézelay, who had been sorely tried by the counts of Nevers on numerous occasions, still looked upon the count as their defender.[4]

Events at Vézelay conform to this general picture. We have already seen that as early as 1026–1027 the count of Nevers had intervened vigorously in

---

[1] *Major Chronicle* 3 §7.

[2] See *Major Chronicle* 2 §5, §12, and §16 for the count's claim and the abbot's denial of it and 4 §40 for the monks' acknowledgement that he is their defender and patron. Note that in his letter to William, abbot of Vézelay, Herbert of Bosham refers to the abbot's defender (*defensor*); see Appendix C.

[3] On the history of advocacy see Introduction above at 6nn.1 *et seq.* and Boudrillat (1931: 1220–42).

[4] See *Major Chronicle* 4 §40.

the affairs of the monastery. The next recorded contact between the church and the count also concerned the election of the abbot of Vézelay. Apparently William II, count of Nevers 1098–1146, tried to intervene in the process that led to the election of Renaud as abbot in 1106. Perhaps because the latter was supported by Cluny, where he had been a monk since 1088, the count had to acknowledge defeat and admit that he had no right to interfere in the process of election, as a document recorded by Hugh of Poitiers makes clear.[1] It may have been this setback that embittered William II, for the rest of his long rule as count shows him consistently hostile to Vézelay, despite his otherwise good reputation as a pious man. Two papal letters of 1117, one warning William not to oppress or attack Vézelay and the other seeking the assistance of neighboring bishops for its protection, are early evidence of his antagonism.[2] Another letter, almost certainly written at the same time to Abbot Renaud, explains the nature of the oppression: the count was turning up at the monastery with any number of men and demanding hospitality for himself and his retinue; he was insisting on his right to decide disputes between the abbot and the inhabitants of Vézelay; and he was demanding that the abbot appear in his court if a quarrel arose between the two of them.[3]

Thus well before the abbacies of Pons and William that occupied the attention of Hugh of Poitiers, the main matters of dispute between the count of Nevers and the abbot of Vézelay had been established. The count's demands were typical of those of other advocates. He wanted procuration for himself and his retinue whenever he came to Vézelay; he tried to make good a claim of judicial competence over both the abbot himself and the men of the church; and he wanted to be consulted when an abbot was elected. The first of these demands was the most resistant to compromise. The count's claims to jurisdiction over the abbot and his men were easier to fight off, and the abbot's triumph in this matter can be traced in Books 2–4 of the *Major Chronicle*. Despite apparent temptations to accede to the count's demands, Abbot Pons, bolstered by the pope's order that he not compromise, had by 1155 consolidated the church's right to "decide its own cases and those of its dependents in its own court, possessing full authority; nor ever or anywhere did the will of any lay or clerical person intercede in its right to judgment."[4] William IV made some endeavour to force the abbot to appear before his court, but he did not press this, or his insistence on being consulted over abbatial elections, very strongly, reserving most of his energies for the question of procuration.[5]

---

[1] See *Major Chronicle* 4 §4.

[2] Charters 17 and 18.

[3] This letter, not in the Auxerre manuscript, is printed by Huygens (1976: 299). Note the following remarks on hospitality or procuration: *Ut videlicet quotiens eum illuc venire contigerit cum qualicumque sotiorum numero voluerit in hospitali domo suscipiatur et de rebus monasterii quandiu ibi manere censuerit procuretur.*

[4] *Major Chronicle* 3 §7. The count's claims to judicial competence are found in 2 §5 and 4 §8; the working out of the issue is shown in 2 §5, §10, and §11, 3 §7, and 4 §20 and §25. The pope's intervention is recorded in 2 §11.

[5] *Major Chronicle* 4 §20 for William IV's judicial claims and 4 §4 for his interference in the election of Abbot William.

The difficulty with procuration was in arranging a compromise that was acceptable to both sides. The abbot was willing to come to an agreement, no doubt because it was the general practice to grant hospitality to one's defender and because it had in fact clearly been granted to William II early in the twelfth century; but just how frequently the count was entitled to it and what the monetary equivalent of any one occasion of hospitality should be could not readily be determined. The main disputes arose after the compromises of 1155, which saw the abbot's success on the question of judicial independence, and were fuelled by William III's renunciation of casual procuration after his near fatal shipwreck in 1148.[1] His son William IV, spurred on by his mother Ida, pressed the monastery almost constantly, virtually from the moment of his father's death, on the subject of his right to obtain procuration from the monastery. In 1163 he rejected his father's renunciation of unannounced procuration and launched that long series of attacks on the monastery which led eventually to the monks' self-imposed exile and voyage to Paris to appeal to the king. Throughout the dispute the count's main aim seems to have been to exact as much money as he could in commutation of the procuration that he claimed.[2] Unfortunately, the details of the deal that was finally worked out and that saw the count and abbot become close friends can not be recovered because of the torn parchments. It is clear, however, that the monks clung stubbornly to their rejection of the count's claims.

In the complicated story of the dispute between the abbot and the count two points in particular can be noted. Firstly, it should be remembered that Hugh of Poitiers' account of what happened is not an impartial one. The monks of Vézelay were too intimately involved in these tumultuous events to report them dispassionately; furthermore, they were divided in their loyalties, perhaps with justification:[3] it is clear, for example, from allusions made by Hugh, that the counts were quite justified in asserting that they were entitled by custom to some of the rights they claimed. Hugh admits, in passing as it were, that the monastery had been paying William II for protection and granting him benefices in return for his support.[4] Later, in his castigation of the Cluniacs, he acknowledges that after the appointment of Alberic as abbot in 1131 the count of Nevers had been invited to Vézelay and allowed to exact profits of justice, to make frequent claims of procuration, and to impose burdensome charges.[5] In short, the later claims by William IV that he was merely trying to reinstate customary rights were not without justification.

The second point to be noted concerns the tactics employed by the two

---

[1] *Major Chronicle* 2 §7 and §8. Note that the text of §7 has been tampered with to make it read as though the count foreswore all rights of procuration, although it is clear from later chapters that he did not give up his right to procuration at Easter and on the feast of Mary Magdalene. See *Major Chronicle* 2 §10 and 4 §19. Note the discussion in Chérest (1863: 1:132n.4).

[2] There are financial negotiations recorded in §19, §48, and §67 of *Major Chronicle* 4 as the two parties try to hammer out a compromise.

[3] See the note on *Major Chronicle* 4 §41:272n.2 and Hugh's own hints of opposition in 1 §7.

[4] *Major Chronicle* 2 §4.

[5] *Major Chronicle* 4 §6.

sides during their prolonged dispute. The various counts, beginning with William II in 1119,[1] themselves, or by way of their accomplices, would on occasion harass the men and lands of the monastery, block the roads leading to Vézelay, lay siege to the monastery, or physically attack the monks or the monastery. The abbots, although on one occasion employing mercenaries,[2] usually rely upon spiritual weapons, such as excommunication or the symbolic overturning of the right order of the world by suspending services, covering crosses and altars, or even, as a last resort, leaving their monastery to show that their persecution is so unbearable that they are forced to break the basic monastic commitment to stability.[3] Both these sets of tactics were standard in disputes between monks and laymen at the time: a dispute could not be resolved by an appeal to law but only by arbitration, and so each side tried by whatever means were available to force the other party to a favorable compromise.

Thus in the *Chronicle* the laity interfere with the monks and disrupt their lives to such an extent that they will be forced to come to an agreement. The monks, on the other hand, try to isolate the layman, in a ritual way, from both God and man in order to win the support of the faithful and force their opponent to agree to a compromise. There is no question of one side trying to overcome the other utterly: both parties have to continue to live side by side and have constant dealings with each other, and so the various arbitrators who try to mediate attempt a solution from which each party can gain something. That is why the monks continue to regard the count as their protector, despite all the evidence to the contrary, and why even as the monks are heading into exile the ruthless Ida tries to dissuade them.[4] Of course, the absence of a decisive conclusion and the search for a compromise meant that arbitration was never conclusive and, as the example of Vézelay shows well, that conflict could easily break out again.[5]

* * * * * * * * *

TRANSLATIONS of the two early secular confirmations of the immunity of Vézelay follow, the first (A) from G. Tessier, *Recueil des actes de Charles II le Chauve, roi de France*, Paris 1952, vol II 183–184 and the second (B) from R. H. Bautier, *Recueil des actes d'Eudes, roi de France (888–898)*, Paris 1967, 41–45.

(A) [7 January 868 Pouilly-sur-Loire]

In the name of the holy and individual Trinity. Charles, by the grace of God, king. If we look with favor on the beneficial vows of those noble and illustrious men who are faithful to us and grant our consent to their just and reason-

---

[1] Charter 57.

[2] *Major Chronicle* 3 §3.

[3] Cf. the *Rule of St. Benedict's* criticism of *gyrovagi* in §1.

[4] *Major Chronicle* 4 §40 and §56.

[5] On the settlement of disputes in twelfth-century France see Cheyette (1970), Geary (1986), and Langmuir (1970).

able requests, we are exercising the customary duty of a king, we make them readier in their faithful service to us and, we do not doubt, we ourselves will benefit by passing more happily the course of this present life and by obtaining more easily the rewards of future blessedness.

Let the sharp mind of all who are faithful, now and in the future, to the holy church of God and to us learn therefore that the illustrious Count Gerard, who is most dear and pleasing to us, has approached our highness and made it known that, inflamed by the torch of divine ardor and out of love and honor for God and our Lord Jesus Christ and his holy mother the ever virgin Mary, he has, with the agreement of his most noble wife Bertha, built a monastery on property he possesses in a place called Vézelay (*Virzelliacus*) in our kingdom of Burgundy in the county of Avallon within the parish of the town of Autun, and that he has had it dedicated to the honor of Mary the holy mother of God and that he has established holy nuns there to serve God perpetually and that, for its defense and protection, he has subjected it to God and his blessed apostles Peter and Paul, namely the holy Roman see. In this connection (*unde*) he has placed before our eyes a privilege for that monastery strengthened by the authority of the apostolic see; but for greater durability he has besought our highness to confirm by the command of our authority what has been established by the holy see.

Granting consent to his just and reasonable requests we demand and declare that whatever the apostolic see by the privilege of its authority has determined will endure justly and reasonably in connection with that monastery should remain undestroyed in our day and in the future and should be observed unimpaired by our successors and by all practitioners of the Christian faith. Whatever the illustrious Count Gerard and his wife Bertha have together agreed to grant and will in future grant to that monastery from the properties they possess justly and legally by hereditary right, by purchase, by royal gift, by exchange or by any form at all of gain or acquisition (*quolibet attracto vel acquisito*), which are not objected to by anyone, and whatever has been justly and legally granted or will be granted in the future to that holy place by those fearing God, should endure and remain undisturbed for the benefit of and to fulfil the needs of that place; and the monastery itself should stand under the protection of our immunity and that of our successors so that no public judge nor anyone with judicial power should ever at any time dare to come to or presume to demand entry to (*ingredi audeat aut exactare presumat*) any of the churches, places, fields or remaining possessions of the monastery in order to hear any cases or to exact any unjust fines or to demand any lodgings or victuals (*mansionaticos vel paratas*) or to take away any people to serve as pledges (*fidejussores*) or to demand any tolls or to punish (*distringendos*) unjustly any of its men living on its land, be they free or slave, or to ask for any payments or unlawful taxes (*ullas redibitiones aut inlicitas occasiones*). But whatever the fisc could exact from there we grant wholly, for the sake of an eternal reward, to the relief of the poor and for the use of the holy nuns living there.

Moreover, however long the illustrious Count Gerard and his most noble wife Bertha live, they should hold, rule and manage that monastery under usufruct, assigning one pound of silver to be rendered annually by that monastery to the apostolic see. After both of them have left this life, the holy nuns of that monastery should elect an abbess from among themselves according to the rule (*regulariter*) and under the regulation of the apostolic see so that they might serve God more freely and more devoutly and implore the mercy of God perpetually on behalf of us and our wife and our children and the state of the whole kingdom. That this confirmation of our authority should have unchallengable strength in our day and throughout the future ages of our successors we have validated the bottom of it (*subter eam firmavimus*) with our own hand and ordered it to be sealed beneath with the impression of our ring.

Sign (Monogram) of the most glorious King Charles.

Given on the seventh of January, in the first indiction, in the 28th year of the reign of the most glorious King Charles. Enacted at Pouilly-sur-Loire. Joyfully in the name of God. Amen.

(B) [10 July 889 Paris]

In the name of the holy and individual Trinity. Odo, king by the mercy of God.

If we incline our ear to the just requests of the servants of God that are made to our serenity and bring them into effect by giving help to any pious petition, we do not doubt at all that this will enable us to obtain more easily an eternal reward and remuneration and to live more freely in this present life. Wherefore let the diligence (*industria*) of all those faithful to the holy church of God and to ourselves, both present and future, know that Odo, venerable abbot of the monastery of Vézelay, has approached our highness and besought us to take his monastery with everything pertaining to it under the guardianship of our immunity and under royal protection, to the end that what is contained within the order of our predecessor of divine memory, Charles the august emperor, and in the privilege of our one time lord and father, John the universal pope, should remain undestroyed and inviolate. Under the same conditions of immunity we accept the castle which has been built there as a result of the persecution of the pagans and order that it always remain free from the encroachment of any trouble. This monastery is situated in the county of Avallon on the river called the Cure and was built in honor of God and our saviour Jesus Christ and his mother the ever virgin Mary and the blessed chiefs of the apostles, Peter and Paul.

We earnestly agree and offer our free assent to this pious request and decree that the said assembly and castle with the whole of their possessions and those things formerly offered there by the faithful at the disposition of divine grace should be taken under the protection of our immunity. Therefore we direct and command that no count or viscount or any secular judge or any of our *missi* who are passing through should take lodgings by force (*potestative mansiones accipiat*) in that monastery or castle or any of the villages pertaining to it; nor should they presume to demand from it victuals (*paratas*) or fines or traffic tax (*cespitaticum*) or bridge toll (*pontaticum*) or annual tribute (*inferendas*). But the servants of God living in that monastery should be allowed to exist safely and calmly and to pray without the annoyance of anyone disturbing them for the mercy of God on behalf of us and the state of our kingdom and also our father and our mother and our beloved wife.

But if—and we believe that this is not likely to happen—any man, no matter what secular power he is endowed with, should presume to act against this document (*preceptum*) of our immunity and greatness or to dishonor it or to violate it in any way, let him be coerced by a penalty of six hundred *solidi* and pay half to our fisc and the rest to the church against which he has brought suit.

So that this inviolable decree of ours should remain strong and secure in future times we request our successors to take pains perpetually to preserve as strong and undestroyed those things which are here being strengthened by us, just as they would want what they themselves have decreed legitimately to be held to firmly by their successors. That this command of our authority should, in the name of God, possess even fuller vigour and strength we have strengthened it with our hand and ordered that it be sealed underneath with the impression of our ring.

Sign of Odo (Monogram), most glorious king.

Throannus the notary has confirmed it in place of Eblo.

Given on 10 July, in the sixth indiction, in 888 AD, in the second year of the reign of our Lord, the most glorious king Odo. Enacted in the city of Paris. Joyfully in the name of God. Amen.

[B] The Communal Revolution and Serfdom at Vézelay

The so-called "communal revolution"[1] or "movement" of the twelfth century was, in the country where it can best be studied,[2] and where "the spirit of association was most widespread,"[3] a transitional, rather than a permanent institutional phenomenon. Defined in its classic sense as the movement "by which cities emancipated themselves from the temporal rule of the bishops"[4] and/or the counts, and established this emancipation in the form of autonomous elective magistracies operating in accordance with a charter setting forth the rights and privileges of the various groups and individuals in the urban area, the process certainly led to some glorious episodes in western history, whether the defeat of twelfth- and thirteenth-century Hohenstaufen imperialism in Italy, or the later Italian Renaissance itself. It also became incor-

---

[1] Butler ([1906] 1969: 54).

[2] *Cambridge Medieval History* (1964: 5:624).

[3] Ibid.

[4] Butler ([1906] 1969: 54). Petit-Dutaillis ([1947] 1970: 79, and cf. Dhondt [1952]); Vermeesch (1966: 14); Black (1984: chap. 4); Berlow (1987: 137ff., 152–53 and n.8 [citing, among other references, E. W. Dow, "Some French Communes in the Light of Their Charters," *American Historical Review* 8 (1903): 641–56]). See also Appendix E below and, for a review of the problem of the origin of communal franchises, see Joris (1988).

porated into the mythology of the French Revolution—whereby in the middle ages "the towns were supposed to have joined forces with the king against their common enemy, the feudal nobility"[1]—and into that of Marxism—whereby the towns were depicted as solvents of the feudal order, as the framework for the rise of a capitalist bourgeoisie and free market industrial relations.[2]

The phenomenon in France, however, served to mark the uneasy passage from feudal anarchy—the environment in which the communes were formed in the period c. 1075-1175 AD—to the new monarchical order. It was the king, ultimately, who guaranteed communal peace in towns like Laon and Vézelay (that is, both within and without the royal domain) and it was the king who, in the end, decided the fate even of fiercely independent towns such as Toulouse.[3]

Hence, the interest of the communal movement in France is episodic and microcosmic, characteristic of what Victor Turner might have termed a "liminal" period of transition, from one structure (Carolingian monarchy) to another (Capetian monarchy).[4] This "liminal" period (c. 1075-1175 AD) loosened bonds in many ways: not only did town populations become to some extent mobilized, but clerical splinter groups and renegade individuals preaching crusade, anti-sacramentalism, and millenarianism roused rural and female groups to new stages of self-conscious action which changed the face of Europe.[5]

At points of crisis and combustion the make-up of social groups and the cohesive bonds within societies are laid bare in unique ways. The microcosmic "crisis"-driven investigation of social cohesion has produced merit-worthy studies in the medieval field, whether of Flanders in 1127 AD[6] or Montaillou in the early fourteenth century.[7] Vézelay is no exception, despite the somewhat peripheral position of the town in relation to the major centers of ferment in the period. That the burghers of Vézelay *were* drawn into the "communal revolution" is made plain from a classic passage in Hugh of Poitiers' chronicle.[8] The *Minor* or *Little Chronicle* gives the date of 1156 for this development[9]: fashionable ideas of civic association seem thus to have reached Vézelay some time later than they did areas both to the north and to the south; there is no trace of such notions in the 1137 disturbances, nor at any earlier time in the town's history. The contrast between the two major episodes of communal cohesion in the town's twelfth-century history is thus important and deserves some comment.

---

[1] Mackrell (1973: 9) and cf. above Introduction 4n.5. Also: Pullan (1966: §18, 264–67), Arnold (1991: 57–58) and below n.3.

[2] See Introduction 4n.5 above, and Dobb ([1946] 1963: 70-83).

[3] Above n.1; Martinet 1ff.; Mundy (1985); Petit-Dutaillis (1964: 196ff.); Reynolds (1984: 178); Scholz (1971); Appendix F below.

[4] Turner (1969).

[5] Blake and Morris (1985); Cohn (1970: chap. 3); Coupe (1987); Dalarun (1985); Duby (1974: part 3), (1985); Moore (1980), (1986), (1987); Nelson (1972); Ward (1985), (1989), (1990).

[6] Ross (1960) and cf. Dhondt in Cheyette (1968: 268ff.).

[7] Le Roy Ladurie (1980) and cf. his study of Romans in the sixteenth century (1979).

[8] Below, *Major Chronicle* 2 §19.

[9] See the translation from the *Minor* or *Little Chronicle* below.

The Accord of 1137 AD[1]

Both Dockès and Duby[2] have commented tellingly on the growing seigneurial pressure exercised upon the peasantry in the productive agricultural
regions of Europe during the eleventh century. "Banal" rights—the lord's
power to demand that his dependents use his mills, ovens, and wine-presses,
perform onerous labor for him, and pay him arbitrarily determined percent-
ages of their crop, and other dues, in kind or cash, upon pain of judicial fine
or military coercion—determined social relations in the period across broad
areas of Europe.[3] "It is known (writes Dockès)[4] that lords profited hand-
somely from their mills, and more generally from the power of the ban (mills,
ovens, presses, cattle, to say nothing of the administration of justice and the
power to strike coinage). Taken together, these profits came (during the eleventh and twelfth centuries) to account for a far larger share of the lord's
income than the dues he received from his land." Indeed, argues Dockès,[5]
"while the great water mills that were forced on the peasantry by the power
of the ban, by coercive means, did indeed represent one form of technologi-
cal progress (since they increased the productivity of the miller's labor), they
were not the only possible form but rather the type enforced by existing
social relations ... the lords drove out the hand mills, destroyed them and enforced use of the banal water mill in their stead ... large scale milling machinery was inextricably bound up with the new feudalism."

The condition of serfdom was thus not only expensive and burdensome for
the victims, but also entailed considerable restrictions upon social mobility—a
comital enquiry into the possible (but obscured) servile origin of leading
bureaucrats in Flanders in the 1120s, was enough to produce an outrageous
murder and a considerable measure of social chaos.[6] R. W. Southern[7] has
stressed the two-sided nature of serfdom—its benefits for the victim, its theological and ideological justifications (no less a figure than the Pope was content to call himself *servus servorum dei*)—as well as its costs. Our evidence suggests, however, that serfdom was routinely seen as degrading and restrictive
during the "liminal" period here under consideration, and individuals went
to considerable lengths to evade its limitations—as indeed they had apparently
been doing for some time.[8] No doubt the temptation to evade the bonds of
serfdom grew sharper with the enhanced prospects for social and economic

[1] See Graham (1918: 55–59); Berlow (1971: 33, 170-87, 248ff.) and (1980: 136ff.);
Chérest vol. 1, chap. 3 (Huygens [1976: 38–59]); Bastard (1851: 347–52).

[2] Dockès (1982), Duby (1968: 224ff.), (1974: parts 2 and 3), (1982a: parts 3 and 5), etc.

[3] On the word "ban"—*bannum*—see Niermeyer (1976: 81–84).

[4] (1982: 183). F. Haverkamp (1988: 210).

[5] (1982: 176, 179–80). See too Bloch (1967: chap. 5, esp. 152ff.).

[6] "The pious count [writes Galbert of Bruges], wishing to reestablish proper order in
his realm, sought to find out who belonged to him, who were servile and who were free
men in the realm" (Ross [1960: 96]). The Vézelay annalist knew of these events. See below
Annals or *Minor Chronicle* s.a. 1127, and Van Caenegem in Bachrach (1990).

[7] 1953: 102-3.

[8] Lopez ([1959] 1965: #23b, p. 37) (M. G. H. *Leges* 4, *Constitutiones et acta publica
imperatorum et regnorum* [Hannover 1893: 1:47–48]).

mobility offerred by the twelfth-century courtly market for literacy and related skills.[1]

An analysis of the document presented as Appendix B below reveals much about the tensions within the *potestas* of Vézelay and much about the machinery for negotiations and adjudication that contemporaries had available to help prevent recourse to violence in such disputes.[2] In the year 1137 an abbatial/episcopal tribunal adjudicated a dispute between the abbot of Vézelay and his "burghers" (*burgenses*[3])—that is, the inhabitants of the *burh, burg, bourg*, or fortified, walled, built up area, rather than the *surburbani* or *rustici*, or villagers in the outlying parts of the Vézelay *potestas*.[4] The abbot clearly wished to prevent a recurrence of disputes by drawing up some form of notarial record of the hearings before the tribunal in which the matters disputed and the resolutions arrived at in each session would be clear for future generations. Abbot Alberic, says Berlow,[5] "had taken the initiative in setting up the inquiry in order to settle arguments of long duration. Burghers were present but the text does not state whether their arguments were presented by their own representatives or by the abbot or monastic officials on the basis of complaints which they had heard."

The background to the "charter" of 1137 is provided in §28, where it is stated that the burghers and the country-dwellers had entered into a "confederation and conspiracy" against the abbot and his church, presumably while negotiations over disputed issues were proceeding. Thus even in 1137 new

---

[1] Ward (1979: 67), (1988), and (1990); Jaeger (1985); and above Introduction 10n.4. On manorialism, banal monopolies, slavery, and serfdom generally in the period see Berlow (1980); Bloch (1961: part 5, chaps. 18–20), (1964), (1967: 82–123), (1975); Dockès (1982); Duby (1968), (1974: part 3), and in Benson and Constable (1982: 249–54); Hilton (1973: chap. 2); Pounds (1974: chaps. 5–6). Bloch's (1964) article is particularly relevant to the study of the communal revolution: it shows a group of peasants seeking to avoid the taint of serfdom by due legal process. See also Barthelemy (1984), J. Boussard, "A Serf in Anjou at the End of the 11th Century," in Thrupp (1967: 124–26), and Jordan (1986).

[2] See clauses 3, 18, 27, and 41 of the *Accord*. For the 1106 AD recourse to violence see Introduction 3n.1.

[3] On the word see Niermeyer (1976: 108). Guibert of Nogent refers to *proceres, clerus atque burgenses: De vita sua* [*Memoirs*] (ed. Labande, 64).

[4] The inhabitants of the *poté* of Vézelay seem to have been divided roughly into three groups: *suburbani* or *rustici*, residents of the town itself with employment mainly in the fields, and town residents whose employment lay mainly in the walled city (money-changers, stall-keepers, retailers, administrators, monks and clergy, etc.). It would seem that the 1137 compromise was more favorable to the first two classes of citizen than the third, and it would also seem from the evidence that it was the third group, or sections within that group, who provided the major revolutionaries in 1152. The protagonists of the commune seem to have been drawn in the main from the class of money-changers, retailers, and lay abbatial administrators. Berlow (1987: 150–51) asserts that the c. 1200 urban charter granted the burghers of Vézelay (see above Introduction) "clearly distinguished them from the populace of the surrounding countryside." She thinks the burghers can be divided into two groups—an upper elite of merchants and money-dealers whose welfare depended upon good relations with the seigneurial lord, and "local tradesmen who were potentially the most active element in the revolt and were in direct contact with the rural populace which provided the most volatile element in the rebellion." For the various terms used to describe towns in the medieval period see Lombard-Jourdan.

[5] 1971: 177. See also below, 79.

forms of mutual political action were becoming visible, even if, at this stage, the institutions of a commune were absent[1] and the mechanism of tribunal, hearing, and charter eventually prevailed in their stead.

It is significant also that the burghers, through delegates, swear that they never made a conspiracy against the abbot (§42). What relationship was there between the seven delegates chosen to "swear" and those who put the case of the burghers before the tribunal? Berlow[2] suggests that various clauses in the 1137 *Accord* seem to support the idea of some burgher "body already exercising jurisdiction in the market-place before whose power the abbot was forced to bend, even if he refused to acknowledge its existence." A shadowy form of "magistracy" may thus already have emerged among the burghers of Vézelay. Hugh of Poitiers himself refers to "the elders among the people who seemed to be their heads."[3] Although this refers to the year 1152, it seems specifically to imply a group different from the communal magistracy just formed.[4] Berlow suggests that a confraternity of the Holy Spirit may have been the seed of burgher organizational structure and strength.[5]

It is worth noting, too, that *some* form of representative institution for the burghers and country-dwellers was proposed in 1137[6]: democratically elected community representatives to supervise the making up before the dean and provost, of the *tallia* or "arbitrary tax taken by the lord from all inhabitants of the town: a tax moreover, which on account of its capricious nature proved incompatible with mercantile pursuits and prevented the growth and prosperity of the community."[7] This small move towards representative institutions was, however, thwarted by the abbot.

Evident too, in the *Accord*, is a move on the part of the burghers towards setting up an urban judicial tribunal which would have jurisdiction over the *rustici*.[8] This attempt to withdraw the *rustici* from the abbot's seigneurial,

---

[1] Berlow (1971: 267): "It is therefore highly significant that the term commune was not used in 1137."

[2] (1971: 269–71).

[3] *Major Chronicle* 2 §20, and cf. §17: *potiori parte hominum Vizeliacensium* and 3 §2 for a "senate" of "elders."

[4] Berlow (1971: 273) writes: "Although the earliest reference to this group occurs with regard to this meeting in 1152, it is likely that they existed at an earlier date. The agreement of 1137 between the abbot and the burghers was discussed primarily on the basis of customary practice and it may be that the spokesmen for the burghers at these hearings were in fact the 'elders,' the body whose authority on local customs was recognized. If so, judging from the information available on those burghers present whose names were given, in 1137 the 'elders' represented the local elite, either by virtue of profession or family." Bourquelot (462) insists that *natu maiores* "dans la langue du droit romain et du droit du moyen âge, signifie magistrats et dignitaires." See Berlow (1987: 148).

[5] See Duparc in Cheyette (1968: 349); Berlow (1971: 376), and below *Major Chronicle* 2 §19.

[6] *Accord* §§34 and 52.

[7] Stephenson ([1954] 1967: 41–42). "The abolition of the *taille* . . . was one phase of the great social revolution that was already well under way in France by the opening of the thirteenth century" (ibid., 43).

[8] §§39 and 51.

feudal justice in favor of inclusion within a town-based burgher tribunal was naturally rejected by the abbot.

The disputed matters in 1137 may be grouped into the following categories:

* Disputes between the abbot and burghers regarding the fruits of burgher-rustic labors and regarding access to the land for cultivation, fishing, grazing, and viticultural purposes: payment of tithes/tributes from the agricultural/viticultural/pasturing activities in which the burghers were engaged; disputes over ponds, common lands, other properties title to the revenues of which was unclear: §§4, 5, 9, 10, 12, 13, 17, 18, 19, 21, 22, 24, 26, 35, 36, 37, 38, 48, 49, 50, 53, and 54.

* Urban activities, specifically those associated with markets and commerce, and those where the natural economic interests of the burghers clashed with the abbot's interpretation of his seigneurial, proprietorial rights. As Berlow indicates,[1] the new wealth of the district related particularly to these activities, and the competition to control them, on the part of *all* parties (burghers, count, abbot) was intense: hire of houses to pilgrims and guests, fraud on the part of the moneyers, rental of moneyers' and merchants' stalls by the proprietary lord, and rental of market places: §§6, 7, 8, 11, 20, 32, 47.

* Banal rights, or economic monopolies enforced by and through the abbot's ban: §§16, 25, 40, 55, 56.

* Practices which derived from and emphasized the servile or serf-like status of the burghers and rustics.[2] The document actually mentions freemen among the populace subject to the abbot, and from this it can be deduced that the issue at stake here was not so much the lifting of servile bonds over serfs, as the abbot's persistent tendency to consider "his men" (the "townsmen of the church") as serfs, or at least as subject to the sorts of restrictions characteristic of servitude.[3] Some of the burghers no doubt *were* serfs, and the count addresses the burghers as a group as if they were serfs, that is, as if they were "unfree."[4] Yet the word "servitude" is more a threat than a reality: the abbot accuses the count of seeking to reduce the townsmen to servitude to himself, and flatters the burghers as his own *fideles* (i.e., "free vassals")

---

[1] (1971: 179).

[2] §§14, 23, 29, 30, 31, 43, 44, 45.

[3] Bourquelot (1852: 458): "Mais il leur restait le nom de serfs. . . ." Bloch (1961: 264–65): "The lord was apt to lay claim, even in defiance of custom, to the exercise of an arbitrary authority: 'he is mine from the sole of his feet to the crown of his head,' an abbot of Vézelay said of one of his serfs. . . ."

[4] *Major Chronicle* 2 §17. Cf. also Thierry (1851: 312), describing the inhabitants of Vézelay: "all serfs belonging to the abbey of the Magdalene, the inhabitants of Vézelay had gradually acquired the ownership [*propriété*] of several domains in the neighborhood, and their servitude, diminishing with the passage of time, was little by little reduced to the payment of *tailles* and *aides*, and to the obligation to carry their bread, wheat and their grapes to the public oven, mill or press belonging to or rented out by the abbey." Also p. 345: "The inhabitants of Vézelay became again (after the events of 1155 AD) serfs of the church of St. Mary, but not, doubtless in the same rigorous way as before (1155); for, now as always, servitude was limited by the will and the courage of those who underwent it. If the period of complete independence for the Vézelay citizens had been of short duration, we should not be in any haste to accuse them of a lack of constancy. . . ."

promising them "salvation and liberty."[1] Recall the situation in Flanders scarcely ten years before the Vézelay *Accord*.[2]

The *Accord* seems to have left the seigneurial, banal structure of the abbot's power more or less intact, and the authority of the lesser abbatial officials unimpaired.[3] Some regard had, however, to be paid to the interests and the grievances of the burghers and certain measures were adopted to protect their interests. However, a residue of resentment remained to serve as tinder for later agitators to ignite.

The Formation of the Commune[4]

Hugh of Poitiers points plainly to Hugh of St. Peter as the focus of the agitation[5] that led to a more serious outbreak of burgher discontent in the town of Vézelay, and the description he gives of this servile migrant to the town is accurate for the type of mobile, talented, lowborn servant/trader/*ministerialis*[6] who appears in our documents among the earliest leaders of the urban movements towards autonomy from feudal restrictions. Hibbert comments:

"Two processes are involved in the formation of the (new, urban) patriciate, the internal transformation of an old dominant class and the recruitment of new families from the more successful merchants and artisans, who were often immigrants or the descendants of immigrants . . . in the earlier stages of town development there was often a class between the actual lords on the one hand and agricultural workers, craftsmen, petty traders, porters, innkeepers and the like, on the other. . . . The economic position of the group was intimately associated with the possession of land and feudal office. At the same time its members were willing to take advantage of any opportunity to improve their position—by leasing their land or renting the buildings they had constructed on it, by letting out stalls in the market place, by farming mints,

---

[1] *Major Chronicle* below 2 §18.

[2] Above 31n.6. See also the perceptive remarks of Bloch (1975: 75ff.; 1961: chap. 19, esp. 262–63): "Subject for generations to chevage and to several other 'customs' which were generally held to be inconsistent with freedom, the members of several burgher communities of northern France in the thirteenth century refused nevertheless to allow themselves to be treated as serfs. . . ."

[3] Among these we may mention the following: Peter the prior, Garnerius the subprior, Hugh the chamberlain, the cellarer (whose name has not been preserved), the cook Benedict (a lay oblate?), Bardelin the forester (a layman), the prefect Hugh (who exercised jurisdictional power in the monastery), the *decanus* (who, often with the prefect, carried out various duties such as assessing the *taille*, registering marriages, assessing the character of the guards for the vineyards selected by the burghers, supervising the division of the harvest, and receiving various payments and servile dues), the marshal, or constable (who supervised the stables), Rodulf the sacristan (who kept the official weights of the town, amongst other duties), and others (later to include an almoner [*helemosinarius*] and a refectorian [*refectorius*]).

[4] Graham (1918: chaps. 3 and 5); Bastard (1848; 1851: 352ff.); Bourquelot; Berlow (1971: chap. 4, 248ff., esp. 317–41, 375–82); Chérest (1862: 1: chaps. 4–7, Huygens 1976: 60-137). Berlow (1987: 155n.45 rebuts those historians who deny the existence of a commune at Vézelay.

[5] *Major Chronicle* 2 §9.

[6] Bloch (1967: chap. 3). See Arnold (1985) and (1986).

tolls or mills from the lord, by raising loans wherever required, and by engaging their capital in commercial and industrial enterprises beyond the scope of lesser men. Two things would happen to such a group, made up of quite wealthy men, used to freedom and possessing initiative, men accustomed also to running the affairs of the town on the lord's behalf, or at least to being consulted by him. What more natural than that they should be in the lead of movements for freedom from seigneurial control? The new municipal powers created economic and political opportunities of which they were in the best position to take advantage. Psychologically, socially and politically they were in the most suitable position to conduct a successful attack. Secondly, these men would probably have had an interest in trade from the earliest times. As seigneurial officers many of them were well-placed for controlling supplies to one of the best of the early markets, the feudal households. . . ."[1]

We may compare this description with Augustin Thierry's description of Hugh of St. Peter: "The extent of his commercial connections put him in touch with the barons of the region (*contrée*) and even with the count of Nevers who was always pleased to welcome him and to receive presents from him. Obliged to live in a land of servitude (*pays de servitude*), Hugh of St. Peter bore ill his new condition and aspired to establish in the town (*bourgade*) of Vézelay a free government on the model of the great communes which flourished with such éclat in Provence, the county of Toulouse and along the Mediterranean coast. . . ."[2]

Hugh clearly did seem intimate with the count of Nevers and sought every pretext to use the latter's ambition to control the wealth of Vézelay and to administer justice to its inhabitants as a means of promoting his own power in the town.[3] A more blatant example of the type is Hugh Letard,[4] whom, though a tenant-in-chief of the monastery of Vézelay and of probable servile origin, the count "made his provost at Châtel-Censoir." In all this we are reminded of the fraternity between the count of Soissons some forty years earlier and *quidam rusticus Clementius nomine*, who lived in a village near Soissons and was considered by the count to be the wisest of men.[5] This same Clement drove the inhabitants of Soissons into the arms of the bishop, and for his pains (whatever they were), was dubbed a heretic, a weapon Pons seems to have been curiously reluctant to use against his own recalcitrant townsmen.[6]

The count of Nevers, in accordance, it would seem, with the fashion, proposed to the burghers of Vézelay the formation of a sworn confederacy under his protection[7] and after an initial refusal, and prompted, it seems, by a radical element in their midst,[8] the "execrated commune" was established under

---

[1] Hibbert (1953) as reprinted in Tierney (1974: 162–63). Cf. also Verhulst.

[2] Thierry (1851: 313).

[3] Thierry (1851), the sentence following that just translated: "This liberal thought was not without an element of personal ambition. . . ."

[4] *Major Chronicle* below 4 §§22 and 71. Cf. also §54.

[5] Guibert of Nogent, *Memoirs* (*De vita sua*) 3 §xvii (ed. Labande [1981], 428).

[6] Wakefield-Evans (1969: 101ff.).

[7] *Major Chronicle* 2 §17.

[8] Ibid., 2 §19, 3 §3 and cf. the list of names at the end of 3, especially those who

the patronage of the count, who chose its leaders/magistrates (called "consuls"[1]).

The innate weakness of the communal movement at Vézelay is suggested by the preponderant role that the count was thus forced to play in its inception,[2] and even by the (one would have thought unnecessary) advice to the people to break the abbot's banal power by using their own mills.[3] It is clear from Hugh of Poitiers' account that although the leaders of the communal revolution and the count had reasonably sophisticated goals, the burghers were concerned mainly with their tithes, poll-taxes and other servile dues, and the consequences of the abbot's banal monopolies.[4]

Berlow[5] believes the burghers may have nominated *their own* magistrates and that Hugh of Poitiers is demeaning their role by his reference to comital appointment: "His [Hugh's] account is hardly conclusive evidence as to the means of selecting the communal officials at Vézelay."[6] Bourquelot considers that the word "consuls" everywhere "implique l'élection populaire; tout concourt à prouver qu'il en est ainsi pour Vézelay."[7] In support of this view it should be pointed out that another Vézelay monk who later moved to St. Germain-des-Prés, in his own account of these events, which he inserted in a biography of King Louis VII, written c. 1171–1173 AD, castigates the *superbia* of the *burgenses* who "swore together that they would no longer undergo the lordship of the church" and "made amongst themselves a commune against their lord abbot, with the assent and counsel of the count of Nevers [*communiam ... adversus dominum suum abbatem ... assensu et consilio comitis Nivernensis*]."[8] The language here certainly suggests that the townsmen needed little encourage-

---

"swore to kill the abbot and constable" (*Guilelmi conestabuli*, Huygens [1976], 511).

[1] Thierry (1851: 320): "This particular influence from the Midi region on the little town of Vézelay can scarcely be explained other than by the presence of Hugh of St. Peter, this foreigner who had come to establish himself, with a zeal and capacity superior to those of his new fellow citizens." Berlow (1987: 144) denies that the term *consul* indicates the influence of southern France: the word is also used in central and northern France to describe the office of count (cf. the curious fragment of a "History of Anjou," not unlike the *Brief History* translated below, found in Halphen/Poupardin (1913: lxxxix) *cum tenuissem consolatum Andegavinum*. The use of the term *consul* in the *Major Chronicle* to describe secular (feudal) dignitaries in the Vézelay region, however, does not really support Berlow's view here. As a term for civic magistrates the word is overwhelmingly southern and Italian in context.

[2] *Major Chronicle* 2 §19.

[3] Ibid., 2 §24.

[4] Ibid.

[5] 1971: 319–20.

[6] Ibid., 320. Berlow considers (322) that the advice given by the count in regard to how the townsmen might bake their own bread and grind their own grain is a rhetorical exaggeration inserted by Hugh of Poitiers to discredit them: "this inconsistency in the narration of events by Hugh of Poitiers casts serious doubt on the sequence of events he presented" (323).

[7] Bouquelot 461; contrast Bastard (1851: 359).

[8] *De Glorioso rege Ludovico Ludovici filio* or *Historia gloriosi regis Ludovici*, ed. A Molinier (1887: 174–76, and cf. xxxv–xxxvi on the circumstances of authorship; Chérest 1:212–15; Huygens (1976: 112ff.) discusses the work. The *coniuratio* or "swearing together" was fundamental to new institutions in the Middle Ages: cf. Oexle.

ment from the count, though they were happy enough (largely, in all probability, because of his own urgings), to receive his counsel and agreement.

However, without wishing to imply that the townsmen were altogether unimportant stooges for the count,[1] the tentative nature of the "communal revolution" at Vézelay and the rather wild and random nature of the acts of violence committed against the abbot and his officials do seem to confirm the picture being presented by the chronicler Hugh. Even Berlow[2] describes the townsmen as "complete novices at self-government." The social origins of the communal leaders also suggests rusticity and lack of sophistication.[3] The same conclusion is recommended not only by the evident defeat of communal aspirations at Vézelay, but also by the curious absence of links between the burgher revolutionaries and heresy, and by an equally curious failure of the burghers to respond when the heretics *did* finally enter their town[4]: then, as at Soissons in the second decade of the century, church and populace closed ranks to exclude the "alien filth" of heresy. In other areas heretical ideas served to sharpen popular resistance to abbatial or episcopal seigneuries.

Links between communal and heretical dissent are, however, fragile and difficult to assess. Frederick Engels made the obvious initial assumptions when he asserted (in 1850) that "all the generally voiced attacks against feudalism, above all the attacks on the church, and all revolutionary, social and political doctrines, had mostly and simultaneously to be theological heresies" or (in 1894) that "the first rebellions of oppressed peasants and especially urban plebeians (in) the middle ages ... like all medieval mass movements, inevitably wore a religious mask and appeared to aim at the restoration of primitive Christianity in the face of rampant corruption, but very solid mundane interests were always concealed behind the religious exaltation."[5] Since Engels's time assessments have varied,[6] and the recent comments of Stephen Johnson are therefore very pertinent:

"The situation at Vézelay, like that in any medieval community, grew out of custom and precedent. Local conditions were important. In Laon the

---

[1] Bastard (1848: 548; 1851: 364).

[2] 1971: 323.

[3] See *Major Chronicle* 3 §7 below, and the comments of Latouche in regard to the situation at Le Mans, in Appendix E below. Berlow (1987: 150-51): "Merchants involved in long-distance trade and money-lenders, those representatives of the newly developing commercial class, were conspicuous by their absence [at Vézelay]." Indeed, argues Berlow, such persons as may be said to have represented these latter groups in Vézelay society, "rather than being the revolutionary bearers of progress on the political scene, were, instead, a conservative force, swept into power in the wake of popular uprisings which they then contributed to control ... the sharp division between rural and urban society, which characterized the later medieval world was the indirect result of, not the cause of, the communal movement."

[4] Ibid., 4 §78 below.

[5] *Peasant War in Germany* (1926; NY: 1966, 1976: 42); *History of Primitive Christianity*, in *Marx-Engels, Pre-Capitalist Socio-Economic Formations, a Collection* (Moscow: Progress Publishers, 1979) 483-84. See too Russell (1965: 232): "Dissidence was incontrovertibly bound up with the great communal movement of the 11th and 12th centuries when the towns revolted against their lords, who often were bishops."

[6] See Evans (1931), Cohn (1970: chap. 3), Russell (1965: chap. 9), and Nelson (1980).

bishop and nobles were against the commune, in both Amiens and Soissons a bishop supported the commune against the count, while at Vézelay the count supported the commune against the abbot. In spite of the fact that resistance to communes was strong, especially among churchmen, the episcopal cities were among some of the earliest communes, for example, Cambrai, Arras, Noyon. Communes were generally regarded as challenges to established rights, an overthrowing of God's order and a threat to finances. In general, reports to the Holy See confirm this atmosphere of distrust. However, in spite of this, relations between church and commune were not always hostile. Local conditions sometimes encouraged the formation of communes by church authorities, usually as a method of reestablishing order or a means of overcoming secular power. Such was the case at Beauvais, Amiens, Noyon, Soissons and Senlis. It is in the light of these temporal relations that the spiritual relations of church and laity must be set. It is obvious that many conflicts grew out of the temporal affairs of the church and that these conflicts neither constituted heresy nor, necessarily, led to heresy. . . . It is important to note that the lower strata of society did not produce heresy, either consciously or accidentally, but because of their social and religious condition they offered enthusiastic reception to charismatic leaders in both town and countryside during the eleventh and twelfth centuries. In short, the poor were incited to heresy, and in towns where traditional means of authority were weakened, or in rural areas where the presence of authority was lacking, this incitement went relatively unchecked. Cohn points out that it was amongst the poor that preachers claiming to be a semi-divine being or a messiah gained their greatest acceptance. . . .[1] Is it therefore possible that without Arnold of Brescia, the episodes of communal violence associated with his name in Brescia and Rome during the 1130s and 1140s would have been cases of communal conflict only, with no hint of heresy? In the years before 1167 in Vézelay, the townsmen, in their pursuit of communal privileges, committed acts of violence and sacrilege against the clergy and church, but, in the absence of any charismatic reformer, the conflict was neither directed towards nor perceived as heresy by either the clerical authorities or the rebellious townsmen. One is thus tempted to ask whether Brescia, Rome, Le Mans and Antwerp would have been other Vézelays but for the presence of Arnold, Henry and Tanchelm."[2]

Certainly Vézelay in the 1130s, 1140s, and 1150s was off-course for leading charismatic heretical figures, and it seems to have abounded with formal, ecclesiastical leadership; perhaps too its urban/industrial development was limited when compared with districts such as Lombardy, Flanders, and southern France. However, *some* significance must be attached to the fact that the burghers of Vézelay did *not* seek to demolish the *spiritual* authority of their abbot, even at the height of their zeal to demolish his *political* and *economic* authority. Were the Vézelay communards simply beginners in the matter of contesting ecclesiastical power, or were they, at bottom, conservatively pious?

What, in sum, does the Vézelay instance contribute to the debate about the

---

[1] Cohn (1970: 51).

[2] Johnson (1989: 34–35, 52, 46–47) (slightly emended). See Appendix E below for the case of Le Mans.

communal movement in twelfth-century Europe? In the past, leading scholars and writers seem to have thought it offered great insight: in 1825 Francois Pierre Guillaume Guizot (1787–1874) made a translation of the Vézelay *Major Chronicle* for inclusion in a *Collection des Mémoires relatives à l'histoire de France*. Guizot's vast output as an historian, and his extensive career in politics (leading up to his tenure of the prime-ministership of France under King Louis Philippe 1840–1848) prevent the student from finding any useful notice of his concern with the Vézelay chronicle in any of the standard works on his career,[1] but it is worth noting in the present context what seems to have drawn the politician/historian to the twelfth-century work. Guizot's own preface alerts us to his primary interest: "It is one of the extremely rare chronicles which assist us to understand the origin of the communes and their struggles with their powerful neighbors ... we do not possess details so exact and animated about any other commune, unless it be Laon, where Guibert of Nogent is our guide...."[2] In the same period of his life, the first half of the 1820's, Guizot wrote the original lectures later published as his *History of the origin of representative government in Europe*, and the preface he wrote to this work, after the abortive 1848 revolution, betrays his concern for "the alliance of free institutions with hereditary monarchy" ... "the union of monarchy and liberty ... [where] lies our haven."[3] Is it too far-fetched to see in the Vézelay story exactly these elements: the struggle of the townsmen against their abbot for free institutions, the intervention of the monarchy as the guarantor of the "liberty" of the church, the very monarchy that had already begun to emerge as the guarantor of communal liberties,[4] the very monarchy that was the ancestor of that under which Guizot himself, born of an honorable protestant family, served?

Monarchy and bourgeoisie played, in fact, crucial roles for Guizot. "Monarch and burgher [writes Weintraub[5]] were indispensable as the vectors in the process of action and counteraction which produced the first flowering of European civilization in the twelfth century.... *La grande société* [initiated by the twelfth-century bourgeoisie] ... was the finest and the most precious

---

[1] For example, Johnson (1963). See also Weintraub ([1966] 1969: 75ff.).

[2] Guizot (1969: 7). Guizot "was a prodigious consumer of documents and labored extensively on behalf of the systematic gathering of sources" (Weintraub [1966/1969]: 104).

[3] Guizot (1852: vii). Weintraub ([1966] 1969: 77, 90).

[4] See Appendix F below. Weintraub (93) points out that when Guizot passed beyond "the early formative centuries of European civilization, the period from the fourth to the tenth century"—a period with which his historical researches were much preoccupied—"he concentrated upon the 'real revolutions,' the great crises, those axial points where a new experiment in balancing the tendencies was undertaken." To some extent, the Vézelay events must have formed such a crisis in Guizot's mind. Cf. Weintraub (105) for Guizot's interest in "royal ordinances and town laws": "it was his habit to intersperse his lectures with extensive quotations from his sources." Compare Ralph Miliband, *Marxism and Politics* (Oxford, 1977: 189; as cited in Graham Maddox, *The Hawke Government and Labor Tradition* [Penguin, 1989]: 185) " ... the civic freedoms which, however inadequately and precariously, form part of bourgeois democracy are the products of centuries of unremitting popular struggles...."

[5] See 110ff.

result of the civilizatory process.... The third estate was for Guizot the symbol and the representative of such a society.... Until the twelfth century this 'principle of society' had no effective spokesman. Then the towns and the communal movement became its vehicle in the medieval context. In the towns and in the free association of the communal movement those men came together who could not find satisfaction in the stationary life of the rural districts and who were not willing to bow to the assertion of private will by force.... From 'weak, despised, almost imperceptible beginnings ... by continuous movement and incessant labor' the middle class had built up modern society. Order and liberty were fruitfully balanced."

Guizot was not alone in these interests. In his *Lettres sur l'histoire de France*, the earliest edition of many of which dates back to 1820, Jacques Nicolas Augustin Thierry (1795–1856) devotes three chapters (letters) to the Vézelay story, told in more or less summary form from Hugh of Poitiers' *Major Chronicle*, but *not* using the French translation by Guizot, which was presumably not available in 1820. In the preface to the first collected edition of his *Lettres*, Thierry mentions the two themes with which they are in the main concerned: "la formation de la nation française, et la révolution communale"[1]: *twelve* of his letters are devoted to the history of the medieval communes, and a thirteenth is entitled "On the history of national assemblies."

For these early French historians, then, working in the wake of the anti-feudal French revolution and under the restored "liberal" monarchy, the origins of free institutions formed an important topic, and the long and detailed narrative contained in the Vézelay chronicle was too good an illustration of what was involved in the struggle against feudal institutions to pass by without close attention and translation for "popular" consumption. The generations immediately following Guizot and Thierry continued this interest: the debates of Léon de Bastard and Bourquelot seem quaint to us nowadays, but whether or not there actually *were* communal institutions at Vézelay in the 1150s seemed important in the 1850s. Modern historians have retained some interest in these topics, but their concerns are wider and they are less passionate advocates of the revolutionary or constitutional cause. For many (to quote Witt) "there was little about the communes that was revolutionary in intent."[2] "Even in the most independent, rich, and splendid cities of Italy very few revolutionary ideas about society and politics seem to have been produced before the fourteenth century," argues Susan Reynolds.[3] At Le Mans, St. Quentin, Beauvais and Noyon "communes were formed about 1081, 1099, and 1108 respectively, and they seem to have been formed along the same lines. All were recognized by outside authorities to a greater or lesser degree

---

[1] Thierry (1851: 1).

[2] Witt (1971: 984), speaking for such historians as Vermeesch (e.g., 1966: 109, 112), Kennelly (1963), and others—see Head and Landes (1987: 385ff.)—who find the general context of the "peace movement" more enticing than the framework of often violent anti-feudal "revolution." Contrast Petit-Dutaillis ([1947] 1970: 73ff., 78–79, etc.).

[3] (1984: 156). See, however, the strictures of L. Genicot in *Le Moyen Age* 92 (1986: 448).

5

INTRODUCTION

and all look pretty unrevolutionary."[1] "What townspeople wanted when they formed communes and took oaths, then, was not a new 'right of association' but better protection for themselves, individually and collectively, against oppression. Inevitably that meant asking for greater freedom to run their communities, but since all government was supposed to be consultative, since officers were supposed to be appointed with the consent of the governed, and since towns tended to develop autonomy as they grew in population and wealth, the first demands to appoint their own officials may not always have seemed very revolutionary. The degree of revolution depended more on the attitude of lords to the first, often modest, demands that towns made than on the nature of the demands themselves."[2]

This last is the point we should grasp, and it is well illustrated at Vézelay. Where ecclesiastical lords dug in their heels and insisted upon their divine autonomy and liberty to dominate their seigneuries without let or hindrance from anyone, revolutions tended to be inevitable. Thus, at Vézelay, the abbot and his advisers are once again[3] seen to be swimming against the tide of change in twelfth-century society: upholding notions of ecclesiastical liberty that were themselves shrill and new, they were nevertheless, in the perspective of time, bastions of the sort of feudal privilege that the later revolutionaries of 1789 were to sweep away forever.[4]

In the final analysis, however, the reader of these pages can only be invited to make up his or her own mind as to what was at stake at Vézelay in the middle of the twelfth century, and how important it was. Each historical episode is a moment in time in its own right, and no more deserves to be elided into a rounded generalization applicable to an era or country than does any one individual deserve to be elided into a statement about others. As Guizot himself said, we have no fuller and more circumstantial account of the anguish and violence associated with the clash between groups, individuals, and classes in a crucial century of change than the Vézelay story: may our readers step into the past as boldly as did Francois Guizot and Augustin Thierry, and let them not be daunted by the cautions of the modern academic!

[C] Culture in Twelfth-Century Vézelay

The Sermons of Julien of Vézelay

A reader whose knowledge of Vézelay in the twelfth century was confined to Hugh of Poitiers' chronicle might think it a very worldly place. All its energies, it would seem, were devoted to its struggles with those various enemies

---

[1] Reynolds (1984: 176). See Appendix E below for Le Mans.
[2] Ibid., 182.
[3] See the remarks made towards the end of the Introduction, above.
[4] See Mukherjee and Ward (1989).

who attempted to infringe upon its liberties. Any intellectual skills the monks had, such a reader might think, must have been devoted to poring over ancient charters in the hope of finding further confirmation of its cherished liberty. Of that pursuit of spiritual peace and understanding which had animated St. Benedict a reader will find little mention in Hugh of Poitiers.[1] The more general intellectual ferment summed up by historians with the phrase "the twelfth-century renaissance" does not seem to have made any great impact on our author either.[2]

Such conclusions, however, would underestimate even Hugh of Poitiers, to say nothing of his contemporary Julien, of whose sermons something will be said below. These two monks demonstrate that learning and culture were not ignored in the pursuit of political ends. The monks of Vézelay did not devote all their energies to squabbles with rivals, nor did they ignore the traditional monastic love of learning. Theirs was not a great center of intellectual achievement, but they did not fail to train their monks and novices in the seven liberal arts. Important evidence of their cultural concerns is provided by the physical remains of the churches of Vézelay, which offer convincing evidence that the monks there were abreast of architectural and sculptural trends that have left a lasting testimony of a grandeur that speaks of the twelfth century's conception of man and his relationship to God.

Hugh of Poitiers shows himself to be a competent, if rather plodding, writer of Latin, one with a wide vocabulary and a thorough knowledge of grammar and syntax. He was very familiar with the Bible and gives intimations of an acquaintance with some common tags from standard classical authors, even if he did know these only through convenient anthologies and not through first-hand acquaintance.[3] More significantly Hugh shows himself to be at ease with the whole series of complex legal wrangles in which Vézelay was embroiled. He uses legal jargon confidently and grasps easily the legal principles at stake in the various conflicts on which he reports. His legal train-

---

[1] On monastic spirituality generally, see Leclercq (1961). On Benedict himself, see, apart from his *Rule*, the *Life* by Gregory the Great to be found as Book 2 of his *Dialogues*. For an analysis of the conflict between secular and spiritual concerns in the twelfth-century abbey of Christ Church at Canterbury, see Scott (1972).

[2] For a conspectus of recent views and references to the substantial literature on this theme see Benson and Constable (1982). Note that another Poitevin, Aimery Picaud, around 1140, at Asquins (below the hill of Vézelay) wrote a major pilgrimage work, the celebrated *Liber Sancti Iacobi* or *Codex Calixtinus* Huygens (1976: xxiv n. 40). Books 4 and 5 of this codex are now available to Italian readers as: *Compostella: Guida del pellegrino di san Giacomo; storia di Carlo Magno e di Orlando*, trans. D. Tuniz (Milan, 1989), whilst Book 5 has long been available in both French and the original Latin (Vielliard [1938] 1978). Michel Huglo (*Scriptorium* 43 [1989]: 152-55) summarizes "Le symposium de Pittsburgh sur le codex Calixtinus de Compostela" (Univ. of Pittsburgh 3-5 Nov. 1988). Cox: ". . . during the abbacy of Alberic, Aimery Picaud, while representing himself as Olivier d'Asquins and serving as the priest in the church of Saint-Jacques at Asquins, located at the foot of the Vézelay hill, wrote the famous *Liber Sancti Jacobi*. . . . It is also possible that the author of the epic *Girart de Roussillon* was living and writing at Vézelay during the first half of the twelfth century, a deduction based on the detailed attention given in the poem to the construction of a magnificent church of the Magdalene there."

[3] Some of these classical tags are recorded in the notes to the *Major Chronicle*. For a compilation of the most common of such tags see Walther (1963-70).

ing exemplifies an important[1] current of the "twelfth-century renaissance." These intellectual skills must have been developed in the monastic school where he would have received his early education: there are sufficient indications in the *Major Chronicle* itself and in the sermons of Julien of the existence of such a school—indeed all monasteries needed to educate their novices in the elements of Latin.[2]

Apart, however, from Hugh of Poitiers, there are only two other twelfth-century writers from Vézelay whose work is extant. The first of these is abbot Renaud, who wrote a prose *Life* of his uncle, St. Hugh, abbot of Cluny, and a metrical summary of his *Life* in some two hundred verses.[3] These are valuable works which, although they contain standard hagiographical themes and miracle stories, cast interesting light on Hugh's activities as a church builder, a monastic reformer and an influential figure in Western Christendom.[4] There is one reference to Vézelay in the *Life*, with Renaud asking rhetorically: "Who returned the church of the blessed Mary Magdalene at Vézelay to its former state of regular order, but that blessed man?"[5] But Renaud's writing must be seen as a product of Cluny, where he spent the years between his profession in 1088 and his promotion to the abbey of Vézelay in 1106, not as a reflection of the interests of Vézelay. Indeed, so great was his devotion to Cluny that, possibly in deference to the Cluniac custom of denying the title abbot to the heads of dependent houses, he began his *Life* by disclaiming the title abbot of Vézelay: "For all the sons of the church of Cluny, your brother Renaud, not so much abbot as servant of the church of Vézelay, wishes salvation in the Lord."[6]

The other Vézelay writer whose works survive is of more relevance to an understanding of the environment in which Hugh wrote. This is Julien of Vézelay, twenty-seven of whose sermons survive, preserved complete in two manuscripts and selectively in some eight others.[7] Although he was not educated in Vézelay and in fact probably came there quite late in life,[8] Julien delivered all the sermons that are preserved, in the chapter at Vézelay[9] and, perhaps more surprisingly, the sermons themselves were collected and pub-

---

[1] See, for instance, Brooke (1976: 75–89) and Haskins ([1927] 1970: chapter 7).

[2] The record of the papal hearing of 1151 refers to *Hugo de Scola Virzeliacensis monacus et presbiter* (*Major Chronicle* 1, §4; Huygens [1976]: 401); see below for the evidence from Julien's sermons; on the situation generally see Leclercq (1961).

[3] Both printed in *PL* 159, cols. 893–906 and, for the metrical summary, cols. 905–10. Renaud's *Life*, praised by Barlow for its independence, is analysed along with other *Lives* in Barlow (1980).

[4] Hugh's participation in the Council of Rheims (1049) and his role in the conflict betwen Gregory VII and the emperor Henry IV are described in cols. 903–4, for instance.

[5] Col. 899C.

[6] Col. 893B.

[7] The manuscripts are described in Vorreux (1972: 29–39). See Saxer (1975: 202ff.).

[8] *Sermon* 24 contains all that we know of Julien's life. In it he refers to his early entry into the monastic life and the numerous monasteries in which he had served before coming to Vézelay. See also the discussion by Vorreux (1972: 8–11).

[9] *sermunculos, quos in capitulis dixeram*. See Julien's remarks in the prologue to his *Sermons*, ibid., 42.

lished at the instigation of Abbot Pons.[1] This encouragement of a sermon
writer shows a different Pons from the crusader of the *Major Chronicle*, whose
whole-hearted defense of Vézelay's interests against anyone who might challenge them would seem to have left him little time or energy to take note of
Julien's sermons. But clearly he was not interested solely in the material welfare of his monastery; his concern was also to foster its spiritual well-being.

Most surprising, for anyone familiar with the turbulent history of the monastery in the twelfth century, is the fact that there is no reflection of this
turbulence in Julien's sermons. They read like sermons delivered to an audience whose sole concern was its spiritual well-being, not the latest attack by
the count of Nevers or the outrageous demands of the burghers. There are
only a few oblique hints in the sermons that a knowing reader might interpret
as a response to contemporary events. Towards the end of *sermon* 1, after a
long excursus on the importance of silence, there are a couple of sentences
in which Julien castigates those who seek to sow discord among the brothers
by complaints and grumbling.[2] The aside seems somewhat out of place, particularly in its emphatic position almost at the end of the sermon, and could
have been prompted by contemporary events: that there certainly was dissension among the monks is revealed by the events following Abbot Renaud's
departure and by the conspiracy against Abbot William recorded in Book 4
of the *Major Chronicle*. *Sermon* 3 contains another warning to those who would
seek to divide the monks and disturb their fraternal peace: they will not
inhabit the heavenly Jerusalem.[3]

It seems that the troubles that beset Vézelay concerned Julien only in so far
as they might disturb the internal discipline of the monastery. Of external
events with which we are familiar from the *Major Chronicle* only one is mentioned in a sermon. This occurs in *sermon* 23 on the text of John 12:31 ("Now
is the judgment of this world; now shall the prince of this world be cast out").
Here Julien discusses judgments of various kinds: the Last Judgment, the
need to judge oneself, the judgment of the monastic chapter and, finally, that
judgment of the world exercised by the one who has the power of the sword.
When a guilty person is apprehended by one who has the power of the
sword, the guilty either has his eyes torn out or is decapitated or is mutilated
or is hanged. It is surely right to see here a reference to the grisly blinding by
the monks of a man who had insulted one of their number, an event which
so angered the count and had such a dramatic impact on the lives of the
Vézelay monks.[4]

This shocking blinding aside, Julien makes no reference to the troubled
events of Pons's abbacy. What then is the subject matter of his sermons? To

---

[1] Also in the prologue: *Rogatu plurimo caritas vestra [Pontii] me compulit, sermunculos . . . colligere et . . . redigere.* Ibid.

[2] *Sermon* 1, ibid., 64, *quanto vanior est detrahentis, murmurantis, seminantis inter fratres
discordias.*

[3] *Tu si murmuriosa aut inuida vel iracunda mente a fraterna pace divideris, non habitas in
Jerusalem . . . ;* ibid., 98.

[4] *Sermon* 23, ibid., 528. See *Major Chronicle* 2 §8; Huygens (1976: 425). On the other
hand, the count was delighted at the excuse presented by the blinding to intensify his
persecution of the monastery.

a large extent they exemplify the remarks of an anonymous contemporary of his: "In church we receive doctrine, in chapter, discipline."[1] Julien was most particularly concerned with urging on his auditors the importance of their moral behavior: sins are castigated, virtues upheld and the rewards for each plainly spelled out.[2] A special concern of his is the souls of adolescents in the monastery.[3] A number of sermons are specifically addressed to them, and several others contain warnings to young monks to be wary of the sin of lust, to which they are especially susceptible—but lest the older monks become complacent he does not neglect to remind them that the memory of fornication can tempt them to sin, even within the holy walls of the monastery itself.[4]

Sermon 13, designed especially to appeal to the young monks grappling with the Latin language, is a good example of a sermon of moral exhortation.[5] It is based on the text of Psalm 36:27, "Avoid evil and do good" (*Declina a malo et fac bonum*). By playing ingeniously on the ambiguity of *declina*— avoid or decline (grammatically)—Julien was able to give a thorough disquisition on sins and their avoidance and at the same time to reinforce the elements of Latin grammar. The sermon begins with a comparison between the five declensions of Latin and the five types of sins which must be avoided; Julien first analyzes these in some detail and then points out that *istae declinationes* (these avoidances) have, like the declensions of grammar their *casus* (cases/falls). The first *casus* is the nominative in grammar, pride among the sins, then the genitive case and disobedience engendered by pride, and so on through the six cases of Latin grammar. By the end of the sermon his listeners have been given a comprehensive analysis of sins and how to avoid them, their interest maintained as much by speculation about how the analogy would be continued, as by the subject matter.[6]

This sort of extended allegory was not Julien's usual style; more common was his practice of taking a text for his sermon and then proceeding through it word by word drawing out its moral and allegorical significance. A typical example of this is *sermon* 7, on Genesis 49:20 ("Out of Asher his breed shall be fat, and he shall offer dainties to the kings"). Asher is interpreted as symbolizing Christ, who was rich (fat) in mercy, and so examples of Christ's

---

[1] Quoted by Lebreton (1955: 119). "*In ecclesia doctrinam, in capitulo disciplinam suscipimus.*"

[2] See, for example, *sermons* 23–25 on virtue and its rewards and 12–14 on sins and 21 on the Last Judgment. Apart from these, all the sermons contain fervent moral exhortations.

[3] See, for example, *sermons* 13, 15, 17, 18, and 26. Julien offers a definition of *adolescentia* in *sermon* 17; it is, he says, equivalent to *iuuentus* and is the age between one who is a baby/child and one who is old/senile ("*adolescentia vel iuuentus . . . vitae humanae mediatrix est, duas antecedentes, id est infantiam et pueritiam, duasque sequentes, senectam et senium . . .*" [ibid., 364–66]).

[4] *Sermon* 14, ibid., 242–44.

[5] On the allegorical method exhibited in this and most of Julien's other sermons see Leclercq (1961); Smalley (1970: esp. 1–36). Note Julien's own criticisms of the Jews for their concentration on the literal meaning of the Scriptures (". . . *stultitiam Judaeorum qui, Scripturarum superficie contenti . . . ,*" etc.), *sermon* 18, ibid., 376.

[6] *Sermon* 13, ibid., 264–84. Compare Ziolkowski (1985).

mercy are given; the bread is really the body of Christ and is for the spirit not the body; this leads to a discussion of the importance of preparing oneself to be worthy of receiving the bread: There is also a brief discussion (springing from bread being the body of Christ) of the contrast between faith and reason and of the doctrine of substance and accident; the kings are defined not in political terms but as those who rule their own body (that is, their king-dom) justly and with discipline: "the tyrant of sin who threatens to overthrow you must be fought off with prayer, fasts and vigils; if you do not succeed, the dainties will not be offered to you, you will be told not to touch them."[1]

This crude summary should provide good evidence of what a flexible form the monastic sermon was. The freedom to interpret texts allegorically and morally meant that any biblical text provided opportunities for the preacher to discuss important moral and theological questions. In the same sermon monks could have right behavior urged on them and be instructed in the finer points of contentious theological issues. All this was achieved without sacrificing fluency of expression and naturalness of tone—Julien's sermons have some of that mellifluous quality characteristic of the sermons of his greater contemporary St. Bernard of Clairvaux.[2] Homiletic sermons of this kind were soon supplanted by the much more rigid school sermon, which an-nounced its own structure, proceeded step by logical step, summarizing as it went, towards its triumphant and logical conclusion. The latter may have been more pleasing to the dialectician, but did not give as much satisfaction to the rhetorician.[3]

The freedom of organization and interpretation that Julien's form allowed enabled him to combine moral teaching and doctrinal analysis in one sermon. Generally, as in the two sermons described above, moral exhortation predom-inated, but the collection does contain some sermons in which theological in-struction seems to have been the main purpose. There are firstly those sermons written for particular festivals—Easter, Pentecost, Ascension, for in-stance[4]—and expounding their theological significance. But even here Julien took the opportunity to exhort his auditors to right behavior: *sermon* 10, for Easter, dwells on Christ's crucifixion and his final triumph, but in it sinners are reminded vividly of the terrible punishment that awaits them.[5]

Can any conclusions about Julien's audience—the monks of Vézelay—be drawn from his sermons? Apart from the obvious, but important, point that the monks were not so embroiled in the political and ecclesiastical struggles of their monastery as to neglect their spiritual welfare, nothing surprising emerges. There was obviously a flourishing school in the monastery and a good number of young monks; more strangely, some of the monks seem to have been illiterate, although this must presumably be interpreted to mean

---

[1] *Sermon* 7, ibid., 170–92.

[2] For a good example of the eloquence of Julien's style see *sermon* 1. St. Bernard's sermons, renowned for the beauty of their style, have recently been re-edited by Leclercq. Some relevant issues are discussed in Leclercq (1962, 1966, 1969).

[3] See Rouse (1979) and Murphy (1974: chap. 6).

[4] *Sermons* 10, 11, 12.

[5] *Sermon* 10, p. 212.

unable to write rather than unable to understand Latin.[1] Alongside the latter there must have been many monks whose appreciation of Latin was quite sophisticated. It was these who would have appreciated the grammatical analogy cited above and enjoyed the other plays on words in which Julien indulged.[2] It must have been to these monks too that Julien recommended the reading of Plato's *Timaeus* and certain works of Cicero and Seneca. Certainly, he noted especially the profundity of their ideas and their relevance to the living of an honest life, but he did not neglect to comment on the beauty and eloquence of their style.[3] In short, while there is no evidence of a particularly rich literary culture at Vézelay in the twelfth century, the sermons of Julien indicate that the monastery was not culturally impoverished.

The chief glory of Vézelay's cultural achievement in the twelfth century, however, can still be seen today in the physical remains of the wonderful church of Mary Magdalene, although its medieval bases were overlaid by the "restoration" of Viollet-le-Duc in the mid-nineteenth century. In particular, the nave and side aisles and the sculptured capitals and doorways, especially the central tympanum, "the most marvellous Romanesque doorway in France,"[4] provide wonderful evidence of the skills of the masons and artists who worked on this basilica (the *maior ecclesia* or "greater church" of Hugh) in the first half of the twelfth century. To do justice to so important a Romanesque building "a whole volume and especially large and numerous drawings and pictures"[5] would be needed, but all that can be done here is to identify the various churches of Vézelay and to give a timetable of their construction.

The building of the main basilica, the church of Mary Magdalene, was begun by Abbot Artaud, who was probably inspired by the building program at Cluny where he had been a monk, although the style of architecture at Vézelay incorporates features which distinguish it from the work done there.[6] The original Carolingian church was inadequate to accommodate the crowds of pilgrims who flocked to worship at the shrine of Mary Magdalene, and so in about 1096 Artaud initiated work on a new church. Of Artaud's church, which was dedicated on 21 April 1104, little survives: probably only the transept, as the choir was demolished and replaced in the late twelfth century and the nave had been left in its original Carolingian state to ensure continuity of

---

[1] *Sermons* 2 and 21. Vorreux (1972: 25) doubts that any of the auditors were quite unable to understand Latin; but Lebreton (1955: 123) thinks it possible that they were and cites an unpublished sermon of Maurice de Sully on the same theme.

[2] *Sermons* 11, 17, 18, and 25.

[3] *Sermon* 18, p. 378, *ut taceam eloquentiae leporem et cultum*.

[4] Graham (1918: 36).

[5] Vogade (1987: 31).

[6] According to Aubert (1966: 447), the church belongs to a type different from that of the major church in the area, that of Cluny. Instead of three stages (main nave arches, blind arcade or triforium, and clerestory, with barrel vaults), Vézelay has two stages (main arcade and windows) and is groin-vaulted. The Vézelay nave is less than one-third the length of the (whole) Cluny III church, and, according to James (1986: 293), "Vézelay was the first large church in France to be built with the nave and aisles covered by groin vaults." For further detail, see Conant (1966: 187, 192–93, 209–11, 215–16, 218, 245, 390, 463). On the stages of construction for the abbey church of the Magdalene, it is essential now to consult Saulnier-Stratford. See also Cox in Aspects [F] below.

worship. What is clear is that the construction must have been an expensive undertaking because Artaud himself was assassinated two years after its dedication, a victim of the townspeople's resentment of the heavy financial burden that they had been forced to bear to ensure its completion.

Further building work was required soon after, as a result of a disastrous fire in 1120 which killed a number of pilgrims and destroyed the Carolingian nave of the church. Artaud's successor Renaud began the construction of the nave in about 1120, and it was brought to completion during the abbacy of Alberic, probably in about 1140. It survives today as an outstanding example of Romanesque architecture, its beauty bearing witness to the vision of its designer and the skills of its builders. The work of the narthex was somewhat later, 1140–1150, and the choir was completed at the end of the twelfth century.[1] In short, throughout most of the first half of the twelfth century, while the monks were arguing with the count of Nevers, the abbot of Cluny, and the bishop of Autun, their church was being transformed into an inspiring basilica. They cannot have been indifferent to this work and their pride in its success may have been another factor that promoted the self-confidence that enabled them to take on these challenges.

But the grandeur of the nave and the narthex does not exhaust the artistry of the church of Mary Magdalene. The superb and detailed sculptures on the capitals and doorways of the church provide a lesson in art as theology: biblical characters and scenes are brought to life from the stone of Burgundy. The most famous of these sculptures is the renowned central tympanum on the main central doorway, which depicts "the serene, majestic vision of the Ascension combined with the Mission to the Apostles."[2] Although there has been disagreement about the interpretation of the tympanum, its splendor is beyond dispute. Some historians have seen the learned theology of Peter the Venerable behind the complex thought that the sculptural program manifests, on the grounds that he was prior at Vézelay before he left in 1120 and was surely consulted by Abbot Renaud, who was closely tied to Cluny where Peter had gone, when the abbot was planning the sculptures which were begun in about 1125.[3] Be that as it may, the reader must bear in mind that the deliberations of the monks and the various confrontations that involved them took place in a magnificent and finely decorated church whose construction had taken decades and involved great labor and cost.

---

[1] Apart from the references in the previous note see also Seidel (1981), Duby (1966), Calmette and David (1951), Delautre (1981), Berlow (1981: 327ff.), and Graham (1918: 34–46). Cox: ". . . since Hugh (of Poitiers) . . . represents the burghers as wishing to 'drive away tax collectors' [*exactores*], it is likely that (Pons) was trying to increase the abbey's revenues in various ways. These were the years that saw the construction of the splendid narthex and the new ribbed vaults in the tribunes of the basilica, which could well explain the need for more money (Robert Branner, *Burgundian Gothic Architecture* [London 1960: 193])."

[2] On the sculptural progam at Vézelay see Salvini (1969: illustrations 42 and 44–45, and pp. 315–16); Vogade (1987); Beckwith (1974: 214–18 and 252 [from which comes the quotation in our text]); Katzenellenbogen (1944); Taylor (1980); Brooke (1984: 92–93); and Berlow (1981: 330ff.).

[3] See Salet and Adhémar (1948: 132ff.) and Katzenellenbogen (1944: 151).

It is not just the church of Mary Magdalene that bears witness to the wealth
that flowed into Vézelay in the twelfth century and the cultural capital into
which that wealth was turned. To the same half century that saw the construction of the grand basilica belongs the building of the churches of Saint-
Étienne and Saint-Pierre-le-Haut (*Sanctus Petrus Superior*), both in the town but
separate from the monastic buildings. The latter was almost completely de
stroyed in the nineteenth century but the former still survives in part and
bears witness, with its remarkably vaulted interior of "great simplicity and
purity of style,"[1] to the aesthetic achievement of the town.[2] Also mentioned
in the *Major Chronicle* is the "Church of the Pilgrims," the location of which
has puzzled historians, some arguing that it was the narthex or porch of the
basilica itself,[3] others that it was the present nave of the basilica,[4] and still
others claiming that it was the chapel of the Hostelry which was also in the
main basilica.[5] The other church frequently mentioned in the *Major Chronicle*
is Saint-Père-sous-Vézelay (*Sanctus Petrus Inferior*) which was below (hence its
Latin name) the hill on which the town of Vézelay is situated—in the *Major
Chronicle* people are said to go down to or come up from it.[6] The present
church is described as "a beautiful and elegant Gothic Church of the 13th
century"[7]—"an unexpected bonus of coming to Vézelay ... a gem of Gothic
architecture ... the first sight of the shameless flamboyance of its tower
makes you catch your breath."[8] It is to the remains of these various churches
that we must look to help understand the cultural and religious ideals that inspired the monks of Vézelay when they were not plotting against their various
enemies.

---

[1] Vogade (1987: 26).

[2] The church of Saint-Pierre-le-Haut was within the town walls of Vézelay, halfway
between the basilica and the St. Stephen Gate. The nave was constructed c. 1150,
collapsed 1587, was restored, and remained in service until the revolution. In 1814 the
nave and choir were demolished (nowadays a car-park!), and the bell tower was transformed into a public clock tower in 1859. Saint-Étienne (dating from the early twelfth
century) lies immediately to the right as one ascends the principal street of Vézelay from
this gate. Secularized and partly demolished, the church had become by the nineteenth
century a warehouse and merchant's hall. See Vogade (1987: 27–28).

[3] Guizot (1969: 230–31) and Chérest.

[4] Berlow (1981: 333) and Graham (1918: 43).

[5] Huygens (1976: 149, 489, and 680); Salet and Adhémar (1948: 25 n. 2). Pierre
Baudouin kindly informs us by letter (1989): "Viollet-le-Duc a fait disparaître au XIXe
siècle dans sa restauration les traces du choeur des moines qui s'avancait fort avant dans
la nef: les quatres dernières travées étaient voûtées en gothique et formaient un seul
ensemble avec l'abside. Aujourd'hui seule demeure la dernière travée à titre de témoign-
age archéologique. Face à cette 'église des moines' se trouvait donc 'l'église des pélerins'
des six premières travées auxquelles nous pouvons ajouter la galilée. Point n'est besoin
d'inventer, comme Francis Salet, une nouvelle église qui n'a jamais existé."

[6] See *Major Chronicle* 4 §18 and §19 for instance.

[7] Vogade-Pouyaud, 31.

[8] Unless you find it covered with bagging and scaffolding (as one of the editors of the
present volume did recently!). Speaight (1990: 137).

[D] Relics and Pilgrimage at Vézelay

Next on the route which goes to St. James of Compostela past St. Léonard, the most meritworthy body of the blessed Mary Magdalene must first be revered by pilgrims, and justly so. For this is that glorious Mary who, in the house of Simon the leper, sprinkled with her tears the feet of our Saviour, dried them with her hair, and, kissing them, anointed them with her own precious perfume. It was for this that her many sins were forgiven her, since she greatly cherished Jesus Christ, her redeemer, the lover of all people. This is she who, after the Lord's ascension, left the coast near Jerusalem with the blessed Maximin, Christ's disciple, and other disciples of the Lord, for Provence, travelling by sea to the port of Marseilles. In this region she passed for some years an unmarried existence and eventually was buried at Aix by the same Maximin, now bishop of that town. After a very long time, a certain celebrated person, blessed for his adherence to the monastic life, Badilo by name, transferred her precious remains from Aix to Vézelay, where she has rested in honorable burial right up to this day. In that place a vast and most beautiful basilica and an abbey of monks is established. There sinners are forgiven their sins by God, for the love of her, sight is returned to the blind, the tongue of the mute is released, the lame are rendered upright, the possessed are exorcised and ineffable boons are bestowed upon many. Her holy solemnities are celebrated on July 22nd.

[*Liber Sancti Jacobi*, ed. Vielliard (1938/1978) 50–52.[1]]

Why were so many people interested in the affairs of Vézelay? To some extent the struggles that engaged the energies of the abbot and the monks—against their advocate, against their diocesan bishop, against Cluny, and against the citizens of their town—were taking place all over Europe. Other local quarrels, like those at Vézelay, also drew in the pope and the king; but that all these tensions and the attention of all these forces came to a head at Vézelay, which was rather out of the way even then,[2] suggests special circumstances. The proud determination of a community which was fiercely jealous of its rights accounts for the resistance of the monks to their ecclesiastical and secular enemies, just as the passion for independence of the burghers explains their violent rejection of abbatial authority. But these strong communal loyalties themselves have to be explained. The key to the monks' pride and the burghers' self-assertion was Vézelay's possession of the relics of Mary Magdalene, whose cult became popular in the eleventh century and flourished through-

---

[1] See below Appendix D n. 1 and *MGH Scriptores* 7 (Hannover 1846) 464.

[2] See the maps in Cohen (1980), which reveal that Vézelay was at the start of a pilgrimage route to Compostela but was not otherwise linked by convenient and frequently used roads to northern France.

out the twelfth century.[1] These were the very years of Vézelay's greatness, when
its wonderful church was built and its citizens prospered.

Vézelay's growth from the nondescript town of the mid-eleventh century to
the religious center where the Second Crusade was preached and excommunication pronounced against Henry II by Thomas à Becket coincided with the
great age of pilgrimage. All over Europe, churches which possessed the relics
of venerated saints were besieged by pilgrims seeking miracles, cures for illness, forgiveness of sins, or divine assistance of some other kind.[2] On the
feast-day of the resident saint and on other important church festivals the
crowds were at their greatest, but any unusual event could encourage the
hopeful to flock to a church.[3] A particularly vivid account of the multitudes
that might pour into a pilgrimage town is the following description of the
pilgrims visiting the tomb of St. Trond. "Such was its [the tomb of St.
Trond's] fame that for a good half mile around the little town all roads leading to the tomb and even fields and meadows were daily crowded with
pilgrims of all classes, ranging from the nobility to the humblest peasants,
above all on feast days. Those who, because of the great press, could not find
lodgings made shift to dwell in tents or shelters hastily put together with
branches and curtains.... Words fail to enumerate the offerings placed on
the altar. Nor can we give an account of all the beasts, horses, oxen, cows,
pigs, sheep and ewes brought thither, in number like the sands of the sea.
Nor can we assess the quantity and value of the fine linen, wax, bread and
cheeses. To gather in all the silverware and the pieces of money which poured
in without cease until nightfall several sacristans had to labor without
cease."[4] Even granting the hyperbole of this account it provides an indication
of what a financial boon pilgrims were to a town.

What were the pilgrims seeking? Above all they sought the help of the saint
whose relics were in the possession of the church being visited. There were,
of course, other motives for undertaking a pilgrimage—as a penance for sins

---

[1] See Saxer (1959) and Appendix D below.

[2] On saints and pilgrimage see Sumption (1975), Brooke (1984: chaps. 2-3), Ward
(1982), Finucane (1977), Weinstein (1982), Wilson (1983), and the bibliography in the
latter.

[3] *Major Chronicle* 4 §21 and §51 contain incidental accounts of the fervor that could be
aroused by relics. The *Compostela Guide* mentioned above (Aspects [C] 43n.2) and cited in
part at the head of the present chapter, is further evidence of the great popularity of relics
and pilgrimage. See also the role that relics played in oaths: *Major Chronicle* 4 §75 below.
See too P. J. Geary, "The Ninth-Century Relic Trade" (Obelkovich [1979: 8-20]); NCE, s.v.
"pilgrimages" and Solt (1987: 167ff, 205ff.). Cox: "Under Charlemagne a regular campaign had been mounted to give relics a central role in both secular and ecclesiastical life.
In 801 and 813 the canons of the council of Carthage (401 AD) were cited in support of
a requirement that all church altars contain relics, and each parish was ordered to institute
celebrations on the feast days of the saints whose relics were preserved there (Geary
[1978: 20, 42-44]). In 803 Charlemagne decreed that all oaths for whatever purpose be
sworn either in a church or upon relics, rather than upon beards, rings, or other such
objects (as had been ancient Germanic practice), and his throne at Aachen was filled with
compartments for relics." The ninth century thus saw a greatly increased demand for
relics and the Vézelay founders themselves applied to the pope in search of authentic
relics for religious foundations.

[4] Duby (1986: 1:94).

committed or even as an escape from the narrow confines of ordinary life, for instance—but most pilgrims came to venerate saintly relics. A saint was thought to inhabit the church which possessed his or her relics and so the pilgrims who worshipped at that church would win the favor of the saint.[1] Of course, to guarantee that favor and to ensure a favorable hearing of the pilgrim's particular request an offering would be made at the saint's shrine. The popularity of relics created a great demand for them and led to competition among churches as to which had the authentic relics of favored saints; nor was the theft of relics unknown, or considered a crime.[2] Although some saints were popular throughout the middle ages—Rome, Jerusalem when it was accessible, and Compostela were favorite destinations—other cults would arise suddenly, flourish, and then lose popularity as other saints became fashionable. Thus, in England the martyrdom of Becket created a new and formidable rival to established pilgrimage centers.[3] Vézelay flourished in the twelfth century because the relics of Mary Magdalene proved to be a potent attraction to pilgrims and the town became the starting point for one of the popular pilgrimage routes to Compostela.[4]

Puzzlement about the presence of such relics at Vézelay is not new. The author of the *Miracula* of Mary Magdalene, writing probably in the late eleventh century, responded to what must have been a matter of discussion even then. "Many people ask," he wrote, "how the body of St. Mary Magdalene, whose native land was Judaea, could have been translated to Gaul from a land so far away. To such doubts we may return a brief reply. All things are possible to God...."[5] In fact, a rather more lengthy explanation of this curiosity was developed at Vézelay and in its final perfected form, as recorded in the thirteenth century, is translated in the present volume as Appendix D. That there clearly was a need for such a justification is borne out by later events which saw Mary Magdalene reclaimed by the church of St. Maximin, whose monks produced a counter story to the Vézelay account.[6] Pilgrims wanted to believe in holy relics but were not totally credulous—one of the reasons for the decline of Vézelay as a destination for pilgrims was believed to have been the monks' reluctance to exhibit, and so confirm the presence

---

[1] Note that it is as a "pilgrim of my blessed lady Mary Magdalene" that King Louis VII declares that he will protect Vézelay (*Major Chronicle* 4 §57).

[2] On the theft of relics, see Geary (1978).

[3] See Cheney (1973: esp. 351 and 357–58), Sumption (1975: 150–51), and the discussion in Scott (1981: 28–29).

[4] See Cohen (1980); Vielliard ([1938] 1978: 2); note too how William III fits in a journey to Compostela between raids on the properties of Vézelay (*Major Chronicle* 2 §11). On the pilgrimage to Compostela see NCE, s.v. "Santiago de Compostela," and V. and H. Hell, *The Great Pilgrimage of the Middle Ages: The Road to St. James of Compostela* (London 1964). Cox also cites Roger Collins, *Early Medieval Spain: Unity in Diversity 400–1000* (NY, 1983: 236–38).

[5] Quoted in Brooke (1984: 92). On Vézelay and the rise of the Magdalene cult, see the supplementary essay of E. L. Cox in Appendix D below. Further material on Vézelay, Autun and relics will be found in Cox's essay in Aspects [F] below. For the Magdalene cult in the context of eleventh-century popular spirituality, see Delaruelle in *L'Eremitismo* (235ff.).

[6] On the rivalry between Vézelay and Saint Maximin near Marseilles, see Geary (1978: 90–95).

of, the Magdalene's relics[1]—and so it was important to be able to give a plausible account of the acquisition of one's relics.

The origins of the cult of Mary Magdalene can be traced to the middle of the eleventh century. A privilege of Pope Leo II dated 27 April 1050 "is the earliest official recognition of the cult of Saint Mary Magdalene at Vézelay, the cult which was to make Vézelay famous throughout western christendom."[2] The setting for the emergence of the cult of the Magdalene at Vézelay is one of monastic decline and reform, comital intervention, famine, plague, and struggles between factions associated with the choice of a successor to Abbot Herman in 1037, which culminated in the appointment of one Geoffrey, not of the Vézelay monastic community. Geoffrey was noted for his devout piety and in his time pilgrims began to frequent Vézelay, attracted, it seems, by the notion that some iron chains discovered in the monastery (and perhaps abandoned there by serfs fleeing forced labor in the nearby iron mines?) were left there by imprisoned soldiers—later freed—who had prayed to the Magdalene for release from their chains. Such a dedicatory practice—so it was imagined—became common and derived support from the idea that the Magdalene herself had been redeemed from "the chains of sin."[3] Although chains were not at the time an accepted attribute of Mary Magdalene, and although her cult was not very popular—Vézelay was, in fact, one of the earliest examples of the introduction of her cult into France—Vézelay became the site

---

[1] See Sumption (1975: 216); this failure reinforced "certain hesitations and scruples as to the authenticity of the said relics."

[2] Berlow (1971: 86). Cox (using Saxer [1959] and other sources): "Until the eleventh century there is no mention of Mary Magdalene, or any part of her, at Vézelay, nor was she then commonly to be found in Western Europe ... the Venerable Bede, apparently relying upon Greek texts, seems to have been the first Christian writer in the West to enter her name into a martyrology with 22 July as the date of her commemoration, and in the ninth century prayers in her honor first appear in sacramentaries. The earliest evidence that cults in her name existed in northwestern Europe dates from the tenth century at Exeter (which claimed to have one of her fingers) and at the church of St. Steven in Halberstadt. In France the earliest sanctuaries known to have been dedicated to Mary Magdalene were at Bayeux (attested by 1027) and Verdun, where the church built in her honor there in 1024 was, according to legend, constructed over the site of an oratory in her name that had supposedly existed in the time of Clovis. From this point on interest in Mary Magdalene began to spread. Sanctuaries dedicated to her were founded at Reims, Cohémon and Besançon between 1034 and 1050, and it is during this same period that the earliest evidence appears attesting to a cult of the Magdalene at Vézelay." Cox also cites Faillon ([1855] 1865) and Louis (1946) on the development of the Magdalene cult in this period.

[3] Luke 7:48. St. Foy was also "particularly famous for her success in securing the release of prisoners who applied to her for help, and she ordered them to bring their chains as an offering to her tomb at Conques. Bernard (of Angers, whose *Libellus Miraculorum Sanctae Fidis* was written between 1020 and 1060 AD) informs us that soon there were so many chains at the abbey that the monks had them melted down and made into iron doors. The similarity between this tradition and that which was developing somewhat later at Vézelay, where the chains brought to Mary Magdalene's tomb were made into a wrought-iron railing, is surely too close to be merely coincidental, and, by the mid-eleventh century, the monks of Conques, as if to reciprocate, had introduced the cult of Mary Magdalene in their own church as a result of the popularity of the cult at Vézelay" (Cox, citing Geary [1978: 94, 169–70], Louis [1946: 1:159], and Berlow [1971: 88–100]).

of her relics, and a collection of miracle stories soon developed illustrating the power of these relics to save believers from death or illness. Within a very short time the association between Vézelay and the relics of the Magdalene had become widely known and the consequent pilgrim traffic greatly bene-fited the abbey's economy: "the pilgrimage to the Magdalene ... was almost an instantaneous success, although it was not until the end of the eleventh century that it received official blessing."[1]

The monks were fortunate in their choice of a patron because they were able to take advantage of a general Burgundian ground swell of emotion in regard to the Magdalene, which dated back at least to the abbacy of Odo at Cluny (926–944), who had composed a homily in honor of her.[2] The first French sanctuary to the Magdalene was at Verdun in 1024 but, although Vézelay seems originally to have been dedicated to Christ, the Virgin, and Saints Peter and Paul, by 1060 Pope Stephen could proclaim that the monas-tery possessed the Magdalene's tomb. This papal recognition can be seen as the climax of a lobbying campaign directed at the papacy by Abbot Geoffrey to prevent other centers from achieving pre-eminence in the worship of the Magdalene.[3] The *Book of the Miracles of the Magdalene* from which we derive our knowledge of the circumstances surrounding the growth of the Magda-lene legend at Vézelay, was apparently composed between 1037 and 1043 in the first flush of Geoffrey's abbacy. Whatever the exact circumstances of the origin of the cult, it is clear that by the end of the eleventh century Vézelay had been recognized as the possessor of the remains of Mary Magdalene.

Once the presence of these relics had become widely known and accepted, the golden age began for the monastery and the town. The *Major Chronicle* provides a clear insight into the effects of pilgrimage on a popular pilgrimage center; there are many accounts of pilgrimage as experienced by the pilgrims themselves and we find a lot of evidence of the importance which churches attached to the possession of the relics of a favorite saint,[4] but there are few accounts of the ramifications of the pilgrim phenomenon as rich as the story of Vézelay. Even before looking at the impact of pilgrims on the town itself we may begin by noting the importance of the roads along which pilgrims had to travel to reach the relics. Control of these roads, or at least the absence of hostile control of them, was vital for the pilgrim church. No one was more aware of this than the counts of Nevers who knew that one of the most disruptive tactics they could employ in their struggles with the abbot was to impede traffic along the roads to Vézelay. Such tactics seemed guaranteed to ensure papal intervention as the monks strove to keep the roads open and to maintain their source of income. There are five papal bulls preserved in the Auxerre manuscript which date from the twelfth century and which deal with the issue of unimpeded pilgrim traffic on the roads leading to Vézelay.[5]

---

[1] Berlow (1971: 103; cf. also 97).

[2] Saxer (1975: 182). Evans (1931a: 103–4).

[3] Saxer (1959: 65ff.).

[4] See Scott (1981: 27–31).

[5] *Charters* 15 in 1103, 26 in 1144, 55 and 56 in 1148, and the charter in *Major Chronicle* 4 §33 from 1165.

When the dispute between Pons and William II was being arbitrated there was a complicated discussion about control of the various roads around Véze-lay as both parties sought to establish their rights over them.[1] There was more at stake than just movement along the roads; another point of conten-tion was the levying of tolls along the roads; pilgrims, in theory, were exempt from these, but in practice they were often exacted.[2]

A related issue was the charges imposed on merchants and traders who set up their stalls in the roads and market places of Vézelay. These were a rich source of income for the abbot, who claimed the right to collect such dues, but a source of resentment for the merchants who had to pay them.[3] Al-though the count of Nevers tried to intervene in this dispute on the side of the merchants[4] it was a battle fought essentially between the abbot and the burghers. With the related issue of the accommodation that the abbot de-manded the merchants furnish for guests during the major festivals of Easter and the Feast of Mary Magdalene, these charges formed the most important of the complaints that were resolved in the *Accord* of 1137. In essence the problem was that the greatest profits could be made by merchants during these important festivals when the town would be flooded with pilgrims and that the abbot wanted to take advantage of this himself. Hence he demanded more for the right to set up stalls or benches on the roads and insisted that some houses which would otherwise be let out for profit should be put at the disposal of the church to house its important guests.[5]

As the passions that these quarrels aroused suggest, a lot of money flowed into Vézelay as a result of the pilgrim traffic. The monastery's share of this came directly from offerings and from the various charges that the abbot was able to levy as the controller of the town. It was this wealth that financed Artaud's building program at the beginning of the century and the rebuilding of Vézelay after the terrible fire of 1120 which destroyed the old nave and killed a large number of pilgrims.[6] As a result of this wealth, an obscure hill-top town which had struggled for survival in the first centuries of its exist-ence became one of the glories of Romanesque architecture and a fitting loca-tion for St. Bernard's dramatic preaching of the Second Crusade. But it was not only the church that benefited from the pilgrim traffic; the whole town, especially its merchants, profited from it. Someone had to provide the pilgrims with food, drink, and shelter and, especially, to change their money, since visitors from all over Western Christendom, all with different curren-cies, would be among the worshippers. Clearly it was not just travelling mer-chants who met these needs: the presence of an active group of local mer-

---

[1] *Major Chronicle* 2 §5 and §6.

[2] *Major Chronicle* 4 §33; see also Sumption (1975: 177); as an example of the protection offered to pilgrims see the letter of Hugh, archbishop of Lyon, to Ivo, bishop of Chartres, in which the former places an interdict on a royal official who had arrested a pilgrim on his way to Vézelay (*Recueil* 14:792–93).

[3] See the 1137 *Accord*, paragraphs 32, 33, and 47.

[4] *Major Chronicle* 2 §5.

[5] On the issue of accommodation, see paragraphs 6–8 and 18 of the 1137 *Accord*.

[6] See Sumption (1975: 214) and Brooke (1984: 93).

chants is clear enough from the *Major Chronicle*, and there is also evidence from the 1137 *Accord* that the town itself had grown during the twelfth century, presumably as more and more traders were attracted by the possibility of profiting from pilgrims.

Perhaps the best evidence of the wealth that could be won from the pilgrim traffic is provided by the career of the money changer Simon de Souvigny. He came to Vézelay in 1138 with Pons, by whom he was granted, contrary to the wishes of the monastic chapter, the right to set up a money changing booth.[1] By 1155 he had become one of the wealthiest citizens in the town and a leader of the opposition to his former patron, Pons. He had, moreover, so won the support of the local nobility, presumably by lending them money, that they wrote letters to Pons in support of Simon, beseeching the abbot not to vent his anger against the money changer. To no avail, however, as the abbot had the outworks, ramparts, and a tower of what must have been a substantial building destoyed, as an example to the other burghers.[2] Even this assault on his home did not diminish Simon's influence nor, apparently, seriously affect his wealth. He continued to be one of the leading citizens of the town, a key figure in negotiations, and one whose lodgings were still sufficiently opulent for him to be able to offer hospitality to the count, William IV, and his mother.[3] The key to Simon's rapid success must have been the speculative gains he would have been able to make as a money changer, at the expense of pilgrims and merchants.[4]

The riches that poured into the coffers of the church and merchants of Vézelay are the most obvious result of its popularity as a pilgrimage center. Even more interesting, however, and perhaps a corollary of the great wealth, is the growth in self-confidence and self-assertion of the mercantile and monastic communities at Vézelay. Even before the formation of the commune which is described in Books 2 and 3 of the *Major Chronicle* the inhabitants of Vézelay had shown that they would not easily be cowed by the abbot despite his legal control over the town. Abbot Artaud was murdered by some of them because, according to Count William IV, he attempted to increase modestly the feudal burdens imposed on them.[5] In fact, the dissatisfaction of the burghers had probably been building up over the years during which Artaud oversaw expensive architectural works at the church. It was probably the constant financial demands on the citizens to support this building work that underlay their resentment. Certainly it is clear that they had developed a strong enough sense of corporate identity to plan and undertake this crime, as later they formed a commune and negotiated with both the count and the abbot over matters concerning their rights. Equally clear is the monastic community's strong sense of corporate identity. Throughout most of the events described in Book 4 of the *Major Chronicle*, as William IV oppresses the

---

[1] See *charter* 70.

[2] *Major Chronicle* 3 §6.

[3] See *Major Chronicle* 4 §20, §51 and §52.

[4] On the importance of money-changers in towns of the period see Chérest 1:75, Hibbert (1953), and Lopez (1953).

[5] *Major Chronicle* 2 §17.

monastery and threatens them, the monks are forced to deal with him themselves in the absence of Abbot William. But they prove to be determined
champions of the rights of their monastery and sufficiently self-confident to
abandon their house and go into exile without feeling that they need consult
their abbot. During negotiations with the count they are on one occasion
more forthright in defending their rights and more courageous before the
bluster of the count than either the abbot or a visiting Roman cardinal.[1] This
corporate self-confidence can be explained by the protection afforded the
monks by Mary Magdalene and by the prosperity that came to them and
enabled them to build so magnificent a church. That church which had been
honored by the preaching of the Second Crusade could not idly allow its
rights to be undermined. The link between the monastery's prosperity and
the protection of Mary Magdalene is shown strikingly at the time of the
monks' exile. Hugh of Poitiers has a bystander cry out in terror: "O glorious
and blessed mistress Mary Magdalene, why do you endure such acts? What
support may we sinners hope for from you, when you allow your servants to
suffer such injury?"[2] A saint was expected to protect and support physically
the church which contained his or her relics and the failure to do so was considered a failing by the saint.[3] One of the reasons for the challenges to the
authenticity of the relics at Vézelay in the thirteenth century was that the
monastery had fallen into some decline, something which suggested that perhaps it did not really have Mary Magdalene looking after its interests.[4] But
when her support was unchallenged and the monastery flourished, the monks
were assured in their role as the keepers of her shrine and felt confident
enough to resist all their enemies.

[E] MS. Auxerre 227—Contents and Historiographical Context

Introduction

If political and social turbulence stimulates an interest in history, it is not to
be wondered at that the twelfth century is one of the great ages of history-
writing.[5] More history, arguably, was written and copied during the so-called

---

[1] *Major Chronicle* 4 §25.

[2] *Major Chronicle* 4 §56.

[3] See Geary (1979), who explains that the humiliation of relics was in part a punishment of the saint herself.

[4] See Introduction pages 12–13 above, Appendices D and H below for the thirteenth-
century developments. For further discussion: Berlow (1971: 34, 38, 86ff., 119); Chérest
1:22ff. (Huygens 1976: 10ff.); Graham (1918: 28ff.); Saxer (1975: 18ff.); Stock (1983: 64ff.);
Van Engen (1986: 296); Vogade (1987: 50ff.).

[5] Cf. the comments in Breisach (1985: 103). In general: Smalley (1974); Breisach
(1983); R. W. Southern's various papers in *Transactions of the Royal Historical Society* S.5
vols. 20–23 (1970–73).

"twelfth-century renaissance" than at any other time in history, prior, perhaps, to the later, Italian, Renaissance. Whether we take notice of available
statistics—such as the fact that more copies of Josephus, Orosius, and Cassio-
dorus's *Historia Tripartita* have survived from the twelfth century than from
any other period before the age of printing (more, in fact, than from the
whole total of centuries between 500 and 1100 AD, and more by far than
from the thirteenth and fourteenth centuries taken together [1])—or whether
we simply observe the great variety of historiographical activity in the period,
we cannot avoid the conclusion that the twelfth century was an age of great
crises—church and state, Norman and Anglo-Saxon, serf and lord, monk and
bishop (to name but a few of the competing contestants)—that stimulated the
recording and writing of history in an unprecedentedly comprehensive
manner.[2]

Recent historical scholarship has not failed to pay court to the historiographical interests of the century, whether in the form of fine editions,[3] translations,[4] inspired sallies,[5] summaries,[6] collections of essays,[7] overviews,[8]
reviews of recent work,[9] close studies of individual writers,[10] or definitive,
analytical monographs in the *Annales* tradition.[11] In all this volume of scholarship, the unit of focus has invariably been the individual piece of historical
writing. This is a natural enough reflection of the "author" and "individual"
consciousness of the modern cultural mentality[12] and not an improper response to the survival of numerous works from the period that do represent
consciously composed, or "authored" historical writings. There are, however,
two problems with this emphasis. In the first place, it stresses precisely the
format most susceptible to the "rhetorical manipulation" so unpalatable to
the modern historian.[13] In the second place, and correspondingly, it ignores
a format that lies closer, perhaps paradoxically, to the pattern of historio-

---

[1] Guenée (1980: 271).

[2] Cf. Davis (1981: 272) on Romuald of Salerno, and Breisach (1985: 106) and (1983:
chap. 9) for right relations between *sacerdotium* and *regnum* as a great "crisis" and theme.

[3] For example Alessio (1982), and cf. Ouellette (1982).

[4] A translation of Suger's *Life of Louis VI* is expected from the hand of John Moorhead
(University of Queensland). See too Fisher (1979) and Mortensen (1987). Scott (1981) is
particularly pertinent here: "one of the responses of the monks (to the challenges
mounted by the crown, nobility and secular clergy against their way of life) was a literary
recreation of it, in the form of saints' lives, cartularies and histories" (3). Consider the job
William of Malmesbury was called upon to execute for the Glastonbury monks, and their
attitude towards his execution of it: as at Vézelay, the sanctity of a monastic church
needed to be buttressed by every possible relic and document, whether "forged" in the
modern sense or not.

[5] R. W. Southern, as cited above n.1.

[6] Hay (1977); see the review by R. Ray in *Speculum* 54 (1979): 577–80.

[7] For example, Davis (1981), Breisach (1985), and Morgan (1982).

[8] Breisach (1983).

[9] Ray (1974).

[10] See Thomson (1987).

[11] Guenée (1980). Select bibliography only is cited here and above.

[12] Foucault, "What Is an Author?" in Bouchard D. (1977: 113ff.).

[13] See Breisach (1985) and Ward (1977d).

graphical interest evident in the modern, "objective," school, the format described by Guenée as the "dossier,"[1] the collection or assemblage of works, some authored in the modern sense, some authored but abridged, and some not authored in the modern sense at all (for example, a cartulary). Guenée describes the "constitution d'un dossier" as:

> a normal step in historical research and one which results naturally in the *florilegium* or the compilation which marks its completion ("une étape d'autant plus normale de la recherche historique qu'elle prépare tout naturellement le florilège ou la compilation qui en marque l'achève-ment").

Such assemblages were often peculiarly monastic and they illustrate the extent to which monasteries were perceived as essentially historical institutions whose privileges were rooted in past time, manifested at various points in subsequent time, and destined to ensure their inmates and possibly also the world that benefited from their profession, a future beyond time. In their "factuality" and distance from the rhetorical prose of the more ambitious medieval historians, these assemblages are an important anticipation of modern historiographical attitudes. Leclercq[2] and others[3] have shown how dear history was to monks, for whom the historical record was evidence of the working of God in the world. The fragile status of monks in society could be maintained only by constant conservation and evocation of past charters, acts of donors, and precedents establishing privileges. Being "cut off from the world" by their profession, monks found it more difficult to maintain social contacts and the day-to-day visibility and respectability that could alone ensure tranquil possession of rights and land in the medieval context. To be sure, the most successful monks and monasteries abandoned the possibility of remote isolation for just such contacts,[4] but even so, the tension between the monastic profession and the social basis of power and privilege in the period presented monasteries with an impasse they sought to resolve by an assiduous cultivation of history, and historical authority or precedent.

This cultivation of the past is evident not merely in the historical works composed by monks, or the *florilegia* of historical writings they put together—all of which have been studied in some detail of late[5]—or in the cartularies—forged or genuine—assembled to buttress claims and privileges, but in the col-

---

[1] Guenée (1980: 114). Huygens (1976: xxvii) also uses the term. For another Vézelay "dossier" see Saxer (1975). Note also the *Liber Sancti Jacobi (Codex Calixtinus)* above, Aspects [C] 43n.2.

[2] Leclercq (1961: 190ff.) and (1970: 57–86).

[3] See, perhaps most recently, Guenée (1980: 45ff.) and Nichols (1983).

[4] See Lynch (1975) and (1976). Of the monastery of St. Denis, Bernard of Clairvaux wrote: "the cloister of the monastery was often crowded with soldiers ... business was done there ... it echoed to the sound of men wrangling, and ... sometimes women were to be found there. In all this hubbub," asks Bernard, how could anyone attend "to heavenly, divine, and spiritual things?" James (1953: 112, letter 80).

[5] See for example Leclercq (1961); Thomson (1987); Ray (1974: 41n.23, 56n.81, etc.); and in Shriver (1974: 119–34, "Orderic Vitalis on Henry I: Theocratic Ideology and Didactic Narrative"); Lewis (1987); Vaughan (1986); etc.

lections of "raw" (so to speak) materials that have survived to our times, and combine all three types of historical record in a manner that demonstrates with painful clarity the motivation behind the study of the past in monastic circles.

These collections demonstrate, in fact, a great paradox inherent in the monastic phenomenon, a paradox that it is worth restating: founded to make manifest a disdain for the secular world and the history to which the secular world was attached,[1] monasteries yet became peculiarly dependent upon the time-conscious secular world and its history. Their survival, in a world progressively structured against them, depended upon benchmarks hammered into the hard rock of history; like mountain climbers, they inched their way from piton to piton towards the summit of their salvation, each piton representing a landmark in the establishment of right, privilege, autonomy. Material relevant to the polemical purpose of monasteries defines itself as history not just by the internal genre characteristics appropriate to each piece, but by inclusion in collections which illustrate both the witness of *historia* (the letter [in an exegetical sense], the foundation of monastic autonomy), and also the witness of "virtù," the monastery's store of grace, magic, miracle. This latter was time-bound too, though recent work has shown a lack of sensitivity towards what we today would call the historical aspects of the miracle stories.[2] The consanguinity of miracle stories, discussions of legal privilege and "history" might not be recognized today, but the collections represent what monks thought was most useful from the past of their abbey. Thus a monk of the Bec priory of Conflans-Ste-Honorine compiled an autograph manuscript over a period of forty years, containing sermons and eucharistic proof-texts (c. 1100), miracle stories (c. 1099–1129), discussions of the monastic profession and the community's legal relations with the secular world, a (lost) *summa*, a legal treatise *De libertate beccensis ecclesie* (c. 1136, a legal recast for polemical purposes of Milo Crispin's *Vitae abbatum*) and further miracle stories concerning a local (Merovingian) martyr.[3] Such collections demonstrate what formal "authored" works of history sometimes obscure, the precise cutting edge of history, its polemical—or in the case of combinations of computistical material, geography and history,[4] practical—utility. They also evince a tendency to let raw materials mingle with worked up narratives, a tendency sometimes found in a "composed" work, for example, Rahewin's continuation of Otto of Freising's *Gesta Frederici*.[5] It is not therefore entirely true that Anselm of Canterbury's contemporaries "almost to a man" favored "the use of a narrative scheme."[6] If we restrict our vision in the main to

---

[1] Cf. Markus (1970), Hanning (1966: chap. 1).

[2] Carter, "The Historical Content of William of Malmesbury's Miracles of the Virgin Mary," in Davis (1981: 127ff).

[3] See Gibson, "History at Bec in the Twelfth Century," in Davis (1981: 171ff., and 169).

[4] Davis (1981: 215).

[5] See references cited at Breisach (1985: 150n.11). Rahewin's *Continuatio* is translated in Mierow (1953).

[6] Davis (1981: 200).

authored works in the modern sense, this might be so, but the collections
speak for a sense of history that transcends the narrative structure, or at least
is content to leave the focus only partially on the historical narrative. Valerie
Flint has recently proposed that the association of material within Honorius
of Autun's *Imago mundi* and within manuscripts containing it, reveals a
tension in contemporary minds between the notion of a future determined by
astrology and magic, stars and dreams, and "a way of recounting the past in
such a way as to hope to submit that future to the control of Christian man."[1]
Here then, the association of works in a collection reveals something about
the contemporary sense of history (and its urgency) which is not to be
discerned necessarily from a consideration based only upon the individual
piece within the assemblage.

The monastic historiographical project in the middle ages was, it has
recently been pointed out,[2] peculiarly conducive towards the assemblage:
monastic historiography, says Guenée[3] is "collective, elle est le fruit d'un
travail d'équipe"; the equation of "historian" with *scriptor, confector, composi-
tor*[4] distanced the monastic historian—as indeed it did the notarial historiog-
rapher[5]—from the authored, composed text in the modern sense, from the
"truth-warping" effects consequent upon the creative use of rhetoric in the
language of history, and thus, inadvertently as it were, gave rise to an important anticipation of the "fact" or "document" based "objectivity" that forms
one of the cardinal characteristics of modern historiography. It is indeed no
accident that both Rahewin, and the Hugh of Poitiers of the *Vézelay Chronicle*
Book 4, though they are continuing a *History* from which raw documents have
been purged or in which they have been digested, are driven to include large
undigested slabs of documents in their work: here the mentality of the "dossier" triumphs over that of the (medieval) rhetorical historian.

Alerted by these examples and observations, we may well be encouraged to
look more sympathetically at the associations of texts and themes in the
manuscript historical collections, in order to detect the scope of the urgent
motivations that lay behind the medieval, and in particular, the twelfth-
century study of and sensitivity towards history. An excellent starting point is
provided by MS. Auxerre, Bibliothèque Municipale, 227, an historical collection that has been subjected to a great deal of attention since at least the
seventeenth century when it was first printed. In all this, however, the signifi-

[1] Davis (1981: 231) (V. I. J. Flint, "World History in the Early Twelfth Century: The
Imago Mundi of Honorius Augustodunensis," 211–38).

[2] Guenée (1980: 46ff).

[3] Ibid., 49.

[4] Ibid., 50.

[5] Ibid., 67: "l'histoire des bureaucrates est surtout une histoire fondée sur les documents originaux"; affirmation of the use of original sources is common—Guenée (1980:
91ff.)—but some historians were closer to the primary sources—Guenée (1980: 109ff.)—than
others. On monastic historiography, cartulary, and chronicle, see Bautier (1970: 816–22);
Blake (1962); Davis (1958: xiii); Duby (1982a: parts 1 and 4); Gransden (1980); Hay (1977:
49–50); Hearne (1720); Stenton (1913); Stevenson (1858); Van Engen (1986: 289, 298).
More importantly, for a chronicle/cartulary closer in time and spirit to the Vézelay
chronicle, see Scott (1981).

cance of the manuscript for twelfth-century monastic sensitivities has not been fully commented upon. Guenée in his monumental study, for example, devotes but six lines to the manuscript. It is the purpose of the present volume to present in English a conspectus of the entire contents of MS. Auxerre 227, an outstanding twelfth-century historical "dossier," in order to illustrate the urgent historical sense that accompanied the compilation of such historical dossiers in the period and to facilitate analysis of the relationship between that historical sense and the historical sense found in more conventional "authored" works. MS. Auxerre, in fact, illustrates both senses. It is itself a "dossier," but the major *Chronicle* within it illustrates what was worked up from the "dossier."

Contents of the Auxerre Manuscript and Arrangement of Material in the Present Volume

The Auxerre manuscript—described fully in the introduction to Huygens (1976) and printed there in its entirety (195–607)—was executed with considerable care, as is evident from the spacious script and the frequent use of color, especially in the fine miniature of the founders of the monastery of Vézelay, with its Byzantine influences (Huygens pl. 1 and pp. xv–xvii; Berlow [1971: 213]). It is a copy, probably, of the autograph itself [Huygens xxii]. The latter apparently stood incomplete at the death of its compiler, Hugh of Poitiers, in 1167; at that point, our manuscript, the Auxerre manuscript was made, and additions to it began [Huygens xxvi]. The stages of compilation of the copy and the various hands involved have been set out by Huygens (xiv, xxvi etc.) and need not detain us here. The copy was probably completed within a very few years of the death of Hugh (Huygens xix)—although it sustained additions as late as the fifteenth century (Huygens xviii)—and was executed at Vézelay itself (Huygens xxii). For its vicissitudes between the end of the Middle Ages and its appearance at Auxerre see Huygens (xxxiiiff.).

A summary of the contents of MS. Auxerre 227 follows.

Folios 1–17v contain *Annales*, of which the last entry dates from 1316 AD, and the first records the birth of Christ. See Berlow (1971: 19, 21) and *Annals* below for a digest of the early entries and a translation of the twelfth-century entries. On chronicles and annals in the Middle Ages see Hay (1977: chapter 3); Holdsworth and Wiseman (1986); Jones (1943); Poole (1926). Huygens (1976: xxvif.) discusses the authorship of the *Annales*. They are sometimes referred to as the "Little (or Minor) Chronicle."

Folios 18(a) to 19v(a) contain a *Brief History of the Counts of Nevers*. This is an odd mixture of apparently semi-legendary material and dry genealogical information. The history of the area of Nevers in the ninth and tenth centuries is invoked with tales of a duel caused by adultery, a lecherous bishop and his brave nephew, and a feast for three of France's most powerful counts. When he reaches the eleventh century and the historical counts of Nevers, the writer confines himself to a summary of the various counts' marriages and offspring. Huygens (1976: xxviii) is not persuaded that Hugh of Poitiers is the author of this short work.

Folios 22–63 contain a collection of (mainly papal) acts and privileges compiled, probably, after Pons's victory over the commune in 1155 (Huygens

[1976: xxviii–ix]). This cartulary contains the most important documents for the monastery's struggle to assert its independence against its various enemies. In particular, Count Gerard's charter of foundation, his letter to the pope and Pope Nicholas I's privilege issued in response to the count's letter are given pride of place. There follow numerous papal letters confirming the liberty of Vézelay and other letters relevant to its struggles against its opponents.

There are other manuscripts containing charters relevant to the history of the abbey of Vézelay apart from MS. Auxerre 227. An important collection (MS. Florence, Bibl. Med. Laur. Plut. 14, 21, Huygens [1976: xxxii]) contains a number of royal acts, one of which (issued by Louis IV d'Outremer in 936 AD and substantially repeating the provisions of earlier Carolingian monarchs [Huygens (1976: 267nn.23, 25)]) mentions the very *castellum*, built by the abbot and monks of Vézelay "on account of the persecution of the pagans" to which Huygens charters 5–8 refer (cf. Huygens [1976: 262]), and in similar terms. It decrees that the *coenobium* situated in the *pagus* of Avallon on the river Cure *in honoratione dei et salvatoris nostri Iesu Christi eiusdem genetricis semperque virginis Mariae beatorum apostolorum Petri et Pauli principum*, and the *castellum* with all its appurtenances and offerings by the faithful be received *sub nostra immunitate seu tuitione ... ut nullus comes seu vicecomes aut aliquis ex secularibus iudicibus vel ex missis nostris discurrentibus in prefato coenobio vel pretitulato castello cum omnibus villis ad ipsum locum aspicientibus potestative mansiones accipiat aut paratas seu freda aut cespitaticum vel pontaticum aut rotaticum* (a toll on wheeled vehicles—Niermeyer [1976: 922]) *vel inferendas ab eo exigere presumat sed liceat servis dei in eodem sepe dicto coenobio degentibus secure ac quiete vivere* (for translation cf. above, 28). It is surprising that Hugh of Poitiers did not see fit to include these privileges in *his* cartulary.

The collection and preservation of the documentary records of their abbey's privileges and possessions were matters of high priority for the many monastic historians who, as mentioned earlier, were busy in the twelfth century. Even when writing a history of the kings of England, for instance, the English historian William of Malmesbury recognized the importance of charter evidence[1] and when he concentrated on the history of particular monasteries he became an indefatigable antiquarian as he pored over old records.[2]

William was not alone. Many English monastic houses produced local histories during the twelfth century and nearly all of these took the form of a charter-chronicle: deeds and privileges of the house formed the basis of the history, linked together with more or less fluent prose depending on the skill and inclination of the writer.[3] A variant on the theme involved forging appropriate documents or tampering with existing ones to make them accord with the writer's beliefs about the past of his monastery.[4]

---

[1] See Stubbs (1887–89).

[2] See his *De antiquitate Glastonie Ecclesie*, in Scott (1981); also his account of his own monastery in Book 5 of Hamilton (1870).

[3] See the discussion in Scott (1981: 10–14) and note the use of the term "chronicle-cartularies" in Davis (1958: xii). See too, Chibnall (1976).

[4] For some discussion of the widespread practice of "forgery" in the twelfth century see Morey and Brooke (1965), and for an account of a particularly elaborate forgery see Davies (1973).

The same phenomenon occurred on the Continent. Here too, monks zealously collected the records which justified their privilege and their owner-ship of their estates. Hugh the Poitevin may have had a more exciting story to tell than most but he was not alone in compiling the documentary back-ground to it, nor was he the only monastic historian upon whose chronicle events from the wider world intruded.[1]

Folios 64–73v contain the first book of the *Major Chronicle* or *Vézelay History* or *Vézelay Chronicle* (the work is without title in the MS). Book 1 records an important episode in the ongoing dispute between the diocesan bishop(s) and the monastery over powers the bishops thought were theirs—on the basis of comprehensive diocesan power relating to their episcopacy—and from which the monastery thought it was exempt owing to the peculiar nature of its foun-dation and documentary privileges: "any question about the benediction of an abbot, the ordination of monks or clergy and the consecration of the mon-astery and other churches within the territory of Vézelay. Their monks and clergy might be ordained [the abbey protagonists argued] by any catholic bishop and they might send to any catholic bishop for the chrism or holy oil which was consecrated on Maundy Thursday and used especially in the sacra-ments of baptism and confirmation."[2] If the monastery happened to pass over its nearest diocesan neighbor and select a more remote bishop to per-form any of these tasks—as it claimed it had the right to do—the local diocesan bishop might complain of a breach of his ancient diocesan privileges. Book 1 of the *Major Chronicle* opens in 1140 with the accession of Humbert to the bishopric of Autun.[3] Autun alleged that another bishop (Elias of Orleans) had invaded his rights at Vézelay. The settlement of this dispute was followed by the outbreak of a similar one, initiated by a new and powerful bishop of Autun, Henry (1148–1170),[4] brother of the local duke of Burgundy. The aggression of Bishop Henry against Vézelay led to violence, eventually ending in a papal settlement, beginning 18 November 1151 AD, and dragging on until well into the year 1154 AD. The interest of Hugh the Poitevin's account of the adjudication of this dispute lies in his careful use of a notarial transcription of the depositions in court of the parties of both the abbot and the bishop, to which he seems to have had access.[5] The aim of the witnesses was to adduce evidence to support or contradict the thesis that the bishop of Autun had legal, canonical, jurisdiction over Vézelay by right, to the exclusion of the rights of other bishops and of the abbot himself. Thus it was important for the abbot's witnesses to prove that the abbot had invited *other* bishops to per-form duties within the monastery, and that he in his court had exercised full judicial competence in cases affecting the residents of the Vézelay *potestas*. The abbot sought to prove that the bishop of Autun had no established right

---

[1] The Continental local histories have not been studied as closely as the English ones, but see Bautier (1970). Also relevant is Chibnall (1984: 181–220).

[2] Graham (1918: 81), and see her chap. 4 in general.

[3] See *Major Chronicle* below 132n.1, and Graham (1918: 82ff.).

[4] See *Major Chronicle* below 133n.2, Bouchard (1987: 387), and Graham (1918: 84ff.).

[5] Graham (1918: 85), *Major Chronicle* below at 143n.3.

to compel attendance at his synods by the Vézelay clergy, and various other matters were raised to test the judicial and jurisdictional competence of plaintiff and defendant in the seigneury of Vézelay. In the end, the bishop, afraid that a definitive papal judgment might clip his wings and those of his successors for all time in the matter of diocesan "rights" over Vézelay, settled "out of court" and a mutual stand-off or "peace" was arranged enabling each church to "save face" and leaving to the abbey the somewhat uneasy enjoyment of its customary autonomy.

Folios 73v–123v contain the *Major Chronicle* or *Vézelay History* Books 2–3. If Hugh the Poitevin thought his labors as court chronicler to the abbot had ended with the settlement of the dispute involving the rights of the diocese of Autun, he was wrong. What became the second and third books of his *Chronicle* recorded perhaps the most interesting and lively events so far—the adjudication of the case against the rights of advocacy supposedly exercised by the counts of Nevers, and the communal "revolution" instigated against the seigneurial control of the abbot by the count and his stooges among the serfs and *cives* of Vézelay, the "abbot's men." At stake here were lucrative revenues as far as the counts of Nevers were concerned: the rights to the profits of justice over the inhabitants of Vézelay (since the counts' claims included the right to exercise justice over the inhabitants of the monastic *poté* in the comital courts), exemption from abbatial tolls on the lucrative commercial traffic attracted by the prosperity of the abbey and its relic cults, the right to impose tolls on commercial traffic along the principal routes to and from the town of Vézelay (consequent upon "ownership" of the roads in question),[1] the right to "hospitality" for themselves and their retinues whenever they visited their "protected" monastery,[2] and related rights, such as the right to tax the abbot's traders and purchasers in lands subject to the counts' power. Book 2 relates the disputes between Count William II of Nevers[3] and the abbot which were adjudicated before the abbot of Clairvaux, the lord of Thil-en-Auxois, and others on the eve of the second crusade (1146).[4] The dispute seems to have ended in another dubious "stand-off" whereby the counts William II and his son William III "promised in the presence of St. Bernard and the bishop of Auxerre that neither they nor their men would hinder merchants and others who were on the road to Vézelay."[5] Hugh's account suggests that the disputes were interrupted by the retirement to a (Carthusian) monastery in 1147, and death in 1148 of William II, and the departure on crusade of William III (1148), following an adventure in connection with which he vowed to surrender some of the "rights" his father had extorted from the monastery.

The remainder of Book 2 deals with Count William III's reluctance to abide by his vow, especially in the light of an outrageous incident involving the exercise of the abbot's seigneurial power over someone whom the count

---

[1] See Graham (1918: 70ff.) and *Major Chronicle* below 159n.1.
[2] See *Major Chronicle* below at 143n.2, and above Introduction and Aspects [A].
[3] See above, Introduction, Aspects [A], and below Aspects [F].
[4] See *Major Chronicle* below 160n.2.
[5] Graham (1918: 72).

claimed as a dependent, and who should in any event have been afforded a hearing before at least the abbot's court.[1] The dispute over who had the right of justice concerning the people of Vézelay flared up, and at this point the townsmen enter the picture, seduced by the count's desire to add their grievances against the abbot[2] to his own, as a basis for their transfer of allegiance from the abbot to himself. Amidst episodes of demagogic eloquence and spiritual and economic blockade of the town and its appurtenances, a temporary stand-off was arranged pending Pons's consultation of the pope concerning the count's case late in 1151 AD. Here the subject matter of Books 1 and 2 briefly overlaps.[3] Following Pons's return from Rome with papal advice to the effect that he suffer no diminution of abbatial autonomy by appearing in the count's court to settle outstanding disputes with the count, the latter subjected Vézelay to a close blockade and urged his men to destroy the abbey's possessions. After a brief but inconclusive flirtation with the possibility of justice at the king's court, Pons appealed to the papal legate, Cardinal Jordan, but through him could obtain from the count no more than a truce for the coming festival of St. Mary Magdalene. The count was eventually successful in persuading key agitators among the townsmen at Vézelay to transfer their allegiance from Pons to the count, who helped them to establish a fashionable commune with appropriate magistrates.[4] Thus the Vézelay *cives* joined the widespread movement to throw off, commute, or in other ways control the servile obligations and arbitrary seigneurial authority that so hindered their social and economic activities. Thus they joined the wider mainstream of history, earning for themselves a footnote in Charles Petit-Dutaillis's *Les Communes françaises!* The patronage of the count seems to have been crucial for the townsmen, and under his auspices they took over the seigneury of Vézelay and severely harassed its monks, while the abbot, refusing to return to the town, tried various expedients to restore his control, including excommunication of the townsmen and interdict of the town—both sentences that proved difficult to impose in practice, scenes of profanity and violence accompanying their public promulgation. By early 1153 AD, partially by way of the mediation of the abbot of Cluny, Pons's brother, an uneasy stand-off had been arranged involving the count's dissolution of the commune. This situation was blown apart by the belated arrival of the pope's letters extending the sentence of excommunication to the lands of the count (dated 19 December 1152), addressed to all and sundry, secular and religious, and by the abbot's injudicious arrest of certain burgesses who had apparently been attending the count's court, in defiance of the terms of the recent stand-off.[5] Pons was clearly now going for broke, and the new papal hard line, dragooning count, townsmen, bishops, and other secular potentates alike, provoked scenes of armed violence in the abbey. At this point in Rose

---

[1] Below *Major Chronicle* 2 §9 and Graham (1918: 75ff.).

[2] See the 1137 *Accord*, Appendix B below.

[3] Below *Major Chronicle* 2 §14. Graham preserves chronological accuracy here by adverting at this point to her account of the matter of Book 1 (her chapter 4).

[4] Petit-Dutaillis ([1947] 1970: 104 and 305n.215); below *Major Chronicle* 2 §19.

[5] *Major Chronicle* below at 196n.6.

Graham's account of Pons's abbacy, her text becomes a virtual translation of Hugh the Poitevin's *Chronicle*.[1]

Autumn (1153) and Book 3 brought the king to Vézelay and powerful persons intervened to persuade the pious Louis VII to support the beleaguered abbot. Pons, however, continued his balancing act by declining at this stage the possibility of royal justice, considering that even a royal decision in the matter might prejudice ancestral abbatial autonomy. By the end of 1154, however, fighting a battle on two fronts—against the bishop of Autun, whose cause was now manifestly failing, and against the count—Pons decided that royal justice was better than no justice, but the resultant settlement compromised important points of abbatial autonomy and soon came violently unstuck. Pons fled town, was nearly murdered, and obtained a promise of royal redress set down for June 1155. The town of Vézelay erupted into rapine and pillage and the townsmen, with comital assistance, besieged the monks in the fortified abbatial residence behind the abbey church. All parties prepared for a showdown and the king gave orders for mobilization of the royal army. A measure of common sense, however, prevailed among the leaders of society, and the local bishops arranged a further parley before the king at Montargis.[2] Here, and at further subsequent parleys, the abbot's rights were slowly restored and the count was forced to maintain face with the townsmen by extraordinary subterfuge and duplicity, which produced widespread confusion and chaos in and around Vézelay. The abbot countered by raising a seigneurial army, by further petitioning the king, by further negotiations with the *potentes* of the area, and finally by forcing his way back into power with an offensive that culminated in a series of Hollywood-like scenes— the abbot's furious demolition of the house of a major communal conspirator while the luckless culprit himself "sat by the fire in the very house with his wife and children,"[3] and, shortly before, the extraordinary scenario of the count, disguised as a pilgrim to St. Denis, forcing his attentions upon the monarch there and pleading emotionally on behalf of the townsmen who were now enduring a savage battering from the triumphant abbot.[4] The Book concludes with a complete restoration of the abbot's seigneurial and spiritual powers, with compensation from and punishment of the communal conspirators, and a fascinating appended list of the names of the latter, with the damage they did to the abbey duly itemized.

Early 1156, therefore, saw the troubled monastery returned to some semblance of calm. Neither comital nor communal aspirations, however, were scotched, nor was any one of the victorious powers—whether king, pope, abbot, or bishop—clearly and unequivocally the long-term master of the situation. Nevertheless, for Hugh the chronicler, right order had at last prevailed, and the ancient order stood forth pristine again; "the struggles of the

---

[1] Graham (1918: 106ff.).

[2] *Mons Argisii* (Huygens [1976: 495, 1158 and 663 s.v]). For a profile of the bishop of Auxerre, who arranged the parley at Montargis, see Bouchard (1979: chapter 4).

[3] See *Major Chronicle* below 3 §8.

[4] See *Major Chronicle* below 3 §5.

abbots of Vézelay which, while of tremendous dramatic value, have only limited interest for the historian" (!),[1] were, so it seemed, over.

Folios 124–187v contain the *Major Chronicle or Vézelay History* Book 4. After some prefatory remarks about the purpose of the book, Book 4 begins with the papal schism following the election of Alexander III in 1159 (§1). Soon after his election Alexander comes to France where his election is not recognized by the Cluniacs. As a result abbot Hugh of Cluny is excommunicated (§2).

After the death of Abbot Pons on 14 October 1161 William of Pontoise is elected as his successor but William IV, count of Nevers, tries to have his election annulled and to prevent his arrival at Vézelay. His election is confirmed by the papal legate, however, and then by the pope himself (§3–§5).

An account is given of Cluny's efforts, previously successful, to obtain control of Vézelay; this domination is finally ended when Pons obtains a charter from Alexander withdrawing Vézelay from the control of Cluny (§7–§8).

A servant and confidant of Pons, William of Montréal, who tried to steal valuables the night the abbot died, is imprisoned by Abbot William. He flees to Count William but is forced on the testimony of witnesses to return to the abbot. Because of him the count's men pillage the lands of the monastery of Vézelay (§8–§9).

Louis VII becomes disenchanted with Pope Alexander and, with Count Henry of Champagne as intermediary, begins negotiations with Frederick Barbarossa toward a resolution of the schism in August 1162. Louis is tricked by Count Henry but saved from his difficulties by the intransigence of Rainald, archbishop of Cologne. Subsequently, in February–March 1163, Louis is reconciled with Alexander (§10–§14).

A report of the papal council at Tours in May 1163 follows (§15–§16).

In June 1163 Count William demands hospitality from the monastery of Vézelay although the count's own father had renounced that right. Abbot William refuses and so the count's men invade the town of Vézelay. Peace is made in July 1163 and the count publicly renounces the right of unannounced hospitality (§17–§19).

Soon after, the count charges the abbot to appear in his court for not paying dues of salt. The abbot refuses and so the count's men invade the town again, demanding that the burghers renounce their allegiance to the abbot. The abbot, when his advice is sought, pretends to agree to this but delays further and appeals to the pope and the king (§20).

About this time, a monk of Vézelay, seeking alms, carries around relics, which are responsible for some miracles at Labroye (§21).

Hugh Letard, one of the count's men, plunders the possessions of the monastery. A letter from the pope on 7 December 1164 fails to move the count (§22–§24).

The parties meet at Auxerre in the presence of papal legates. All the abbot's supporters are afraid of the count and only Prior Gilo speaks out and

---

[1] Berlow (1971: 16).

asserts that the abbot denies being bound by any law of the count's. The count is angry, but a truce is declared (§25–§26).

A short account is given of Thomas à Becket, archbishop of Canterbury (§27).

Hugh Letard continues to despoil the monastery's possessions at the instigation of Countess Ida, the mother of William IV. The abbot seeks out the pope again in May 1165 and makes a powerful appeal to him, threatening to reject his monastery's links with the papacy. The pope writes to the count, ordering him to cease his vexations of the monastery and to appear before him, or at least before the archbishops of Sens and Bourges. He follows this up with letters to the archbishop of Sens and to various bishops with a command that the count is to be excommunicated if he makes no amendment to his behavior. He also writes to the king, asking him to force the count to make satisfaction to the monastery, and to the abbot, notifying him of the tenor of his other letters (§28–§34).

Hugh, archbishop of Sens, tries to mediate between the count and the abbot but the former refuses to make good the losses incurred by the monastery. Angry at his excommunication he comes to Vézelay in July 1165 but is shunned by the monks (§35–§37).

Peter of Auvergne, a former abbot of Tonnerre and now a monk of Vézelay, plots with a number of supporters to have himself declared abbot in place of William. They gain the support of the count, who harangues the monks in chapter, in late July 1165, about the abbot and his dishonoring of the monastery. Prior Gilo defends the abbot (§38–§40).

The two parties appear before the archbishop of Sens, at which time the count seeks a postponement of the case and gives hostages as a pledge that he will restore the confiscated possessions of the monastery. Peter of Auvergne, who is one of the representatives of the abbot at this meeting, shocks the others by siding with the count (§41).

On his return to Vézelay Peter meets the other plotters again before setting out to see the pope. Meanwhile, on 31 July, the abbot also returns to Vézelay and discovers the plot against him. When he reveals it publicly all the conspirators except two repent (§42–§43).

The abbot and the conspirators arrive at the papal court early in August; the abbot is received with honor but the plotters are turned away. Then the pope orders Archbishop Hugh of Sens and Bishop Stephen of Melun to hear the dispute between the abbot and the count. A meeting before the two at Joigny and a later one at Bassou resolve nothing, and so in early November the excommunication of the count and his mother is publicly proclaimed in church and the bishops who have dealings with the count are notified (§44–§50).

An account of a fire at Vézelay, which reveals a number of valuable relics (§51).

On 26 November 1165 the count, the countess, and their armed followers enter the town of Vézelay. They order the burghers to renounce their oath of allegiance to the abbot and the monks to hand over the keys of the monastery. The latter refuse and so the count's men invade the monastery and the church; they even prevent the monks from collecting their bread. The monks decide to flee from the monastery. They do so, ignoring the countess's plea to return, and make their way to Paris, where Louis receives them kindly (§52–§57).

The abbot joins the monks and on 7 December they plead their case before the king and his court. The king promises to help them once he has heard from the count (§58–§59).

Meanwhile, at the request of the countess, the abbot and she meet before the archbishop of Sens. But meetings on 18 December and 3 January 1166 achieve nothing and so the abbot and the count meet before the king on 13 January. The count agrees to return the monastery's possessions in the condition they were in a week before the departure of the brothers and to keep the peace. The monks return to Vézelay (§60–§64).

The count makes further claims for hospitality owed him but the abbot refuses even to respond while the count is still excommunicate. An attempt by the archbishop of Lyons and Archbishop Thomas à Becket to mediate fails (§65).

The count breaks the truce he has promised to uphold and so the abbot appeals to the king again. The latter reprimands the count and orders him, in early April 1165, to reinstate the truce (§66).

A further attempt to mediate, by the counts of Troyes and Blois, fails and so Louis orders both parties to appear before him at Moret on 22 April. At this meeting the abbot agrees to abide by the king's decision, but the count will not so agree. This angers the king but he takes no action (§67–§70).

Hugh Letard invades the lands of the monastery, plunders its possessions and harasses its men. The abbot complains to the king of the attack and Louis orders the count to appear before him on 5 June. But the count successfully seeks a postponement of the meeting (§71–§72).

An account of the genealogy of the Capetians (§73).

Both sides finally appear before Louis and agree to abide by the decision of the archbishop of Rheims and the count of Troyes in early October. Louis agrees to a further postponement because he needs the count's help in a campaign against the count of Chalons. Finally they appear before Louis on 10 November 1166 and a peace agreement is reached between the abbot and the count (§74). (Unfortunately the terms of the peace can not be established because they are outlined on those folios that have been cut.)

Louis comes to Vézelay with his court. Stephen, abbot of Cluny, comes too but arrogantly refuses the hospitality of Abbot William. For this he is condemned by the whole court (§75–§77).

An account of some heretics captured at Vézelay concludes the book (§78).

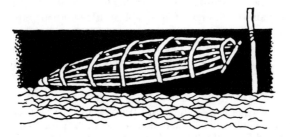

Fig. 2. A medieval fish-trap (from Ward [1977c: 16]).

[F] The Main Protagonists of the *Major Chronicle*[1]

The abbots of Vézelay:

Little is known of the abbots of Vézelay before the twelfth century, and that mainly from the *Annals*. The abbots who appear in the *Major Chronicle* are:

Artaud (Artald), 13th abbot of Vézelay, 1096–1106, a Cluniac monk. Began construction of the abbey church we see today in place of the smaller Carolingian basilica (so Guizot; Berlow [1971: 121] says Artaud concerned himself with the choir and other areas rebuilt in the thirteenth century and no longer visible). Increases in imposts to cover costs of construction provoked a riot in which the abbot was killed (1105–1106), the assassin (Simon) taking refuge with the count of Nevers and the bishop of Autun. See Berlow (1981: 328); Bouchard (1987: 431); Chérest 1:283ff.; Huygens (1976: 143ff.); Graham (1918: 54); and *Major Chronicle* 2, 162n.7 below.

Renaud, Raynald de Semur-en-Brionnais, 1106–1125/28 was the son of Geoffrey III of Semur and a nephew of Hugh the Great, abbot of Cluny. He entered Cluny with his parents and sister in 1088. His election as abbot was approved by the king and the pope, but the count of Nevers was hostile although unable to exert influence over the decision. He took his revenge in 1119 when his men sacked the abbey! Renaud was archbishop of Lyon 1125–1128. For controversy concerning the length of Renaud's abbacy, see Chérest 1:285ff. (Huygens 1976: 144ff.); Bouchard (1987: 360–61, 389, 431); Berlow (1971: 153ff., 167; 1981: 329); below *Major Chronicle* 2, 162n.1 and 165n.4; Guizot (1969: 226).

Baldwin, 1125–1129, and *Gerard, 1130*, are known only from incidental references. It seems more than likely that both were opposed by the Cluniacs. See Berlow (1981).

Alberic, 1131–1138, imposed on the abbey by Cluny and Innocent II; had been sub-prior of Cluny before his appointment to Vézelay. He became cardinal-bishop of Ostia and papal legate after his abbacy at Vézelay. He was a friend of St. Bernard of Clairvaux and accompanied the latter on preaching tours against heresy in Brittany, Toulouse, and Albi. In 1146 he was at Vézelay assisting with the preaching of the Second Crusade. See Guizot (1969: 227–28); Bouchard (1987: 431); Berlow (1981: 336); Chérest 1:290ff. (Huygens 1976: 148ff.).

Pons (Pontius) de Montboissier, 1138–1161, one of the eight children (seven reaching maturity) of Raingarde (whose intimate counsellor had been Robert of Arbrissel) and Maurice, was the brother of Peter the Venerable (abbot of Cluny 1122–1156 and formerly prior of Vézelay), of Jordan (abbot of La Chaise-Dieu and later cardinal and papal legate in France), of Herman (prior of Cluny under abbot Peter and later abbot at Manglieu), and of Heraclius (archbishop of Lyon [1153–1163]). He was also related to count William III of Nevers. The evidence of Peter's letters suggests that Pons's character left something to be desired; certainly there was no obvious fraternal love be-

---

[1] The tables and genealogies in Bouchard (1987: 255ff.) are invaluable in the present context. On the Burgundian nobility and monasticism in the period see Bouchard (1987: 34ff. and parts 2 and 3); on the Burgundian bishops 32ff. and chap. 2; on the medieval Burgundian nobility in general 26ff., chap. 1 and 251; on the counts of Nevers 33ff.

tween the two. See *letters* 16 and 91 in Constable (1975). Berlow (1971: 189) speaks of Pons's "selfish pettiness," likening him to a "spoiled child." Both Pons and his brother Peter had been educated at Vézelay and it could be argued that the abbey's most flourishing period coincided with Pons's abbacy. Constable suggests that Pons was born about the turn of the century and thus would have been in his 50s during the events related in the *Major Chronicle*, below, Books 2–3. He was clearly a proud aristocrat, conscious of his monastic rank and perhaps irked by his lack of secular rank. He undoubtedly felt that a person of his connections and monastic position ought not be overawed by a mere local count. The litigious defense of Vézelay's privileges seems to have suited his temperament. See Guizot (1969: 220–21); Berlow (1971: 155ff., 187ff.); Graham (1918: chap. 2); Bouchard (1987: 411, 431); Chérest 1:114ff. (Huygens 1976: 60ff.) and 295ff. (Huygens 1976: 151ff.).

William of Mello, 1161–1171, was from the noble family of the lords of Mello and had been abbot of Saint-Martin-de-Pontoise before his election to the abbacy of Vézelay.

The counts of Nevers:

An outline of the family of the counts of Nevers can be found in the *Brief History* and this can be supplemented by the account in Bouchard (1987). See also Lespinasse (1909–1914) and Sassier (1980). The counts who figure actively in the *Major Chronicle* are:

William II, 1098–1146, who made a journey to the Holy Land after the fall of Jerusalem in 1101 and, on his return, continued his long period of rule before abdicating in favor of his sons in 1146. Despite his squabbles with the church of Vézelay he was generally thought of as a pious man and was well regarded by Bernard of Clairvaux (see Bernard's *Letters* 230–231, trans. James [1953: 309–10], but cf. below *Major Chronicle* 2, 158n.6).

William III, 1146–1161, who married Hugh of Poitiers' bête noir, Ida, the sister of the countess of Champagne. He went on the Second Crusade with Louis VII and while he was in the Holy Land his wife acted as regent for him. He died in 1161 and was buried at Saint-Germain d'Auxerre.

William IV, 1161–1168, was knighted only in 1159. He married Aanor, the sister of the count of Flanders, and died in the Holy Land in 1168. He was buried at Bethlehem.

For Countess Ida see below, *Major Chronicle* 4, §56 291n.2.

The bishops of Autun:

Norgaud, 1098–1112, had been precentor of Autun before his election.

Stephen I, 1112–1139, had been a canon of the cathedral of Autun before his election. His nephew, and later successor, Humbert, served as archdeacon under him. He retired to Cluny after retiring from Autun.

Robert of Burgundy, 1139, was one of the brothers of Odo, duke of Burgundy. He was dean of Langres before his election to Autun.

Humbert, 1140–1148, was the nephew of his predecessor Stephen I. He was appointed archbishop of Lyon in 1148 and retired in 1153 to La Grande Chartreuse, where he lived for at least another sixteen years.

Henry of Burgundy, 1148–1170, was another brother of Odo, duke of Burgundy. He had been archdeacon of Autun since at least 1140.

[G] The Central Actors in the Vézelay Story

E. L. Cox

Artaud, from all available indications, was an energetic, perhaps even aggressive, individual, and as a Cluniac, he may well have been inspired to try to emulate at Vézelay something of the worldly grandeur which Cluny had attained under Saint Hugh. By 1088 even the pope was a former Cluniac monk, and Hugh had embarked upon his most ambitious project yet, the construction of a great new abbey church at Cluny that when completed would be the largest church in Latin Christendom. The prosperity in Vézelay's fortunes during the last half of the eleventh century and the greatly increased attendance at the services there on major holy days both justified and made possible a similar effort at Vézelay, where the old abbey church was deemed no longer adequate. Artaud therefore began the building of a new church which was sufficiently near completion to be dedicated in 1104; but this achievement apparently did not make for harmonious relations between the monks and the townsmen. If later evidence is accurate, it was the abbot's efforts to ease the financial strain on the monastic community that created the animosity. It seems that Artaud sought to reduce the cost of providing for guests at the abbey by trying to require those who had houses in the town to assume the burden of furnishing accommodations for such persons at least twice a year, on Easter and on the feast of the Magdalene.[1] This was in fact to impose a double burden upon the burghers by requiring them to pay for the visitors' expenses while at the same time foregoing the income they would otherwise have received by renting out the available space.

The conflict between the monks and the burghers reached a climax in 1106 when, under circumstances that remain obscure, Abbot Artaud was murdered. According to Hugh the Poitevin, one of the murderers was Simon, the son of Odo, the abbot's provost in Vézelay; and according to Pope Lucius II another was a relative of one Steven, who in the 1140s was a cleric at Auxerre.[2] Some, if not all, of the assassins managed to escape from Vézelay after the deed had been done, and Pope Paschal II was scandalized to learn that they were being harbored by the inhabitants of neighboring parishes. From Italy, in October 1106, he dispatched a circular letter addressed to the "bishops of Gaul," in which he deplored this situation and ordered that the malefactors be exiled or excommunicated.[3] These would seem unusually mild punishments for the murderers of a Cluniac abbot, which suggests that the question of blame was much more complicated than it appears to be on the surface; and the apparent unwillingness of the ecclesiastical authorities to prosecute the assassins suggests that the murderers enjoyed a good deal of sympathy.

The new abbot, Raynald de Semur [Renaud], was a nephew of Hugh of Cluny and he received the papal benediction in person at the Council of

---

[1] See the *Major Chronicle* 2 §17 below. The vexed question of hospitality for the abbey's guests was one of the points at issue in 1137 also.

[2] *Major Chronicle* 4 §22; Berlow (1971: 122-23).

[3] Below, *Cartulary*, no. 19 (Huygens [1976: 302-3]).

Guastalla in October 1106. He was understandably reluctant to take up his new position at Vézelay without taking precautionary measures to ensure his safety, and these required time for preparation. According to Vézelay *Annals,* Raynald did not enter upon his duties as abbot until 1108, and he apparently went first to Cluny upon his return from Italy.[1] As a former Cluniac monk, he quite naturally turned to his monastic colleagues there for advice and support before undertaking to deal with the problems of his new assignment, and when he did finally arrive at Vézelay he was accompanied by a group of monks from Cluny, as if preparing to institute major reforms.[2] Among them was a monk, Tezelinus, who remained Raynald's companion for the rest of his life, and very possibly Peter de Montboissier, the future Abbot Peter the Venerable of Cluny, who became *seniorum doctor et custos ordinis* as well as prior of Vézelay before he left in 1120. Peter's younger brother Pontius might also have been in this group of Cluniacs, although he would still have been quite young at the time.[3] In addition to furnishing himself with support from his Cluniac brethren, Raynald also seems to have enlisted the help of Count William II of Nevers. This formidable personage was a descendant of the Count Landry who had expelled Abbot Herman and his monks from Vézelay back in the 1020s, and Vézelay was located just within the northeastern boundaries of his dominions. As one of the most powerful princes in the region, ruler of the three counties of Nevers, Auxerre, and Tonnerre, William was the logical source of military support and choice as advocate—but a dangerous one. Such persons were not likely to offer their assistance without something being given in return, and William was later accused of having taken advantage of the situation to greatly expand his claims on the abbey. He had apparently initially challenged the election of Raynald because his prior consent had not been secured, and he expected monetary contributions whenever an abbot entered or left office. At some unspecified subsequent date the count was induced to renounce these pretensions, doubtless under pressure from both the papacy and the Cluniacs, since they obviously violated the ancient privileges granted to both Vézelay and Cluny.[4] But Abbot Ray-

---

[1] Berlow (1971: 153-55). [The *Annals* (translated below) only say, in fact, e.a. 1108, that "Renaud shines greatly [*prefulget*] as abbot"—eds.]

[2] The epitaph on his tomb particularly emphasized his service as a "restorer" of the abbey of Vézelay.

[3] Although it is certain that Peter the Venerable did spend time as a monk at Vézelay, the length of his stay and the dates are very uncertain. After he became abbot of Cluny (in 1122), he wrote to his brother Pontius [Pons] fondly recalling the ten years they had once spent together thinking and speaking only of divine subjects and ignoring the temptations of the world. It has usually been assumed that the ten years in question were spent at Vézelay, but this is by no means clear. See Constable (1967: 1:23; 2:243-44); and Berlow (1971: 156-57), who disputes Constable's conclusions. The evidence for Pontius's early stay at Vézelay is Hugh the Poitevin's description of him as having been "nourished since boyhood" by Mary Magdalene. See the *Major Chronicle* below 4 §3.

[4] See the *Major Chronicle* 4 §4. Paschal II, who like Urban II was also a former Cluniac monk, was at La Charité-sur-Loire in March 1107 for the consecration of the new church there, which Count William also attended. In the count's renunciation statement he calls these pretensions "perverse custom[s] which I have been exercising in the abbey of Vézelay," but since William II only became count in 1099/1100, Raynald's election would

nald was later accused of having, without consulting his monks, given the count permission to levy tolls on Vézelay people using the route to Auxerre, which suggests that this was also part of the price he had to pay in return for military assistance when he arrived to take charge of his troubled monastery.[1] In the arbitration of 1137, moreover, the burghers of Vézelay contended that it had been Abbot Raynald who, in the presence of Count William, had settled the question of providing for the abbey's guests by agreeing that their obligation would be limited to housing only members of the count's entourage, and even then only once every four years.[2] All this strongly suggests that the new abbot felt obliged to make major concessions both to the count of Nevers and to the burghers of Vézelay in order to pacify the disaffected groups who had been roused to fury under Abbot Artaud. Raynald did not give in on everything, however. Later testimony also reveals that Count William had tried to get toll-free status for his people at Clamecy when they came to trade at the Vézelay markets and fairs, but that he had agreed to drop that demand in return for a cash payment....[3] Count William II of Nevers' intervention in Vézelay's affairs, with or without any invitation from Cluny, could easily be explained by his need for money and his concern to prevent so illustrious a place from falling under the sway of his rival, the duke of Burgundy, whose provost at Avallon was only a few miles away.[4] William may have subsequently matured into a "personnage pondéré," as Pacaut affirms,[5] but in his earlier years he often displayed that curious mixture of piety and brutality that characterized so many members of the warlord class in the Middle Ages. In 1099, when he may not yet have reached the age of twenty, he attacked the abbey of Molesme in the county of Tonnerre and set it on fire, a deed for which he was officially pardoned two years later and after which he became a great devotee of the abbey.[6] In 1108, when Raynald de Semur was taking up the reins of abbatial government at Vézelay, William was assisting the new king of France, Louis VI, to take up the reins of royal government in the Île-de-France. This doubtless helped to divert his attention from possible interference in Vézelay's affairs, and during the next few years, while Raynald was handling problems over the church of Bulles in the Beauvaisis, complaints against the monks of Fleury, and claims to property at Crisenon, William was participating in Louis VI's military expedition against

---

have been his first opportunity to interfere in an abbatial election. Whether this is just loose terminology, or whether in fact previous counts of Nevers had been enforcing such patronage rights at Vézelay is not clear. Count Landry's expulsion of Abbot Herman in 1027 is the only previous case of a count of Nevers interfering in the governance of the abbey.

[1] Raynald's concession of these tolls was affirmed in testimony given before arbiters at Bessy-sur-Cure in 1146. See the *Major Chronicle* below 2 §5.

[2] Appendix B below §7.

[3] The *Major Chronicle*, below 2 §5.

[4] This concern was articulated in so many words by Count William IV in 1165, and in 1166 the abbot did in fact seek the assistance of the ducal provost of Avallon when the men of Nevers were besieging Vézelay. *Major Chronicle* 4 §§56, 72.

[5] Pacaut (1964: 87).

[6] Louis (1946: 149).

Thomas de Marle.[1] On his return, in the summer or autumn of 1115, he was captured by one Hugh Mansellus and imprisoned for the next four years at Blois. William was thus in no position to cause trouble for the monks at Véze-lay; but shortly after his release in 1119 a band of men led by his provost of Monceaux and officers of his court launched an apparently unprovoked attack on the abbey in pursuit of, among other things, military supplies.

Considering that on 21 December 1117 the pope had already written to the count forbidding the demands he was making, and to all the neighboring bishops ordering them to protect Vézelay from exactions and injuries of this kind, it is likely that this attack was the count's way of punishing the monks for their refusal to comply. The fact that the count had just been in prison suggests that he may also have been trying to raise ransom money, which would go far toward explaining the evident animosity of the attackers toward their victims.[2] The attack is also strong evidence that the monks under Abbot Raynald were by no means disposed to surrender their historic liberties to the count of Nevers, however formidable his powers of coercion, nor was the abbot himself. In April 1119 Raynald obtained royal confirmation of Vézelay's privileges from Louis VI, and early in 1120 he secured a similar confirmation from the new pope, Calixtus II.[3]

In 1120 disaster of another kind was to afflict the population of Vézelay. On the eve of the great feast of Saint Mary Magdalene, when the church and all available space in the town were overflowing with pilgrims, a terrible fire broke out, which apparently burned the church to the ground. The Vézelay *Annals* record the event without details, noting only that many men and women lost their lives; and the *Chronicle of Saint Marian of Auxerre,* where the catastrophe was still being commemorated thirty years later, added only that the fire had broken out at the hour of vigils, in "that twilight between day and night."[4] As far away as Saint-Maixent in Poitou a chronicler reported that "the monastery of Saint Mary Magdalene at Vézelay was burned with 1,127 men and women," but he unfortunately gives no indication of how he had obtained such precise information at such a distance from the event. Both the extent of the casualties and the extent of the damage thus remain unclear, but there is general agreement that at least the nave of the abbey church was destroyed, and possibly some of the conventual buildings as well.

This was the kind of calamity likely to bring the whole community together, however, and the pretensions of the count of Nevers were forgotten as the monks and townsmen alike joined in the effort to replace the ruined structures with a nave of surpassing magnificence. We need not rely upon such

---

[1] Berlow (1971:157); Lespinasse (1909: 1:281–85). Lespinasse is mistaken, however, in dating William's release "in the autumn of 1119" (282), since Bishop Cono's letter makes it clear that he was present at Vézelay in February of that year.

[2] Huygens, *Cartulary,* no. 17, no. 18 below (Huygens [1976: 299–301]). This explanation seems to me much more persuasive than Berlow's hypothesis (1971: 158–60) that the crisis was caused by the monks' refusal to grant toll-free status to the count's men of Clamecy.

[3] Berlow (1971: 160).

[4] For the sources on the fire and the arguments among modern historians over what got burned, see Berlow (1971: 160–65).

colorful accounts as that by the author of *Girart de Roussillon* (although he
may well have been living in or near Vézelay during this period), who depicts
pious pilgrims—and even Countess Bertha herself—as endlessly climbing the
hill of the Magdalene laden with mortar and stone and buckets of water to
aid in the construction work.[1] The masons' marks that have been found on
the stones of the basilica show that although some of the heavier work may
have been done by *corvée* labor, the stone workers at least were apparently
free men paid on a piecework basis.[2] Once begun, the reconstruction of the
great church advanced rapidly, supported by a growing population and no
doubt hastened by news of the new cathedral also being built in the 1120s at
nearby Autun. For Bishop Steven de Bâgé had recently acquired the church
of saints Mary and Lazarus at Avallon from the monks of Cluny and had
transferred the relics of Lazarus to his episcopal seat, where a splendid new
church to house them would soon replace the old cathedral dedicated to
Saint Nazaire. The idea that Autun was preparing to compete with Vézelay's
Mary Magdalene for the pilgrim traffic through Burgundy by thus "showcas-
ing" parts of her brother can only have fired the builders at Vézelay with
added zeal. Just when the magnificent nave the visitors admire today at
Vézelay was completed is not known, but it is known that in the autumn of
1131 Pope Innocent II granted special indulgences to all who would visit the
shrine of the Magdalene on her feast day and the octave following. This was
very likely an effort both to publicize the rebuilding of the church and to
swell offerings to help pay for it; and in January 1132 the pope came to
Vézelay in person to participate in the consecration of the new "Church of
the Pilgrims" by Bishop Steven of Autun.[3] By 1138/39, when Aimery Picard,
author of the famous guide for pilgrims to Santiago de Compostela, was
about to leave Asquins, at the foot of the Vézelay hill where he had been living, the basilica could be described as a "huge and beautiful" church.[4] By
that time, however, Raynald de Semur was no longer abbot of Vézelay....
Despite the attempts by the monks of Vézelay to choose their own abbot regardless of the wishes of Cluny,[5] the pope and the abbot of Cluny were
resolved that Vézelay should remain subject to Cluniac supervision. Their
choice for abbot was Alberic, sub-prior of Cluny, who was therefore "intruded" by force in 1131. Alberic was a man of wisdom and moderation who was
to have a distinguished career as a collaborator of Saint Bernard and as cardinal-bishop of Ostia after he left Vézelay in 1138; but the monks of Vézelay
were adamant in refusing to receive him. According to Hugh the Poitevin,
"nearly all of the brothers of the monastery" had to be "bound in chains"
and exiled to houses "in Provence, Italy, Germany, Lorraine, France, and

[1] *Girart de Roussillon* (Paris: Hackett, 1953: 427).
[2] Berlow (1971: 255–57).
[3] Louis (1946: 179–81); Berlow (1971: 165–66). There is some doubt among scholars
concerning the so-called "Church of the Pilgrims." Salet (1948) has argued that it was a
separate church altogether, located beside the hostelry at the entrance to the abbey
enclosure, and no longer in existence, rather than simply another name for the basilica
itself. On the "Church of the Pilgrims" see above Aspects [A].
[4] See the beginning of Aspects [D] above.
[5] See Aspects [A] above.

Aquitaine," and their places at Vézelay taken by "foreigners"–that is, no doubt, by a colony of monks from Cluny.

Once established at Vézelay, the new abbot set about putting the affairs of his abbey in order after the chaos of the preceding years. He met with Abbot Hugh of Pontigny in the presence of Bernard of Clairvaux and Matthew, cardinal-bishop of Albano, in 1133 and, probably on that occasion, arranged to cede Vézelay's priory of Chaalis near Senlis to the abbey of Pontigny in return for an annual rent. In 1135 he ceded to the monks of Ham in the diocese of Noyon the church of Mary Magdalene there, and received from the bishop of Noyon the church and tithes of *Fraxinus*.[1] Alberic also arranged an amicable settlement of disputes with a local lord over their respective rights to properties and serfs at Bessy-sur-Cure; but his greatest achievement was the arbitration of 1137 that aimed to resolve peacefully a number of difficult issues that had arisen in Vézelay itself.[2] The hearings on these issues consisted of at least two sessions in which both the abbot and the burghers were allowed to explain their grievances to a panel of arbiters, who then withdrew to consider how they should be settled. Alberic made it clear that his chief concern was to follow the established traditional practices, which the preceding period of confusion had no doubt enveloped in some obscurity, while at the same time allowing for a fair exercise of the abbey's rights in new circumstances where tradition was no longer an adequate guide. The first panel of arbiters included the bishop of Auxerre, the abbots of Pontigny, Reigny, and Trois-Fontaines, and the prior of Clairvaux,[3] and these were able to settle some of the questions at issue. A second day of hearings was then scheduled before the same group of arbiters, to whom were joined the abbot of Corbigny and, at Alberic's special request, Count William of Nevers. "Several others" were also present, and when the final decisions were reached on all of the outstanding issues, a dozen men listed by name were called upon to participate.[4] Since most of these can be identified as vassals and familiars of the count of Nevers, it is possible that the final arbitration took place at William's court. Although this court of arbiters was thus made up of seigneurial lords, there is every indication that the burghers were given ample opportunity to air their views, and the resulting decisions are remarkably even-handed.

The charter of 1137 makes it clear that the town of Vézelay had greatly increased in both size and wealth since the time of Abbot Artaud, and that the ambitious building program since 1120 had greatly depleted the abbey's resources. Alberic's predecessors since Abbot Artaud had apparently been unwilling to risk antagonizing the townsmen by adjusting the terms on which the abbey's revenues were based so as to take the new affluence into account, and Alberic's energetic measures to do so had brought the community to the brink of rebellion. . . .

---

[1] Berlow (1971: 173–76). *Fraxinus* has eluded attempts to identify it.

[2] Quantin (1854/60), below Appendix B, above 31ff.

[3] The text here is defective. Appendix B §3. The last arbiter is given as "Geoffrey, prior of Clairvaux," and the gap following his name may mean that there were other arbiters on this first panel as well.

[4] Appendix B below §27.

On 3 April 1138 Abbot Alberic was removed from the abbey of Vézelay by Pope Innocent II, who consecrated him as cardinal-bishop of Ostia and thus attached him to the papal curia. In his seven years as abbot, Alberic had done much to reconcile the aspirations of his lay subjects with the rights and concerns of his monks, and to restore harmony and discipline in a monastic community that had been rife with dissension. Peter the Venerable was fearful that the Vézelayans might fall into chaos and strife again if the strong hand of Alberic were removed, and he wrote to Innocent to protest against his removal. "I shall not presume to remind you in detail of the condition in which he found that house when he was installed there by us in your name, or of what he has accomplished since then. You have heard tell of it, but we have been able to assess it in person. You know it, perhaps, but we know it better still. That monastery standing upon an arid mountain and shrouded in shadows he has made fertile in good works and resplendent with the brightness of a justified renown, so much so that in our country, except for Cluny, Vézelay knows no rival among the houses of our order, and one can truly say with the psalmist, 'Behold a fertile mountain, a mountain filled with abundance, a mountain where the Lord is pleased to dwell!'"[1] Abbot Peter's protests went unheard, however, and it was necessary therefore to provide the abbey of the Magdalene with another pastor who would be capable of continuing Alberic's good works. The choice fell upon Peter's own younger brother Pontius [Pons], then monk at the abbey of San Michele della Chiusa, high on a rocky cliff overlooking the road from Turin to the Mont Cenis pass into Savoy. Pontius was probably the fourth or fifth of the seven sons of Maurice II de Montboissier, the head of an important baronial clan in the Auvergne, whose grandfather, Hugh *Dissutus* (Hugh "the Unstitched"), is thought to have been the founder of the abbey at La Chiusa.[2] The pious energy of the great-grandsire was to bear ample fruit in Pontius's generation, in which no fewer than five of the brothers became churchmen of rank: Heraclius as archbishop of Lyon (1153–1163); the rest as abbots, of Cluny (Peter the Venerable, 1122–1156), of La Chaise-Dieu (Jordan, 1146–1157/58), of Manglieu (Armannus, c. 1152/53–?), and of Vézelay (Pontius, 1138–1161). A more immediate source of inspiration for these young men in their choice of ecclesiastical careers was no doubt, as in the case of Saint Bernard, the example of their mother, Raingard. Nothing certain is known about her family, but according to her son Peter, despite her youthful beauty and her marriage, she had always yearned for heavenly things "like a prisoner of liberty, like an exile for his homeland."[3] The cares and responsibilities of presiding over the household of an important castle and a family of eight boys were never permitted to interfere with Raingard's fascination with religion, and the least reputation for piety—or simply the appearance of someone in clerical garb—was sufficient for her to insist upon a visit. "Monks she received with enthusi-

---

[1] Constable (1967: 1:193; *Letter* 64).

[2] Ibid. 2:235–36, 244. The curious surname "Unstitched" apparently derived from his frequent fits of generosity, in which he would tear the stitches out of his clothing in his eagerness to give the garment to someone in need.

[3] Ibid. 1:158; *Letter* 53.

asm, hermits were brought by force to the castle, all those whose ecclesiastical garments or pious renown were commended to her attention were obliged, even against their will, to accept her hospitality." Even before the birth of Peter she was in communication with Saint Hugh of Cluny and then with Saint Robert d'Arbrissel, the founder of the famous double monastery of Fontevrault; and shortly after her husband's death in 1116/17 she became a nun at the Cluniac convent of Marcigny, where she died in the odor of sanctity in 1135.[1] The new abbot of Vézelay thus belonged to a family whose members were as distinguished for their contributions to Christianity and the Church as they were for their lineage and aristocratic connections; but they did not always dwell together in perfect harmony. For a son without a religious bent, life with Raingard must have been somewhat trying, and there is some indication of friction between the lay and ecclesiastical brothers in the family. In a letter written c. 1141, Peter the Venerable refers to a quarrel that had erupted between Heraclius, then provost of Saint-Julien-de-Brioude, and Eustace, who was probably the youngest of the brothers.[2] Later, in the early 1150s, when Eustace had become a knight and the only Montboissier brother still in secular life, he began to attack the priory of Sauxillanges and Peter had to get Pope Adrian IV to place that monastery under the protection of the archbishops of Lyon and Vienne. The reasons for Eustace's behavior are unfortunately unknown, but since the Montboissier family had long been patrons and benefactors of Sauxillanges, it is possible that the hostilities had something to do with Eustace's attempts to establish or maintain what he regarded as his rights and privileges there, much as the counts of Nevers were trying to do at Vézelay during those same years.

Pontius [Pons] was clearly destined for an ecclesiastical career from very early on, as his years of schooling at Vézelay (and perhaps also at Sauxillanges or even Cluny) indicate, but he may not have been altogether happy about it. The company of a distinguished older brother like Peter would have made a great deal of difference for a young man unsure of his vocation, but when Peter left his post as prior of Vézelay to become prior of the Cluniac house at Domène near Grenoble in 1120, Pontius seems to have felt abandoned. The only source of information we have on this period of his life is to be found in a rather remarkable letter written to Pontius by Peter at some point after his installation as abbot of Cluny.[3] In it he approves of Pontius's pilgrimage to "the tombs of the martyrs" (presumably in Rome), but defends himself against Pontius's complaint that he had forgotten his younger brother now that he had risen to so "majestic" a position. Peter was reproached for not having written in a very long time and for not having sent Pontius a tunic he had apparently been promised. The abbot of Cluny excused himself for the delay in writing and promised to send the tunic, but he in turn reproached Pontius for having abruptly departed without so much as a word of farewell. "Your conduct is the subject of all the conversation here," wrote Peter. "It

---

[1] Constable (1967: 2:238–39).

[2] Ibid. 2:241.

[3] Ibid. 1:22–23 (*Letter* 16, which can be dated no more precisely than between 1122 and 1138, not, "a few years after" 1122, as Berlow affirms).

seems inexplicable. What! You, my brother in God and my blood brother according to the laws of nature, you my most intimate friend, you abandon me like a refugee, you escape like a criminal, like a thief in the night, out of hatred or out of scorn for me, without even saying goodbye!" Peter then went on to remind his errant sibling of the almost ten years the two had lived together, years filled with exchanges of confidence, with fervent discourses on spiritual matters, with aspirations for eternal life, with contempt for all worldly things.

It would be fascinating to know more about the circumstances to which this letter refers, but unfortunately additional information is not available.[1] Perhaps Pontius had been present at Cluny for his brother's installation as abbot, felt neglected and ignored, and returned to his cell at San Michele della Chiusa full of resentment that he had not been given a share in his brother's good fortune. Or perhaps this letter should be dated later, in the 1130s rather than the 1120s, shortly after the death of their mother, Raingard, in 1135. On that occasion Peter wrote to his brothers about their mother's life, and Pontius might have come back to France to be present at his mother's funeral. If Pontius were unhappy with his life as a monk at San Michele, such a visit would have been an opportunity for him to apply to his brother for a more congenial position, and the failure of his petition could explain both his reproaches and his strange behavior. Such a visit, however, would have served to remind friends at Cluny, and perhaps also at Vézelay, of his availability. Who proposed Pontius for the vacancy at Vézelay in 1138 is not known, but it is quite possible that the initiative came from the community at Vézelay itself, since Pontius combined the advantages of a past familiarity with the place through his years of schooling there and the required connection with Cluny, both as a Cluniac monk and as a brother of the abbot.

This attempt to recapture the "real" Pontius de Montboisser, especially during the years prior to his election as abbot of Vézelay, may appear excessively speculative, but so many conflicting judgements have been passed upon him during and since his own time that some effort to place them in perspective would seem in order. For Constable, who viewed him above all as a difficult younger brother of Peter the Venerable, Pontius was "certainly the most notorious" of the Montboissiers; and he quotes the judgement of De Lespinasse, whose vantage point was the history of the counts of Nevers, that Pontius was the sort of man made "to shine at the head of an army more than in the calm of a cloister."[2] For Berlow, concerned above all with the economic and social conditions in and around Vézelay at the time, Pontius was "a spoiled child" of "selfish pettiness" who even in full maturity was "totally lacking in ... *caritas*...."[3] René Louis blamed Pontius for antagonizing

---

[1] Berlow's denunciation of Pontius (1971: 188–90) seems to me rather extreme—perhaps an over-reaction to Hugh the Poitevin's overly favorable bias—considering the total absence of all information on the circumstances.

[2] Constable (1967: 2:243–44).

[3] Berlow (1971: 189, 194).

all the parties with whom the monks had had good relations by 1138,[1] and
Chérest, foreshadowing De Lespinasse's opinion, pronounced him "born for
command and domination" and affirmed that "he would have shone at the
head of an army or of a province as much as, and perhaps more than, at the
head of an abbey."[2] Chérest, however, went on to say that it was not that
Pontius was lacking in piety or in religious zeal, but only that during a career
so full of agitation and turns of fortune, the "humility of the Benedictine"
more often than not gave way to the impetuous passions of the feudal grand
seigneur. Chérest also points out that this was what was expected of an abbot
of Vézelay by 1138, where it was hardly a question of humility or renunciations of worldly grandeur. For the monastic community at Vézelay, he wrote,
issues of hierarchy took precedence over issues of discipline, and temporal
questions over questions of religion. "In other words, Vézelay was not purely
and simply an abbey; it was also—it was above all—an ecclesiastical principality,
and that is why Abbot Pontius deserved to be the choice of the monks of the
Magdalene." If Pontius had in fact been unhappy with his life as a simple
monk—if, as we have surmised, his temperament was more akin to that of his
youngest brother, Eustace the warlord, than to that of Peter the Venerable—
then his sudden change of fortune in 1138 was a heaven-sent opportunity.
Now at last he occupied a position that would challenge to the utmost his
abilities and his character alike. At the request of his brother Peter, Pontius
received the benediction from Steven de Bâgé, bishop of Autun, who soon
after resigned his episcopal dignity and retired to end his days at Cluny.[3]
One non-monastic aspect of Pontius's temperment was an evident fondness
for money-men. On or shortly after his installation at Vézelay, apparently
without consulting his monks, the new abbot granted to one Simon from
Souvigny in the Bourbonnais special permission to establish a money-dealing
business adjacent to his house in Vézelay.[4] Souvigny was already well known
as the location of the earliest of the Cluniac mints, and Simon soon became
enormously wealthy, with a wide-ranging clientele that included many magnates in the region. The concessions made to Simon were later ordered revoked by Pope Adrian IV on the grounds that they constituted an illegal alienation of abbey property, and the monks destroyed his place of business in
1155 in the aftermath of the Vézelay rebellion. But Simon's prosperity seems
scarcely to have been affected—a decade later he was still in a position to offer
hospitality to the countess of Nevers in his Vézelay mansion. Again, in his
final years, Pontius fell under the spell of an ingratiating young man named
William de Montreal, who seems to have built up a lucrative money-lending
operation making use of abbey funds. He even appropriated treasures stored
in the abbey's *armaria* and the chapter's seal, which he hid in his own Vézelay

---

[1] Louis (1946: 180).

[2] Chérest 1:119–20.

[3] See *Major Chronicle* below 1 §5.

[4] *Major Chronicle* 3, 212n.5 and Appendix B note to §11; Berlow (1971: 313, 315–17);
Chérest 1:39–42, 62. Chérest believed that Pontius was once prior of Souvigny and that he
brought Simon with him when he came to Vézelay.

townhouse, presumably for use in further banking operations.[1] Despite his admiration and fondness for the abbot, Hugh the Poitevin indignantly reports that Pontius followed William's unworthy counsels in everything, and that only his death led to William's exposure and disgrace.

Pontius assumed the reins of government at a propitious moment. The arbitration of 1137 had brought peace to the community and the count of Nevers, who had participated in the arbitration, had left soon after to accompany Prince Louis to Bordeaux for his marriage to Eleanor of Aquitaine in July. Louis VI died at the beginning of August, and Count William, like the other great vassals of the crown, was expected to be present when the new queen was crowned at Christmas in Paris. These events seem to have occupied the count of Nevers during the last months of Alberic's tenure at Vézelay, and although William was apparently present at Vézelay for Pontius's installation, a feisty new bishop of Auxerre, Hugh de Mâcon, was to occupy him thereafter with his demands for the restoration of property and rights which the count was accused of having taken away from the church of Auxerre under an overly complaisant episcopal predecessor.[2] At Autun Steven de Bâgé, after presiding over the construction of the new cathedral of Saint Lazarus, brother of Mary Magdalene, which was consecrated by Pope Innocent II in 1132, and after giving his blessing to the new abbot of Vézelay, resigned his see and was replaced by Robert de Bourgogne, the fourth son of Duke Hugh II.[3] Robert, however, died in July 1140, so for the first two years of his abbacy Pontius had nothing to fear from the diocesan pretensions of the church of Autun....

While the monks of the Magdalene were fending off the efforts of their diocesan bishop to compromise their liberties, they were also fending off the encroachments of the count of Nevers. In the 1140s William II was an old man in his sixties with aspirations to make an edifying end as a Carthusian monk, but he was by no means always so ready to make an end of his seigneurial pretensions.[4] He did, in 1143, confirm all of the possessions of the Cluniac house at La Charité-sur-Loire, renounce all judicial authority over the abbey and its environs, and give up his rights to collect tolls or demand hospitality in their *villas*. Yet these generous impulses were nowhere evident when the retirement of Bishop Fromont from the see of Nevers led to a spirited three-way struggle among candidates to succeed him. William stub-

---

[1] See the *Major Chronicle* below 4 §8.

[2] William's presence is attested in *Major Chronicle* 1 §5 below. On Auxerre, see Bouchard (1979: 54ff.).

[3] The *Dictionnaire de Biographie française* 13 (1975), "Etienne de Bâgé," gives the date of his retirement as 1136, as do many other authorities. But his participation in the installation of Pontius, which cannot have been earlier than April 1138, shows that he was still acting as bishop then. Constable (1967: 2:194) gives 1138/39, and Huygens (1976: 677) gives 1139 as the correct date for Steven's retirement, which would seem confirmed by Hugh's chronicle.

[4] De Lespinasse (1909–14: 1:293). The desire to become a Carthusian is expressed in the 1143 charter to La Charité. The choice of Carthusians, rather than Cistercians or Cluniacs, suggests that William's many dealings with the monks of those orders had not persuaded him of their spiritual superiority.

bornly ignored the protests of Saint Bernard, who denounced him for "fraud" and "artifice," and he finally managed to get his own man into the office. At the same time the count was engaged in a bitter conflict with Bishop Hugh of Auxerre over the administration of justice in the city of Auxerre.[1] This time Saint Bernard was asked to arbitrate in the dispute, and in 1145 William finally accepted a settlement that made him the bishop's vassal for several castles, gave the bishop jurisdiction over his own *familia* and all clerics in Auxerre, and compromised the count's rights to city taxes and tolls, guards in the nearby vineyards, and exploitation of nearby woods.

With all of these threats to his authority coming from churchmen in his dominions, it is perhaps not surprising that William should have been in no mood to welcome similar threats from the community at Vézelay. Abbot Pontius, however, perhaps with the knowledge of William's recent concessions to Vézelay's sister house at La Charité, apparently chose this moment (1143–1145) to protest against the monetary exactions that the counts of Nevers had become accustomed to levying upon his abbey. . . .

Conventions of the Present Volume

We have aimed at some sort of fidelity to the often stilted and just as often overflowingly purple original, while introducing a measure of freedom at different points for the purpose of easier comprehension by English readers. We have retained the "chapter titles" of the *PL* edition of the Latin text, for the sake of easier consultation and comprehension. These are not in the Auxerre manuscript and are not always entirely appropriate. The numbering of these "chapters" is our own.

Introductory editorial remarks or summaries/paraphrases, etc., included for the sake of continuity, have been placed between square brackets to distinguish them from the translated passages. The original Latin for some words and phrases, where provided within the translation, is placed within square brackets, or else is added as a footnote. Expansions/alternatives/words added for clarity, the occasional editorial "comment" *en passant*, have sometimes been inserted in the translation between square brackets.

The translations of the 1137 *Accord*, the *Brief History*, and the *Major Chronicle* are as complete as the present state of the manuscripts will allow. The *Cartulary* has been partly calendared and partly translated in full.

The *Minor Chronicle* or *Annals* has been translated in full only for the twelfth century. Earlier entries have been summarized in tabular form (see Fig. 15).

The notes attempt to give the original Latin for all contentious or interest-

---

[1] Ibid., 295; Bouchard (1979: 53–55).

ing or significant words and phrases. They also supply in summary form material designed to enable a reader to comprehend the text and to secure further information in regard to persons places, events, institutions, etc., mentioned in the text. We are indebted for much information to the notes appended to the Guizot-Vogade translation, to the excellent and meticulous annotations of R. B. C. Huygens, and to the valuable annotations Professor Eugene Cox prepared for his own translation (see Preface above). We are grateful for the opportunity of having access to this material and have, here and there, reminded the reader of the source of our information. Professor Cox's material has in every case been acknowledged, and usually quoted verbatim.

All works listed in the General Bibliography—to be found at the end of the volume—are cited elsewhere by name or abbreviation and, where necessary, date of publication only. A few bibliographical items of minor importance are not listed in the General Bibliography: they are given in full where they occur. Proper names have caused insoluble confusion (see Huygens 1976: xl). In general we have tried to give English equivalents if only to indicate the meaning of some of the names. Doubtless most persons in the twelfth century would have carried names in the dialect of their region, which in many cases would have sounded more like their modern French equivalents than either the notarial Latin in which the church laboriously kept its records or the modern English of the present translation. Sometimes, therefore, where it was available and seemed more natural than the English, we have used a French equivalent. Names for which we could suggest neither an English nor a French version are left in the original Latin but italicized. In passages cited from or written by E. L. Cox, the reader will find the form of a name preferred by Professor Cox, even if it differs from our own practice. For the resultant miscegenation we apologize, but can do no better.

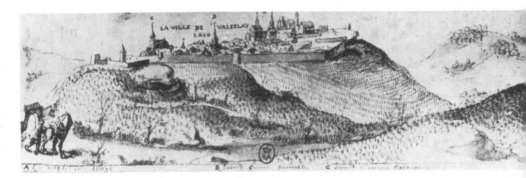

Fig. 3. Vézelay in 1610 (from Guizot [1969], by permission of F. Vogade): A: Basilica, chapel of St. Nicholas, abbatial château and its outbuildings; B: Church of St. Peter; C: Church of St. Stephen. Below, left, the bridge en route to Clamecy. Note the good condition of the ramparts, towers, and gates, and the hillsides planted with vines.

Fig. 4. The abbey church of the Magdalene at Vézelay as it is today (J. O. Ward).

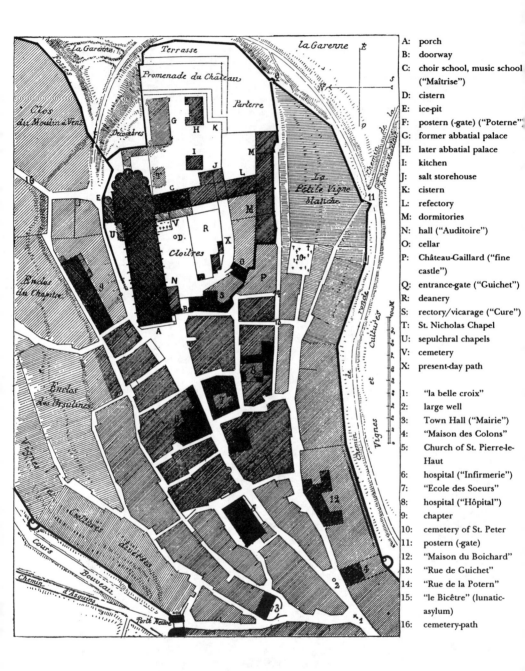

A:	porch
B:	doorway
C:	choir school, music school ("Maîtrise")
D:	cistern
E:	ice-pit
F:	postern (-gate) ("Poterne")
G:	former abbatial palace
H:	later abbatial palace
I:	kitchen
J:	salt storehouse
K:	cistern
L:	refectory
M:	dormitories
N:	hall ("Auditoire")
O:	cellar
P:	Château-Gaillard ("fine castle")
Q:	entrance-gate ("Guichet")
R:	deanery
S:	rectory/vicarage ("Cure")
T:	St. Nicholas Chapel
U:	sepulchral chapels
V:	cemetery
X:	present-day path
1:	"la belle croix"
2:	large well
3:	Town Hall ("Mairie")
4:	"Maison des Colons"
5:	Church of St. Pierre-le-Haut
6:	hospital ("Infirmerie")
7:	"Ecole des Soeurs"
8:	hospital ("Hôpital")
9:	chapter
10:	cemetery of St. Peter
11:	postern (-gate)
12:	"Maison du Boichard"
13:	"Rue de Guichet"
14:	"Rue de la Potern"
15:	"le Bicêtre" (lunatic-asylum)
16:	cemetery-path

Fig. 5. Plan of town and abbey of Vézelay
(from Vogade [1987: 41–42], by permission of F. Vogade).

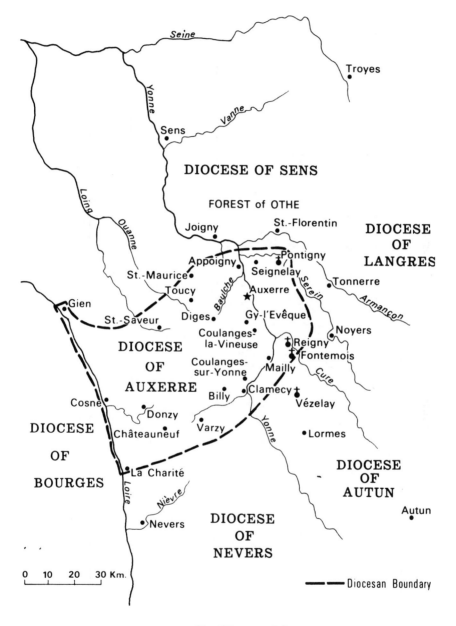

The Diocese of Auxerre

Fig. 6. The Diocese of Auxerre (from Bouchard [1979: 7],
by permission of the Mediaeval Academy of America).

CENTURY / SUBJECT MATTER	1–100 A.D.	101–200 A.D.	201–300 A.D.	301–400 A.D.	401–500 A.D.	501–600 A.D.	601–700 A.D.	701–800 A.D.	800–900 A.D.	901–1000 A.D.	1001–1100 A.D.	Total Entries
Religious and Christian history in general; Israel	17	1		4	5	3	4	1	1		5	41
Imperial history (mainly regnal dates)	10	6	15	10	7	6	10	9	2	1		76
Islamic History							2					2
Papal events (mainly regnal dates)	3	9	14	10	13	24	21	5	19	28	18	164
Secular Latin culture	3	1						1				5
General secular history (famines etc.)	2						3	3	5			13
Portents and geographical or astronomical phenomena (earthquakes, fires, etc.)	2						1	2	5	3	7	20
National affairs (almost entirely French)					3	4	9	35	[See immediately below]		7	51
Frankish imperial affairs									7	12	10	29
Dukes/local counts										7	9	16
Local Vézelay history									7	6	9	22
The French Church										3	2	5
Normans in England											3	3
Imperial Germany										5	5	10
TOTAL ENTRIES	37	17	29	24	28	37	50	56	46	65	68	457

Fig. 7. Tabular summary of pre-twelfth-century entries in the *Annals, Minor or Little Chronicle* (MS. Auxerre 227, fols. 1–17).

Annals
[Annals or Minor or Little Chronicle]

[Folios 1–17 of the Auxerre manuscript are occupied by a series of annals, beginning with the commencement of the Christian era. The entries for the twelfth century are translated here in full, to give an idea of the scope of the *annals* and because they are the ones of most interest to historians of the town of Vézelay.

The entries for the earlier centuries are more conventional and their changing contents and emphases can be assessed from the accompanying table (Fig. 15), which gives in the left hand margin a brief classification of subjects, at the top the century, and below that the number of entries for that century dealing with the subject matter indicated at left. Each entry is listed only once, under its dominant content heading. An entry represents a separate sentence as printed in the Huygens edition: the layout for the translated portions approximates the layout in Huygens's edition, and in the manuscript itself. For detailed notes on the translated portions, the reader is referred to Huygens 1976: 224–33.]

Entries for the Twelfth Century [Huygens 1976: 224–33]

Dedication of the church of Vézelay built by Abbot Artaud.	1104	The storms are so fierce that buried bodies are thrown up from the ground.
	1106	Henry V is emperor over the Romans.
Paschal [II] comes into France.	1107	He held a synod in Troyes.
	1108	Renaud vigorous as the abbot of Vézelay.
	1109	Philip [I] king of the Franks dies and is succeeded by Louis [VI].
	1111	Emperor Henry seized Pope Paschal and threw him into chains.
Raging winds destroy houses and woods.	1116	William [II], count of Nevers, is taken at Annay-la-Côte [*Annacum*]. In the monastery of Déols, a boy appeared on the altar instead of the host, in front of the chalice, as a certain monk was celebrating mass.
There was an earthquake.	1117	
Calixtus is pope. Matilda, queen of the English dies.	1118	William, the son of King Henry of the English is drowned.
In this year in the monastery of Vézelay many men and	1120	

women are consumed by fire.[1]
The order of Premonstraten-
sian Canons begins. Honorius
is pope.

	1124	Baldwin is abbot of Vézelay.
	1125	Lothar, duke of Saxony rules.[2]
	1127	Charles, count of Flanders is killed by his own men using a stratagem.[3]
William duke of Aquitaine dies.	1128	Philip, a boy, is crowned while his father lives.[4]
Innocent is pope. Alberic is abbot of Vézelay.	1130	A spear appeared in the sky and a wondrous sign on the moon. The boy Philip is suffocated. There is dissension in the Roman Church. Peter Leone is condemned and Gregory, also called Innocent, is accepted by the Church and comes into Gaul. He holds a synod at Clermont-Ferrand and another at Rheims. He consecrated[5] Louis the son of King Louis.
Henry, king of the English dies and Stephen his nephew rules. There is night at the third hour of the day.	1135	
	1136	A horrible sign appeared four days before the nones of March.
	1137	Louis, king of France dies and his son Louis reigns. William, duke of Aquitaine dies, whose daughter Eleanor King Louis had previously wed.
Alberic passes on and Pons is ordained abbot of Vézelay. This man, the brother of Abbot Peter of Cluny, is drawn from the monastery of Saint-Michel-de-Cluse [San Michele della Chiusa—above 80].	1138	
	1140	Hugh of St. Victor dies.[6]
	1141	Hugh, duke of Burgundy dies; his son Odo succeeds.
Celestine is pope for six months. Lucius [II] is pope.	1142	Ice breaks the bridges over the waterways.
	1144	A voice is heard speaking from the earth in Gaul at Choisel.

Eugenius is pope.   1145   The town of Edessa is taken by the pagans.[7]

King Louis takes the cross of a journey to Jerusalem at Vézelay, during Easter, and the greatest multitude does so with him.[8]   1147   The king went to Jerusalem.

1150   King Louis returned from Jerusalem.

1151   A serious famine.

1152   Count Thibault [II of Champagne] dies.

Anastasius is pope.   1153

Bernard, abbot of Clairvaux, dies.   1154   A boy is born and in the pupil of one of his eyes, written in normal characters [*naturaliter scriptum*], is read "man of God" and in the other "a good man."

Hadrian is pope.   1155

1156   The burghers of Vézelay formed a depraved commune [*pravam communiam*] against the abbot Pons and their lords the brothers of the monastery of Vézelay. Forced by King Louis, they abjured it [by swearing an oath of loyalty] in his hand.[9]

With Pope Hadrian dead there is a schism in the papacy. Octavian is repudiated and Roland, called Alexander, is accepted by the Church.   1158

Abbot Pons of Vézelay dies and William, abbot of [Saint-Martin-de-] Pontoise is ordained in his stead.   1161   Count William dies.

1162   A conference is held between the king and the emperor and Duke Odo [II of Burgundy] dies.

1163   Council of Tours.

Philip, son of King Louis is born.   1165   William, count of Nevers and his mother Ida are excommunicated on behalf of the church of Vézelay. Pope Alexander returns and is installed at Rome.

The count makes peace with Vézelay and takes up the cross.   1166

The *Populicani* are burnt at Vézelay.	1167	Emperor Frederick flees from Italy [Fuhrmann (1986: 160).
The burghers of Vézelay conspire against the Church.	1168	The aforesaid count dies at [St. John of] Acre.
	1169	The city of Catania is destroyed in an earthquake.
In this year, about the time of the Feast of the Apostles Peter and Paul, a great earthquake occurred lasting fifteen days in the lands across the sea. Many towns and forts of both Christians and Saxons and the greater part of the walls of Antioch collapsed.	1170	
	1171	Abbot William dies. His successor, Gerard, is joyously installed.
Lucius [III] is pope.	1184	
Urban III is pope.	1185	
Gregory VIII is pope.	1187	Henry, king of the English dies and his son Richard succeeds him.
Clement III is pope.	1188	In this year, around the [time of the celebration of the] translation of [the relics of] the Holy Martin, the city of Acre and many other cities and fortified centers [*castella*] were taken by Saladin, and the cross of the Lord was taken along with the king; and in the same year around [the time of] the Feast of St. Michael, the holy city of Jerusalem was taken by Saladin and all were either captured or put to the sword.
Celestine III is pope.	1190	
William *de Brene* [Brienne] with his army burnt Asquins, Précy-le-Sec, and Blannay, and several others of our localities.	1196	
Pope Celestine dies. Innocent succeeds.	1197	
Abbot Gerard dies. Hugh succeeds.	1198	Richard, king of the English dies. John, his brother receives the kingdom.[10]

Notes to the Entries

1. On this fire see Graham (1918: 42); Berlow (1981: 329). Note that the annalist makes no reference to the murder of Abbot Artaud in 1106!

2. *imperat*, i.e., rules as "emperor," though Lothar III (1125–1137 AD) was not crowned emperor until 1133 AD. See Hampe (1973: chap. 8), Barraclough (1957: 155–58), Fuhrmann (1986: 116ff.), Haverkamp (1988: 135ff.).

3. See Ross (1960).

4. Philip, son of Louis VI of France, associated in the government of the realm 14 April 1129, dies 13 October 1131.

5. *iniunxit*. On the schism of the 1130s see Stroll (1987).

6. Cf. Taylor (1961).

7. Runciman (1952: 2:225ff.).

8. Ibid., 247–63.

9. This date is incorrect. See below *Major Chronicle* 2 §19 (between 1151 and 1153).

10. There are another twenty or so entries covering events down to the year 1316 AD and dealing with similar subjects, that is, the succession of kings, counts, dukes, pontiffs, and abbots, local wars (such as the *guerra* of Count Guildo of Nevers and Forey and Countess Matilda against the church of Vézelay and the burghers of the ville recorded for the year 1230 AD), crusading affairs, miracles, Sicilian events, matters relating to saints and relics, disputes between townsmen and the church of Vézelay (see entry for 1250), ecclesiastical councils and the like.

Fig. 8. The Church of St. Stephen as it is today (J. O. Ward).

Brief History
[A Short History of the First Counts of Nevers]

c. 880–1149   [Folios 18–19v: Huygens 235–239]

The castle of *Nivedunus*, which is now called Nevers [*Nivernus*], is situated on the river Nièvre at the furthest edges of Burgundy, and just below it flows the river Loire, which divides Celtic from Aquitainian Gaul. In the most distant past that castle resembled nothing more than a tiny hamlet. It was ruled by Count Rather,[1] who held it by right of homage [*iure hominii*] from the lordship of the count of Burgundy. On one occasion the accusation was levelled against him by the knight *Alicherius* that he had violated the marriage bed of his lord; whereupon he took part in a duel with his accuser on the island which is known today by the name of the victor.[2]

Rather brandished his spear and struck *Alicherius* beneath his jaw, piercing his mouth. "Let that mouth which spoke so freely atone for its lies," he cried. "It is certainly not atoning for lies," said *Alicherius*, "but for keeping quiet for so long about your adultery." With these words he rose up fiercely and struck Rather, who fell down, beaten and condemned, and soon died.

Then for a long time the castle remained in the hands of the count of Burgundy,[3] who held it by right of lordship. At that time the king of the Franks died and left a very young son who, it was decided by the common counsel of the chief men of the Franks, was placed under the guardianship of Richard the Justiciar, to whom was committed care of the whole kingdom. And Richard brought up the boy with piety and love and ruled the kingdom with justice.

There was a castle in the territory of Nevers named Metz-le-Comte, which was very secure because of its fortifications and its location and very rich in the number of its men. The inhabitants of this castle, the worst of men, used to devote themselves to banditry and would rob, capture, and kill travellers who passed by. When news of their wickedness came to the ears of Richard the Justiciar, he collected a large army and besieged the castle. Augier [*Hildegarius*], bishop of Autun,[4] was among the chief men and bishops from all over Gaul who attended this siege.

This man, born in Poitiers, was the deacon of the king of the Franks.[5] Once when he was tempted, as men are, it happened that the king, rising from his sick bed at night and lying by a window, saw Augier dallying with a

---

[1] The only other reference to Rather is in a charter of Varennes; it is discussed by Chaume (1977), who suggests that he is to be identified with count Roger, nephew of Count Hugh II of Bourges (d. 892).

[2] This island is unknown; nor does it survive in toponymy.

[3] This was Richard the Justiciar (880–921), tutor of his nephew Louis III, the blind (born 880), who was the son of Richard's brother Boso, king of Burgundy-Provence (died 887).

[4] Augier, bishop of Autun, 875–893.

[5] Charles the Bald, 840–877.

young girl in a corner of the palace. The king was greatly astonished at this because Augier's sobriety and respectability had commended themselves to the king, and so he warily awaited the outcome of the affair. There was a lot of snow on the ground and so as Augier left, the young girl followed him and smoothed over his footsteps with her hand, walking backwards so that she also eliminated her own tracks. So, marvelling at the cunning of the woman, the king returned to bed.

When the king had risen in the morning and was attending divine service, he saw that Augier, who as it happened should have been reciting the gospel reading,[1] had appointed a vicar and did not approach the altar himself. The king wanted to test whether Augier would abstain out of reverence for the sacraments, and so he called him and ordered him to put on the holy vestments and perform the appropriate office, as was his duty for the week. Augier, who was aware of his sin, began humbly to dissimulate and, when the king insisted, said that he was unwell. The king then became more and more insistent while Augier offered more and more excuses, until the king's warnings turned to orders and his orders to threats against Augier, who, moved more by fear of God than of a man, finally left the church, repudiating the king's orders and anger.

When the solemnities of the mass had been completed, the clerics of Autun, now without a bishop of their own, met the king as he was leaving and offered to him, in the custom of their forefathers, the episcopal insignia, namely the ring and the staff, and beseeched him to give them a bishop. At once the accompanying palace officials, wise as regarding affairs of the flesh [though] not in regard to divine affairs, each began to cry out for his own candidate. But the king was divinely inspired and at once ordered Augier to be called, to the terror of the courtiers [*aulici*], who feared that in his indignation the king might drive him out of the palace—for Augier was loved by all. As he stood shaking before the king, the latter called him aside and jokingly said to him: "I would gladly have saddled up the fair mule you were riding last night if you had let me know beforehand." The terrified Augier feared that he had been reported on or seen by the king and so threw himself at his feet and cried out: "I have sinned and am as a man who is fallen," But the king said to him: "Take particular heed now and, just as you put reverence for God before fear of me, in future put the fear of God before your own pleasures lest, while you rightly fear sacred things because of your transgressions, you are considered guilty because of your transgression and negligence of the duty you owe." Then, calling together the clergy of Autun and all his nobles, he handed over to Augier the ring and the staff and committed to him the care of the bishopric of the church of Autun.

It was while he was ruling that church with skill and prudence that Augier came with the others to the siege mentioned above; and with him was his nephew Landric. The army approached the castle [of Metz-le-Comte] and attacked it boldly. When the lord of the castle saw that he could not hold out, he prepared a great feast for the citizens and, while they were all lying

---

[1] *ebdomadarius evangelii.*

around, he himself stood up, pretending to be weary, mounted a horse in secret, and escaped through the middle of the army. All the quickest [soldiers] sprang up and pursued the fugitive but were unable to catch him. It happened, however, that Augier's nephew, Landric, who was commanding some cavalry,[1] encountered him, struck him a blow from his horse, and led him captive to Augier's tent. Since a priest ought not hand anyone over to his death, Augier hid the knight and sent his horse to the leader of the army. When the leader asked for the knight the reply was given that in his keenness to hold the horse their knight had neglected [to seize] that knight. So servants were sent to search Augier's tent; and the knight, who was discovered, and his horse were hung from a gibbet, and the captured castle was handed over to Augier's nephew, Landric, as his possession.

Landric married into the Angevin line and his wife bore him a son named Bodo, whose godfather was Bodo of the Mountains. When he grew up Bodo asked his godfather to give him something. His godfather replied: "What do you want given to you, my son?" "I want you," he said, "to grant me as much land as shall be shaded in one day by that nearby mountain." After gaining this request the young man began to get up early in the morning during summer to lay down the boundaries of his property all around, as they were marked out by the shadow cast by the very low sun. There he built a castle, called Monceaux-le-Comte, extended his father's borders and fathered a son named Landric.

This Landric became a man of great generosity who entertained almost anyone, be they noble or unknown, who passed by hastening on the way to the gates[2] of the blessed apostles Peter and Paul.[3] In his day people from all over Gaul and Britain[4] used to throng to those gates. Landric too, together with many other princes, on one occasion undertook the same pilgrimage. The others included the counts of Poitiers, Anjou and Burgundy.[5] As these three were returning home with Landric they celebrated Easter Monday at Viterbo, where they spent three days to relieve the burden of their journey. On the second day, Easter Tuesday, Landric, the son of Bodo, prepared a feast for everyone and when they had risen after the meal the count of Poitiers invited Landric to come with him back to the land of his ancestors, where he would load him up with great gifts. When Landric returned thanks to him, the count of Anjou said, "You ought rather come with me as it is your mother's family inviting you." In response the count of Burgundy said, "Why would he leave the land of his father to wander here or there when I can and want to enrich him there more than enough?" In reply Landric said to the count of Burgundy, "It is true that you can do a great deal. So I ask that you deem me worthy of the grant of that insignificant island, the castle of Nevers, so that when the dignity of a count has been granted to me honor

---

[1] *qui preerat cursariis.*

[2] *limina.*

[3] I.e., Rome.

[4] *omnis Gallicana et Britannica natio.*

[5] William II or III of Aquitaine, Fulk (III) Nerra of Anjou (987–1042), and Henry I of Burgundy (d. 1002), although none of the three is known to have made such a trip.

will redound to you and I will keep safe control of an inheritance adjacent to your own." The count of Burgundy replied, "I grant what you want and hand over the county of Nevers to you and your heirs, saving the right of homage [*salvo iure hominii*]."

This Landric,[1] the founder of the family, became count of Nevers and began to expand his borders in every direction. He had a son named Renaud,[2] who was joined in marriage to the sister of King Robert, the son of Hugh Capet, and thereby joined the county of Auxerre to that of Nevers. It was for the sake of this county that he engaged in a war with the duke of Burgundy,[3] in which he was killed at Seignelay, leaving both the triumph and the family inheritance on his death to his son William.[4]

William maintained the county for almost fifty years by the practice of warfare, with so much zeal that within all that time he would not have been able to tally up as much as even one year altogether in which he had kept the peace. Even when his blood was being let or he was relieving some other bodily care,[5] he did not enjoy a lesser crowd than fifty knights as his familiars in his company at table. He was so rich in possessions that he always had 50,000 *solidi* in his treasury, out of which towards the end of his life he built the basilica of Saint-Étienne outside the walls of the city of Nevers.[6] He expanded his borders into the territory of Langres, adding the county of Tonnerre to the counties of Nevers and Auxerre, making one county of the three. He fathered two sons, William and Renaud, of whom the former obtained control of Tonnerre and the latter had possession of Mailly-le-Chateau and Hubans, both noble towns. But both of them died before their father.[7]

William of Tonnerre had one daughter[8] from his wife and she was joined in matrimony to Aimon of Bourbon; while Renaud's first wife was the only daughter of the count of Forez[9] and she presented him with a daughter who was married to Miles of Courtenay. On the death of his first wife, Renaud married again, to the daughter of Lancelin of Beaugency, who bore him a son named William.[10] When Renaud was dying he sent his son into the care of his father. When he too died William took over as ruler of Nevers, Auxerre, and the province of Tonnerre and expanded his borders around the Loire and Allier rivers. Although he was an exemplary upholder of justice, he was the first to try to appropriate the monastery of Vézelay to himself, by citing

---

[1] Landric, the first count of Nevers, 991–1028. On him, and this account generally, see Lot (1903: 1–17).

[2] Renaud, count of Nevers 1028–1040. His marriage to Adelaide joined him to the Capetian dynasty.

[3] Robert I, duke of Burgundy (1031–1075).

[4] *hereditatem sanguinis*: William I, count of Nevers (1040–1098).

[5] The text seems to be corrupt here.

[6] Saint-Étienne of Nevers was founded in 1097.

[7] William's dates are unknown; Renaud died on 5 August 1089.

[8] Alsinde, wife of Aimon II of Bourbon.

[9] Ida-Raymonde, daughter of Artaud V de Forez.

[10] William II, count of Nevers (1098–1147); his mother was Agnes, daughter of Lancelin of Beaugency.

unheard of customs. He fathered William and Renaud,[1] who both advanced in military service (*militia*). When they had taken the road to Jerusalem with Louis, the king of the Franks, and the duke of Aquitaine, their father exchanged his earthly goods for heavenly ones and joined the Carthusians.[2]

[Two thirteenth-century hands then add a brief note about a sentence passed by the abbot of Vézelay and confirmed by Pope Innocent IV against the town and people of Vézelay who refused to right a wrong perpetrated against the abbot.]

[An intercalated fragment in a fourteenth-century hand extols the virtues and praises the deeds of Hugh of Maison-Comte, abbot of Vézelay 1358–1383.]

Fig. 9. Abbey Church of the Magdalene and the Church of St. Peter
from the northwest (J. O. Ward).

---

[1] William III, count of Nevers (1147–1161) and Renaud, count of Tonnerre (1147–1148).

[2] The two left with Louis VII in August 1147. Renaud died in 1148, but William returned 1149/50. It was his wife Ida who acted as regent while he was in the Holy Land. William II died at La Grande Chartreuse on 20 August 1149. For a comparable account of the "growth of government" in central medieval France see Southern (1953: 80ff.), Painter (1961) and Bachrach (1990: 29ff. and with literature there cited).

Cartulary

[Folios 22–63 of MS. Auxerre contain a collection of acts and privileges designed to illustrate Books 1–3 of the *Chronicle* that follows them. These are printed as the "cartulary" in Huygens (1976), but were labelled Book 1 of the *History* in the *PL* edition.]

CHARTER 1   858–859 AD

In the name of the holy and individual Trinity, the Father, Son, and Holy Ghost, the instrument or testament of Count Gerard, the founder of the monasteries of Pothières and Vézelay, begins, a testament confirmed and strengthened forever by subsequent privileges of apostolic authority that will follow.

To all the faithful of Christ who await the blessed life with piety, love, and fervent desire and who maintain Christian unity everywhere by obedience to the teachings of God, to those living now and those to come, who will be victorious through their strong bond of love and will succeed each other in the church of the saints up till the end of time, I, Gerard, raised to the honor of count by a gift of divine piety and by means of glorious royal clemency, give greetings. By a wish and desire shared by my beloved and living wife, Bertha, it has pleased us both together, thanks to God's inspiration, to establish from our possessions and the estates to which we hold titles, a memorial to our Lord God, where constant praise can be offered to him. And since our lords and masters, [*seniores*] who have most generously promoted us in honors and dignity—that is our emperor and master, the most clement Louis, and our glorious mistress and queen, Judith, and their son, also our lord and master, Charles,[1]—have greatly increased our possessions by their pious bequests, it has seemed only right to us, encouraged by our love for them, that we should found a certain place where constant prayers of thanks might be offered for their welcome gifts and where God might be solemnly and perpetually beseeched for their salvation. For we are not forgetful of the benevolence to us of our lord and master Louis Augustus, of Judith our mistress and queen, and of their son Charles, likewise our lord and master, who is presently ruling us; but we also want to return due honor to our forebears and parents, Leuthard and Grimild and the most beloved Hugh and Bava, and their sons and daughters worthy of love, both those who are sleeping with the Lord and those who are still alive, who are linked to us by blood, marriage, or even friendship, namely those most famous counts Leufred and Adalard, so that there might be constant prayers and intercession for them by which atonement might be made for their sins, so that there might be a lasting remembrance of them throughout succeeding ages in that place which we have founded with Christ's help, and so that a perpetual memorial will survive too

---

[1] That is, Louis the Pious and Charles the Bald.

to the kinsmen to whose possessions we succeeded by hereditary right and to all others, including all our friends and all the faithful generally, and so that prayers will be offered for all of them in common through the ages.

Therefore I, Gerard, together with my most beloved wife, have established and built, out of pious and faithful devotion, a monastery as a habitation for the servants of God in a suitable and appropriate place, and by gifts and offerings from our goods and possessions we have provided whatever is necessary to sustain those worshippers of God and to enable them to practice their religion. With pious and careful foresight, as befits the power that God bestowed on us, and with a most ready will we have offered these same things which we received from his hand as a way of conveying our thanks for his benefits. Therefore, we have established and founded this place of our devotion, in honor of our Lord Jesus Christ and out of veneration for the apostles Peter and Paul, on the river Seine, in a field facing the estate known since antiquity as Pothières, in the county of Lassois, in the kingdom of Burgundy, so that the venerable house of prayer there will be filled with the vows and supplications of the faithful and so that the heavenly way of life of those living under the strict rule and institutes of the blessed Benedict will be pursued and sought after with absolute determination and profound ardor. And we have conferred on it these estates: the very one near which the monastery is situated, Pothières, or that part of it which we inherited, or which our master King Charles granted to us by the authority of his own command, or which has been added to our possessions there through any other legitimate agreement, together with all its appurtenances and whatever pertains to it anywhere; in the county of Sens, Sixte with everything pertaining to it and all its appurtenances and the estate of Villemanoche with everything pertaining to it and all its appurtenances; Veron and Villiers-Louis too in the same county with everything pertaining to them and all their appurtenances; similarly, in the same county, in the estate of Le Pechoir, situated on the Yonne, absolutely everything that we acquired from our lord's vassal, Ydlinus, and whatever belongs to Le Pechoir—everything, in short, over which we rule there or over which our power is known to extend; and whatever is rightfully ours in the county of Troyes.

In similar fashion we have founded, with the same zeal and devotion, in honor of our Lord Jesus Christ, another monastery, as a dwelling for handmaidens of God living under the strict rule and institutes of the blessed Benedict, in the place or land called Vézelay, in the county of Avallon, in the kingdom of Burgundy, and we have granted it these estates: the very one in which the sacred and venerable monastery is situated, which we gained by exchange at the initiative and command of our mistress and glorious queen, Judith, in the presence of our lord and master, the emperor Louis of pious memory; and whatever pertains to that estate which that most clement emperor presented and granted to us, confirming it by an edict, we have consigned to that monastery, whatever appurtenances pertain to that estate wherever they be.[1] We have also granted it the estate of Dornecy and *Cisternæ*, Fontenay-près-

---

[1] The clumsiness is in the original: *ad eandem villam respiciens ... quae ubicumque respiciunt ad eandem villam pertinentia. ...*

Vézelay, *Molnitum,* and whatever we have acquired in the county of Avallon or Tonnerre, together with all the appurtenances of the estates, wherever they are or whatever county they are in.

Therefore absolutely everything that we have acquired or have been able to acquire in the above-mentioned estates and lands, we have brought together for those sacred places and monasteries and linked together for the concord and usefulness of those who serve God there, only reserving the usufruct for ourselves while our life in the flesh continues; and we take under our own care the defense and protection of those monasteries. And so whatever has been granted in our religious offering to the monastery of men and whatever, at God's inspiration, shall be bestowed or added in the way of goods, services, or commodities of any kind or shall be offered at any time whatever by any of the faithful, should remain untouched, by virtue of the continued strength of this present testament of ours, without any services or actions being owed to any other, with the exception of the allowances and necessary expenditures of those who serve the Lord there, except that each year, as a gift to the most reverend seat of the blessed apostles, to which we have subjected those same places, two pounds of silver should be offered to the blessed bishop of the city of Rome, to teach, by the example of this free and voluntary act of charity and office of humility, what gifts should be offered daily. Let the monks live free from other tributes in quiet service of the rule, solemnly offering to God the gift of prayer on behalf of our most glorious masters and notables, Louis Augustus and Charles his son, and our mistress of outstanding memory, Judith, and Hermengarde and also Hermentrude, the venerable wife of the notable Charles, and also for [the souls of] their fathers and mothers, sons and daughters, both those living and those at rest with the Lord, and for us too and our sons and daughters living and dead, and for all our friends, and for the whole multitude of the faithful. This monastery and the other named above, together with everything granted to them, we submit to the blessed apostles at Rome and, by the witness of this charter we have granted, we commit them in perpetuity to the holy bishops of that eternal city, those who in the place of the apostles have throughout the years that followed held that see, to rule them, command them, and administer them—yet not so that they have license to give them as a benefice or alienate them to anyone—so that through their painstaking zeal and watchful direction the religion of piety and honesty shall always increase there to the glory of God, as our devotion intends, and the fruit nourished there will incline more and more to God.

We want especially to emphasize that whenever the abbot or abbess of one of those monasteries handed over out of our consideration for religion and our respect for God to the holy apostles passes from this life, the congregations which God has wished to be in those venerable places should have the power conceded to them, after they have consulted and been advised by holy men, of choosing, with the Lord's help, as their next head, a person of good behavior and reputation from out of their own company [*consortio et collegio*], with the approval of the bishop who at the time has deserved the Apostolic See. Moreover, the state of the monastery's wealth should always be considered in connection with receiving brothers or sisters, lest with an excess of numbers the congregations—may it not be so—decay from their heavy burden. And we stress most strongly and insist and adjure that no one ever be permitted to alter our vow of poverty or to disturb it by a perverted attack on its order. But if anyone should so presume—which we do not think will happen—let him be condemned by order of our lord and master, the pious King Charles; our Lord God will return him retaliation worthy of his deed; and, unless he recovers his senses, let him incur an eternal punishment by the sentence of the bishop of the holy city as a sacrilegious thief of holy things and a stranger from the flock of the people of God. Through our Redeemer we beseech all of you, holy fathers and bishops, always to deem this work of our devotion worthy of your promoting and helping in every way. Finally, our pious and beloved servants of God living in the monasteries founded by us with such pious zeal ought to be advised to be fervent and alert in their careful devotion to religion and ought to show themselves in everything to be ministers of God, not giving offense to anyone by disparaging the most religious and sacred order of their ministry, so that the bishop of the Holy See may be their ruler and their diligent consoler and helper, with the result that, united in faithful love and religious obedience to the head and members of the church, they may deserve to be closely joined to the very head of the whole body, that is Christ. So that this testament, executed by us with all piety and devotion, will possess an unchallengeable validity throughout all time, we have ordained that it be fortified by the subscriptions of our own hand and of the following illustrious men.

Sign of Count Gerard and sign of his wife Bertha, who offered this gift to God for the relief of their souls and confirmed it by preparing this deed and ordered it be confirmed. Sign of Ava, their daughter, who, having heard of her parents' wishes and the offering they made to God, confirmed and agreed to them. Sign of *Saimarus*. Sign of Thierry. Sign of *Dimo*. Sign of *Aivertus*. Sign of *Fanuel*. Sign of *Fredebertus*. Sign of *Baimarus*. Sign of Ralph. Sign of *Widericus*. Sign of Gérard. Sign of *Sigibertus*. Sign of *Rotardus*. Sign of *Gislemarus*. Sign of *Abbo*. Sign of *Gauzselmus*. Sign of *Auzgarius*. Sign of *Airbaldus*. Sign of *Optadus*. Sign of *Berno*. Sign of *Walfarius*. Sign of *Odolardus*. Sign of *Atho*. Sign of *Odobertus*. Sign of *Ardulfus*. Sign of *Austoricus*. Sign of *Bercharius*. Sign of *Amalbertus*. Sign of *Raganaudus*.

CHARTER 2   March 863

The letter of Count Gerard to Pope Nicholas about apostolic rule and protection begins.

To the most blessed Nicholas, apostolic father of the most sacred see and special father to us, Gerard, raised to the honor of count through the gift of the omnipotent God and by royal clemency, and our most beloved wife, Bertha by name, [send greetings].

We want it to be made known publicly to your beatitude and to the clergy and all the people of the sacred city that, at the inspiration of the Lord, we have together been pleased, by a joint vow, to make an offering, most devoutly and readily and as a sign of our faith in our Lord Jesus Christ, out of the richness of our patrimony—for the Lord has given us a generous portion of possessions—and on account of our love for him and as eternal assistance for our souls. Except for those possessions which have been reserved for the succeeding generations of our family, we make God himself and his most blessed apostles Peter and Paul heirs to the rest of our possessions, and we establish the apostles as perpetual intercessors before God. And since by the aid of the one who dispenses all good intentions and is the inspiration for every holy vow, we have added to our devotion by constructing out of the possessions of our patrimony monasteries and dwelling places for the servants of God in an appropriate and convenient place, and with pious and thoughtful care have provided, out of those same resources which God has granted us, whatever is necessary for the support of those servants of God and for the cultivation of religion, we donate and subject them to the most sacred and reverend place and city where the eternal memory of the most blessed apostles Peter and Paul is celebrated, so that they may have a lasting guardian and protector of their order and their religion and so that the fruit of our devotion may last forever. We commit them to the rule of the most holy bishop of that city so that this most blessed bishop might manage and govern them with ecclesiastical piety and firmness, with the proviso that he will never grant them as a benefice to anyone except those to whom, after taking counsel, we ourselves have indicated in the record of our gift it ought to be granted and whom this same writing will indicate below.[1] To fulfil our most ready devotion and our deepest wish in Christ, we establish a church of God from our inherited possessions by a legitimate donation, testified to legally; and we set down and found a venerable and sacred place for our offering, in the name of our Lord Jesus Christ and out of veneration for the most blessed apostles Peter and Paul, so that the servants of God, professing and living by the rule of the blessed Benedict, will have a dwelling place by the river Seine on the land facing the estate anciently known as Pothières, in the county of Lassois in the kingdom of Burgundy in the parish of the city of Langres, so that the venerable house of prayer there will be filled with the vows and supplications of the faithful, and so that a heavenly way of life will be sought and longed for with absolute determination and profound ardor by all of them. Our goods and the possessions of our patrimony, which came to us by succession or as an affectionate gift from our generous parents, or which our most generous king and exalted master Charles deigned to confer on us by his command, or which were transferred to our jurisdiction by a suitable purchase, we have, with God helping us completely to fulfil our devotion, transferred and given back by a legitimate donation in a legal testament; that is the land or estate in the county of Lassois, in the neighborhood of which the monastery is situated, and whatever part of Pothières was inherited from our parents, or came to us as a grant on the authority and command of our pious king, or was added to our possessions there by any other legitimate agreement, together with all its appurtenances and whatever pertains to it anywhere. In the county of Sens, Sixte with everything pertaining to it and all its appurtenances; likewise the estate of Villemanoche with all the appurtenances that pertain to it. Absolutely everything at all, as we have declared, that we have

---

[1] Perhaps not surprisingly, no list of those entitled to hold the monasteries as a benefice survives.

acquired or that we have been able to acquire in those estates, we have joined together for that sacred place and monastery and for those who will serve as soldiers of God there and we have united these properties forever to serve the monks usefully and in concord, reserving for ourselves while we remain in the world of the flesh only the usufruct, in return for which we will act as guardians and defenders of that place. Again we have similarly enriched and endowed, out of our possessions and by a shared vow, another equally venerable and sacred place, for the honor of the same God and our Lord Jesus Christ and out of veneration for his mother the most blessed virgin Mary, in the place or land called Vézelay in the county of Avallon and the kingdom of Burgundy, and we have granted it these estates: Vézelay itself, in which the sacred and venerable monastery is situated, which we acquired by exchange from the emperor Louis of most pious memory, and whatever pertains to the same estate that the most clement emperor himself gave to us, fortifying it with the confirmation of his edict—in short whatever pertains to that estate we have consigned to the monastery. Also the estates of Dornecy, *Cisternæ*, Fontenay-près-Vézelay, and *Molnitum* and whatever we have acquired in the counties of Avallon and Tonnerre, with all the appurtenances of the above estates wherever they are or whatever county they are in.

And whatever we have granted to the above-mentioned places, monasteries, or churches, whatever has been conferred there by our offering or added by us, through God's inspiration, by way of goods or services or any kind of commodity, or has been offered at any time at all by any of the faithful, all this we decree, on the basis of the continued strength of our authority and by the writing of this testament, should remain free of all services or exactions owed to any others, except for the allowances and necessary expenditure of those who serve the Lord there, reserving the usufruct to us only while we live, except that each year, as an offering of charity to the most reverend see to which we have subjected those monasteries, two pounds of silver should be offered by each monastery to the blessed bishop of the city, as a way of teaching by this example of a free and voluntary act of charity and work of humility what gifts should be offered daily. Let no bold person, nor any person at all ever presume to try to seize or diminish this sacred donation by attacking it or to appropriate it by illegally transferring it by proprietary right to his own use; but, in fear of terrifying judgment, let everyone allow to remain undisturbed what was performed by us out of divine respect.

And so, most blessed bishop, these venerable living places of the servants of God, as well as those serving God there or those who will serve God there, we commend and subject, with all the devotion of our soul before God, to you and your successors, because of our reverence for the most blessed apostles to whose place and duties you have been elected. To ensure that our avowed wish is administered with stability, we commit them in perpetuity to the zeal of your apostolate, so that you will deign to govern, protect and defend them in every way with paternal ecclesiastical piety and a merciful hand, lest they be handed over as a benefice contrary to our vow to anyone except those indicated in the written testament; and may you charge your pious successors, by calling the divine majesty as a witness and by holding up the fearful contemplation of that future judgment when there is no doubt that each of us will have to convey an account of his behavior before the judgment seat of Christ, to preserve my gift with unshakeable strength by their paternal and apostolic authority. We throw ourselves at your feet with every effort of humility, in the hope that we may deserve to have it happen, as far as the goods we have offered to the Lord with complete devotion and confirmed with a legal testament are concerned, that the servants of God in the monasteries we have constructed and the congregation of nuns, who depend at all times on your blessing, should rightly administer them in accord with our devotion and our wish and, protected and defended by you, should live according to the rule and by their own law, owing nothing beyond charity to anyone, and subject in servitude to no one except the chief of apostles and his vicar. And after our death—for as long as our life goes on we want these monasteries to remain under our care, with your blessing—may present and future tranquillity be provided by God's mercy for those who are there now and for all those whom divine grace has added there or will add there. Whenever the abbot or the abbess from the congregation that God has wished to be in those venerable places passes from this life, those congregations should have the power conceded to them, after they have consulted and been advised by most holy men, of choosing as their head a person of good behavior and reputation from out of their own number or company, with the approval of the bishop who at that time has deserved the apostolic see; that person should, according to the rule of the order of St. Benedict, willingly look to the rights of the monastery, internally and externally, and should, with the Lord's grace being granted, boldly assert them.

But because, with the flourishing of evil, the charity of many people has flagged and greed has seized control of everything, we greatly fear that after our death somebody, either the bishop of the diocese, who has not been granted the right of ordination nor any right to rule over that place, or one of the more powerful men, or some other person, persuaded by wickedness or driven by greed, will try to disrupt the congregation of the servants of God or of the handmaidens of God or will try to unsettle their observance of the rule or will strive to change the abbot or the abbess whom the congregation has, according to the rule, elected, or will presume to exercise illegal control over the monasteries or over the possessions which were bestowed permanently on them by us, for this reason we request, most reverend paternity, for God's sake, that your beatitude not hesitate to offer help in any way at all and that your sanctity charge your pious successors, calling the divine majesty as a witness and in fearful contemplation of future judgment, to protect them with unshakeable strength by their paternal authority. And we request that your authority suspend from communion with the church as an embezzler and assailant of sacred goods anyone who has dared defile so sacred a donation to God and at once condemn such a person with a severe ecclesiastical censure. Let no one, aroused by the most perverse greed, ever be able to change or overturn part of the above-written pious wish, which was inspired by our religious devotion to God and which we have most trustingly commended to you before the Lord and his holy apostles, without at once undergoing an appropriate canonical and apostolic judgment and, with the apostles rendering him return for his iniquity, let him be punished and condemned by a fine of three hundred pounds of gold, as has been inserted in our testament.[1]

Moreover, humble and submissive with our whole soul, we beseech you, holiest father, and your successors, through Christ our Lord, through his virgin mother, through the blessed apostles Peter and Paul, and through all who illuminate the whole church of God with their blood, to bring help in your special capacity as father, with pious and enthusiastic zeal, to the inhabitants of those monasteries handed over to your paternity and reverence and never to allow what we have committed to your protection with the best hopes to be granted as a benefice or to be alienated by exchange. May you piously deign to maintain our offering complete and leave it and hand it over to your successors, that they might maintain it in the same way; and may you continue to occupy yourself worthily by protecting with your pious blessings the brothers and sisters whom we place in your hands, by defending them against attackers and by ensuring that they remain safely at peace and in fruitful leisure, so that you receive your reward from Jesus Christ our Lord, who crowns his saints with an eternal gift.

So that its strength will remain unshakeable for all time, we have decreed that this letter expressing our will, this testament of our offering, which we have made with the deepest piety and devotion, should be strengthened by the subscriptions of our own hands and those of the following illustrious men, and we have sent it to be kept safe and in eternal memory in the archives [*bibliotecis*] of the blessed apostles.

Signs of Count Gerard and Bertha his wife, who offered this gift to God for the salvation of their souls and, once the deed had been executed, strengthened it and ordered it to be strengthened. Sign of Ava, their daughter, who having heard of her parents' wishes and the offering they made to God, confirmed and agreed to them. Sign of *Saimarus*. Sign of Thierry. Sign of *Dimo*. Sign of *Aivertus*. Sign of *Fanuel*. Sign of *Fredebertus*. Sign of *Baimarus*. Sign of Ralph. Sign of *Widericus*. Sign of Gérard. Sign of *Sigibertus*. Sign of *Rotardus*. Sign of *Gislemarus*. Sign of *Abbo*. Sign of *Gauzselmus*. Sign of *Auzgarius*. Sign of *Airbaldus*. Sign of *Optadus*. Sign of *Berno*. Sign likewise of *Berno*. Sign of *Walfarius*. Sign of *Odolardus*. Sign of *Atho*. Sign of *Odobertus*. Sign of *Ardulfus*. Sign of *Austoricus*. Sign of *Bercharius*. Sign of *Amalbertus*. Sign of *Raganaudus*.

---

[1] In fact, this stipulation is not found in the original testament (charter 1). This entire paragraph, and, to a lesser extent, the previous two paragraphs, and portions of the final section of the testament (above charter 1) seem to match rather too closely the attacks on the abbey described in the *Major Chronicle*, below, 1 §2 and 2 §1 et seq. for the modern historian to resist the impression that the cartulary has been "edited" to better serve the abbey's mid-twelfth-century purposes. See Huygens (1976: xxxi) and below *Major Chronicle* 4 §4 p. 231n.1. Compare the situation at Glastonbury (Scott [1981]) and note Davies (1988).

CHARTER 3   May 863

Privilege of Pope Nicholas [I]

Bishop Nicholas, servant of the servants of God. To the religious woman
dedicated to God, who, through the divine will and providence, has been appointed in the monastery which was built and endowed with riches in the
place or field called Vézelay in the county of Avallon within the borders of
Burgundy by you, Gerard, our most famous son and illustrious count, and
our most noble daughter Bertha, in the name of our Lord Jesus Christ and
out of veneration for the most blessed virgin Mary, mother of the son of God
and our Lord Jesus Christ, and to all those ever after who will hold the position of abbess in that same monastery after her. For the relief and future
reward of your souls you have made the Holy Roman Church the proprietor
of that monastery and of everything that pertains to it by law and you have
bestowed this on the most blessed Peter, prince of the apostles, through the
charter of your donation.

When the hearts of Catholic men, which ought to be encouraged to certain
acts by the admonitions of bishops, are so kindled by an ardent desire, after
the divine mercy has intervened, that those same acts are in fact willingly
sought out by them, their wishes ought to be granted with alacrity and a joyful soul, the more so if what they wish for would have had to be asked for if
they had not been willing to do it. And so in accordance with your petition
we confer, in a decretal backed by our apostolic authority, and concede, confirm, and decree the following privileges for the benefit of the monastery
honoring our Lord Jesus Christ which you, devout in your religion, have
founded in the parish of the town of Autun in the place and kingdom named
above, so that no king, no bishop, no one endowed with any dignity, indeed
no one at all will be permitted, whatever the cause or the occasion, to diminish or remove, to direct to his own use, or to grant in any way for any other
apparently pious cause, as an excuse for his own avarice, anything which has
been granted as an endowment to that monastery by you or by anyone else.

But we want—and by our apostolic authority we command—everything that
has been offered there or will be offered there by you or by those who succeed in that place to the office of abbess or to the religious life or by those
who make an offering there for the relief of their souls, to be possessed unharmed and untroubled from this time on for the use only of those for whose
maintenance and government they were granted and will be granted, to be
employed by them in any way at all, with this condition: none of our successors in this holy see, which through the Lord's doing we serve, should ever
under any circumstances at any future time undertake to give any of its possessions as a benefice to anyone or to exchange them or grant [*concedere*]
them in return for payment [*sub censu*] or retain them for himself, with the
single exception of that payment of one pound of silver[1] which—in accord
with the charter of your gift in which you have made the holy mother church
the proprietor of that monastery—our successors will receive every year. In

---

[1] This due has been reduced by 50% since charter 2!

return for this they will take care to provide against all attacks, with the vigilance of an anxious pastor, the assistance of their pious paternity to that monastery and its abbess and the nuns who live there under the Rule of our holy father Benedict.

Moreover, we decree that on the death of the abbess of that monastery no one is to be ordained there, by cunning or surprise, except one who has been elected with the agreement of the nuns, in accord with their fear of God and the regulations of the Rule of the blessed Benedict. The bishop of this Apostolic See should provide for her ordination or, at the suggestion of the nuns, agree to her being ordained. We also add here, in order to eliminate the possibility of avarice, that no one, be he priest, king, or one of the faithful, should dare to take anything in the form of gold or any other sort of payment or even a gift, on the occasion of the ordination, by himself or any other person, of the abbess or of any clerks or priests, or for giving the chrism or for the consecration of the church or for any other spiritual or temporal service or for any other cause pertaining to the monastery. Nor is the abbess herself to presume to give anything for the sake of her own ordination, lest in doing so what is offered or has been offered to that pious place by the faithful is used up. The diocesan bishop, unless invited by the abbess of that monastery, is not to celebrate a public mass there or establish any [liturgical?] stations in that monastery, lest the peace of the handmaidens of God be disturbed by crowds of people in some way or other; nor should he presume to demand any food or lodging [*paratas aut mansionaticos*] from that place. Yet as far as space and resources permit, not only do we not deny that the accommodation and bounty that the apostle teaches should be shown to everyone, ought to be shown freely there to the faithful and to monks and nuns; we definitely urge it. Yet moderation ought to be observed in the size of the congregation so that there are neither so many nor so few inhabitants that penury or destitution is inflicted on the place. We decree that everything contained in this charter of our instructions and commands is to be preserved forever for all those who succeed you, who retain the usufruct of that monastery which you built and handed over to the holy Roman church, and for those who have a legitimate interest in the matter [*vel eis quorum interesse poterit*]. But if any priest, judge, or secular person, knowing that we have set down this charter, tries to act against it, let him be struck with an apostolic anathema and be deprived of the dignity of his power and honor and let him know that he will stand before the divine judge as guilty of the wickedness he has perpetrated; and, unless he restores those things that he has wrongly removed from the monastery or rectifies his presumption or weeps with appropriate penitence for his unlawful deeds, let him be a stranger to the most sacred body of God and our Lord and Redeemer Jesus Christ and let him be subject to strict revenge at the eternal judgment. But let the peace of our Lord Jesus Christ be with all those who preserve justice in that place so that they gain the fruit of their good actions here and, at the last judgment, find the reward of eternal peace.

Written by the hand of Sofronius, deacon and notary of the Roman church, in the month of May.

Given by the hand of Tiberius, chief dignitary [*primicerius*] of the Roman See, in the reign of Louis, the son of Charles the Great.

CHARTER 4   19 September 878
[Pope John VIII to Odo, abbot of Vézelay, and the whole community. The pope confirms the arrangements made by his predecessor, Nicholas I (charter 3). He notes that he is addressing monks, not the original community of nuns, who had to leave because of frequent attacks from the world outside.[1]]

CHARTER 5   23 January 897
[Pope Stephen VI to Odo, abbot of Vézelay, and the whole community. The pope confirms the arrangements set out in charters 3 and 4. He extends the arrangements to include a recently built fortification,[2] constructed for the security of the monks and their servants against the attacks of pagans and disloyal Christians.]

CHARTER 6   18 May 908
[Pope Sergius III to Odo, abbot of Vézelay, and the whole community. The pope takes the monastery under his protection and confirms its privileges. He decrees that Aripert should be Odo's successor.]

CHARTER 7   8 January 933
[Pope John XI to Aymon, abbot of Vézelay, and the whole community. The pope confirms the arrangements of charters 3 and 4 and their extension to the fortification of charter 5.]

CHARTER 8   4 February 943
[Pope Marin II to Guy, abbot of Vézelay, and the whole community. The pope confirms the privileges described in charters 3, 4, 5, and 7.]

CHARTER 9   28 November 973
[Pope Benedict VI to Eldrad, abbot of Vézelay, and the whole community. The pope confirms the privileges in charters 3 and 4. He confirms the gift of the tithes of four churches to the monastery by Gerard, bishop of Autun.]

CHARTER 10   12 December 975 or 976
[Pope Benedict VII to Eldrad, abbot of Vézelay, and the whole community. The pope confirms the privileges of charters 3 and 4. He also confirms the gifts of charter 9.]

CHARTER 11   986
[Pope John XV to Eldrad, abbot of Vézelay, and the whole community. The pope confirms the privileges of charters 3 and 4 and the other stipulations of charters 9 and 10.]

CHARTER 12   1000–1001
[Pope Sylvester II to Robert, abbot of Vézelay, and the whole community.

---

[1] On this document, see below 360n.3.
[2] It was built between 881 and 889 AD.

The pope confirms the privileges of charters 3 and 4. He repeats the stipulations of charters 8 to 11.]

CHARTER 13   27 April 1050
[Pope Leo IX to Geoffrey, abbot of Vézelay, and all his successors. The pope confirms the privileges of all his predecessors.][1]

CHARTER 14   27 February 1076
[Pope Gregory VII to Berno, abbot of Vézelay, and all his successors. The pope confirms the monastery's privileges.][2]

CHARTER 15   Rome, 30 October 1103
[Pope Paschal II to the clergy, the knights and the other lay people of France. The pope has heard, but scarcely believes, that (Norgaud) bishop of Autun is preventing pilgrims from going to Vézelay and making offerings. He threatens sanctions if the bishop does not desist.]

CHARTER 16   Rome, 25 October 1116
[Pope Paschal II to Renaud, abbot of Vézelay. The pope takes the monastery under his protection and forbids anyone to interfere with the abbot.]

CHARTER 17   Préneste, 21 December 1117
[Pope Paschal II to William II, count of Nevers. The pope warns the count not to oppress or attack Vézelay. It should remain undisturbed, as Count Gerard proclaimed.]

CHARTER 18   Préneste, 21 December 1117
[Pope Paschal II to Daimbert, archbishop of Sens, Hugh, bishop of Nevers, Stephen, bishop of Autun, Josserand, bishop of Langres, and Hugh II, bishop of Auxerre. He asks them to protect and ensure justice for the abbot and brothers of Vézelay.]

CHARTER 19   Guastalla, 25 October 1106
[Pope Paschal II to the bishops of France. The pope complains that the killers of Abbot Artaud of Vézelay are being protected. They must be exiled or excommunicated.]

---

[1] This is the first charter to contain a reference to Mary Magdalene: the monastery is said to exist "in honor of our Lord, Jesus Christ, and out of veneration for his mother, the blessed apostles Peter and Paul, and the blessed Mary Magdalene."

[2] Charter 14 is incomplete due to the loss of a folio. Huygens is not sure whether the loss is accidental or not (1976: xxix–xxx). Sassier (1986: 69–70) argues convincingly that the folio was torn out deliberately after the declaration by Pope Alexander III of Vézelay's independence from Cluny. He thinks that as well as the end of charter 14, which would have referred to the role of the abbot of Cluny in the election of the abbot of Vézelay, two other charters from the time of Cluny's control over Vézelay, those of popes Urban II and Paschal II, were also torn out at the same time.

CHARTER 20 Provins, 27 January 1131
[Pope Innocent II to Stephen, bishop of Autun. The pope charges him to bless in the pope's name, Alberic, sub-prior of Cluny, as abbot of Vézelay.]

CHARTER 21 End of 1140–September 1143
[Pope Innocent II to Humbert, bishop of Autun. The pope commands him not to molest the abbot and brothers of Vézelay but to see justice done if they complain about any of his parishioners.]

CHARTER 22 Rome, 6 May 1140–1143
[Pope Innocent II to Pons, abbot of Vézelay. The pope had ordered Pons to appear before Godfrey, bishop of Langres, and Bernard, abbot of Clairvaux, to answer a complaint of Stephen, a canon of Auxerre. But having heard Pons's case he retracts that command and orders that the statute of his predecessor Paschal II remain in force.]

CHARTER 23 6 May 1140–1143
[Pope Innocent II to Godfrey, bishop of Langres, and Bernard, abbot of Clairvaux. On the same subject as charter 22.]

CHARTER 24 Rome, 22 March 1144
[Pope Lucius II to Gervase, abbot of Saint-Germain at Auxerre. Pons, abbot of Vézelay, has complained that Gervase has had Pons's men captured and handed over to the count of Nevers to be imprisoned. Pons gave pledges and a gospel text for their release. The pope orders the return of the gospel and the absolving of the pledges. Any complaint that Gervase has should be taken before Godfrey, bishop of Langres.]

CHARTER 25 Rome, 8 April 1144
[Pope Lucius II to Pons, abbot of Vézelay. The pope confirms the command of charter 19. He particularly forbids Stephen, a cleric of Auxerre, who has already complained about Pons (charters 22 and 23) from molesting the church of Vézelay.]

CHARTER 26 Rome 22 May 1144
[Pope Lucius II to William II, count of Nevers. The pope orders the count to restore to Vézelay the use of its ancient road.]

CHARTER 27 Rome, 19 November 1144
[Pope Lucius II to Bernard, abbot of Clairvaux. The pope commands him to warn William II, count of Nevers, not to insist that the abbot of Vézelay answer a complaint in the count's court. The count should take the matter before legates. The pope will not allow the monastery to be oppressed.]

CHARTER 28 1145–1146
[Pope Eugenius III to William II, count of Nevers. The pope has heard that the count insists that Abbot Pons and the brothers and burghers of Vézelay leave their town to seek justice. He commands that this should cease.]

CHARTER 29   Beginning of 1152

Eugenius [III], bishop and servant of the servants of God, greetings and apostolic blessing to his beloved son, nobleman and count, William [III] of Nevers.

It ought not to have escaped your notice how great was the devotion your father displayed towards the apostolic see and all that he knew belonged to it, or how zealously he cherished it and took care to foster and sustain it. For this reason blessed Peter honored and advanced him while he lived and increased his landed possessions, placing him—so we believe—when his fleeting life came to an end, in the company of holy men, opening the gates of the heavenly kingdom to him and surrounding him, happy in the eternal palace, with throngs of saints. Our predecessors too, loved him with due affection and helped him with alacrity in his moments of need. We too, in our day have cherished with paternal goodwill your person and your house, as if both were a special part of the household of blessed Peter; we have honored you and always taken the initiative in this on the authority of God, just so long as you have been prepared, adhering to the example of your parents, to love your mother the holy Roman church with filial devotion and to take care to cherish and maintain all that belongs to her. We are led therefore to wonder at the complaint of our beloved son Pons of Vézelay that you attempt to infringe the ancient freedom of that monastery of Vézelay which is known without any doubt to belong, from the very beginning of its foundation, in every way, to the very jurisdiction[1] of blessed Peter. [We marvel] that you contrive to impose on that same son of ours, the abbot, novel customs and unwonted exactions, unmindful of the sentence of anathema pronounced by so many of our great and holy predecessors in their letters of privilege, against all persons who would disturb or harry that same monastery. Thus since the place itself is seen to lie within the guardianship of blessed Peter and hence especially within our own area of protection, and since we cannot—nor should we—suffer any lessening of the abbey's freedom and immunity, we command your nobility through these present words to let that monastery enjoy its freedom and to refrain entirely from molesting the already mentioned son of ours, Pons, abbot of the place. But if you insist on pressing your case, we offer you all the equity that your rights demand[2] and we wish you, together with our aforementioned son Pons to come before our beloved son John, legate of the apostolic see, who is about to return to those parts with the Lord's help, and to submit your case to the processes of justice. If by chance the same legate should be delayed in returning to your districts—we do not think he will be—we would like the same matter to be discussed and set straight, in accordance with the dictates of justice, in the presence of our venerable brothers Samson archbishop of Rheims, Ernoul bishop of Luxeuil, and our dearest son Bernard abbot of Clairvaux. If, however, you are unwilling to agree to this judicial process and continue to press and harass the above-mentioned abbot and the brothers of the abbey who fight there for the Lord, we shall have no recourse but to exercise our guardianship of the

---

[1] *utique ad proprium ius.*
[2] *quantum equitatis ius exigit.*

patrimony of the blessed Peter and free the monastery in question from your improper oppression, using our own resources and the assistance of those loyal to the church.

CHARTER 30   Beginning of 1152

Eugenius [III], bishop, servant of the servants of God, to his dearest son in Christ Louis [VII], illustrious king of the Franks, greetings and apostolic blessing.

The highest achievement of kings is to cultivate justice, to guard and love with due devotion the churches of God that lie within their gift,[1] and not to allow naked power to exercise itself against their subjects but to uphold what is equitable. How correctly and how specially the monastery of Vézelay, from the moment of its foundation, has belonged to the Apostolic See, and with how great care it has been protected in the fullness of its freedom and immunity by the Roman pontiffs, the kings, and other princes who bestowed favors on the same place[2] right up to our own times, through the zeal and deliberate care of our predecessors and your parents, the unharmed status of the same place today clearly declares and its neighbors near and far recognize. Now however, the nobleman William [III], count of Nevers, lowering the high standards of his parents, strives to infringe the monastery's liberty and to impose novel customs and unwonted exactions on our beloved son Pons, abbot of the place in question, paying no attention to the sentence of anathema which is clearly proclaimed in their letters of privilege by so many and such holy Roman pontiffs against those who would disturb or harry the same monastery. Since therefore the place itself is known to be without doubt within the jurisdiction of blessed Peter and under his protection and our obligation to defend, and we cannot—nor should we—suffer any lessening of justice in the matter, we command your nobility through these apostolic writings that you make the aforesaid count desist from his harrying of the monastery in question and leave it alone in its liberty. But if he wishes to continue pressing his case we ourselves offer him all the equity that his rights demand, and in the presence of our beloved son John, legate of the Apostolic See, who is about to return to those parts with the Lord's help, we wish our aforementioned son abbot Pons to attend for justice on that same case. If by chance the same legate should be delayed in his return—we do not think he will be—we would like the same matter to be discussed and set straight, in accordance with the dictates of justice, in the presence of our venerable brothers Samson, archbishop of Rheims, Ernoul, bishop of Luxeuil and our dearest son Bernard, abbot of Clairvaux. If, however, the aforesaid count is unwilling to do this and to cease from harassing the abbot himself and the brothers of the abbey who fight there for the Lord, we shall have no recourse but to exercise our guardianship of the patrimony of the blessed Peter and free the monastery in question from the oppression of the same count, using our own

---

[1] *in suo iure.*

[2] *eidem loco indulte.*

resources and the assistance of those loyal to the church. Therefore, since we cannot [operate] through [any] more eminent and devout a vassal [*fidelem*] and defender of the church [than yourself] we urge you more strongly to devote your energy to our request and firmly to call back the count himself from his audacious presumption and entirely to prohibit it.

CHARTER 31   1152–July 1153

Eugenius [III], bishop, servant of the servants of God, to his dearest son in Christ Louis, illustrious king of the Franks, greetings and apostolic blessing.

Relying upon[1] the sincere love and paternal affection we have shown you frequently in letters and face to face [we point out] that if at any time on any case we happen to appeal to your energies [*strenuitatem*], you ought to attend the more carefully to our prayers, or rather the prayers of St. Peter operating through ourselves. But, since we wrote to your nobility on the matter of the harassment which the count of Nevers is known to have inflicted with tyrannical presumption upon the monastery of Vézelay against God and all justice, the count has subsequently oppressed the monastery more vehemently and savagely than before: he has assailed it and, with the perfidious burghers of the place itself, has not ceased from impugning it and strives to acquire—though in vain—the rightful allod and patrimony of the same prince of the apostles. We do not know why this should be the case: either you have been unwilling or have neglected to deflect the aforesaid count from his audacious presumption, though we requested you to do so in our mandate, or the count himself has set at nought your warning and the lordship of your power.[2] But since we cannot—nor should we—ignore such unpunished and immoderate wickedness, we command your nobility through repeated writings and we most assiduously pray that you strictly warn the aforesaid count to make good in their entirety the losses which he is known to have inflicted on the already mentioned monastery, and to leave the place alone in its peace and freedom. But if he thinks that he has some just claim on the monastery we shall request him afterwards to show what this is. If, however, obdurate in his pertinacity, he spurns this course of action we ourselves shall institute a sentence of excommunication—without remedy of any appeal—against his person and the persons of the burghers of Vézelay. All divine offices will be prohibited in his lands except for the baptism of children [*puerorum*] and the administration of penance to the dying. Wherefore we command by the authority of these present words, that from now on you abstain from dealings with him as if he were excommunicate and you prohibit utterly under your ban the burghers themselves from taking part in any holy days[3] of your kingdom. If any are found so doing, you should issue orders out of a zeal for justice that they be apprehended and despoiled of their goods as breakers of their oath and disturbers of the church.

---

[1] *pro . . . prerogativa.*
[2] *potestatis tue dominium.*
[3] *burgenses ipsos ab omnibus feriis . . . prohibens.*

CHARTER 32   Ferentino, 26 January 1151

Eugenius [III], bishop, servant of the servants of God, to his most venerable brother, Hugh [III], bishop of Auxerre, and Godfrey, bishop of Langres, and to his dearest son Bernard, abbot of Clairvaux, greetings and apostolic blessing.

The administration of the Holy See, to which we are, though undeserving, devoted, puts us under an obligation to all churches, and just as we rejoice in their peace and tranquillity, so, if anyone should disturb them with unwonted molestation and oppressions, we grieve with paternal affection, and are concerned to provide for them in goodwill, as much through our own efforts as through those of our brothers. We hear, moreover, that our son William [III], count of Nevers, strives to burden the venerable monastery of holy Mary Magdalene of Vézelay against justice and beyond ancient custom, in that he constrains our beloved sons Pons, the abbot, and the brothers of that place and their burghers to go out of the town to seek or obtain justice, against the statutes of privilege granted by the Apostolic See.

Since, therefore, the monastery itself is within the jurisdiction of blessed Peter[1] and lies under the patronage and defense of the holy Roman church, we cannot, nor ought we, fail to render it justice. It is for this reason that we command you through the present writings to see to it that you strictly [*districtius*] warn the count on our behalf to the effect that he for the future [*de cetero*] constrain neither the abbot nor the monks nor the burghers to go out of the aforesaid town [*villam*] for reasons of this kind. You should inform him that if he continues to do this, we shall have no alternative but straightly to avenge the insult to blessed Peter.

CHARTER 33   1145–1148

Eugenius [III], bishop, servant of the servants of God, to his beloved son in Christ the nobleman Odo [II] duke of Burgundy greetings and apostolic benediction.

It is recognized to pertain to the industry of Catholic princes to cherish venerable places devoted to God with wonted affection, to love them and to defend them from the incursions of depraved men. How specially the monastery of the blessed Mary Magdalene at Vézelay belongs to the jurisdiction of blessed Peter—entrusted to the guardianship of the Apostolic See from the outset of its existence—everyone near and far recognizes. So it is that, trusting greatly in your nobility, we have judged that the same monastery and all that belongs to it should be the more carefully commended to your energies, and we ask by way of the present letter that you love the place itself with respect and devotion, that you protect it from the harassment of those who strive to infringe or disturb its ancient liberty, and that you maintain and defend the place out of reverence for ourselves and blessed Peter. We write in the same vein to Archibald [VI] of Bourbon and Count Thibault [II of Champagne].

---

[1] *beati Petri iuris est.*

CHARTER 34   June 1144—beginning 1145
[The legate Alberic, bishop of Ostia, to Pons, abbot of Vézelay. The legate has written to Count William II on Pons's behalf. But if the count continues to be stubborn Pons should do nothing contrary to the monastery's privileges or liberty.]

CHARTER 35   1152
[Pope Eugenius III to Godfrey, bishop of Langres. He commands Godfrey to order Count William III to make good the losses of Vézelay and to leave it in peace. If this is not done within thirty days he is to excommunicate the count and burghers and notify other bishops of his action.]

CHARTER 36   19 December 1152
[Pope Eugenius III to Hugh, archbishop of Sens, Godfrey, bishop of Langres, Thibault, bishop of Paris and Henry, bishop of Troyes. The pope orders them to forbid the reception in their parishes of the burghers of Vézelay who broke faith with their lord, the abbot. Anyone who catches them should despoil them of their goods.]

CHARTER 37   19 December 1152
[Pope Eugenius III to Odo II, duke of Burgundy, and to various other Burgundian nobles. On the same subject as charter 36.]

CHARTER 38   24 October 1150
[Pope Eugenius III to Henry, bishop of Autun. The pope commands the bishop to have his men restore the property stolen from Vézelay and make good the damage done to it. Any pecuniary complaint that the bishop has against the monastery will be dealt with by Hugh (III), bishop of Auxerre.]

CHARTER 39   24 October 1150
[Pope Eugenius III to Odo II, duke of Burgundy. The pope commands the duke to make satisfaction to the monks of Vézelay for the damage done to them and not to molest them in future. Hugh (III), bishop of Auxerre will hear any complaint he has against the brothers.]

CHARTER 40   24 October 1150
[Pope Eugenius III to Hugh (III), bishop of Auxerre. The pope orders the bishop to mediate between Henry, bishop of Autun and the monks of Vézelay if there is a financial dispute between them.]

CHARTER 41   24 October 1150
[Pope Eugenius III to Pons, abbot of Vézelay. The pope sends him copies of charters 38 and 39. He commands him to appear before Hugh (III), bishop of Auxerre, if summoned, and to observe his judgment on any pecuniary matters.]

CHARTER 42   3 April 1148
[Pope Eugenius III to Odo II, duke of Burgundy. The pope commands him to stop molesting the church of Vézelay.]

CHARTER 43 Ferentino, 23 February, 1151

Eugenius [III], bishop, servant of the servants of God. To his beloved son Pons of Vézelay, abbot, greetings and apostolic blessing.

Our venerable brother Henry of Autun, bishop, coming into our presence, laid his complaint against you, in our sight and in that of our brothers. The brother whom you had sent to us was also present. The complaint was to the effect that certain [rights] which his church has possessed peacefully in your monastery right down to the present day, you contrive to take away from him against justice and that you reply in your own words [*viva voce*] that you will do absolutely nothing on the bishop's behalf. Since therefore it is very much our special duty to banish the scandals of brothers, and to uphold their just rights for each, we instruct by means of the present document that, unless you and that same brother of ours have come to an agreement in the meantime, you come into our presence on the next octave of blessed Martin,[1] either yourself or by way of deputies with adequate powers,[2] together with the muniments of your abbey, especially the documents of foundation, and that you be prepared to make answer on these matters. At the same time we entrust to your sense of responsibility that in the presence of our venerable brother, Hugh [III], bishop of Auxerre, you do justice concerning those things which you and your men hold unjustly and to the disadvantage of the bishop of Autun from his men, since we have given similar instruction to that same brother of ours, the bishop of Autun, that he should equally do justice in the presence of the same men concerning [*ex*] those things which his men have taken away from your men. In the meantime too, we wish that the bishop [of Autun] suffer no harassment on the subject of his possessions.

CHARTER 44 29 January 1152
[Pope Eugenius III to Godfrey, bishop of Langres, Stephen, abbot of Reigny, and Peter, abbot of (Saint-Philibert de) Tournus. The pope commands them to hear the case between Henry, bishop of Autun and Pons. They should record what the witnesses say under oath and send it to the pope. The form of the oath is prescribed.]

CHARTER 45 1152
[Hugh, archbishop of Rouen, to Pope Eugenius III. He reports that the bishop of Autun attacks Vézelay. One of the bishop's complaints is that no other bishop has the right to confer orders or consecrate altars there. But the archbishop and other bishops have done so, in accordance with the monastery's privilege. He beseeches the pope to preserve its liberty and dignity.]

CHARTER 46 27 January 1153
[Pope Eugenius III to Henry, bishop of Autun. The pope commands the

---

[1] 18 November 1151. This is the hearing described in Book 1 of the *Major Chronicle* below; see especially §4.

[2] *per sufficientes responsales.*

bishop to appear before him to discuss his disagreement with Pons and to explain his attacks on the latter and his support of the excommunicated burghers. In the meantime, on pain of suspension, he is not to molest the abbot nor to offer spiritual services to the excommunicates.]

CHARTER 47   Segni, 20 June 1152

Eugenius [III], bishop, servant of the servants of God, greetings to the bishop of Autun.

The activities [*opera*] which have come to our hearing since you left our presence, concerning your own person and those who take orders in everything from you, have confirmed the words you yourself used in our presence while you were tarrying with us. You then said that you would prefer the whole monastery of Vézelay to be destroyed rather than that it should not be subject to your command. Indeed, the urgent complaint of our son Pons, abbot of the same monastery, has recently been brought to us, to the effect that after you departed from the Apostolic See you harried him and the church entrusted to him in many ways, as much by your own actions as by those of your servants; furthermore you incite any others you can to multiply his losses and worries. Your brother too,[1] at your instigation, rages violently against the church [of Vézelay] and its possessions with damnable presumption: he does not permit his men to go in their accustomed manner for the sake of prayer to the monastery [of Vézelay], he seizes and plunders the men of the monastery, and certain of those who are under his sway burst forth with such rash presumption that they do not hesitate to lay violent hands on the monks themselves. You are further alleged to have aroused the count of Nevers to persecute the same church to such an extent that beneath the blast of such a hurricane of harassment the aforesaid abbot, our son, and his brothers can scarcely find a tranquil place to attend to divine service. Now since these allegations are extremely serious they ought not go unpunished or unexamined: accordingly we have decreed that a statement about them be entrusted to our venerable brother Godfrey, bishop of Langres. We thus instruct you by the authority of what we have written here that when you are summoned by him you present yourself to him and make a full and reasoned response on all these matters to the enquiry [*inquisitioni*] that he will make.

Moreover, you will announce in full public congregation of the church with candles lit that those parishioners of yours who have been shown to have laid violent hands on anything belonging to the monks or clergy of the monastery [of Vézelay] itself, are excommunicate, and you will order them to be shunned as excommunicates throughout all your diocese until such time as they present themselves to our apostolic sight, armed with letters from you, to make satisfaction for the great excesses they have committed. For the rest, take particular care by every precaution not to inflict presumptuous harassment on that aforementioned brother of ours or his church, either yourself

---

[1] The brother of Henry, bishop of Autun, was Odo II, duke of Burgundy.

or any one under your orders. Otherwise we will punish on God's authority both yourself and your church in such manner that all who hear will be given to understand what a serious thing it is to wish to engross [*occupare*] through tyranny those things which ought to be available [*provenire*] to anyone by canonical judgment.

Given at Segni on the twelfth day before the kalends[1] of July.

CHARTER 48   1152–July 1153

Eugenius [III] to king Louis [VII].

We have commanded your nobility in other writings to restrain by every attention the count [William III] of Nevers from molesting the church of Vézelay which especially pertains to the jurisdiction [*ius*] of blessed Peter. But lo!—and we do not speak without grave affliction in our mind—we do not know whether your magnificence has neglected to advise him in that direction or whether he has been unwilling to obey your order; for, after we sent our writings to you for this purpose, the same count oppressed the same church very harshly and he has not refrained from terrifying the brothers tarrying therein for the service of God with threats and wearing them out with insults, either himself in person or through those who stand beneath his sway.

Surely, even without our frequent admonition you ought to offer protection to that church, as indeed to all the churches which in the land stand entrusted to you by God, and to defend them very zealously against the incursions of the depraved, especially persons who take their orders from you. We do not, however, despite all our petitions and prayers, see the church of Vézelay freed from all its troubles. Wherefore, we advise your magnificence through apostolic letters and prayers to the effect that, as you place your faith in our love for you, you straightly restrain the same count from troubling the church of Vézelay and its possessions and compel him so to warn his men with all care. Again, if the count believes that he has a just complaint to make against the church itself or its possessions, he may rely upon us, to whom the care and governance of the same church especially pertain, to make an appropriate and equitable response to his demand either ourselves or else through judges to whom we delegate the matter.

CHARTER 49   Beginning of 1153

[Pope Eugenius III to Godfrey, bishop of Langres. The pope commands him to investigate Pons's complaint that certain priests have been ministering to the excommunicates of Vézelay. If it is true they are to be suspended and sent to the pope.]

---

[1] In the ancient Roman calendar the *kalends* were the beginning of the month.

CHARTER 50   End of 1152
[Pope Eugenius III to Peter, abbot of Cluny. The pope commands him to grant the monastery of Souvigny to Pons, his own brother, as long as he is in exile.]

CHARTER 51   26 January 1151
[Pope Eugenius III to Hugh, archbishop of Sens. The pope commands him to mediate between Pons and the brothers of Vézelay and Manasses, bishop of Orleans, who, they say, has seized back a church granted to them by his predecessor.]

CHARTER 52   26 January 1151
[Pope Eugenius III to Manasses, bishop of Orléans. The pope commands him either to restore the church he is said to have wrongly seized from Vézelay or to plead his case before the archbishop of Sens.]

CHARTER 53   28 January 1152
[Pope Eugenius III to G., abbot of Cure. The pope commands the abbot to appear before Stephen, abbot of Reigny, about Pons's complaint that he has seized rights in the village of Précy-le-Sec and has refused to pay money owed to two burghers of Vézelay. He is to abide by the abbot's decision.]

CHARTER 54   28 January 1152
[Pope Eugenius III to Stephen, abbot of Reigny. The pope commands him to call together the two parties in the dispute of charter 53 and to mediate between them.]

CHARTER 55   5 April 1148
[Pope Eugenius III to Ida, countess of Nevers. The pope commands her not to prevent merchants and other people from going to Vézelay.]

CHARTER 56   1148
[Bernard, abbot of Clairvaux to Ida, countess of Nevers. Bernard advises and requests her not to prevent merchants and other people from going to Vézelay.]

CHARTER 57   February 1119
Conon, bishop by grace of God of Préneste, legate of the Holy See, to Hugh, bishop of Nevers, his venerable and beloved brother, greetings and fraternal love in Christ.

We would like to make known to your beloved self what happened to us after you left our presence. The very day we parted from each other, we [for our part] hurried with our chosen leader, by the mercy of God, to the region of Lyon. Before we arrived at Lyon, moreover, the lord [Humbald] archbishop of Lyon assented to our candidate[1] and subscribed [allegiance] at

---

[1] *electioni nostrae.*

Lyon.[1] There in solemn procession he received the lord pope Calixtus and ourselves with great honor. [Gerard] the bishop of Angoulême also, before he departed from us, had subscribed and humbly given himself in obedience to the lord pope. Then we came to Vienne, where on the Sunday before Lent the lord pope was crowned. When, moreover, we had left him and come to Vézelay, we discovered that the rumor which we had somewhat apprehensively gathered from popular report was true. We were apprehensive, I should say, not only about the church of Vézelay, whose peril is that of the mother church in Rome, for Vézelay is a special daughter of Rome, but also about [William II] count of Nevers himself, whom we love well enough: the count's retinue [*clientela*] broke the gates of the Vézelay cloister and plundered it, despoiled the bodies of the saints Lazarus and his sister Martha and the holy martyrs Andeolus and Pontianus by hurling stones at them; they broke also the [reliquary] cross in which there was a fragment of the true cross [itself],[2] they beat the monks and stoned them, and they took one of their number aside, and, thrusting their hands under his monastic habit, dishonored him. For all of this we advise and command you by apostolic authority to meet with the count on our behalf[3] and warn him to proceed to make satisfaction for such an act of sacrilege. But if he says he was not party to this disgraceful action, accuse him of complicity,[4] since when he himself had come to Vézelay on the same day and found there all the sacrilegious persons who had committed the shameful acts, he neither of his own accord nor prompted by the abbot—as many of his own men can testify—desired to render either justice, honor, or satisfaction to the church of Vézelay on behalf of his own retinue. For this reason he should fear the judgment of the most holy pope Lucius which is found, addressed to the bishops of the Gallic and Hispanic dioceses, in the first of his decretals and states in part: "It is undoubtedly the greatest sin that the goods of your churches and the offerings of the faithful, which you indicate are being harried by certain grasping persons, should be taken away from you and your churches; Holy Scripture itself says 'who takes something away from a father or mother and says it is no sin, participates in murder.'" In this case our father is without doubt God, who created us, and the mother is our Church, which gave birth to us spiritually in baptism. The prophets, the apostles, their successors, and the decrees of all the Catholic Fathers forbid that these things should occur and judge all such presumptuous acts to be sacrilege. Following these examples we, by apostolic authority, anathematize all such presumptuous persons who plunder churches and alienate their resources, and in association with you drive them from the doorstep of the holy mother church, judging them to be condemned for sacrilege. We include in this not only those who commit the heinous acts, but also those who are in alliance with them. For the same penalty embraces both

---

[1] In the matter of the disputed papal election, the anti-pope Gregory VIII having been proclaimed pope by the emperor Henry V in 1118. See Kelly (1986: 163–65).

[2] *de ligno domini.*

[3] *ex parte nostra.*

[4] *de consensu eum arguite.*

the agents and their accomplices."[1] Likewise Pope Symmachus decrees against those who invade churches: "In general, whoever presumes to confiscate, covet, or invade ecclesiastical property with dangerous and violent infestation, should be struck with perpetual anathema, unless the swiftest satisfaction is made to the church in question. Similarly also those who have held onto the rightful possessions [*ius*] of a church either as a consequence of some gift from a prince, or of an invasion by any potentate or else by using tyrannical power, and have bequeathed—as we hear is done—such things to their sons or heirs as if they were their own hereditary possessions, [such persons, I say,] should be struck with perpetual anathema, unless, admonished by the pope and having recognized the true situation, they swiftly return the things of God. For we consider it iniquitous that we be judged rather as the guardians of charters than as defenders of things entrusted to us, the latter having been enjoined upon us. "[2]

But if the count himself spurns the privileges of the church of Vézelay, let him give ear to the words of Pope Anacletus, third in line from blessed Peter: "The holy apostles by command of the saviour himself, have laid down that the privileges of churches and priests should remain for all time."[3] Also in secular laws we read this caution: "If the privileges of a venerable church are violated by any rash aggression, or are ignored through neglect, a triple fine must be paid according to the sanction of the laws of the church in question and for our part a triple fine for breaching our ban must be paid."[4] Likewise in another place: "Sacred, religious, and holy things should be appropriated by no one. For what belongs to divine jurisdiction[5] should become part of the goods of no one."[6] Similarly against those who break down the gates [of churches], Justinian says: "Holy things such as walls and gates are in a certain fashion within divine jurisdiction and must not be appropriated by anyone. So too we declare that the walls [of churches are] holy, and that on pain of death[7] no one should construct any unauthorized building within such walls."[8] We do not, however, dearest brother, wish to exaggerate the significance of what has been done, in case we end up passing judgment on someone who is not, in fact, guilty. We would, therefore, like you to announce to the same count that he should make satisfaction to us in our hand[9] for the sacrilege perpetrated by his men, whose names are listed below, and he should do this no later than the middle of Lent, and for the future he should desist from troubling the church with his infestation. If he does not obey us

---

[1] Quoted from the *Decretals* (3.140) of Ivo, bishop of Chartres. See *PL* 161.230.

[2] Also from Ivo's *Decretals* (3.148; *PL* 161.232). Compare the preoccupation in charters 1–3 above with the possibility that wrong-minded persons might turn Count Gerard's and Countess Bertha's endowments into hereditary benefices.

[3] Quoted from the Pseudo-Isidorean *Decretals*, ed. Hinschius (1863: 73 [XV]).

[4] Ivo's *Decretals* (16.298); *PL* 161.959.

[5] *divini iuris.*

[6] Ivo's *Decretals* (3.193); *PL* 161.244.

[7] *pena capitis.*

[8] Ivo's *Decretals* (3.193); *PL* 161.244.

[9] *in manu nostra.*

in this, we will, in accordance with the judgments of the holy texts included above, strike both him and his lands with the sword of anathema. We will set a date after which the anathema will come into force, though we are reluctant to have to apply this action.

There follow the names of those who were seen taking part in the sacrilege in question:

Renaud, provost of Monceaux-le-Comte and his brother Nicholas; William the marshal; Payen the butler; Peter the pantler; Odo the chamberlain [*camarlancus*]; *Petiz* of Monceaux-le-Comte [*Moncelli*]; Thibault the cook; William provost of Cercy-la-Tour; *Croslebos*; Renaud nephew of Manfred of the Gate; Beraldus of Monceaux-le-Comte; the two sons of *Aimbertus* of Monceaux-le-Comte; John *Deli*; *Tardet* of Monceaux-le-Comte; Séguin of Monceaux-le-Comte; Guichard brother of Walter the butler; Berger of Monceaux-le-Comte, who is called by that name; Godric of Clamecy with seven friends, and many others whom, until we can name them separately, we leave to be punished by their own consciences, if they do not make worthy satisfaction themselves.

CHARTER 58   25 December 1153
[Pope Anastasius IV to Hugh, archbishop of Sens, Godfrey, bishop of Langres, Thibault, bishop of Paris, and Henry, bishop of Troyes. He orders them to prohibit the treacherous burghers of Vézelay from attending fairs and markets in their parishes. Anyone who catches them can despoil them of their goods.]

CHARTER 59   Rome, 25 December 1153

Bishop Anastasius [IV], servant of the servants of God, to his beloved sons, the noble men Odo [II], duke of Burgundy; Count Henry [I of Champagne]; Archibald [VI] de Bourbon; William [I], count of Chalon; Raymond, the brother of Duke [Odo II of Burgundy]; Renaud, count of Joigny; Geoffrey of Donzy; Renaud de Rougement; *Dalmacius* of Luzy; Anseric of Montréal; *Salo*, viscount of Sens, with his sons Guérin and Burchard; G., viscount of Chateau-Landon; Guy of Vergy; Odo of Thil-en-Auxois; and Hugh of Mont-Saint-Jean, greetings and an apostolic blessing.

We believe that it was some time ago now when it came to your notice that because of the gross cruelty and barbaric tyranny which they have exercised against their lord, our beloved son Pons, abbot of Vézelay, and against that monastery, and which they continue to exercise still, the lying and treasonous burghers of Vézelay have been cut off by the sword of the divine word from the body of Christ, that is the church, like rotting limbs, at the command of Pope Eugenius of holy memory. They consider this to be nothing, imagining that their fraudulent power will prevail against the Lord, and they still persist stubbornly but not with impunity in their wickedness, believing perhaps that the protection of the Apostolic See will eventually be withdrawn from that church. So we judge their wickedness severely, although in our anger we still retain some mercy and have not considered for the moment raising our hand

more threateningly against them. Yet we enjoin your nobilities in this apostolic letter to forbid absolutely in the fairs and markets of your lands the
acceptance of the above-mentioned burghers, as lying traitors and excommunicates, and indeed to order any of your men who find them to seize them
and confiscate their possessions.

CHARTER 60   Rome, 25 December 1153

Anastasius [IV] to Peter, archbishop of Bourges.

We believe that your fraternity must recognize, because of your own greatness, the gross cruelty and barbaric violence that [William III] count of
Nevers still continues to inflict on the monastery of Vézelay, as if his own
power could prevail over the Lord and his bride the holy Church. Although
our predecessor, Pope Eugenius [III] of holy memory, had prepared the
antidote of the Holy See against this cruelty and had wanted to reprove the
count, the latter has not deserved to be cured of his illness because it has
penetrated into the feelings of his heart, which has become foolish and blackened so that, as the prophet says, looking he does not see and perceiving he
does not understand at all what belongs to God. Therefore since we, who
have, by the dispensation of divine mercy, succeeded Eugenius in the Apostolic See, are forced to defend the monastery of Vézelay as an allod of St. Peter,
and yet, with fatherly love, long for the salvation of the count and of all
Christians, and since we have great confidence in your fraternity's prudence
and honesty, we enjoin you in your charity through this present letter severely
to press upon the count that he should without any delay completely make
good the losses which he has inflicted on the monastery and leave it in peace
and freedom. Also command the count in our name not to compel the abbot
of Vézelay to appear before him to render justice to any of his men, unless it
has been established beforehand in the abbot's own court that such a one has
been refused justice. If the count has disdained to carry out your commands
within thirty days you should make your way, in the company of religious and
prudent men, to a place from where the news will easily carry to his ears and,
gathering together a crowd of people in church and lighting the candles, you
should solemnly declare on apostolic authority and without the right of any
appeal a sentence of excommunication against the persons of the count and
the treasonous burghers of Vézelay and you should forbid the celebration of
any divine offices, except for the baptism of children and the last sacraments,
in all the count's lands. In addition we enjoin you to announce clearly in
letters in our name to our venerable brothers Hugh, archbishop of Sens,
Geoffrey, bishop of Nevers, Godfrey of Langres, Henry of Autun, Henry of
Troyes, and Alan of Auxerre, bishops, that that sentence ought to be observed. Moreover we have enjoined them in apostolic letters to ensure that
after your announcement that sentence is absolutely observed in all their
parishes. Will you ensure that the letters which we have sent to our brothers,
the bishops of Langres, Autun, Nevers, and Auxerre, are delivered to them by
your messengers?

CHARTER 61 Rome, 25 December 1153

Anastasius [IV] to King Louis [VII].

Since we and the holy Roman church have been hearing many good things about your royal magnificence for a long time now, we have loved your nobility in every respect, as have those who preceded us in the office of the apostle, and we who are still alive, thanks to the divine will, do love you and want to increase your honor in every way we can, as God permits. Therefore, dearest son in Christ, like our predecessor, Pope Eugenius [III] of holy memory, we too send you an apostolic letter on behalf of the monastery of Vézelay, instructing and requesting you in the name of the Lord to impress strongly on [William III] count of Nevers, who continues to vent his anger against that monastery with barbaric cruelty, that he should strive to right all the wrongs that he is known to have inflicted on it and should leave that place in peace and in its liberty. If he is confident that he has a just case against the monastery, he can soon obtain that justice by our decree. But if, rigid in his obstinacy, he disdains to act on our words, we have instructed that a sentence of excommunication, against which there is no possibility of appeal, be pronounced against the count himself and against the burghers of Vézelay, and that none of the divine offices, except baptism of children and the last rites, be allowed in any of his lands. Therefore we charge you, through the person of the bearer of this letter, to keep away from the count if this should happen, as from an excommunicate, and by your own ban to forbid those burghers access to all the fairs in your kingdom and, zealous in your pursuit of justice, to order that they be seized by whoever finds them and despoiled of their possessions, like perjurers and schismatics. Moreover we additionally charge you in your diligence not to oppress that monastery in any way because of the false suggestion of any person but rather, out of reverence for us and the blessed Peter, to strive to defend it against all its enemies as the patrimony of the prince of the apostles. Finally, we do not want to hide from your devotion that we have issued a command to our beloved son, the abbot of Vézelay, that he is not to dare make any concession at all to the count about this monastery of ours.

CHARTER 62 Rome, 25 December 1153

Anastasius [IV] to the bishops of Gaul.

When, at the instigation of the devil, people commit sins which have the effect of unloosing vengeance, they should suffer so severe a rebuke that the punishment will teach them how serious their actions were and the fear of such an ecclesiastical rebuke will inhibit others from any similar presumption. It is for this reason that our predecessor, Pope Eugenius [III] of blessed memory, sent an apostolic letter to you, my brother [Godfrey] bishop of Langres, instructing you severely to warn [William III] count of Nevers to come to his senses about the monstrous tyranny which he has exercised with barbaric cruelty over the monastery of Vézelay, which definitely belongs to the jurisdiction of St. Peter, and, if he refused to desist from such madness, to pronounce a sentence of excommunication against him and the burghers of Vézelay and to proclaim an interdict over the lands of the count. But we have heard, to our great amazement, that for certain reasons the pope's command has not yet been completely carried out, and so, since we have by the disposition of divine clemency succeeded him in the apostolic office, we are forced to follow in the footsteps of our predecessor and defend that monastery as the special patrimony of St. Peter, by issuing orders to our venerable brother Peter, archbishop of Bourges, to warn the count that unless he compensates the monastery fully for the damage he has inflicted on it and leaves it at liberty and at peace, the archbishop, on our authority, will impose a sentence of excommunication on the count himself and on the burghers of Vézelay, who have actually committed these villainies, and will prohibit the celebration of the divine offices, except for the baptism of children and the last rites, throughout his lands. And so we order you by the authority of this letter strictly to observe that sentence, after it has been announced to you by the archbishop, and to ensure that it is observed without violation throughout your parishes.

Given at the Lateran on 25 December.

CHARTER 63   Rome, 25 December 1153

Anastasius [IV] to Pons, abbot of Vézelay.

In the grief, persecution, and distress which you have suffered for the sake of the church committed to you and for the sake of justice, we suffer with you in your devotion with paternal sympathy and, as much as God permits, we want to render you acceptable assistance. So it is that, in accord with your wish and request, we have taken pains, as your devotion requested, to send to the archbishops and bishops of the kingdom of the Franks and to the king, counts, and barons, letters, the contents of which you can clearly learn from the copies. If therefore, beloved son in Christ, you are exposed to distress for the house of Israel you must hope that the Lord will give you aid in your distress and will snatch away from all affliction those who trust in his mercy and lead them by his grace to the door of peace. Continue therefore, my son, as before and do not hesitate to set yourself up as a wall of strength around your monastery; indeed, you should resolve to contend vigorously against those who have completely denied the faith and whom we have ordered to be bound with the chains of excommunication until they have been excommunicated, and if by chance they want to call you before the law on any matter, you should definitely not reply to them without consulting us. In addition, our command is that you be prevented by apostolic authority from daring to make any concession, except on our instruction, to [William III] count of Nevers in the matter of our church of Vézelay, which is known to be a rightful allod of St. Peter.

Given at the Lateran on 25 December.

CHARTER 64   1153–1155

To his lord Pons, abbot of Vézelay, his brother Macharius, abbot of Fleury, wishes the peace which is proclaimed for men of good will.

After reading your letter and considering its contents carefully I am writing to you whom I love, to tell you what I consider wisest. If it is proposed to you that you buy peace, so that the burden of your great distress is relieved, your foes humbled, and your supporters delighted, it seems to me that it should be bought even at a very high price, as long as your church would maintain its own proper status and its privileged liberty would not be impaired. Furthermore, it seems very hard to be so suspicious of your brother [Peter the Venerable] that you refuse his arbitration just because the count [William III] entrusts himself to him completely. And so, having weighed up the various options and their value, we advise you to wait for the messengers whom you sent to the lord pope and, on their return, to show to the lord abbot[1] the reply of the pope and the privileges of your church and then finally to submit your affair confidently to his arbitration. For we do not believe that he will make a judgment contrary to or in opposition to your privileges or the instructions of the lord pope.

CHARTER 65   First half of 1154

Louis [VII], by the grace of God, king of the Franks and duke of Aquitaine, to the venerable Pons, abbot of Vézelay, greetings and our grace.

It is not fitting for a king to be too harsh and to refuse forgiveness to anyone imploring it sincerely. We understand that it was at your request that our faithful Archibald [VI] de Bourbon and his wife, our aunt, have interceded with us on your behalf. Obedient to them and for the sake of the honor of God, the sanctity of your church, and our own reputation, we completely dismiss any enmity we had felt against you and drive away any cloud of rancour; and we kindly receive you henceforth into our grace and take your affairs under royal protection.[2]

CHARTER 66   Sutri, 21 May 1155

Hadrian [IV], bishop, servant of the servants of God, to his venerable brothers the bishops [Godfrey] of Langres, [Henry] of Autun, [Geoffrey] of Nevers, and [Alan] of Auxerre, greetings and an apostolic blessing.

So greatly has the wickedness of [William III] count of Nevers against the special daughter of the Apostolic See, the church of Vézelay, increased, as your fraternity knows, that it would surely be seen as too remiss if his wickedness were to remain unpunished. Moreover, besides those evils which for a long time now he has been rashly attempting to inflict on it [the church] by inciting the burghers to persecute it and by various other means, he has

---

[1] That is, Peter the Venerable, abbot of Cluny.

[2] See the beginning of Book 3 of the *Major Chronicle* below for a brief account of the cause of the king's anger against Pons and of the circumstances of the intercession of the Bourbons.

recently established his own knights and some of his friends' men in the town of Vézelay and has seized control of that town to suit his own wishes, contrary to the rights of his ancestors, and has even dared to foster the burghers in their conspiracy and perjury against our beloved son, Pons, abbot of Vézelay. Indeed, our predecessor, Pope Eugenius [III] of holy memory, sharing the distress and suffering of that church with paternal affection, and afire with due fervor at the wickedness of the count, cut him off with the scythe of the divine word[1] from the body of Christ, which is the Church, and forbad the celebration of divine offices throughout his lands. But since the count has surrendered to his disgraceful inclinations and turns the eye of his mind away from consideration of his eternal damnation, so that despite this scourging he has not been able to be restrained from his wickedness, we command and enjoin you by this very letter to warn him severely that he should remove his guards from the town of Vézelay, that he should right the wrongs that he has inflicted on the church, that he should restore to the abbot the charter of agreement which he had extracted in opposition to the privileges of our predecessors and to the liberty of the church, that he should offer no help or support to the burghers in their conspiracy against the abbot, and that he should promise on oath that he will not offer any more military support to that commune. But if, within thirty days of your warning, he has disdained to perform what you set down, you are to renew the sentence of excommunication against his person and the sentence of interdict on his lands and to instruct that it be observed rigorously by everyone.

Given at Sutri on 21 May.

CHARTER 67   Sutri, 21 May 1155

Hadrian [IV] to the bishops of Gaul.

Your fraternity has been notified, and we certainly know, how maliciously the men of Vézelay have conspired against their mother and sovereign, the church of Vézelay, and how bitterly they have attacked her and her possessions. So our predecessor, Pope Eugenius [III] of happy memory, who was very moved both at their arrogance and by the suffering of the church, bound those sacrilegious men by a severe ecclesiastical sentence. But that alienated them and they became worse, and, scarcely desisting at all from their hatred, indeed displaying their true feelings, they actually began to make even heavier attacks against their mother, having become like those of whom the prophet says, "You struck them but they did not sorrow, you destroyed them but they refused to accept correction."[2] Even if we remain silent now about the other things they had done earlier against the church of Vézelay, there is the recent attack in which they rampaged through the monastery's stores, breaking casks, pouring out wine and smashing everything and even dared to extend their violence to the monks themselves. We sorrow at all these acts of those wretched men, who have fallen into a pit of perjury, sacrilege, plunder, and

---

[1] *divini ... verbi falce precidit*; cf. Isaiah 18:5: *praecidentur ramusculi eius falcibus.*

[2] Jeremiah 5:3.

other sins, and we sorrow that we do not see any of you take up the shield of justice and stand up to help that monastery; so that it is fitting for us to lament and say with the prophet, "There is not one, of those dear to her, who will console her."[1] Therefore, since it is to us especially that that church looks for protection and defense, we neither can nor ought overlook its suffering, and so we command and enjoin you by this present letter to stop procrastinating and to hasten to warn those burghers severely that they should restore to the abbot and brothers what they have taken, that they should repair the damage that they have inflicted, that they should make appropriate compensation for the injuries they have caused and that they should submit themselves faithfully again to the dominion of the church. But if they disdain to carry out what we have laid down after you have issued your warning, you are to excommunicate without any avenue of appeal all those who were the perpetrators of this malice—who will be denounced to you by the abbot—and you are to prohibit the celebration of the divine offices anywhere in your episcopates where any of those burghers goes, as long as he is there, and if any of them should happen to die he is not to be buried among Christians. But so that they do not escape temporal punishment, you are to enjoin all of your parishioners strictly not to admit them to their markets, and not to dare to have any association with them, either in trading or in any other way, but to avoid them as excommunicates and, whenever they do come across them, to seize them and, out of a love of justice, not to hesitate to plunder their possessions, so that, even if unwillingly, they will be forced to acknowledge their subjection and fidelity to their master. For it is proper that new antidotes be prepared for new diseases.

Given at Sutri, 21 May.

CHARTER 68   Sutri, 21 May 1155

Hadrian [IV] to King Louis [VII].

It is not appropriate to give you lengthy advice about the protection of men of religion and the veneration of holy places. No admonition is necessary to this end since that fire which the Lord came to earth to incite inflames your soul, so that there is not one among the great rulers of the world who is considered in the eyes of the whole church as more commendable in these matters than you. Yet although you extend the protection of your power to all the churches that have been established in your kingdom, we want you to show yourself particularly attentive to the church of Vézelay as it pertains especially to the jurisdiction of St. Peter and is enduring great persecution and oppression from the perfidy of its own burghers. Nor is your prudence unaware of how for some years they have been conspiring against our beloved son, Pons, abbot of Vézelay, with the support of [William III] count of Nevers and have dared to seize the church's possessions and then even to drive out the abbot himself. For this they deserved to be banished from the

---

[1] Jeremiah 1:2.

body of the Lord, that is the Church. Moreover, recently they attacked and burst into the church where they broke down doors, rampaged through workshops, poured out wine, tore off the monks' clothes, took away sacramental ornaments, and even had the temerity to molest violently the monks themselves and the servants of the house. Therefore, since their wickedness could not be restrained by the severity of an ecclesiastical judgment, and to date has not been set right despite a just and canonical censure, it requires to be checked by your hand and needs to be corrected by your vigour. And so we ask, advise, and exhort your magnificence in the name of the Lord, and enjoin you for the remission of your sins to advance with a strong force to Vézelay, burning with zeal for justice and inspired by the monastery's suffering and our own urging, and to compel the burghers to foreswear the commune which they have formed and to make themselves once more faithful subjects of our beloved son, Pons, abbot of Vézelay as their lord; and you should make them restore what they have removed and repair the damage they have inflicted and you should wreak such vengeance against all who were the ringleaders in this wickedness that all who succeed them, contemplating the possibility of like vengeance, will not attempt to raise their heads against their lord or to commit any similar perfidy against the sanctuary of the Lord.[1]

Given at Sutri on 21 May.

CHARTER 69   1155

[Hadrian (IV) to King Louis VII of France:]

We are pleased and grateful and we commend your magnificence highly for your performance of pious deeds, for our beloved son, Pons, abbot of Vézelay, has revealed to us in an account he forwarded that, out of love of God and reverence for our letters, you have diligently assisted him in accordance with the duty of your royal dignity and you have offered him aid and advice against those persecuting him and his monastery. And since the intention of good men is more fully directed towards beneficial deeds the more they are so encouraged, we ask your highness through this apostolic letter, and enjoin you for the remission of your sins, to love and honor that abbot even more willingly out of love of God and reverence for the blessed Peter and ourselves, and to defend that monastery against the attacks of our beloved son, [William III] count of Nevers, and of any others, so that the brothers living there will perpetually intercede with the Lord for your salvation and that of your kingdom and so that we will offer our thanks to your royal nobility. And since the burghers at Vézelay have become so proud, especially because of the stone houses which they have fortified and raised up against our son the abbot and the church of Vézelay, that our son can not remain in his monastery because of their persecution, we ask your magnificence to have those very houses destroyed so that the pride of the burghers

---

[1] Note the ideological value of the ambiguity of *dominus*: Lord (God) or (feudal) lord. Disobedience toward one's feudal lord can be equated with an offense against God.

will be beaten down and, as a result, the church of Vézelay will not have to be vexed by them.

CHARTER 70   Benevento, 21 November 1155

Hadrian [IV], bishop and servant of the servants of God, to his beloved sons, [Pons], the abbot, and all the brothers of Vézelay, greetings and an apostolic benediction.

In as much as your monastery is known to pertain particularly to the juris-diction of St. Peter, so it is proper that we should labor more attentively to guide it and glorify it. But it has come to our attention, oh abbot, beloved son in the Lord, that at the beginning of your prelacy, when you had not yet taken note of the tenor of your papal privileges, you conceded to Simon of Souvigny the right of establishing a money-changing booth,[1] despite the protests of your brothers and contrary to the tenor of your privileges from the Apostolic See. Therefore, since we cannot allow the possessions of your monastery to be diminished by any thoughtlessness, or the privileges of our predecessors to be violated, we order you by this present letter, if things are as we say, quickly to take that right of money-changing back into your own hands as the property of your church and by no means to presume to sell, give, or alienate in any way anything that is part of the monastery's property. Otherwise you should know that severe vengeance will be taken against you.

Given at Benevento, 21 November.

Fig. 10. Seal of Countess Ida of Carinthia, wife of Count William III of Nevers (from Guizot [1969], by permission of F. Vogade). See *Major Chronicle* 4.

---

[1] *tabulam nummulariorum.*

The Vézelay History by Hugh of Poitiers
[The Vézelay Chronicle—The Major Chronicle]

Book One

1
Why The Author Has Attempted Such a History

[1575D/395]

The grace of divine goodness, having human infirmity at heart in many and various ways, granted man, among the other quite innumerable advantages deriving from its beneficence, the material assistance of letters, whereby the industry of those at hand might be spurred on, the sympathy of those absent aroused, and the posterity of future generations instructed. And since oblivion, the enemy of all wisdom, was often wont to intercept the memory of all particularly useful things, the custom developed from antiquity of handing down the memorials[1] of the Fathers to the notice of later ages by the medium of letters,[2] or sounds, as it were, that could be seen. We too, as far as our meager talent has allowed us, have imitated this custom, and, in brief compass for the utility of many, have busied ourselves with the task of describing the oppressions which our church has so constantly suffered throughout the many annual circuits of time on account of the liberty implanted in it from birth. In [our history], while we have sought brevity, we have wholly fled the haughtiness of arrogance: for if, in accordance with what the substance of our subject demands, we were to belabor the exact truth of every little detail, we might seem somehow to weaken belief in what we say—few would credit the obvious enormity of the danger[3] afflicting our church—whilst what should to some extent serve the cause of historical integrity, an incredulous reader might attribute to loquacious boasting. With this in mind, therefore, we have chosen a dignified middle path[4] so that an integrated understanding of

---

[1] *mandare ... monimenta*. The latter word combines the CL sense of "memorial, monument, tomb, chronicle" (cf. Horace *Odes* 3.30) with the later sense of "archives, muniments" (as in Huygens 398.129 below).

[2] *litterarum apices*: from Aulus Gellius, *Noctes Atticae* 13.31(30).10 and 17.9.12.

[3] *periculum* can also mean "lawsuit," an appropriate overtone in view of the legal wrangles incurred in defending the church of Vézelay's autonomy. Guizot (1969: 10) translates: "we would fall, without any doubt, into this enormous danger of appearing in manner less worthy of faith."

[4] *sic medio tramite incedimus* (between excessive zeal, which could be seen as loquacity, and dogmatic brevity); *procedere* and *incedere* are somewhat elaborate words for "to go, advance, procede"; the latter has overtones of measured solemnity or exultation and on *procedere* see Postgate (1950: 2 [book 1, poem 2, line 10]; 52n.1). *Trames* is a poetic or elevated word for "pathway."

things might emerge and no trace whatsoever of falsity be visible. Assuredly, however aware we may be that we are little suited, scarcely adequate, to these tasks, we have yet been aroused by charity towards our church, and invited too, or rather, as I should say, strongly urged by a sense of obedience to our reverend Father, the venerable abbot Pons, who, although the most recent in time[1] of his predecessors, yet, in defense of the liberty of his church he is justly thought to be first among all the ancients [*antiquorum*]. For, although his predecessors have effected more in terms of the acquisition of lands and construction of buildings, he has certainly labored more than all those in the course of valiantly guarding the church, safe, whole, and unharmed, from those who sought to plunder and overturn it. It is less indeed to have something to guard, than to guard something you have.[2] But now, advancing to my task, I will have done with these introductory matters.

2
The Privileges of the Church of Vézelay. Humbert, Bishop of Autun, First Tries to Overturn These Privileges

[1577B/395. 34]

1140–1145

Now the church of Vézelay, nobly born, and even more nobly nourished in its youth, stood, in its inborn liberty, head and shoulders above all the other western churches. At the very moment of its foundation it was placed under the patronage of[3] the most blessed Peter, key-bearer of the kingdom of the heavens, nobly assigned by its most noble founders to his sole and unique Apostolic See, and furnished[4] with a dowry of perpetual liberty by the highest and apostolic pontifex of the time, Nicholas. His successors, adhering up to these times to the path chartered by his piety, strengthened the church in their privileges with apostolic authority and Roman dignity. They decreed that the church of Vézelay should remain entirely immune from all subjection to any person or church, just as if it were the particular right and allod[5] of blessed Peter. Accordingly, indulging the church with the clemency and apostolic liberty inherent in the Roman privileges, they allowed it to receive ecclesiastical offices, such as the holy ordination of its monks and clerics, the consecration of churches and altars, the blessing with chrism and holy oil,[6]

---

[1] *tempore . . . novissimus.*

[2] Cf. Ovid *Ars amatoria* 2.13.

[3] *attitulata.* See Niermeyer (1976: 68 §5).

[4] *subarrata: subarr(h)are* means "to pledge, espouse, endow, promise." See charter 3 above.

[5] *proprium ius et alodium.* See Guizot (1969: 220n.3). On *alodium* see Niermeyer (1976: 36–38).

[6] *sacri ordines monachorum vel clericorum suorum et basilicarum seu altarium consecrationes, crismatis vel sancti olei gratiam.* On "orders and ordination" see Cross (1974: 1004–6, esp. 1005): "Traditional theology . . . holds that the sacrament of orders can be validly conferred only by a duly consecrated Bishop acting as the minister of Christ and the successor of the Apostles." On "chrism" see Cross (1974: 277). For the bishop in the

and other things of this kind, wherever it chose, from any Catholic bishop of
any province. Thus, its innate liberty heralded abroad so effectively and
thoroughly, Vézelay presented to its fellow churches a truly enviable situation.

After several hundreds of years, however, a certain Humbert, presiding
over the church of Autun,[1] contrived to infect the beauty of liberty with the
wart of spotty servitude.[2] At that time Vézelay was governed by the venerable
Pons, the blood brother of Peter of Cluny and Jordan of La Chaise-Dieu, both
abbots.[3] Pons, of noble stock, and possessed of a most noble church, invited,
as was customary in a church enjoying such liberty, Elias, bishop of Orleans,[4]
and humbly beseeched him to perform holy ordinations for him. Elias,
observing the privileges emanating from Roman authority, very devoutly gave
assent to Pons's humble request[5] and promoted several monks and some
clerics to holy orders in the basilica of the church of Vézelay. He had no
sooner done so than the bishop of Autun, much put out, pronounced the
ordinations which the clerics had obtained null and void.[6] Innocent [II], of
good memory and at that time apostolic pontiff of the Roman See, reproached Autun's mad temerity; he restored to their orders the clerics suspended by Autun, and commanded him not to presume further to profane
the laws [iura] of the Roman church.[7] Then Autun, having tasted apostolic
indignation, came to regret what he had begun, but was too ashamed to
repudiate it. Nor did he cease to provoke the abbot until, frustrated in every
one of his attempts, he submitted to an adjudication[8] that had been arranged
by the abbot of Cluny and other upright persons. Between both churches he
[the abbot of Cluny] then refashioned, at the instigation of the above mentioned venerable abbot Pons, a state of pristine peace.

---

church at this period see Barraclough (1933), *Cambridge Medieval History* vol. 6, chap. 16
and Zacour (1969: chap. 8).

[1] Humbert was bishop of Autun from 1140. He was related to the counts of Nevers
and initiated the cult of St. Lazarus at Autun to rival that of the Magdalene at Vézelay;
Bouchard (1987: 387). On an analogous initiative in regard to the cult of St. Lazarus, at
Angers, see Moore (1987: 57).

[2] *nevum maculose servitutis*. Cf. Cicero *De natura deorum* 1.28.79, *macula naevus*.

[3] Pons was seventeenth abbot of Vézelay. See Aspects [F] above. Peter the Venerable
(1092–1156), as abbot of Cluny, was the leading monastic figure of the day, apart perhaps
from St. Bernard of Clairvaux himself. According to Katzenellenbogen (1944) Peter played
a large role in the design of the celebrated Pentecost tympanum in the narthex at Vézelay.
Jordan, brother to Peter and Pons, was abbot of the Benedictine monastery of La
Chaise-Dieu and later cardinal and papal legate in France (Bouchard [1987: 411]).

[4] Elias was bishop of Orleans 1137–1146, when he was deposed for simony.

[5] *devotioni eius devotius acquievit*.

[6] *quos adepti fuerant ordines clericis interdixit*: the construction suggests that it was only
the "orders" that were rendered null and void: the clerics themselves would not have been
placed under excommunication or interdict.

[7] Charter 21 above, dated end 1140–September 1143. Innocent II was pope 1130–
1143, but for the first eight years of his pontificate his authority was challenged by that of
the anti-pope Anacletus; he was at times a refugee in France. See Kelly (1986: 167–69).

[8] *in manu Cluniacensis . . . proposite liti renunciavit*. The reconciliation took place around
1145; Graham (1918: 83).

3
Henry, His Successor, Brother of the Duke of Burgundy, Harasses the Church in the Same Way [1578A/396. 76]
c. 1143–1145

Humbert was of most distinguished stock and resplendent in piety and uprightness of life. Consequently, when the church of Lyon suffered the loss of its own archbishop[1] it sought him as a replacement. Humbert accepted the dignity and Henry, brother of the duke of Burgundy[2] assumed the episcopacy of Autun. It was not long before those who had fostered[3] the earlier long-standing discord began to work on Henry, making every effort to renew their slanders against the liberty of Vézelay, slanders which had slumbered for some time now. They found ready ears. Henry, moreover, confident of the might of his family connections and his wealth—he was equally pre-eminent on both counts—was a man of quite singular capacity in his efforts to bring about change. He sought to win Vézelay into his own jurisdiction,[4] to reduce it to the status of a subordinate parish within his diocese, as was the case with other churches, and to make it obedient to his synods. But he could not wrest the club from the hand of Hercules;[5] he could not counter the protection of God and the patronage of Mary Magdalene,[6] the blessed lover of God. Nevertheless, as far as he could, he quite plainly left nothing untried in his urge to usurp for himself what had been granted to blessed Peter alone. Blind cupidity in fact persuaded him that all he now desired with so great an appetite could easily be obtained. Consequently Henry pressed[7] the above-mentioned worthy abbot Pons, who had taken the cause of his church upon his own shoulders,[8] first in the matter of the execution of synodal decrees, then in regard to the examination of clerics and priests, and finally concerning the business of ecclesiastical sacraments. On all these counts he demanded from Pons acknowledgement of his proper jurisdiction.[9] But the abbot replied that he was the guardian of the church of Vézelay, not its legal advocate,[10] and, in fact, in so far as the rights of his church were concerned, he was the vicar of the apostolic paternity: he would not therefore engage in litigation with the

---

[1] *antistite.*

[2] Graham (1918: 83–84), Bouchard (1987: 256, 260, 386–87).

[3] *incentores*: for *incentor* Lewis & Short give "one who sets the tune, a precenter, singer/inciter exciter."

[4] *in ius proprium.*

[5] A proverbial expression (Huygens [1976: 397]).

[6] See Aspects [D] above and Appendix D below.

[7] *compellans*: can also mean "summoning to court."

[8] *qui causam aecclesiae in ratione sua acceperat*: "who had taken up as his own the cause of the church" (Cox); "had taken up the cause (case) of the church from motives of his own"?

[9] *iurisiusticiam*: Huygens (1976: xxxix n.111) observes that the word *ius*, in the prose of Hugh of Poitiers, frequently combines with other words to express several aspects of the judicial power of the abbot of Vézelay and the count of Nevers.

[10] *tutorem aecclesiae non actionarium.*

bishop on any of these points, without the lord pope's knowledge. Thus repulsed, the bishop desired to extort by violence what he could not gain surreptitiously by means of legal prosecution.[1] He began therefore to infest the church, to oppress its men, to plunder its possessions, and, as far as he could, to attempt everything to the disadvantage of the church. Considering his own power insufficient for the accomplishment of all the ventures he had in mind, Henry incited his brother the duke and also his other brothers to a hatred of the church. In this way he gathered together and hurled towards the ruin and overthrow of the church virtually the entire aristocratic might of Burgundy.[2] The abbot, however, attaining a constancy of mind and displaying his characteristic patience, spurned, smashed, annulled, and annihilated as if they had been from the first pointless and futile, all Henry's attacks.

4

There Is a Dispute Before His Highness the Pope Concering the Immunities of Vézelay. The Bishop of Autun's Case Fails   [1597A/397. 114]

c. 1145–1151

The most holy Eugenius was now presiding over the universal church. When he heard of the madness with which Autun strove to violate the chastity of his special daughter, that is, the church of Vézelay, he repeatedly admonished him, reproached him and threateningly warned him of the danger of losing his episcopal office unless he recovered his senses.[3] Autun therefore, frustrated in his particular ambitions and doubting the efficacy of his own power by itself, went to the Roman curia and, inventing falsehoods and composing verisimilitudes,[4] laid a complaint against the abbot, asserting that those things which he was demanding from the church of Vézelay, the church of his own see had held without the calumny of any controversy by entitlement of established custom[5] right down to the present day. But the most clement pope Eugenius, keeping in mind at every point the dignity of apostolic authority and the integrity of truth,[6] demurred,[7] set a day for each party, informed the abbot of the fixed day and instructed him through a mandate

---

[1] *actionali prosecutione.*

[2] *quasi potentatum totius Burgundie*: doubtless exaggerated. Note the importance in the *History* of key concepts: *potentia, ingenita (innata/ingenua) libertas, servitudo, discordia, mos, jus (proprium, jurisdictio), possessio,* etc.

[3] Eugenius was Pope 1145–53 AD. See charters 28–33, 35–55 above, especially 38 and 43–46, which concern the dispute between Autun and Vézelay, and Kelly (1986: 172–73).

[4] That is, pleading his case using *veri similis narratio* (*Rhetorica ad Herennium* 1.9.16).

[5] *per longi temporis prescriptionem*: a legal phrase implying "prescription, right created by lapse of time" (Latham [1965: 369]). Eugenius summarizes Autun's complaint in charter 43 above.

[6] *salva integritate veritatis*: Hugh is careful to point out that his own ends, the ends of Vézelay, and those of the pope happen to coincide with *veritas.*

[7] *deferens*: a legal term meaning "to enter a demurrer; seek a delay in the proceedings."

written in the spirit of piety to present himself or proctors with full powers,[1] together with the muniments of the church, before the pope on the appointed day to answer the charges laid against him. Both parties, therefore, with sufficient, and, as it seemed to each, proper accompaniment of witnesses, presented themselves before the universal curia, confident that the papal examination[2] would result in their obtaining the goal of their case.[3]

Meanwhile Abbot Pons, rightly to be styled "tenacious of justice,"[4] gaining entrance to the pope, complained that he ought not enter upon legal suit at all, or submit to any judgment on this matter: his perpetual possession of the church of Vézelay was guaranteed by the hand of the pope himself, and, as was attested in several ancient Roman privileges of the same apostolic authority, he was constituted heir to it by testament of perpetual liberty. To this the pious apostolic[5] replied that the more conscious the abbot was of the justice of his case, so the more freely and fairly ought he too to seek out the examination of a court: he should be in no doubt that in so far as his case would always be clearly the stronger when the balance of the judicial pendulum had been weighed, it would emerge unscathed from every difficulty associated with the trial.[6] Even if the abbot's case somehow were to suffer harm from thoughtless prejudice—and the pope trusted that this would not eventuate—then he did not doubt but that violent judicial findings deriving from prejudice could in the event be overturned by the authority of the [papal] privileges.[7] The abbot, reassured by this reasoning, agreed to undergo trial, and each party now presented its case.

In this presentation it was established by definition that Autun could prove no legal point deriving from proprietary right,[8] none from possession of [the right of] investiture,[9] none from entitlement of established custom[10]—on which the bishop especially relied—none even from usufruct or legacy.[11] He could rely only upon largesse or permission, granted in accordance with the

---

[1] *per sufficientes responsales.* For this phrase see, for example, *per se vel sufficientes responsales monachos*: "in person or [through] competent representative monks," Thomson (1974: 80–81). The mandate referred to is charter 43 above, dated 23 February 1151.

[2] *examine . . . tanto.*

[3] *finem . . . causae suae*; the *finis cause*, a technical term: see Cicero *De inventione* 1.5.6 and Häring (1964: 284); also Fredborg (1988: 53).

[4] *iustitenax*: see Juvenal *Satires* 8.25: *iustitiaeque tenax.*

[5] *apostolicus*: the regular twelfth-century word for "pope." Cf. Ullmann (1961: part 1) and Cross (1974: 75–77).

[6] *ab omni questionis nodo*: *nodus questionis* is a common phrase, found in Cassian, Augustine, and Boethius. For *quaestio*, see Cicero *De inventione* 1.13.18.

[7] What is meant here? Was the pope promising to override the determination of his own court if necessary? Such a preliminary meeting with Abbot Pons, canvassing some hint of "undemocratic" procedure, forms an interesting parallel to the meetings St. Bernard called before the council of Sens and the trial of Gilbert of Poitiers at Rheims: Chibnall (1956: 17–19) and cf. Klibansky (1961: 1ff.); Häring (1966).

[8] *in qua prosecutione definitum est Eduensem nichil ex proprietario iure*: cf. *Ad Herennium* 1.12.21 *definitione causa.*

[9] *ex investitionis possessione.*

[10] Cf. 134n.5 above.

[11] *ex fructuario seu legatario.*

custom of the liberty of Vézelay to any bishop of any province. The abbot, on
the other hand, based nothing on entitlement of established custom, nor
legacy,[1] nor any other use by alien acquisition,[2] but said that the church of
Vézelay had always possessed the liberty in question solely by proprietary
right and by ancient investiture of perpetual possession.[3] He ended his
oration[4] very adequately[5] by stressing that this liberty was not the result of
enfranchisement appropriate to a freed person,[6] but on the contrary was
innate in the church, had been born with it, had grown up with it and had
endured unimpaired in the church right down to the present day. Since each
party moreover was strengthening its allegations with witnesses, the court
gave its opinion[7] that the witnesses produced should corroborate their testimony by taking the oath.[8] The form of the oath was this, that each party
would reveal any true information it possessed relative to the case of either
side, that falsehoods would be entirely banished. Thus the abbot produced his
witnesses, bound by the oath. The manner of their deposition [*testificationis
modus*] was as follows.

5

The Witnesses of the Abbot Tell What They Know of the
Church's Rights   [1580B/399. 172]

1151

Gerard, prior of *Albornensis*, said under oath: "Before I became a monk I was
present at a council which Pope Paschal held at Guastalla[9] and I saw that
there he blessed Abbot Renaud of Vézelay. After I became a monk at Vézelay
the same abbot sent me to Auxerre[10] with Peter Aribald, cleric, and several
other monks, Guibert, Achard, Aimon, and I took the four orders as far as

---

[1] *nec longi temporis prescriptionem nec legatarium.*

[2] *alienae acquisitionis usum.*

[3] *ex proprietario iure et antiqua perpetuae possessionis investitione.*

[4] *peroraret*: a technical term for the final part of an *oratio*.

[5] *sufficienter*: that is, Pons "perorated" in accordance with the advice of the classical
rhetorical manuals: he both summed up and induced sympathy by emotional or moving
discourse. Hugh's report of the *peroratio* (which he must have heard, or derived from an
eyewitness) makes clear that it was a clever piece of rhetoric, based on the *topos* of an
accumulating climax: *Ad Herennium* 2.30.47 et seq., 4.25.34 (*gradatio*).

[6] *non libertina emancipatione.* See Jordan (1986).

[7] *ex sententia consessus.*

[8] *iurisiurandi sacramento.* Cf. the note on the two kinds of *iusiurandi* in Wahrmund
(1962: 93). The form of oath here is called by Aegidius *promissorium, quod concipitur super
futuro, in quo promittitur aliquid dandum vel faciendum vel non dandum vel non faciendum.*

[9] October 1106. The priory of *Albornensis* (Cox, "Alborne"; Guizot [1969], "Albano")
is not otherwise known. Paschal II was pope 1099-1118. The Council of Guastalla (a town
in northern Italy) was convoked to renew ecclesiastical censures against laymen who
claimed the right of investiture for ecclesiastical benefices. For Paschal's privileges in
regard to Vézelay see Charters 15-19 above. See Kelly (1986: 160-61) and Wilks (1971:
69-85).

[10] These various incidents show that the bishop of Autun was regularly bypassed and
thus that the abbot of Vézelay could employ the services of other bishops.

the subdiaconate, and Peter Aribald was ordained, but I do not remember what particular order he received. At another time I was ordained subdeacon[1] by the same Bishop Humbald.[2] Afterwards the bishop of Angers, coming to Rome, consecrated the chrism and holy oil at Vézelay in the greater church[3] and I am quite sure that the chaplains of the same town received that holy oil and chrism. The same bishop of Angers also ordained me deacon and other monks as well, together with certain clerics of the same town[4] in their turn. I do not, however, remember the names of the clerics. And the same abbot sent me and the monk John to Hugh bishop of Nevers,[5] who consecrated us as priests. And when I was at [the church of] Saint-Jacques-d'Asquins[6] in the obedience of Vézelay, I saw William Barzelier, envoy of the Abbot Renaud, going to Auxerre for chrism, and, returning thence, he entrusted the chrism to me while he took a short rest that night. Afterwards the same envoy, taking it back from me, deposited it at Vézelay. At another time I saw Amicus of Lormes sent by Abbot Renaud to the same Bishop Hugh for chrism, and he returned with it. In the time of Abbot Renaud a certain parishioner [*parochianus*] of his, Stephen Aicaphit went to Jerusalem, and since he remained there for seven years [*septennio*], his wife married another man. Later, however, the said Stephen returned and sought out his wife again. She denied him, whereupon he brought her before Abbot Renaud and there, once the case was known, she was restored to her husband by the judgment and authority of Abbot Renaud, and, with the assistance of Peter, chaplain of Saint-Pierre-le-Haut, the adulterer and adulteress received penance from the abbot."[7]

Hugh, prior of Moret[8] said under oath: "Bishop Matthew of Albano [*Albanensis*] ordained me subdeacon and several other monks in the chapel of St. Lawrence at Vézelay in the time of Abbot Alberic,[9] while the pope Innocent was at Auxerre.[10] I also saw in the time of the same abbot that Archbishop Hugh of Rouen consecrated the altar of St. Gilles [*Egidius*] in the

---

[1] The subdiaconate was one of the five minor clerical orders in the church. The major orders were the diaconate, priesthood, and episcopate; see Cross (1974: 1318).

[2] Bishop of Auxerre (1095–1115) (Bouchard [1987: 389]).

[3] *in maiore aecclesia*. The *ecclesia maior* was normally the cathedral church; in this case the abbey church of the Magdalene. For the lesser churches in Vézelay see Aspects [C] above.

[4] I.e., Vézelay.

[5] Hugh III, bishop of Nevers 1110–1119; see Bouchard (1987: 401).

[6] Asquins/Esconium, the root word being "aqua"—water, referring to the village springs. The village is located two kilometers from Vézelay and was under the authority of the abbot. See Aspects [C] above n.2.

[7] Saint-Pierre-le-Haut lay within the town walls of Vézelay (Aspects [C] above). For jurisdiction and procedure in the enforcement of the church's decrees in marital and sexual matters, see Brundage (1987: 223ff., 253ff., 319ff., 409ff.). For the "crusader's wife" see Brundage (1967).

[8] Moret, eleven kilometers from Fontainebleau, where Louis VII decided the dispute between the abbot of Vézelay, the *cives* of the town, and the count of Nevers. See below Book 4 §74.

[9] Alberic, sixteenth abbot of Vézelay; see Aspects [F] above.

[10] 1131 and 1132 (Huygens [1976: 400]).

greater church, and I saw the marriage of Hardouin and Cécile, about which there was a great controversy, confirmed by the authority and judgment of Abbot Alberic of Vézelay, with the assistance of Walter, bishop of Chalon-sur–Saône: and the father himself and his young son were from a parish of Autun, that is, Glaine.[1] Garnier, subprior at Vézelay, took me to Auxerre and there I was ordained into the priesthood with several monks of our monastery by Bishop Hugh [II], who had been abbot of Saint-Germain.[2] Afterwards, when I was chamberlain,[3] I had Hugh [III] of Auxerre, who had been abbot of Pontigny,[4] ordain fourteen monks at Auxerre, acting on a request from Abbot Alberic.[5] Stephen, bishop of Autun consecrated the altar of Saint-Andéol[6] placed in the choir of the monks, and I heard Stephen, bishop of Autun saying to the count of Nevers that he had come to give the benediction to Abbot Pons at the summoning of Abbot Peter of Cluny and of the monks of Vézelay, and this took place in the chamber of the abbot. I also saw Geoffrey, bishop of Chartres, and Hugh of Auxerre, who had been abbot of Saint-Germain, frequently celebrating masses in the church of St. Mary Magdalene, on her feast day,[7] with Stephen of Autun present and raising no objection."

Anselm, monk of Vézelay, said under oath: "I saw Abbot Pons commit the church of Saint-Père-sous-Vézelay,[8] spiritually and temporally, to a certain priest Bernard, and in this chapter. The same man entrusted to the priest Guy the church of Saint-Pierre-le-Haut in regard to spiritual and temporal matters, in full chapter [*praesente capitulo*]:[9] and the same abbot commended to the priest Andrew the church of St. Stephen,[10] likewise in the chapter; and all these things happened after the agreement[11] which was made at

---

[1] Walter II of Sercy, 1126–58 (Bouchard [1987: 392]; Huygens [1976: 647] gives Walter bishop of Chalon-sur-Saône's dates as 1128–56).

[2] Fifty-third bishop of Auxerre, 1115–36. Nephew of St. Hugh of Cluny. A monk of Cluny, he was sent to put order into the affairs of the abbey of St. Germain of Auxerre, of which he became abbot. Bouchard (1987: 389 and 1979: chap. 2); Crozet (1975: 264) gives 1116–36 as the dates of "Hugues II de Semur."

[3] The *camerarii* were administrators of monastic property and expenses. Niermeyer (1976: 120): "treasurer, head of financial administration, chamberlain." See Knowles ([1949] 1962: 434).

[4] Hugh of Mâcon, fifty-fourth bishop of Auxerre (1137–51), formerly a Cistercian. He had been deputed to head the Cistercian colony of Pontigny which had been established with twelve monks in 1114. He was the first Cistercian to become bishop, as Eugenius III was the first to become a pope. Crozet (1975: 265) gives 1136–51 as the dates of "Hugh III de Mâcon."

[5] Huygens (1976: 400.221) takes this last phrase with the following sentence, against *PL* and Guizot (1969), but the sense requires otherwise.

[6] On the circumstances that led to the acquisition of the relics of St. Andéol, see Guizot (1969: 229n.23).

[7] 22 July. The right to celebrate masses on a feast day was especially significant.

[8] *Sanctus Petrus Inferior*. "Saint Père" is an alternative for Saint Pierre or St. Peter (*Sancti Petri ecclesia*), to whom the church was dedicated. The village was part of the estate of Vézelay, and is easily visible from the elevated plateau behind the abbey itself.

[9] Guizot (1969) omits this sentence (by haplography?).

[10] The various churches of Vézelay are discussed in Aspects [C] above.

[11] *concordia*: probably at the end of 1145 (Huygens [1976: 401]). The relevance of this

Moulins. Bishop Matthew of Albano ordained me into the diaconate, with three other monks in the chapel of St. Lawrence. Hugh [II], bishop of Auxerre, who had been abbot of Saint-Germain, ordained me into the priesthood with several others at Pontigny. I have seen Henry, bishop of Autun and several others received at Vézelay with a procession."

Hugh of Souvigny, monk and priest said under oath: "Elias, bishop of Orleans, ordained me into the priesthood with several other monks, in the greater church at Vézelay, and he did the same to Guy, who is now chaplain, and Renaud Rialte, in my presence. In the very same year of my ordination I saw the messenger of Abbot Pons, Durand by name, going for chrism and oil to Bishop Fromond of Nevers and returning with the chrism and oil. Since it is the custom of the monastery of Vézelay that no cleric of the town should go to a synod without the abbot's permission, I saw, at the time of a synod, that Abbot Pons called before him Sado and Peter Aribald, greater chaplains,[1] and instructed them not to go to the synod, and they obeyed him. And when priests on the day before the feast of All Saints sought the abbot's permission to go to a synod, the abbot did not grant it, and they did not go either. I saw Arnulf of Ferrières on the abbot's command go to Auxerre for chrism and oil, and return with it, six years ago, after the agreement previously mentioned.[2] After the agreement I also saw the altar of St. Michael in the greater church blessed by [Arch]bishop Hugh of Rouen, and after the agreement,[3] I saw Hugh of Auxerre make ordinations at Vézelay. I also saw three cases of matrimony laid before Abbot Pons: that of Obert Saltarell and Elizabeth, that of Aimeri the wax dealer and the daughter of Blanchard the tailor, and that of the brother of Drogo[4] and the daughter of Peter the merchant. These were all concluded [*terminari*][5] by the authority of the abbot. In the case of Obert and Elizabeth, the advocate was Herman who is now archdeacon and archpriest of Avallon." Concerning the presentation [*donatione*] of the three churches this same man said emphatically what Anselm the monk of Vézelay had said.

Hugh of the school [*de Scola*], monk and priest,[6] said: "In the time of Abbot Alberic, Prior Hugh of Moret led me with several others to Auxerre, and there had us ordained, myself into the subdiaconate and the remainder into several other orders, by Hugh, who was abbot of Pontigny. In the time of Abbot Pons, Elias of Orleans, the bishop, ordained me into the diaconate, and several others into different orders, including Guy who is now greater chaplain, and Renaud Rialte, the latter two becoming priests. This was done

---

agreement is discussed in Aspects [A] above.

[1] *maiores capellanos*. A chaplain is a priest who has the charge of a chapel; the greater chaplain is the most senior of a number of chaplains.

[2] See 138n.11.

[3] See 138n.11.

[4] *et fratris Drogonis*. The abbot's exercise of jurisdiction in matrimonial disputes was in defiance of episcopal authority. See the discussion in Aspects [A] above and 137n.7 above.

[5] See Niermeyer (1976: 1020); or "annulled"? See below 140n.4.

[6] See Huygens (1976: xxiii). Hugh of the school of Vézelay. Is this the author of the present history?

in the greater church. And in the time of the same Abbot Pons, I saw Humbert of Lyon, then of Autun, called by the abbot of Vézelay into the Church of the Pilgrims,[1] ordain several [monks], some into the priesthood, others into the diaconate, others into different orders. I also saw Hugh, archbishop of Rouen consecrate the altar of St. Michael, in the greater church, after the peace had been refashioned [reformatam]. In addition, I saw Hugh of Auxerre ordain the two Geoffreys into the subdiaconate." Concerning the presentation [donatione] of the three churches, the same man said straightly[2] the same things that Anselm and Hugh had said. "I saw Humbert, who is now archbishop of Lyon and Henry, who is now bishop of Autun in the town of Vézelay. Sometimes they were maintained as guests in the greater church, sometimes they took lodgings in the town at their own expense."

Ours[3] said under oath concerning the chrism and oil the same as Hugh of Souvigny, and he said the same concerning the synod. Concerning the examination and the determination of the marriage cases,[4] he said[5] the same as Hugh, except that he made no mention of the archpriest of Avallon.

Benedict, the abbot's cook, said under oath the same things concerning the marriage of Hardouin and Cécile as Hugh the prior of Moret, and concerning the marriages of Obert and Elizabeth, Aimeri the wax dealer and the daughter of Blanchard the tailor, and the brother of Drogo and the daughter of Peter the merchant, he said[6] the same as Hugh of Souvigny the monk and priest.

Alegreth, under oath, said the same concerning the matrimonial cases of Obert Saltarell and Elizabeth, and Aimeri the wax dealer and the daughter of Blanchard the tailor as Hugh of Souvigny and Benedict the cook had said;[7] and he also said a certain woman went to Jerusalem and when she had delayed there her husband sought another wife.[8] The wife, returning, claimed her husband again, and when the case was made known in the presence of the abbot Pons himself, she was returned to her husband by the judgement and authority of the abbot. He did not, however, remember the names of those concerned.

---

[1] See Aspects [C] above.

[2] prorsus. For de donatione trium ecclesiarum see text above at 138nn.8–10, and text immediately following 139 at n.5.

[3] Ursus: "Bear."

[4] de questionibus et terminationibus matrimoniorum. See above 139n.5.

[5] Literally "says." The use of the present tense here and in other places in this book suggests that Hugh's report of proceedings could have been copied from a notarial original.

[6] The abbot's rights in disputed jurisdictions are reinforced by many witnesses.

[7] This repetition emphasizes how contentious jurisdiction over marriage disputes was.

[8] An example illustrating the complications that could ensue from a long pilgrimage. See the case of Stephen Aicaphit above, at 137n.7.

6
The Witnesses of the Bishop of Autun Are Brought Forward. [1583A/402. 311]

1151

With the abbot's witnesses removed, Autun offered his own, and the first was the abbot of Sainte-Marguerite.[1] He said under oath that he had seen priests of Vézelay at the synod of the bishop of Autun on several occasions, but he did not know whether they went there all the time, or simply made occasional appearances;[2] he had seen Sado, Peter, and Bernard, and, in the time of [Bishop] Stephen, Sado and Peter, and, in the time of [Bishop] Humbert, Bernard. He did not know whether they had attended under orders or of their own will,[3] nor could he remember whether he had seen them together or not.[4] "But often I have heard [he said][5] the monks saying that they did not go to the synod under compulsion: I heard a complaint when the monks of Vézelay did not come, but I heard no penalty or satisfaction. I know the priests suspended by Autun were restored by the lord pope and I saw his letters. In the reformation of peace I heard the abbot promising that he would henceforth be a faithful friend of Autun, and that he would act towards him as his predecessors had acted towards the predecessors of the bishop. I saw that the abbot showed this bishop the privilege of Eugenius,[6] and then the abbot of Cluny said to the bishop of Autun in the presence of Pons, abbot of the same monastery,[7] 'When there is need, go to Vézelay and act as bishop.' "[8]

John, prior of Saint-Symphorien,[9] said under oath: "I saw that Humbert, bishop of Autun, celebrated mass at Vézelay, and delivered a sermon in connection with some ceremony."[10] In the time of the synod he saw Sado and Peter at Autun, and believed that they had come for the synod. Concerning the reformation of peace, he said that he heard it said by someone that the bishop would go to Vézelay and would perform his office there, and this after the reformation of the peace.

---

[1] Founded in the eleventh century by the counts of Vergy, near Beaune (diocese of Autun), with a community of Augustinian canons regular. The abbot's name (Huygens [1976: 410.627] was *Obertus.*

[2] The text should perhaps read here "*utrum* continue *et* assidue *annon* ignorat."

[3] *an debito vel voluntate.*

[4] *si simul non reminiscitur.*

[5] The text suddenly breaks into direct speech, without any introductory word.

[6] This privilege is lost (Huygens [1976: 403]).

[7] It is interesting that the abbot of Cluny urges the bishop to act against the interests of his own (Cluny's) brother.

[8] Words inspired by Paulinus of Milan, *Vita sancti Ambrosii* (ed. M. Pellegrino [Rome, 1961], 60), as noted by Huygens.

[9] A bishop of Autun in the fifth century AD established a basilica of canons regular in honor of St. Symphorien, situated on the spot where St. Symphorien was supposed to have been martyred. The abbey received monks in the tenth century and was reformed by the Benedictine monks of Fleury-sur-Loire in the eleventh century.

[10] *et hoc quadam sollennitate.* Latham (1965: 443) gives for *solennitas* "solemn service, mass," Niermeyer (1976: 978) "written deed."

Everard, archpriest [of Avallon], said under oath: "I saw Stephen, bishop of Autun on Easter Day and on the feast of St. Mary Magdalene celebrate the greater masses at least twice. On the day of St. Mary Magdalene when Autun celebrated the masses, the bishop of Chartres was there, and he delivered a sermon to the people. The bishop of Autun gave the blessing. The same Stephen dedicated the Church of the Pilgrims when Pope Innocent [II] was at Vézelay. I do not remember when this took place. The same man dedicated the altar of the monastic choir and the altar of the chapel of St. Stephen. I saw that he blessed Abbot Baldwin[1] and heard that he blessed [Abbot] Alberic at Auxerre, and I saw Pons blessed by him. I saw ordinations of monks and clerics take place at the hands of the same Stephen, in the Church of the Pilgrims. I saw this once. I saw Belin, Angilbert, Sado, and Bernard, chaplains of the lower church, and Peter Grael, Blain, Sado, Guy, of the upper church, come to the synod continually, except for two years: this present year, and the one in which there was discord between Humbert, bishop of Autun and Abbot Pons over orders celebrated there by the bishop of Orleans. I am referring to a period of thirty years."[2] He said the same as the abbot [of Sainte-Marguerite] on the subject of the chrism and oil, as also concerning the peace, except that he did not say the words "go to Vézelay." Afterwards, however, he saw the bishop confer orders there once,[3] "and I saw two clerics, Bonami[4] and Peter, wishing to be ordained, carrying letters of Autun to Auxerre, and I saw two chaplains of St. Stephen [of Vézelay] and Saint-Jacques-d'Asquins come to the synod at Autun, and this indeed once.[5] I, Archpriest Everard, saw the transgressions of two clerics punished. The clerics concerned were Blandin, sub-chaplain, and Mainard of Asquins. And I saw Angilbert chaplain of Saint-Père-sous-Vézelay receive the cure of souls[6] from Lambert, the archpriest of Avallon, and Bernard the cure of souls from Humbert of Autun, and I heard him saying that he hoped that the abbot would not find out. Peter, Andrew the chaplain, Sado,[7] and Walter of Asquins handed their own parishioners over to me for the administration of penance as a result of offenses. This they did often. In consequence of an ancient custom of the land, I saw parishioners from the town of Vézelay come to the church of Avallon one by one, over a period of forty years, from their various homes, and there each one of them bestowed upon the church a coin or a measure of wax. I saw Sado and Peter receive the cure of souls from Stephen, bishop of Autun. I saw Renaud, archbishop of Lyon perform ordinations there, of both monks and clerics. I saw that the abbot of Vézelay used to send his monks for ordination to any bishop he wished. I saw the instrument of the

---

[1] Omitted in Guizot (1969) and *PL*. For the significance of this omission and the abbacy of Baldwin, see Berlow (1981) and Aspects [C] above.

[2] *pro ordinibus . . . et hoc per xxx annos.*

[3] Here the report breaks into direct speech again.

[4] "Goodfriend."

[5] *et hoc vel semel.*

[6] *cura animarum* = "cure of souls" = duty of a curate or parish priest or clergyman, who has charge of the souls of his parishioners.

[7] Huygens (1976: 673) gives the name as Sado, Sadonis, Sadus.

founder:[1] I read it before the lord pope Innocent, and it contained the clause that the monastery should be free from all pecuniary exaction except a pound of silver which was offered annually to the church of blessed Peter. When I had read this, the lord pope said to the bishop: 'Go, perform your duty.' And I saw that the church of Saint-Père-sous-Vézelay every year, for the past forty years, paid to the church of Autun, five solidi as a procuration fee."[2]

Arnulf said under oath: "I saw that Bishop Stephen blessed a certain altar in the church of St. Stephen." Yet he did not know what altar it was, since there are many there.[3] The same man blessed an altar of the choir in the church of St. Mary Magdalene. He also blessed the Church of the Pilgrims while Pope Innocent was there. The same man, in the same church, as he recalled,[4] also performed ordinations of the monks and clerics of that town,[5] and of others in his episcopate. "And when I was archpriest in Saulieu[6] I saw Bishop Haganon [of Autun] going to Vézelay to perform ordinations and I saw clerics returning who were saying that they had been ordained. I heard that on the following day, after the ordinations, he dedicated the church at Asquins. Bishop Stephen celebrated the greater masses at Vézelay on the days of the Resurrection of the Lord and of St. Mary Magdalene, and the bishop of Chartres delivered the sermon and the bishop of Autun gave the blessing; this happened on several occasions in my presence. I have seen the priests of Vézelay for thirty-five years continuously coming to the synod of Autun: the names of some are as follows: Blandin, Sado, Peter Grael, Peter Aribald, Guy. I saw Bishop Norgaud [of Autun] received by the monks of Vézelay with a procession. I saw that Stephen blessed [Abbot] Alberic at Auxerre"; but he did not remember the church in which he did so.

Walter, archpriest, said under oath that Bishop Stephen blessed Abbot Pons and the altar in the choir. On the subject of the peace he said the same as the others; the bishop afterwards, he said, performed ordinations in the church of Saint-Père-sous-Vézelay, and confirmed all there. He, Walter, very often saw the priests of Vézelay come to the synod of Autun, among others, Guy and Bernard, who are chaplains now;[7] and Stephen received the five *solidi* procuration fee for ten years, and each family paid one coin for crosses.[8] He saw this once, and heard about it many times. He also heard that the abbot of Vézelay could send monks to any bishop he wished for ordination.

Walter the priest said under oath that for thirty years past he had seen Vézelay clerics seek chrism from the archpriest of Avallon, except in two

---

[1] *instrumentum fundatoris*: see charter 1 above.

[2] *pro parata*. Procuration is discussed in Aspects [A] above.

[3] The frequent insertion of third person remarks and the rapid alternation of first and third persons in the depositions suggest that Hugh is using a notarial record of the trial proceedings.

[4] *sicut credit*.

[5] *villa*.

[6] In *Sedeloco* = Saulieu, Côte-d'Or. This witness's memory is long, as Haganon was bishop of Autun from 1055 to 1098 (Huygens [1976: 632]).

[7] The text says only *qui modo sunt*. Huygens (1976) adds *capellani* and Guizot (1969) translates "who are still alive."

[8] *nummum pro crucibus*. See below 144n.5 and above n.2.

years: the present, and the year of the discord. He did not know who the
envoys were. He also saw the Church of the Pilgrims blessed by Bishop
Stephen, whilst Pope Innocent was in the town. He did not know when this
was. An abbot was there, but he did not know his name. The same bishop
consecrated the altar in the choir of the greater church, but he did not know
which consecration preceded which. The same witness saw Landri, Peter, and
Angilbert come to the synod at Autun, and they did this for thirty years. He
saw Angilbert receive the cure of souls from the archpriest of Avallon. For
thirty years he saw Peter Grael, Sado, and Blandin, with their successors come
to a synod. The same witness saw the church of Saint-Père-sous-Vézelay pay
the procuration fee to the ministers of the bishop for thirty years. He also saw
Blain and the chaplain Sado[1] punished by the archpriest of Avallon for their
transgressions; he also saw Mainard and Walter of Valterie[2] similarly punished. He heard too that the abbot of Vézelay used to send monks for ordination wherever he wished.

John Gentil said under oath that for the last thirty years he had seen[3]
clerics of the churches of Saint-Père-sous-Vézelay and Saint-Pierre-le-Haut
come to a synod, but not every year. He had seen Angilbert of the lower
church receive the cure of souls from Lambert, archpriest of Avallon, and had
heard Peter, Aribald, and Sado saying that they had received the cure of souls
from Bishop Stephen, but he had not seen this. He had also seen the chaplains
of Vézelay receive chrism from the archpriest of Avallon and Montréal[4] for
thirty years, but not every year; he had seen Peter Grael seek an archpriest from
Bishop Stephen in synod, and the bishop had granted the present one; concerning the transgression of Blain he said the same as the others; he had seen cross
pennies[5] paid and he had also seen the chaplains of Vézelay bring their own
parishioners to receive penance from the archpriest of Avallon. Concerning the
dedication of the Church of the Pilgrims he said the same things. Concerning
the celebration of masses by the bishop he said the same as the others.

Bonami said the same on every point as Gentil, except for the present year
and the year of the discord.

Geoffrey said under oath that several times during the episcopacies of
Stephen and Humbert he had seen Sado and Peter, and Bernard and Guy,
during the episcopacy of the latter, come to a synod; and he saw a certain
cleric of Vézelay seeking a license to ordain from the bishop.

Constantine under oath said that often he had gone to synods with clerics
from Vézelay, and that a certain cleric of Vézelay was ordained by letters
from the bishop of Autun.

Geoffrey, bishop of Nevers, said on the Holy Gospels:[6] "I have seen the

[1] *Idem vidit Blainum capellanum Sadonis [sic] puniri....*

[2] *de Valteria*; Guizot (1969: 24): "Gautier de la Gauterie."

[3] For variety we have used both perfect and pluperfect tenses; the Latin usually
presents only the perfect.

[4] Montréal (the Royal Mount), 27 kilometers from Vézelay, fief of one of the most
powerful houses in Burgundy and allied to the duke of that province. Speaight (1990:
151–54).

[5] *vidit denarios crucis solvi*; cf. above 143n.8.

[6] *coram positis sacrosanctis Evangeliis.* See Huygens (1976: xxiii). Geoffrey, bishop of

bishop of Autun, called Stephen, received at Vézelay as bishop, both when summoned and when not summoned. Sometimes he was entertained[1] at the expense of the monks, sometimes at his own expense, and on the feast of the blessed Mary Magdalene, he often celebrated solemn masses with certain other bishops present. Once, while the bishop of Autun was celebrating solemnities, the bishop of Chartres delivered a sermon. I saw Stephen give the blessing to Abbot Alberic at Auxerre,[2] and consecrate the Church of the Pilgrims whilst Pope Innocent was at Vézelay. At another time the same Stephen blessed the altar in the choir of the monks, at another time that in the church of St. Stephen. I was present when peace was re-established between the bishop of Autun and the abbot of Vézelay, through the mediation of the abbot of Cluny. At the conclusion of this re-establishment, Autun was told, 'Go to Vézelay and perform your duty.' But whether the abbot [of Cluny] said this or some other for him, I do not remember. At another time Abbot Pons came with Bishop Humbert of Autun from Vézelay.[3] After the bishop had preceded him into Autun the abbot was received into the city with a procession by the bishop and his clerics, and then proceeding to the chapter of Autun Cathedral he promised friendship and love to the bishop according to the custom of his predecessors."

Humbert [archbishop] of Lyon said, with the Holy Gospel placed before him, "When I was bishop of Autun, I went to Vézelay without being summoned and in the greater church I celebrated the solemnities of the masses at Eastertime, believing that I was exercising my episcopal right, and I delivered a sermon to the people, and I pronounced a blessing with a certain other bishop present." Concerning the concord he said exactly the same as the bishop of Nevers, except that according to his testimony the abbot said to him, "Go and do at Vézelay what your predecessors were accustomed to do." "Afterwards, summoned to Vézelay, I performed ordinations, both of monks and of the clerics of the town, and of certain clerics of my diocese. And at another time, performing ordinations at Autun, I examined and promoted clerics of Vézelay, with other clerics of my own, according to custom. And as long as I was bishop, the clerics of Vézelay came each year to my synod, or sent an excuse. The archpriest of Avallon brought to me a certain burgher of Vézelay who had dismissed his wife because of her sterility. I instructed him that he should compel the burgher to take back the wife, because justice demanded it."

And so, having given their testimony, the witnesses of Autun retired to their quarters. If their depositions are carefully weighed, they are found to demolish rather than to support the case of the bishop of Autun. Indeed, the celebration of masses, the consecration of altars, the conferring of orders, the

---

Nevers (1146–59), Bouchard (1987: 401). Guizot (1969: 231): Geoffrey assisted in the translation of the relics of St. Lazare to Autun in 1147 and was sent by Louis VII to the count of Nevers to get him to cease his depredations against the monks of Vézelay. See charters 60 and 66 above.

[1] *procurabatur.*

[2] *Altisiodori*: the author frequently uses a genitive of place; see Huygens (1976: xxiii).

[3] *ab urbe.*

dispensation of benedictions, the request for holy oil or chrism, and other things of this kind may all be conceded by free permission to a neighboring bishop of an adjoining province as much as to a bishop of more distant parts, quite in accordance with the authority[1] of the liberty of Vézelay. Privileges therefore enjoyed in common by the bishop of Autun, along with other bishops, cannot by any means be yielded to Autun as his peculiar right. Again, because witnesses testified that the clerics suspended by Autun were restored to their orders by apostolic liberty, the case of Vézelay is completed and that of Autun entirely destroyed. To say that the clergy of Vézelay have attended the synod of Autun, have requested from him the license to ordain, have received the cure of souls from him, have paid what they owed under procuration, have led their parishioners for penance to the archpriests, all these things smack of priestly fraudulence, and betray the temerity of Autun— if one may be permitted to speak thus. Because they admit that these things took place without the full understanding and agreement of the church of Vézelay, they bring upon their own heads a serious charge that they have relied upon clandestine deception.

After the witnesses on both sides had testified as we have set out above, the highest apostolic lord decreed that the dispute in this prolonged lawsuit should be settled by his judgment.[2] However, since complete panic argues a patent sense of guilt, it often happens that a mind borne down by an aware-ness of impending perils is forced to adopt expedients that in a condition of peace it would scorn to anticipate. And so, with his case on the point of settlement,[3] the bishop of Autun, conscious of his rash position, grew anx-ious. Roman equity[4] in a matter involving examination of the justice inherent in claims to jurisdiction[5] was no longer hidden from him. Consequently he began to waver, he became unable to keep up his pretenses, he requested that the judgment be put off on the grounds that he still had several most effec-tive supporters of his case who, overcome with exhaustion or age, could not endure the burden of a long journey to court [as attendance in the capacity of a witness required]. But if a suitable place and time for an action some-where within Gaul were to be offered him, he would produce these witnesses without fail, and when their testimony had been heard, in the pope's pres-ence, at the time he stipulated,[6] the bishop promised that he would without hesitation submit to the apostolic decision, unless a desirable peace had al-ready been concluded between himself and the abbot. But the abbot of Vézelay, thinking about this unnecessary stay in the proceedings,[7] felt that

---

[1] *arbitrium.*

[2] *ut iudicio tantae litis controversia dirimeretur.*

[3] *in articulo discriminis.*

[4] *Romana aequitas.* Guizot (1969) translates "l'équité de la cour de Rome," i.e., canon law, papal *decreta,* rather than "equity" as in Roman law.

[5] *in censura dumtaxat iurisiusticiae.*

[6] Guizot (1969) takes this thus: "promising besides that after their depositions he would come back without fail into the presence of the pope, at a time he might fix, to submit himself to the apostolic sentence."

[7] *supervacaneam comperendinationem.* Lewis & Short cite Seneca, Pliny, Aulus Gellius, Tacitus, and Cicero for the latter word, with the meaning of deferring the time of a trial

the bishop of Autun was placing more trust in the passage of time than in the worth of his case. Accordingly, he began at once to demand the justice to which he was entitled and a judgment of his rights.[1]

Apostolic clemency, however, prevailed and in the end judgment was postponed. A day was fixed for the reopening of the case and neighboring bishops were designated to hear the evidence of Autun's new witnesses, namely, Bishop Godfrey of Langres, Abbot Peter of [Saint-Philibert de] Tournus and Abbot Stephen of Reigny.[2] To these the pope gave written instructions that at a suitable time and place, they reopen the case between Autun and Vézelay, hear the witnesses which Autun should bring forward legally under the form of the prescribed oath, and send the transcript of this testimony to him, properly authenticated by the impression of their seals, in time for the agreed day of judgment. The text[3] of this letter is contained above in the series of letters which the pope kept, addressed to different persons, in connection with the preservation of the liberty of Vézelay. For Pope Eugenius, of incomparable memory, devoted a respectful attention to possible future needs.[4] He instructed that the testimony of both parties be written together in three copies,[5] of which he gave one to the bishop and one to the abbot, while he filed the third with his own archive bureau.[6] His intention was that if by any chance either before himself or before one of his successors, this same dispute should be reactivated, the written testimonies of the earlier hearing would, as if living witnesses,[7] refute all novelties, and any witnesses newly brought forward would not deceive a changed gathering of court personnel.[8] At the conclusion of these proceedings, each party returned to its own region.

Autun, however, having obtained his desired delay, began to dissemble over his earlier propositions and to buy time, completely neglecting the agreements he had made with the highest bishop of Rome in return for the stay in proceedings. As a result the abbot bore ill the delays and saw in them not only an impediment to his own case, but an endless prolongation of the suit. He consequently sought out the bishop of Langres, who had chanced one day to come to Vézelay, and asked him about the instructions of the lord pope. The bishop replied that he wished the person who had proposed the action would ask such a question, for in general, silence regarding a lawsuit amount-

---

to the third day or later; and Ambrose, for a delay in general.

[1] *iusiuris vel iurisiudicium*: cf. Huygens (1976: xxxix n.111) on these reduplicative terms.

[2] Godfrey and Stephen were both Cistercians. See Crozet (1975).

[3] *tenor*. The letter referred to is charter 44 above.

[4] *pia sollicitudine futuris precavens eventibus.*

[5] *in triplici scedula.*

[6] *suis scriniis.*

[7] *ac si vivae voces.*

[8] *iudicum vel agentium*. Note that the opposition between "written" (*prescriptae testificationes*) and "oral" (*suppositi testes*), i.e., the old and the new, is clearer than the translation here implies, for the words "of the earlier hearing" are not in the original: it is a case of contrasting existing written depositions and new, oral ones. This passage is of importance for the evolution of papal legal and archival procedures: it struck Hugh as novel that a record of a trial decision be kept by the pope. See Ullmann (1975: 148–49).

ed to a withdrawal from it.[1] Autun himself had certainly said nothing to him so far on the matter.

In the meantime holy Eugenius, of holy memory, apostolic lord of the Holy See, went the way of all flesh. His successor as vicar of the Holy Roman Church was Anastasius.[2] Learning this, the abbot of Vézelay feared that his old enemy would present himself before the new pope; he therefore swiftly wrote to Anastasius explaining in what high esteem all his predecessors had held the church of Vézelay, right down to the present. He went on to beseech the pope, on the example of his forefathers, the Roman bishops, to protect the church of Vézelay, as the peculiar right and allod[3] of blessed Peter, from the incursion of enemies, especially, at present, from the rash presumption of the bishop of Autun. He described to the pope how the case—as much the pope's as his own[4]—was aired in the presence of his predecessor Eugenius, of pious memory, but had remained without conclusion because the bishop sought a delay for the day of judicial decision. Finally, he prayed that the pope in his piety might appoint a new day for judgment in his own presence— since the former had lapsed with the death of Eugenius—and might see fit to announce this to the bishop of Autun.

7
At Length Peace Is Entered On Between the Abbot and the Bishop of Autun   [1588D/409. 588]

1154

The divine apostolic father, therefore, acceding to the prayers of the advocate[5] of a church linked to himself with such special ties, instructed that both parties reopen their case, and set the date for both as the fifteenth day after Easter,[6] unless it should, in the meantime, chance that peace had been refashioned between the churches on the basis of a common agreement. On that day it was hoped that the matters Anastasius's predecessor had left unfinished might, with God acting through the pope himself, be brought to a worthy conclusion. At this the bishop's tortuous neck turns in upon itself, as if stricken with unexpected darts,[7] and, already despairing of his case, he approaches his brother the duke[8] and immediately begins negotiations on the

---

[1] *cum plerumque tacendo liti renuncietur.*

[2] Eugenius died 8 July 1153; Anastasius IV succeeded on 8 July 1153 and died 3 December 1154.

[3] A phrase used elsewhere in the *Major Chronicle* and also in the charters. Cf. Niermeyer (1976: 36–38): *alodis.*

[4] *tam illius quam sua.* We have adopted Guizot's translation, but the meaning could be "as much the bishop's as the pope's," or "as much the bishop's as the abbot's."

[5] *patronus,* "protector" or "legal advocate"; i.e., Pons.

[6] 18 April 1154.

[7] *Tunc nodosa cervix sese contorquens utpote insperatis perculsa spiculis.* Note historic present used in the whole sentence (below n.2). Huygens (1976: 410.593) cites *opus imperfectum in Matthaeum* 42; *(MPG: 56.867): nodosam cervicem. . . .*

[8] Odo (Eudes, Eudo) II (1143–62). According to Guizot (1969: 232) until the four-

subject of such a peace[1] with him who had sometimes helped him to oppress others. He began in fact, to fear that while he gaped after the rights and possessions of the abbot, he might end up losing both his own and the abbot's. He therefore renounced his duel with the abbot and gave thought to a reformation of peace. Thus the bishop, who himself had hitherto striven to usurp what did not belong to him [*aliena*], now, with the mediation of others, hastened to consult his own real interest. The duke, for his part, afraid that his brother's malice might be mistrusted, brought to the bishop's assistance men of a religious life and honest reputation, namely the abbot of Cîteaux and several others of the same order. These monks came to Abbot Pons at Vézelay as supplicants and offered the prayers of the duke. On behalf of the bishop they put before the abbot the need for peace, and demanded its reinstitution. The abbot of Vézelay could not rebuff them, since in men of ample spirit the gentleness of clemency is always associated with the rigor of rectitude.

Pons, therefore, though he had not yielded to the arrogance of the bishop's overweening pride, yielded to him when he came as a humble suppliant. With the mediation of those mentioned, peace was refashioned at the hands of the duke between both churches: every dispute was settled,[2] kisses of mutual friendship were exchanged, and treaties of perpetual peace entered upon. The bishop had the composition of peace written in his own chancery hand and strengthened with the protection of his seal,[3] in the belief that it would in this way be better guarded by succeeding generations, as the following exemplar reveals:

Let it be known to this and future generations that I, Henry, in the name of God bishop of Autun, by the advice of religious persons and of certain brothers of our church, wish the lawsuit and dispute aired for so long between Autun and Vézelay to be settled by amicable agreement in such a way that both I and Pons, abbot of the aforementioned church, should remain and persist in worthy peace and concord, saving the rights and privileges of each church, in my lifetime. The above mentioned transaction or composition I decree to be kept firm as long as I live, to such a degree that after my death no prejudice should be suffered hence by either church. The witnesses of both parties are: William, abbot of Fontenay; Hugh, abbot of La Bussière; Peter, abbot of Saint-Jean-des-Prés; Obert, abbot of Sainte-Marguerite; master Obert, Séguin de Ligny-le-Châtel; Gilbert, prior of Oisy; Gerard Buca; Hugh de Monceaux-le-Comte and many others.

These things are all that our own meager talents and our desire to be brief and accurate would allow to be put together concerning the liberty of the

---

teenth century, the bishoprics of Burgundy recruited their prelates from the most noble families of the region. See Bouchard (1987: 260, 256).

[1] *ducem aggreditur et iam cum fratre agit de pace sua.*

[2] *pacificatur.*

[3] *manus suae formatam fecit quam et sigilli sui munimine corroboravit.*

church of Vézelay. A broader account, perhaps, but not a truer one, must be assigned to a period of greater leisure.[1] As far as accuracy is concerned, we have, I believe, performed an adequate service for the sons and lovers of this church. Our brevity has moreover taken care to cater to those who mock this sort of writing. For many, indeed, are wont to become enraged at those who write useful things, seized with envy, perhaps, of the things recorded, or unaware of them. Now, since the wise man in his leisure is seldom at leisure and judges the leisure of another to be a challenge to him, it is by contrast especially characteristic of a fool to ascribe to leisure whatever is the result of careful study. Taking this attitude on its own merits, we have travelled via an abridged path, and hurriedly brought our discourse[2] to an end. For though we belong to the younger generation in our church, our devotion towards it is not the less thereby if we devote our abilities, such as they are, with the most upright of motives, to the advance of the church. We have no fear that our church will furnish us with strength, as it has done with will and grace, provided that we are able to pass our time without dispute. There are indeed some among us who seek their own advantage, instead of the rewards of duty itself. Like mercenaries[3] rather than sons of the church, they pursue their own gain. We have engaged our mind[4] so far cleansed[5] of such an approach, that we have bestowed our attention on these things out of respect for the common good pure and simple, on behalf of the common good and for the advancement of the common good. We have, in sum, placed our hope in Him alone and have looked to Him alone who decrees that no virtue goes unrewarded[6] from the beginning right up to eternity.

---

[1] On the implications of this phrase and the division of the *Major Chronicle* into books, see Huygens (1976: xx).

[2] *Quod sui precio pensantes, compendio usi cursim stilum exegimus.*

[3] Phil. 2:21. According to the Gospel of St. John (10:12-13), "The mercenary is one who is not the shepherd ... he sees the wolf coming and leaves the sheep and flies. ..."

[4] *nos ab hac specie adeo mentem defecatam gessimus.*

[5] *mens defaecata* is a phrase of Paulinus of Nola and *animus defaecatus* is from Ambrose (Huygens [1976]).

[6] Huygens (1976) cites Anianus, *in Matthaeum* for this phrase. Despite the evidence that certain phrases in Hugh's full blown *conclusio* are drawn from biblical and late antique sources, the style displayed in the passage is clearly modelled on the *mediocris figura* of the *Ad Herennium* (4.9.13). The author has chosen to stress the *brevitas* and *veritas* of his *narratio* (Huygens [1976: 410.632]), which may be taken to represent the *brevis* and the *dilucida/verisimilis* of the rhetorical manuals (e.g., *Ad Herennium* 1.9.14). The writer also clearly alludes to factions within the monastery, and hints that there were elements who opposed an accurate record of the church's struggle for liberty. Are these connected with those who tried to foment a revolt against Abbot William or with the elements who later mutilated the volume by tearing two groups of folios in half? For similar factions see Thomson (1974) and Butler (1949).

Book Two

Pons, the most celebrated in virtue of the abbots of the realm,
Ruled his sheep in turn,
And while he sets before them the path to an upright life,
And oversees the church entrusted to him,
A crowd, more crowded than any,[1] stirs up envy,
The seditious hand of serfs against their lord.
A mob armed with guile, a duke and a path to treachery,
A mob driven to break down the gates, to plunder homes,
A mob that dares to hurl assaults at holy buildings,
And to lay hands on holy things, seeking the death of their lord.
What woeful cup of evils, disasters, ravings would then have overflowed,
Had not the wise abbot swiftly brought help?
If, O reader, you wish to know the causes of all these things,[2]
Follow the journey of this book's pages.
These pages our Hugh, a Poitevin by birth, chose to weigh up in mind,
And to set down with his hand, for you, without recompense.
Read carefully; you will soon see how well, how wisely,
And how brilliantly the work takes its course, in proper order.
Be still, envious tongue, enemy of virtue, whose great sin
Is always to wish to harm the good.

1

The Author Begins His Work at the Order of Abbot Pons

[1590D/414]

A most famous proverb is related of a certain Greek, and said to have been
found on the tripod of Apollo: know thyself, and see thyself as thou art.[3]
There is nothing clearer in human nature, nothing of greater value, nothing,
finally, more excellent. It is through these qualities, indeed, that man is, by a
singular prerogative, preferred to all sensible creatures, and is joined also, by
a bond of unity, to those incapable of sensitivity. To know oneself, moreover,

---

[1] *turba turbatior omni.* According to Huygens (1976: xx, xxv), this poem is written in a
contemporary hand (corrected by two other hands, twelfth- and thirteenth-century
respectively) in a blank space left by the writer of the *History.*

[2] Virgil *Georgics* 2.490. The standard of composition of this poem is very poor. The
choice of words is dictated by the meter and the poet does frequent violence to good
sense in order to complete the line. The poem, like an overture, touches upon some of
the main themes of the book that follows; for example, line 10 refers to the communal
revolution against the abbot of 1152 AD. The meter is elegaic.

[3] An inscription engraved upon the Temple of Apollo at Delphi in antiquity, attributed
to the pre-Socratic philosopher Thales, and chosen by Socrates for his motto (Huygens).
See de Burgh (1953: 1:116).

is to know and to understand the condition of one's proper dignity; to see oneself as one is, is to cultivate that same dignity of condition with the sincerity of faith and the practice of piety.[1] In regard to what we have in mind[2] concerning the first of the aforementioned two injunctions, that is, knowledge, know that we have treated the dignity of Vézelay, as far as we could with brevity, partly in the earlier book of this work. There, while we have taken great care to give the matter the attention it deserves[3] and not to bandy words,[4] we have navigated like a ship slicking through the slopes of a calm sea, well aware that the worthy reader would infer the weighty nature of the business at stake from the simplicity of our words.[5] However, certain parties, relying upon daring rather than placing their confidence in virtue, have attempted to tear with the mouth of a dog and to mangle with bestial foot the clothes[6] of the aforesaid liberty or dignity, that is, the possessions of the church. As a result, our most serene and strenuous father, the venerable abbot Pons has seen fit to entrust to far distant future ages, through these writings, how and in what way through divine providence the strivings of a rival have come to nothing, and the church has shone forth from the depths of its very misfortunes.[7] Nor have we bent our labors to these things in an idle manner, as if doing what came naturally to us. The time we have devoted to this task, instead of to other forms of learning, has been assigned by virtue of a vow we made. In fact, we have been especially moved as much by the probity of our own generation as by the use we may be to future generations; nor has the dignity of our mother church been far from our minds. We have been moved too, by the unimpeachable command of the aforesaid father, who, for this same liberty and dignity has striven to the point of bloodshed.[8] This valiant crusher of crime did not[9] obtain his goal, but there was at no stage anything lacking in his total devotion to the immunity of Vézelay and his neglect of his own welfare in the interests of the welfare of the church.

For several years, then, the abbot blazed with a chaste love of the church

---

[1] *sinceritate fidei et pietatis cultu;* cf. Augustine, *De peccatorum meritis et remissione,* 3.13.23.

[2] *supponitur quod intendimus. Supponitur* is a standard phrase in contemporary school commentaries and the *intentio auctoris* is a standard ingredient in the medieval *accessus ad auctores.* Cf. Häring (1964: 22).

[3] *res commendare.* On "praise and blame" among the rhetors see, e.g., Cicero *De inventione* 2.59.177, *Ad Herennium* 3.6.10 *et seq.*

[4] *non verba iactitare.*

[5] *superficie verborum pondus negocii.* On the topos of "weight" = simplicity of words, and on medieval historical prologues in general, see Ward (1985: 103ff.).

[6] Boethius *De consolatione philosophiae* 1.1: *eandem tamen vestem violentorum quorundam sciderant manus.*

[7] On Hugh of Poitiers, the author of the *History,* see Huygens (1976: xxiv–xxv, 413. 15), and the Introduction to the present volume. Note that the *History* here appears to have been a "commissioned" work.

[8] Hebrews 12:14, for the phrase *ad sanguinem.*

[9] *licet votum sceleris percussor non optinuerit.* A curious statement in view of the outcome of events as recorded at the end of Book 3 below. What was Pons's *votum?*

that was his bride; he arranged its rights with very dutiful care, and administered them most strenuously. However, fortune began to envy him and he
came to feel certain that the church would be violated by the wart of some
depraved confusion.[1] When this came about he stood firm like a true zealot
for the house of Israel,[2] put himself in the way of the false eyes of envy, and,
though it meant many hazards to his own life, rendered the purity of that
liberty, which was his bride, clearer and plainer for all to see. We will take
care to make this known,[3] keeping in what follows to our customary brevity,
so that those of the present generation might have a source of enjoyment,
and those of future generations a model for emulation. God has aided our
weakness, and the authority of that same father, the abbot, has strengthened
our insignificance. It is a characteristic of the pious that they exert themselves
for common rather than private utility; thus we have found our hands full
providing for the profit of future generations and extending the garment of
charity right down to the heel. This is a worthy work, worthy reader, and it
should be read worthily; I am speaking now in an undertone, and would have
any detractor remove himself. If our efforts displease anyone, he will be seen
as a false pretender [*adulterinus*], if he is still worthy of the name of a son [of
the church], or else as little better than a household rouse-about,[4] in fact an
enemy of the church. If the ancients found it pleasing to hand down to
memory old wives' tales[5] and monstrous portents, solely for the display of an
elegant talent, and if these are not infrequently and not without profit read
in our own day, then we believe it will be much more acceptable to future
generations and much more to their profit to know not only the truth of
things that have taken place, but also their worthwhile outcome. We do not
say such things right away as if disdaining the test of brotherly charity, but
rather that those things which by chance have poured from our pen to excess
should be cut away, and those things likewise that have escaped our notice or
have not fitted the brevity of our style, should be supplied.[6] If then on both
counts, we clearly interpose a simple approach we need not blush at our
poverty, nor shirk the burden of so great a labor.

---

[1] *nevo . . . pravae commixtionis constuprari;* cf. Huygens (1976: 396.55), *Major Chronicle* 1
§2 above: *nevum maculose servitutis*: at least the author is consistent in his polemic! This use
of *naevus* is late imperial.

[2] Ezekiel 13:5.

[3] *compendium propalare curabimus.*

[4] *vernaculus*: "of or belonging to homeborn slaves," the rabble of slaves; buffoon or
jester in Martial (in the plural); *vernacula* = a female household slave in Martianus Capella,
Ambrose. In CL, "native," "domestic," "indigenous," i.e., Roman (Lewis & Short).

[5] Horace: *Serm.* 2.6. 77-78.

[6] *stili . . . compendium.* The author, in this tortuous sentence, is simply saying that his
earlier remarks should not be taken to imply that he felt no need for criticism or comment
from his brethren; in fact the latter are invited to prune what is superfluous in the author's
narration, and to supply anything it lacks. With this invitation the author is no longer worried
about his own shortcomings, nor is he afraid to tackle the task that lies before him.

2

Concerning the Nobility and Immunity of the Church of Vézelay. The Origin of the Liberty of Vézelay [1592A/415. 61]

The church of Vézelay over the years grew powerful, being protected by the prerogative of liberty deriving from the gift of the founder and from the dignity of Roman authority, and being the chapel of the blessed loved one and servant of God, Mary Magdalene, whose relics and special seat are there, and whose name, known splendidly to all, is celebrated the world over and adored. Many people as a consequence have flocked to the place from all parts and, as much by their number as by their affluence in worldly goods, have rendered the town of Vézelay illustrious and conspicuous.[1] The farms too, in so far as they were very ample and close to each other, made the location such a delightful site, and so very rich, that it attracted admiring gazes right up to the borders of the district, and stood out above all others the world over in splendor.[2] These physical possessions were joined in compact unity to the church, as body is to head,[3] by the particularly important and peculiar charity of proprietary law, and as a consequence the church shrank from admitting in any part of it the participatory tenure [*participium*] of any lord or company [*societatis*], as if this would be profane and an incentive for arrogance. It held fast, through apostolic favor, to the allodial condition bequeathed it by the will of its founder and bent its neck in contract of service to none, unless to the apostolic pontiff. If anyone of pure intent and without fraud would contemplate the full liberty of the church of Vézelay he should thoroughly digest the foundation charter and the privileges emanating from the primordial and ancient authority of the Roman pontiffs: the venerable Nicholas, both Johns, Benedict, another Benedict, Leo and Sergius, Stephen and Marin, and also Urban, of divine memory, who, drawn from the order of Cluny to the administration of the Apostolic See, wished the privileges and decrees of his predecessors in favor of the liberty of the aforesaid monastery of Vézelay to be inviolate, firm, and unshaken, and accordingly confirmed them by the protection of his own authority.[4] When these docu-

---

[1] See above Aspects [D] for the importance of pilgrims to Vézelay.

[2] This is not entirely an exaggeration, as will be confirmed by any modern-day visitor to the area. Agriculture (including viticulture) played a preponderant role in the lives of the Vézelay burghers, and their prosperity was evident in the twelfth century. Today less than 4% of the Vézelay region is characterized as "arid." See the 1137 *Accord* below (Appendix [B]).

[3] Guizot: "the whole body was so straightly and intimately united to the church that formed its head ..." (1969: 38). The Latin reads literally, "joined ... to the very head of the Church" (not the abbot!). The phrase comes from Ephesians 4:15–16. On the body metaphor in politics see Gierke (1958: 22ff.), Kantorowicz (1957), and Black (1984).

[4] See on all these, charters 3–10, and Huygens nn. ad loc. The privilege of Urban is lost. The frequent appeal to these charters in the *Major Chronicle* makes clear the rationale behind their presentation in the form of an appended cartulary in MS. Auxerre 227.

ments have been carefully perused, any impression of contradictory elements or factors[1] arguing contrary conclusions must be set aside as fictitious or surreptitious,[2] since it is impious and sacrilegious to imagine that the apostolic fathers would pronounce any decision that was internally inconsistent, or could provide grounds for the allegations of an opposing party. To go back to the beginning of the monastery we find that Count Gerard, of happy memory, together with his pious wife Bertha, out of fear for the Lord and regard for the salvation [*salutem*] of themselves and their dependants, founded a monastery on the river Cure,[3] with an entirely unencumbered allodial status of its own,[4] and established there a congregation of handmaidens of God.[5] This monastery, with all its appurtenances, he wholly made over by testamentary deed of perpetual possession[6] to the most blessed apostolic lords and to their successors on the Roman See to be ruled and defended for ever. He entirely removed from this grant any license by way of beneficiary power to alienate by donation or change of legal status.[7] However, as a result of the incursions of the Saracens,[8] the aforementioned monastery was entirely overthrown. The count then rebuilt it on an adjacent hill, where the fortified hamlet [*castello*] of Vézelay was situated, lest hostile envy prevail over his initial pious intentions. At the same time he effected a change of sex and instituted a community of monks, the first abbot of whom was Odo.[9]

3

Summary of Apostolic Privileges [1593A/417. 108]

The Roman See welcomed the count's great display of devout piety with joyful satisfaction, and resolved to register the monastery itself as a rightful allod belonging peculiarly to blessed Peter, and to strengthen it with the favor and gift of apostolic authority. The Roman pontiffs then, in their indulgence, conceded and confirmed privileges of this type by decree of their own apostolic authority. They ordained that no emperor, king , bishop, or person of any rank should, on any pretext, diminish or make off with, or apply to any use of their own, or alienate in favor of any other pious interest that might serve

---

[1] *contraria vel repugnantia;* cf. Quintilian *Institutes of Oratory* 4.2.60.

[2] *ficticia et surrepticia.*

[3] The river "Cure" has its source in the forest of Anost and flows some 112 kilometers before joining the Yonne at Cravant.

[4] *in proprio et liberrimo alodio suo.*

[5] 867 AD. The convent of Benedictine nuns was founded in honor of St. Mary Magdalene. On the nunnery and its context see Skinner (1984: 90ff.).

[6] *dato testamentario libello perpetuae possessionis.* See charter 1 above.

[7] *beneficiaria potestate . . . dandi aut mutandi licentia.*

[8] Huygens (1976: 416): "actually, Normans, about ten years after the death of Count Girard in 877 AD."

[9] Charters 4, 5, and 6 are addressed to Odo, whose dates must therefore be c.878–c.908. No documents that were written to or by the religious women who inhabited Vézelay before the monks survive. See below Appendix G.

as a mask for their own avarice, the things legitimately conveyed to that same monastery by the count himself from his own possessions[1] or by anyone else. Instead, those who in the same place lived the religious life, were to enjoy these possessions in unimpaired quiet, on this condition, that no Roman pontiff should ever, in any place, permit any of those possessions to be given in the future as a benefice to anyone, exchanged, granted in return for a payment,[2] or retained [in any other way].[3] The Roman See should, however, upon annual payment of but one pound of silver by the same monastery, in the tradition of the will,[4] strive vigilantly, with pastoral care, to provide it with the benefit of papal support[5] against all infestations. The Apostolic See also ordained that when an abbot had been elected by the common consent of the brothers, without resort on the part of any to shrewd cunning, or by the counsel of the senior part of the same monastery,[6] and had been approved by the Roman prelate, no pontiff, no king, nor anyone of the dependants [fidelium] of any ecclesiastical or secular personage, either himself or by means of an agent, should dare to receive anything for ordaining an abbot, or monks, or clerics, or priests, or for dispensing chrism, or for consecrating the basilica, or for the provision of any spiritual or temporal service,[7] nor should he dare to lay legal claim on his own behalf to any of the special rights of the church of Vézelay.

With the apostolic privileges arrayed in this manner, the majesty of the kings of the Franks, too, looked kindly upon the same monastery, and, viewing favorably the prayers of the illustrious count Gerard, the king determined that the monastery should have an edict to this effect,[8] that whatever the Apostolic See had resolved to enforce by decree should endure undisturbed for all time without the smallest contradiction. The king instructed that no secular person nor any royal agent[9] should receive lodgings[10] in the afore-

---

[1] *de proprio.* If this is to be taken with *iure*, then the meaning would be merged with "legitimately."

[2] An annual rent could imply legal tenure.

[3] *quiddam ... cuiquam beneficiare, commutare aut sub censu concedere vel retinere ... pateretur.*

[4] *in testamento traditionis.* Possibly "with custom as evidence/upon the guarantee of tradition/by force of custom."

[5] *piae paternitatis suffragium.*

[6] According to the provisions of the *Rule of St. Benedict* (Huygens 1976: 64.1).

[7] *"spirit(u)alis vel temporalis obsequii."* These provisions are based on charter 3.

[8] The charter issued by Charles the Bald is dated 868, but Hugh actually summarizes two royal diplomas in what follows, dated 877 and 889 respectively. The charters are extant today (see Huygens [1976: 417.138/153n]) and are translated at the end of Aspects [A] above. The charter of Louis IV, 936 AD substantially repeats the exemptions that follow (cf. above Aspects [E] (b) on MS. Auxerre fols. 22–63).

[9] *missus.* Cf. use of the term in the Carolingian period: Loyn and Percival (1975: 73ff., 79ff., etc).

[10] *mansiones acciperet.* Guizot: "n'établît aucun manoir" : "establish a manor-house"/ "accept (control of) manors?" Cf. charter 3: *mansionaticos ... exigere.*

said monastery, or in the aforesaid fortified town, or in the villages[1] pertaining to the place itself or to its power, and should not demand from it the payment of fees in lieu of procuration,[2] or fine,[3] or traffic tax,[4] or bridge-toll,[5] or tributes.[6] Whosoever might dare to take lightly this decree of immunity should be compelled to pay a fine [*multam*] of six hundred *solidi*, half, indeed, to the royal fisc, and half to the church for which the king had instituted the action. So that this instruction of his authority should obtain a stricter observance, the king strengthened it with his own hand and signed it with the impression of his seal.[7]

4

Several Interests Envy the Liberty of Vézelay. William [II], Count of Nevers, Tries to Usurp the Rights of the Monastery of Vézelay [1594A/418. 154]

1144

Under so full and free an immunity, therefore, the new plant blossomed[8] forth on its fresh turf, and the fertile green shoots of its branches attracted interest across many provinces. However, among the other faults which human nature contracted in the transgression of the first parent, the stain of envy infected most deeply the race of man, and, as a consequence, many ecclesiastical and secular powers in adjacent lands, corrupted by this pest, strove to spoil the garment[9] of the church's liberty, and to deprive the aforesaid monastery of the glory of its nobility. They conspired together in secret colloquies[10] towards mutual evil, and putting their conspiracies into effect[11] brought on the ignominy of their own confounding. At different times, either all together or one after the other in turn, they strove to vex the peace of the holy monastery, to trouble and perturb it, and did not fear to

---

[1] *pretitulato castello seu villis.* On the *villa* see Latouche (1966a: part 3, chaps. 3–4).

[2] *paratas.* See Aspects [A] above.

[3] *freda.* See Niermeyer (1976: 453): fine, punishment. For a different meaning ("frith," "woodland," "pasture") see Latham (1965: 201–2).

[4] *cespitaticum* : Guizot : "droit de regain," second growth/crop. Niermeyer (1976: 173): "traffic tax for compensating damage done to fields and meadows."

[5] *pontaticum* : Guizot : "droit de péage sur des ponts." Niermeyer (1976: 812): "pontage, bridge-toll."

[6] *inferendas* : Niermeyer (1976: 531–32): "a tribute in kind or money exacted yearly by the fisc," "a present given every year to churches and monasteries."

[7] A thirteenth-century hand has added as a gloss : "several of the later kings of the Franks added that whatever the fisc might demand from the abbey, should be restored to it for the salvation of the souls of their forebears and for the sustenance [*alimonia*] of the monks" (Huygens [1976: 418]).

[8] Psalm 143:12.

[9] See 152n.6 above.

[10] Psalm 11:3.

[11] Psalm 72:8.

give offense to the great authority of the outstanding fathers of the same monastery in numerous and various ways. They spewed forth against the most distinguished and most prudent abbot Pons of our own day the entire poison of their most vicious malignity, and, spewing forth everything that the vile and viperine powers of their own depravity could effect,[1] they weakened, exhausted and annihilated themselves. The fact was that the abbots of Vézelay, with their devout sense of duty,[2] frequently used to pay, in a spirit of most liberal indulgence, voluntary court to the counts of the city of Nevers, on account of the frequent incursions of impious men, in order that they might the more devotedly protect the church against all aggressors, the church which was in no point of right beholden to the counts, and which was busily bestowing upon them gratuitous benefices.[3] But the degenerate mind[4] always abuses good deeds,[5] and is often rendered more prone to insolence by services freely received. An ungrateful person will never ascribe a service rendered to goodwill.

Thus it came about that William, later to become a Carthusian monk, while he held the consulate[6] of the state [*civitatis*] of Nevers, insolently abused the payments[7] and other benefices provided by the church, and kept trying to exact from the church through tyrannical force a number of allegedly customary prerogatives.[8] These demands were prejudicial both to peace and to the liberty of the monastery. The abbot Pons, so worthy of veneration [*venerandus*], spurned the count's insolence, denied with reasons what was unjustly demanded, and prudently kept control of what was being demanded with menace. Taking this rebuff extremely ill, the count of Nevers worked himself up into such a state of complete anger that he diverted the royal ways from Vézelay[9] and prohibited public traffic from the town. The abbot of Vézelay

---

[1] Luke 11:29 and Matt. 3:7.

[2] *pia quippe Vizeliacensium abbatum sollicitudo.*

[3] It had been customary since the time of Gerard of Roussillon for the count (after c. 1000, of Nevers) to regard himself—at the abbey's request—as secular *avoué* of the house (Guizot 1969: 237). On this term (*advocatus ecclesie*) see below 160n.5 and 173n.6 and Benton (1970: 157, 159). According to Guizot (1969: 240) in exchange for "protection" by the count under the heading of "droits de garde" the count claimed the right of free lodging at the abbey with his suite, or a payment in lieu. See Introduction, especially 6n.1, and Aspects [A] above.

[4] Cf. Lucan *Pharsalia* 6.417 and Vergil *Aeneid* 4.13.

[5] *beneficiis*. The *beneficium* means both "good deed" and "fief": see Mierow (1966: 182–83). See below n.7.

[6] *consulatum*, i.e., *comitatum* or "county." William II, count of Nevers and Auxerre (1080–1149), was an intimate of kings Louis VI and VII, the latter of whom tried to make him regent of France, with Abbot Suger, during the second crusade. He had led an army of 15,000 men to the Holy Land before 1104 when he returned to France, following the failure of his expedition. Bernard of Clairvaux described him as one who misappropriated the goods of the church "like a lion awaiting a favorable moment to leap upon his prey" (Guizot [1969: 237]). See Bouchard (1987: 346–47).

[7] *salariis atque aliis aecclesiae beneficiis.*

[8] *nonnullos consuetudines* : Guizot: "redevances" (rents). See Huygens (1976: 299), charter 17 above.

[9] I.e., diverted public traffic from the royal ways (*stratas regias*), blocked them, forced

was unable to bend the count from his proposed course, either by favor [*beneficium*] or earnest prayer, and consequently brought notice of the oppression of his monastery to the Holy Apostolic Mother, the Roman See, and set forth by what tyranny the count was pestering the allodial rights[1] of blessed Peter. The lord pope, as a result, wrote and reiterated his warning[2] to the same count, that he should desist from pestering his [the pope's] special daughter, the church of Vézelay. He advised him to show proper reverence for blessed Peter by respecting the peace and liberty of the church, enjoining him not to presume to usurp apostolic rights, lest he stand out as an enemy and violator of the universal church. If he believed, wrote the pope, that any right in the same monastery belonged more properly to himself, he ought not be distrustful of[3] apostolic favor, provided that he did not vex the quiet of the church; if on the other hand he acted otherwise, he should not be unaware that he would have to bear the burden of the apostolic rod. The pope[4] also admonished[5] the abbot of Vézelay by apostolic authority not to cede any of the monastery's rights to anyone at all, and not to go beyond the boundaries set by his predecessors. He was instructed to place all his faith in the assistance of God and blessed Peter, and to strive manfully for the church, lest, if he should permit its integrity to be spotted, he would stand out as the betrayer of that [apostle's] integrity.

---

traffic to by-pass Vézelay. See charter 26 above, Huygens (1976: 312 lines 8–10) and Berlow (1971: 293): "it was along the route to Auxerre that the count of Nevers maintained a toll station and his repeated blockades of the routes to Auxerre were expressly for the purpose of intercepting merchants and peddlers coming and going from Vézelay." Vézelay, it should be noted, "was *not* located on a major commercial highway" (Berlow [1971: 288]), a fact not lost on the car-less modern tourist, to his/her cost. Commenting on the communal revolution of 1152, Berlow (1971: 336) remarks that "None of the leaders' names suggest distant origins or connections with the developing commercial centers of western Europe ... however [287], the Fairs at Vézelay, by the time of these events, were certainly attracting business to the town." See too (for the significance of fairs and solemnities) *Major Chronicle* below 160n.2, 164n.1, 175n.5, 180n.3, 219n.7, and Aspects [D] above. Guizot (1969: 242–43n.64) lists and describes the commercial routes that lead to Vézelay. See below 162n.2, 163n.1; Graham (1918: 70ff.); Cohen (1980); Chérest 1:88ff. (= Huygens 1976: 46ff.).

[1] *ius vel alodium.*

[2] *reiterato* Huygens (1976: 419.196): "there is only a single letter on this subject, charter 26" (above).

[3] *non diffideret.*

[4] *idem presul.*

[5] This letter is not extant.

5

Arbitration of the Controversy between the Abbot of
Vézelay and the Count of Nevers. The Latter Puts his
Case, the Former Replies and Refutes It   [1595B/419. 210]

1146

For a long time therefore, the dispute between Vézelay and Nevers dragged
on. Finally it came to this: the count and abbot agreed to present themselves
respectfully and harmoniously for a ruling by the abbot Bernard of Clairvaux,
Hugh of Thil-en-Auxois,[1] and others whom these two wished to summon to
the adjudication. Whatever decision on the matters at issue these persons
were unanimously [*concorditer*] to arrive at, the abbot and the count were to
observe to the letter. And so, on the holy feast day of Easter[2] the count came
to Vézelay with all the aforesaid persons. Almost all Gaul had assembled at
the abbey in greater numbers than usual, to take part in the frequent opportunities for prayer and at the same time to show their reverence for the most
pious and religious king Louis the Younger,[3] who, intending to make a
pilgrimage to Jerusalem, accepted there, on his own shoulders, the standard
of the cross of the Lord. When they had all arrived at the grange of the
church called Bessy,[4] on the day appointed, the fourth day, that is, of the
octave of Easter, the count proceeded to his calumny in this manner:

> The church of Vézelay is in my advocacy.[5] I wish that whenever I com-
> mand the abbot, he will do justice before me and my men according to
> the sentence of my court.[6] This he ought not refuse. And if anyone
> should wish to speak against the abbot on the grounds that he has
> refused him justice, the abbot ought to defend himself at the dictation
> of my court.

---

[1] On Bernard of Clairvaux, see Cross (1974: 162), Evans (1983), and Williams (1952).
Hugh II was the lord of Thil-en-Auxois.

[2] 31 March 1146, the dispute having erupted in 1144 when Pons refused the customary tributes to the count. The ceremony that acompanied Louis' assumption of the cross
and the preaching of the crusade in the plain of Asquins below the hill of Vézelay by St.
Bernard of Clairvaux (from a wooden tribune which was constructed so as to magnify the
voice and which survived in the basilica down to the eighteenth century) was grand and
emotional.

[3] See Guizot (1969: 239–40n.55), who cites Luchaire in his *Les Premiers capétiens*: "of
all the judicial processes involving a decision of the crown in a dispute between the lay
feudality and the abbeys during the eleventh and twelfth centuries, the longest, the most
complicated, the most replete with dramatic episodes, was that brought by the abbey of
Vézelay against the commune and the count of Nevers. This affair occupied a great part
of the reign of Louis VII. It required an almost incalculable number of meetings and
assemblies on the part of the king."

[4] Near Arcy-sur-Cure. The "day appointed" was Wednesday 3 April 1146. The
property at Bessy-sur-Cure was acquired by Vézelay between 1103 and 1106.

[5] *in advocatione mea*; see above 158n.3 and above Aspects [A].

[6] *michi et hominibus meis secundum iudicium curiae meae iusticiam faciat.*

The abbot replied that he was in no way bound to do this, since he did not hold the abbey of Vézelay from the aforesaid count. Again, since he was a monk, priest, and abbot, he did not wish to subject himself to lay court decisions [*laicali iudicio*] nor was he obliged to undergo sentence at the hands of lay persons either on his own behalf, or on behalf of his monks. The count repeated his demand that the men pertaining to the church of Vézelay[1] came within the ambit of his own justice and insisted that as often as it should please him to command the abbot, the latter should lead his men to the count's court to undergo imposition of a court decision. The count also claimed that if any dispute arose between the abbot and his men, no settlement was to be entered upon in the court of the abbot except at his [the count's] hand. The abbot replied that the church of Vézelay had not been founded by the count, nor by his ancestors; the men of Vézelay were not, he went on, of the count's fief,[2] nor did the abbot or church hold them from the count; and therefore it was an indignity to expect that they should undergo justice at the court of the count, for they were not of his benefice.[3] Concerning the count's claim that peace with the burghers could be made only in the count's presence and by his hand, the abbot said that he had heard nothing more unjust or contrary to all truth and justice, since peace was the common property of all, and the blessed feet of the those who preach the Gospel proclaim peace publicly from the divine scriptures and from [the writings of] the holy fathers. Moreover, there was not to be found any such custom in the church from the earliest times.[4]

Again the count said that his men of Clamecy, when they came to the fairs and market of Vézelay, and laid down their merchandise in the street, were wont to say that they were immune from the customary dues paid by other men; and yet, he claimed, the toll-collectors of the abbot[5] were violently wresting those same customary dues from them. The abbot replied to this that he held the streets from antiquity for his own use, that no one had any exemption from his rights, and that since all men who came to the fairs and market of Vézelay willingly paid a toll according to the kinds of their merchandise, he made the same request—that they pay the customary dues—of any persons who did not say by what justice they claimed to keep their tolls.

---

[1] *homines Vizeliaci ad aecclesiam pertinentes.* Guizot (1969: 240-41n.57): not the serfs of the church, but the whole population of the "poté" (*potestas*, "principauté féodale"), especially,of course, the burghers. The serfs of the church were formerly free or semi-free individuals who had voluntarily given up their liberty in favor of a bishopric or abbey. The "poté" itself consisted of a *seigneurie* comprising several villages inhabited by servile families—attached by inheritance to the soil (*servi adscripti glebae*). See Bloch (1961: part 5, chaps. 18-20), (1975), and Jordan (1986). For further discussion see Aspects [B] above.

[2] *de feodo suo.*

[3] *de cuius . . . beneficio*; parallel to *de feodo suo.*

[4] For the "blessed feet of those proclaiming peace" see *Romans* 10:15. On the church's sponsorship of "the peace" from the eleventh century onwards see Mackinney (1930) and Head and Landes (1987).

[5] *teleonarii abbatis.*

Then Hugh of Thil-en-Auxois testified that the count had no right in this complaint, since in the time of Lord Renaud, abbot of Vézelay,[1] later archbishop of Lyon, a complaint was lodged on this matter by the count himself; but, having received money from the abbot by the hand of Hugh-en-Auxois, that is, Hugh of Thil, the count himself entirely abandoned the complaint and faithfully promised that in future he would never renew it.

The count then laid claim to the road[2] which stretched from Asquins to Blannay, and to that from Précy-le-Sec[3] and to others reckoned from boundary markers and crosses right up to Vézelay. To this the abbot replied that the street of Vargigny,[4] which the count demanded from Asquins to Blannay, was [the property or fief] of Hervé of Donzy[5] and Savary of Vergy, lords of Châtel-Censoir,[6] and they themselves had given it and sold it, with all its appurtenances, that is, running waters and springs and other things [which] they possessed by hereditary right in allod, to Artaud,[7] abbot of blessed memory, and to the church of Vézelay, and, on the altar of the blessed apostles Peter and Paul, they offered it in the presence of many to the apostles themselves, to God and to blessed Mary Magdalene, with all its appurtenances. This territory the church of Vézelay had possessed in its entirety[8] peacefully and so far quite without any calumny, for forty years and more by hereditary right. The abbot had robbers hanged there, [who had been] seized on the public way; he [had] executed justice on other malefactors, and if anything was found there, he had quietly kept possession of it, without violence. Again, the land of Précy-le-Sec was an allod of the duke of Burgundy which certain knights had held [in fee], and these knights had given and sold it to the blessed Mary Magdalene. From that time, therefore, right up to the present, both the church and abbot of Vézelay held and possessed in peace without any interruption all that land itself, the public way within the town, and beyond it all its public ways and paths. Concerning this and other things mentioned above, the abbot named several witnesses whom he had: namely Martin, and his brothers of Précy-le-Sec, and many others living in the town, who said that they had apprehended on the street six robbers bearing false money and had sent them to the provost at Vézelay to have justice done. In particular, [they said that they] had delivered to Renaud, a monk of

---

[1] Renaud de Semur, fourteenth abbot of Vézelay; see Aspects [F] above.

[2] *strata*. Earlier: *platea*; later: *via*.

[3] Twenty kilometers from Vézelay between Voutenay-sur-Cure and Joux-la-Ville.

[4] Destroyed town on the site of Gué-Pavé between Asquins and Blanney. Vézelay was given land at Vargigny between the river Cure and the public road in 900. The 1137 *Accord* (Appendix B below) § 24 refers to a dispute about fishing near Vargigny.

[5] The baron of Donzy, a vassal of the bishop of Auxerre, controlled important territories to the north-east of Vézelay.

[6] *castrum Censorii*, fifteen kilometers from Vézelay, in the Yonne valley. Speaight (1990: 126–27).

[7] Thirteenth abbot of Vézelay; see Aspects [F] above.

[8] *totam ex integro*.

Précy-le-Sec who was staying there at that time, an ox found on the public way without a lord, as if it came within the jurisdiction of the church. All these things the aforesaid men were prepared without delay to prove. Concerning the other roads, that is, from Fontenay-près-Vézelay, and from Crai, and from Mont-Tirouet, and from other places stretching right up to Vézelay, the abbot replied that his predecessors had exercised [the right of] justice over them without dispute for a long time and frequently since these same roads pass through the area controlled by the church.[1] Concerning all of which he had many witnesses: Guinimer once dean, Gerard the present dean, Hugh provost, Renaud Dautran, Renaud of Saint-Christophe, William of Pont-sur-Yonne and his brother John, Arnulf of Ferriéres, Robert of Montreuillon, Guy the forester, Durand of the village of Lovet, Durand of Chastenay, Constantine provost of Fontenay-près-Chablis, Stephen provost of Blannay, Aimon the moneyer,[2] Bonami of Châtel-Censoir, Geoffrey Bertin, Blanchard the tailor, Stephen Beurand, Odo the handsome,[3] and many others. All these assertions were confirmed by the highest pope to be held fast for ever, and whoever would molest either the abbot or the church on these issues was interdicted under anathema. These then, were the complaints of the count and the counter arguments with which the abbot refuted them.

6
The Objections of the Abbot and the Responses of the Count
[1597C/422. 318]

1146

After this, the abbot complained of the aforesaid count that he was turning away all pedlars and merchants[4] along the public way from Auxerre to Vézelay and not allowing them to proceed to Vézelay. The count replied that he had in fact done that formerly and had not met with any opposition from any abbot on the matter. The abbot made the rejoinder that the road which leads to Vézelay was at once royal, public, as old as the Nevers route and safer, and that it was unjust that the count should call back travellers from the way which seemed easier and better to them, especially when a considerable number were in the habit of making the journey more for the sake of prayer than for commerce. Again, the abbot complained of the toll-collectors of the count [*de theloneariis comitis*] who assiduously raided the abbot's men passing through Auxerre, saying that the abbot on three holy festivals, that is, Easter,

---

[1] *per viam aecclesiae transeunt.* See above 158n.9.

[2] As with other tradesmen and specialists, a street was normally occupied by and named after the money-changers, who had charge of currency exchange and the commerce in precious metals, and enjoyed some considerable social prestige. Compare "Change Alley" in modern Singapore. See Lopez (1953).

[3] *Odonem Pulchrae Similitudinis.*

[4] *institores et mercatores.*

Pentecost, and the feast of Mary Magdalene ought to put them [the toll-collectors] up with all their friends and give to each of them one pound's weight of wax as a toll[1] for the wine from Auxerre which he was wont to buy.[2] The count replied that the aforesaid servants [*pueri*] of his did have this right from the church and that it had been granted by Abbot Renaud. The abbot said to this that he did not know this custom and, if indeed it existed, it had not been done by the advice of the chapter and for this reason he felt that it was neither sure nor stable, nor ought to be.

7

The Sons of the Count Together with the King Set Out for Jerusalem. The Count Himself Dons the Garb of a Carthusian Monk and Is Later Devoured by a Dog

[1597D/423. 339]

1147

When the most pious King Louis the Younger, about to set out for Jerusalem, had taken up the sign of the Lord's cross, many, aroused by the fame and example of this act, seized upon a transmarine pilgrimage. Among these were the two sons of the count of Nevers, that is, William and Renaud. Attaching themselves to the royal company [*comitatui*] they undertook the same journey. Their father too, himself desiring to change his former life for another, took the habit of religion and finished his life among the Carthusians. But since he had unjustly afflicted and vexed the glorious tomb, most holy for its religion, of the venerable nourisher and handmaiden of God, Mary Magdalene, he bequeathed the punishment for his crime and the avenging of his injustice to his heirs.[3] For Renaud, whom it befell in a shameful manner to experience the wretchedness of captivity, was unhappily constrained to servitude among the barbaric race; thus, his father, who had tried to deprave the liberty of the church of Vézelay, tasted the opprobrium of servitude in the person of his son.[4] Moreover William, heir to the paternal consulate and crime, when he

---

[1] *pro pedagio*. Cf. Niermeyer (1976: 781): *pedagiare*—"to levy toll upon a person."

[2] The whites and reds of Auxerre were considered in the Middle Ages to be the best of the Burgundian wines. See Benton (1962), Guizot (1969: 243n.66), and in general Speaight (1990: 375ff.).

[3] An interlinear gloss of the twelfth century has added that William was punished by being devoured by a dog. Cf. the (non-medieval) rubric to the present chapter. Cox: "Huygens has omitted from his edition of the Latin text the statement 'he was devoured by a dog,' which was inserted by a later writer between the lines of this sentence and the one above it in the Auxerre MS. Chérest 1:68n, however, notes that the addition is nevertheless in a twelfth-century hand and thinks it ought to be included. He agrees that it could have been added simply for melodramatic effect, but points out that it is possible that William II did, in fact, die following an accident involving one of the ferocious watch dogs which the Carthusians employed to guard their herds. Bouchard (1987: 342, 347) gives the corrected date of his death as 1149."

[4] Renaud count of Tonnerre, second son of William II of Nevers, participated in the

was returning from Jerusalem, suffered shipwreck, so that his very life was in danger. However, when he had made public his father's actions[1] and had realized that all were on the point of death,[2] he was advised by his entourage to give up, for his own welfare and that of his companions, what his father had appropriated for himself by usurpation from the monastery of Vézelay, against right and religion.[3] Finally he gave way before the imminent danger, and, before witnesses, swore on oath that he would henceforth demand from the monastery no procurations for the feasts of Easter, or the death of the blessed Mary Magdalene. Without delay, by the wondrous virtue of God and with the intervention of his beloved, the blessed Mary Magdalene, the ship in which he was travelling was suddenly seized out of the narrow straits of jagged rock onto which it had fallen, and, passing across the turbulent sea, was brought to a quiet shore.

8

The Count, Saved from Shipwreck, Makes a Vow to the Chapter of Vézelay [1598C/424. 368]

c. 1150

In the meantime the excellent abbot Pons took care of the territories and family of the aforementioned count of Nevers, protecting them from attacks on all sides. He was moved by the feeling that in this way the interests of his own monastery might best be attended to, and also by the fact that the same William was joined to him by the affinity of blood relationship.[4] When the

---

second crusade and fell at the hands of the "Saracens" in the defiles of Laodicea. See Bouchard (1987: 347).

[1] *rebus autem expositis.*

[2] *cum iam in articulo mortis omnibus constitutis.*

[3] Phrase from Sallust *Catiline* 15.1. Note that in the following sentence there are six or seven letters erased after "procurations"; see Aspects [A] 24n.5 above for the implications of this. Cox: "Chérest 1:132n surmises that [the scratched out letters] were the words *nisi in*, which would completely change the meaning of the passage. William III would have renounced all procurations [board and room at the abbey's expense or payments in lieu thereof] *except* at Easter and on 22 July. Chérest's emendation seems to be supported by later passages in the chronicle that do strongly suggest that these procurations had never been surrendered, but only the 'extras' that had come to be demanded in addition over the years. See later where the renunciations are specified as *salaria* and *cibaria* [below 166n.5], where the count and his entourage took up residence in the abbey on the feast of Mary Magdalene in 1150, 'as was customary' [below § 10] and where the renunciation 'of these occasional dues' is specified [below 4 §19]."

[4] Geoffrey II of Semur, the father of Geoffrey III de Semur (who married Ermengard and was himself the father of Renaud abbot of Vézelay [162n.1 above]) married "a woman named Adelaide," the daughter, perhaps, of either Count Renaud of Burgundy or Count Renaud of Nevers ([1987: Bouchard 360]); their daughter Raingarde de Semure (cf. the Raingardis mentioned by Bouchard [1987: 411], who does not, however, index the lady)—according to Guizot (1960: 244), where "Geoffroy de Semur" is erroneously stated to have been the "frère de Renaud, abbé de Vézelay" [cf. Bouchard 1987: 431])—married Maurice de Montboissier, whose two children were Peter the Venerable and Pons of Vézelay; cf.

count returned from Jerusalem, after his shipwreck, the abbot went to meet him, showing him all honor, and adequately eased the situation of poverty with which the count found himself heavily oppressed. Then he handed over to him his household and belongings unharmed, with all his possessions as they had been,[1] and, not long afterwards, even brought the enemies of the count into favor again, by satisfying their grievances.[2] The count was then invited to Vézelay, summoned before the brothers, and advised to pay to God what he had vowed. He appeared before them, but secretly was devising stratagems in his mind.[3] Having entered, therefore, the chapter of the monks, he explained to them his shipwreck, declared under confession that he had been freed by the intervention of blessed Mary Magdalene, paid the vow which he had made in return for divine favor, and remitted, conceded, and confirmed with the agreement of his wife and son William [still under age],[4] and in the presence of innumerable others, the payments or provisions[5] usurped by his father. Later, when the count had become embroiled in an increasing number of wars, Abbot Pons helped and assisted him in them all, hoping that in this way he could tame fierce minds,[6] minds bent on the headlong usurpation of the rights of others. Indeed although the count burned with a total urge to attack the church, he was yet restrained by the overflowing good deeds of his relative and feared some disadvantage if he attacked the man who was so accommodating towards him.[7] But a vicious streak was too deeply ingrained in his character and he devoted every waking

---

Graham (1918: 47–50). Cox: "The kinship tie between Pontius (Pons) de Montboissier and William III of Nevers remains obscure. Chérest 1:115–18 believes that it derived from the marriage of Geoffrey II of Semur with an Adelaide de Nevers (who is unidentified), a union that produced Raingard, wife of Maurice II de Montboissier, the parents of Abbot Pontius (Pons) and his brothers. Unfortunately, however, there is no documentary evidence to support such a version of Raingard's lineage, and although it has been repeated by many modern writers (most recently by Vogade [Guizot 1969] 244–45), it has not been accepted by specialists. See Giles Constable (ed.), *The Letters of Peter the Venerable* (Cambridge, Mass., 1967) 2:238."

[1] *incolumem familiam cum totius immunitate possessionis suae.*

[2] *cum satisfactione.* Following Niermeyer (1976: 940), the translation could be "with the payment of compensation."

[3] Phrase from Virgil *Aeneid* 4.563.

[4] An attempted erasure in the MS (Huygens [1976: xxi]).

[5] *salaria vel cibaria,* Guizot translates "soit en argent soit en denrées" and Niermeyer "provisions and corn." Latham has "larder" or "salary/payment" for *salarium.* See 158n.7 above.

[6] This is in fact plural, but Guizot takes it in the singular, referring to the count. The translation we have adopted would suggest that the abbot hoped, by supporting the count, to strike a blow for general peace in the neighborhood. Huygens suggests that the phrase "tame fierce minds" is a reminiscence from Boethius's *De consolatione philosophiae* 3 m.5.2: *qui se volet esse potentem/animos domet ille feroces.* Cf. Hugh's language: *sperans mitigare se posse feroces animos. . . .* However, Boethius clearly intends the plural to refer to the subject: "who would himself be powerful must tame his own fierce spirits. . . ."

[7] Highly compressed. Literally: "the which [i.e., benefits] yielding he was afraid to attack for some disadvantages"; *quibus obsequentem verebatur impetere aliquibus preiudiciis.*

moment to the problem of how he might obtain the opportunity of vilifying either the abbot or the church. At the same time, men of iniquity, whose hearts were ovens of impiety,[1] grieving at the loss of the very many opportunities for indulging their lust,[2] which they used to enjoy at the banquets which were frequently showered upon the count at Vézelay,[3] began to turn the mind of the prince, ready as it was for all evil, and suggested[4] that he make up the loss, which he had incurred of his own will, by the renewal of the old lawsuit against the abbot or by the initiation of a new one.

9

Hugh of St. Peter, Author of the Persecution Carried Out against the Monastery [1599B/424. 401]

1150

There was a certain alien[5] at Vézelay, it turned out, whose name was Hugh of St. Peter, ignoble [*ignobilis*] by birth and habits and endowed rather meagerly by nature, but wealthy from the profits of his expertise in the manual arts.[6] This man, being of keen wit and versed in every wicked device, began to woo the count with gifts at one moment, and to raise his hopes with

---

[1] *clibanus*: this is the word used of the communal ovens, or manorial ovens, for the baking of bread. Huygens suggests the word "iniquity" has biblical overtones: 1 Macc. 3:6 and Luke 13:27.

[2] *questus suae libidinis*: cf. Boethius *De consolatione philosophiae* as cited 166n.6 above line 3: *nec victa libidine colla.*

[3] *quae comiti frequenter Vizeliaco exhibebantur*; these hangers-on apparently shared in the "procurations" that the count had just renounced: their aim was to renew the procurations.

[4] Present tense, as is *circumveniunt* (here translated as "began to turn the mind"), for dramatic effect. For the background see Cox: "Count William had given in under pressure with evident ill-will, but for the time being he was not in a position to avenge himself. On his return from the Holy Land he learned that an alliance was in the making between two of his most inveterate enemies, Count Steven of Sancerre and Geoffrey of Donzy, lord of Gien. William tried to forbid the marriage between the count and Geoffrey's daughter that was intended to consolidate their alliance, and his complaints caused the matter to be appealed to the royal court for arbitration. While all this was happening, an incident occurred at Vézelay that offered Count William an excuse for reopening the old jurisdictional quarrel with the abbey. One of the monks whose task it was to oversee the abbey's forest preserves, while making his rounds encountered a peasant illegally cutting wood and attempted to apprehend him. . . ."

[5] *advena genere.*

[6] *manus arte docta mechanica.* The "mechanical arts" in Hugh of St. Victor's *Didascalicon* 2:20 include fabric-making, armament, commerce, agriculture, hunting, medicine, and theatrics; see Taylor (1961: 74ff.); Huygens (1976: xviii, and 425.403/04 n.). A contemporary hand adds this marginal note: "*Ars mechanica* is a very general term referring to whatever, beyond the liberal arts, is performed as rural service, such as construction, weaving, provisioning. It is called mechanical because it is impure and has degenerated from the liberal arts." See Berlow (1971: 330ff., esp. 334), and E. Whitney, "Paradise Restored: The Mechanical Arts from Antiquity through the Thirteenth Century," *Transactions of the American Philosophical Society* 80 (1990): I.

fraudulent expectations at another, to the effect that he should extort from
the church the rights of justice, that is the right of judgment, of taking up and
examining the suits of the men of Vézelay.[1] For this worst of men was
hoping to direct the affairs of the whole village[2] by securing, through the
favor of the tyrant,[3] the right to decide the cases of the men of Vézelay.[4] To
this end he therefore began to associate with himself in clandestine conspiracies several persons equally as depraved as himself who were to put his proposed malignity into practice, to devise a betrayal [of the men of Vézelay into
the hands of the count] under the pretext of defending their liberty, and to
prepare cunning stratagems under the pretext of piety: the prospect of affluence, it seems, always breeds insolence in degenerate minds. For when a man
is able to effect more with riches than another is with natural talents, he
comes to prefer himself even to the children of royalty, and, forgetting his
true nature, glories in his private wealth and struts grandly, his true condition
visible to all, his inanity evident.[5]

A certain monk of Vézelay, therefore, doing a circuit of the possessions of
the church, happened to come upon this Hugh, one of whose companions
was illegally cutting wood in a certain grove which was under the jurisdiction
of the church.[6] The monk wished to seize the axe from him as proof of his

---

[1] *iusiusticie seu iudicii dirimendi vel examinandi causas hominum Vizeliacensium.*

[2] *se principari vico.*

[3] *per gratiam tiranni.* On the contemporary implications of the term *tirannus* see Rouse
(1967), Nederman (1989).

[4] *optio iurisjudicii.* Huygens (1976: xxxix). For the sociological type of communal
conspirator to which we should assimilate this Hugh and the later mentioned Letard (see
below Book 4 §22) and his ancestor, Simon–son of Odo, provost of Vézelay and serf to
the church, killer of Abbot Artaud in 1106–see Hibbert (1953). Compare the position of
Bertulf in Flanders in 1127 (Ross [1960: 96ff.]), or that of the serf Theudegaldus (Thiégaud) in Guibert of Nogent *De vita sua* 3 §8 (ed. Benton, 175; ed. Labande, 341), or that
of the *iuvenis Guilelmus* (*servus conditione et moribus*), below *Major Chronicle* 4 §8. See
Berlow (1980: 138). Thierry (Guizot 1969: 245) says Hugh was a native of the Midi of
France, although there is no evidence for this (Berlow [1987: 143–44] denies Hugh's link
with southern France). As his name suggests, he may have been born in St. Père-sous-Vézelay. Chérest (quoted Guizot 1969: 245) supposes that Hugh's "mechanical" talents had to
do with the construction of water wheels and associated works for grinding and milling (a
seigneurial monopoly). See above Aspects [B], below *Major Chronicle* 4 §54, etc.

[5] See *Major Chronicle* 1, 130n.4 above for *incedens.* Compare the career of the provost
Bertulf in the chronicle of Galbert of Bruges (Ross [1960]).

[6] Guizot translates, "a certain monk of Vézelay, doing a circuit of the properties of the
church, came by chance into a forest which belonged to our jurisdiction; and, having
found there an individual who was cutting wood, a thing forbidden in the forest, he
wished to take away his axe, as proof of the crime." On the event, which seems to have
taken place in July 1150, see Huygens (1976: 71ff.) and Guizot (1969: 245–46). Chérest
translated *eum* (Huygens 1976: 425.19)–which can only, if the text is not corrupt, refer to
Hugh–as "l'un des habitants." So, too, do Berlow (1971: 199), and Graham (1918: 75–76).
Because *eum* can refer only to Hugh and because subsequent events (for example 2 §24
below) make clear that Hugh could not have been the victim of the blinding, we have
assumed that *quendam* must refer to a companion of Hugh, and have translated accordingly. Cox: "According to David Boudin *Page d'histoire du moyen-âge, suivi de faits datant de la
Renaissance et des siècles suivants en ce qui touche la Bourgogne et particulièrement les bourgs de*

guilt, but the culprit, having turned around, struck the monk heavily and threw him down with this assault from the horse on which he was sitting. The monk then, disgraced by the receipt of this injury, returned home [*ad propria*] and revealed to the supporters of the monastery[1] the insult that he had endured. They, unwilling to put up with such an indignity, came by night to the house of the man [who had been cutting the wood] and, gouging out his eyes, brought down upon him a night of perpetual blindness. When the count found out about this he suppressed his joy at having found an opportunity for vilifying the abbey but threatened the perpetrators of this deed with perdition. Gradually giving birth to a wickedness that he had long ago drafted in his heart, he arranged to renew the lawsuit which his father had allowed to slumber.

10
The Count Raids the Goods of the Monastery [1599D/426. 432]
1150

The solemn feast of the blessed beloved of God, Mary Magdalene had come around and, seizing the moment, the count, when he had taken up residence

---

Dornecy, Vézelay, et autres circonvoisins (Auxerre 1893: 44–46), the true story of this incident was quite different and was suppressed by Hugh the Poitevin out of concern for the abbey's reputation. On the basis of research in unspecified archives amid *vieux parchemins et mémoires particuliers*, notably a chronicle by one Jehan Colon of Chamoux, Boudin asserted that in reality the monk whose task it was to patrol the abbey's woods between Dornecy and Chamoux was a stalwart youth of very considerable physical prowess and high lineage. He was wont to frequent a hostelry known as the *True Cross* at Chamoux, whose proprietor, one Graind'orge, had recently been married to a 'frisky lass from the Morvan well made to delight a man of taste,' who had been, and continued to be, the monk's mistress. The blinding incident was the result of Graind'orge's discovery of their liaison, and the victim was not an illegal wood-cutter, but the wronged husband, whose mutilation was avenged some time later by the murder of the monk at the hands of Graind'orge's kinsmen. According to Boudin, Jehan Colon also recounted another incident which Hugh the Poitevin took care to avoid mentioning in his chronicle, an incident involving the cousin of the 'belle Morvandelle.' This young woman, 'grasse et plantureuse jeune fille' [Guizot] like the first, was taken up by one of the high dignitaries of the abbey. She was accordingly disguised as a monk and lived with him in the monastery for several years under the name of Brother Apollinaire" (shades of Pope Joan!). "Vogade, in the notes to his edition of Guizot's translation of Hugh the Poitevin's chronicle [Guizot 1969: 245–46] reproduces these stories as if they were matters of established fact, but they cannot be verified. Nothing is known of a chronicle by Jehan de Colon, although a family by that name was prominent in Vézelay at least as early as the late fifteenth century, and Boudin offers no information either as to its date or as to its provenance. Boudin himself was a former commissar of police in Paris who originally came from Dornecy, a village some ten miles west of Vézelay, and who apparently devoted his retirement years to local history. He produced his own version of the history of Vézelay, and although he was apparently unaware of Chérest's research, he does quote translated passages from Hugh the Poitevin's chronicle. The tone is consistently hostile to the monastic community, however, which suggests a willingness to accept such accusations as those attributed to Jehan Colon regardless of their provenance."

[1] *clientibus monasterii.*

in the guesthouse of the monastery, as was his wont,[1] ordered his servants [*servos*] to stand before the doors in order to prohibit the entry of the abbot, should he happen to come by to pay a visit. The servants duly carried out these orders and barred the abbot from the threshold saying that the count was detained in conference within. The abbot, repulsed, sustained this insult with patience and though he suspected evil from the ungrateful man, nevertheless kept an open mind. Later, however, when the count was at Clamecy,[2] the abbot advanced towards him and asked him the reason for the insult which the count had offered him. The count alleged the offense to the blinded man, to which the abbot replied that the man was not under the count's jurisdiction. The count, however, insisted that the man was his very son, and gave the name of his mother.[3] Smiling, as if at a joke,[4] the abbot asked the count whether he would deign to accept justice from him [the abbot].[5] When the count replied in the negative, the abbot again asked insistently whether the count would return to amity either at the hand of his own friends and servants or by his own hand.[6] When the count refused, the abbot asked him again whether it would unavoidably fall to him to watch over himself and his possessions against the count. The latter replied that this would in fact be necessary and the abbot, recognizing that a feud was inevitable,[7] left him.

The count sent his henchmen [*satellites*] into a certain possession of the abbot and laid it waste, taking many animals and much spoil. At once the abbot beseeched the count to return to him what he had taken away, but the latter simply poured forth at last his full—hitherto hidden—poison and demanded that the abbot should seek justice in the count's court when summoned by him on any point. The abbot replied that this demand was entirely contrary and adverse to divine law, the customs of the church, and apostolic decretals. He said further: "It is a disgraceful and disgusting thing to me[8] that the liberty of the monastery which flourished for a very long time under many fathers right up to the present circumstances, should perish and be condemned to servitude because of the affinity which links you and me. What you propose is offensive not just to our kinship but to nature since you con-

---

[1] *ex more.*

[2] Clamecy, being twenty-three kilometers to the east of Vézelay, implies a rapid scene change which is inadequately signalled in the Latin.

[3] *at ille filiolum* ("his very own dear son") *suum hominem esse dixit, hoc est ab utero matris denominatum*: the count doubtless means to imply that the companion of Hugh was one of *his* serfs.

[4] *arridens abbas quasi ludo.*

[5] I.e., recognizing that the abbot had jurisdiction in the relevant wood (in which the incident occurred).

[6] Literally; that is, confirming some pact of concord by a gesture of clasped or enfolded hands. See Bloch (1961: plates 2–3).

[7] *diffidatus abbas ab eo recessit.* See Niermeyer (1976: 331).

[8] Cf. Cicero *De officiis* 1.27.94 and *De finibus* 3.4.14 (Huygens).

trive, though a mere man, to subvert to your own purposes the laws of God, instead of preserving and amplifying them, safe and undiminished; for I am your relative and kinsman. It is open to all to see how inhuman it is of you to repay my good deeds with such opposite coin, how you strive always to offer me nothing but insult while I offer you honor and munificence. However, though I promise you favorable compliance [*obsequium*] on other matters, you must know that I intend to yield you nothing in regard to the present demand."

11

The Abbot Makes Every Effort to Conciliate the Count, But in Vain [1600D/427. 473]

1150-1151

Having heard this, the tyrant became enraged; he uttered many threats, hinted at worse, and bent himself wholly upon the destruction of the church. The abbot sent messengers to appeal for help against him from the Roman See. In the meantime, by the mediation of friends, he sought peace from the count: he pleaded elaborately that he did not deserve the count's malignity; he made out the case for harmony, with the dignity of the church and the legal status of its privileges intact. Immediately many colloquies took place in a variety of districts between a large number of great magnates, and various were the opinions expressed. Finally, however, the peace of friendship was not forthcoming since everywhere the torch of discord was rife. As soon as the tyrant learned that the abbot had sent his legates to Rome, he at once despatched an expedition throughout the farms and possessions of the monastery of Vézelay, comprehensively invading, plundering, abducting, and spoiling whatever the church possessed by law in the counties of Nevers or Auxerre. The monastic provosts and the procurators[1] in charge of various offices he compelled to promise faith to him through oaths[2] to the effect that in no matter should they obey the monks or make answer to the abbot or his men on any account. He exerted every effort, indeed, with shrewd cunning, to pervert the legates of the abbot from their purpose, in the hope of extorting some words of concession,[3] even if they were unwilling. But the abbot, with his customary prudence, and taking into account the precarious state of his affairs, promised satisfaction on the matter of [judicial] competence to the count, received back what he had lost and bestowed many gifts and presents on the count who was about to depart for the oratory of Saint James of Compostela.[4] But what abundance of good things could possibly stop the

---

[1] *prepositos . . . procuratores.*

[2] *per sacramenta pollicite fidei coegit*: perhaps seeking to make them his vassals?

[3] *aliquod cessionis verbum.* Cf. previous note.

[4] Compostela: see Cross (1974: 325), s.v. "Compostela." Compostela was traditionally

voracity of cupidity? To be sure, a corrupt mind knows nothing other than to
pervert the upright or to see evil in them.

Finally the count returned from Spain and fixed a day for the abbot by
mandate so that on those accusations made against him[1] he could obtain the
judgment of the count's principal court[2] in the presence of its president, the
count himself. But, he to whom the staff of St. Peter had been committed
could not be entirely unaware of the constancy and magnanimity of St. Peter!
The abbot, therefore neglected the mandates of the tyrant, and the count at
once gave orders by the framing of an edict that no one should enter Vézelay,
whether under pretext of trade, of travel or of pilgrimage; nor should anyone
go forth from Vézelay to the public fairs or market. Whoever should dare to
make light of the published edict would be judged open to legal pillage at the
hands of any they met. The townspeople,[3] besieged in this way, began to
hear some of their number whisper in secrecy, with furtive voices, that the
author and at the same time the cause of all these evils was the abbot himself,
who was pressing them with new and unjust laws and arousing against them
the fury of the tyrant, within whose territory they were enclosed, to their peril
and destruction. The whisperers were preaching that they would all be at last
happy and blessed if they rejected the yoke of the church and offered themselves as chattels to the will of the count.[4] If they did so they would not have
to fear enemies outside the monastery and would brush away from their
doors, like the least of flies, the monastic tax collectors.[5] They even, when
there was need, would contend on equal terms [*equipollenter*] with the abbot

---

supposed to be the burial place of James the apostle, son of Zebedee, elder brother of St.
John (Cross [1974: 723, 742]). Hence "Santiago (= Sanctus Jacobus, St. James) de Compostela." Note the curious mixture of piety and impiety on the count's part. Southern (1953:
86) notes the same characteristic in the history of the counts of Anjou: "In them the
alternation of headlong violence with abrupt acts of remorse and atonement, which
characterises the early feudal age, has its full play."

[1] *de quibus foret interpellatus.* See Niermeyer (1976: 550–51). Cox supposes that "the
'charges' in question here were presumably accusations of injustice in the case of the
blinded woodcutter, whose cause was apparently being championed by dissident burghers."

[2] *curiae principalis.*

[3] *vicani*; but clearly the inhabitants of Vézelay are meant.

[4] *sese manciparent comitis arbitrio.* Cf. Niermeyer (1976: 633) (*mancipium* §3): "the word
is used even for ecclesiastical tributaries whose serfdom is marked by rather slight
charges": implied, perhaps, is the notion that the *vicani* would enter into a chartered
agreement with the count (since the abbot was proving unamenable to any such arrangement) to commute servile or serf-like dues and arbitrary exactions into a fixed tax. Cf.
Guibert of Nogent *De vita sua* 3 §7 (ed. Benton, 167; ed. Labande, 320).

[5] *internos exactores.* "Flies" (*velut exiguas muscas*): see Cicero *De oratore* 2.60.247 (Huygens). See Guizot (1969: 246n.74) for a graphic depiction of the plight of the serf of the
region. Cf. also the *Accord* of 1137, translated below as Appendix B. For the "new and
unjust laws" mentioned above see Berlow (1980: 138ff). Like the count of Flanders,
murdered in 1127 by his rebellious "serfs," Pons seems to have been trying to control the
movement away from serfdom on the part of his dependents. His motives may have
derived from fiscal or manpower problems.

in court, since the majority, leaning on the bolder elements, would withdraw themselves from the control of the unwarlike few. Nor did it escape the count that they were muttering such things among themselves, for Hugh the Profane[1] bore him these impious tidings. The count embraced the stratagem of Hugh, whereby he was advised that if he were to come to Vézelay and have some word with the villagers on the subject of deserting the abbot, sensing his opportunity, as it were, in a judicious way, there could be no doubt but that the more influential and numerous faction of the citizenry, who favored the count, would at once give him their hands in homage[2] if they were recompensed by a treaty[3] whereby he would offer them everywhere his protection and help. The count [therefore] came to Vézelay, went unexpectedly to the monastic guesthouse,[4] from where he called the villagers to him in secret, persuaded them that desertion was desirable, and beseeched them to throw in their lot with him against the abbot, saying that there was nowhere they could protect themselves against his anger, but that in peace they need not fear him as their lord.

12
The Count Persuades the Burghers of Vézelay That They Should Withdraw Themselves from the Domination of the Abbot [1602A/428. 531]

1151

The count began: "You see how the abbot alone strives to hinder the welfare of you all,[5] though I am the legitimate advocate and guardian of this church.[6] In disdaining to answer his calumniators before me as judge and advocate, he is in fact demanding back from me the right of justice, he is seizing what belongs to another.[7] And who could bear such outrageous arrogance, nay, iniquity, that anyone, claiming his own right, should keep back the rights of another without discussion? What case can I mount against those plundering your goods when the abbot retains, like a tyrant,[8] judicial compe-

---

[1] *Hugone prophano*; i.e., Hugh of St. Peter (above §9).

[2] *manum deditionis.*

[3] *recompensato federe.*

[4] *in hospitio monasterii.*

[5] *communem salutem.*

[6] *legitimus advocatus et tutor huius aecclesiae.* See Aspects [A] above.

[7] *dum preripiendo quod iuris est alieni, iusiusticie quidem a me repetit quod ipse calumniantibus me iudice vel advocato exequi dedignatur.* We have turned this sentence around considerably to make sense. Cox translates: "for while he is seizing what is rightfully another's, he demands from me a jurisdiction that he disdains to make use of, namely, my judgment or advocacy in prosecuting his accusers."

[8] Cf. above 168n.3. The polemic associated with the word "tyrant" evidently cut both ways in these disputes.

tence over them? In the final analysis," he said, "it is better to exercise power
than to be always seeking it. In regard to the nature, extent, and scope of our
power, however, nothing can be clearer than a proven case. But monkish
prayers, even if they don't deserve rejection, are usually of slight efficacy. It
is of some importance to you, therefore, how you vote on this issue.[1] By
favoring ourselves, by sharing in our power, you need have no care for the
now empty prayers of the monks or the futile resources of the abbot because
you will have free and untrammeled egress and ingress whatever your destination, and you will enjoy security for your persons and your property forever."

13

The Brothers of Vézelay Beseech the Count to Desist
from What He Had Begun   (1602C/428. 549)

1151

Saying these things and breaking down into sobs, he poured forth the tears
of impiety, which he drew from the well of filthy cupidity.[2] The abbot, seeking to avert the eventuality of so ill-advised a suggestion [as that which the
count had put to the people of Vézelay], convoked a gathering of the brothers and admonished them to go before the count, prostrate themselves down
to the ground[3] and beg him all together to have pity on them and spare the
church. These sons [of the church], obedient to the fatherly admonition, left
their table and fell together before the feet of the tyrant and piteously
demanded that he spare them, for the love of God and out of reverence for
his handmaiden [the Magdalene], and that he refrain from perverting with his

---

[1] There is an echo here of Lactantius *Epitome* 66.7 (Huygens [1976: 428.545n]). It is
difficult to make sense of the count's speech and the translation may not be correct. He
seems to be arguing that he has jurisdiction in the case of the person apprehended in the
grove with the axe. The abbot, by refusing justice at the count's hands deprives the count
of any ability—so he claims—to redress the depradations (the blockade, the incursions) he
has carefully engineered against the church and its possessions. The abbot is portrayed as
the source of the evil because he cannot make good his right to do justice, let alone any
justice that might flow from the proper exercise of this right. Until it is decided who has
judicial power over the *vizeliacenses*, no tranquillity can be obtained. The count offers the
cives a formula. Note that in these mock speeches, Hugh of Poitiers follows out the
dictates of classical and medieval rhetorical and historiographical theory: see Ward (1985:
146ff.). Hugh is simply working up into dramatic, persuasive form arguments he was told
were used, or which he himself heard used, or which he felt were appropriate to the
occasion. Cox translates: " 'Who can bear such arrogance, indeed such wickedness, as
someone demanding his own rights who withholds without discussion the rights of others?
What recourse can I have in the face of those who are despoiling you if they tyrannically
retain all jurisdiction? In the end,' he said, 'it is much better to have some power than to
have to petition ceaselessly. What our power is worth, how great and extensive it is,
nothing shows better than the argument of experience. The prayers of the monks, even
when they do not deserve to be rejected, are usually weak and without effect. In which
direction, therefore, do your wishes incline you? It is important for you to decide.' "

[2] Lewis & Short (1933) give an instance from Tertullian of use of the word *caenulentus*.

[3] *solatenus*. Guizot (1969: 56): "dans la poussière."

seductions their men, the men of the church.[1] His snake-like form[2] concealing no dove-like mind, the count replied humbly to them that he required of
them nothing more than that, just as they claim their own rights, they should
in like manner maintain others' rights as interpreted by him [*per manum
illius*]. "And I am marvelously stunned," [he went on], "at the notion of
equity that could spawn such massive insolence; I marvel that you should
arraign others when it is I who am judge and advocate; I marvel too that you,
when others do the arraigning, should disdain to follow out the obvious
course of justice before me as advocate and judge. I am not zealous to seduce
your men or call them from your allegiance—as you charge—but those whom
by custom and by right I everywhere guard and defend from all, I decree
should be cleared or brought to book[3] by proper and public judgment of my
court. For whoever," [he added], "seeks to recover what is his own, ought in
justice concede the rights of another."[4] The brothers then replied to this that
in accordance with the long-established custom of their fathers and the
apostolic statutes, they denied no one what was just. At this the whole house
was at once filled with a confused clamor.[5] Again the brothers, since the
solemnity of the feast of the blessed Mary Magdalene was at hand,[6] pressed
the count to grant them a truce of some days whereby they might celebrate
the festal days midst the public throng. To this he replied that they could
hardly ask such a thing since he was not confining them by siege nor were
they being led into captivity. They went on, however, thus: "You have prohibited under threat any stranger from coming into Vézelay, as you have prohibited us from going out for the sake of supplies. We protest that we are
unjustly besieged by such a wretched situation." Eventually, a little confounded by the pleas of so many brothers, he granted a truce of eight days and
immediately departed, leaving incomplete his schemes of treachery.[7] The
brothers then, though not with the accustomed throng, went ahead and celebrated the festal days with no inferior rite. When the ceremonies had finished, the bishop of Auxerre was summoned and the abbot set out to the
count, to whom he made known the apostolic mandates by which he had
been ordered to go to Italy for the purpose of terminating the calumnies of

---

[1] *suos vel aecclesiae homines*: the citizens of Vézelay whom the count has just attempted
to persuade to his side, rather than, perhaps, "the brothers [*monachi*] and the men of the
church [*cives*]."

[2] The effect here derives from the similarity between "colubrino" (*corpore*) and
"columbina" (*mente*). Cf. the provisions of the *Rhetorica ad Herennium* 4.20.27 et seq.

[3] *purgatos vel iustificatos.*

[4] Huygens (1976: 429. 569–70 matches 428. 533–34). The count touches on his major
themes again, addressing the abbot. See 174n.1 above.

[5] *domus confuso clamore repleta est*: See Jeremiah 2:26: *confusi sunt domus Israel*, and Isaiah
22:2: *clamoris plena*, etc.

[6] 22 July 1151.

[7] Or: "his schemes for the betrayal [of the abbot] having been spoiled": *infecto
proditionis negocio.*

the bishop of Autun.[1] He then beseeched the count to guard the monastery
of his relative and its appurtenances just as he, the abbot, had faithfully preserved the count's rights as if they were his own and had held them intact
against every incursion while the count had been away on pilgrimage.[2] He
should undertake this task in good faith and faithfully protect the abbey until
the abbot's return from Rome. He promised besides that he would persuade
the lord pope to permit Vézelay to take part in a court hearing at Nevers,[3]
and, if he was successful in this, he agreed to make a deposition concerning
all matters in dispute. Moreover, so that the truce mentioned above might
endure sure and unshaken, the abbot offered the count money: sixty pounds
from the public mint.[4]

14

When the Count Has Ratified the Truce the Abbot Sets Out for Rome Where He Triumphs over the Bishop of Autun. The Pope Advises the Abbot to be of Good Heart Against the Count [1603C/430. 598]

1151–1152

Thus the tyrant, moved by the prayers [of the monks], lured by the promises
and spurred by the gifts [of the abbot], conceded the truce that had been
demanded, and for the rest promised that he would be a faithful friend to the
church, if the abbot would give effect to the pledges he had made. And since
nothing comes more easily to a duplicitous mind than lying,[5] the count made
many promises, few of which he kept. However, since charity knows no
deceit, is full of hope, and lifts up the heart of all,[6] the generous simplicity of
the faith of the abbot placed trust in what the count said. Having set out,
finally, for Rome[7] and having entered the universal court,[8] he triumphed
over the calumny of the bishop of Autun before the highest pontiff, so effectively that not the smallest hair of his head fell into disorder.[9] Autun, thus
confounded, became so dejected that, inventing subterfuges to avoid trial of

---

[1] See charter 43 above.
[2] The second crusade, presumably, rather than the count's visit to Compostela,
mentioned above by Hugh in §8.
[3] *subire audientiam Nivernensis.* Cox: "*Audienciae* were special judicial assemblies over
which important territorial lords presided more or less regularly and usually in person."
See below 177n.1 and Niermeyer (1976: 71).
[4] Guizot (1969: 53), "une somme de soixante livres en monnaie de cours" = *pecuniam
sexaginta librarum monetae publicae.*
[5] Cf. James 1:8 (Huygens).
[6] Cf. 1 Cor. 13:4–7 (Huygens).
[7] 18 November 1151 (charter 43 above).
[8] The papal court. This is a reference to the hearing described in *Major Chronicle* 1
§§4–6 above.
[9] Literally: "that not even the hair of his head wavered (due to) anything."

his rights,[1] he demanded a postponement.[2] Afterwards the abbot had an audience with the pope at which he laid bare the vexation which the count of Nevers was visiting upon himself and the abbey of Vézelay, over which, up to now, blessed Peter and the Roman church had enjoyed the most untrammeled of proprietary rights. The abbot,[3] who could not be swayed by the pleas of the mighty, nor tempted by the intimations of friends, nor won over by flatterers, nor influenced by gifts, nor coerced by ecclesiastical censure, addressed the pope thus: "Apostolic prudence must decide what is to be done, whether, indeed, its liberty is to give way to the wantonness of a tyrant, or not. Perhaps it will turn out that when the lustful madness of this enemy has run its course, he will bestow upon the church peace, and the protection of an eternal guardianship." "Quite the contrary," replied the apostolic father, "for if the priest of Vézelay,[4] no less, shall be compelled to undergo trial in a secular or popular court, not only will the monastery be deprived of its peace, but the whole ecclesiastical order will be entrapped in the noose of extreme confusion. We shall, therefore, reprove the count, whom we have already warned, and urge him, as we have already done once before, to desist from this insolence, laying it down that if he should dare to seek for himself any rights over your monastery, he should accept them from judges appointed by us and should leave alone what belongs to another.[5] If, however, he should spurn our piety, lo! the collar, lo! the reins, lo! the sword of St. Peter with which the ear of his contumacy may be cut off! In brief, we want your watchfulness to be especially fortified by apostolic authority, lest in the affairs of the monastery—which involve the rights of Saint Peter—you should yield to anyone on any point, or lest you should betray, by any pusillanimity, the liberty with which your church was born and which has been, since then, considerably built up by apostolic favor. For however remote from us you are, we will not hold you, vigilant as you are for the rights of the Holy See, in lesser favor [but rather we shall bestow on you] the care and authority which becomes a son [of the church]."

[1] *audientiam iurisiudicii subterfugiens*. Cf. above 176n.2.

[2] *dilationem*. Cf. above *Major Chronicle* 1 § 6 at 147n.1.

[3] Guizot translates *is* (Huygens [1976: 430. 613]) as referring to the pope. Such a translation, however, requires an unannounced change of subject from *is . . . flectitur*—the pope—to *inquit*—the abbot.

[4] *vizeliacensis sacerdos*, i.e., Pons.

[5] The advice to which the pope refers is the letter which is charter 29 above.

15

The Count Spurns the Apostolic Letters and Stirs Up the
Bishops of Burgundy Against the Monks   [1604B/431. 637]

1152

Armed with such advice, the abbot returned rejoicing to his monastery with the blessings of the curia. However, when he had given the apostolic instructions to the count, the latter spurned them, vilified them, rejected them out of hand and replied that he owed nothing to the abbot, from whom he held nothing. The count then inquired if the abbot had obtained from the Apostolic See, as he had promised, permission to lay his suit before the count's court and accept the judgment of that court.[1] "I have kept the promise I gave you," said the abbot, "but I was forbidden to fulfil my vow."[2] The count choked with rage and, ablaze with gall, again prevented Vézelay commerce [*commeatum*] from having free right of egress and ingress. Afraid of the prospect of making war on the monks by himself, he stirred up the satraps [*satrapas*][3] of the province, that is, Gibaud de Saint-Verain,[4] Itier de Brèves, Geoffrey d'Arcy,[5] and their accomplices, encouraging them, wheresoever they should meet with the men of Vézelay, to fall upon them, to seize and appropriate their goods, to show the monastery of Vézelay no mercy, to plunder its possessions, to spread calumnies about its abbot, to fill any shortage of their own with the supplies of the church [of Vézelay]. And so, like dogs, they overran the farms of the monastery from all directions, they killed the monks, took away their clothes and shamefully abused them, plundered all their personal effects, and at the same time raided the flocks, herds, and serfs [*servos*] of the church. No piety restrained them; everywhere clerics were cut down, priests were foully handled, wayfarers were stripped of their possessions, pilgrims were captured, noble matrons were raped. In the midst of all this the patience of the church of Vézelay could only be marvelled at and more wondrous still was the magnanimity and steadfastness of the prudent abbot Pons. On the one hand it was the count of Nevers, on the other the

---

[1] *audientiam et executionem iurisiudicii curiae suae.*

[2] Psalms 53:4 and 77:1 (Huygens). Cf. §13 above at 176n.2.

[3] Cf. Judges 3:3, *satrapae Philistinorum.* The word *satrap(e)s* is of Persian origin and though found in classical Latin is commoner in biblical and later Latin.

[4] Faithful and important vassal of the count of Nevers (d. 1174), cruel but liberal and courageous and descended from a family with a good record for pillaging pilgrims, travellers, and churches. Gibaud lived up to the reputation of his house and plundered Vézelay lands, with the acquiescence of count, duke, and bishop, harassing at the same time other abbeys in the region. Between 1154 and 1161 he even revolted against his own overlord.

[5] Lord of Arcy-sur-Cure, 18 kilometers from Vézelay. In the end a benefactor of Vézelay (his brother became abbot there in 1171), but along the way one of the count's more vigorously persecuting henchmen. See on both these lords Guizot (1969: 246–47), below 201n.2 and Appendix H. On the famous grottos of Arcy-sur-Cure see Speaight (1990: 127–28).

bishop of Autun; here the tyrants hurried around on all sides like wild beasts, there it was the lords of the land:[1] one spirit united them, they assailed in concert, they provoked the abbot, worried the church and infringed its rights to such an extent that whatever met with a hostile band was usurped completely. But the more calmly the abbot, with his generosity of spirit and innate nobility, bore these indignities the more iniquitously did the evils weigh down upon him.

16
The Abbot Shows the Privileges of Vézelay to the King
and Implores Protection from Him   [1605A/431. 668]
1152

Eventually, the abbot, feeling that the evils were multiplying on all sides, came to the king, seeking help from him against the count. The latter, asked to explain his cause, replied to the king: "I hold and possess the advocacy and the guardianship[2] of the monastery of Vézelay, with the uses pertaining to it, from my fathers and ancestors, by right of matrimony and by the concession and favor of your pious father and your own Serenity, [and I have done so] right down to the present—without any complainant speaking against it. I am entirely at a loss as to why rights inherited from my fathers over so long a period should be made a matter of calumny against me."

The abbot, in reply, said: "The church of Vézelay, nobly founded by the illustrious count Gerard, was more nobly dedicated [*attitulata*] and ascribed [*adscripta*] to the name of the blessed apostles Peter and Paul by the same man, assigned to them by right, entrusted to their governance, committed to their protection. Moreover, by the mediation of the pious count Gerard himself, it was considered worthy of endowment with such prerogative of privilege from the most excellent kings of the Franks, that they themselves remitted whatever royal rights had prevailed there from antiquity, with the result that no power or person whatever could lay claim to any right or custom, regardless of the type or occasion of demand, whether arising out of piety or gift.[3] Instead, the church should endure free from any condition of servitude, or demand to fulfil an obligation. To corroborate this claim, we have ready, if your Serenity will deign to hear it, the privilege of your ancestor Louis."[4]

The privilege was read through and the king asked the abbot whether he

---

[1] *duces terrae.*

[2] *advocationem sive tuitionem.*

[3] *muneris.* Guizot (1969): "soit de piété soit de generosité."

[4] According to Huygens (1976: 432.689n) an act of Louis IV d'Outremer is in question here. See his note to charter 6, lines 23–25 (in Huygens's edition). Curiously, the abbatial cartulary contains no royal acts before that of 1154 (charter 65). For these see Huygens (1976: 432.682n). Presumably they did not favor Vézelay—hence, perhaps, the hostility of the king's court to the abbot's cause mentioned immediately below. See above §3.

would place his confidence in the king's enquiry and act in accord with the royal decision on his claims. The abbot, considering carefully the fact that the court was hostile to him and favored the party opposed to him, feared to entrust himself to a decision that might not go his way, lest the church, whose only true judge was St. Peter, should suffer prejudice now that it had gained some brief respite. In the end he begged the royal Loftiness, to order the tyrant to cease infesting the monastery of Vézelay, and to accept the right of the legate[1] of the Holy See—or whomsoever the pope had commissioned as his agent—to decide the matter. While the count was derisively denying [the truth of] all that the abbot had said, the latter, bidding the king farewell, returned to his monastery.

When he learned that John, cardinal-priest of the Roman church, to whom the Apostolic Father had delegated[2] the suit between Nevers and Vézelay, was returning from England after the fulfillment of a mission, Pons sent to meet him a request to come to Vézelay as swiftly as he could, since the church there was destitute of all help and threatened with isolation. When the cardinal-priest had received the envoy of the abbot, he accelerated his progress and instructed both parties, that is, the abbot and the count, to meet him at Auxerre. Hearing too, that Cardinal Jordan had been assigned as legate to the Gallican Church, John also wrote to him urging him to come to Vézelay post-haste, that they might together celebrate the forthcoming feast of the blessed Mary Magdalene there.[3] When both parties, the count and the abbot, had come together at Auxerre with John and Jordan, the legate kindly and affably encouraged the count to let his claims rest and make peace with the abbot, lest, by pursuing a case against the vicar of Christ and St. Peter he should be proved to be a manifest enemy of God and in this way a persecutor of the Church, like Saul of old. "But in fact if you continue spurning us," he went on, "you would not really be a worthy imitator of Saul, for he, when he had made trial of the one who rebuked him, at once followed the Master."[4] But when the count broke his pretense by contemning these worthy admonitions—since he again prohibited public egress from or access to Vézelay—the

---

[1] *iusiudicii . . . susciperet.* Cf. Huygens (1976: xxxix).

[2] On the system of judges-delegate in the period see Duggan (1963); Barraclough (1968: 104ff.).

[3] 22 July 1152. Cox: "The cardinals in question were John Paparo, cardinal-priest of San Adriano (1151–54) and Jordan, cardinal-priest of Santa Suzanna (1145–54). John of Salisbury offers highly unflattering portraits of both Jordan and John Paparo in his *Memoirs of the Papal Court* (Chibnall [1956: 12, 71–72, 75–78]). John is accused of accepting bribes while on a mission to France in 1148, and of threatening to create sedition in Rome during a dispute with the pope in 1151, 'for he (John) was ingenious in planning stratagems. . . .' Jordan, a Carthusian monk, is depicted as a religious hypocrite with a scandalous reputation for avarice and dishonesty, which earned him several humiliating rebukes. There is a scathing denunciation of Cardinal Jordan in the letters of St. Bernard of Clairvaux, but John Paparo is described as 'a credit to his ministry' (James [1953] no. 355)."

[4] I Samuel 13:11–14; 14; 15:10–31, etc.; Acts of the Apostles 9.

cardinal sought a truce from him for the purpose of celebrating the solemnities of the blessed Mary Magdalene in the wonted manner, with feast-day worship amidst the assemblies of pilgrims and locals. With some difficulty a truce was obtained for a week and Cardinal John and Abbot Pons came to Vézelay, where they were joined by Jordan, cardinal legate of the Gauls. They spent the holy days at Vézelay together.

17
The Count Tries to Turn the Church's Subjects at Vézelay from Their Subjection [1606B/433. 727]

1152

In the meantime the count, having returned from the king, came down to Vézelay and occupied the level spot where King Louis, about to become a pilgrim (of the Lord), had taken up the sign of Christ's Cross.[1] When the more influential[2] among the men of Vézelay had gathered together to hear him, he spoke to them thus, summoning forth profuse, impure tears from his cupidinous eyes, with a pretense of compassion: "O most illustrious men, so famous for your great prudence, so vigorous in your fortitude, and so rich with the proper gains of your great talents, I really grieve to see the wretched condition of your status: in appearance you are the possessors of many things, but in fact you are effective lords of nothing: you do not even enjoy a trace of the freedom that is your birthright. When I see before me such superb farms, such excellent vineyards,[3] such copious streams, such abundant meadow, such fertile fields, such dense woods, such apple orchards, such conspicuous dwellings—all of which the area itself places within your grasp,[4] without your being able to enjoy the fruits of them at all—when I look upon all this, I say, I have compassion on you, in no small degree. I am at a loss, I am thoroughly stunned. Where now is your once famed valour? To what degree of sloth has it sunk? You men, who once killed the most prudent—and liberal enough—abbot Artaud, just for two billetings a year![5] Yet you put up

---

[1] *crucis Christi tropheum sustulerat*: the plain of Asquins on the northern slope of the town, where St. Bernard had preached the second crusade. See above 160n.2.

[2] *potiori parte hominum Vizeliacensium.*

[3] On the qualities of the wines of Vézelay see Guizot (1969: 247n.79). Cf. also below 186n.6.

[4] *quae ipso situ in circuitu vestro sunt omnia.*

[5] *ob duas tantum domorum stationes.* Niermeyer gives, among less likely meanings for the last word: "temporary residence, siege, castle ward/feudal service, dwelling house, stall in a market," but the reference is probably to the long-standing dispute over rights of hospitality: 143n.2, 157n.2 above and the 1137 *Accord* (Appendix B below) §§ 6, 7, 8, etc. Berlow (1971: 123) translates, "because of a matter of two requisitions of houses": Artaud had required that the burghers receive the guests of the monastery at Easter and during the feast of the Magdalene. Cox: "The *statio* was the obligation to furnish accommodations for guests of the abbey and pilgrims of note visiting Vézelay ... for the householders [of Vézelay] the *statio* represented a double hardship: not only the expense of providing for

in such a stupid manner with this foreigner from Auvergne, this man who is
ferocious when he is in town, cruel when he is absent from it, arrogant in his
speech, plebeian in his habits, this man who battens off your goods, and even
your very life itself:[1] I can only compare [this insanity] to that of the wild
beasts. Finally, for the progress and consummation of your destruction, your
lord abbot contrives to seize away and take from me the right of legitimate
advocacy, by which I am charged to guard you and make answer for you; your
abbot does this that he might the more freely impose upon you in your destitute state extortionate customs.[2] For these reasons, dearest ones, I appeal to
your prudence and magnanimity, that you take counsel in this moment of
pressing necessity, and withdraw allegiance [*declinetis*] from that man, who
debauches himself in so tyrannical a manner where you are concerned, knowing that with myself on your side, no mischance will befall you, just as you
know that if on the other hand you show loyalty to my adversary, there will be
no salvation for you. But if, however, you swear among yourselves a mutual
confederacy[3] and take an oath of loyalty[4] to me also, then, wherever you
enjoy my guardianship, I will strive to free you from every corrupt exaction
that might arise from evil customs, and I will defend you against the violent
incursions of evil men."[5]

18

The Citizens of Vézelay Decline to Offer Agreement to
the Count   [1607A/434. 766]

1152

Having said these things, with frequent interruptions of simulated expressions
of grief, the count was silent. The men of Vézelay, in reply to him, said: "We
have sworn fidelity under oath to our lord, and however iniquitously he
abuses us, we think it nevertheless wrong to betray our loyalty. Indeed, when
we have become more certain of our counsel,[6] we will reply to you in your
presence on these matters at a predetermined day in a nearby place." Then,
coming to the abbot, they told him what the count had said and asked what
advice he could give them on the matter. The abbot spoke thus: "It cannot
have escaped your wisdom, my faithful ones [*fideles mei*] that the count has

---

the visitors, but also the loss of the income they would normally have received from
renting out any spare room."

[1] I.e., Pons. This description of Pons is so unfavorable that it suggests a measure of authenticity: perhaps Hugh heard what the count was alleged to have said from an eyewitness, or even heard it directly himself.

[2] *exactorias consuetudines.*

[3] *mutuam confederationem.* See Aspects [B:II] above.

[4] *iurantes ad me quoque fidelitatem servare volueritis.*

[5] Compare the features of the *gravis figura* for *orationes* in *Rhetorica ad Herennium*
4.8.12 and note the use of such *colores* as *repetitio, similiter cadens, gradatio*, etc.

[6] *consilio initio certiores effecti.*

one reason and one alone for carrying on his enmity with me: he wishes to ensnare you more fully in servitude to him by terminating my lordship over you, a lordship characterized by complete liberty.[1] I myself have labored unceasingly up to now for your liberty and if it is your wish to repay me with so impious a return of ingratitude that you would not fear to become the betrayers of myself and the church, your mother, then, even though alone, I will endure, though full of groans and confused, the damage to the church and your own destruction, whilst you and your children will pay forever the penalty of betrayal. However, if, relying upon wise advice, you will prudently consult your best interests and keep without hesitation the loyalty you have sworn to me and to the church which nourished you with its own milk[2] and brought you up, and labor constantly with me against all attackers, for liberty and salvation and your own glory and upright reputation, I will spare no efforts for you, never doubting that favorable times will follow unfavorable and that after the many storms of trials and upsets, we shall be given the serenity of peace at some stage or other."

The citizens [*illi*], however, replied: "We believe and hope all things will turn out as you anticipate. Nevertheless it seems advisable to us that you should give up the lawsuit against the count and yield to your adversary, entering into a peace with him. But, if you think otherwise, we are still certainly yours and will remain so. Do not doubt that we stand by you as loyal dependants [*fideles*], everywhere and in all things." The abbot answered : "It is not I who initiate any lawsuit—I simply make reply and defense [to the count who] involves me in a lawsuit. Again, if I were to yield to my adversary in the present case, I would be signing with my own hand a document of the maddest cowardice and constant confusion. In fact, I have often sought peace, by prayer and by service;[3] even more often have I offered peace; with the most insistent frequency have I demanded it, but I could not procure it from that son of discord. If then, as you say, you stand on the side of our common salvation, I pledge my every effort towards your salvation and liberty, and, together with you, I will undergo every misfortune and blind chance, placing my trust in virtue and justice."

---

[1] *erepto quod plenum est libertate dominio*. On this curious notion of "liberty" see Tellenbach (1966: chap. 5).

[2] Isaiah 1:2 (Huygens).

[3] *tam prece quam obsequio*, the latter term probably implying not only "good turns," such as looking after the count's goods and family while he was away on crusade, but also "feudal service"—attendance at the count's court.

19
Conspiracy of the Young Men Against the Abbot[1]

[1607D/435. 806]

1152

With these words the abbot dismissed them. But lo! Wicked men flocked
forth, pouring out venom long hidden in the lurking-places of their cruel conscience, and, gathering to themselves a vast throng of criminally inclined
youths, drew up and confirmed a mutual pact [foedus] of wickedly conspiratorial intent against their lord, that man of most just moderation and inborn
piety, betraying their hitherto pretended loyalty and cutting themselves off
from the church their mother. Gathering on the day fixed and at the determined place, they formed a confederacy with the tyrant and foreswore their
legal lord.[2] Swearing one by one their mutual loyalty to an execrated commune,[3] clasping the hand of the tyrant and conspiring against their chief in
order to throw off from their necks the yoke of the church's liberty, they
transferred their loyalties to the count, who swore that he would never, ever,
fail them in advice or help, whatever the emergency. The count then chose
for them leaders or magistrates whom they decreed should in fact [et] be
called consuls.[4] This development did not escape the betrayed[5] lord abbot,
nor the cardinals, who, as was said, had been summoned to the festival.

20
The Cardinals Try to Deter the Townsmen from What
They Had Begun

[1608B/435. 822]

1152

Then the elders among the people, who seemed to be their heads,[6] came

---

[1] See Graham (1918: 97). Berlow (1971: 321) asserts that "the prominence of the
young men prior to the formation of the commune suggests the creation of a local militia
to take over local peace-keeping functions. After the return of the abbot in 1155, arms
and shields were found in the houses of the rebels who had fled."

[2] *confederati sunt tiranno, legitimo domino suo abiurato.*

[3] *paciscentes ad invicem per manum tyranni execratam communiam.* Cf. Bloch (1961: plates
2 and 3). Compare the language of Guibert of Nogent *De vita sua* 3 §§7 and 10 (ed.
Benton [1970: 167 and 183]; ed. Labande [1981: 320, 360]).

[4] *constituitque illis principes vel iudices, quos et consules appellari censuerunt.* Elsewhere
Hugh uses the term *consul* to describe the natural leaders of Burgundian society (*comites,
duces,* etc.), but here the southern French and Italian practice of applying the name to city
magistrates is at the bottom of the matter, together, of course, with the prestige of the
term used in classical documents and histories to describe the ancient Roman republic's
most prestigious officers. See Bastard (1848: 538ff.), Berlow (1971: 321), and Reynolds
(1984: 170ff.).

[5] The *PL* text has *praedictum,* "aforesaid"; Huygens reads *proditum,* "betrayed."

[6] *maiores natu quique capita populi esse videbantur.* See the important note in Huygens
(1976) to 435. 822-23, and the discussion in Aspects [B] above.

before the cardinals, and, relying on the authority of their perfidious act, demanded that certain customs which the townsmen felt were both novel and tyrannical be rescinded. The cardinals replied to them: "Since it is our duty to offer to you all equally as sons of the Roman church, our careful solicitude, we will persuade the abbot, with all our compassion and goodwill to effect a result that joins peace and your advantage to every upright and proper consideration. We are aware, moreover, that the abbot is of such a gentle disposition that, lending an ear irrevocably to our advice, he will grant with clemency whatever the principles of equity[1] demand. But, your present course of action compels him in defense of common liberty and your welfare to risk the greatest of danger. It is therefore necessary for you to bring to him the pledge of your assistance in all things and to work with him for your own sakes. As things are now, you endanger your entire welfare. If any taint of conspiracy should attach to any one of you against your lord the abbot—and we can scarcely believe this—then it must at once be abjured, purged, corrected. Then, whatever just complaint you have can be settled with due regard to the rights of the church." The abbot also spoke to them: "You can see," he said, "how gravely I am oppressed and harried by the count, to whom you have given your hand, conspiring mutually against me, to your ruin. It is therefore iniquitous that, joined together in evil strength, you should seem to grasp—rather than ask for—a remission [of certain customs]; it is, I say, iniquitous that you should have as a remission what has been extorted and exacted. But if you completely abandon the evil arrangements into which you have entered, you will not only deserve a remission, but also a pardon, as befits our gentleness." But the townsmen, shouting out together, said they would not meet these conditions but rather would carry forward their rebellion against the church.

21

The Cardinals, Having Discussed the Controversy Ineffectively, and Repelled by the Count, Go Away

[1608D/436. 851]

1152

The cardinals next begged the count to put the discord to rest and quell the anger in his heart towards the abbot. He pretended to listen to them, but when they had pleaded with him for a long time, swore that he would admit no concord at all until he received everything which he claimed was his right in law. Then, after a while, the abbot complained in the presence of the cardinals, of his enemies, Geoffrey of Arcy and others whom the count had impelled towards destruction of the church. The count replied that those men were not members of his household [*familia*] nor his soldiery [*militia*] and for

---

[1] *ratio aequitatis.*

that reason perpetrated this outrage to the abbot of their own will, not at his—the count's—direction.[1] The cardinals then decreed that they be smitten with the sword of anathema[2] as devastators of the church. The count opposed this judgment, saying that they were his men and that he would produce them for the carriage of justice if the abbot would reply to himself and to the townsmen on the items the latter had objected to.[3] A day was therefore fixed at Chablis for examining those things about which the count had made wrongful accusations and the cardinals set out from Vézelay on the ninth of the month, in great fear, keeping the abbot between them on account of the conspiracy of the traitors [*infidelium*] who had sworn to kill him. When they reached Chablis the cardinals commanded the count to set forth his case. When he had done so he demanded that the abbot, whom he had summoned to the case, submit himself to justice, as much on his [the count's] own account as on account of the men of Vézelay. To the cardinals and other wise men who were there, it did not seem fit that such things should be demanded of an abbot. Justice was instead offered to the count according to the tenor of the apostolic precept. The count, however, refused this justice, unjust as he was, refused this judgment, villain as he was.[4] Apostolic letters were read out in his presence, in which a sentence of excommunication against him was promulgated, unless he came to his senses. The count was very indignant at this and for a long time refused the cardinals a safe-conduct through his lands. The notable people who were there were at length able to persuade him with difficulty to allow them a permit. He would not, however, issue the abbot a permit of safe-conduct[5] unless he agreed to go directly back to Vézelay. The abbot was not minded to go back there since his own wicked men had conspired against him. The bishop of Nevers took the abbot in his train, on the instruction of the cardinals from the Holy See, and led him from the church of Chablis right up to the dock at Saint-Ayeul.[6] Pass-

---

[1] Despite Hugh's assertion above 2 §15 *instigat satrapas!*

[2] On "anathema" see Cross (1974: 50).

[3] *ad interpellata*; possibly, "the items the latter had wanted remission of." Note the contrast between *nec de familia nec de militia* and *homines suos esse*. Cox translates *homines* here as "vassals," but elsewhere as "men."

[4] *ille autem iusticiam ut iniustus et iudicium ut iniquus recusavit.*

[5] *dextras fiducie.*

[6] According to Huygens (1976: xviii n.16) the scribe of MS. 227 has here confused *portus Sancti Maioli* (the name being given in honor of Saint Mayeul, abbot of Cluny, who re-established strict observance of the Benedictine rule in the monastery of Saint-Germain) with *portus Sancti Aioli*, Saint-Ayeul being a hermitage in the commune of Guillon, Avallon district, near which was situated a ford across the Serein and which is referred to in Chablis, described in the current English Michelin *Guide to Burgundy-Morvan* as the "Golden Gateway" to Burgundy, "the wine capital of Lower Burgundy" (in the sixteenth century there were more than 700 vineyard owners in the district) is situated on the river Serein, one of the tributaries of the Yonne (which is itself a tributary of the Seine), about 20 kilometers east of Auxerre and about twice that distance north of Vézelay, which is situated on the Cure, another tributary of the Yonne. Between Vézelay and Avallon lies the Cousin, a tributary of the Cure. Hugh's language at this point (*Quem assumens episcopus Nivernensis ... ab ecclesia*

ing through there the abbot turned his course to Montot,[1] where he remained for some days.

22

The Townsmen of Vézelay Adhere to the Count   [1609D/437. 888]

1152

The traitorous men of Vézelay, for their part, adding sacrilege to perjury, adhered to the count, and forgot their benefactor[2] [the abbot] who enriched them when they were reduced to need and beggary, and filled their hands with all good things when they were homeless and without resource; forgot, I say, God himself, and, turning from him, worshipped Gods whom they knew not,[3] submitting their necks to the count, and other tyrants of the province, giving themselves and their goods to them, and, fornicating in the pride of their eyes, they stained the holy seed,[4] as much as was in them, and adul-

---

Iabliaci eum eduxit et ad Portum usque Sancti Aioli perduxit. Quo permeato ad Montetum . . .) suggests that the abbot left the church in Chablis (probably St. Martin, the collegiate church of the canons of St. Martin of Tours, and near the Serein, or else St. Pierre, further away from the Serein—see Speaight [1990: 67–70]) and was conducted to the harbor (of Chablis?) as far as Saint-Ayeul. This would have the abbot and bishop of Nevers travelling by boat along the Serein, some 40 kilometers to the hermitage of Saint-Ayeul, "situated on a hill which looks to the north over the hamlet of Perrigny, itself about one and a half kilometers from Montot [*Montetum*], a dependency of Vézelay" (Huygens [1976: xxviii n.16]). Huygens, however, takes *ad portum usque Sancti Aioli* to mean "as far as the harbor near Saint-Ayeul," and it, in the knowledge that the river Serein was no more navigable in the twelfth century than it is today, considers that *portus* must mean a "ford" rather than a harbor, and that the bishop and abbot travelled by road between Chablis and St. Ayeul. Given the meandering course of the Serein this seems very likely: the road perhaps led from Chablis to Noyers and down to Montréal (on the route from Montbard to Avallon) near which the "ford" across the Serein lay. The modern road system from Noyers to Guillon crosses the road from the D905 route between Tonnerre and Montbard some 6 kilometers before Guillon. About halfway between that intersection and Montréal, en route to Avallon, one would have crossed the Serein. There are, therefore, two anomalies in the text of Hugh's chronicle at this point: the reference to a *portus* when a ford is meant and the description of the *portus* as that of St. Maiolus (Mayeul) rather than St. Aiolus (Ayeul). For boat/river transport elsewhere in the *Major Chronicle*, see below 4 §§56–57.

   [1] A hamlet in the commune of Guillon (Huygens). The abbot would thus have been some 25 kilometers west of his town of Vézelay. Cox observes as follows: "There is considerable divergence among scholars as to which place is meant here. Constable thinks it was Le-Montet-aux-Moines near Moulins, but there was a property called *Montetum* (now Montot) belonging to the abbey of Vézelay and located a dozen miles northeast of Avallon in the duchy of Burgundy. Vogade [Guizot (1969: 249)] identifies Montetum as the Montot located near Annay-sur-Serein, but this identification agrees neither with what is known of Vézelay's holdings, nor with the abbot's need to get well into the territories of the duke of Burgundy and away from the region dominated by the count of Nevers-Auxerre, as he made his way to Cluny in southern Burgundy."

   [2] Isaiah 51:13.

   [3] Deut. 32:17–18.

   [4] *semen*, i.e., the nurturing seed or shoot from which they sprang, as sons of the church: see the "blossoming plant" image used in Hugh's chronicle of the "liberty of Vézelay" above 2 §4.

terated the chastity of the incorruptible church. The tyrant himself, over and above all the evils which he had caused the monastery, seized whatever lay beyond the boundaries of the town, and inflicted many other evils full of cruelty and barbarism. To the above he added the fostering of those deserters of God and the Church[1] against all justice and apostolic privileges, and himself impelled them to these things with various promises and blandishments; he himself incited them with threats and terrors, promising in addition that he would never make peace with the abbot, never agree to the concord the abbot wanted, without them.

23

The Townsmen of Vézelay Plunder Everything Belonging to the Abbot, Harry the Monks and Overturn Buildings [1610A/437. 905]

1152

Relying therefore on the count's help and conspiring by his counsel, the townsmen went forth like mice from their holes, red hot with evil,[2] rose up against the church their mother and like an abyss overwhelmed her, like the sea engulfed her[3]—the townsmen [oppidani], or those who are called burghers [burgenses], who once passed for sons of the church and are now become her enemies, the more troublesome for being so intimate. Once they had found out that the abbot had secretly departed from them,[4] they violated the holy temple of the church, occupied its towers, stocked them with guards, food, and arms, and, adding insult to injury, inflicted disgraceful wrongs upon the monks, servants of God and their lords, and shut them up hidden to all behind the walls of the monastery, lost to all human help and deprived of all necessities, allowing none to go forth, anywhere, without an escort. On top of all this, they invaded the servile farms [colonias], usurped as well the rights of the monastery and its accustomed revenues, plundered several houses belonging to the church, and destroyed farms, mills, and every kind of equipment [suppellectilem], sparing neither movables nor immovables in their fury, smashing the fortifications and enclosures of the monastery to the ground. By day and by night they hatched plots, schemes, ambushes, and malignant machinations in the market-places,[5] conspiring to a man and daily threatening graver evils on top of wrongs, the worst of evils on top of graver ones.

Meanwhile the most vigilant abbot Pons set out for Cluny,[6] where the

---

[1] I.e., the townsmen of Vézelay.

[2] prorumpentes torrentes Belial; cf. Judith 14:12 and 2 Kings 22:5.

[3] Jonas 2:6.

[4] Cf. above §21.

[5] conciliabulis; cf. Psalms 82:4.

[6] On Cluny and its relations with Vézelay see Aspects [A] above. Guizot (1969: 249n.83b) provides some information to illustrate the power and might of the abbey of

cardinals and legates of the Holy See had gathered with many religious and upright persons. When he had made known to them what vast evils the profane citizens of Vézelay had inflicted on his monastery, he beseeched them to seek from the abbot of Cluny—his brother in fact—that the latter grant him a small cell where he could go in safety and search for peace. His hearers took compassion on his affliction and beseeched the abbot of Cluny to bestow pity and compassion on his own brother, placed as he was in the greatest of straits, and, in order to relieve his exile, graciously to concede to him the monastery of Souvigny[1] until his tribulations were quieted. The abbot of Cluny, nodding assent to their petition, promised to do so shortly when a suitable place had been located.[2] Abbot Pons then suggested to his brother and the senior monks of Cluny that they should press the cardinals to promulgate a sentence of anathema on his sacrilegious and perfidious betrayers at Vézelay and their backers. They baulked at this, however, and prevaricated a little, but the cardinals saw fit to expedite the matter about which the abbot was insistent.

24

A Sentence of Excommunication and Interdict is
Pronounced Against Them [the townsmen]   [1610D/438. 945]

1152

A sentence was therefore pronounced which cut off the infamous malefactors, violators of holy things, and betrayers of themselves, from the body of Christ, that is the Catholic Church, by the sword of anathema. The abbot begged them [the cardinals], since they had seen his case with their own eyes[3] and had felt it with their own hands, to explain it wholly to the lord pope. He entrusted his own envoy into their hands, to bring back the sentence of the universal pontiff upon the count, and returned to Montot with the sentence (*libellum*) of excommunication against the traitors at Vézelay. When he sent the sentence of the Romans to Vézelay and commanded it to be read, the priests, gathering together in one of the chapels of Saint-Pierre-

---

Cluny in the twelfth century. It commanded 1,450 subordinate houses ("priories") and numbered 10,000 monks throughout France, Germany, Italy, Spain, and England. Its abbot carried the title of "abbot of abbots" and the adage was popular stating that "wherever the wind blows, the abbot of Cluny collects rent." The abbey of Cluny itself sheltered some 18,000 poor in a year. See Speaight (1990: 332–38), Evans (1931a), and Schmitt (1984: 501).

    [1] An important priory dependent on Cluny. Pons had made his debut into the monastic life there. In charter 50 above Pope Eugenius III commands Peter of Cluny to grant the monastery of Souvigny to Pons while he is in exile.

    [2] *explorato loco congruo:* Peter evidently felt Souvigny was not suitable or available. See below §25. Pons's action in thus deserting his abbey is curious.

    [3] Luke 24:39.

le-Haut,[1] expounded the sentence to the whole people and anathematised publicly those who were designated by name, placing an interdict on the rest, including the entire vill, as far as the celebration of divine office and the other gifts of grace bestowed by the church were concerned, excepting only baptism of the very young and administration of confession to the dying. Certain of the sacrilegious townsmen were enraged and attacked the priest who read out the sentence. The first of these was Odo de l'Étang[2] who threw off his coat and went looking for stones to throw at him; then David Long-beard[3] and his son Robert loosed their coats and pulled off their clogs[4] in order to hit the priest, and, had not others intervened, would have broken him into a thousand pieces. As it was, the priest, fleeing towards the altar, scarcely escaped the hands of the impious townsmen. On the following day, the leaders and fomenters of all this evil found the great doors of the church taken off their hinges and the entrance obstructed with brambles. These leaders, Hugh and Peter, both with the cognomen of St. Peter, took away the thorns and put the doors back on their hinges.[5] They carried off the goblet, bible, and priestly vestments from the church of St. Stephen, in the course of which they injured a cleric who was resisting their sacrilege. Afterwards, with a great shout of fury, they broke into the monastic cloisters and grievously as-sailed and abused the prior, Hilduin and certain brothers who were assisting him, protesting about the excommunication and demanding a pause in the hostilities with a great deal of arrogance. When the prior was unwilling to ac-cede to this demand, the townsmen made answer to him thus: "Since you ex-communicate us without cause, we shall provide you with one. We shall no longer pay to you the tithes [decimas] poll-tax [censum], and other accustomed dues." Then they had recourse to the count and complained of the sentence of excommunication. "I cannot," he said, "do much about that: they will ex-communicate me too if they wish." The townsmen then said: "But how will we grind our grain and bake our bread? The monks will not let us use their mills".[6] The count returned with "Go and light up an oven [clibanum] from your own wood and bake the bread. If anyone tries to stop you, burn him alive. If the mill-operator obstructs you, crush him to death with the mill-stone."

---

[1] See Aspects [C] above.

[2] Odo de Palude, Eudes du Marais. See Berlow (1980), and Huygens (1976: 666, s.v. palus). *Palus* and *marais* both = "march, bog," and *étang* = "pond, pool." Étang, according to Huygens, was a hamlet some kilometers to the south-west of Vézelay.

[3] David *Longabarba, Longue-Barbe.*

[4] *patinos suos.*

[5] The removal of the doors and their replacement with brambles were part of the ritual associated with interdiction. For Hugh see above §9. This is the first mention of St. Peter, who is described—as far as can be discerned from the mutilated folios of Book 3 of the Major Chronicle at this point (Huygens [1976: 474. 473–75])—as *accinctus balteo ... istius factionis dux et signifer* ("girded with his sword-belt ... the leader and standard-bearer of that infamous faction"), and is mentioned again at 3 §3 below (as is Hugh) and several times in the list of names at the end of Book 3.

[6] Literally: "the monks do not want to grind with us."

25

The Townsmen, Not Heeding the Excommunication, Assail the Monks with Insults   [1611D/440. 988]

1152

Excited by these and similar replies, the townsmen returned to redouble the evils. Thus it happened that whatever losses, injuries, or adversity they selected, they inflicted upon the monastery. They expelled the servants [*pueros*] of the church from their houses, harried them with whips, and with much boasting vowed that they would beat the monks to such a degree that even their very feet would require absolution. Entirely rejecting, therefore, the power of the abbot or the church over them, they set at nought the sentence promulgated against them and, taking not the least pains to avoid entering the holy church, they accumulated their sins, neither fearing God, nor revering his sanctuaries. The prior complained of all these doings, and others of the kind, in the presence of the count. He, uttering depraved and perverse remarks, replied that the townsmen had done well, and, speaking out in exaggerated tones, said "Would that we could get rid of all the monks and destroy the monastery completely! Why did the abbot excommunicate them?" Then, extracting a hair from the garment he was wearing, he added, "If the whole hill on which Vézelay stands were to be plunged deep into an abyss, I would not give this hair to get it back. I put you in charge of the treasury of the church; take care that you set guard over the oblations,[1] lest the abbot should have or get hold of anything therefrom. It is because of the abbot[2] that I wish the burghers to dissipate everything, to scatter everything, especially those who are in league with him."[3] It happened too that the townsmen themselves buried a man who had died while the anathema was still in force, without a priest; they sounded the bells[4] themselves and drove the priest from his house.

While the abbot was delaying at Montot,[5] news was brought to the abbot of Cluny that the abbot of Vézelay, sending to Rome, would ask the highest pontiff for the monastery of Souvigny.[6] The abbot of Cluny took this ill[7] and put off executing his promise[8] by prevarication. He feared, moreover, that an

---

[1] *oblationes*; gifts of the faithful (Niermeyer [1976: 728]).

[2] *cuius gratia*, referring back to *ille* (Huygens [1976: 440. 1006]), presumably the abbot (so Guizot).

[3] *illos qui de ipsius confederatione sunt.*

[4] Niermeyer (1976: 871 § 2), *signa pulsantes.*

[5] He must have returned there after his visit to Cluny, §23 above.

[6] Graham (1918: 102).

[7] As is hinted at §23 above.

[8] To give Pons a suitable cell for repose and tranquillity (§23 above). Cox notes that Pons was, in fact, installed as abbot at Souvigny in 1152 at the request of Eugenius III, but Anastasius IV ordered the withdrawal of this concession in 1154.

anathema might perhaps be promulgated against the count and his land and
that this would endanger the several monasteries under the care of Cluny in
the territory of the count. He therefore entrusted to the count, by way of his
own intimate servants, the following advice:[1] "All of us who choose the name
of Christianity cannot entirely escape apostolic censure. You will have done
well, therefore, if you commit yourself to trust in good hope, and make peace
with the abbot of Vézelay by our mediation. It will be our duty so to consult
the interest of both sides that some profit should accrue to you from the
peace." Having accepted such advice, the count acquiesced and sent another
senior monk,[2] Bernard, prior of Saint-Étienne [at Nevers] to the abbot of
Vézelay, whose death the count thirsted for more than he did for all the vari-
eties of spiced wine.[3] The prior, therefore, coming to the abbot, proclaimed
the latter's vigorous constancy and magnanimity, but asserted that if his
pertinacity should be softened by his virtue, it would do his monastery no
harm at all. In the same spirit he encouraged the abbot to be of good cheer
in his adversity as an assurance of the uprightness he would display in
prosperity. He pointed out that the fortunes of war were always uncertain,
and that nothing, he felt, was more secure, more calming, more sure than
peace, however difficult it might seem at present to obtain. Nevertheless he
declared the count would grant a peace, by way of a pact, if the abbot would
deign to receive it through the mediation of the abbot of Cluny. One ought
not hold in suspicion someone born and bred of the same blood:

A relative [*identitas*], however closely related, [who is] resisting like an
enemy,
Will, having forgotten his own interests, remain true if judgment is left
to him.[4]

26

They Meet at Luzy Where Peace Is Discussed[5]   [1612D/441. 1039]

1152

The abbot placed his trust in the prior and believed that prejudice could not

---

[1] See Constable (1967: 2:13n.57).

[2] *quasi sempectam Bernardum: Rule of St. Benedict* 27. 2–3. Cox: "A sempect was a
Benedictine monk who had been in the order for at least fifty years and was exempt from
the more onerous monastic duties."

[3] *cuius mortem sitiebat pigmentis omnibus prestantiorem.*

[4] The last lines, within quotation marks, are in hexameter verse, though no source is
known for them and their tortuous construction suggests Hugh is again trying his hand at
literature: *cum sit affinis repugnans identitas hostis, / immemor ipsa sui se iudice victa manebit.*
Cox translates: "one ought not to be suspicious of someone born of the same blood, for
although a relative in opposition is the same as an enemy, kinship with itself as judge,
forgetting enmity, will remain." See too charter 64 above.

[5] Graham (1918: 103); Guizot (1969: 75).

enter into it when his whole case rested so squarely on justice. There gathered together, therefore, the abbots of Cluny and Vézelay, and the count of Nevers at Luzy,[1] a town in the diocese of Autun. Also present were Stephen, abbot of San Michele della Chiusa[2] and [Peter][3] the abbot of Moissac,[4] and also some other weighty Cluniac personages. When all these had sat down together and several ill-merited requests had been unjustly made by the count, those who had gathered to play the role of advocate, under an appearance of piety and favoring the opposing party rather than the party with whom justice lay, composed a draft of peace,[5] inimical to the liberty [of the church of Vézelay], liable, indeed, to promote its servitude, and bound to prove quite unstable. They then urged Abbot Pons to accept what brotherly love and friendly disposition[6] had arranged concerning a peace. In this way he would buy time and satisfy the present necessity, consoling himself with the thought that his opponent would secure less than he wished for. The abbot wisely put to them on a number of occasions the reverence they ought to have towards the holy[7] and the degree to which his probity would be compromised by the suggested arrangements and repeatedly begged them not to press him in this way, lest impiety [= the count] should seem to derive profit at the expense of the servants of piety [= the abbot and the monks].[8] Then the count asserted roundly that if the abbot would acquiesce in the arrangements suggested by such a throng of friends, he himself would dissolve the commune or sacrilegious confederation of the abbot's men, and utterly abolish it, and would establish the abbot back in his monastery, safe and sound, with the fullest rights of lordship preserved for him. But since many points were still being debated and the abbot was insisting upon his objections, accommodation gave way to confusion. At length, intending to take further counsel later at Nevers,[9] they set an end to this discussion and conclusion of peace. The tyrant therefore sent to the leaders of the traitorous conspiracy and ordered them to take an interest in a future concord. The abbot also instructed the prior and certain other brothers of his monastery to

---

[1] Twenty-eight kilometers southwest from Autun, a fief of the count of Nevers. "This medieval town is a pleasant spot on the banks of the Alène on the southern edge of the Morvan region. The 14th century tower of the barons of Luzy still stands on the highest point" (Michelin, Burgundy-Morvan, 106). Luzy lies south of the main road between Autun and Nevers, en route to Moulins.

[2] Founded by the great-grandfather of Pons.

[3] Gap left in MS for insertion of name, Peter, which was not, in fact, filled in.

[4] Affiliated with Cluny in the eleventh century, but founded in time of Dagobert (623–39 AD).

[5] *quandam formam pacis.*

[6] *socialis dispositio.*

[7] *numen.* See Lewis & Short (1933) for the associations of this word.

[8] This sentence has been much expanded in translation.

[9] *tandem inito consilio Nivernis.* Guizot (1969: 76): "l'assemblée ayant tenu conseil s'ajourna à Nevers." Possibly: "on the advice of the count of Nevers" See the beginning of the next section of the *Major Chronicle.*

meet him, having first consulted all the monks in assembly to see whether
they felt the peace arranged between himself and the count by the abbot of
Cluny[1] should be approved. The monks democratically and unanimously
resolved to write[2] to their lord and most vigilant father [to the effect] that
whatever his fatherly providence decreed or established would remain sure,
firm, and undisturbed, as far as they were concerned, saving only their own
rights and privileges and those of the liberty of the church.

27

The Monks of Cluny Also Cause Trouble   [1613C/442. 1074]

1152

As the peace-makers were now assembled at Nevers, the count sent certain
gifts and various goblets to Abbot Pons to make a display of his simulated
pacific inclinations. Seeing this, the sacrilegious traitors[3] were confused and
feared that they had been deserted by their tyrant. The count then went to
the abbot of Cluny and was advised abundantly by him concerning the
refurbishing of the peace with his [the abbot of Cluny's] brother. But he [the
count], with many protestations swore that he cherished none more dearly
than the abbot [of Vézelay]; nevertheless, the latter should not expect anything from him [the count] which would not minister to his [the count's]
profit and reputation, and, saying these things on his knees, while grasping
the abbot of Cluny's hands with both his own hands, he wiped away the
dirty[4] tears with which his fraudulent face was copiously suffused. Meanwhile,
since the monks of Cluny were secretly entering into some dealings concerning the peace arrangements and were keeping all the colleagues of the abbot
[of Vézelay] at a distance from their own meeting, the monks of Vézelay
became suspicious and some of them, afraid that under the appearance of
peace some prejudicial and ignominious condition would be imposed upon
them all, had an audience with the abbot of Cluny. On the authority of God
and his apostles and on behalf of the Vézelay Chapter, they denounced and
repudiated the recent developments, lest anything contrary to the rights, dignity and privileges of the monastery should be worked into the conditions of
the peace. The abbot of Cluny grew angry at this and instructed that his
departure be arranged. Calling his brother to him he upbraided him thus:
"What do you think you are doing? Why do you so rudely dishonor me? Do
you think I am mad—or a child? I work day and night for your peace and
quiet; I watch over without hesitation your interests and success, but you, for
your part, destroy what I have accomplished; what I accumulate, you dissi-

---

[1] *per iam prescriptam manum.*
[2] *qui pari et unanimi sententia rescripserunt domino suo. . . .*
[3] I.e., the townsmen of Vézelay.
[4] *lutulentas lacrimas*: see Lewis & Short (1933) for the associations of the former word.

pate, what I collect, you disperse, and what I acclaim openly for the sake of bringing you peace, you secretly undo by vilifying me. Since then, my labors seem of no use to you, bear your own burden yourself." The abbot of Vézelay marvelled at this outburst and asked who would have dared [to prompt the abbot of Cluny] to say such things. The monks of Cluny told him: William, surnamed of....[1]

[At this point in the Auxerre manuscript someone—possibly in the thirteenth century, and possibly to obliterate or confuse the record of certain names and developments—has cut some 26 folios in half, from top to bottom. Approximately half of each line has survived, enough to get the sense of developments but too little to permit a useful translation. To fill in this gap, therefore, we have taken the liberty of reproducing in an edited form, the reconstruction of events from the extant fragments of the Vézelay chronicle, from letters and other sources, to be found in Graham (1918: 104-17). To this we have added passages from Professor Cox's summary of the same events. See also Huygens (1976: xiii–xiv, xx–xxi, xxxviii and 85-137 [= Chérest]), Guizot (1969: no. 88, p. 250). Berlow (1971) argues persuasively that the mutilation probably occurred within about half a century of the writing of the *Major Chronicle*, when the rights of the count of Nevers over Vézelay—the subject of the mutilated pages—were still being disputed. There would be little point in such vandalism after 1213 when the abbot of Vézelay officially recognized the count of Nevers as protector of the monastery. The fragments from folios 91-116 of the Auxerre manuscript are printed in Huygens 443-96, with notes.]

[28]

1152–1153

"Pons was willing to make peace with the count, and they adjourned to the Cluniac monastery of La Charité on the Loire, twenty-four miles from Nevers, to draw up the settlement, which was then drafted by Thibaut [*Tetbaldus*] one of the count's clerks. The leaders of the burgesses were willing to abjure the Commune[2] and pay an indemnity, but could not pledge the rest of the burgesses without consulting them. Every one set out for Vézelay, and on the road there was a further dispute about the clauses which gave the count rights in Vézelay. Abbot Peter the Venerable abandoned his task of mediating between his brother and the count, and rode home to Cluny. Meanwhile Pons was expecting an answer from Rome to letters which he had written before the conference at Luzy, urging the pope to excommunicate both the count and the burgesses. As they had not arrived, he signed the agreement. The

---

[1] The fragmentary text of the chronicle at Huygens (1976: 443. 1104ff.) suggests a certain William "arrogantly" advised the abbot of Cluny along these lines.

[2] *confederationem abiurant*; Huygens (1976: 443. 1114 and cf. 445. 1188), *solutoque vinculo perfidae confed[erationis....*

burgesses came out to meet the count, who persuaded them to submit to Pons and give pledges for the payment of a considerable sum of money for damages.

"There was peace for a short time. However, when the abbot's servants tried to prevent certain persons from trespassing in the woods and damaging them, they offered violent resistance. The burgesses pulled down the house in which their pledges were kept and set up the commune again.[1] Pons appealed to the count for help.[2] The latter offered at first[3] to come to Véze-lay to judge between the abbot and the burgesses, but when Pons refused this suggestion,[4] the count was persuaded to summon the leaders to appear before him. According to the historian of Vézelay, the conspirators numbered three thousand.[5] Unfortunately Pons again damaged his cause by an act of violence and injustice, for he arrested the burgesses when they were on their way to the count's court and got new pledges of submission from them by force.[6]

"The people of Vézelay were goaded to fury. When Pons attempted to ride out of the monastery he was driven back by men armed with swords who tried to batter in the gates. The bishop of Nevers was at Vézelay, perhaps to keep the Easter festival in this year, 1153, and he calmed the people. The

---

[1] *domum ubi repositum pignus.* Huygens (1976: 446.1214; 1219): ... *nec communiam abiurabant.*

[2] Cox: "There was a meeting at the abbey of La Charité (Huygens 443.1112) and reference to a 'charter of Nevers' (Huygens 443.1129-30); but the passages which ensue suggest that these did not result in an acceptable treaty. There are charges of deceit and allusions to misunderstandings over the meaning of a charter drawn up by one of the count's secretaries (Huygens 444.1135-1151), and the abbot of Cluny apparently withdrew in a rage (Huygens 1152); but it seems that some kind of agreement was reached later between the count and abbot Pontius (Pons, Huygens 1154-1160). Conversations followed between the count and the 'conspirators' at Vézelay in which the count adjured them to return to obedience to the abbot, since he had made his own peace (Huygens 1163-1167). There was a meeting between the count and the rebel faction at Asquins (Huygens 445. 1175) where the latter claimed to be unable to pay what was probably a large fine imposed upon them (Huygens 1178). Soon after, violence erupted again; the 'sons of the church' and its officials were treated with contempt, the abbot's woods were damaged, and the house where things taken in pledge were kept was destroyed down to its foundations (Huygens 446.1202-1215). The abbot left for Tonnerre to complain of all this to the count (Huygens 447.1252-58), who apparently went to Vézelay and tried to persuade the rebels to submit. They refused, and amid strange apparitions and supernatural portents of disaster (Huygens 1252-58), abbot Pontius (Pons) again went to meet the count, at Ligny, and begged him to deliver his church from its oppressors (Huygens 448. 1259-1261)."

[3] Huygens (448.1261ff.): the count's speech seems to read: "I know that the common people [*plebeios*] and ... are inclined to every evil and cannot be dissuaded except by force, yet, if, with all pusillanimity set aside ... you should command me to come to Vézelay to ... decide the matter of the calumny, doubtless [you would secure a resolution of your problems and your enemies] would cease to kick against you. . . ."

[4] An invitation to the count to come and judge the case would constitute a tacit admission of the count's authority and so would compromise Vézelay's claims to judicial autonomy.

[5] Huygens 448.1274.

[6] *forte offendit aliquos ... pignus extorsit* (Huygens 448.1286-87).

count arrived and complained that sometimes the abbot invoked his protection and sometimes repulsed him. He had heard news of the coming sentence of excommunication, for the letters of Eugenius III, dated 19 December 1152, were delivered about Easter. He refused to help Pons against the burgesses, and promised them his help and protection.

"Eugenius III espoused the abbot's cause very hotly. If the count did not make restitution to the monastery for all the wrongs which he had done and leave it in peace and liberty within thirty days after the summons, the pope commanded the bishop of Langres to excommunicate the count and the traitorous burgesses[1] of Vézelay, and put all the count's lands under an interdict and send the papal letters to the bishops of the neighboring dioceses to see that the sentence was observed everywhere.[2]

"The pope had heard from Pons that the archpriest of Avallon and two priests had given communion to burgesses of Vézelay, knowing that they were excommunicated. If this had really happened the bishop of Langres must suspend them from their offices, and send them to the pope to answer for their presumption. He rebuked the bishop of Autun, who had allowed and even ordered the priests of his diocese to celebrate the sacraments for the burgesses whom he had incited against Pons. If any burgess of Vézelay should come to any place in the diocese no priest might celebrate the sacraments in his presence.

"In letters to the archbishop of Sens and the bishops of Langres, Paris, and Troyes, Eugenius III bade them prohibit the presence of any of the perjured traitorous and excommunicated burgesses of Vézelay at any fairs or markets in their dioceses and command their people to seize the burgesses and spoil their goods.[3] He wrote in the same vein to the duke of Burgundy, the count of Champagne, and their vassals.[4] Thus the burgesses were touched in their persons and their pockets as well as outcast from the Church.

"Eugenius III wrote to the bishop of Langres, not only because he had known him when they were both monks at Clairvaux, but because the bishop was such a near neighbor of Abbot Pons that he heard of all that happened at Vézelay. The choice was unfortunate for Pons. Bishop Godfrey was always hostile to Vézelay, and he had no wish to offend the count of Nevers. He was at Vézelay at Whitsuntide, but he put off sending the summons to the count and taking proceedings as the pope had commanded.

"On 8 July Eugenius III died. He was succeeded on 12 July by Conrad, bishop of Sabina, a Roman by birth, who took the name of Anastasius IV."

---

[1] Cf. Huygens (1976: 455.1495) for the phrase (*perfidis burgensibus*).
[2] Charter 35 above.
[3] Charters 36 and 49 above.
[4] Charter 37 above.

Book Three

Sept.– Oct. 1153

[Book 3 of the History begins at this point (Huygens [1976: 459] where Hugh commences with his usual lofty prefatory tone, "Among all the virtues of the mind . . .") "with a eulogy of Abbot Pons, praising in particular his equanimity as a man neither puffed up by prosperity nor cast down by adversity. He had apparently decided to withdraw to the abbey of Souvigny at this point, and while he was away negotiations among the contending parties resumed" (Cox). Graham (1918: chap. 6).]

[1]

1153–1155

"In the autumn of 1153 King Louis VII arrived at Vézelay on a pilgrimage to the shrine of St. Mary Magdalene when Pons was at the priory of Souvigny,[1] where he had gone to pray at the tomb of St. Mayeul,[2] one of the great abbots of Cluny. The burgesses of Vézelay made insinuations against their abbot, and the king sent the count of Nevers to summon Pons to appear before him. The abbot was afraid that the king was now prejudiced against him, so he tried to come to terms with the count, who refused to parley with him, saying, 'Every discussion with you is endless and peace is as fragile as a spider's web.'[3] He rode back in haste to the king and reported that the abbot had not followed him. The king was very angry and ordered the abbot to pay all the expenses of lodging for himself and his train at Vézelay on the ground that he had the right of procuration in all monasteries.[4] Pons consulted the monks in chapter and offered to pay the expenses of a voluntary procuration without recognizing the king's new claim to demand it as a right. Some months later the king's mother Adelaide de Savoy and her sister, the wife of Archibald de Bourbon, an enemy of the count of Nevers, came on a pilgrimage to Vézelay.[5] Afterwards Archibald and his wife interceded with the king

---

[1] See 2 §23 above.

[2] 2 §21, at 186n.6 above.

[3] Huygens (1976: 461.64–65 and 64n) for Jerome (*Commentary in ps.* 89) as source for the phrase about the spider's web.

[4] Huygens (1976: 461.78–81): *rex ergo iratus . . . suae abbati mandavit qua regis . . . ret et sumptus regalis expensae . . . curaret. . . .* It is a pity that these early initiatives of the crown in regard to peace beyond its domain fall within the mutilated portion of the *Major Chronicle*.

[5] Huygens (1976: 100) (Chérest). Cox: "At this point the king's mother, Adelaide de Savoie, and her sister Agnes, wife of lord Archimbald of Bourbon, arrived at Vézelay in execution of some religious vows, accompanied by Agnes's husband and Constance, the king's sister, who in 1154 married count Raymond V of Toulouse (Huygens [1976: 462.110–12]). They were implored to intervene with the king on the abbey's behalf, which

for Pons, and early in 1154 Louis VII wrote to him, 'Whatever cause of offense we have against you we pardon it altogether, and we banish the cloud of all our rancor and for the rest we kindly receive you into our favor, and all that belongs to you we take under our royal protection.'[1]

"Soon after his reconciliation with the king, Pons received a letter from Anastasius IV dated Christmas Day, 1153.[2] The pope had heard from him that the bishop of Langres had failed to execute the mandates of Eugenius III. At the abbot's request the pope had written letters to archbishops and bishops of France, the king, counts, and barons, as he would see from the copies enclosed. 'If therefore, my beloved son in Christ, you suffer tribulations for the house of Israel,' he wrote, 'you ought to hope that God will give you help from tribulation and will bring you by his grace to a haven of peace. Show yourself to be a most strong wall of protection for your church as you have been in the past.' In conclusion he forbade Pons to yield anything to the count of Nevers without his mandate.

"Among the papal letters was a mandate to the archbishop of Bourges[3] to summon the count of Nevers forthwith to make restitution to the monastery of Vézelay and to warn him not to summon the abbot before his court unless the abbot had denied justice in his own court. If the count did not obey the summons within thirty days, the pope commanded the archbishop to excommunicate the count and the traitorous burgesses of Vézelay and put all the count's lands under an interdict. He wrote in the same strain as Eugenius III to certain bishops and barons of France, and asked the king to ban the burgesses of Vézelay from all the fairs of his kingdom, and have nothing to do with the count if he came under the sentence of excommunication. The count should have justice if he first obeyed the papal mandate.[4]

"The pope's intervention brought about the settlement of the long quarrel between Pons and Henry of Burgundy, bishop of Autun. The latter was summoned to appear at Rome a fortnight after Easter, 1154, so he made peace before then.

"Louis VII offered to come to Auxerre and hear the cause between the abbot, the count of Nevers and the burgesses of Vézelay. Pons was very anxious to get his support, but he hesitated to recognize the king's right to give judgement in the case, as he feared that the claims of the crown might be even more prejudicial to the independence of the monastery than those of

---

they did, Archimbald of Bourbon acting as the chief mediator. The monks produced the document signed by William III of Nevers's 'own hand' and with his own seal attached (Huygens [1976: 463.128–31]), in which, 'while in danger at sea,' he gave up the *salarium* and *procurationes* that he was now trying to reclaim. As an old enemy of the counts of Nevers, Archimbald of Bourbon was more than ready to support the abbey's case, and he succeeded in reconciling Pons and Louis VII as well."

[1] Charter 65 above.
[2] Charter 63 above.
[3] Charter 60 above.
[4] Charters 58, 59, 62 above.

the count. He was able to decline the king's offer on the ground that the pope had commanded the archbishop of Bourges to act without delay. But he was doomed to fresh disappointment. The archbishop did not wish to make an enemy of so near and powerful a neighbor as the count of Nevers, so he said that he did not have enough information about the wrongs of the contending parties and took no further action.

"There was despair in the monastery. Pons commanded the monks to bar the doors of the church, strip the altars of their ornaments, and toll the bells. Very few of the people cared.[1] The count again beset the roads and turned back merchants and pilgrims, while the leaders of the burgesses assumed a still more threatening attitude. Nothing was left to Pons but to invoke the king's help. Louis VII was ready to intervene, and he summoned the count and the burgesses to appear before him at Auxerre in December 1154.

"Pons then formally accepted the king as sovereign arbiter and recognized his jurisdiction, but the representatives of the Commune hesitated on the ground that they had no mandate from their fellow-burgesses, and must go back to Vézelay to take counsel with them. In this answer the king saw a sure proof of their guilt. 'I swear by Bethlehem, by the cradle of our Lord, by the crown I wear,' he exclaimed, 'that the just cries of the Church have not resounded in vain. I shall know how to mete out rigorous treatment to insurgents and contumacious persons such as you, and you will undergo the chastisement which your crimes have deserved. Meanwhile depart. I will no longer endure your presence.'[2] The king's anger increased as he listened to the abbot's tale of outrage, and he promised to visit Vézelay. Pons sent a message to prior Hilduin bidding him put all the ornaments back on the altars, decorate the church as for a festival, and come out in procession with the monks, priests, servants, and any of the people who were still faithful to him, to meet the king and his train.[3] The count of Nevers rode off in haste and advised the burgesses to make a formal act of submission to the king. Louis VII sent for them as soon as he arrived and commanded them to obey the abbot as their lawful lord.

"The result of the king's visit was a truce with the count. The abbot of Cluny was anxious to bring about a lasting peace, and two other brothers of Pons, Jordan, abbot of La Chaise-Dieu and Heraclius, archbishop of Lyon, and his friend, Macharius, abbot of Fleury,[4] also persuaded him to make

---

[1] There seems little justification for this remark in Huygens (1976: 465.180ff.). Cox: the fact that the archbishop of Bourges, the papal legate assigned to the case, "declined to promulgate apostolic sanctions against the count suggests that William's case may have been a good deal stronger than our chronicler cared to admit."

[2] Huygens (1976: 466–67). Huygens (1976: 467.241): *sed per Bethleem dei et per coronam.*

[3] Huygens (1976: 467.270ff.).

[4] See charter 64 above, Guizot (1969: no. 88b, 250) and Chérest 1:203–5 (Huygens 1976: 107–8). Macharius was the nephew of Alberic, sixteenth abbot of Vézelay. He was *literatus* and amassed an important library at Fleury. Cox, following Constable (1967: 2:268), suggests that since Archbishop Heraclius was with Peter the Venerable at Cluny

terms with his enemy; both parties sealed a settlement early in 1155. The chronicler suspects Cluny's motives, fearing that its abbot was afraid that his influence at Vézelay would decline if the monastery was in royal hands. Anastasius IV died on 3 December 1154, and was succeeded two days later by the cardinal bishop of Albano, Hadrian IV. When he heard of this settlement he declared that it was contrary to the privileges of his predecessors, and he commanded the count to give it back to the abbot.[1] Pons had consented to recognize that Vézelay was under the protection of the count, who soon found an opportunity to exercise his right. A neighboring baron[2] persistently raided the lands of the monastery, so the count sent armed men into the town where they lived by plunder and stirred up the burgesses against the abbot.[3] As the count paid no heed to remonstrances, Pons sent messengers

---

March 2 1155, the meeting at which the events here related occurred must have taken place in Lent 1155—in February.

[1] For Hadrian's letters see charters 66–70 above. Cox's summary of these events reads: "Louis went to Vézelay, summoned the count and the townsmen to appear before him, and with Pontius at his side informed them that both the monastery and their abbot were now placed under his safeguard (*tuitio*). They were warned hereafter not to molest the monks in any way and to obey their lord the abbot faithfully, which led our chronicler to exult that the wicked had thus now been caught in their own snares, for God had taken pity on the monks' afflictions and come to their rescue (Huygens [1976: 468–69.273–310])." At this point Hugh the Poitevin accuses the Cluniacs of intervening, apparently in an effort to re-establish their dominion over Vézelay, 'one of the foremost of the churches (once) subject to them' (Huygens [1976: 469.313]), and fearing to lose all chance of doing so if the abbey passed into royal patronage. They seem to have made common cause with the count of Nevers, who also stood to lose by the transformation of Vézelay into a royal abbey; but abbot Pontius (Pons), 'ever vigilant' (Huygens 335), soon learned of the 'deceitful intrigues' going on around him. His good friend Mac(h)arius, abbot of Saint-Benoît-sur-Loire, went to speak with the count (Huygens 325–332), and Jordan, abbot of La Chaise-Dieu, was sought as a mediator, apparently between his brothers Pontius (Pons) of Vézelay and Peter of Cluny (Huygens 470.339–342). A meeting took place at Dornecy in which both sides agreed to make peace and put aside all rancor and resentment, and the agreement was confirmed by the archbishop of Lyon (Heraclius of Montboissier, the fourth brother) as well as by persons (probably the abbots) of Cluny and La Chartreuse (Huygens 355–549)."

[2] Huygens 470.361: ... *Godfridus ... exinde multa ei mala inferebat ... su[bvertere, fame illud satagebat ... ob]sidione illud capere. Misitque plures ... is, qui negociantes a presidio prohiberent ... exis]timans autem habere se oportunitatem ... t satellites suos Vizeliaco, quasi iure ... per divorcia villae armata manu incedebant viduas spoliabant, vi[rgines ... ad scelera provocabant*; which, perhaps, means something like "Godfrey then brought many evils upon the abbey and bent every effort to subvert it by starvation and to take it by siege. He sent several of his men for parleys, but they were prevented from approaching the abbey's citadel, so, thinking to find an opportunity for conquest he sent his henchmen into the abbey as if it was his right to do so and they made sport with the widows and virgins, provoking the citizens to crimes...." For this Godfrey (Geoffrey d'Arcy?—Cox: "probably Geoffrey of Arcy-sur-Cure, a vassal of the count of Nevers and an old enemy of the abbey") see above 2 §15.

[3] Cox describes the reaction to Geoffrey's ravages thus: "The abbot and monks in desperation sent some of the elders of the monastery to describe their intolerable situation to the count and beg him to order the withdrawal of these men, who had now invaded Vézelay itself and turned even the monastery into a 'den of thieves' (Huygens 471.370-86). The count received them with 'savage countenance' and after roundly cursing

to Hadrian IV to ask for help in this fresh trouble. Meanwhile there was a
dispute about the possession of some land between the abbot and one of his
men, and he decided on a trial by battle.[1] Crowds gathered in the cemetery
of the town to witness the duel between the abbot's champion and Robert the
Baker. Hugh of St. Peter incited the mob to attack the monks, and threw the
first stone himself. The abbot, the prior, and some of the monks escaped to
their fortress, which stood apart from the monastery, but the people broke
into the monastic buildings, forced open the wine casks, poured away the
wine, destroyed everything on which they could lay hands, including, apparently, archives,[2] and assaulted the monks and their servants.[3]

---

the abbot (Huygens 389-90), apparently accused them of inflicting lawsuits upon him and
therefore of being themselves responsible for the hostilities between their people and his.
He sent the elders back with the usual promise that all would be well if the monks
recognized his rights as they should, and he then despatched messengers of his own to
them. The brethren were celebrating Easter Vespers (1155), and after they had finished,
they listened to the count's response (Huygens 471-72.392-406). As usual, the monks
replied that they could not comply with the count's wishes, which ran contrary to their
own rights and privileges, whereupon the count again sent his men into the suburbs of
Vézelay, which they plundered for several days (Huygens 472.407-21). Appeal was again
made to the king, and a company of knights and foot-soldiers established themselves at St.
Père-sous-Vézelay (Huygens 422-29). It is not clear whose men they were, but the leaders
of the Vézelay commune took advantage of the confusion to stage another uprising, no
doubt counting upon the support of William III." At this point (Huygens 473.438) a list
of names is provided: "David of the monastery, Hugh the Bread-kneader (*Fricans Panem*—
Berlow [1987: 148] 'Hugh Frying-Bread' and cf. her note 110 p.160 on the link with the
name 'Frangipane').... -nus Pelet, Christian *Crassadona* (Fatgift?), P-... Robert *Caligalaxa*
[Bootmaker? Cox: "Loose-boots?"], Felix, Hugh G—... (the) cleric, Renaud, Joscelin and
Clement... William his son, Robert Baker (*de Furno*), Aimo of St. Christopher... Renaud
the charioteer (wagoner, groom, hostler, *auriga*), Renaud Daudet... Peter Galimard...
the sons of the provost of—... Odo de l'Étang (*de Palude*), Ralph Niger... —of the Fort
(castle), Joscelin of the Towers, Gai-... the bastard (*adulterinus*; see Niermeyer [1976: 23]),
Guy of the Fountain, T-... *Tornodoro* (Tonnere), Claude of St. Père... John Gerard,
Gerard the Dalmatian, Bernard... who bore the hostile standards on the day of the
contradiction... [cf. Huygens 489.952 *preferente signa Bernardo*] all these with their
innumerable accomplices..." (Cox: "among whom were one Eustace and his brother
Simon, a banker, who had prospered greatly through his connections with the abbey
during the time of abbot Pontius [Pons] (Huygens 473-74.457-466). Another notable
figure was Peter de Saint-Pierre (St. Père), 'leader and standard-bearer' of the rebel faction
[Huygens 474.474-90], who played a major role, according to our chronicler, in the
resumption of secret meetings and a renewed determination among the burghers to fight
for their commune"). On Pons's interest in local bankers see Berlow (1987: 153n.16).
Compare 204n.1 below and the list of names at the end of the present book.
   [1] Huygens 476.553: *ut duellii cer[tamen....* On trial by battle and the ordeal see Lea
(1892) portions re-edited by Peters (1973 and 1974).
   [2] *Scrinia quae erant in claustro:* Huygens 478.615.
   [3] Huygens 478-79. Cox: "At this juncture a dispute of a more specific nature arose
between the abbey and Robert *de Furno* (listed above among the trouble-makers) concerning a certain piece of property claimed by both. Abbot Pontius (Pons) decided that the
matter should be resolved by judicial duel, and when Robert began to fear the outcome,
the populace of the town was invited to attend the contest with weapons hidden under
their coats so that if Robert's champion failed, they could come to his assistance (Huygens
476-77.549-83). These developments were reported to the abbot, who ordered his most
faithful men to guard the abbey gate towers, exclude all outsiders, and post watchmen

"A few of the faithful inhabitants of the town and the neighboring villages joined the abbot in the fortress. His messenger escaped the armed men of St. Père-sous-Vézelay who were guarding the roads and carried the abbot's urgent appeal for help to the count of Nevers. The count would do nothing, but the bishop of Nevers hastened to Vézelay, got into the fortress, and cheered the garrison. Then he went out and harangued the burgesses and persuaded them to agree to a seven days' truce.[1] Pons eluded the sentinels and went to the king, who was then at Corbeil; the latter cited the contending parties to appear at the Council of Soissons, which met in June 1155. Pons carried the king's message to the count of Nevers, and then went to visit his brother, Heraclius, archbishop of Lyon.

"At the Council of Soissons the king decreed a general peace for ten years to be extended to all churches, cultivators of the soil, and merchants, but it was an ineffectual measure.[2] The abbot of Vézelay was represented by his proctors. His brother, the abbot of Cluny, made a strong appeal on behalf of the monastery of Vézelay, but there were very divergent views among the bishops and barons. The king favored a further delay and charged the archbishop of Sens to make a fresh and full examination of the case, and then to deliver judgement. Pons decided to go to Lyon, but on his way there he was attacked at Autun and barely escaped with his life.[3]

---

around the town cemetery where, appropriately enough, the duel was to take place (Huygens 477–78.583–600). The parties all assembled there on the appointed day, but what happened in the duel is not entirely clear. What is clear is that insults were soon followed by blows and stone-throwing led by Hugh de Saint-Pierre (St. Père), which forced the monks and their men to flee into the abbey enclosure. They took refuge in the citadel (*arx*) while the rebels pillaged the church, invading the cloister, destroying archives and vestments, breaking holy vessels and trampling the contents underfoot. They put to the sword anyone they encountered and did not spare even the abbot's horses, which were widely admired for their elegance (Huygens 478–79.601–26). The citadel held out against attackers, but mayhem reigned elsewhere: monks were slaughtered, the oblation strong-boxes were broken open and the money collected for the poor was carried off, wine jars were smashed, and the wine spilled out (Huygens 628–48). Reinforcements for the monks reached them by night from the countryside, but the rebels summoned armed forces from St. Père-sous-Vézelay to help them blockade the abbey citadel (if anyone escaped, a bell was to be rung so that the beseigers could give chase: Huygens 653–67)."

[1] Huygens 481.701. Huygens 480.684: the abbot calls upon the count to exercise *advocationem vel tuitionem seu defen[sionem . . . aecclesiam in periculo . . . quo] audito tirannus valde gavisus est. . . ;* the count, it seems, made light of the abbot's predicament (*per nugacissimum quendam*) and prevented his own men from assisting the abbot against the *burgenses*.

[2] Graham cites "Lavisse, *Histoire de France* vol. 3 part 1, 34" here.

[3] Cox: "Raymond, a brother of the duke of Burgundy, apparently offered his services as a mediator at this point (Huygens 482.723–24), but abbot Pontius (Pons), frustrated by the ensuing lack of progress, escaped from Vézelay and went to the king, to whom he described all the evils which the abbey had recently suffered. He was therefore present at the royal assembly at Soissons on 10 June 1155 (Huygens 739–49), which Louis VII had summoned specifically to discuss the ways and means of curbing private warfare, and at which 'almost all Gaul' was present, including William of Nevers. The problems of Vézelay were therefore a subject of discussion at Soissons, but not everyone agreed that the rebels or the count were wholly at fault (Huygens 483.760–44). A 'new race of Pharisees' now made its appearance: a group of prelates, including the bishops of Langres and Auxerre

"While Pons waited at Lyon for the return of the messenger whom he had sent to Hadrian IV, he heard of a fresh outbreak of violence at Vézelay. The burgesses held that the abbot's flight was a breach of the truce, so they raided the crops and cattle of the monastery. The valiant prior Hilduin and the monks prepared for a siege in their fortress, and they were joined by some of the abbot's peasants, archers, fishermen, and carters, who climbed up the ramparts by ropes in the darkness. The garrison was very small, a hundred against five thousand, according to Hugh the Poitevin.[1] The burgesses failed

---

and the archbishop of Tours, took sides against abbot Pontius's representatives, so the king imposed upon the archbishop of Sens the task of mediating (Huygens 778-83). At this point Pontius decided to take refuge with his brother Heraclius of Lyon, but while he was stopping over in Autun a group of clergy, including members of his own entourage, apparently decided to detain him. Declaring that his pride and arrogance were the cause of all their troubles (Huygens 484), they thus sought to avenge the abbot's enemy, the bishop of Autun, as well as themselves. They gathered together a great multitude of the abbot's foes and by night surrounded the vicar's house, where he was staying. They broke open the stables, took away the horses, and prevented anyone from entering or leaving. The abbot thought of taking refuge in the nearby basilica, where the night offices were being sung, but he was prevented from doing so. Finally, the Vézelay brethren joined him and the vicar arrived to appease the tumult. Pontius was subjected to further accusations of 'repeated and enormous arrogance' (Huygens 485.840-41), but he answered by representing himself as a monk of the apostolic pontiff (Huygens 846) and warned them of the consequences of interfering with the discharge of his business. At this point canons, presumably from the cathedral of Saint-Lazare, including one Anseric and Bertrand the precentor, arrived, denounced the rioters, and reminded them that their behavior would bring their whole church, including their superiors, into disrepute (Huygens 850-72). Bertrand then sought to excuse their behavior to the abbot as the effervescence of youthful spirits and asked that they all not be blamed for the sins of a few. The abbot was then escorted between 'a wedge of enemies' out of the city to Lyon, where he was comforted and encouraged by his brother the archbishop while awaiting the return of the envoys he had sent to Rome (Huygens 872-80)."

[1] Huygens 490.979. At 489.970ff. it seems the revolutionaries set fire to a part of the abbey: ... *acerrime impugnantes torq[uebant ... sagittas ac spicula balistarum in eos, ... a parte basilicae sancti Iohannis Baptistae ... abbatis incenderent* (perhaps "fighting bitterly they were winding up their seige engines and hurling bolts and darts at them, and coming out from part of the basilica they burned the ... of St. John the Baptist ... of the abbot"). Huygens (489.972n) thinks that it is not possible to determine upon what the genitive *Sancti Iohannis Baptistae* depends and denies that any part of the abbey (*maior ecclesia* or *basilica*) is meant or any of the lesser churches in Vézelay (for which see Aspects [C] above). Cox: "presumably the narthex (of the abbey church) which has a large sculpted figure of Saint John the Baptist on the trumeau. ..." At 487.893 Hugh gives a list of names of those who *interfuerunt obsidioni cum fratribus:* "Hugh Sarre and Josmer his brother, very strong indeed ... Gerard Pichonius, Durand ... of Clamecy and his son Guy, William ... -bert the cardinal, Hugh the cleric on the crossbows (*balistarius*) ... (also) on the crossbows, John the donkey operator (*de Asinariis*), John ... -sina, Durand the little baker boy (*Furnerellus*), Gilbert ... the wine servant (cellarer, *pincerna*), Durand the Sexton, S- ... John Fisher (*piscator*), Garnier (Guérin, Warren?) Fisher (*piscator*), R- ... the wagoner (*auriga*), Owen (*Auhinus*) the wagoner, Amiet the donkey driver (*asinarius*) ... of the bakery (*Pistrino*, of the mill?) Ernoul the cook, Christian the janitor ... of the pasture (Niermeyer [1976: 770],—or the 'pastrycook'? *de Pasticio*), Peter *de Fureis* (to do with thieves harnesses, ferrets??), Bernard ... Renaud son of Benedict the abbot's cook, Simon ... his brother, Peter of Auvergne (*Arvernicus*), Peter the eavesdropper (? *Auriculatus*–Niermeyer [1976: 72-73], possibly 'counsellor') ... Bernard son of Payen, *Guasconius* the boy...." Cf. 201n.3 above.

to take the fortress by assault, but the garrison had no sufficient store of food for a long siege; the bread ration was used up and they had nothing left but some meat. The first messenger who was sent to tell the abbot of their plight was caught by the burgesses, who executed him and nailed his head to a tree facing the fortress.

"At last the abbot's messenger arrived at Lyon with several letters from the pope, dated 21 May 1155. Hadrian IV[1] commanded King Louis VII to go to Vézelay and compel the burgesses to abjure the Commune, return to their subjection to their lawful lord, and make restitution for all the damage which they had done. He urged the king to inflict such exemplary punishment on the leaders that succeeding generations should never raise their heads against their lawful lord. In a letter to the bishops of France he grieved that no one of them had taken the shield of justice and arisen to help the church of Véze-lay. They must cease to be lukewarm and hasten to admonish the burgesses to make restitution and return to their allegiance. If, however, the burgesses paid no heed to their mandates, the abbot would send a list of the names of the leaders, and the bishops must excommunicate these men at once. He repeated the instructions of his predecessors to enforce the interdict and the excommunication, and prevent the burgesses from trading anywhere. He gave to the bishops of Autun, Langres, Nevers, and Auxerre the hard task of com-pelling the count of Nevers to obey the pope's command; if he proved con-tumacious, they must renew the sentence of excommunication against him and see that the interdict on his lands was observed.[2]

Louis VII determined as a matter of principle to support his bishops and abbots against the burghers as his father had done.[3] He summoned the

---

[1] See charters 68 and 69 above. Graham points out here Hadrian's possible sympathy for Pons against the burghers in view of his unfortunate experiences with the Roman communal revolution of the time: see Greenaway (1931) and 219n.2 below. Petit-Dutaillis ([1947] 1970) considers charter 68 major evidence for the existence of a commune at Vézelay. See Aspects [B] above. Cox's summary of this siege is graphic: "It was on a Sunday as the sun went down that one John Rufus and a companion gave the call to arms with trumpets, and the rebels marched up to the abbey walls behind a banner borne by one Bernard. One of the elders tried to parley with the leaders who apparently demanded that the monks send away their reinforcements. When the latter refused to do so, the monastery was attacked by a great multitude of people with arrows and crossbow bolts and rocks thrown from catapults (Huygens 489–90). Balistas were brought up, part of the abbey was set on fire, and even the most strongly fortified buildings were assaulted by an attacking force said to number five thousand men, whereas the monks numbered scarcely a hundred (Huygens 490.979). The roofs of the abbey buildings were shaken, no doubt by the battering rams; monks were killed, wounded, and subjected to many indignities (Huygens 490–91). Some women who tried to bring bread to the besieged were caught and publicly executed; but although deprived of human help, the monks of course received 'abundant divine help,' notably in the form of a bread miracle (Huygens 490.993–1008) which replenished their supplies. Meanwhile, the hostilities continued, led by the most wicked Aymon de Saint-Christophe. One band of rebels cut off the head of a captive from the monastery, then propped the body up against a tree with the head on and amused themselves by uttering blasphemies (Huygens 492.1052–57). Letters (dated 21 May 1155) now arrived from Rome. . . ."

[2] Charters 66 and 67 above.

[3] Graham cites Luchaire (1890: 276–79) here. Cox's summary of the final portions of

count of Nevers to come to Sens with representatives of the burgesses of
Vézelay, but as he appeared without them, the hearing was adjourned, though
not without the count being urged to bring the burghers back to obedience.
Neither the count nor the burgesses appeared at Chaumont, so the king
began to prepare for a punitive expedition. The count garrisoned his strongholds, but at the same time he urged the bishops of Auxerre and Langres to
intercede for him. The bishop of Langres refused, but another bishop was
willing to act with the bishop of Auxerre. At their request the king abandoned the expedition and summoned all parties to appear before him at
Montargis. There abbot Pons told the story of the trial by battle and the
attack on the monastery in which the sanctuary was defiled and some of the
monks and servants were killed."

[At this point the folios in the Auxerre manuscript are complete again and
the story can be continued in the words of the chronicler. The abbot of Vézelay is speaking (Huygens 496.1199ff.)]:

2

1155

... when I was administering the rights of the church during the peace and
truce your reverence [= the king] had arranged for the monastery, it hap-

---

the mutilated folios is satisfyingly full: "The count of Nevers and others accused of
harboring the seditious were accordingly summoned to present themselves before the king
at Sens, where the count was asked why he had broken the king's truce (Huygens
493.1085-1100). He replied that he could not be held responsible for what the men of
Vézelay did; and when he was asked why he had not brought the leaders with him, he
answered that they were not his men but the abbot's, and therefore that it was up to the
abbot to bring them to justice (Huygens 493-94.1101-7). This time Count William's
arguments were not accepted. He was reminded that he had publicly taken the men of
Vézelay under his protection and that he had encouraged them to rebel. It was therefore
his responsibility to restore them to obedience by returning to Vézelay and bringing the
rebel leaders back with him to a new meeting, to take place at Chaumont (Huygens
494.1107-17). William was to promise on oath no longer to encourage the rebels or to
offer them asylum on his lands, and to do all he could to bring about the dissolution of
their commune. When Count William returned to Vézelay, however, and the burghers
went to him to learn the outcome of his discussions with the king, he reassured them,
saying that their cause and his were one and the same (Huygens 1117-27). Consequently
neither he nor they appeared at the appointed time and place, and the king, enraged,
summoned his magnates and gathered an army (Huygens 1127-33). The count also
assembled a well supplied army, but asked the bishops of Auxerre and Langres to try to
appease the king's wrath. Since the bishop of Langres could not—or would not—do so, he
sent in his place as a favor to the count a man 'capable of every species of deceit' and
'excessively greedy for money' (Manasses de Garlande), who, according to our chronicler,
had forced the venerable Hélie of Orleans to resign his see so that he could have it for
himself (Huygens 495.1136-46). The count of course willingly sent this 'wolf in sheep's
clothing' along with the bishop of Auxerre and the abbot of Les Roches (a Cistercian
house near Cosne in the Nivernais) to intercede on his behalf with Louis VII, who with
great regret finally agreed to dismiss his army and accept the scheduling of yet another
conference (Huygens 1146-59)."

pened that I undertook a lawsuit with a certain serf [*servo*] of the church concerning a possession of the church itself, which I judged would be decided by combat in a duel.[1] But, as the time for the ordeal arrived, these very men who are present now before you turned to sedition, went to meet me and my brothers and servants, put us to flight unsuspecting and unprepared as we were, violated the cloisters of the monastery, scattered the ornaments, plundered the utensils of various kinds, broke the wine butts, poured out the wine, pillaged everything of value, kicked open and polluted the sanctuaries [*sanctuaria*], put our monks and servants [*famulos*] to slaughter, and sought me out for murder. Had they found me, they would have cut me into a thousand pieces.[2] Then they besieged us, unused as we were to battle, smashed our houses, overturned the mills, and took complete possession of whatever they could lay their hands upon. Insulting the royal majesty, they sated themselves on the punishments they dealt us. At length, having obtained an opportunity and again at the apostolic command, I fled to you, my principal defense, and you must now judge my situation.[3] Accordingly, relying on the judgment of your equity, I require satisfaction from the townsmen: the price of my blood and that of my monks, the price of the death they would have inflicted on me, and compensation for the damages my house has suffered, saving in all things your rights and those of the Apostolic See,[4] the injury to which I am neither able nor bound to forgive in any way." With these words he fell silent.

The tyrant, the count of Nevers, then got up and spoke up for the traitors, saying: "It is common knowledge that the town of Vézelay is crammed with a motley crowd of people,[5] many thousands in number, and that the men [of

---

[1] *duellii certamine.* See above 202nn.1, 3 and, for the duel as a solution to the question of servile status in the time of Otto III (996–1002 AD), Lopez ([1959] 1965: 38) (MGH, *Leges* 4 *Const. et acta publica imperatorum et regum* [Hanover, 1893: 1:47–48]). For the right of an abbot to order judgment by duel see the example of Saint-Michel de Tonnerre, to whom Count William of Nevers specifically grants such a right; Chérest 1:217–18 (Huygens [1976: 114–15]), citing Quantin vol. 1 no. 174, 296–99.

[2] See the fate of the bishop at Laon in the second decade of the century, cut to pieces by the revolutionary serf Thiégaud: Guibert of Nogent, *De vita sua* 3.8. *Sanctuarium* means "sanctuary" or "reliquary" or "relic" (Niermeyer [1976: 397]).

[3] *ut in presentiarum est cernere.*

[4] Cf. Ezekiel 3:18. Graham (1918: 124) translates: "I come to you for justice. I ask from these men the price of my blood and the blood of my people, of my death which they sought to compass. I ask for damages for the losses of my monastery, saving your rights and those of the people, for I cannot and may not overlook these wrongs." Cox has: "Accordingly, standing in the court of your Equity, I call them to account for the blood of me and mine, and my death, which they sought; and I prosecute them for the damage done to my house, saving royal and apostolic rights in everything, for I neither can nor should excuse such injury."

[5] *promiscui vulgus esse refertum;* cf. Exodus 12:38. The sense seems to require that *refertum* be followed by a genitive (as normal in Classical Latin: Lewis & Short, s.v. "refercio" 1544 (ß)) and that *vulgus* be a genitive singular in agreement with *promiscui*. The same phrase, *promiscui vulgus*, is found in 4 §18 (Huygens 530.714–15), where again it seems to be genitive. Huygens (1976: xxii, n.35) suggests that the author, on the analogy

Vézelay] are not of the same quality or value. Most of the residents of Vézelay are foreigners [*adventicii*] from many different regions and they bring with them different enthusiasms [*studia*], settling their affairs on impulse [*studio*] rather than by law. It would be quite wrong to impute to the superior natives,[1] beyond criticism in respect to every law and in reputation, whatever faults the transient crowd should be proved to have committed. Otherwise justice is not just if the just and the impious are equally blamed with a crime. But since the mass of the people[2] is everywhere more numerous and for that reason stronger in some ways than the senate [*senatus*], what blame could possibly attach to the very few and most reputable of the citizens, those concerned solely with the regulation of their household affairs, when even the authority of a prince cannot suppress popular movements?[3] Thus, if it be pleasing to royal government, let the authors of the crime be named by the abbot so that censure may be justly brought to bear upon them, as defendants, without involving the innocent." The tyrant, on these points, received this reply: "Since it is proper for citizens, by natural and lawful right, to guard and defend and keep safe from all danger their lord and prince and not to shrink from voluntary death for his safety, those who saw that it was his moment of need and defrauded him of solace and assistance, should be accounted not innocent men, but betrayers and deserters of their lord—and judged as such. Thus, it is the responsibilty of the leaders[4] to pay for whatever the vulgar band[5] nefariously committed, spurred on, assisted, and endowed by them." Thereupon, all, without distinction, who had not left Vézelay with the abbot, nor gone to join the brothers besieged in the monastery, nor borne them help, were charged with treason, faithlessness to their lord, sacrilege, perjury, and homicide.

After this the first article [*capitulum*] of the judgment of the king was pronounced, to the effect that the abbot should offer proven testimony[6] concerning the losses to himself or the church, and whatever was legitimately proven should be wholly restored by those charged with the capital crime. To this article the abbot objected: "Since it is clearly agreed that those men, by reason of the savageness of their pertinacity, have been excommunicated and anathematized by three popes, it seems to me incorrect for a lord to make faith with his faithless serfs,[7] to swear an oath with perjurers, to offer testimony to the profane, to make law for those who hold law in contempt."

---

of *promiscui sexus*, may have treated *vulgus* as a fourth declension noun.

[1] *electis indigenis.*

[2] *plebs.* In the previous sentence we find *erroneum vulgus* ("transient crowd"). Cf. too the next note and 201n.5 above.

[3] *plebeios motus.* I.e., if the king cannot suppress uprisings one can hardly expect the "elders" (Senate) of the people of Vézelay to do so.

[4] *a capite ipsorum.*

[5] *plebeia manus.*

[6] *testificando probaret.*

[7] *dominum servis fidem perfidis . . . facere.*

The bishop of Langres[1] replied to him: he always and everywhere opposed the cause of Vézelay, and with Humbert of Tanlay, the archdeacon of Nevers, had, at the urging of the count, bent his advocacy to the cause of the treasonous burghers.[2] "Even though [he said] a sentence [of excommunication] may have been recently promulgated, we do not consider these men bound by the law appropriate to excommunicates until they are denounced, called upon, and published by the Church generally and we are not sure that this has yet happened."[3] To which the abbot said: "The lord [bishops] of Sens, Paris, and Troyes are to hand, and they have, upon the order of the apostolic pontiff, named and published these men as sacrilegious traitors." These bishops testified that they had so acted but the abbot was persuaded to offer his proof,[4] which would—it was agreed—have no injurious effect on his rights. But since the officials and ministers of the church, through whom proof was to be offered, were not all present, the meeting was adjourned to the following sabbath when all present and absent would meet at Moret.

3

They Meet Again at Moret. Judgment Is Brought Against
the Count of Nevers and the Perfidious Townsmen of Vézelay

[1616A/498. 1277]

1155

It was the day named after Mars [Tuesday] that is, the third day of the week. When all those who were required had met, they went out with the king and all the nobles[5] into a grove set above Moret. There the abbot presented the gist of his proven losses: 160,000 *solidi*, not counting losses to his groves and waters, the insult of the treachery, the lives of those killed, and the sacrilege involved in violating the holy church. Having heard these things, they [the citizens of Vézelay] conscious of their crime, disturbed and worried, at once turned to flight, not awaiting proof. Unknown to the king, they went back to their accomplices and consorts in crime. The abbot, at the order of the king, set forth his proof in the presence of the count and his above-mentioned supporters. However, when the king realized that the perfidious [citizens] were

---

[1] See Crozet (1975). Cox: "The bishop of Langres was Geoffrey de la Roche-Vanneau from 1137 to 1161, when he resigned and withdrew to Clairvaux, where he died on 8 November 1165. He was a fourth cousin to St. Bernard and the first abbot of Fontenay." See E. Brouette in the *Dictionnaire de biographie française* 5 (Paris, 1982).

[2] *causam proditorum burgensium.*

[3] For procedures of excommunication at the time see below 280n.2.

[4] *probationem.* See *testificando probaret* in the previous paragraph.

[5] *optimatibus.* See §2 above for references to *plebs/senatus*, etc. The early books of Livy's *Histories* (e.g., 3.8ff., 6.18ff., 37ff., etc.) are replete with constitutional and political struggles between the *senatus* (cf. Huygens 497.1234), the *plebs*, and *patricii* (*optimates*); the author may have these, or similar, in mind in these pages.

absent and without permission had rashly avoided the royal court, he spoke thus: "Happily the abbot has proved the justice of his case, and the traitors have confirmed their treachery; wherefore, since they have cut themselves off from justice, let a sentence appropriate to their guilt be carried against them." The archbishop of Rheims then spoke: "We have dictated one chapter [of their sentence] and were ready to pronounce others if the citizens had waited and shown themselves worthy of judgment. But since, in their insanity, they have cut themselves off from all right of justice, we pronounce, according to the dictates of the king's judgment, that the count of Nevers, who is present as a result of his fidelity to the king,[1] should apprehend the profane traitors by force and bring them for punishment to the king, wherever the latter will have commanded. The property of the citizens, movable and immovable, should be assigned by the count to the abbot as restitution for the losses he has suffered." Asked whether he would undertake execution of the sentence thus pronounced by the king himself, the count replied, "I will." When Langres tried to upset the judgment, Rheims replied to him: "If the judgment just elaborated seems unjust to you, I challenge you to attend an audience at Rome, where, before the highest pontiff and universal judge, you may air any grievance you have." "I will not take up that right of appeal at all," Langres replied, "nor do I refute the judgment of the king, but approve what seems good to his equity, as I ought." Again, therefore, the king asked the count whether he would undertake the judgment concerning bringing the traitors into custody. Nevers replied: "If my lord king commands, I will; but I ask that the citizens be granted the deferment which I, trusting in royal piety,[2] granted them." The king replied to him, "I clearly order and by my royal authority, on account of that fidelity by which you are sworn to me,[3] instruct that what is here laid down, you complete, omitting nothing of the sentence. In regard to the deferment it is up to you, for neither to you nor to the citizens will anything be conceded by me: you must execute my judgment by next Sunday."

4

Unwillingly the Count, Having Agreed to Carry Out the Sentence, Strives to Set It at Nought in all Ways and Labors to Give It No Effect   [1616D/499. 1319]

1155

After two days in conference at Moret, the assembly dissolved. The abbot, bidding farewell to the king and his nobles and friends, came towards Vézelay and stayed at Givry[4] until the nominated Sunday. The tyrant, however, griev-

---

[1] *de fidelitate regis.*

[2] *ex fiducia regiae pietatis.*

[3] *plane iubeo et auctoritate regia pro fidelitate, qua michi iuratus es, precipio quod. . . .*

[4] 10 kilometers north of Vézelay, en route to Sermizelles (the current railway station

ing over the impious citizens whom he had incited to conspiracy and provoked to crime, to whom he was sworn, whose resources he had drained because they had placed their trust in him,[1] and by whose help he hoped to obtain the lordship[2] of the monastery of Vézelay, and grieving also that he had been so potently and publicly defeated by the abbot, confused, confuted and triumphed over in his folly—not only his own, but that of his henchmen and accomplices—all as the abbot had wished, felt terribly dejected[3] and gave thought to how he could provide for the condemned and alleviate their despair. But since a confused mind is without power of reason, his counsel— by God's disposition—was foolish;[4] thus, attempting to provide for the condemned common people, he brings the decree[5] to the church and, reluctant [to enforce the decree] and heedless [of the consequences of evading its impact], he provides help to the oppressed but seeks to effect it through a stratagem: while holding out the noose, he [yet] himself lightens the burden for [his] ally [the people]; he is hooked by the goad,[6] evilly sated by his desires.[7] Therefore he sent forth his henchmen, ordering them to proclaim through heralds to all the townsmen and villagers, on the authority of the count, that they should all flee together with all their movable possessions, wherever they could, to any one of his fortified places where they would least expect him to come, since the judgment of the king required him on the following Monday to seize all who could be found within Vézelay and to take them, though he was unwilling, to the king in Paris for punishment.

God then sent terror into the hearts of those men,[8] and all who were adversaries [of the abbey] fled, every one of them, from the least to the greatest, leaving their houses, wives, children, possessions, and merchandise, so that absolutely no one from so many thousands remained at the break of day: the town, as if it had been invaded and plundered by enemies, was bare and empty.[9] The shrewd and cunning count, thinking that the abbot would not

---

for Vézelay) and Auxerre. Vézelay, Givry, and Avallon form a triangle. Speaight (1990: 281 and map 277).

[1] *ob fiduciam sui.*

[2] *dominium.*

[3] *affligebatur animo.*

[4] *infatuatum est consilium eius:* see 2 Kings (Sam.) 15:31: *dixitque David: infatua, quaeso Domine, consilium Acitophel* ("and David said: O Lord, I pray thee, turn the counsel of Acitophel into foolishness").

[5] *consultum:* a word originally found in Classical Latin in the longer form of *senatusconsultum,* a decree of the Senate. The verbs in this and the following period are in the present tense in the Latin. Both Guizot and Cox translate *consultum* as "counsel" (*secours*) and read the rest of the sentence as if the count was actually helping the monks without knowing it. We have inclined to the more formal reading of *consultum* in view of the heavily classical language of Hugh's account in this part of his narrative—see above 209n.5.

[6] I.e., spurred on in his evil intents. See Augustine *In Psalmos* 102.9.

[7] *male satur cupito.*

[8] Ecclesiasticus 36:2.

[9] Compare events at Laon: Guibert of Nogent, *De vita sua* 3 §11 (ed. Benton [1970: 184–90]; ed. Labande [362–76]).

dare to enter his monastery without himself [the count] being present,[1] made
a show of inactivity.[2] The abbot, however, despising the count's folly, at once
proceeded in triumph to Vézelay on the nominated Sunday, around evening,
and gained possession of his monastery. There was great exultation in the
church since the adversary was confounded and the enemy contrite. Then the
tyrant sent his henchmen to Vézelay, as if to keep favor with the king by
carrying out the latter's mandates, and instructed them to seize the profane
citizens whom he had ordered to leave the place. These henchmen, having entered the town, said to the abbot that their lord the count had been waiting
some time for the abbot's envoy, in order to conduct him into his monastery
with all honor. They marvelled that the abbot had been so ill-advised as to
enter the monastery without regard to the movements [*motus*] of his enemies.
Moreover, they said that they had been sent by their lord to exercise the
revenge that had been agreed upon against his adversaries at the command
of the abbot. The abbot replied: "I heard your lord was ill and did not wish
to be burdensome to him. Trusting myself instead to God and the blessed
Mary Magdalene, whose cause I honor with all my prayers, I received, at the
hand of God, what the envious foe was trying to snatch from me. But you
know from whom you have been sent: if he has instructed you to do anything
it is up to you whether you do it or not. For my part I will patiently await the
outcome." In reply they said that they had been sent to apprehend the men
of the village [*homines vici*, i.e., Vézelay], but, having gone in, they had found
no one except women and their little children. He [the abbot, then] said to
them, "Did the four of you expect to apprehend so many thousand citizens?"
Someone then said to them:[3] "Indeed, if you have come to capture the perfidious traitors, you will find almost eighty hiding like bandits in the nearby
wood." But they replied: "We have another journey to make; our path does
not lie in that direction." With this sort of prevarication they went away; the
trickery of the master is proved by the cunning of his pupil. Then some of the
brothers went out with the young servants of the monastery in arms,[4] and
broke the [money-changer's] table of the impious Simon,[5] and the porch of

---

[1] I.e., for the abbot's protection.

[2] *simulavit languorem* may imply feigned illness (Cf. Huygens 501.1364: *infirmaretur*),
but the latter implication probably represents the abbot's tactful interpretation of the
count's inactivity.

[3] Guizot translates "one of the abbot's men," but the Latin reads: *et dixit illis quidam.*

[4] *quidam de fratribus armate cum pueris iuventutis.*

[5] *tabulam impii Simonis.* Guizot (1969: no. 92, 251) says: "one of the three leaders of
the communal insurrection, with his brother Eustace, and Hugh of St. Père. Originally
from Souvigny in the Bourbonnais, he seems to have come as a young man to Vézelay and
to have enjoyed the support of Pons who gave him a money-changer's counter (*comptoir*)
despite the opposition of the (abbey) chapter. His success must have been resented by the
chapter because in 1155 Hadrian IV ordered that the privileges that Pons had granted him
be revoked, on the grounds that they were prejudicial to the rights of the chapter." See
charter 70; see also the 1137 *Accord* (Appendix B below) §§32–33 and 46–47 with notes.
Berlow (1971: 315) writes that "Simon of Souvigny was probably the wealthiest man in

his house, which he had built in defiance of the command of the brothers and against right. Putting his faith in the conspiratorial faction he had held onto this porch[1] up to now, against the wishes of the church. Going on from there, they demolished the wine-presses[2] which the impious Hugh the Bread-kneader and the foulest Hugh of St. Peter had fraudulently erected in the basements under their houses. The impious citizens were by now spread out through the towns and localities belonging to the tyrant, who ordered his henchmen and provosts to keep them concealed, to pardon them, and to show them every kindness, insisting only that [the citizens] be kept from the presence of the count himself. The rest were scattered and wandered all about, exposed to ambush, plunder, and captivity. Resourceless and unsettled, they lived in a nearby wood, building huts for themselves there, and from these, plying the trade of bandit, they used to fall upon travellers and pilgrims. Hunted by day, they escaped contact with their pursuers by resorting to their friends in very well fortified places. By night, however, from their bases in the already mentioned wood, they would send scouts into the village, disguised as pilgrims, to bring back to them the necessities of life and any information they could gain. These exiles assembled at Corbigny,[3] and planned an attack designed to regain by force the homes they had willingly abandoned when so panic-stricken.

5
The Abbot Assembles an Army to Resist the Perfidious Townsmen [1618C/501.1400]

1155

Then the abbot collected an army from beyond his seigneury,[4] a most powerful band, comprising skilled bowmen and balista-operators.[5] Retaining some soldiers[6] within the monastery,[7] he divided the rest up, with his own servants,

---

Vézelay around the mid-twelfth century. At the beginning of his term in office, Abbot Ponce (Pons) had granted him a moneydealer's counter on very liberal terms. Pope Adrian (Hadrian) later referred to this concession as contrary to ecclesiastical practice which prohibited the gift, sale or alienation of property of the church and instructed Ponce to revoke the grant." See Cox in Aspects [F] above, and below at 218n.2 and Appendix B n. to §11.

[1] *vestibulum domus.*

[2] *torcularia:* 1137 *Accord* (Appendix B below, §§ 4, 9–10, 19, 26, 30, 35–36, 48, 53, 55).

[3] Twenty-seven kilometers south of Vézelay. On the lands of the count of Nevers, who exercised the right of advocacy over the celebrated abbey of Saint-Léonard there, a comparable "seigneurie" to that of Vézelay. Corbigny, Vézelay, and Clamecy form a triangle.

[4] *externum exercitum:* mercenaries, "routiers" ("soldiers by profession, plying their trade along the major communication routes").

[5] *homines doctos arcu et balista.*

[6] *militibus* (Guizot [1969]: "chevaliers," "knights"). The term is the normal CL one for legionaries, foot-soldiers, but by the twelfth century, had come to be applied to the horsed

and placed [them] in the fortified points [belonging to] the worst of his
opponents so that by such an action, the impious citizens, who were hoping
to attack the fortifications of the abbey by a similar action, might be repelled.
These troops were ordered to patrol by turns, day and night, making the
rounds of the town and surrounding farms. Whomsoever of the fugitives they
managed to seize, they punished by wretched imprisonment or mutilation of
the limbs.[1] Thus the church obtained its deserved right of justice, without
being compelled to make suit at the court of the tyrant for it. Abbot Pons
avenged the church on his worst adversary, Hugh of St. Peter, instructing that
everything he owned should be plundered, all his goods confiscated, all his
buildings overturned, his house, his mills, his system of ponds, everything
which his haughty determination had accumulated, to the great advance of his
power.[2] And thus were all his possessions destroyed, making him a parable
and a proverbial tale for future generations.[3] In addition, however, the just
censure of the abbot's revenge touched other servants of the sedition, utterly
destroying their houses, which were burnt to the ground, and plundering
their possessions which they had made such evil use of. Those involved were:
Aimon of Saint-Christophe, surnamed the Madman [*insanus*], Peter surnamed
of St. Peter, Aimon of Phalèse, Robert the Baker,[4] Renaud Daudet, Walter
the Norman, Robert of Stonyfield, Durand the Glutton, Alard, Claude, and
Peter Galimard. In the case of others, that is, Eustace, Simon, Durand Alburg,
David, and Hugh the Bread-kneader and Felix and their other accomplices,
the abbot's piety lead him to moderate their sentence, and only their wines
were poured away by the faithful of the church.[5] Shields and arms of various
types were found also among the spoils from the plundered houses. The
culprits were for the most part thrown into chains until the judgment of the
king might decide upon them. Thus the pride of the impious was humbled,
and the insolent boorishness[6] of the men of Vézelay acknowledged itself subdued. The tyrant too, saw that justice was prevailing and impiety confused
and that there was no way that he could be of any help to those who had

---

warrior. See Duby (1974: part 3); Duby (1982a: chap. 13); Flori (1975).

[7] *castrum.* Guizot (1969): "dans le château (des abbés)?" The abbot's palace, built of
sombre, austere, and vast construction c.1120, on the terrace behind the basilica, above
the plain 156 meters below, was demolished late in the eighteenth century. (See Guizot
[1969: 252 and plan, 48ii], Vogade, *Vézelay* [1987: 15, 40].)

[1] Compare the tortures inflicted by Thomas of Marle (Guibert of Nogent, above
211n.9) and, for the significance of mutilation, Ward (1981: 104n.31).

[2] *domus et molendina stagnaque aquarum, quae multo fastu extruxerat et exaltatus fuẹrat
usque in celum*: cf. Matt. 11:23 and Luke 10:15.

[3] Cf. Ezekiel 18:2–3.

[4] Guizot (1969): "Robert du Four," *Roberto de Furno* = the Robert the Baker of 201n.3
(Niermeyer [1976: 458]: *furnus* = "stove"). See in general the list of names at 201n.3 and
204n.1, and at the end of *Major Chronicle* 3.

[5] *a fidelibus aecclesiae* = serfs of the church.

[6] *rusticitas*: much used (with related forms and words) in the classical writers to suggest
an absence of civilized (literate) culture (*urbanitas*).

been deceived [in the trust they placed in him]. He stood in some fear of them and could not tolerate their sight, for they accused him of cowardice and he was tortured by his conscience. Nevertheless, he forbad the impious who were anxious to return [to the fidelity of the abbot] from making satisfaction in accordance with the judgment of the abbot, and promised them on oath that he would bring an acceptable peace to them. Since he was confounded in his attempt to intercede for them, and lest he seem to assist them against his oath [to the king] he conceived of a plan to thwart God, [a plan that was] blasphemous to the maintenance of piety: he took up the staff and wallet of one seeking the shrines of St. Denis, whose solemnities were close at hand,[1] and set out for the king. When the king asked his purpose, he lied that he had come as a pilgrim to the blessed martyr Denis. Then, seizing a chance to talk with the king, he fell at his feet and with much emotion begged the king to spare the exiled citizens of Vézelay, and to spare the monastery itself since if the town was destitute, the monastery too would be desolate. He promised, swearing and calling all to witness, that he would bring those men into the presence of the king and that they would satisfy the abbot and the church in accordance with the judgment of royal piety and would make a treaty of perpetual peace.

6

The Count Suggests Many Things Fraudulently to the King and the Abbot Agrees to Them [1619D/503.1453]

1155

Moved then by such pleas, the king fixed upon a day for the count, at Auxerre, the third day after the Feast of All Saints.[2] He then sent all the count's petitions and promises to the abbot and asked that in the meantime the latter spare the houses of the citizens until the day fixed for the proposed concord. Hearing these things, the abbot at once informed [Macharius, abbot of] Fleury and the rest of his friends of the mandate of the king and the agreement of the count and asked that they be with him at the proposed conference. However, the other nobles whom the king had notified of the conference on the Vézelay case refused to come, saying that they would not be present at any conference with the count of Nevers. Hearing of all this, the tyrant wished to make further use of his impudent wickedness and hurried again to the king, asking that the day and place of the proposed conference on the Vézelay case be cancelled and [the date] be brought forward, claiming as his excuse the opposition of his enemies, against whom he ought to defend him-

---

[1] 9 October 1155. The king would certainly be in Paris for the occasion. On the fairs of St. Denis in the Middle Ages see Evans (1966: 262) (the Lendit fair in June), Van Engen (1986: 279ff.), and *Cambridge Economic History of Europe* 2, index, s.v. "Fairs–of St. Denis."

[2] Thursday, 3 November 1155.

self. He hoped that thereby he might meet the abbot and easily bend him to his persuasive intentions[1] since he would be unprepared and without his friends. But the abbot, his mind well accustomed to false schemes, could not be deceived so incautiously. However, the king believed the count and wrote to the abbot instructing him to be present on All Saints Day at Saint-Julien-du-Sault for the conference,[2] ready to make and receive peace if the appropriate agreements were forthcoming. To this the abbot, who had begun to take counsel, replied that he could not meet the king as quickly as all that; indeed, he had summoned his friends to the day first designated and would make and accept peace by their counsel if the appropriate agreements were forthcoming. He asserted that it was not fitting that he should proceed with a conference on so great an issue alone (i.e., without his friends). The king heard this and agreed that the abbot's reply was just. Consequently he ordered that the original details be adhered to.

7

On the Agreed Day at Auxerre the King, the Abbot and Others Meet. The Townsmen of Vézelay Are Once Again Condemned   [1620B/503.1481]

1155

On the determined day, Thursday after the Feast of All Saints, the king and the abbot met together at Auxerre with their nobles and friends.[3] The count also came, attended by the villagers of Vézelay. On the following day, which is named after Venus [Friday], the king sat down and asked the burghers what they wished to do. But they replied that they would do everything as the good pleasure[4] of his mercy desired. The king's judgment, therefore, required that the conspiracy and mutual confederacy which they had made and whatever agreement they might have made among themselves, should be entirely abjured; furthermore, they should either seize those who had been responsible for killing the servants of the church, wherever they could find them, or else, they should reveal where they might be found, either by clamor or some other disclosure.[5] They should, moreover, swear upon holy relics, fidelity and

---

[1] James 3:17.

[2] 1 November 1155: *apud sanctum Iulianum de Saltu,* "Saint Julien-des-Bois," Saint-Julien-du-Sault (*de Salice,* "of the Willow," Huygens [1976: 674]), about 20 kilometers south of Sens, slightly less than halfway from Sens to Auxerre. Speaight (1990: 56–57): "the name commemorates a legendary leap by the saint to escape his pursuers."

[3] *optimatibus et amicis.* The abbot of Vézelay's case makes clear the truism that in politics (as elsewhere) success depends not on "right" or "justice" but on the weight of friends and connections.

[4] Ephesians 1:9.

[5] *aut clamore et indicio quo,* by "hue and cry." In the pre-conquest English lawcodes a person against whom an act of theft (*furtum*) had been committed could summon his neighbors and get his goods back by direct action. From this "pursuit" (*secta*) arose the

[devotion to the] life and welfare of the abbot's person and his men, the church and its men, and they should pay 40,000 *solidi* for the damage the abbot suffered; they should also destroy the fortifications and outworks of their houses by, at the latest, the Feast of St. Andrew.[1] They were to swear that they would do all these things wholly, and in good faith. The [townsmen] then, their [proud] necks broken,[2] tamed and humbled, promised that they would do all these things and swore that they would venerate and protect the abbot as their lord. Those there at once made very solemn confirmations[3] of the oath that had been agreed to. Their names were: Guibert of Toul,[4] Hugh the Bread-kneader, Durand Alburg, and almost forty others. The abbot returned to Vézelay with his men, once perfidious, now loyal.[5] They entered the town with him, exulting with happiness and dancing for joy, and lived in peace, wild beasts now tamed. When those townsmen who were still dispersed all around outside heard of the condition of peace, they rejoiced and returned, pouring in daily in troops, to take the oath [*ad iusiurandum*]. The abbot next set up treasurers [*quaestores*] from among the townsmen, who would demand from each the payment imposed by the royal judgment. The management of the collection was to be as follows: each person's possessions were to be valued for the purposes of fulfilling the oath to the king, and the sum total was to be reckoned in pounds,[6] payment to be made to the value of a tenth part, so that for an evaluation of twenty *solidi*, two would be paid. There was not a one who would resist or voice an objection, since the horn of their pride was banished and the rod of their fortitude was wasted, and the liberty of the church was re-established at the hands of the outstanding abbot Pons, all prostitutors of its chastity being routed. Nevertheless, by dissimulation they neglected to pull down the outworks of their houses since this instruction scandalized them, like a thorn boring a hole in their eyes.

---

later development of the "hue and cry," as the recognized means of pursuing a thief. This civic duty was enjoined in thirteenth-century English statute law.

[1] 30 November 1155.

[2] 1 Kings (Sam.) 4:18.

[3] *iuramenti sacramenta.*

[4] *Guibertus Leucensis*: Huygens (1976: 504.1501n and 649, s.v. Guibert).

[5] *iam de perfidis factis fidelibus.*

[6] *ut appreciatis per obligationem iusiurandi singulorum possessionibus redactisque in summa pensitationibus de libra persolveretur pars decima. Libra:* "standard weight of gold or silver" (Niermeyer [1976: 609]). *Pensitatio,* a post-classical word, can mean either "payment" or valuables with which payment was to be made. Our translation is somewhat conjectural, and the meaning may be ". . . and with the sum of the payments worked out, a tenth part of the total valuation in pounds was to be paid . . . ." According to Guizot (1969: 252n.98) it is a matter of £ (= L[*ibra*]), s(*olidi*–20 per £) and d(*enarii*–12 per "s"). The *libra* would be money of account. See *Cambridge Economic History of Europe* 3 [1963: Appendix, 576–602]).

8

The Abbot Blames a Citizen Who Refuses to Subject
Himself to His Decrees   [1621B/505.1520]

1156

With the Kalends of the Lord's Nativity complete[1] the abbot summoned the
citizens and advised them that, according to the composition of the peace,
they should complete what they had not yet done, that is, destroy the fortifications around their houses. And he appointed a deadline for them to
comply with the requirements of the peace. He warned and threatened them
when they began again to dissemble, that if they failed to comply with the
requirements of the peace any further, they would feel the brunt of his wrath.
Moreover, the abbot was continually receiving begging letters from the nobility of the region, especially on behalf of Simon [the Money-changer], to the
effect that the abbot should not wrap up his mercy in anger[2] where Simon
was concerned, but should instead take pity upon him and make an exception
of his house, which was the cause and beginning of the evils. From this cause
the impious Simon himself, vaunting too much confidence in the favor and
familiarity of the princes of the land, spurned the abbot, who was trying to
persuade him to demolish what he had built with evil, and added insult to
injury by building ramparts and the foundations of a tower. The abbot then
realized that the mark of contumacy and the glory of pride lay in the townsmen's houses; consequently he summoned the rustic multitude from the
possessions of the monastery[3] and on the Sabbath after the day of the presentation of the Lord [in the Temple][4] sent them with some of the brothers
against the house of the impious Simon. This band tore down entirely the
outworks of the house, the ramparts, and the tower, while Simon sat by the
fire in the very house, with his wife and children. Seeing this, the other townsmen grew mightily afraid and, blushing with mortification, gave pledges for
the destruction of their fortifications within the determined period.

---

[1] After 1 January 1156.

[2] Psalm 76:10. On Simon, see above 212n.5.

[3] Cf. Guibert of Nogent, *De vita sua* 3 §7: *ex episcopalibus villis plurimo accito rusticorum agmine* (Labande, 334; Benton [1970: 173]).

[4] *et sabbato post Ypapanti domini*: Candlemas, 4 February 1156. Our translation is that of Guizot (1969).

9

At Length in the Year 1155 the Church of Vézelay Obtains Its Liberty and at the Request of the Abbot Ordinations Are Conferred [1621D/505.1544]

1155-1156

In the eleven hundred and fifty-fifth year of the divine incarnation,[1] in the first year of the apostolic pontificate of Nicholas who is called Hadrian,[2] with Louis [VII] the Younger reigning actively as pious king of the Franks, rest was given to the church of Vézelay at the hands of the outstanding and most famous abbot Pons, foremost in stock, character, and dignity. The church obtained its fullest and most unrestricted liberty, as much in private as in public matters.[3] In private matters, the good bishop Alan of Auxerre—although the abbot's great rival was still alive—was invited by Pons to confer holy orders[4] at Vézelay in the oratory of the blessed and always Virgin Mary mother of God on the Lenten Sabbath in the month of March,[5] with the assistance in the monastery of the cardinal-subdeacon Odo of Goodhouse.[6] After an inspection of the authority of the Roman privileges, three acolytes, one subdeacon and four deacons were created. The bishop also promoted to the grade of priest six brothers in the presence and with the help of Stephen, abbot of Reigny. In the following year, the year after the peace and the victory, two bishops, Le Mans and Evreux, coming to Vézelay from Rome with the abbot of St Albans for the celebration of Holy Easter,[7] performed the office of Holy Vigils at the request of the venerable Pons and solemnly celebrated holy ordinations. Evreux ordained doorkeepers, exorcists, lectors, and

---

[1] The beginning of the medieval year, probably being reckoned at this time from 25 March (Lady Day, Feast of the Annunciation), would make the dates given at 218nn.1, 4 and 91 above "1155" in medieval terms; the date given at note 5 below is according to the medieval year (Huygens [1976: 505.1555/56n] "d'apres l'*Ordo Romanus* . . ."). See Poole (1934: 1–27).

[2] Nicholas Breakspear, canon at Avignon, then bishop of Albi, was the only Englishman ever to obtain the papal throne, as Hadrian IV, 1154–1159. See Kelly (1986: 174–75).

[3] *forensi negocio.*

[4] *ordines.* Huygens (1976: 505.1552n) thinks the *emulo* ("the abbot's great rival") refers to Bishop Henry of Autun. The Latin reads: *nam in privato, superstite adhuc emulo, invitatus est a predicto abbate Alanus Altisiodorensis pius episcopus. . . .* On this Alan see Bouchard (1979: chap. 4; see 76ff. for relations with Vézelay and the counts of Nevers). The point of the present § is to demonstrate Vézelay's ecclesiastical independence of the bishop of Autun.

[5] 19 February 1155 (see Huygens [1976: 505.1555–56n]). See n.1 above.

[6] *Odone de Bonacasa*: Guizot: "Othon de Bonne-Chaise," or Odo of Goodhouse (*casa* = house). See further Huygens (1976: 506.1556n). Cox: "In modern reckoning the ordinations described here took place on 19 February 1155, and Odo de Bonacasa was in fact a cardinal-deacon, of San Giorgio in Velabro (1132–1162)."

[7] 15 April 1156. Cox: "The bishops of Le Mans and Evreux were William (1143–1187) and Rotrudus (1138–1165) respectively, and the abbot of Saint Albans was Robert of Gorham."

acolytes in the oratory of Mary, Mother of God.[1] Le Mans ordained seven subdeacons and one deacon, consecrating besides five priests. And in all this the
adversary was silent, his throat choked with envy, cast down by the authority
of justice. On the same Sabbath Abbot Pons received holy chrism from the
archpriest of Auxerre. As for public matters, the church obtained the free
right of judgment over the perfidious betrayers and rebellious serfs, not
because of right [*iure*] or custom [*consuetudine*], but out of necessity, at the
hands of the king, by apostolic authority. Then, at the hand of Abbot Pons,
it decided its own cases and those of its dependants in its own court, possessing full authority [*potestative*]; nor ever or anywhere did the will [*arbitrium*]
of any lay or clerical person intercede in its right to judgment [*iurisiudicii*].
Thus all calumny was annulled, since confusion and ignominy possessed the
calumniators, and the enemy failed, while the just prevailed.[2]

[The rest of folio 122 is blank; on fol.122 begins a list of names,[3] as follows:]

These are they who pulled up the vines of the dean and other vines:
Robert Caligalaxa [Bootmaker? Cox: "Loose-boots," Berlow (1987: 144)
"Littleboot"]
Peter of St. Peter
Peter the Deaf [*Surdellus*]
Odo de l'Étang [*Odo de Palude*, of the Marsh]
Geoffrey Quint [*Quintini*][4]

---

[1] *in oratorio theotocon Mariae.*

[2] Habakuk 1:4.

[3] See Berlow (1971: 23, 324ff.) and (1987) for the significance of this list. On names
in the twelfth century see Benton (1982), Kedar (1973), and Emery (1952) who remarks
(46) that "the use of the surname was becoming normal in the late 12th century in the
Catholic Mediterranean lands" and warns against any assumption that the bearer of a
geographical surname actually hails from the area indicated. A similar caution may be
issued in regard to occupational names. The names listed below may all be followed up in
Huygens (1976: "Index Général," 632ff.), but seldom is much information provided other
than references to the occurrence(s) of the name in the text. See also the lists of names at
201n.3 and 204n.1 above, and 4 §71, Appendix B §§18 and 42 below. Names/words left
in the original are put in italics. The list of names seems to have been added into the MS
by a hand different from that which wrote the previous folios. See Huygens (1976: xx–xxi)
and Bastard (1848: 549n.1). Berlow observes (1971: 341) that in general "the names of the
rebels show very little evidence of the active participation of the commercial and business
class but rather indicate that the revolt involved a broad spectrum of regional society,
including peasants, villagers, tradesmen, members of the class of officials
and even the petty rural nobility." See the comments of Latouche on the commune of Le
Mans, below Appendix E. The names are set out below as in Huygens (1976).

[4] Niermeyer (1976: 880) gives *quintana*: "screen, zone, country-seat," and *quintum*:
"tribute consisting of a share of one-fifth of the crop". Cf. also "quintaine/quintain"
(mock-jousting–Latham [1965: 389]: *quintina*). See further Latham (1965: 389). *Quintana*
is the Italian name of the September jousting festival (*giostra*) held in modern Foligno. A
description of "The Quintain" (in fifteenth-century English) will be found in Guilford
(1920: 48–49). Berlow (1987: 144): "Geoffrey Quentin."

Peter Galimard
Renaud Daudet
Robert the Baker [*Furnerius*]
Robert de Crux-la-Ville [*de cruce*, of the Cross]

These ones are the uprooters:[1]
Heribert [*Arbertus*] White [*Blancus*]
Walter Haytread [who treads the hay, Berlow (1987: 147) "Walter Treading Hay"—*Galterius Calcans Fenum*]
Robert, his brother
Thomasset
John, son of Renaud *Peerel*
Maurice of *Champel* [Littlefield?][2]
Meschinus de Nancapra [Nanchèvre[3]]
Birthday's son [*Filius Natalis*]
William of the Staircase [*de Scalario*]
Charles
William *Beroardi*[4]
Little Walter [*Galteriolus*] of Nanchèvre
Robert *Champerrus* [Field ?][5]
Walter the German
Guy of *Burgaraudo*[6]
Robert the Norman
Clement
Thierry and his son
Lambert Tevin
Briccius
[*Amicus*] the son of Bernard de Pont-sut-Yonne [*de ponte*, of the Bridge]

---

[1] *extirpatores*, i.e., those who pulled up vines, trees, etc., presumably to be distinguished (somehow) from the first group of names; possibly those in the first list were the leaders.

[2] Huygens (1976: 661) suggests "Champeal, Champeau(x)"—Maurice of the Meadow(s). See below Appendix B §18 n.

[3] A hamlet some kilometers east of Vézelay.

[4] The use of the genitive here, as in *Quintini* above suggests the possibility of a "son of" indication ("Fitz").

[5] See n.2 above. Berlow (1987: 144): "Robert Champereux." On this personage, and on others in the list, Berlow writes (1971: 341): "the names of other rebels suggest a relationship with the monastic officialdom, such as Renald, the grandson of Robert the Chaplain, and the Prefect Stephan, perhaps the same man as the Prefect of Blannay who testified in 1146, who was charged with keeping a column and two beams from the smashed mill of Pâtis. The name of Johah, son of *paganus* Seguin, indicates the participation of a member of the petty rural nobility, perhaps the Seguinus Grosso who witnessed the agreement of 1137. Another rebel, Robert Champerrus, may also have witnessed the agreement with other petty nobles."

[6] Huygens (1976: 650) says, "probably the hamlet of Bourguerault, today called Bergros."

Hugh son of Goodfriend [*Boneamicae*][1]
Elmo [*Aalelmus*]
Stephen *Regard*
Her[i]bert nephew of Hugh of St. Peter
Robert *Erraudi*[2]
Landric his brother. Renaud his brother
Andrew son of *Ermenre*[3]
The son of Landric Duck [or Bigship: *Canardi*]
Renaud *Bricio*
William King
John Christopher
John Shepherd [*Bergerius*]
Walter son of Renaud Daudet
Renaud nephew of Robert the Chaplain[4]
John *Anelia*
Robert Crossbowbolt [*Quarrellus*, "Robert Quarrel," Berlow (1987: 142)]
Robert Guilers
The two sons of Mary Galerna[5]
Michael [*Michelet*] who has the almoner's tax[6]
Simon the Stammerer [*Balbus*]
Iunanus son of Payen [*paganus*] Seguin[7]
Robert Cheese
Barbinus Golos [= the Glutton ?]
Robert Jerusalem[8]
John Wastel Cake[9]
Claude's son

These were the ones from Vézelay [who went] to the vineyard of Arnulf de Ferrières:[10]
Robert *Caligalaxa*
John *Pucinus*
Pons the Little [*Ponciolus*] nephew of Robert
Bruno the Little [*Bruniolus*] the servant of Robert

---

[1] Matronymic?
[2] Cf. later Robert *Arraudus*.
[3] See n.1 above.
[4] See 221n.5 above.
[5] See n.1 above.
[6] Money, dues; *censum*.
[7] See 221n.5 above.
[8] Cf. Berlow (1987: 146): "the name of Stephan [below 226n.3] Jerusalem is probably a nickname, perhaps referring to a resident who had visited the Holy Land."
[9] *Gastellus*—Berlow (1987: 147): "John the Pastry-Cook."
[10] *de Ferrariis*—not from Ferrara; cf. "Bois des Ferrières" near Vézelay: Berlow (1987: 145).

Bruno Daniel
Dodo the reseller [*revenditor*] of hay

These are the ones who took the annual corn rent [*annonam*] from Metz-le-Comte:
John Wastel Cake
Renaud son of Hugh of St. Peter
Lambert son of Robert the Baker
His brother Renaud
Champerrus [Field?][1]
Michael [*Michelet*]

These are the ones who have [taken] of the flour [*de ista farina*]:
Hugh of St. Peter, one pint [*sextarium*][2]
Peter the Deaf, one q[uart] [*quartarium*]
Robert *Caligalaxa*, one pint
Peter of St. Peter, one pint
Peter Galimard, one pint
Renaud Daudet, one pint
Michael [*Michelet*] and John Wastel Cake, one pint
Robert de Crux-la-Ville,[3] one peck [*modium*]
Nivard, one peck

These six[4] took eleven pigs, killed them in the house of Robert Crossbowbolt and divided them up among themselves:
Robert de Crux-la-Ville
Nivard
Renaud Daudet
Peter Galimard
Geoffrey Quint
Odo de l'Étang
Peter of St. Peter
Robert *Caligalaxa*

These ones took hens, capons, geese, pigeons with the above six:
Robert *Guilers*
William King
Robert *Arraudus*[5]

---

[1] See 221nn.2, 5 above.
[2] See Isidore *Etymologies* 16, sect. 26, *de mensuris* on these measures, and Latham (1965), Lewis & Short (1933), Niermeyer (1976), etc. under the words in question.
[3] "Robert of the Cross," Berlow (1987: 145) and cf. above 221.
[4] Eight are named!
[5] *Arraudus* probably = *Erraudus*. Cf. above 222n.2.

Landric Goodgift [*Bondons*]
Ronald [*Ranaldus*] his brother
John Shepherd
John Christopher
Bollerius his brother
The son of Renaud Daudet
The nephew of Robert the Chaplain[1]
The two sons of Mary Galerna
Geoffrey Quint has two geese and three capons
Odo de l'Étang, two hens
Robert *Caligalaxa*, four
Peter of St. Peter, five
The son of Hugh of St. Peter, eight
Peter the Deaf, two
Renaud Daudet did the division
Robert the Baker, eight
Robert de Crux-la-Ville, four
Nivard, five
The grooms [*garciferi*] ate others

These are the ones who broke [Cox, "into"] the granary [Cox, "barn" *grangiam*] of *Pasticio*:[2]
Durand *Golos* [= the Glutton?]
Roger *Golos*
Robejais
Alard of the Lion's Spring
Nivard who has from it fifteen *cabrones*,[3] two beams, and two ridge caps[4]
Stephen *Papeiai*
Robert de Crux-la-Ville
Stephen *Regard*
Stephen the Provost [*prepositus*] who has from it one column and two *crabrones*[5]
The son of Constantine King
Walter the Fat
Thibault of Asquins [*Tetbaldus de Esconio*]
The sons of Renaud de Pont-sur-Yonne

---

[1] See 221n.5 above.

[2] Huygens (1976: 666): "unidentified locality." Berlow (1987: 142): "the men who destroyed the grange of Pâtis."

[3] Iron clamps?: *grabones, crabbones, scrabbones*, etc. Cox: "for *cabirones*, rafters?"

[4] ? *pennas*—gables? pinnacles? steeples? Cox: "long beams (*pennas* for *pannas*?)."

[5] See n.3 above. Berlow (1987: 147) "other rebels bore names suggesting some connection with the monastic regime, such as ... the Prefect Stephan, who was accused of appropriating a column and two beams from the mill of Pâtis, which the rebels had destroyed...." Cf. her n.104 for a link with the 1137 *Accord* (Appendix B below).

These are the ones who broke the dean's mill:
Robert *Champerrus* ["of the Field?"][1]
The four brothers Haytread
Maurice of *Champeal*[2]
Her[i]bert White
Walter the German
Amicus, the son of Bernard of the Bridge
Thierry and his son

These are the ones who broke the mill of the granarian[3]
The four brothers Haytread
Maurice of *Champel*[4]
Thierry and his son
Robert *Champerrus* ["of the Field?"][5]
Lambert Tevin
Hugh son of Goodfriend [*Bonami, Bonae Amicae*]
The son of Martin *Ermenre*[6]
The three nephews of Hugh of St. Peter
The sons of the same Hugh
Michael [*Michelet*]. Stephen Jerusalem
The two sons of Mosca [*Muschete*]
John Wastel Cake

These are the ones who absconded with the annual corn rent from the grange
of St. Père-sous-Vézelay:
John Wastel Cake
Iunanus son of Payen [*paganus*] Seguin
Simon the Stammerer
Michael [*Michelet*] who has from there four pints and one-hundred-and-fifty
pieces of pannelling [? Cox, "boards," *de lambrois*] with which he clad [*clausit*]
his house
William son of Galerna[7]
John Wastel Cake [*Gastellus*]
The two sons of Galerna
Lambert son of Robert the Baker
The son of Renaud Daudet

---

[1] See 221nn.2 and 5 above.
[2] Ibid.
[3] Overseer of the granary, *granetarii, granatarii*. Cox: "grange-master."
[4] See 221n.2 above.
[5] See 221nn.2, 5 above.
[6] See 222nn.1, 3 above.
[7] See 222nn.1, 5 above.

These swore to kill the abbot:
Hugh of St. Peter and his son Renaud
Peter of St. Peter
Robert *Caligalaxa*
Aimo the Madman
The two sons of Mosca
Jocelyn. *Attonet*
Michael [*Michelet*]. *Champerrus*[1]
John Christopher
William King
Hugh son of Goodfriend
The son of Martin *Ermenre*[2]
Robert *Arraudus* and his brother Landric
Renaud Moses
John Shepherd
Stephen Jerusalem[3]

[These swore] to kill the constable [*conestabuli*] William:
Iunanus, son of Payen Seguin
Michael [*Michelet*]. Gerald [*Giradus*] *Verret*
Claude's son. Robert *Arraudi*. W. King
Bollerius. The son of Renaud Daudet

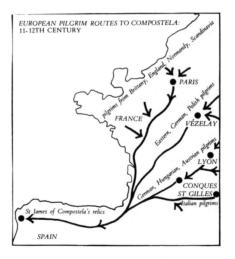

Fig. 11. European pilgrim routes to Compostela eleventh–twelfth centuries
(from Ward [1977c: 8]). Cf. also Evans (1966: 66).

---

[1] See 221nn.2, 5 above.
[2] See 222nn.1, 3 and 225n.6 above.
[3] Cf. 222n.8 above.

Book Four

As fathers enrich their sons[1] with the increase of their gains and wealth, so our ancestors in their foresight have enriched the knowledge of posterity by the writing of books commending the example of their deeds. For by being transmitted in writing, that which is past is, so to say, joined to that which is to come, for the written word sets before us afresh such things as have vanished with the passing of years.

And so, as we have described in the foregoing books the dignity, origin, and liberty of the church of Vézelay, and the troubles which it untiringly endured in defense of its rightful liberty, we now turn our pen to matters as yet unmentioned—not to supply a gap but merely so that what we saw and heard should be set out. We shall describe the honorable conduct of pious forebears, who ought to be imitated by pious sons, lest they neglect to preserve those things which their ancestors acquired for them by their strenuous sagacity and by going to great pains.

Now after all those who assailed the liberty of the church of Vézelay had been vanquished, Abbot Pons of revered and ever-to-be-venerated memory attained the summit of untarnished dignity; as though by renewed right he utterly and completely abolished whatever had been slavishly introduced by envy or error, and having attained peace, he ruled his monastery quietly for five years with the rod of equity.[2]

1

In The Year 1159 a Schism Arose in the Church [1623B/512. 19]

1159

In the year of the incarnate word 1159 there arose, alas! a foul dissension within the Roman church. For, on the death of Pope Hadrian, Roland, chancellor of the sacred bureau, was elected in general council and by unanimous assent. While he was humbly declining to take on himself so great a burden, Octavian, one of the apostolic cardinals and one of the city's noblest senators, fraudulently seized the apostolic insignia for himself and (O the wickedness of it!) usurped the apostolic honor: neither divine nor human law overawed him, even though he had no more than three followers of his schism in the whole apostolic consistory, namely Aimar, bishop of Tusculum, Guy of Cremona, and John of Santa Martina. Two of these, Aimar and John, met their death during the schism before the schismatic himself died. When the rest of the cardinals learnt of this schismatic usurpation, they left the city at once with their candidate, who had in the meantime taken the name Alexander and been consecrated by Humbald, bishop of Ostia.[3] There began a

---

[1] *2 Cor.* 12:14.

[2] *Hebrews* 1:8.

[3] The schism that developed on the death of Hadrian lasted for eighteen years and

grave schism in the western Church, the German emperor favoring Octavian, who took the name of Victor,[1] and the king of Sicily[2] backing the Catholic Alexander. Alexander sent his legates, William of Pavia, Henry of Pisa, and Otto of Tulliano Carcere,[3] into France and the British Isles, to King Louis VII of the Franks and to King Henry II of the English, as well as to the whole church in each realm. When these men had passed through Italy and had not been received by the monastery of Cluny, Abbot Pons of Vézelay of worthy memory became the first among all Frenchmen to receive them, and commended the catholic election of the orthodox Alexander to all the princes of both orders.[4]

2
The Cluniacs Refuse to Support Pope Alexander. They Are Excommunicated   [1623D/513.47]

1161

When Alexander's election had been recognized in both these kingdoms [i.e., England and France], the legates wrote to the Cluniacs asking them to accept it. Now the ruler of Cluny at that time was Hugh,[5] a man prudent in his actions and of a straightforward disposition. When the chapter had been convoked, as is customary with such matters, he consulted his brothers about recognizing Alexander. The brothers, however, detested the pastoral rule of their father Hugh, and being unable to fasten their envious teeth into his innocent person, they employed a cunning plan and forbad him on oath to receive either the Catholic or the schismatic party, lest by favoring the vanquished they should incur the odium of the victor, as happens in such cases. To counter any suggestion on the abbot's part that this advice might turn out to be harmful rather than advantageous, they all promised unanimously to follow it and to submit to the outcome with the abbot, whatever adversity might befall them all. Now because the papal legates were afraid to come to Cluny

---

was resolved finally by the Treaty of Venice in 1177 (Thomson [1975]). It resulted in a fierce struggle for support between the partisans of Alexander III (1159–1181) and those of the emperor, Frederick I Barbarossa (1152–1190). It was the latter's opposition to Alexander's election that forced him into exile at Sens for one and a half years, between October 1163 and Easter 1165. Alexander had been a professor of law at Bologna and had written a commentary on Gratian and a work of theology influenced by the teachings of Abelard, before being made a cardinal in 1150. See Baldwin (1968), Barraclough (1968), Ullmann (1972) and, on the schism of 1130, Stroll (1987). Notice the broad scope of the present book of the *Major Chronicle* compared with the focus of Books 1-3.

    [1] Victor IV, the anti-pope, was elected, like Alexander, on 7 September 1159. He died on 20 April 1164. His successor, the anti-pope Paschal III (1164–1168), was his elector Guy of Cremona. See the appropriate entries in Kelly (1986).

    [2] William I (1154–1166).

    [3] This is probably San Pietro in Carcere, later called the Mamertine Prison. (See the *Blue Guide to Rome* [London, 1979] 110.)

    [4] *universis utriusque ordinis principibus*; that is, the leaders of both the lay and the ecclesiastical orders.

    [5] Hugh III, abbot of Cluny, 1158–1161 had been claustral prior at the time of his election.

and to pronounce sentence against the schismatics, they sent Henry, then bishop of Beauvais, later archbishop of Rheims. Because he was King Louis' brother they thought he could travel more safely in those parts and wield the sword of the apostle Peter delegated to him by Alexander through the agency of the legates. Henry, having arrived at Luzy and met with the Cluniacs, was preparing to place them under sentence of anathema, but he delayed at the request of Dalmacius[1] and other princes of that land. Instead he wrote to the Cluniacs, exhorting them to reconsider and to recognize Alexander as the other French monasteries had done; otherwise he would no longer delay pronouncing a sentence of excommunication, by the papal authority delegated to him, against both them and all their followers as well. They were assigned a day to present their case at Melun, but neither the abbot of Cluny himself, detained by the fraud of his monks, nor his proctors arrived. As a consequence, certain of the abbot's rivals took a stand against him, namely Thibault prior of Saint-Martin-des-Champs, who had once held office as prior, second only to the abbot, in the monastery of Cluny, and many others who were considered the chief men of his church. They accused their abbot as parricide sons accuse a father, removing the blame of being schismatic from themselves and saying in fact that they would commit themselves and the monasteries entrusted to them to the subjection and protection of the Catholic pope Alexander. At the urging of these men Henry publicly excommunicated Abbot Hugh of Cluny and all his dependants and supporters.[2]

3

After Pons, Abbot of Vézelay, Had Completed His Life, William, Abbot of Pontoise Was Chosen to Replace Him

[1624C/514.85]

1161

Our Pons of holy memory, worthy to be called abbot, had been summoned to this meeting, for certain people were striving to have him promoted to the abbacy of Cluny and Hugh expelled. But the blessed and glorious handmaiden of God, Mary Magdalene—to whom as a devotee Pons had always shown devoted obedience—would in no way allow him to be snatched away from her candlestick, which had shone forth so splendidly, and she held on bodily to him whom, raised from boyhood and conceded to her by Michael prince of angels,[3] she had appropriated and consecrated entirely and absolutely to her-

---

[1] Dalmacius of Semur-en-Brionnais, the lord of Luzy, was related to Abbot Pons through the latter's mother.

[2] Hugh was deposed as abbot in 1161 and actually left the monastery in 1163; see Brooke and Morey (1967: 192). There survives a letter from Hugh to Gilbert Foliot, bishop of London, in which Hugh explains his vacillation over the papal schism. In essence he argues that because Cluny has possessions both in lands controlled by the emperor and his supporters and in lands controlled by the supporters of Alexander it must be very careful not to alienate either party. See Robertson (1881: 5:29–32).

[3] Before becoming abbot of Vézelay, Pons had been a monk of San Michele della Chiusa, near Turin.

self. Nor would she suffer the enemy of the liberty[1] of her sepulchre to boast of him [Pons] even for an hour in case, acting contrary to his own principles, he [Pons] who had fought for his country, as it were, should attack his country, or in case malice should lay virtue prostrate by virtue, or evil overthrow probity by probity. For he was detained by an unexpected illness and in the twenty-fourth year after his ordination he went the way of all flesh.[2] Being buried before the sepulchre of the maidservant of Christ's sepulchre amidst the deep grief of his monks, he was transported, as we may believe, lest the glory of human probity should alter his way of thinking. As soon as he had been taken up, the brothers of the monastery of Vézelay, with one voice and unanimous assent, elected as their father a man of noble birth and conspicuous probity, one instructed in sacred disciplines from his youth, both at Vézelay itself where he was now received, and in the house of Cluny. The new abbot, William, had been abbot of Saint-Martin-de-Pontoise, where he had ruled for fifteen years, enriching the monastery with many possessions and buildings.[3]

4

The Count of Nevers Puts Up a Barrier So That The Election Cannot Come Into Effect. The Agreement of the Count Ought Not Be Required in the Election of Abbot

[1625A/514.110]

1161

In those days Count William [III] of Nevers—son of William [II] of La Chartreuse, son of Renaud de Hubans, son of William [I], son of Renaud, son of Landric who was the first of this line to receive the lordship of Nevers from the duke of Burgundy—this count, I say, after he had inflicted on the church of Vézelay those many injuries which are partly contained in the preceding books, became violently ill, and began to drain the chalice of divine vengeance.[4] When William [IV] his son heard that the Vézelay monks had elected an abbot for themselves, the young man, who in his native insolence had determined that everything should be ordered by his will, came to Vézelay full of great rage and fury, and annulled this election made by the brothers in his

---

[1] Cluny, of course, which the chronicler sees as the great enemy of the liberty of Vézelay.

[2] On 14 October 1161.

[3] William of Mello was abbot of Vézelay from 1161 to 1171. He was of the noble family of the lords of Mello and was the uncle of William of Mello and Renaud, the almoner of Vézelay, both mentioned later in this book. Cox: "The Mello clan were, in fact, an ancient and powerful family with its base in Picardy. Raynald de Mello, son of Dreux, had founded the priory of Mello and placed it under the jurisdiction of Vézelay."

[4] Count William (III) of Nevers died on 21 October 1161. William IV, his eldest son by Ida of Carinthia, ruled from then until his death on 24 October 1168. Apart from his struggles with Vézelay he was also involved in wars against the barons of Donzy, the counts of Joigny and Sancerre, and the bishop of Auxerre. He took up the cross in 1167, along with his brother Guy, and died of the plague a year later. William IV would have been perhaps 15-16 years old in 1161 AD.

absence and without consulting his [William IV's] father; he also posted guards to prevent any of the Vézelay monks going to their abbot-elect. But with what depraved and unreasonable advice he did this, is made clear by our muniments from the Roman pontiffs and the privileges of the kings of the Franks; even a document of his grandfather, who assailed with similar arrogance the election of Abbot Renaud, later archbishop of Lyon, declares as follows:[1]

> I, William, count of Nevers resign to God and his blessed apostles Peter and Paul, and to the blessed Mary Magdalene, a certain evil custom, which I have been exacting from the church of Vézelay, namely that from now on the consent of myself or my heirs or successors need not be sought for the election of an abbot there; but the church may have whomsoever they have elected, so that none of our men may be able to challenge anything or exact anything from the church, because our consent has not been sought. And I promise that I will not lay further charges concerning the entry or exit of any abbot [from office].

5

The Cardinal Legate Confirms the Election. The Abbot Enters Into Possession   [1625D/515.137]

1161

So the Vézelay monks, disregarding the young count's unjust accusation, sent Renaud de Mello[2] to summon their abbot-elect. When he had come, the abbot-elect did not want to enter the monastery, nor to be received by the brothers in solemn procession, lest his entry should seem not to have been made through the door[3]—for this kind of translation from monastery to monastery, or from church to church could in no way be seen as authentic without the knowledge of the Roman pontiff. So the Vézelay monks wrote to Cardinal Otto, legate of the Apostolic See, through Geoffrey the guestmaster,[4] notifying him of the manner of the election, and the person elected. When he had read through their papal privileges, the cardinal approved the election as legal, and in his capacity as papal delegate confirmed it as valid, and on behalf of the lord pope he committed the care of the church of Vézelay to the abbot-elect, through the agency of Peter of Pisa, dean of Saint-Aignan-d'Orleans. So Abbot William entered Vézelay to the applause of all the populace, and was received by the brothers in solemn procession; with him were the abbots Macharius of Fleury, Thibault of Saint-Germain-des-Prés, and Stephen of Reigny. A few days later he sent the same Geoffrey and his

---

[1] There is no other record of this document.
[2] Renaud de Mello was the nephew of the newly elected abbot William and the son of Dreux de Mello who had just acquired a seigneury at Saint-Bris, near Auxerre.
[3] See *John* 10:1-2.
[4] *per Gaufredum hospitalem*. As well as furnishing the guest rooms, the guestmaster was responsible for shoeing and obtaining veterinary treatment for the horses of the monks and the pilgrims.

clerk John the Italian to Pope Alexander with letters from the chapter describing the process of his election, with letters from the king of the Franks, even with letters from the king of England, and from the above-mentioned abbots, commending the mode of election and the person of the abbot-elect.

6

Pope Alexander Reaches His Palace. He Hears an Account of the Abbot's Election and Renews the Abbey's Privileges. The Cluniacs Usurp Rule of the Monastery of Vézelay

[1626B/516.160]

1161-1162 (1130-1131)

Meanwhile Pope Alexander, to avoid the snares set by the schismatic Octavian, crossed the sea to Genoa. Hearing this, the messengers from Vézelay went there. Honorably received there by Alexander, they were with him in his palace for several days. Sitting together with the whole assembly of cardinals, in the presence of a great multitude from many realms, Alexander listened to the representatives of the monastery of Vézelay, received the letters which they had brought with them, declared the ordination of Abbot William valid, and gave to him and all the brothers of that house a privilege in which, following the examples of the former Roman pontiffs, he ordained that the brothers of the monastery of Vézelay, on the death of their abbot, had the right of free election in choosing a successor, and that no one should presume to demand at all or usurp for himself the right to grant assent to that election, for any reason, even on the pretext of religion.[1]

This very liberty, which the church of Vézelay had held quietly and unassailed for almost three hundred years from the very beginning of its foundation, and by which the brothers had put at their head fathers chosen indifferently both from among themselves and from the brothers of other monasteries, the Cluniacs, rising up long after, had tried to snatch away and arrogate for themselves. They arrogated to themselves first the assent to, then the actual right of election, adducing an apocryphal privilege[2] under the name of Pope Paschal II to the effect that Paschal had committed to them the care and ordering of the church of Vézelay. For this reason Vézelay suffered a terrible outrage in the reign of Innocent II as a result of an attempt to reclaim its original liberty: by the violence of Innocent and the count of Nevers a certain Alberic was forced on it by the Cluniacs,[3] and nearly all of

---

[1] Alexander's confirmation of the liberty of Vézelay inspires Hugh to give an account of events that occurred thirty years earlier when the monks tried to resist Cluniac domination.

[2] Despite his description of this privilege as "apocryphal" (*furtivum*), Hugh tacitly acknowledges its legitimacy by publishing below the bull of Alexander III which revokes it. See Huygens (1976: xxix) and above *Cartulary* §14 and n., and Chérest 1.26 n.3 (Hugens [1976: 13 n.3]: the bull is authentic and dated to 1102 AD).

[3] See charter 20, above. The background to this dispute is discussed in Aspects [A] above. Hugh's reference here to Vézelay's "attempt to reclaim its original liberty"

the brothers of the house were bound in chains and ignobly dispersed throughout Provence, Italy, Germany, Lorraine, France, and Aquitaine, while foreigners sneaked onto the freest of all soil, gathered together as though under Sennacherib, coming from everywhere, but all Samaritans in their false belief.[1]

Now because in its time of temptation, arrogance puffed Cluny up—although it had until then stood out as a very special member of the Roman church—and it had turned away from Roman unity, apostolic justice quite rightly decided that the church of Vézelay, uterine sister of the blessed Peter, should never again be subjected to the calumny of schismatics. The Catholic pope Alexander, after all, enjoyed by God's disposition the exercise of the blessed Peter's keys as much as Paschal or any other of his apostolic predecessors—those keys by which whatever happens to have been put forward under color of religion as committed or bound may be reckoned to be released or dissolved because the merit of the faith [recommends it].

To return to my theme, the liberty of the church of Vézelay was endangered by Cluniac insolence, not merely in the matter of elections, but in its totality. For at the same time as these foreigners were using up a great abundance of the church's possessions and were permitting its goods to be plundered by the natives of the neighborhood, they invited the count of Nevers, and under the guise of friendship gave him the opportunity to exercise unaccustomed tyranny and unheard-of customs: a careless and stupid decision ignoring their rightful liberty. In their times were introduced the exaction of unowed profits of justice,[2] frequent claims on their hospitality, burdensome charges,[3] and the submission to evil customs, through all of which in our time our church has been reduced almost to nothing.[4] For, stealing in little by little, this pestiferous disease of servitude to the Cluniacs and to the

---

(Huygens [1976]: 516.185–86 *reclamando libertatem ingenitam*) is a veiled allusion to an apparent attempt on the part of the monks at Vézelay to exploit the confusion at Cluny surrounding the early years of Peter the Venerable's abbacy (1120s AD) by appointing their own abbots Baldwin and Gerard (See Berlow [1981] and James [1953: 223]—Bernard of Clairvaux writing to Innocent II in the 1130s: "with what a strong hand was that noble monastery of Vézelay set in order! The majesty of the apostolic see did not even consider giving way one inch to the insane rabble of armed people, to the frenzied fury of undisciplined monks, or to what is more powerful than all this, the forces of Mammon"). Cox asserts that in 1125 Peter the Venerable had to obtain from Pope Honorius II a bull forbidding eighteen Cluniac houses, Vézelay among them, to elect abbots without his permission.

[1] *qui quasi sub Sennacherib undecunque congregati unum superstitionis Samaritanorum nomen fecere.* On Sennacherib, king of Assyria, see 2 Chron. 32:1, John 8:48. Cox also cites 2 Kings 24–41, though the ruler here is Shalmaneser (Shalmander). Cf. also 2 Kings 18:9–13. For an analysis of the incident, see Aspects [A] above. Hugh now returns to the events of 1161–1162.

[2] *indebite iusticie.*

[3] *occasionumque gravamina.*

[4] See *Major Chronicle* 2 §4, (Huygens [1976: lines 181–86]). Note that this is an admission that some of the rights claimed by the count had, in fact, been possessed by his father. In contrast to *Major Chronicle* 1 §2 and 2 §4 above, Hugh seems here to be admitting that there *was* considerable customary precedent for what Pons and William of Mello were opposing.

count's tyranny infected all the senior men of that time from the sole of their feet to the crown of their head,[1] until the arrival of Abbot Pons of blessed memory, whom the rich soil of Auvergne, nourisher of illustrious men, produced for us, and that man of whom we are now to speak, William of Mello, who came of the virile stock of the great Charles of La Roche-Mello. These men, true sons of their true mother, each sorrowed at her misfortune and fought in defense of justice for her to the point of the shedding of blood.

Now Pope Alexander, leaving Genoa, landed at the port of Maguelonne.[2] He was met by Abbot William of Vézelay, who like his predecessor Pons, received the first fruits of the apostolic legation, not without envy on the part of his own men and certain magnates. It was he, first among all the French prelates, who welcomed the high pontiff as he stepped ashore and found grace in Alexander's sight and was magnified by him before a multitude of the whole Roman church. When he had examined again the testament of Count Gerard and had matched the muniments containing ancient privileges with recent ones, Pope Alexander, in consistory at Montpellier, by common counsel and consent and with the advice of all the bishops, priests, deacons, subdeacons, and cardinals, confirmed the immunity and liberty of the church of Vézelay and its freedom to elect or substitute an abbot, as set out in the following copy:[3]

7

Pope Alexander Confirms the Privileges of the Church of Vézelay and Removes It From the Power of the Cluniacs

[1627D/518.240]

1162

Alexander, bishop, servant of the servants of God, to his dear sons William, abbot of the monastery of Vézelay, and his brothers both present and future, who have professed the monastic life. In perpetuity.

The holy Roman church, which responds to each man according to the quality of his merits, is accustomed to act with more kindly grace towards those whom it finds to be faithful sons, and is wont to adorn with especial honor those whom it observes to be more fervent in its service. Pope Paschal, our predecessor of good memory, as we have learnt from a privilege of our immediate predecessor, Pope Calixtus of happy memory, is known to have committed the monastery of Vézelay, which by law belongs specially to the blessed Peter, to the church of Cluny, noting the fervor of religion which existed in it [Cluny] at that time, and that religious life had disappeared for the most part from the monastery of Vézelay. And Pope Calixtus confirmed

---

[1] Isaiah 1:6. This powerful account of Cluniac oppression and expansionism, culminating in the biblical metaphor, allows Hugh to mention his two heroes, abbots Pons and William.

[2] On 11 April 1162. Note the pope's busy travel schedule.

[3] This charter was issued in 1162. Note that unlike Books 1-3 of the *Major Chronicle*, the relevant documents for which were gathered together in the *Cartulary* that precedes the history, Book 4 incorporates its documents within its text. The privilege of Calixtus II referred to is dated 12 January 1120 (Cox).

this by the privilege of his authority, namely that on the death of the abbot who was then in office, another should be substituted by the common agreement of the brothers, or of the more sensible portion, and with the advice of the abbot of Cluny. However, noting carefully the constancy of devotion and the firmness of faith which both you and Abbot Pons of Vézelay of blessed memory have shown towards the Roman church in this stormy time, and considering how manifestly the church of Cluny has erred in this time of trouble, and how, falling from its original state of religion and good behavior, it has alienated itself from the Church's unity, while your monastery remains most stable in devotion and faith towards the Church, with its religion thoroughly restored to it by God's grace, we have, with the unanimous advice of our brothers, ordered that commission which our predecessor Pope Paschal issued to be recalled, so that both churches may be seen to receive the fruit of their merits. We ordain that your monastery should in no way be subject to the church of Cluny, nor be held answerable to anyone at all except to the church of Rome; and thus you may always have freedom of election, so that neither the advice nor the consent of the abbot of Cluny is required. On the contrary, we wish you to be provided with an abbot set over you whom the brothers elect by common consent, or by the advice of the wiser minority, in the fear of God and in accord with the Rule of the blessed Benedict, and whose ordination the Roman pontiff has planned, or to whose ordination he has consented at the suggestion of the monks of that place. And so that this decision shall be always and inviolably observed in the future, we confirm it by apostolic authority, and fortify it by the privilege of this present writing, ordaining that no man is to infringe or contravene this page of our constitution in any way. If anyone presumes to attempt this he shall be admonished two or three times, and unless he compensates for his presumption with fitting satisfaction, let him lose the dignity of his power and honor, and let him know himself subject to divine judgment for perpetrating such iniquity, and let him be cut off from the most sacred body and blood of our Lord and God Jesus Christ, and be subject to the strict vengeance of the last judgment. The peace of our Lord Jesus Christ, however, be upon those who obey it, that they may here obtain the fruit of their good action, and receive at the hand of the great Judge the prize of eternal peace. Amen.

8

After Being Generously Received By the Pope, the Abbot Returns to His Church. His Reputation Undermines Those Who Hate Him [1629A/519.295]

1161

After Abbot William had been with Pope Alexander for many days, he returned home endowed with the pope's grace and blessing, and with the favor of the whole Roman church. On his return he was received with great glory by his brothers and by all the people in a solemn procession, with the streets decorated and the burning of incense. When he had offered a prayer, as the custom is, he gave two precious silk cloths and two excellent carpets [to the church], whereupon all the enemies of the liberty of the church of Vézelay were put to confusion. But there arose certain gossiping fellows, men whose nature it is to envy the good fortune of honorable men, and they began to slander Abbot William to the young count [for his father had passed away], suggesting that William had wasted all his church's goods and had given incalculable sums of money to the Romans.[1] They said that it was impious to ruin so noble a church, and that this impiety would recoil deservedly on the head of the count, for he was supposed to be the church's protector and defender but did not oppose so great a spoliation of it.

Now there was a young man named William, son of Peter of Montréal, one of the youngest of Abbot Pons's servants[2] but keener in intellect than the rest. Being quick on the uptake and agreeable in his willingness to serve, he found such favor with Pons, that he excelled all the other household servants [aulicos] in his powers, and boasted virtual second place after the abbot in giving orders: whomsoever he shut out was shut out, and whomsoever he admitted was admitted; whomsoever he excused was excused, and whomsoever he condemned was condemned; just and unjust, money [munus] or merit, grace itself, the best of all fortune's gifts—these things counted for nothing without William's favor. Men whose age and wisdom had once made them Pons's close friends now became strangers. In his immaturity he was becoming more and more presumptuous and began to slander even the brothers, accusing his own masters, although a serf [servus] in his condition and manners; and since all others were shut out, he alone abused the favor of his lord—who was his lord in name alone.[3] Good and bad were worth the same price to him, for he devoted himself entirely to enlarging his own possessions at the expense of the poor. Abusing his master's trust, he returned thirty for every hundred pence, and received one hundred pence for a single penny,[4] multiplying his worth exceedingly with many possessions and inestimable wealth; everyone's fate was in his mouth. Content [to achieve his goals] by abusing the trust of one man only,[5] he aroused the hatred of everyone both inside and outside the monastery. A man arrogant, proud, and base, he had no time for honest and well-intentioned men, but accused them and soiled their reputations. To such an extent did he deceive the pious father's simple goodness by his cunning flattery, that everything was directed by him in whatever way he pleased. But after this young man, elated and above himself

---

[1] Abbot William almost certainly had paid for the recognition of the abbey's privileges. The need to oil the wheels of the papal court with money was a common complaint of contemporary satirists. See for example, Thomson (1973 and 1978), Yunck (1963).

[2] inter ministros . . . etate quidem iunior sed ingenio acrior. Every monastery had numerous servants; in fact, the servants would almost certainly have outnumbered the monks. At Cluny, there were so many servants that their idle chatter seriously disturbed order and their pilfering of goods for their relatives depleted the abbey's resources.

[3] solus solo nomine domini sui gratia abutebatur. Hugh implies that William of Montréal did not treat the abbot as his lord, but merely called him lord.

[4] de penuria pauperum dilatare terminos suos . . . pro centenario tricenarium reddebat et pro denario centenarium recipiebat. Cox suggests the context is money-lending using abbatial funds, but the figures are vague and may simply imply large scale fraud and peculation of abbey funds. Cf., however, §9 below (Huygens [1976: 524.462–63]): hac etenim pluribus in locis fenerata.

[5] unius tantum gratia abutendo contentus. . . .

to a wonderful degree, had grown in insolence rather than in maturity for four years, suddenly in one moment of a single night the miserable wretch cracked and crumbled, and became as though he was not—and would that he had never been! For when Abbot Pons of happy memory had breathed his last, this traitorous serf, who from sorrow ought to have remained in his place, neglected the last rites and immediately took his keys, ransacked the cupboards, and carried off on the quiet whatever he could snatch. After he had repeated this most sacrilegious theft several times, he was noticed by the brothers and captured. Asked about the abbot's treasure, and about a golden candlestick which the late empress Matilda,[1] mother of King Henry of England, had given to the monastery of Vézelay, he denied all. But when his house had been searched, and the brothers had obtained from his servants the key which he denied having, they discovered the candlestick which he denied possessing, the abbot's seal, and the chapter seal which he had kept hidden from the brothers for two years. The next morning he gave the brothers sureties for £500 against the execution of justice by the future abbot, who was elected unanimously on the same day that the blessed Pons was buried, Friday, 14 October, in the year of our Lord 1161.

Meanwhile that profane William of Montréal went to the young count, who was involved in the ceremonies surrounding his own father's death—for his father had ended his earthly life a week after the death of the pious Pons—and when he had prepared the way by many lies, he promised the new count £80 and 17 silver cups if he would lend him his aid against the Vézelay monks, and in addition two marks of silver [which he would give the count] each year by way of commendation [*pro commendatitio*]. In return the count promised him aid against everyone, as he had asked.

So after the abbot-elect William had been solemnly received, everyone cried with one voice against William of Montréal, who, relying on the count's help, refused to submit to the law. So he was seized on Abbot William's orders and thrown into prison. Then, employing his usual cunning when he saw that the aid for which he hoped was not forthcoming, he began to entreat the abbots of Fleury and Paris, who had come to the new abbot's instalment, and, under the guise of confession—which it is unlawful for priests to disclose—he revealed all that he knew of the treasures demanded from him. He swore that he would abide by their decision on the charges laid against him if the new abbot would agree. The latter, bowing to their entreaties and advice, said that he too would do as they asked. At once, that very evening, holy relics were placed on the abbot's staff [*in virgulto abbatis*], and the impious William, brought forth from prison, swore on the relics that he would do whatever the abbots decided the next morning, and that in the meantime he would not escape. But what faith can be placed in perfidy? For there can be no trace of truth where there is no foundation of faith. As the common saying has it:

---

[1] Mathilda, widow of Henry V, emperor of Germany, had remarried Geoffrey Plantagenet, to whom she bore the future Henry II of England. She had given a golden chandelier with seven branches to Cluny (Huygens [1976: 521.347/349n]); had she given another to Vézelay?

"No trust can be placed in a known enemy";[1] and no credence is to be given to a traitor's oaths: the impious man swears with his mouth, his mouth speaks justice, but in his heart he speaks from the wickedness of his heart, and falling into the abyss of evils he spurns justice and follows the proposal of the impious. Just so, that scoundrel William, scorning his oath and even disregarding the trust of those who had stood surety for him, shamelessly perjured himself that very night by flight.

When Abbot William heard of this and ascertained that the criminal had gone, he immediately sent his servants to the home of the fugitive traitor, had the grain and wine, vessels and cloths and all the furniture of the house carried off, and exacted the promised sum of £500 from those who had gone surety. Now the sacrilegious man fled secretly to the count, who received him and a few days later led him back to Vézelay. Upon this the abbot demanded to know why the count had received this fugitive liar of his, and why he had led him back into Vézelay, contrary to the custom of the vill, for the law did not permit him to receive a man commended to the monastery,[2] nor to furnish an enemy of the vill with a safe-conduct back to it. In order to decide these and other complaints a day was fixed at Reigny. When they had met there, the abbot first complained that the count had received his liegemen[3] contrary to the custom of the church, and then he asked that this fugitive of his, William of Montréal, who was one of the church's most important serfs,[4] should be handed over to him at once, since the serf was guilty of treason and perjury. Then the count called on his chief men to assess this charge, which alleged the breach of a lawful custom. They all stated unanimously that the count had no right to protect any serf of the church of Vézelay, either against the church, or in any other way. The count immediately sent the slippery William away, and ordered him to return to his rightful lord and to abide by the latter's orders in all matters. When William saw that he could do nothing about it, willy-nilly he submitted to the abbot's orders, and, having sold his house and some of his possessions, freed his sureties from their obligation.

9

The Monks of Vézelay Pour Out Prayers to God for the
Sick Count of Nevers. Nonetheless He Shows Himself to
Be Ungrateful   [1631C/523.419]

1162

After this it happened that the count sickened nigh unto death. Abbot William was filled with compassion for him, and although hated by the count, he served him as well as he could, out of kindness, and prayers went up to God every day on his behalf in the church of Vézelay. But when, by those prayers, the count

---

[1] See Ecclesiasticus 12:10.
[2] *commendatitium hominem monasterii.*
[3] *homines suos commendatos.*
[4] *capitaneus servus aecclesiae.*

regained his strength, the ungrateful man forgot all the benefits which the church and abbot had gained for him. Giving ear[1] to slanderous gossip he considered how he might find opportunities to vex the abbot and monastery. So he wrote to the abbot ordering him to send him the money which the profane William of Montréal owed him [the count] by virtue of a promise. In addition, he gave orders to the messenger who carried this letter, that if the abbot delayed giving him the money, or played for time, he was to lay waste the abbot's lands immediately. So one Sunday a messenger, who was said to be Geoffrey of Melun, handed the abbot a letter from the count about this matter. The abbot immediately replied to him that he did not owe the count any money at all, but that if indeed that impious William owed the count something, then the count should demand it from him without hesitation. Geoffrey replied that it made no difference to him, so long as he carried out the count's command one way or another. "Will you then on this Lord's Day pillage our property?" asked the abbot. "No," said Geoffrey, "but I shall not be able to delay execution of my master's orders beyond tomorrow. However, if you wish to send someone to my lord, I shall gladly accompany your messenger myself and plead your cause." So after he had been entertained by the abbot at Chamoux, he took with him the abbot's messenger, a certain monk, to meet the count. During the journey Geoffrey parted from the monk, and coming to Châtel-Censoir, chose some strong young men, and on that very same Sunday towards evening they raided all the flocks of the abbot's sheep at Chamoux, where he had eaten with the abbot that same day. But it was not long before divine vengeance caught up with him. For less than a week later he went out of his mind, and leapt from the window of his house into the Yonne below; he was dragged out half-dead, but then tried to cut off his own testicles; and so his unworthy life ended in madness and death.

Now all the brothers and the whole populace of Vézelay began to complain of that utter scoundrel William [of Montréal], for it was because of him that they were exposed both to the enmity of such a great prince and to the pillage of their goods. So the abbot ordered William either to pay the count what he had promised, or at least to make good the damage which the church had suffered. Since he refused to do either, he was loaded with chains and flung into prison. Although clapped in irons and surrounded with darkness and the stench of the dungeon he could not forget the amount of money involved; on the contrary, he thought it sweeter to undergo every kind of torment, rather than part with his money freely. For the sake of his money, lent out at interest in many places, he gladly endured the dirty prison and pangs of hunger, and what is more, the injury to his reputation. When at length he was forced by the rigors of his long imprisonment to make peace by selling some of his possessions again, he became like a wolf among sheep,[2] cheating his neighbors, accusing the poor and slandering the rich. The count too, not satisfied with the suffering caused by William and the evil he had already inflicted, preyed on the herds and men of the monastery of Vézelay. For, as the common proverb has it: "Any opportunity suffices him who wishes to inflict harm"; and so, far from relying on a just cause of com-

---

[1] *patulas aures*; cf. Horace *Ep.* 1.18.70: *patulae . . . aures.*
[2] See Matthew 10:16 and Luke 10:3. Also see Horace *Odes* 3.18.13.

plaint, he sought any opportunity to subject the church to his lordship [*dominio*] and despoil it of its rightful liberties [*ingenita libertate*].

10
King Louis of the Franks Supports Pope Alexander But
Is Rebuffed By Him   [1632D/524.474]

1162

At this time the western Church was still suffering its grievous schism. Now Count Henry of Champagne[1] favored the emperor's side. On the other side, King Louis of France sent his legates, Thibault [*Theobaldo*], abbot of Saint–Germain-des-Prés and Cadurcus, his clerk, to meet the Catholic pope, Alexander; but as Alexander received their legation with less enthusiasm than they had hoped for, they turned back and came to Vézelay. There Abbot Thibault sank upon a bed of sickness and died on 24 July, and was buried inside the door of the church of St. Mary Magdalene, whose monk he had been. When King Louis heard that his legates had been rejected he was angry and repented of having embraced Alexander and spurned Victor, and he wrote about these things to Count Henry of Champagne, through Bishop Manasses of Orléans, while the count was hurrying to the side of the German emperor. Heartily thankful at having found such an opportunity, Count Henry suggested to the emperor that he should arrange a meeting with the king, together with the chief magnates and prelates of both their realms, promising on oath that when the king [Louis] had heard an inquiry into the elections of both popes, conducted by persons of both realms, he would abide by his [that is, count Henry's] advice. And so the conference was appointed to meet at Saint-Jean-de-Losne, a town situated on the Saône, on the French border.[2] It was arranged that the Catholic Alexander and the schismatic Victor should be present at the conference, and that they should discuss their elections before the whole Church.[3]

---

[1] Henry I, count of Champagne and Troyes (1152–1181), the eldest son of Thibault (*not* the Thibault who appears in the next line of the *Major Chronicle!*), whom he succeeded, married Marie de Champagne, daughter of Louis VII and Eleanor of Aquitaine. While still only count of Meaux, he had accompanied Louis VII to Palestine where he distinguished himself as one of the most courageous of the king's followers. As count of Champagne he rendered homage to the king of France, to whom he remained very close, despite his support for the emperor and the antipope against Alexander III.

[2] *in finibus regni Franciae.*

[3] On this conference, for which the Vézelay chronicle is one of the most important sources, see Heinemeyer (1964), Munz (1969: 228–32), Pacaut (1970: 107–9) and Fuhrmann (1986: 157–58). Alexander had alienated Louis, whose support he considered certain, by accommodating too readily Henry II of England because the pope considered his support more important at the time. Cox: "Louis' anger against Pope Alexander has been explained as the result of actions taken by the pope to win the support of Henry II of England. Henry was eager to seize control of the Vexin, a militarily important region on the frontier between Normandy and the Île de France, which was eventually to go to the Plantagenets as the dowry of Marguerite de France, daughter of Louis VII and Constance of Castile, who was betrothed to Henry's eldest son. Since the prospective bride and groom were, respectively, only two and five years old in 1160, the French considered

11

Acting on Sounder Advice the Pope Sends Messengers to the King and They Calm His Spirit [1633B/525.497]

1162

When Alexander heard this, he sent messengers, Bishop Bernard of Porto and Hyacinth his deacon, to King Louis, and they calmed the king's anger and arranged for a friendly discussion. As a result Alexander and Louis met at Souvigny,[1] a town [*vicus*] of the monks of Cluny. There King Louis asked Alexander to attend the pre-arranged meeting; or, if he could not tolerate the presence of the emperor, at least to come to its vicinity, as far as the castle of Vergy, which was impregnable. But as Alexander would not agree to this the king said to him: "I myself will lead you there and back, keeping you as unharmed as my own body." Since Alexander would still not agree, fearing the emperor's wiles, the king said: "I am amazed that, conscious of the justice of your position, you should avoid this testimony to your innocence and hearing of your cause." Then the king left to go to the pre-arranged conference with the emperor, as yet unaware of the conditions which Count Henry had made with the emperor on his, the king's, behalf.

12

The King Meets and Talks with Count Henry of Champagne Who, as a Supporter of the Emperor, Opposes Pope Alexander [1633D/525.514]

1162

When the king had come to the castle of Dijon, Count Henry met him and then for the first time revealed to him the conditions which he had agreed to with the emperor, saying: "Out of reverence for your majesty, and thinking of the good of your realm, my lord king, I have arranged a conference on the Saône where you, my lord king, and Emperor Frederick will meet together with the bishops, abbots, and chief men of both your realms, in the presence of your pope and the emperor's pope. There, the most respected ecclesiastics and knights from both realms will be chosen, so that they may adjudicate each pope's election. If Roland's election be adjudged the sounder, Octavian's will be quashed and the emperor will fall at Roland's feet; but if Victor's election prevail, Roland's will be annulled and you, lord king, will come to

---

the loss of the Vexin to Henry II as a fairly remote and uncertain eventuality; but Henry secured a papal dispensation from Alexander so that the marriage could take place despite the children's ages, and in November 1160, he had them married and at once seized control of the coveted castles in the Vexin. Louis seems to have felt that he had been tricked, and the envoys who 'had been turned away' at the papal court may have been trying to get Alexander to rescind his dispensation for the marriage, something the pope could not do without antagonizing Henry II. See Pacaut (1964: 71–74)."

[1] In the week preceding 29 August 1162; the conference lasted for two days. Note that it was Souvigny that Pons wanted Peter the Venerable to give him while he was in exile; see *Major Chronicle* 2 §23.

Octavian's feet. If Victor absents himself, the emperor will give him up and obey your Alexander, but if, conversely, Alexander remains away, the same will occur, and you, king, will support Victor. And furthermore if your majesty does not agree to these conditions, nor agree to submit to the judges' decision, I have sworn on oath that I shall go across to the other side, and whatever I hold in fee from your royal fisc I shall hand over to the emperor to hold from him henceforward."[1] King Louis was stunned, and replied to this: "I wonder where you got the confidence [*fiducia*] to agree to such things with the emperor without my knowledge and without consulting me?" Henry replied: "You yourself, king, gave me this confidence through Bishop Manasses of Orleans." The bishop, when asked about this statement, began to prevaricate from fear of the king, and left unmentioned the machinations by which he had persuaded Henry to his action. Then Henry produced the king's letter which mentioned that because the royal messengers had been repelled by Alexander, the angry king ordered Henry to go freely to the emperor Frederick and convene a conference of both sides, certain that the king would stand by his advice in all things.

13

Another Discussion, on the Border of the Empire.
The Messengers of the King   [1634B/526.546]

1162

Now Emperor Frederick had built himself a palace of wonderful size at a place on the border of his empire called Dôle. When the French learnt that the schismatic Victor was not with the emperor they rejoiced in his absence. Realizing this, the Teutons or Germans ran and led him there with all haste that very day; and after meeting him the emperor led him out onto the middle of the bridge in the dead of night, and immediately, having as it were satisfied the conditions, went home. But King Louis, pretending to be on a hunting-expedition, travelled through the woods to the place of conference and sent on Josse, archbishop of Tours, Maurice, bishop of Paris, and Abbot William of Vézelay[2] with other chief men of his realm to the imperial messengers, who were waiting there for word of the king. Among the king's party was Count Henry, who because of a familial relationship enthusiastically embraced the party of the schismatic Victor. The royal messengers asked on the king's behalf for an appropriate postponement [*competentes inducias*], because the conditions of the conference had been unknown to him until two days before, and particularly because the emperor had made Count Henry swear that the conditions of the meeting should not be made known to the king in any way before the set date. It would be shameless to arrange such a

---

[1] *quicquid de fisco regis in feodum habeo imperatori tradens, ab illo deinceps tenebo.* An extraordinary threat, showing the weakness of the Capetians at the time in their relations with their chief vassals, and the fluid situation in the Franco-German border areas.

[2] The presence of Abbot William at the conference explains the lengthy account of this episode by Hugh of Poitiers. Cf. also the cardinals' return to Vézelay immediately below.

weighty matter in this rash way. When Emperor Frederick's spokesmen refused the delay which he sought, the king returned to Dijon. The cardinals, whom Pope Alexander had sent there, returned to Vézelay, hoping that the meeting had broken down. The king then appointed men to guard the frontiers of his realm. Early next morning,[1] Count Henry came to the king in the palace of the duke of Burgundy, claiming that the king was in no way free from the conditions, and that as a result he, Count Henry, must perforce secede from him, and deliver himself into the emperor's hand, so that all the land which he had until then held in fee from the king[2] would be handed to the emperor and received back from him, and he would become his man.[3] But, he said, as a favor for the king [*ob gratiam regis*] he had obtained three weeks' delay from the emperor, on condition that the king would give sureties and promise the emperor that he would appear on the requisite day, bringing Alexander with him, there to hear the cause of both popes and to submit to the judgment of worthy men of the empire and his own realm, or else he [Count Henry] would deliver himself into the hands [*tradere vinctum*] of the emperor at Besançon, noble city of the Bisontines. The king agreed and his heart grew faint within him and his spirits fell as he bound himself to perform these conditions, giving as sureties [Odo II], duke of Burgundy, [Thierry] count of Flanders and William [IV] count of Nevers. But every ecclesiastical order, hearing of the king's promise, sorrowed greatly, and all cried in their hearts to the Lord to have pity on his Holy Church and to free the king from the guile of those who were working against him.[4]

14

The Stratagems of the Emperor Are Exposed and the King Withdraws from His Agreement with Him

[1635B/527.590]

1162

So the king went away to the town of Saint-Jean de-Losne,[5] where the emperor was to have met him. But the emperor deceived [Count] Henry and sent his chancellor Rainald, from the church of Cologne, the principal promoter of schism. When the conditions which Count Henry had proposed to the king on the emperor's behalf were repeated before the chancellor, suddenly the divine power assisted its Church and the pious simplicity of the royal majesty. For Rainald, promoter of profane error, replied that the emperor had never said such a thing, namely that he would allow a conference where anyone

---

[1] 30 August 1162.

[2] *totam terram quam de feodo regis tenuerat.*

[3] *et hominium illi faceret.* An extraordinary indication of the "vassal-centered" nature of "feudalism."

[4] Wisd. of Sol. 10:11. Odo II was duke of Burgundy 1143–1162, Thierry count of Flanders 1128–1168 (Cox). The MS contains blank spaces for these names, suggesting that the chronicler could not immediately recall the details or that the copyist of MS. Auxerre could not decipher the original words.

[5] 19 September 1162.

could judge the Roman church, which can be judged only by its own laws.[1] Then the king, full of joy, asked Henry whether the conditions that had just been set out were the ones he had proposed. "They were," he admitted. So the king said: "Look, the emperor, who according to your words ought to have been present, is not here; and now, even his messengers change the wording of the agreement in your presence and before your eyes. Am I not therefore absolved from all its conditions?" "You are," said Henry. Then King Louis said to all his chief men and bishops and abbots who were present: "You have all heard and seen that I have willingly performed all that I was supposed to; tell me, am I not free from all these conditions?" All replied: "You have fulfilled your promise." So the king immediately turned about the swift horse which he bestrode and set off at a gallop. The Germans, greatly disconcerted, followed him, asking him to return to the emperor, who was prepared to execute all that Henry had proposed. But he paid no heed to what they said and, shuddering at the trap which he had avoided, said: "I have done my duty."[2] After the conference was broken off in this way the king returned to his realm.

15

Pope Alexander Is Received by the King in Paris.
He Consecrates the Church of St. Germain-des-Prés.
He Celebrates a Council at Tours   [1636A/528. 617]

1162–1163

The Catholic pope Alexander, fearing King Louis' wrath, crossed Aquitaine to its metropolitan city of Bourges, and wintered in the monastery of Déols at Châteauroux.[3] The following Lent he came to King Louis at Paris. Received honorably by the king, the pope himself carried, according to the custom of the Roman church, a golden rose on the Sunday when "Laetare Jerusalem" is sung.[4] When the Easter solemnities were over he consecrated the monastic church of Saint-Germain-des-Prés, ruled by Hugh de Monceaux-

---

[1] *quae proprie sui juris existebat.*

[2] *Feci quod meum fuit.* A diplomatic triumph for the king after a complex series of meetings and secret machinations. The nub of the matter was the emperor's decision *not* to submit his papal candidate to the kind of assembly mentioned by Count Henry above, §12. Cox: "Munz (1969: 232–33n) challenges our chronicler's chronology of the events at Saint-Jean-de-Losne although it is corroborated by Boso's biography of Alexander III and accepted by Heinemeyer (1964)."

[3] The pope was at Déols from 9 to 24 September 1162 but spent the months from October to December at Tours.

[4] 3 March 1163. The golden rose is an ornament of gold and gems in the shape of a rose. It is blessed by the pope on the fourth Sunday in Lent and then presented to a worthy recipient. The origin of the custom is obscure but it was regarded as ancient in the eleventh century. See Cross (1974: 579). Cox: "On this occasion in 1163 Alexander explained the symbolic significance of the rose: the flower itself signifies Christ the King, the gold His Kingship, the red His crucifixion, the fragrance His resurrection and triumph in heaven. Alexander's presentation of the golden rose to Louis VII was presumably out of gratitude for his support during the schism."

le-Comte, former monk of Vézelay. Abbot William of Vézelay came to Paris to the high pontiff Alexander again to confirm a third time, more fully, his church's liberties and possessions and the immunity of the monastery's ban-lieue[1] as prescribed by the pope's predecessors. To this Alexander readily assented, and gave him a third charter of privilege.

From there Alexander went to the metropolitan city of Tours, where he held a council of all the bishops,[2] of Lyon, Narbonne, Vienne, Bourges, Sens, Rheims, Rouen, Tours, Bordeaux, Auch, and the Apennine and Maritime Alps, a total of 105 persons. Also there were the archbishops of Canterbury and York, and of the Scots and Irish, and abbots and persons of various orders who gladly came from all about. Many German bishops wrote secretly to Pope Alexander, humbly professing their obedience and complete rever-ence to him, as far as the circumstances of time and place permitted. Quite a few from Italy were present either in writing or in person. And Sardinia and Sicily, with all Calabria, all of the eastern Church and Spain humbly bowed the head of devoted obedience to the Catholic pope Alexander.

16
Various Cases Were Debated at the Council, Especially that of the Clerics of Paris Against the Monks of St. Germain [1636C/528. 648]

1162–1163

Present at that council were Abbot Stephen of Cluny and Abbot William of Vézelay.[3] Now the Cluniacs thought to raise an action over the renunciation of their rights over Vézelay; but they were all put to silence by the conscious-ness of their own injustice and of Roman rectitude. They did not dare so much as to voice a murmur, although many similar controversies were raised and settled time and again at this council. One such was the case of the Paris-ian clerics and the monks of Saint-Germain-des-Prés; when it had been fully heard, the pope imposed perpetual silence on the unjust voices of the clerics.[4] After this conciliar synod was dissolved Alexander returned to Bourges, which is the capital of Aquitaine. In the following autumn he moved on to Sens, and there remained for eighteen months.[5] Meanwhile the author of the schism, Octavian, called Victor, was unhappily snatched from this life, and the schismatic party chose in his place Guy bishop of Cremona, who was the first of Alexander's electors to become apostate.[6]

---

[1] *immunitatem banniarum.* (*bannia* is not in Niermeyer [1976]).

[2] The Council of Tours was held on 19 May 1163. See Somerville (1977).

[3] Like the protracted account of the negotiations between Louis VII and Frederick Barbarossa this episode is included in the Major Chronicle because of the presence at the Council of Abbot William (and perhaps also of Hugh of Poitiers).

[4] See Somerville (1977: 59).

[5] Alexander arrived at Sens on 30 September 1163 and remained there until Easter 1165.

[6] Victor IV died on 20 April 1164. Paschal III, the antipope, was elected on 22 April, consecrated on 26 April, and died on 20 September 1168.

17

The Count of Nevers Continues to Persecute the Church
of Vézelay   [1637A/529. 665]

1163

Meanwhile the count of Nevers was gravely persecuting the church of Vézelay, and through certain of its people, who concealed their lies beneath the outward appearance of sheep, he kept trying to defame the reputation of Abbot William and his brothers. Desiring nothing less than the surrender of Vézelay, he was filled with the disease of jealousy against the abbot, who resisted his evil attempts both shrewdly and energetically. The more he resisted the count's accusations and depredations, the more his magnanimity shone forth. For this reason, when the count, who was wasting away within himself from the sorrow provoked by his envy, saw that he was getting nowhere and was not supported by any legal right, he thrust justice aside, spurning honesty and contemptuous of any reverence for religion, and armed himself with the madness of insane rage and tyrannical rashness. Thus after he had labored and sought craftily to work iniquity and had found no cause for afflicting the church justly, he demanded back from the church, against all law and justice, those usurped rights of procuration which his father, after escaping shipwreck, had given back to the church, and which he had confirmed with the agreement of the present count himself and his mother in the chapter house of Vézelay.[1] When the abbot denied what the count was unjustly demanding, the latter ordered a declaration of war. But on the intervention of friends of both sides, they arranged a discussion at the lake of Noyers to see if they could resolve by peaceful means the controversy which had arisen. There, when the count had put forward his demand concerning this particular exaction, the abbot replied that because the count's father had resigned it and he himself had conceded it, it ought not to be reclaimed by him nor returned by the abbot, especially since he [the count] found the church endowed [*investitam*] by his father's resignation and by his own concession. That tyrant, beside himself with rage, came at once to Vézelay in a frenzy of mad anger, on the night before the feast of John the Baptist's birth.[2] He entered the monastery and, finding that the brothers, hearing of his arrival, had locked up the cloisters, rushed in and was himself the first to take an axe and break

---

[1] See above, *Major Chronicle* 2 §8. Cox gives the background in his *History*: "Count William was coping with rebellious vassals aided by his old enemies, the counts of Sancerre and Joigny. Matters reached a climax in April 1163 with a great battle at La Marche, near La Charité-sur-Loire, where the young count of Nevers, now barely seventeen, emerged victorious. This triumph seems to have greatly enhanced his self-confidence and this, perhaps together with a depleted treasury, inspired a fresh attack upon the religious institutions in his dominions. He refused to do homage to the bishop of Auxerre for the properties which his grandfather had recognized as fiefs, and soon he was accused of disposing of episcopal property without consulting the bishop. At the same time, he resumed his efforts to establish his dominion over Vézelay, apparently this time by asserting a right to intervene when the abbot was charged with squandering abbey property."

[2] 23 June 1163.

down the kitchen door. Seeing this, his followers straightaway occupied the
houses around the church, broke down the rest of the doors, knocked down
those monks who opposed them, and entertained their lord that night in the
monastery's guest house from the monastery's substance, against the will of
the brothers. At once the brothers put away the crosses and reliquaries, laid
the altars bare, and stopped celebrating the Divine Office throughout all their
churches.[1]

18
The Pope Warns the Count to Cease Vexing the Church
of Vézelay   [1637C/530. 700]

1163

That night the abbot went to Chamoux, and the following night to Givry.
From there he sent a message to the king, while he himself went to the
Roman pontiff, who was staying at the monastery of Déols after leaving the
council of Tours. But because the king had at that time mounted an expedition against the Auvergnois he did not wish to irritate the count, and so
advised the abbot to put off the proposed lawsuit until he returned from that
expedition.[2] Alexander, for his part, turning over in his mind how the
Church was sickening from the effects of the schism, and fearing lest, if he
took a somewhat harder line with the secular princes, the Church would be
afflicted with yet heavier grievances, simply warned the count by a letter only,
to cease vexing the church of Vézelay, which was the blessed Peter's daughter
and an allod of the Roman church. But the heart of that Pharaoh of a count
was hardened[3] and instead of a font of sweetness it became as hard as a
stone. Spurning both the royal and apostolic warnings, he came to Vézelay on
the solemn feast day of the blessed Mary Magdalene herself,[4] accompanied
by a well-armed and sizeable band of cavalry [*equitum*] and footsoldiers
[*peditum*] and a throng of hangers-on, as though to besiege a hostile people.
As soon as he had entered the town, the brothers stopped celebrating the
Divine Office, and, shutting the cloister doors, softly poured forth befitting
prayers to God separately in the chapel of the mother of God, thinking it
improper to expose sacred things to a sacrilegious person. The abbot descended to St.-Père-sous-Vézelay, and the count, having entered the monastery

---

[1] The count's harassment of the monks and their ritual suspension of normal divine
worship were typical tactics in such a dispute. See Geary (1986) and Aspects [A] above.

[2] Louis' expedition into the Auvergne was a move in his long struggle against Henry
II of England. On the conflict see Pacaut (1964: 179–202, esp. 195–97 on the centrality of
the Auvergne). Cox: "Givry, to the northeast, is on the opposite side of Vézelay from
Chamoux and not at all on the road to Déols. If this is not a mistake in the manuscript it
means that William doubled back and took a much longer road to Déols in order to
circumvent the dangerous dominions of the count of Nevers"; "the expedition in question
was doubtless the one undertaken at the request of Alexander III against the count of
Auvergne and the viscount of Polignac, who were accused of persecuting the abbey of
Brioude. See E. Lavisse (ed.) *Histoire de France* III pt. I (Paris 1902) 45, 61."

[3] Exodus 8:19.

[4] 22 July 1163.

as usual—but without his usual followers—went down to the guest house, and enjoyed from his own provisions the hospitality which had been denied him by the brothers.[1]

19

The Abbot and the Count Agree on Peace After Certain Conditions had been Put Forward. The Count Seeks Forgiveness for Injuries he had Inflicted

[1638B/530. 724]

1163

That night the abbot ascended to the tomb of the blessed Mary Magdalene, where he performed the prescribed rites with appropriate solemnity, as far as possible; and when day began to break he went down to Asquins and offered the consecrated host to God. Renaud de Mello, his nephew, and Durand Alburg, following him, asked him to rest there for a little, since Renaud had sent some people to Givry to prepare necessary food for him. Then Renaud climbed the hill and spoke with the count about coming to terms. So the abbot was recalled, and an agreement was reached that the count would make public satisfaction at the altar for his violation of the monastery, would pay out £20 for usurping the right of procuration, and would concede anew his father's renunciation of the right of casual procuration[2] and confirm it in writing. The count made his brother Renaud and his other brother Guy, and his sister concede all this too, giving promises of their good faith, and as sureties Ignace, viscount of Joigny, Stephen de Pierre-Perthuis, and Hugh de la Tournelle,[3] so that when his brothers and sister reached legal age they should again concede the same renunciation. Out of gratitude for the written confirmation and the keeping of the peace in perpetuity, it was decided that the abbot should give the count seventy pounds and that he should pay for the procuration due that day two hundred and fifty-three pounds, on this condition, that the count should wholly resign his right of procuration on the next feast day, and further that he would not demand more than one hundred pounds for any other procuration. When these things had been arranged and agreed to by both sides, the bells were rung for the sixth hour of the day and the brothers celebrated the rites of the holy feast. Then the count, coming up to the altar, made satisfaction for the injury which the monastery had suffered, and he placed there twenty pounds according to the arrangement for the execution of justice.[4] The next day, entering the broth-

---

[1] *negatamque sibi a fratribus procurationem ipse sibi de suo exhibuit.*

[2] *fortuitas procurationes.*

[3] Pierre-Perthuis was a very powerful fief which pertained ultimately to the count of Champagne, to whom the seigneur of the place owed homage. Stephen of Pierre-Perthuis, lord of Bassou, had taken part in the Second Crusade. Hugh de la Tournelle, faithful follower of the count of Nevers, was the son of Séguin de la Tournelle, himself the faithful vassal of William II and of William III of Nevers. Ignace of Joigny was a brother-in-law of the count of Nevers.

[4] *reposuitque iuxta condictum pro recti executione viginti libras.* It is clear that such

ers' chapter house, before them all, with the abbot presiding, he conceded his renunciation of the right of casual procuration as his father had done, confirmed it in writing, and corroborated it by the affixing of his seal.

20
He [the Count] Initiates Further Strife and Persecution

[1638D/531. 756]

1163-64

After this Count William of Nevers became gravely ill, so that his life was despaired of; but since, when humbled, he poured out prayers to God, at length he recovered, and asked the help of the saints in the oratory of the blessed and spotless Virgin Mary at Le Puy-en-Velay. Then he returned in body to his own country, but in spirit to his acknowledged hatred of Abbot William of Vézelay, whom he ordered to submit to justice in his presence for not having paid him the dues of salt,[1] and to stand trial in his court at Nevers. The abbot replied: "I was hoping that I had made peace with the count over all the quarrels of bygone times; but because I am a simple man and do not appear fully instructed as yet in the customs of this monastery, I shall speak with those of most illustrious birth in this town and with other wise men, and according to the counsel vouchsafed us from on high I shall reply to the count through my own messengers." But Abbo of Le Montgaudier—for he it was who bore the count's message—said to the abbot: "If you care to accept the day which I have named for you on the count's behalf, well and good; but if not, the count will act as though you had denied him justice." On that note Abbo departed and made a worse report to the count than the truth justified.[2]

Now the abbot took counsel and sent his messengers to reply to the count's words. On their way they met some of the count's followers preceding their master, who was on his way to Vézelay in a great rage. Then suddenly the tyrant broke into the monastery, invaded its workshops [*officinas*], and sent his heralds at once all through the towns of Vézelay and Asquins and St.-Père-sous-Vézelay, ordering all the abbey's men to present themselves before him in a body the next day. But they one and all treated his order with contempt. Then he was filled with fury and, contrary to the custom of the town, had his herald proclaim that anyone who did not appear before him would be seized when identified and have his house confiscated. Hearing this everyone was stupefied, and many went to him out of fear. He said to them as they stood before him: "Because the abbot has denied me justice, I have invested myself with my own rights ; so I want you to renounce your abbot and to swear fealty to me, and from now on to execute no customary services for him and his monks." To this the burghers replied: "We have sworn fealty to the abbot

---

arrangements simply systematized the count's "taxation" of the abbey; presumably the abbey valued the symbolic renunciation by the count of the right of casual procuration and the writtten agreement solemnizing it. For the £20 see Appendix F §22.

[1] *de non exhibito sibi salinario.*

[2] *peiora dictis comiti retulit.*

and church and so it seems unjust and most wicked to perjure ourselves, without cause as far as we are concerned. We therefore ask you to give us a few days' grace so that we may speak with our lord and discuss these words with him." "Your lord," said he, "is close by, and you can speak with him at once." "Then permit us to go to him," they said. He replied: "Choose two or three of your number to take your message to the abbot, and bring back his reply to you."

Up rose Simon de Souvigny and Durand Alburg, who both particularly welcomed the count's impiety, and with a few others they came before the abbot, who soon learnt from what they said that the count had detained some of his [the abbot's] followers so that they could not come to the abbot. So the abbot called John the Goatherd and a few senior men of the church and sent them post-haste to the burghers in the guest house, to say to them: "Those of you who owe fealty to the abbot and the church, the abbot demands and orders, by that same faith which you have sworn to him and owe to him, that you should abandon this tyrant and come to him as quickly as you can." And they came at once. When they had discussed at length among themselves the count's demand, the burghers, being in such straits, asked the abbot to consult his own and their best interests, and to try to gain time by agreeing to the day named by the count, under this condition, that he should give the count only what he ought. The abbot agreed with their advice and sent to the count, saying: "Although what you demand is totally unjust, I will nonetheless accept the day which you have appointed at Auxerre, because I have been forced to do so by your unexpected violence and your tyrannous invasion of my house; but there I will do only what is shown to be my duty." The count, frustrated in his purpose—for he had made such conditions in order to transfer Vézelay to his own lordship [*Vizeliacum suo mancipare dominio*]—controlled the impetus of his rage and withdrew at once.

But when the day drew near, the abbot sent some of the chief men of his church to the count at Decize, namely Gilo then prior, Geoffrey the Englishman who was subprior, and Gilbert the almoner. The count told them to follow him to Nevers where he would hear them. When they had done this, they renounced on the abbot's behalf the day assigned him, asking that another be assigned in a nearer locality. When the count refused to accept this renunciation or grant a change of date, they replied: "The lord abbot of Vézelay replies to you through us that he is not bound by any law to obey your orders, and if you want to vex him with renewed violence, he summons you to a papal audience—for the lordship of the monastery of Vézelay rightfully belongs to the pope—and to an audience with the lord king, under whose protection and custody the monastery lies. He appoints the octave of Easter for you to present yourself before Pope Alexander.[1] In the meantime he commits himself and his possessions into the hands of pope and king." When they had said this, they asked his permission to return home, but because he was so angry they did not get it; therefore, retiring a little, they returned to their lodgings in the monastery of Saint-Étienne [de Nevers], which is just

---

[1] 19 April 1164.

near the city, giving the impression as it were that they were going to return to the count's court the next day. But during the night they took horse and returned to Vézelay. The abbot for his part, to avoid the count's insane fury, went off to the Île de France.[1]

In fact, he went to Pope Alexander and related to him in what way and how unjustly the count had vexed him and the church of Vézelay. Then he went to the king and poured into his ears his complaints of the unjust vexation with which the count belabored him. The king, moved both by compassion for the complainant and by Pope Alexander's admonition, assigned the count a date for a conference at Sens.[2] When each had gathered there and many complaints had been voiced by both sides without any path to a peaceful settlement opening up, at the king's request the count in the end postponed the day for the seeking of justice as set out in his summons. Then King Louis passed the feast of Epiphany at Vézelay,[3] where the abbot received him and submitted to him attentively. When he had left, the count, moved by ill-will, summoned the abbot to a day at Auxerre; the abbot, accepting the day as far as it lay with him to do so, sent messengers to the pope to consult him as to what he should do about this. They received his advice, were commissioned discreetly with a secret message, and then returned.

21
A Monk Carries Around Relics of the Holy Saints to Seek Offerings
[1641A/534. 859]

?1164

A certain brother of Vézelay, named Renaud, went out from the monastery which lies near Moret,[4] carrying relics of the blessed Mary mother of God, of St. Blaise, and of other saints, and was making a great collection of alms from the faithful for the building of the basilica of Vézelay. After he had traversed many places and by the divine grace had shed light over the country of Amiens through the many virtues of those saints, he came with their relics to a castle called Labroye. He stayed there for a few days, but finally after many miracles had taken place there through the merits of those saints, and a great concourse of people had gathered on all sides, he decided to depart. However, when the people, as the custom is, took up the relic bier, they were completely unable to take it out of the church. After one man alternated with another, and some gave way to others, and strong men to yet stronger, the lord of the place, named Elmo, with another illustrious man, raised the bier; but neither could they reach the church door with it. And so replacing the bier on the altar, they fell on their faces in prayer. Then one of the brothers who had come with Renaud, named Peter, in his stupid rashness began to beat the bier with his staff, as though to compel the saints to go by blows.

---

[1] *abiit in Franciam.*
[2] 31 December 1163.
[3] 6 January 1164.
[4] The priory of Arborea (or Labroye), which was dependent on Vézelay.

Without delay he was struck by divine vengeance; for he was immediately
seized with paralysis and died a few days later. Now the illustrious man Elmo,
perceiving that this was done by divine decree, gave thanks to God, the
author of all good things, for the gift which heaven had bestowed on him,
and donated a place in his own allod,[1] within the confines of his castle, for
the building of an oratory in which the holy relics might be placed and where
the Divine Office might be celebrated by brothers to the honor of God. And
he ordered that this place should be under the rule and dispensation of the
church of Vézelay, because the saints' sacred relics had been brought there
from that church and by its brothers. When Abbot William was called and
came to this place he brought yet more relics and many precious ornaments
with him, which he left there for the honor of the saints and the devotion of
the faithful people of the area. And that place was named after the adjacent
castle, Labroye. Thus in the midst of waves of persecution of her goods, the
success of virtue always makes good her loss; and the more the Church is afflicted, the more she is enriched.[2]

22
The Count of Nevers Rages Against the Monks
of Vézelay   [1641D/535. 897]

1164

Count William continued to maintain a deep hatred against Abbot William
and because he was unable to achieve what he desired he vented his rage by
plundering the monastery's asses, cattle, and serfs. Now there was a certain
vile man, Hugh surnamed Letard, a tenant-in-chief of the monastery;[3] his
mother in fact was cousin-german to Simon, the son of Odo, provost of Vézelay, also the church's serf, the very Simon who betrayed and smote his lord,
Abbot Artaud of Vézelay.[4] The count made this Hugh his provost at Châtel-
Censoir, and he persecuted the church more than all the rest of the count's
followers. I cannot begin to tell how many times and in what ways he vexed
it night and day. Quite unjustly, he haled the church before the courts; but
although he demanded his rights according to the law, he never gave satisfaction as the law demanded. On the contrary, he claimed legal possession for
himself[5] of whatever he had extorted violently and in defiance of law and
order. So when the abbot again complained in Pope Alexander's ears about
the iniquitous and multifarious oppressions perpetrated against him and his

---

[1] in proprio alodio.

[2] Sicsic inter fluctus persecutionis bonorum semper successus virtutis incrementum capit et
unde magis ecclesie affligitur, inde magis cumulatur.

[3] servus de capite suo monasterii.

[4] See above, charters 19 and 25. Cox: "A servus de capite was presumably a serf subject
to the annual capitation or head-tax, which was usually taken as indicating membership in
the lowest ranks of the servile population—which would give point to our author's use of
the term here. Abbot Artaud had been killed in the insurrection in 1106."

[5] immo pro iure sibi constabat.

monks by the count's followers, Alexander wrote to the count and his mother as follows:[1]

23

Pope Alexander Writes to the Count [Urging] him to Desist from his Attack [1642B/535. 916]

1164

Alexander, bishop, servant of the servants of God, to his dear son the noble man William count of Nevers and Ida his mother, greetings and the apostolic blessing.

Because the monastery of Vézelay is known to belong especially to the jurisdiction of the blessed Peter and to be at our disposition, we have with more frequent zeal directed our attention to its growth and flourishing, and we remain more solicitous of its peace and the conservation of its goods. So it is that, being zealous in all ways for the peace and utility of that monastery, we send your nobility our dear son Peter, a subdeacon, asking your magnitude through the apostolic writing, warning and exhorting you in the Lord, to direct yourself in all ways to the peace and utility of that church, and to the conservation and defense of its goods, out of reverence for the blessed Peter and for us; and to take care to listen to and hear out our subdeacon in this matter; and to restrain absolutely the neighboring nobles and your powerful barons from harming and injuring that monastery. Acquiesce, therefore, in our prayers and admonitions in this matter, that we will be obliged the more efficaciously to listen to your prayers and petitions and grant them useful effect, and the more fervently to favor your honor at all times.

Given at Sens, 7 December.

24

The Count Spurns the Pope's Letter [1642B/536. 938]

1164–1165

Then Peter, subdeacon of the Roman church, came to the count and his mother after the Christmas celebrations at Vézelay and handed them the papal letter. When he had made known to their obstinate ears the apostolic writings and his own exhortation, as a highly educated man, they began in return to disparage the abbot and brethren with accusations and many and varied lies and to defame their good name. When he came to discuss peace proposals with these enemies of peace, he found that there was no possibility of it unless the abbot stood trial in the count's court, contrary to the custom and dignity of his church. When the common advice of the brothers was asked, they all thought as one that they would rather endure the exile of death than be slaves to such tyranny. So the abbot, putting aside any pretense

---

[1] Issued on 7 December 1164.

of delay, accepted the day laid down [by the count], the first day in Lent,[1] and sent to the pope for aid. The pope sent him Hyacinth, cardinal deacon of the Roman church, Peter of Bona his subdeacon, and John his marshal.[2]

25
There Are Discussions About Peace   [1642D/536. 954]
1165

At that time the brothers of Pontoise [fratres Pontisare] were at the papal court, summoned by the Cluniacs because those brothers had sent off their former abbot, William, to Vézelay without consulting the Cluniacs, and had substituted another in his place. But the Cluniacs failed in their claim and did not even presume to present themselves on the appointed day. So the brothers of Pontoise, absolved by the pope, returned home with their liberty intact. In the meantime their abbot, Lecelin, was staying at Vézelay, awaiting the outcome of the affair. In their incredible arrogance the Cluniacs had disdained to involve him in the case, but called up only his monks, as though they had no head, lodging their complaint against the monks only, not against the abbot, as though he were not their abbot. Consequently, Pope Alexander sought an audience with the brothers, not the abbot. But since neither Satan nor any evil obstacle arose,[3] he confirmed the proven liberty of Pontoise with the approval of all his cardinals.

Abbot William of Vézelay met at Auxerre with Abbot Lecelin of Pontoise, and [Peter] abbot of the monastery of Saint-Jean-des-Prés[4] and with many other brothers and friends of the monastery of Vézelay. Also there were the apostolic legates. Frightened by their presence the count at once desired to change the day of his own accord, although until then he had not allowed it to be changed when so asked. About this the abbot consulted prudent men. In reply Hyacinth said to the abbot: "Till now you have been burdened with a tertian fever; do you therefore wish to be laid low by a quartan? No, on the contrary, break free of all ambiguities and act now in defense of your right of liberty." The abbot placed the presentation of his case[5] in the mouth of the abbot of Saint-Jean-des-Prés; but neither he nor anyone else dared to speak out for fear of the count. Seeing this, the sons of the liberty of the church of Vézelay, armed with faith, utterly cast aside all fear and held it unworthy that another should defend verbally their own dignity. So Gilo, at that time prior of the community of Vézelay, rose up and said to the count: "Hitherto the lord abbot of Vézelay has heard your charges, and on certain of them agree-

---

[1] 17 February 1165.

[2] mariscalcum: court dignitary having care of requisitions and housing; Niermeyer (1976: 656). Cox: "Hyacinth was cardinal-deacon of Santa Maria in Cosmedin (1144–1191)."

[3] 1 Kings 5:4. See §3 above.

[4] The same Abbot Peter was a witness to the composition of peace between Vézelay and Autun in 1154. See above Major Chronicle 1 §7. His monastery is also known as Moutiers-Saint-Jean.

[5] verbum suum.

ment is easily reached. The rest he will discuss in his own court,[1] for it is in vain that you believe that he ought to stand trial in your court; on the contrary, he is not bound to you by any law at all." Hearing this the count was seized with great fury and grew red at these words, which were in defiance of his own opinion. The abbot and his followers then went outside away from the count. Hyacinth tried to calm the worked-up prince and pressed for peace; but, meeting with no success, he pleaded for some sort of truce to be given to the church. The count gave in and granted a truce [although in pretense only] until the octave of Easter. [2]

26
The Bishop of Segni Exercises his Episcopal Functions at Vézelay
[1643C/537. 996]

1165

Now when the sacred feast of the Lord's resurrection was drawing near, [John] bishop of Segni came to Vézelay, sent from the very side of the lord pope to visit and comfort the brothers. There he consecrated the sacred chrism and holy oil on holy Thursday and celebrated holy Easter Saturday by conferring ecclesiastical orders, ordaining as priests Henry, Peter, and Humbert, monks of the church, and Gerard, cleric of the town also as a priest; and he ordained three deacons from among the monks, namely Anselm, William, and Geoffrey, and also two subdeacons, the boys William and Guy. Finally, he made Laurence of Moret an acolyte.[3]

27
St. Thomas, an Exile in Gaul, Commits Himself To the
Protection of the King
[1643D/537. 1008]

1165

Now Archbishop Thomas of Canterbury, fleeing King Henry, was in exile at Pontigny.[4] This man, at one time the king's great friend and his chancellor, was conspicuous for his elegance and energy and there had been no one who seemed to have more influence with the English king. However, when he undertook the responsibility of ecclesiastical rule, he took care in all things to prefer God to man. Therefore when the king, like Oziah of old, usurped the rights of the church, he [Thomas] resisted him constantly like another

---

[1] *cetera vero secum ipse tractabit.*

[2] That is, until Sunday 11 April 1165.

[3] The acolyte is a minor official responsible for bearing the candles during worship. John was bishop of Segni c. 1138–1178/79 (Cox).

[4] Thomas à Becket, in exile in France after defying Henry II, was, within a few years, to return to England to suffer martyrdom in his own church of Canterbury. There are some interesting links between Becket and Vézelay. Apart from his attempt to mediate in the dispute between the abbey and the count (see §65), there is also a letter from Abbot William to Herbert of Bosham, one of Becket's party, about how to deal with the heretics of chapter 78 (see *PL* 190. 1462–63 and below §78 315n.1 and Appendix C).

Jonah.[1] For this reason the king was angered and, exchanging his unfathomable grace for implacable hatred, determined to seize him and transfer his goods to the treasury. But the ingenuity of the innocent man anticipated these impious connivings, and secretly crossing the sea with a small following, he came to King Louis of France and committed himself and his men into his hands. The king received him very warmly and freely gave him all necessary assistance. But the archbishop thought that the correct thing to do was to go to Pope Alexander and abide firmly by his advice. When he had come to him and explained the cause of his arrival, Alexander sympathized with him and handed him over to Abbot Guichard of Pontigny, later consecrated by Alexander himself as archbishop of Lyon. King Louis contacted King Henry of England over this and other matters, and the kings arranged to hold a conference together. Because Pope Alexander intended to be at this conference, he came to Paris, but when King Henry knew of this, he repudiated the prearranged conference with King Louis, due to his hostility to Alexander and because of his hatred of Archbishop Thomas of Canterbury. Anyway Alexander had by now received more ambassadors from the Romans, who asked him to return to the see of St. Peter, and so, making his farewells to King Louis, he came to the city of Bourges.

28
Hugh Letard Despoils the Possessions of Vézelay at the Instigation of the Countess of Nevers [1644C/538. 1036]

1165

Meanwhile that most impious Hugh Letard, our serf—evil by birth and character—obstinately persisted in the capture and depredation of the men and goods of Vézelay. Moreover that old Herodias, Jezabel's daughter of the seed of Amalech,[2] Ida, mother of Count William of Nevers, enthusiastically poured the virus of hatred from her plague-bearing mouth into her son's heart. Envious of honesty, an enemy of all goodness, and a promoter of her son's cause she vigorously incited her followers to persecute the monastery of Vézelay. Now massacres, now plundering, now imprisonments, now exiles, now various tortures, now diverse kinds of death, all emanated from this cavern of feminine wickedness; and she did not easily allow free egress to anyone of the city of Vézelay. The brothers had constructed a kiln of lime of wonderful size[3] for the building of their dormitory, and having lit a fire, were dragging wood from the nearby forest by means of carts. That hydra, inflamed with the plague of envy, in her madness sent servants who on the feast of Pentecost stole the horses from the carts which were dragging the wood; thus because of the extinguishing of the fire, the work of the kiln, valued at

---

[1] 2 Chronicles 26:17–20. In a curious mistake the author has written *"Jonas"* for *"Azarias"*; see Huygens (1976: xxiv). Oziah = Uzziah.

[2] See Matthew 14:3 and 1 Kings 19:1–2.

[3] *ratem calcis mire magnitudinis*; there is no justification in Lewis & Short or Niermeyer for *ratis* being anything other than some sort of vessel, although here it does seem to refer to a kiln of some kind.

£100, perished. The viperous son of this hydra, the count, ordered Abbot William's movements to be watched, so that he might be shamed by low servants with the count appearing to know nothing about it.

29
Abbot William Complains Before the Pope on Many Grounds [1644D/539. 1056]

1165

Afflicted on all sides by such ills, Abbot William set out for Pope Alexander and when he had come upon him at Bourges, he explained to him, as far as he could, all the evils which he was suffering from the count and his mother. And he said to him that his cause was the cause of the lord pope and the whole Roman church, under whose jurisdiction his monastery directly stood, and so the pope ought to treat this business of Vézelay as though it were apostolic, especially as that monastery was imperilled for this crime alone: that it acknowledged itself openly to be Roman, and asserted that it was subject to no one, excepting only the bishop of Rome. He added too that if the pope did not succour his beleaguered monastery as quickly as possible, he [the abbot] would surrender to the adulterer as though repudiated [by the pope] and would no longer pay his rightful dues,[1] especially since, in the pope's very presence, the papal statutes and grants of privilege from the Roman pontiffs, both new and ancient, were misinterpreted with impunity; and while the shepherd stood by, the ravening of the wolves went on unhindered. He said also that any liberty that could be torn aside because not a single word of justice was spoken in its defense did not amount to much. Moreover, it was neither from timidity nor arrogance that he had appealed so many times to the pope's ears against the count; indeed, just as often he had bought the latter's favor with prayers and money.[2] But the count, for his part, had ungratefully repaid the abbot with such dire calamities, that now he, the abbot, was forced to almost complete exhaustion and extreme penury. The count had not been content with ransoming the monastery's men or destroying its possessions; he had even deprived the brothers of their daily sustenance for two years now. The abbot continued, saying that although this fact gravely afflicted the monastery, nonetheless he mourned yet more for the injury to its native liberty—that liberty which the count, on the pretext of some payment usurped and stolen away as a result of the negligence of certain of his [the abbot's] predecessors, strove to annihilate completely.[3] That liberality which was offered to the count from time to time out of charity was no longer sought devoutly, as voluntary liberality, but rather was demanded tyrannically as a due service. And whereas before, those few who had come

---

[1] That is, the annual pound of silver; see charters 2 and 3.

[2] *et prece et pretio*; Ovid *Fasti* 2.806.

[3] *quam videlicet libertatem sub optentu cuiusdam usurpati et negligentia quorundam predecessorum suorum surrepti salvamenti annullare penitus contendit.* The *suorum* here could refer to the count's predecessors, but the context suggests that the abbot is explaining the flaws in the count's case.

had been content with what was offered them, now they came as a great army, mouths agape at what they have been able to plunder, so that the procuration of just one visit to the guest house cost two hundred and fifty pounds [*librarum*] or even more.

After saying such things the abbot went further, saying that the church of Vézelay, St. Peter's daughter, had been exposed to all evils, so that now, from the sole of its feet to the crown of its head no health could be found in it. "For it is given," he said, "to all passers-by as a thing to be plundered and despised,[1] and whereas it once seemed most worthy, now it is found so much the more abject; and those who once envied its liberty, now wag their heads in derision over it, and deride the sabbath of the Roman Church[2] which they blame for the surrender of the church of Vézelay." At one time Autun instigates and encourages Cluny against Vézelay, at another it is Cluny encouraging Autun. "It is time," they say, "the head of the Roman See being broken, to gouge out its eyes, and to subject to ourselves that fugitive handmaid, who boasts that she is St. Peter's daughter." And now Autun acts like Moab of old, Cluny like another Idumaea, thinking of Vézelay as another Jerusalem for them to attack, and saying: "This people is stupid, poor, and proud.[3] I therefore, Autun, will crush their pride; you for your part mock their stupidity, and their poverty shall supply us with delicacies. So let us invite Assur with prayers, let us instigate him with persuasions, let us egg on with presents him who will wear down her arrogance with a rod of iron and a strong hand,[4] and because there is neither helper nor defender to free her, let us rend her among us, and let each one bear away his share. You, Cluny, will obtain the citadel, their chapter; I, Autun, claim for myself their altar; and Assur [the count] will pillage the town. And who, holy lord Peter," the abbot went on, "will stand against them? Would that we might emigrate! Would that we might perhaps be divided up! Would that time or times might be appointed for us,[5] when the Lord should perhaps raise up for us an Ehud, skilful with both hands,[6] in whose hand was Israel's salvation! But now we are strangled where we sit, we are subjected to servitude in our own house, and the redemption of time brings us perpetual subjugation. Under the cloud of such ills the weight of all our misery and extreme ignominy grows, because we are slain in our father's sight, we are wrenched from our shepherd's embrace, we are wronged in the presence of our legitimate patron, and because, to sum up the whole affair in a word, we are condemned by the silence of the universal

---

[1] See Ezekiel 16:15 and Isaiah 10:15. This whole speech to the pope is full of biblical allusions as the abbot graphically identifies the three traditional enemies of the abbey's liberty: the diocesan bishop, the abbot of Cluny, and the local count. Is Hugh, in the classical tradition, coining a verisimilar speech that the abbot *could* and *should* have delivered before the pope, or reporting from the abbot's notes (or oral recall), or from his own hearing or that of some other informant(s)?

[2] *derident sabbata Romanae dignitatis:* mock the Sunday religious services of the universal Church. Cf. Lamentations 1:7 and 2:15; Ezekiel 23:38.

[3] Jeremiah 5:4. The "broken head" could refer to the schism.

[4] Psalm 2:9 and Exodus 6:1.

[5] Daniel 7:25 and 12:7.

[6] Judges 3:15. Ehud was left-handed.

judge. At least, if the action proceeded openly, if reason interceded, if law and right or the rule of justice held sway, our losses would be made lighter and we could rejoice that our prejudged suffering was reduced, although according to the verdict of conscience they would not seem the less unjust. But as it is, our cause is bandied about in the mouths of the common folk, and our judgment is written out by the hands of our enemies."

30
Pope Alexander Replies to the Abbot and Tries to Divert the Count from His Attacks [1646C/541.1135]

1165

Hearing these things Alexander was much grieved, as was all the Roman church, and he wrote to the count, ordering him to compensate the monastery of Vézelay for the damage he had caused and to cease his attacks from now on, adding that if he thought that he had a case against the abbot, he should come in person before him [the pope] at Clermont-Ferrand on the octave of Pentecost.[1] There the count should first satisfy the abbot, and then he would receive his own rights from the latter. But the count utterly scorned the pope's mandate; in fact he set ambushes for the abbot, so shutting him in that his horses could not even go out to water! So the abbot sent his clerk John to Alexander; and the count, veiling his contempt, sent Thibault [*Teobaldum*] dean of Nevers, and Archdeacon Humbert and Prior Bernard of Saint-Étienne. The pope, receiving them graciously, inquired whether they had come as the count's competent representatives. When they proceeded to excuses rather than to the execution of justice, he dismissed them and sent them back, writing through them to the count that within a week of receiving this letter he was to restore to the abbot and brothers of Vézelay what he had taken, he was to send back the captured burghers and their hostages free and released from all obligations, and he was to permit them the free entry and exit by the public way that they were known to have had from ancient times; and he was then to present himself before the pope, so that he, the pope, might adjudicate between him and the abbot and brothers. But if it seemed burdensome to the count to come into the pope's presence, then he might go with the abbot to the archbishops of Sens and Bourges, who would restore peace and concord between them. Furthermore he notified the archbishops of Sens and Bourges of the gist of his mandate to the count, instructing them, if the count obeyed his order, that they were to bring about a suitable settlement between the abbot and the count; but if not, he charged the archbishop of Sens alone to proceed according to the tenor of other letters whose contents are as follows:[2]

---

[1] 30 May 1165.

[2] All of the four letters that follow were written on 5 June 1165.

31

[The Pope] Writes to the Archbishop of Sens About
the Affair   [1647A/542.1167]

1165

Alexander, bishop, servant of the servants of God, to his venerable brother
Hugh, archbishop of Sens, greetings and the apostolic blessing.

We believe it has come to your fraternity's notice how that noble man the
count of Nevers and his mother have laid more violent hands than usual
upon the monastery of Vézelay, and how, casting aside all fear and reverence
for God and the blessed Mary Magdalene, whose body reposes in that monastery, they fear not to have their servants raid and lead off horses, cows,
donkeys, and sheep, both from the monastery and from the lands of its obedience.[1] The count has poured threats and menaces upon the abbot of this
place, so that he does not dare to go outside the monastery, from fear of the
danger to his own person. Now because that monastery is known especially to
belong to the right and lordship of the blessed Peter and of us, and is not the
least of the members of the Roman church, we order your fraternity by this
apostolic writing, as you hold dear our grace and that of the blessed Peter, to
try with all diligence to meet with the count and his mother as soon as possible, to exhort them attentively to restore without delay to the abbot and
brothers what they have taken, to make fitting satisfaction for the damages
and injuries they have inflicted, and to cease from further undeserved molestation or vexation of them. Otherwise, within twenty days from your warning,
you are to interdict all their lands from the celebration of the Divine Office,
except for the baptism of children and the last rites for the dying; and if they
still do not come to their senses, you are not to delay pronouncing sentence
of excommunication against their persons. Notify our worthy brothers, the
bishops of Autun, Langres, Auxerre, and Nevers by letter, and enjoin them
firmly on our behalf to do their best to observe strictly this sentence pronounced by you over the lands and persons of the count and his mother,
until they give fitting satisfaction. For we have ordered them through our
letters to fulfill carefully and loyally what they hear from you in this matter by
your letters.

32

A Similar Case Is Put Here   [1647B/543.1203]

1165

Alexander, bishop, servant of the servants of God, to his venerable brothers,
Henry of Autun, Walter of Langres, Alan of Auxerre and Bernard of Nevers,
bishops, greetings and the apostolic blessing.

We believe it has come to the notice of your fraternity how that noble man
the count of Nevers and his mother have laid more violent hands than usual
upon the monastery of Vézelay, and how, casting aside all fear and reverence

---

[1] *tam monasterii quam exteriorum obedientiarum.*

for God and the blessed Mary Magdalene, whose body reposes in that monastery, they fear not to have their servants raid and lead off horses, cows, donkeys, and sheep, both from the monastery and from the lands of its obedience. The count has poured threats and menaces upon the abbot of this place, so that he does not dare to go outside the monastery, from fear of the danger to his own person. Now because that monastery is known especially to belong to the right and lordship of the blessed Peter and of us, and is not the least of the members of the Roman church, we have ordered our venerable brother the archbishop of Sens to try with all diligence to meet the count and his mother as soon as possible, to exhort them attentively to restore without delay to the abbot and brothers what they have taken, to make fitting satisfaction for the damages and injuries they have inflicted, and to cease from further undeserved molestation or vexation of them. Otherwise he is to interdict all their lands from the celebration of the Divine Office, except for the baptism of children and the last rites for the dying; and, if they still do not come to their senses, he is not to delay pronouncing sentence of excommunication against their persons. He is to notify you in his letters and enjoin you firmly on our behalf to take care to observe strictly this sentence pronounced by him over the lands and persons of the count and his mother, until they give fitting satisfaction. And so we order your fraternity by this apostolic writing that when you receive news of this through the archbishop's letter you firmly observe what he has ordained, since you hold dear our grace and that of the blessed Peter, and cause it to be strictly observed throughout your parishes. Otherwise with the Lord as instigator we shall correct severely the transgressor of our orders.

Given at Clermont-Ferrand, 5 June.

33
He Asks the King to Use Force Against the Count
[1647B/544.1240]

1165

Alexander, bishop, servant of the servants of God, to his most dear son in Christ Louis, illustrious king of the French, greetings and the apostolic blessing.

We believe it has come to the notice of your royal highness how that noble man the count of Nevers and his mother have laid more violent hands than usual upon the monastery of Vézelay and how, casting aside all fear and reverence for God and the blessed Mary Magdalene, whose body reposes in that monastery, they fear not to have their servants raid and lead off horses, cows, donkeys, and sheep, both from the monastery and from the lands of its obedience. The count has poured threats and menaces upon the abbot of this place, so that he does not dare to go outside the monastery, for fear of the danger to his own person. Not only does the count invade the public and ancient highway, but he forces travellers to go past a certain castle of his, and on one occasion he took prisoner certain burghers returning from the markets.[1] Now because the monastery is known especially to be subject to the right and lordship of the Roman church, and to the protection of the king's majesty, we ask your highness by this apostolic writing and urge and exhort you in the name of the Lord, for the sake of divine love, and out of reverence for the blessed Peter and for us, instantly to warn the count and his mother, diligently to try to meet them, and even, if necessary, to force them by the royal might to restore without delay to the abbot and brothers what they have taken, to make fitting satisfaction for their damages and injuries, and to cease from further undeserved molestation or vexation of them. Thus you will be found sufficient in the sight of almighty God and worthy to attain a happy reward, and we shall be constrained to give you abundant thanks for your clemency. We also have warned the count and his mother through our letters to try to correct their misdeeds, and to cease utterly from such acts in the future.

Given at Clermont-Ferrand, 5 June.

34

He Reassures the Abbot and Monks of Vézelay About
The Letters He Wrote   [1647B/545.1273]

1165

Alexander, bishop, servant of the servants of God, to his dear sons Abbot William and the brothers of Vézelay, greetings and the apostolic blessing.

When we received your letters and diligently perceived your trials and tribulations, which their contents described, we grieved deeply with the affection of a fatherly understanding. Since we know that your monastery is a particular possession of the blessed Peter[2] we love you in the Lord with deep affection as special and devoted sons of the Church and aspire with a prompt spirit to obtain your prosperity. Therefore we have written about your business to our dear son in Christ, Louis, illustrious king of the Franks, and to our venerable brothers Archbishop Hugh of Sens, and the bishops of Autun, Langres, Auxerre, and Nevers, and to the noble man the count of Nevers and his mother, as will be clear to you from the transcripts of those letters. You for your part should apply your best efforts and attention to this work of correction and, praying diligently and observing your cloister and the rules of religion, should cry to heaven that almighty God will soon put an end to these ills and concede to you peace and desired tranquillity.

Given at Clermont-Ferrand, 5 June.

---

[1] Notice that this sentence was not in the letter to the ecclesiastics. A denial of the right of free use of the highway was obviously seen as a matter of particular interest to the king. There are other, more minor, changes of wording too.

[2] *monasterium vestrum proprium patrimonium beati Petri esse.*

35

The Archbishop of Sens, Made an Arbiter by the Pope, Treats the Case Between Vézelay and the Count [1647C/545.1294]

1165

In accordance with the papal mandate therefore, Hugh, archbishop of Sens appointed a day for the count and his mother, before which they were to restore what they had taken from the church of Vézelay and on which they should come to him and the archbishop of Bourges to reach an agreement with the church of Vézelay. But the count and his mother asked the archbishop of Sens to give them and the abbot a day on which he alone would be present, when they would gladly come to an agreement with the abbot by his advice. As a result the archbishop of Sens and the abbot with his brothers and friends met at Saint-Julien-du-Sault. But the count and his mother sent their messengers, not to make an agreement, but to appeal for a papal hearing. The far-sighted wisdom of Abbot William had foreseen this and just a little earlier he had sent his messenger to the pope with great speed, beseeching him to deny any right of appeal to those who sought subterfuge rather than justice. As soon as he had obtained what he sought, the messenger returned in haste, and four days after the lodging of the appeal he entered Sens, where he found the abbot and handed him the hoped for letter from the lord pope. At once the abbot went to the archbishop and handed him the papal mandate, which stated that unless the count and his mother restored what they had taken to the church of Vézelay within the limit of twenty days prescribed in his recent letter, made satisfaction for the injuries which they had inflicted, and desisted thereafter from maltreating the church, the archbishop should pronounce sentence on their persons and lands according to the gist of the other letters, all right of appeal disallowed. Hearing this the archbishop of Sens was stupefied, astounded at such a quick disallowing of the appeal. He was angry too at being delegated to execute the sentence of the apostolic judge, for he feared the enmity of the count of Nevers.

Now the count was oppressed by heavy debts, and hearing that there was much wealth in an Auvergnian town named Mont-Ferrand [*Mons Ferrandi*], he descended suddenly and unexpectedly on its people, who were at peace and suspected nothing, snatched away all the loot he could from that town, and took the town's lord with him as a hostage for an agreed ransom.[1] And while he was raging there with furious tyranny, the messenger of Archbishop Hugh of Sens came to him and handed him a letter from his lord whose contents are as follows:[2]

---

[1] There is no other record of this attack on Mont-Ferrand, a suburb of Clermont-Ferrand.

[2] Written at the beginning of July 1165.

36

He Threatens a Sentence of Excommunication if the
Count Does Not Restore to Vézelay What He Has Taken
[1648B/546.1331]

1165

Hugh, by the grace of God archbishop of Sens, to his most dear son William, noble count of Nevers, greetings and love.

We received a letter from the lord pope on behalf of the church of Vézelay, which you have oppressed in so many ways, as the monks complain, and at once we sent our brother William[1] to admonish you diligently to restore all that you have taken and to make good all their losses and injuries, and a day was fixed for you to do this. But before that day, so the monks complain, you had twenty-four of their cows taken. On the day which had been fixed for you, you sent us your representatives, who, as became clear, were insufficiently competent, for they did not carry letters from you stating that you would abide by whatever decision they came to. Thus they were unable to proceed effectively in the business. The abbot was asking for full restitution of his goods that had been taken, as the lord pope ordered; or if that was not done within a period of twenty days, as is contained in those same letters of the lord pope, for full justice to be shown to you and your land. Your representatives, on the other hand, said that they would see that a pledge would be given to the abbot, but the abbot wanted nothing less than full restitution. About these and other matters, your men appealed to the lord pope, and so we delayed proceeding with the business. Later the lord pope sent us a letter in which it was enjoined on us that, all delays and appeals denied, if you did not make good all the losses and thefts, we should thereupon pronounce sentence of excommunication on you and your lands. If you do not do this within ten days after you see this letter, we shall pronounce sentence of excommunication, although sad and unwilling, on you and your land by the authority and order of the pope.

37

The Count Is Bound by a Sentence of Excommunication
[1648D/547.1359]

1165

The archbishop of Sens sent a similar letter to Ida, the count's mother. When the prescribed number of days was completed, three days before the feast of St. Mary Magdalene,[2] the count and his mother incurred the papal sentence. Nonetheless the count presumed to come to Vézelay on the feast—to exact his customary procuration, not to show the honor due to the handmaid of God. But the brothers, in their abbot's absence, certainly did not presume to show

---

[1] This William, the messenger mentioned in the previous chapter, was the brother of Hugh, archbishop of Sens, and himself became bishop of Auxerre (1167–1182).

[2] 20 July 1165.

hospitality [*procurare*] to one excommunicated by the lord pope, and even abstained from celebrating the Divine Office in his presence. Very distressed at this, the count wished to apply force to the monastery and the burghers, but he was dissuaded by Miles [*a Milone*, of Noyers] and others of his barons.

38
Certain Base Monks Support the Count's Position

[1649A/547.1370]

1165

The hand of Satan too was added to the oppression endured by the monastery of Vézelay, for he entered into the hearts of certain pseudo-monks, so that, as the exterior calamities seemed not sufficient to annihilate the monastery's dignity, he might totally subjugate its liberty by internal warfare.[1] For a certain Peter, born in the Auvergne and nourished in the monastery from boyhood, was hiding a viper's cunning beneath the simplicity of an ass, or rather beneath the feigning of hypocrisy. And because a cloak of virtue sometimes effectively deceives the simplicity of good men, it happened that he was promoted through each grade of his order up to the priorate of the monastery, until by the influence and support of Abbot Pons of worthy memory he was placed at the head of the monastery of Tonnerre.[2] The unworthy man, raised unworthily to this dignity, at once relaxed the reins of his vices and reduced his house's property to nothing. Moreover, notorious for his attendance on a certain youth named Thibault, whom he had clothed in the sacred habit, he was admonished often by the brothers of his monastery, and often corrected by his bishop Godfrey of Langres. But, as he ignored both the warning and the rebuke, the bishop eventually forced him to forswear that brother's company. Since he had added to his house's dilapidation even the ill-fame of perjury, he was removed by canonical procedure from the care and rule of the monastery of Tonnerre.

After he had been deposed, the worthy Abbot Pons received him with his natural kindness and held him in much honor, although he did not deserve it. After Pons was laid in peace with his fathers, that insane Peter, by soliciting the brothers of the monastery of Vézelay, began to deviate from our sacred liberty and to impede as much as he could the election of Abbot William, whom we are discussing; but the counsel of this Achitophel was in vain, and all the machinations of Satan were dissipated. However, when William had taken up his office, he showed all possible favor to that foolish Peter, who hid his envy, and gave him two cells of the monastery of Vézelay in the country of Auvergne. When he had wasted them he came to Vézelay as though full of merit, believing like a blind man that everyone else was blind too. Abbot William received him honorably and kept him with him for a long time, showing to him hardly less honor than to his own person. Moreover when he went to the court of Pope Alexander he took Peter with him and commended him to

---

[1] See (Pseudo-)Cicero *In Sallustium* 2.7 and Cicero *In Catilinam* 2.13.28 (Huygens).

[2] His appointment took place in about 1140 and he was removed about 1159.

the whole curia, looking after his business as though it were his own. In fact he showed him such favor that not the slightest word of his was without effect upon Abbot William. So it happened that at his entreaty the abbot received and had professed that most evil and impudent Thibault, for whose sake Peter had lost his honor and reputation. As probity even makes use of the evil of dishonest men, so conversely evil abuses the piety of prudent men.

Thus after Thibault had been received, he began to engage in secret discussions and to pervert the hearts of the simpler brothers with nasty whisperings. For he alleged that from one man's hatred the whole monastery was being endangered, and that because of his vices the honesty of the whole church was befouled; that this man, relying solely on his arrogance, feared neither God nor man,[1] but rather abused the simple innocence of the brothers, laughing and making fun of them as though they were children. He had deprived them all of both power and honor as the church's obedientiaries, granting them no more than the bare name and usurping for himself the fruits of their management.[2] "Behold," he said, "this man is called cellarer, that guest-master, another almoner, another granarian, another this or that, but none of this gains them anything, for he alone sells everything for himself. Only that flatterer Vincent, laying claim to the title alone of dean, drags everything behind him with his English tail.[3] Panfagus accompanies him with various flatteries, crying always: 'May the Lord bless you!'[4] Such an abbot, supported by such men, thinks of all others as servants, who neither know nor achieve anything, miserable people who do not get anywhere by their grumbling and who do not dare to complain of their woes. There is not one among them, he [the abbot] thinks, who would open his mouth or whine, or who would oppose himself as a wall for the house of Israel[5] and bear off the blame from Judah and the abomination from Samaria; especially as, trusting solely to bouts of conscience, he takes with impunity from the obedientiaries their accustomed rest,[6] on the pretext of religion, abusing their affection with such arrogance that he repays their devoted services with nothing but ingratitude, thinking he has indulged them enough if he gives them permission to serve him. He compensates their immense services with a smile and single 'well done.'"

By these words and the like he [Thibault] infected the hearts of the stupid, and by such persuasions aroused feelings of hatred within the monastery. His colleague in this stupidity was Geoffrey of Lagny, a man skilled in speech and successful in the arts of persuasion—although more successful in those of slyness. This man, at one time fleeing from the monastery of Bonneval in [the diocese of] Chartres, was accepted, from feelings of compassion, in the mon-

---

[1] Luke 18:2 and 18:4. The man whom Thibault is maligning is Abbot William.

[2] On the obedientiary system, whereby certain estates were allocated to particular monastic officials, see Knowles ([1949] 1962: 431–39). The various monastic officials are described in ibid. 427–31.

[3] *Solus adulator Vincentius, nomen tantum decani pretendens, Anglica post se cauda trahit omnia.*

[4] Panfagus ("Eat-all") is an invented name meant to show Abbot William's corrupt rewarding of favorites and sycophants.

[5] Ezekiel 13:5.

[6] *solitam ... obedientiarum requiem*; but it is not clear what Hugh means here, unless perhaps that he makes them work or perform liturgical service all the time.

astery of Lagny. When he had resided there for some time, pretending to be religious, and had shown himself a Cicero in his oratory and a Cato in his morals, the abbot promoted him to share in the rule of the monastery. Without delay, casting off not the habit but the morals of a monk, he showed himself a monster of all kinds of vices; both in shameful acts and crimes he surpassed not only moderation but even his own reputation. Licentious as he was in himself, to his friends he behaved as another Pyrrhus;[1] in an amazing way this same vessel contained both honey and poison, and poured out filth and savagery. For before a man's face he was pleasant, as one who spoke with the Lord,[2] but behind his back he stung with a tail of slander, like a scorpion. To himself he was another Sardanapalus,[3] prodigal to strolling-players, stingy to honest men, to all, another Proteus. But after he had tainted even the city of Paris with his impurity, and his scrofulous pomposity had induced nausea in every surrounding region, the whole throng of the brothers of Lagny raised a clamor about him, and he was deposed from any part in the oversight of the house and ordered to sit in the cloister.

But since his brothers were still not calmed by this, one Sunday when they were celebrating the Office at the sixth hour and Geoffrey had pronounced that verse of the Psalm: "The ropes of the sinners have bound me,"[4] they all made a rush, laid hands on him, threw him out of the church and, after stripping him publicly, put him to flight through the village. When he came to the bridge over the Marne, fearing the savagery of his pursuers, he threw his remaining clothes into the river and sought relief in hasty flight. After this, wandering about and cajoling people, he was taken by the bishop of Paris and sent to the monastery at Soissons, whose abbot wisely sent him to another house of stricter discipline, a monastery built far away in the district of Austrasia,[5] where this madman's turpitude might be punished more severely and the stench of his infamy more quickly stifled. But with the encouragement of Archbishop Henry of Rheims he later left that place and wandered from house to house, hoping to be able perhaps to deceive one of them by flattery into accepting him. At length, rejected by all, with bowed head he came to Vézelay, went to Abbot William, asked to be received by him and was successful in his request. How devout, how humble, how simple, how affable, how modest, how kindly he appeared unexpectedly to be—the man cannot show off these virtues who doesn't know how to feign like Proteus. For he put on so good a show that neither Cluny nor Cîteaux seemed ever to have contained a more religious monk. What more shall I say? He is raised, he is exalted; he is condemned and suddenly driven out.[6]

---

[1] See Horace *Odes* 3.20. In the Horatian poem Pyrrhus is striving for the favor of a young man.

[2] 2 Samuel 16:23.

[3] See Cicero *Tusculan Disputations* 5.35.

[4] Psalm 118:61. See too the *Rule of St. Benedict*, 18.

[5] *Austrasia*: the name of Eastern Francia in Merovingian times and the heartland of Carolingian power. Here it probably means somewhere in the diocese of Rheims. Cox identifies the monastery at Soissons as St. Médard.

[6] See Ezekiel 20:23 where similar phrasing is used to describe God's punishment of the Israelites.

This is the sort of man who, in league with Thibault by secret conversations and nightly whisperings, solicited, questioned, irritated, instigated, and provoked now this man, now that, to scandalous feelings of detraction and hatred. These men, therefore, conniving together, from the seed of Canaan[1] gave birth to a son of dissension, that material of scandal, that kindling for ill-feeling, that inciter of discord: that bastard Bartholomew, born of a whore's adultery. This boy was received into the monastery through the favor of his paternal uncle, but after many benefits which Abbot William heaped upon him, he was suspended from the office of almoner—his own faults demanded it yet he was more offended than could possibly be believed. His pusillanimity was all the more bitterly provoked by the above-mentioned twins of Satan, as well as by William surnamed Pidet, a man of almost no account, whose hands were crooked and who had often fled from the monastery, and in the very year of this schism had committed murder.

These four[2] harnessed themselves to the four wheels of the chariot of Pharaoh,[3] like four horses. With them were another four whose names I suppress, because they did nothing but make up the numbers, and because when examined they recognized their foolishness and repudiated the madness of their plan. Through these men's efforts, a murmur little by little crept about and infected one way and another the discipline of our sacred order.[4] And then, allying to themselves whomsoever they could entice, they all decided to write to Peter, who had been expelled from Tonnerre and who had gone a few days earlier, with the abbot's grace and blessing, to inspect his obediences in the country of Auvergne. They humbly besought him to come without delay to the aid of the desolated house of Vézelay, saying that all the brothers had unanimously agreed to follow his orders in this time of necessity. Learning of this, Peter came at once quite unexpectedly, making the malignant ones joyful, but filling the rest with much astonishment by his sudden and unforeseen arrival. The plotters of unholy sedition went to him secretly and poured into his ears the poison of the betrayal which they had planned, asking and urging him to take up their wretched cause against the abbot—or rather against the church—dedicating themselves to him, promising that they would be with him till death, and that the greater proportion of the convent would ally themselves with them.

At once inspired by these words, Peter went secretly to the count who, as mentioned earlier,[5] had come to the feast, and made known to him their vows of sedition. The count joyfully exulted at this and faithfully pledged that he would give him and his accomplices the firmest support in all things, horses and money and even, if necessary, safe strongholds anywhere on his lands. And he gave as sureties four knights from among his chief men, who

---

[1] Daniel 13:56.

[2] I.e., Thibault, Geoffrey of Lagny, Bartholomew and William Pidet.

[3] Exodus 15:4.

[4] "Murmuring" is specifically forbidden by St. Benedict in a number of places in his *Rule*; see chaps. 4, 5, 23, and, especially, 34 , which says, in part: "Above all let not the evil of murmuring show itself by the slightest word or sign, for any reason at all."

[5] See above 4 §37. The feast is the feast of St. Mary Magdalene, 22 July 1165.

agreed on oath that the count would carry out his promises to Peter and to all whom he could persuade to join him against the abbot in the count's service. And Peter and Thibault swore to the count that they would hold faith with him against the abbot, that they would ensure that the more significant part of the convent of their church also kept faith with him and that they themselves would later arouse the universal pontiff Alexander against Abbot William. This conspiracy was made on the very day of the sacred feast of the holy lover of God, Mary Magdalene, in the upper chapel of St. Lawrence, by the hands of Stephen of Pontoise, Stephen of Pierre-Perthuis, Miles [of Noyers], and Hugh of Argenteuil. Thus these impious and adulterous men profaned that sacred day, while their brothers and free sons sorrowed and were sad, because they were unable to celebrate the day of their patroness in the usual fitting way.[1] Also present were Cardinal Henry of Pisa, the archbishop-elect of Mainz, and [William] the bishop-elect of Chartres, who outwardly seemed to press for peace, but, moved by the spirit of the flesh, favored more and more the party of the count and his mother.

39
The Count Tries to Entice the Monks to Oppose the Abbot
[1651A/552.1550]

1165

For this reason the count himself, emboldened by the promptings of the traitors, asked permission to enter the brothers' chapter house. When it was granted, he complained about the abbot, who had deprived him of his hereditary right and afflicted him with countless injuries. Although he had suffered all this undeservedly, he declared that what especially distressed him was the desolation of a church which had once been so opulent in its wealth, so bejewelled with honorable members, so strict in its religious discipline, so well known for its charitable hospitality, and which in these and many other good works had at one time excelled all the churches of Gaul after Cluny. Yet that church was now so notorious for its penury in goods, the burden of its debts, the meagerness of its personnel, the ill-fame of its life and the inhumanity of its hospitality, that it had become a by-word not only in various churches, but even among the vulgar throng. All this stemmed from the pride and dissolute-

---

[1] The brothers refuse to celebrate mass because of the presence of the excommunicated count. According to Huygens (1976: 662) Milo (V) de Nuceriis (Noyers: Yonne, ar. Avallon) was the brother of Stephen of Pierre-Perthuis. He is styled by Cox, "Milon d'Argenteuil-sur-Armançon in the Auxerrois." Of the personalities in the next line Cox writes: "Henry of Pisa, formerly a monk at Clairvaux, had been promoted to the cardinalate in 1150 by Eugenius III. The archbishop-elect of Mainz was Conrad von Wittelsbach, who had at first supported Victor IV, then embraced the cause of Alexander III at the Council of Tours in 1163. Chérest 2:51n, 52 n says that he was a relative of the count of Nevers. The bishop-elect of Chartres was William 'aux blanches mains,' the youngest brother of counts Henry of Champagne, Theobald V of Blois and Chartres, and Steven of Sancerre—which therefore also made him a nephew of Ida of Carinthia, countess of Nevers. In 1168 William became archbishop of Sens, then archbishop of Rheims (in 1176) and a cardinal."

ness of the abbot, with the assent of those of the brothers who favored him. "Where" the count went on, "are those serious and upright persons of old, the cellarer, guest-master, sacrist, almoner, and chamberlain, by whose prudence and power this house once flourished? Now there is not one among you capable of aiding his fellow, or of giving advice when sought—all you have retained of the honor is the empty name. In short, the dissoluteness of all of you is clear and well known when, like favoring like, you put up, apparently voluntarily, with injustice.[1] Till now I have borne with my injuries, till now I have suffered the destruction of this church—this church which, because it is mine and under my protection, whether your abbot likes it or not, I shall no longer suffer to bear such shame or so great a burden. I want you to be fore-warned, I want you to persuade your abbot to spare this church from now on, to desist from its destruction, and to restore to me that which is rightfully mine. For I am demanding nothing new, but am reclaiming the ancient rights of my ancestors. For how should I burden with new and unjust exactions the church which I am supposed to protect from the assaults of all men? Finally, I warn you to discuss this among yourselves; otherwise I shall demand from all an explanation for your assent to this man's wickedness."

40

The Prior Replies to the Count   [1651C/553.1584]

1165

After hearing this prior Gilo rose to reply. First he called the seniors of the church and that other Judas,[2] whose betrayal was as yet hid from Gilo, and retired into the oratory of the blessed mother of God, Mary, with the broth-ers and burghers. After they had held counsel, Gilo made this reply: "As you yourself, lord count, have professed and as we both know and wish, you are the protector and patron of us and of this church. We acknowledge with thanks your compassion for our house's desolation and so we beseech your highness with great affection to counsel and provide for this church which is under your protection, both in those matters which are your concern, and those which concern the person of other leaders. Now although internally it flourishes in brotherly peace and concord and is adequately provided with food and clothing, externally, it is burdened by the diminution of its goods and the oppression of certain enemies. We know that it is not yet over-whelmed with debts because, we know, they do not exceed seventy pounds. The gravity of the chapter, the cloistral discipline and the behavior of the per-sonnel seem to us to be flourishing not less than usual. If any rumor of lying scandal is attacking the church, it has been instigated not by an assertion of truth but by the envy of rivals. Moreover, our abbot's character is good and upright, as we both wish and believe, and if anything about him seems other-wise to anyone judging out of hatred, he will be shown up as a liar on the

---

[1] *Iccirco patet in propatulo omnium vestrum dissolutio, cum similes simili faventes quasi gratuitam patimini iniuriam.*

[2] That is, Peter of Auvergne.

scales of reason. For this reason, we rejoice to think and feel the same as he does, as is proper for head and members; and we hope that there is nothing vicious in such common and legitimate agreement of head and members. However, if because of some personal excess or the accusation of an outsider he has provoked in you a just feeling of hate, we are ashamed and much saddened, although until today we were unaware of what that could be or how he could have deserved such hate. So when he comes, we shall admonish him humbly, as should monks their abbot or subjects their lord, to take steps to deserve the favor of your dignity. Finally, we beseech your discretion to spare the church which is, as you say, under your protection, and not to try to destroy it out of dislike for one man. For however much it is subject to its abbot, it is also always devoted to you." Now the traitor Peter sent a message to the count secretly through Simon de Souvigny to speak more gently with the brothers, especially in those areas which seemed to touch on their bad reputation, lest, in persecuting the abbot, he should also lose the favor of the angry brothers.

41

The Count Continues [1652C/554.1624]

1165

Therefore the count replied: "I am not condemning your way of life, but rather deploring the poverty which you have suffered through the dilapidation of your church's goods carried out by the abbot. Hence, as I have said, unless you yourselves look after your affairs and your church, I shall no longer bear such destruction. For although I have not yet been declared excommunicate by canonical order,[1] at your abbot's orders you have ceased celebrating the Divine Office solely because of my presence and, for what reason I do not know, you have not shown me the hospitality [*procurationem*] which the world knows is due to me. As for the church's debt, which you say does not exceed seventy pounds, I know well that between the two seas you owe more than a thousand pounds. Moreover, the attacks by hostile forces of which you complain are the fault of your abbot, for his well known arrogance is such that he will not deal justly with me or any other. However, I am not myself taking you to court, but merely warning you to think again and provide for yourselves. If you do this, you will always find in me a loyal helper in all matters; but if not, that is your concern, for I shall provide for myself." These things he said to encourage the traitors and to incite others to agree with them. After leaving the chapter house, he spoke with Peter the traitor, and they deliberated about how Peter should go to Pope Alexander in person to accuse the abbot, accompanied by the abbot of Bourras,[2] who, under the guise of a sheep, would bite the innocent man the more keenly with a wolf's teeth. So that the cunning of their mutual compact might be concealed, the

---

[1] *Nam cum canonico ordine nondum publicatus fuerim.*

[2] The abbey of Bourras, a filial of Pontigny founded in 1119, is about fifty kilometers from Vézelay. Its founder, Hugh of Thil, lord of Champlemy, Giry, and Luzy, was seneschal at the court of William II, count of Nevers.

count promised Peter that he would have returned to him the money which the church of Tonnerre owed him for the sale of a certain obedience.[1]

The day fixed by the archbishop of Sens for discussion between the abbot and count arrived, but neither the abbot nor the count was on hand. However, Prior Gilo represented the abbot and with him was Peter, still concealing his treachery. When the two parties met before the archbishop at Bassou, Prior Gilo, in the presence of the count's legates,[2] took up the issue of the losses inflicted on the church by the count. But Peter, vomiting forth powerful and fervent treachery, began firmly to accuse Gilo, as if the latter were speaking harshly and irreverently against the count. Hearing this, Gilo and Geoffrey, at that time guest-master, and other brothers who had come there to defend the abbot, blushed deeply. The count gave hostages as a pledge that he would restore the confiscated goods, but in regard to the rest of the points at issue, he asked for another day, and this was granted by the archbishop of Sens, the two of them [the count and the archbishop] preparing for the innocent man a trap into which they themselves would fall. For the archbishop sent a letter of justification to Pope Alexander, asking him to delegate sentence over the count to another judge, lest perchance the savagery of the youthful count be unleashed against him and his people and lest the destruction of one man might involve two in the same fate. For his part, the count prepared to send Peter and some of his important supporters to Pope Alexander against Abbot William of Vézelay. They hoped that, with the archbishop seeking an exemption and the count making an accusation, the pope would delegate judges to hear the cause of abbot and count on the border between their territories. But their aim went astray, and the intentions of the foolish were frustrated.

42
The Prior Explains to the Abbot What Had Happened
with the Count   [1653C/555.1675]

1165

With their business unaccomplished, each returned to his own place. Gilo came to the abbot at Saint-Julien-du-Sault, telling him what had happened at Vézelay three days previously and on the present day, and how impudently his [the abbot's] intimate friend Peter had confounded them before the count and archbishop. At this the abbot was not a little amazed but from the abundance of his grace would give these words no credence. Rather he freed Peter

---

[1] *pro dimissione cuiusdam obedientie.* Clearly some land belonging to the church of Tonnerre (Speaight [1990: 70-74]) had been sold when Peter had been there but the money had not been given to him as it ought to have been. There is another reference to the money owed Peter by Tonnerre in the next chapter.

[2] A contemporary hand has crossed this out and written "in the presence of the count." Similarly, he has crossed out the clause in the first sentence of the paragraph, "but neither the abbot nor the count was at hand." This suggests that Hugh was trying to disguise the fact that the count was present but not the abbot. Hugh tacitly acknowledges the count's presence by affirming that he gave hostages (*comes . . . dedit obsides*).

from all suspicion and ordered him to go back to his house at Salles,[1] after collecting the money from Tonnerre. There Peter was to await the abbot, who was on the point of going to Pope Alexander, or, on hearing from the abbot's messenger, to meet the abbot at Le Puy prepared to accompany him. Now the abbot had sent his clerk John on ahead to the papal court, and he received a letter from him announcing that Alexander was to go overseas on 1 August. Abandoning, therefore, the journey which he had intended, the abbot travelled through the duke's territory, reaching Vézelay on the day after the octave of the blessed Mary Magdalene.[2] All those who belonged to Peter's faction were amazed at the abbot's sudden and unexpected arrival, for they had not expected him to return endowed with his abbatial honor—so some of their prophetic, or rather delirious, companions had predicted.

Now Peter, on the same day, before the abbot's arrival, had gone up to Vézelay. He did not enter the cloister, however, but from the hour of chapter until almost nones, sat in the almonry and spoke with his accomplices and the authors of betrayal. When the hour for dinner was at hand, he was admonished by subprior Geoffrey, once his boon-companion and great friend, to enter the refectory to sup as he ought. But he would not agree to do so. Then William surnamed Pidet, one of the four traitors mentioned above, took bread and wine to a secluded part of the house, and word spread among the brothers that Peter had eaten in the almonry. When this rumor came to Peter's ears, his accomplices said that Renaud de Mello was the originator of this as of many other detractions. Meanwhile Thibault, the fomenter of the whole scandal, was waiting for Peter down in the new small church of the Holy Cross, where he received a horse sent him there by the count.[3] When Subprior Geoffrey had gone up after the meal to meet the abbot as he arrived, Peter called him and said: "Renaud your almoner has accused me falsely of eating in his almonry. But by the saints of God, he has not spoken with impunity! Of late he has become much inflated and does not yet know his place. He ought to have known well enough that whether because of all the monks who are within, or in fact because of the abbot's eyes, I would on no account do such a thing." At these words Geoffrey was stupefied and replied: "Heavens! What are you saying! You who have gained the highest favor and all possible reverence from all the brothers of this monastery should not speak so arrogantly against them, and especially not against our lord abbot, who, as we know, has loved you and honored you as another self." And Peter said: "I don't give a fig for the monks or their abbot!" Geoffrey replied angrily: "You are speaking stupidly and have gone too far, and if I had not borne in mind our mutual friendship, you would not have uttered such things with impunity." Saying this, he turned on his heel.

---

[1] Saint-Germain de Salles was a dependent priory of Vézelay located in the commune of Chantelle near Moulins.

[2] 31 July 1165.

[3] On the *novella basilica Sancte Crucis* see Introduction above, at 12n.3. It appears to have been a grave fault for a monk to eat in the almonry, which must have been reserved for the poor. The almoner was the official responsible for the monastery's acts of charity. Renaud, the abbot's nephew, was the almoner.

Peter, who had entered into an execrable confederation with the impious elements, comforted them saying: "Keep calm and don't allow yourselves to be intimidated; very soon you will have your promised aid." Then he added: "If it happens one way or another that our arrangement is discovered, and a discussion arises about it, take heed that you are not deceived by a fear of threats or of the curse of excommunication. We can be confident of the count's aid, for he swore to us that if he were on a military expedition and our messenger came saying that even the least of our number was held in irons in prison, he would at once lay aside his helmet, take off his mailed shirt, leave his expedition and hasten to succour us with his armed might. Be confident therefore, for I leave you in the count's hands and I shall gain the apostolic favor for you against that stupid William who shall no longer reign over you. So do not fear him who you know will no longer reign over you." After the deceived had ensnared the deceived with these words he left, followed at once by Thibault. The abbot of Bourras, named [Renaud], joined them.

That evening Abbot William entered his monastery, and all the brothers rejoiced as though they had received back their father from exile. But the conspirators, stupefied at the abbot's entrance, so sudden and unexpected, were terrified and confused to the point of distraction. Gathering in the most obscure part of the upper infirmary they began to discuss what they should do. They were addressed by Geoffrey of Lagny, more acute and cunning than any of them. "I know," he said, "that your most constant probity will not be jeopardized by childish fickleness. However, I wish and recommend that what you swore to our lord abbot Peter, you now confirm with the kiss of unity, so that you will not in any way fall away either from him or from each other." And they did so and they spent that night in whisperings and secret discussions.

When morning came, Abbot William climbed up to inspect the laborers who at that time were building the marvellous new dormitory. Meanwhile someone went to Vincent, the dean of the monastery, and said to him: "Take heed for yourself and for the lord abbot, because certain monks of this monastery have made common cause with the count against the lord abbot, and moreover, Peter once abbot of Tonnerre, provisioned by the count, goes with Thibault to Pope Alexander." Astounded, Vincent related all this to the abbot. However, since in his astonishment the abbot would not believe these words, Vincent went away; but another came up at once and taking the abbot aside said to him: "I am your serf and owe no fealty to anyone against you. Begging your pardon, however, for keeping my name a secret, I tell you that some of your monks have conspired against you, and having made an agreement with the count, have sent the erstwhile abbot Peter and his Thibault to the pope against you." He also told the abbot the names of some of the conspirators.

43
The Abbot Recognizes His Betrayers at Last   [1654A/557.1773]
1165

The abbot was more convinced by this and on his return called Vincent the
dean and told him how he had learnt the same things from another's testimony. He therefore summoned Prior Gilo and told him all he had heard. It
seemed incredible to him [Gilo], until he recalled to mind the evil of Peter's
words. Then Subprior Geoffrey was called, and was astounded at what was
told him. Nor was their astonishment at such news to be marvelled at; for the
church of Vézelay had flourished in discipline, peace, and honesty for more
than three hundred years, and until this time no stain of infamy, no rumor of
scandal had polluted her. When Geoffrey had recovered from the shock, he
said: "These things which have been said seem impossible to me. Yet Robert
the refectorer said to me the day before yesterday that someone had said to
him that some sort of evil was growing against this church, which scarcely anyone would be able to curb. When I asked him who had said this, he named
Maurice. 'What,' I asked, 'can this evil be and from where can it come?' He
replied: 'I pressed Maurice about this but could get nothing further from
him.'" Now as meal time was drawing near, the abbot said to those present:
"Let us leave these matters for the moment and let us lift up our hearts,
brothers, to the Lord,[1] imploring his lover and our pious patroness, that by her
merits and prayers we may be snatched from these and all other ills." And he
ordered that hospitality should be shown more solemnly than usual in the refectory. It is wonderful to tell how, hurrying there himself, by chance he gave the
most generous portions to his betrayers; and thanking God they went out.

Calling the prior, subprior, and dean, Abbot William went into his bed-
chamber and said: "The news which you have heard is serious, nor ought it
be shrouded in silence. Indeed it cannot, lest the thin air burst into flame."[2]
"That is true," they said. "What then," he said, "do you think is to be done?"
They said to him: "To begin with call Maurice, who first exposed the path to
this secret evil. For he is a good and innocent lad and of noble birth, and we
have always shown him great affection and favor; nor do we expect that he is
a partner in such a betrayal—and this he may easily prove, by telling us willingly the truth of the matter." So when Maurice had been called, the abbot
said to him: "Sit here, and as we have loved you with all affection both from
yesterday and the day before,[3] tell us the truth about those matters of which
we have already learnt something. For we have been told and we have confirmed from reliable sources, that some people have formed a party against
me and, by the mediation of Peter, once abbot of Tonnerre, and Thibault,
they have made a pact with the count[4] to depose me and nullify this monas-

---

[1] Lamentations 3:41.

[2] 1 Kings 19:12.

[3] *sicut te ab heri et nudius tercius toto affectu dileximus* . . . ; this sounds like a proverbial
phrase since taken literally it refers only to a short time.

[4] *confederati sunt comiti.* . . .

tery's liberty. Whatever therefore you know of this, I charge you to tell us truthfully, out of obedience and under threat of anathema." Maurice replied: "I have not discovered anything certain about these things, except that some brothers who have often complained bitterly of you, lord, warned me to consent to enter a sworn agreement with them that, if they deposed you, I would aid them and keep it secret. I was aghast at the thought of taking such an oath but promised by my word alone that I would take no notice of their deeds nor place any obstacle in their way." So the abbot ordered him to retire for a little, and summoned Renaud de Lézinnes. When he had come and was asked about the conspiracy, he replied: "I was not a part of any conspiracy or confederation, but I was called by Geoffrey, prior of Argenteuil, and the knight Hugh, the lord of that castle [of Argenteuil], into the chapel of St. Vincent, and asked by them to swear to do what they would do. This I did, not knowing what they were planning against you."

After he too withdrew to the side, they called Bartholomew. When he had denied the charges, he was called aside by Gilo and advised by him to acknowledge his personal guilt, which was already evident since he was convicted even on the testimony of his companions. At length, after he had been convicted by many arguments from both sides, not only did he reveal the crime of the betrayal but acknowledged himself as the instigator of the whole faction. Then Peter of Sermizelles and Hildin [*Hildinus*] were called and when they learnt of the charges they revealed the authors and manner of the betrayal. Last of all William Pidet was called. Obstinate in his evil, he was found more obstinate in his confession. And since he did not give in to his companions' arguments, nor to warnings, he was damned with the sentence of anathema. At once he appealed to a papal hearing, just as he and his allies had been instructed by those originators of the evil, Peter, Thibault, and Geoffrey [of Lagny]. But because they were damned, the appeal was quashed, and William [Pidet] was beaten, locked in an inner chamber, and kept there under guard until the morning.

After matins had been celebrated, Abbot William entered the chapter house with his brothers, and when all the guests had been shown out, the aforementioned brothers Renaud [of Lézinnes], Bartholomew, Peter [of Sermizelles], and Hildin rose, asked pardon and renounced the wickedness of their proposed betrayal on the holy gospels. The abbot immediately received them into his favor and gave them the kiss of peace. When William [Pidet] saw that he had neither friend nor helper, he fraudulently pretended to repent. Led therefore into their midst, he confessed and abjured his crime, and thus he was absolved from the bonds of anathema and received with the kiss of peace, as a wolf by his shepherd. But after much had been said by many people, and the count's malice and Peter's stupidity and Thibault's wickedness had been condemned before them all, the talk suddenly turned to Geoffrey de Lagny. He, rising at once in their midst, foreswearing and execrating what he was accused of, denied absolutely everything. Even when he had been convicted by many arguments and by the testimony of his companions and was to be excommunicated if he did not repent, he still did not wish to confess anything. On the contrary, he proposed that he swear on the text of the gospels that he had known nothing of these things. But, disregarding his wickedness for the time, the abbot warned his brothers to beware of such trickery, which certainly got them nothing except the monastery's destruction and the annulment of its liberty. Because he saw that the count had had a finger in this, it seemed necessary to him to resist such wicked attempts. And lest he labor in vain, the abbot exhorted them all as one to bend their minds to works of peace and quiet, silence and charity, and besought them to give themselves to prayer more attentively and to raise their hands to heaven against Amalek.[1] Then, after the customary solemn procession, he offered a sacrifice to God.

Those who had foresworn their sedition[2] wrote to Peter and Thibault to desist from what they had begun, for it was in vain that they kicked against the pricks,[3] especially as their advice seemed from the very beginning to have come to nought. Besides, they themselves, having been found out, had renounced the wickedness foisted on them by those two. They also wrote to the highest pontiff Alexander and to all the cardinals of the apostolic curia, saying how they had been deceived by a certain recalcitrant of all evil days;[4] and they prayed that this man, who was coming to the feet of the apostolic curia against his abbot and mother church, should not be received, and beseeched them that darkness should not overcome the light, nor error confound the truth. Nevertheless, those vessels of iniquity, those sons of Belial, Geoffrey de Lagny and William Pidet, persisting in their poisonous hatred and planning the evils of stupidity, asked the abbot to be permitted to follow after Peter and Thibault so that they might either lead them back or else convict them of the evil of their betrayal at the Roman curia. Truly it is sometimes prudent for the simplicity of a dove to be on guard against a serpent's cunning. For a practiced wickedness seldom fails to give rise to suspicion.

44

The Author of This History [1654C/560.1895]

1165

Having secretly arranged a journey after breakfast, Abbot William then came by night to Avallon, which is a castle of the duke of Burgundy. Going on from there he came a week later to Montpellier, having in his entourage Geoffrey of England, the subprior, Vincent the dean, Franco his chaplain, and Hugh of Poitiers his notary [*notarius*], the writer of the present work. From Varennes Hugh followed the traitors Peter and Thibault, whom he found at the castle named Gannat together with [Renaud] abbot of Bourras, who by that time had already arrived there. Hugh, drawing forth the letter from Abbot William and the whole chapter of Vézelay, handed it to Peter. At this, Thibault, looking at Peter with "glaring eyes,"[5] said: "What have you done, you stupid idiot? Who is this abbot in whose name you received this docu-

---

[1] Exodus 17:8–11.

[2] This refers to those monks who had acknowledged their guilt and had been reconciled with Abbot William.

[3] Acts 9:5.

[4] Daniel 13:52; a reference either to Peter of Tonnerre or to his close friend Thibault.

[5] Virgil *Aeneid* 3.677.

ment? For we don't hold as abbot whoever behaves contrary to his fidelity to the count." And saying this, he snatched the still unopened letter from Peter's hand, threw it on the floor and stamped on it. In reply, Hugh said to Peter and Thibault: "This injury harms not only the abbot, but also the whole convent of Vézelay. So, on behalf of Abbot William and of the whole chapter, I tell you that you must return to Vézelay within four days to answer charges against you; if not, the abbot and convent will promulgate sentence of excommunication against your persons by papal authority; and on their behalf I announce this sentence to you." Then Hugh departed and met the abbot at Le Puy-en-Velay, and told him of the rebelliousness of the traitors. Meanwhile the traitors went on ahead of the abbot, but were recognized by John, the abbot's clerk, and denied entrance to the papal court.

45

The Abbot Is Received With Honor by the Roman Pope.
His Betrayers Are Driven Away   [1655B/561.1923]

1165

The abbot, however, went in to Pope Alexander and was received by him and all the curia with great honor and complete favor. But when the traitors tried to gain entrance to the court, they were thrown out in disgrace by the very doorkeepers as men whose treason was well known. However, the abbot of Bourras entered as if to carry out business on behalf of his own order; but when in fact he began to press the count's case and to espouse the cause of those traitors, as if they were innocent representatives of the church of Vézelay, against the abbot, as though he were a dilapidator of their goods and a subverter of his order, he was expelled at once by Pope Alexander, after being resisted to his face[1] by Humbald, cardinal-bishop of Ostia.[2] Then Henry, cardinal-bishop of Pisa, and the archbishop-elect of Mainz spoke out as much as possible on behalf of the count and the traitors. By these means they managed to compel the pope, who was wearied with so many requests, to write to the excommunicated count. When the abbot heard of this through the secretaries, he went in to the pope and, kneeling, said: "What have you done, my lord? We have not yet obtained full justice, yet already you have recalled the small piece of justice which you have done us!" "How is that?" asked the pope. "By writing," he said "contrary to the apostolic custom, to a man you have excommunicated." "Has the sentence then already been pronounced?" the pope asked. "It has," replied the abbot. The pope said: "Show me your copy of my letter." The abbot gave it to him and Alexander forthwith sent to his secretarial department and ordered that the [above-men-

---

[1] Galatians 2:11.

[2] Cardinal Humbald (Ubaldo 'Allucingoli of Lucca), bishop of Ostia, who had consecrated Alexander pope, succeeded him on the papal throne on 1 September 1184 under the name of Lucius III. His celebrated decretal *Ad abolendam* requiring bishops to seek out and punish heretics, has earned him a secure, if unenviable, niche in the history of the Inquisition. See Peters (1980: 170–73) and (1988: 47 ff.). Lucius III died at Verona on 25 September 1185. See Kelly (1986).

tioned] letter [to the count], which had been obtained by stealth, be retained.[1] When he learned that the archbishop-elect of Mainz had already obtained it, he was very angry and ordered that it be demanded back from him at once. When it had been returned, Mainz went in to the pope and asked that the papal letter be given back to him; but the pope began to accuse him of stealing a letter to which he had no right. Because he thought it shameful that his petition should be denied, Mainz burst into tears. Moved by this, the pope said to him: "Look here, since you want it, you may have it; but it will get you no reward for your kinsman, for we have made another document cancelling the one obtained by stealth." So, when the traitors Peter and Thibault saw that they were getting nowhere, they went home. On their way they were met by William Pidet and Elias—the latter void of learning but full of stupidity—who, returning to their own vomit[2] by resuming the disloyalty which they had renounced, had left the cloister secretly by night, climbing the monastery wall and letting themselves down by ropes. But it happened that the rope broke and Elias fell, hurting his arm.

46
Judges Are Delegated By the Supreme Pontiff　　　[1656A/562.1960]
1165

So, fleeing all through that night and coming to the count, they complained that the abbot had inflicted heavy torments upon them simply because of his hatred of the count. The count gave them horses and money for expenses and sent them after Peter and Thibault. As soon as the two parties had met, they returned together to the court, and watching for the appearance of Pope Alexander—for they were unable to obtain access to him at all—they met him as he was coming out of the oratory. William Pidet, prostrating himself before him, complained that after appealing for a papal hearing he had been beaten and imprisoned by Abbot William. But the pope said: "Are you not one of the excommunicated traitors to your church?" When everyone present shouted that it was so, the traitors were thrown out of the consistory and from Pope Alexander's sight. From then on the abbot cared nothing for them, and did not deign to mention so much as a word about them at the court. He very much desired that the delegation of the papal sentence against the tyrant and his mother should be transferred from the archbishop of Sens, and given to someone else—something which the archbishop himself sought greatly and had asked for in a recent letter. However, because the larger and more important part of the count's lands was in that diocese, the pope did not wish to transfer the delegation of the sentence at all; but that the arch-

---

[1] *et iussit ut surrepticium illud scriptum retineretur.* This incident provides an interesting insight into the practice of the papal chancery. Clearly, by this time the popes were in the habit of keeping copies of all their own correspondence. From §34 above it is also clear that copies were often sent as informative attachments to other letters. The episode above also indicates that procedures for the correct issue of copies existed and were sometimes—as in this instance—breached.

[2] Proverbs 26:11.

bishop might proceed to execute the sentence courageously and in greater
security, he gave him as his colleague Bishop Stephen of Meaux.[1] He wrote
to both of them, that they should meet with the count of Nevers and his
mother to exhort them to come to terms in friendly fashion with the church
of Vézelay, or else they should promulgate the delegated sentence over those
contemptuous ones, with no appeal or reference to any stealthily obtained
document allowed.[2] They were to announce to the bishops of Autun, Langres, Auxerre, and Nevers that they should observe what was ordered in the
letters the pope sent them.

47

The Delegates Meet at Joigny and Place the Count and
His Mother Under an Excommunication   [1656C/563.1990]

1165

On the Monday following the Assumption of the chaste virgin and mother of
God, Mary,[3] the most holy and universal pontiff and Catholic pope Alexander went up to the altar to offer the sacred and life-giving sacrifice to God for
the soul of Ivo, dean of the church of Chartres. While he was completing the
sacrifice, the traitors began to argue with Geoffrey of England [sub-prior of
Vézelay]. Geoffrey went to Humbald bishop of Ostia and told him how much
irreverence the traitors were showing to the lord pope. Turning around, the
bishop of Ostia saw those detestable traitors and said to Alexander: "Why, my
lord, do you allow those profane betrayers of Vézelay to take part in the
divine service, in your very presence?" "Where are they?" the pope replied.
"There they are," said the cardinal. And the pope said: "Throw them out at
once." But since they only pretended to depart, the bishops of Ostia and
Segni at once called the guards and had them expelled from the church. Seeing this, the archbishop of Mainz, who just then happened to be speaking to
the abbot of Vézelay there, left in a great rage and went after them. The
abbot of Bourras too, to whose side these traitors constantly clung, seeing his
purpose frustrated, became very red and withdrew. The traitors followed him
and reported to their lord the count their shame and well-deserved confusion.
But Abbot William did not leave until he had accompanied Pope Alexander
as far as the sea. Then making a favorable journey himself, armed with the

---

[1] An interesting hint of the constraints on ecclesiastical power. Even a senior churchman like the archbishop of Sens was obviously reluctant to impose a penalty on a powerful lord.

[2] *omni surreptitio scripto postposito.* A reference to the letter that the pope had allowed
the archbishop of Mainz to retain. In 4 §37 above, it is said that the count and his mother
incurred a sentence of excommunication. But in §41 the count asserts to the monks that
he has not been excommunicated by canonical order. In §45, however, Abbot William
assures the pope that the sentence of excommunication has already been pronounced. Yet
it seems that it is only in the next chapter (47) that the sentence becomes official. Clearly
there is a distinction between incurring a sentence of excommunication and having it
pronounced. In fact, it appears from §49 that only public proclamation of a sentence
makes it final.

[3] 16 August 1165.

papal blessing, he arrived at Vézelay on the last day of August. After a few days he went on from there to Paris, where he delivered the papal letters to Archbishop Hugh of Sens and Bishop Stephen of Meaux, who at once fixed a day for him and the count at Joigny. When they had met there, the abbot exhibited Vézelay's muniments—privileges of the Roman pontiffs and of the French kings—and Pope Alexander's letter in which he had delegated to these prelates the execution of the composition or sentence. But since many charges had been lodged by both sides, the day finished with controversy still raging. But as soon as the prelates learnt that the count would do anything but agree to peace terms, they pronounced the sentence of excommunication delegated to them by Pope Alexander over the count and his mother.

48
They Discuss the Case Again at Bassou But Fruitlessly.
The Abbot Goes to the King [1657C/564.2026]
1165

On the following day, at the request of the prelates, both sides convened again by the elm at Bassou. After the goods confiscated from the church had been enumerated, certain people tried to bring about an agreement whereby the abbot would condone all these confiscations, the count would make peace with the abbot and the church, and all the other points at issue would be let slide. But the abbot replied: "In that case, what assurance will the count give that he will keep the peace?" They said to him: "He will be bound only by his word; but if you force the count to it, he will swear faith with you with his hand in the hand of these prelates." "And if he breaks faith over this peace he has promised," said the abbot, "who will see justice done on my behalf?" They replied: "You will see." So the abbot would not agree to the writing off of such great losses, but rather insisted all the more that the count should completely give up his burdensome demands for procuration. For by the authority of its founder and of his privileges, the church did not have to grant hospitality [*procurare*] to anyone, except voluntarily and out of charity. The count replied that he would rather be disinherited than relinquish a custom handed down to him from his ancestors. On the contrary, unless the abbot paid him three hundred pounds that very day for the procuration which he had recently denied him, he would not make peace with him. Abbot William said: "I haven't brought my wallet here like a money-changer to a fair! Behold, now the count's excessive tyranny, or rather rapacity, is clear to all, for he exacts three hundred pounds for a single day's procuration. What settlement could last under such a scourging?" Thus, because the possibility of peace was rejected by the count, the meeting broke up. That night Prior Gilo came to Pontigny with the bishop of Meaux, who celebrated the feast of All Saints at Vézelay.[1] Geoffrey the subprior with Renaud the almoner and the rest of their companions went, not without trepidation, to Auxerre, and rising while it was still night, they entered Vézelay the next morning. But the

---

[1] 1 November 1165.

abbot spent that night at Saint-Julien-du-Sault, with the archbishop of Sens and the abbot of Saint-Germain-des-Prés. From there he went to meet the king at Moret, beseeching him from his native piety and out of reverence for the papal mandate to succour the church of Vézelay in such dire and pressing necessity. The king told him that he would never fail St. Mary Magdalene and her servants, but rather would fight for the monastery of Vézelay as though for his own crown Yet the abbot must bear with things for a short time and avoid the mad tyrant's rage, to see if he would extend his activities to include sacrilege. If he did, the king would punish such extreme behavior, as the whole world would witness.

49
The Archbishop of Sens Declares the Count and His
Mother Excommunicate   [1658B/564.2068]

1165

The abbot accepted the king's advice and sent his secretary Hugh to request the archbishop of Sens, according to the papal mandate, to denounce publicly the count and his mother as excommunicate. So the archbishop stood at the sacred altars while the reading from the gospel was concluded[1] and the solemn celebration completed, in the people's presence and with the dean waiting, and then he preached a sermon to the congregation in which he declared to them what heavy damages the count of Nevers and his mother had inflicted on the sepulchre of the glorious and blessed Mary Magdalene, God's lover, famous throughout the whole world. On account of these crimes, he said, "at the lord pope's order we pronounce sentence of excommunication over them both; and unless they repent before the next feast of St. Martin,[2] we declare the whole of their land interdicted from all divine services, except for the baptism of children and the confession of the dying." This sentence Archbishop Hugh notified to the bishops Alan of Auxerre, Bernard of Nevers, Henry of Autun, and Walter of Langres in these words:

---

[1] et expleta lectione apostolica; on this practice see Ordo Excommunicationis in PL 138.1123: Episcopus . . . post lectionem Evangelii clerem et plebem ita debet alloqui. The instructions go on to say that an account should be given to the congregation of the crimes that the excommunicate had committed.

[2] 11 November 1165. In regard to the personalities mentioned in the next sentence Cox writes: "Bishops Henry of Autun and Walter of Langres were both sons of Duke Hugh II of Burgundy, hence uncles of the reigning duke Hugh III. Gallia Christiana XII, 639 identifies the bishop of Nevers as Bernard de Saint-Saulge (1160–1176). See also Bouchard (1987: 401)."

50

The Archbishop of Sens's Letter to the Bishops On the
Same Matter [1658C/565.2086]

1165

Hugh, by the grace of God humble servant of the church of Sens, to his worthy brothers and friends Henry, by the same grace bishop of Autun, Walter bishop of Langres, Alan bishop of Auxerre, and Bernard bishop of Nevers, greetings and affection in the Lord.

We notify your discretion that the lord pope has written to us time and again from Clermont-Ferrand, Le Puy, and Montpellier, with warnings and commands, on the basis of his apostolic authority, about the undeserved damages and wicked oppressions which the count of Nevers and his mother are known to be inflicting upon the monastery of Vézelay and its men. At length he ordered us—as you may see from the gist of his letter which we send you on his behalf—to meet each of them, that is, the count and his mother, as soon as possible, to exhort them with all diligence to restore at once to the abbot of that monastery all that they had confiscated, to make satisfaction for their damage and attacks, and to cease from further raiding and undeserved persecution of it. But if they were to disdain to obey our command within twenty days, we were to pronounce sentence of excommunication upon them and interdict their land wholly from all divine service except for the baptism of infants and the confession of the dying; and we were to order this sentence to be observed inviolably by you on his authority, all appeals denied and all occasions of delay removed. We therefore began to see to the execution of our lord's command and, since nothing has come of our admonition, we have pronounced sentence of excommunication on both persons; but until now we have deliberately delayed letting you know. For we have persisted and worked as hard as we could in our desire to bring about peace between the abbot and the count, together with our worthy brother the bishop of Meaux, to whom the same order was, with that purpose, enjoined by the lord pope. But because our purpose was continually frustrated, eventually we met at Joigny and attempted for two days to bring about a settlement. However, since we did not find the slightest possibility of doing so, we confirmed the sentence long since announced by us on the lord pope's order, and we decree that it is to be held and firmly observed by you on the authority of the lord pope and by our order, commanding that from now on you treat them as excommunicate, and that you publicly announce them to be excommunicate from the next St. Martin's day through all your parish churches, without any delay, and that you prohibit any divine services within their lands, except for the baptism of infants and the confession of the dying. Especially are you to announce this to those priests who are the special chaplains of the count and the countess, his mother, and command them on peril of their orders to beware of transgressing the apostolic order and ours.

51

The Sepulchre of the Blessed Mary Magdalene Catches
Fire. Relics Are Found in a Statue of the Blessed Virgin

[1659C/566.2131]

1165

These were the archbishop's words. But the bishops did not strive so firmly
to observe the sentence laid down by him. Now while Abbot William was visiting the houses subject to him in the neighborhood of Beauvais, he entered
the district of Amiens and came to the monastery of Villeselve on the first
Saturday of Advent.[1] That night there came to him one of his servants,[2]
named Gerald, who told him of the woeful state of the church of Vézelay. For
in the meantime a certain presage both of future calamity and of solace had
occurred at that church. In the vault above the tomb of God's blessed lover
Mary Magdalene such a blaze accidentally broke out that even the supports
[tirannos] above it, which the French call beams [trabes], were burnt. But the
wooden image of Mary, blessed mother of God, which stood on the floor of
the vault, was not harmed by the fire at all, although it was a little blackened.
The silken phylactery which hung from the neck of the image of the infant Jesus
did not smell of smoke, nor did its color change at all, not even slightly.[3]

Hence it was as clear as crystal that the image itself would not have been affected by smoke in the slightest, except by divine dispensation for the purpose of revealing, when it was repaired, the inestimable treasure hidden within it. For when this image was sent to the restorer, he declared that it had, so
it seemed to him, a cunningly hidden little door between its shoulders. When
he heard this, Prior Gilo ordered the image to be carried into the sacristy,
and calling in with him Geoffrey, the subprior, Gervaise, the sacrist, Gerard,
the constable, Maurice, the succentor,[4] and Lambert, the restorer of the
statue, he took a knife and scratched off the paint himself; but they could not
discover any sign of a joint in the uncovered wood. Then he took a little iron
hammer and tried to discover by ear what none could discern with his eyes,
and hearing a sort of hollow sound, the bold man, armed with joyful hope,
piously broke open the little door with his own hands. He found in it hairs of
the chaste Virgin, the like of whom had not been seen before nor has been
seen since, and part of the tunic of the same Mary, mother of God, and a
bone of the blessed John the Baptist. He also found bones of the blessed
apostles Peter, Paul, and Andrew in one bundle, and one joint of the thumb

---

[1] 4 December 1165. The monastery of Villeselve, a dependent priory of Vézelay, was
in Noyon. A contemporary hand has crossed out the author's "Amiens" and written
"Noyon" above it.

[2] unus e pueris.

[3] Obviously the image was a Madonna with child; a silk phylactery must have been
hung from the neck of the child Jesus.

[4] The sacrist "had complete charge of the service of the altar, of the vestments, and of
all the internal decoration and repair of the church." The succentor was an assistant to the
precentor, who was chiefly concerned with liturgical and literary matters. Knowles ([1949]
1962: 428–30).

of the blessed James the Lord's brother, and two bundles of bones of the blessed apostle Bartholomew, and most of an arm of one of the Innocents,[1] relics of St. Clement, and a portion of the hair of the queen St. Radegund; a piece of the vestments of the three boys Shadrack, Meshak, and Abednego,[2] and a section from the purple robe in which our Lord Jesus Christ was clothed during his passion.[3] With each of these items they found individual notes which distinguished one from another; and while all of the notes were so ancient that they could hardly be read, three others were found which were illegible; and of whom they spoke God only knows. Those which could be read they had transcribed, and tied the old notes to the new in testimony. After they had carefully inspected all these things they returned them to the place where they had been before, and placed the statue with these saints' relics over the high altar. Then everyone put on copes and, with all the larger and smaller bells ringing, praised the Creator of all, who had deigned to place in their custody, and for the protection of that place, so many and such illustrious relics.

Then all the people came flocking, both pilgrims and locals, and there was wonderfully great joy and exultation in the church, in the whole town, and in the neighboring countryside, with people hurrying to the joyful celebration from the fields and surrounding villages. Gilo, barely managing to curb everyone's clamor, gestured with his hand for silence and in a few well-chosen words declared the cause of praise and joy, while all wept for happiness. When later they tried to return the image to the vault over the tomb of God's lover, such a throng of people wished to kiss it or just touch it that they were barely able to replace it in its original position intact with all the people around. The monks did not permit the statue to be touched, lest they be accused of avarice.[4] So the divine fire which broke forth was a portent of imminent tribulation, but the finding of the saints' relics indicated that there would be a good end to that tribulation. The monks of Vézelay wrote to their abbot, William, about this to comfort him on the pilgrimage he had undertaken.

---

[1] See Matthew 2:16.

[2] See Daniel 1:7, 2:49, 3:12. St. Radegund, wife of the Frankish king Clothaire, founded a monastery at Poitiers and died 587 AD: Cross (1974: 1155) and Gregory of Tours, *History of the Franks*, trans. L. Thorpe (Penguin Books, 1974), index s.v. "Radegund."

[3] See John 19:2.

[4] Cox explains the reference to "avarice" thus: "Presumably, because of the more or less obligatory offerings that would normally accompany an act of reverence before a sacred relic." On the popularity of relics and the competition between churches for them, see Sumption (1975) and Geary (1978) and Aspects [D] above.

52

In 1165 the Count of Nevers Initiates a New Persecution
of Vézelay   [1661A/568.2203]

1165

In the year of the Incarnate Word 1165, 26 [actually 25: Huygens (1976: 568.
2205n.)] November, the fifth day of the week before Advent, Count William
of Nevers and his mother Ida entered the city of Vézelay with a multitude of
armed men, as if to raze it to the ground. The count turned aside to the monastery's guest house, which lies next to the almonry at the entrance to the
cloister, while his mother, the instigator of all these evils, went down to the
house of Simon de Souvigny. All the inhabitants of the town were terrified.
When the news reached Prior Gilo and all the brothers who were sitting in
chapter at that hour, Gilo took all the keys of the monastery and ordered that
no one was to leave the cloister. The count was quiet all that day. But the
next day, when he saw that none of the brothers would come forth, he asked
mockingly whether the monks were keeping Good Friday by mistake, or
whether they were scorning his presence with their accustomed insolence.
This he said by way of mockery; but it was true that the brothers were celebrating the Good Friday of the imminent recovery of their liberty. For, just as
on the Good Friday of our Lord's Passion the dignity of the human condition
was restored, so through this Good Friday of the brothers' communal exile
tyrannical usurpations were eliminated and the integrity of their [the brothers'] ancient liberty was restored.

The count notified the brothers that he wanted to enter their chapter
house to speak with them. They replied that they could not communicate
with an excommunicate, but, if he wanted to treat of peace, they would speak
to him through their prior. So, taking a few of the brothers with him, Gilo
went and faced the count, who, looking at him with a ferocious gaze, rebuked
him for many things and ended by insisting that they should receive into the
monastery those detestable traitors, Peter and Thibault, and their accomplices. Gilo replied that it was neither possible nor fitting to receive men who
had been excommunicated by the lord pope. But the count said: "These men
are not excommunicate; but because, like prudent people, they did not wish
to be a part of your shamelessness, you have expelled them from among you
although they are innocent." Gilo replied: "We came in peace and to treat of
peace, but you hurl undeserved insults at us; therefore know this for certain,
that we shall not appear before you again to receive such a reward." Having
said this, Gilo returned to the cloister. But the count sent his herald to order
all the burghers [burgenses], with threats, to assemble before him. Some of
them, wise after having experienced his wickedness so many times before,
retired secretly into the monastery via back streets [per abdita], for he had
posted guards to watch the gates, lest any of the burghers enter the monastery.[1]

---

[1] Although in the past the count and the burghers had co-operated to oppose the
abbot, it seems as though by this time some of the burghers had aligned themselves with

53
The Prior Exhorts the Brothers to Be of Bold Spirit
[1662A/569.2243]

1165

Now those who could hope for something, either because they had done him obsequious service or had furtively commended themselves to him, went to the tyrant. At once he ordered them to renounce their oath of fidelity to the abbot and church. But they replied that they would have to discuss this proposal. "Hold your discussion as soon as possible then," he said. He had the guest house doors and the monastery gates locked and sent his chancellor [*cancellarium*] Stephen, Stephen of Pierre-Perthuis, and Fournier de Druyes [–les-Belles-Fontaines, *de Droia*] to order Prior Gilo to give them the monastery keys. But Gilo said: "Is the count our abbot, or the caretaker [*clavicularius*] of this monastery?" "Such is the count's order," they replied. And he: "I shall speak with my brothers about this." Entering the chapter house, where all the brothers were seated again, he addressed them thus: "Lo, brothers, lo, here is the day long ago foreseen by our worthy abbot and by ourselves, and often predicted by you, in which you must not merely discuss but rather make a decision about your liberty and that of your church, and about the danger to all of you in common and to your men. This day is the turning point between servitude and liberty, rest and labor, wickedness and honesty, honor and infamy; whichever of these you choose will constitute an inviolable charter. Till now you have borne with the plundering of your goods, till now you have suffered with patient ear the threats and curses of the impious, as if they were the raging of the winds.[1] In the theater of fortune allotted you, the eyes of all are fixed upon you. Now the very body of your business is in the arena, and there will be no delay, whether you conquer or are conquered. For this tyrant will not be satisfied to tear off your clothes, pull out your hair, flay your skin; he will even try to knock out your teeth. He asks for your keys, that he may boast that he has shut up your liberty in shackles of servitude." At this speech all rose and with one voice demanded, on behalf of the pope and their abbot, that the monastery keys should not be given to the count. And they insisted that they should undergo exile all together for their liberty, leaving behind a few caretakers. To this Gilo replied: "It seems to me unwise to leave our house, as long as its revenues hold out."

54
Servants of the Count Enter the Monastery By Force and Plunder It
[1662D/570.2279]

1165

While these matters were being discussed, Fournier de Druyes left, and taking with him the count's servants, went outside to the lower door of the abbot's

---

the church and were resisting the count's interference in the town.

[1] See Ovid *Metamorphosis* 5.7.

house. Throwing out the cripple who guarded the gate, he took the keys, which by chance hung in the postern of the great door, and occupied both floors of the house, leaving there impious men who took possession of it in the count's name, as though the count had such lordship over the monastery that he could eject the abbot's men and introduce his own at will. Meanwhile the count burst into the cloister by force, with Ignace, viscount of Joigny, who cried out: "Hasten, insolent monks, to make your submission to my lord the count." But when the count hurried to enter the brothers' chapter house, certain people confronted him and compelled him to fall back. The brothers at once left the chapter house and entered the church—in order to await the outcome of the business, not in order to celebrate the divine office there, for the church refrained from this while the count was present—and while they were sitting there, they looked round and saw above their heads the tyrant's followers, who had already invaded the tower of St. Michael through a door they had broken. Preoccupied by the sudden arrival of their enemies, the brothers were unable to resist this unexpected wickedness, and to the more prudent of them it seemed better to give in than to resist, lest by chance they provoke the tyrant's fury and he raze to the ground both monastery and town. Thus the brothers entered the refectory, mixing their bread with tears and their drink with weeping,[1] but they barely tasted their food before going out very quickly to reply to the burghers about the count's demand for a renunciation of their oath. They said to the burghers: "If you consider reasonably, you will prefer honest poverty to the infidelity of riches. For it is better to live honestly with loyalty than luxuriously in the shame of faithlessness. You yourselves will see which is the more sensible. It is, you see, for your sake that we labor, for your cause that we persist in our defense. For what is our habit [staminium], or this little black cowl [nigellum caputium] that you see worth? It is your wealth which they are seeking [ambiuntur], it is at your own head that they are aiming. If, in the manner of a serpent,[2] we expose you—our very members—to the blow, behold, like the head when it is severed from the body, we should [indeed] enjoy some kind of repose! But let such thoughts be far from us. Let it be far from our thoughts to purchase an ignominious peace at the cost of your capitulation! For we do not glory in the tribulations which you suffer for us, but rather we glory in our tribulations for you. Now is the time when you can prove—when you must prove—what loyalty, what alliance, what love has till now united us; and now let not anyone who is our man [qui noster est] allow himself for any reason to be torn from us."

Encouraged by such words, those who had remained faithful stayed with the brothers within the monastery. Hearing this, the count dispersed armed followers among the houses of all the burghers, ordering that they must sustain themselves wholly from the stores of the besieged. And he handed over to those excommunicated traitorous pseudo-monks, Peter and his accompli-

---

[1] Psalm 101:10.

[2] *more serpentino*: an obscure analogy; presumably a lizard is meant, not a snake, with the idea of the regeneration of that part of its body which has been cut off. Or it could just be a reference to low, snake-in-the-grass sort of behavior; see the reference below in §56 to the count's "serpent-like mother."

ces, the convent and rents of Asquins. All the other rents of the monastery he put in the hands of Hugh Letard, provost of Châtel-Censoir, who was a serf of the church from the family of Simon, son of Odo, provost of Vézelay, that same Simon who had slain his lord abbot Artaud. Hugh in turn delegated everything to Maurice of Saint-André-en-Morvan, of the same condition and family. Gilo was informed of this and so when evening fell he sent servants to collect their usual loaves [*debitum furnagium*, Cox, "bread-due"]. They were intercepted by Maurice's wife and the count's servants, who beat them up, took away their bread, and sent them back. Moreover the count even ordered those responsible, who were being held in the provost's house, to be freed.[1] Then, as is the monastic custom, the board was beaten and Gilo entered the chapter house with his brothers and said to them: "Now we are compelled by necessity to do that which reason made us put off. Our houses and those of our men are occupied by the enemy; the rents of which we have need are carried off; and, what is worse than death, low fellows [*garciferi*] together with their harlots tread with their dirty feet the most holy tomb of the lover of God. Now there is nothing to keep us, for both the means to live and honor are denied us. Let sorrow give way gracefully to reason, and let indiscreet desperation be far from us. For what has happened is neither novel nor unexpected. It is almost two years since this thought crossed my mind and I had before my eyes that tyrant's violence and the possibility of future exile, both of which I preached to you all. Moreover, you yourselves often exclaimed the same thing to me and prayed that what we had planned beforehand should be put into effect. And behold! The night of tribulation and the night of that time now urge us, and it is time to turn from words to deeds." At this there was great wailing and weeping[2] among the brothers and servants and the burghers who had fled within the monastery.

55
The Monks, Being Cruelly Harassed, Flee [1664B/572. 2353]
1165

Thereupon Prior Gilo appointed those who were to remain, those who were to go, and those servants who would accompany those who left. Then after they had drunk they appointed sentries to watch over them through the night and took down all the images, crosses, and reliquaries containing the relics of saints.[3] During this dismantling they carefully inspected the icon on the great cross which hung over the altar in the middle of the church and found in it milk of the inviolate virgin and mother of God, Mary. Prior Gilo, amidst the tumult of people coming and going, left secretly during the night and went down on foot to the village of Saint-Père-sous-Vézelay, where he immediately mounted a horse and went to the estate called Pontaubert. After he had

---

[1] The writer seems to have telescoped events here. The servants responsible for beating up the monks must have been arrested and imprisoned in the provost's house, before being freed on the count's orders.

[2] See 1 Maccabees 1:26 and Judith 7:18.

[3] The night of 27–28 November 1165.

rested for a little, Geoffrey the sub-prior and Geoffrey the guest-master came to him from Givry. Sending the latter back, the prior and subprior went to Joigny, making a long detour through Burgundy to avoid the count's lands. In the morning the count, seeing that the brothers were about to depart and were packing their bags, retired to the house of Simon de Souvigny. When everything was ready, the brothers entered the chapter house and, receiving the blessing, each said good-bye to the others with tears. Then they entered the great church, where nearly all the people, with their wives and children were gathered, and prostrated themselves before the tomb of their blessed patroness and committed their cause to her protection. There was a huge noise of weeping and wailing and tearing of hair, so that the clamor of those wailing resounded to the very heavens. It was an unbearable horror to see what could hardly be seen for the sorrow, the confused clamor and the uncontrolled weeping of those who beat the pavement with their heads and breasts. The elements themselves seemed to have some sort of compassion amid such a great calamity, for the sky darkened, the sun's splendor clouded over, the flowing streams froze up, the earth was covered with a continuous rain of snow, and all nature showed a sad face. At length, followed by the weeping and wailing of the whole populace, the brothers, numbering about sixty, went out from the church.

Now the count had already left the town, leaving behind his mother. The traitor, William Pidet, then mounted his horse and galloped after the brothers, saying that the countess ordered them to halt and wait for her. But they pretended not to see him whom they hated, and passing through Asquins, came to the cross of Montjoie,[1] accompanied by the people. There they stopped for a little and, looking back at the church of Mary Magdalene, God's lover, venerated through the whole world, fell on their faces singing, as well as they could: "O solace of sinners!"[2] What weeping, what sorrow there was on the part both of the refugees and the men and women following them, who rolled their heads in the snow there in their agony, no one may tell, since this iron pen of mine is almost completely awash with tears. This mourning—I speak truly—exceeded the mourning at a funeral, for the succession of an heir relieves the sadness of a funeral; but the abolition of succession means the desolation of the heir, a desolation unheard of in our land or our time! A Catholic prince expels innocent monks from their monastery,

---

[1] There were two such crosses (Cox: "markers, crosses or piles of stones") of Montjoie ("Mounts of Joy"). The one of which the chronicler speaks here must have been on a high place, possibly on the hill of Vaudonjon, between Asquins and Brosses ("probably not far from the one that stands today on the road from the valley of the Cure between Le Vaudonjon and the village of Montillot"—Cox). The second was above Fontette. The two crosses of Montjoie served not only to mark out the territory of Vézelay, but above all to incite pilgrims to prayer. The crosses of Montjoie were erected on high places from where the pilgrims would make out for the first time the church, a moment which was particularly favorable for meditation and supplication. All the great places of pilgrimage had their Montjoies: Rome, Jerusalem, Compostela. See *Song of Roland* laisse 92, 88 and n. in R. Harrison, trans., *The Song of Roland* (Mentor, 1970); also Berlow (1987: 159n.88).

[2] First words of a response in the office of Mary Magdalene sung at Vézelay during the vigil of the great festival on 22 July and of the Translation on 19 March.

and his relations cruelly lay waste a place venerated by almost all Christians throughout the world. If it is asked why, liberty is the culprit; if the reason is sought, [the count's] prejudice is brought forward.[1]

56
The Count's Mother with False Tears Feigns Compassion for the Monks and Tries to Persuade Them to Return
[1665B/573. 2404]

1165

While tears and sighs were being poured out on all sides by both the brothers and all the people alike, the tyrant's serpent-like mother, Ida, who had followed the walkers, came near and dismounted, asking with pretended humility to be heard by the brothers. And they, remembering the words of the Apostle: "Do not be vanquished by evil, but overcome evil with good,"[2] rose from the ground and waited. Then, pretending to be in tears, she began to condemn their departure as unreasonable and without cause, for her son loved them and the church of Vézelay most affectionately and was only at enmity with the abbot, by whom he had been unjustly disinherited, although her son demanded nothing from the abbot except what was rightfully his. She added that they ought to remember that saying in the Gospel: "Render unto Caesar the things which are Caesar's, and to God the things which are God's."[3] So she asked them to return, whereupon she would beseech her son to have mercy on them and return the usurped rents of their house, or, if she could not persuade her son to do this, she herself would supply them with their daily sustenance until their abbot should reach an agreement with her son. To these words the brothers replied that it was neither the time nor the place to discuss her son's rights, for it was patently obvious that he had appropriated for himself both what was right and what was wrong; that it seemed foolish to return with such an uncertain hope; that they believed it intolerable

---

[1] *Si causa queritur, libertas criminatur. Si ratio ventilatur, preiudicium contorquetur.*

[2] Romans 12:21. Cox: In 1148/49, after the second crusade, the sons of Count William III of Nevers "entrusted the regency (of the county—William II having retired to the Carthusian order, where he died in 1149 AD) to Ida of Carinthia, wife of Count William III and daughter of Engilbert, margrave of Istria and duke of Carinthia. Her uncle, Frederick of Carinthia, archbishop of Cologne, is thought to have been responsible for the marriage of her sister Matilda to Count Theobald IV of Blois and Champagne, and since Theobald and the count of Nevers were good friends, it may have been Theobald who proposed his sister-in-law as bride for William III. Countess Ida was thus well connectecd in the world of the high and mighty, and, as subsequent events would reveal, she was a woman of strong views and vigorous action. She evidently enjoyed this opportunity to take command of her husband's dominions, for she promptly had a magnificent seal made showing her standing erect and holding a kind of scepter in one hand, with an inscription around the edges giving her name and title. Ida had been especially commended to the protection of abbot Suger, but it was soon a case of others in need of protection from her. She wrote Suger at once asking him to assist one of her men in recovering a debt owed to him at Étampes, and she resumed her father-in-law's policy of harassing travellers bound for Vézelay."

[3] Matthew 22:21.

to depend upon sustenance supplied by another without consulting their
abbot; and that they thought it shameful that they, prebendaries of Mary Magdalene the handmaid of Jesus Christ, should become dependants of her who
had desolated the tomb of their most blessed patroness. Saying this they
turned their backs on the woman and came that night to Brosses.[1]

The next day, when they were hurrying on to Auxerre, they were met by
Arduin, worthy abbot of Saint-Germain [of Auxerre], who besought them to
turn aside to Saint-Germain. When they agreed to this, he returned home to
arrange for hospitality. The brothers entered the city by twos, with their
heads covered, expressing their calamity in the singing of Psalms. This
brought about a great gathering of people from all over the city, with men
and children and women weeping and exclaiming: "Alas! Who has ever seen
such a thing? Who would have believed that such a thing could happen? What
fury,[2] what madness has brought this to pass? O glorious and blessed mistress Mary Magdalene, why do you endure such acts? What support may we
sinners hope for from you, when you allow your servants to suffer such
injury? May all those by whose counsel these things were brought about
perish and be confounded!" Then the tyrant himself arrived on horseback,
and looking at each of them, mocked them saying: "This is how such people
ought to earn their bread!" But the brothers, caring nothing for these things,
passed on with their heads bowed. And being honorably received into the
monastery of Saint-Germain, they rested there that night.

The next morning[3] they went on to Joigny, to the house of Hugh, once
provost, and there they were honorably entertained by Aimeri of Le Puy and
his brother Stephen. From there the brothers hurried on to the town of Sens,
sending their buyers on ahead. And Simon *Infans* having come out for a walk
met them by chance, and learning the cause of the hardship of so many and
such men, was greatly saddened. Coming down towards them he besought
them humbly to come to his house to share his meal. When they had reluctantly accepted, he received them and entertained them honorably. The next
morning he led them to a hired boat—for till now they had proceeded on
foot—and himself brought down a lot of hay for them. They worked hard
rowing all that day and when night fell they just made a little town [*villulam*]
called Misy-sur-Yonne. Since they could not find suitable hospitality there for

---

[1] Night of 28–29 November 1165. Ida's action demonstrates (a) the forceful approach
powerful women could and did take in the Middle Ages and (b) the fact that the monastic
walk-out was serious enough to disturb the count, or at least his mother. Brosses is about
one quarter of the distance from Vézelay to Auxerre; the route passes Asquins and
continues on up the Cure and then away from the river through Vaudonjon, Montillot,
and Fontenille. See map 122–23 in Speaight (1990).

[2] *Quis furor?* Lucan *Pharsalia* 1.8. Ardouin (1148–1174): a relative of his predecessor at
Saint-Germain-d'Auxerre, Gervais de Semur, a nephew of Saint Hugh of Cluny; Bouchard
(1987: 428), *Gallia Christiana* 12.381 (Cox). Of the Benedictine abbey of Saint-Germain
d'Auxerre nothing remains (Michelin, *Burgundy/Morvan*, 45 and Speaight [1990: 81ff.]). It
dates back to a sixth-century AD foundation by Queen Clothild on the site of an oratory
where St. Germanus, the fifth-century bishop of Auxerre was buried. The brothers, as the
text indicates, *had* hurried, covering three times the distance they had on the previous day.

[3] 30 November 1165.

so many persons of such a kind—for they were about eighty souls—[1]they went into the barn of some farmer, crammed with ox dung. Although they had fasted that day, nothing could be found round about except a little common bread and two bunches of garlic, which, however, the brothers ate ungarnished with their own bread and water. It is wonderful to relate how, although they had been afflicted with such hardship, they bore it in high spirits, and embracing exile for liberty's sake, as though it was their fatherland, they put up with the grime of wayfaring by joyful singing.

At first light[2] they returned to their boat, disembarking at Cannes-Écluse. There for the first time they joined Prior Gilo and his companion Geoffrey. From there they came by foot to Moret on 2 December, where they remained for the next two days. They sent on Renaud, prior of Labroye, to Hugh the worthy abbot of [Saint-Germain-des-Prés] Paris, to announce to him their arrival and the reason for their coming to the king. On hearing of it, he was much saddened and with tears in his eyes hurried to King Louis, declaring to him how the count of Nevers, by criminal sacrilege, had invaded that most famous monastery of Vézelay, and with what efforts almost all the brothers of that house had fled to the feet of the royal majesty. The king, moved simultaneously by anger and sorrow, immediately ordered the count to abandon what he had unjustly invaded and to return to the brothers within a week the church, towers, houses, the town, and all their rents and possessions, in that state in which they had been a week before the brothers' departure, to restore what he had destroyed, and to make satisfaction to him [the king] for such heavy injury inflicted on the whole realm. To this the count replied to the royal messengers: "I have dealt with the monastery of Vézelay as my own property [*sicut de meo*], and for this reason [*ex hoc facto*] I do not owe anything to the king." "On the contrary," they replied, "you are accountable for such an outrage committed within the king's fief [*in feodo regis*]." But he became angry and forbad them with threats to appear in his presence again. To this they replied: "We are the king's servants [*servi*], and it is our duty to take your reply to the lord king." At once the count sent to the king John of Orleans, to excuse him for the acts of tyranny which he had perpetrated, saying that he had cared for the public good [*rebus publicis*] on his land, and that the abbot and monks of Vézelay had allied with his enemy the duke of Burgundy and, unless they had been prevented, would have handed over to him the fortifications of their monastery.

---

[1] In §55 there are said to be about sixty of them. The additional twenty could be servants.

[2] 2 December 1165.

57

The Monks at Length Reach Paris and, Pouring Forth Tears, Reveal to the King the Cause of Their Sorrow. They Are Gently Received by the King [1667B/576. 2496]

1165

Meanwhile the brothers rose just as day was breaking on the second Sunday of Advent[1] and, boarding their boat, came to a property of the monastery of Saint-Germain [one time] bishop of Paris. Entering the house of a certain man, they were well entertained by an official named Renaud, who had been sent by the abbot of that monastery and who had just arrived. Then leaving there and betaking themselves to their water-borne vehicle, they came to Paris. The whole city was in a stir, with everyone from the least to the greatest, coming together and weeping. Entering the mother church,[2] the exiles

---

[1] 5 December 1165. The brothers make some twenty-five kilometers per day on foot, as the crow flies; the boat section of their trip (Sens to Cannes-Écluse via Misy-sur-Yonne), some thirty kilometers as the crow flies, together with the further fourteen kilometers to Montet on foot, occupied two days.

[2] *matricem ecclesiam*; the church of the monastery of St. Germain-des-Prés is probably meant. Cox thinks that the Paris Cathedral of Nôtre Dame is intended. However, it would be natural for the Vézelay monks to go to the monastery church; and the phrase *matricem ecclesiam* was probably suggested by the fact that the monks' previous halt had been at an outlying property of the monastery of St. Germain. The "mother church" of St. Germain-des-Prés is, of course, but a short walk from the Cathedral of Nôtre Dame and the king's palace on the Ile-de-Cité. Cox provides the following additional glosses on events mentioned in this and previous paragraphs of the *Major Chronicle*: "I do not find corroborating evidence for the allegation of hostilities between the count and the duke of Burgundy, but after a long struggle William IV had in 1164 finally accepted an arbitrated settlement with the bishop of Auxerre who, like the abbot of Vézelay, had also appealed to the king against him and had been prepared to place his bishopric under royal protection as a counter-move against the count. This may help explain Count William's uncompromising frame of mind at this point in his dealings with Vézelay. The bishop of Paris at this time was the famous Maurice de Sully (1160–1196), the builder of the present cathedral of Nôtre Dame. The reference in our text is to Saint Germain, bishop of Paris in the sixth century and founder of the abbey that in the eighth century became Saint-Germain-des-Prés." On Maurice see J. W. Baldwin, *Masters, Princes and Merchants: The Social Views of Peter the Chanter and His Circle* 2 vols. (Princeton, 1970), index s.v.v "Maurice of Sully." From *Major Chronicle* 1§7 above it seems the dukes of Burgundy were rather allies of the count against the liberties of Vézelay than the other way round. Cox points out that the conflict with the bishop of Autun "had incurred the enmity of the whole ducal House of Burgundy, whose head, Duke Odo II, was married to Marie de Champagne, daughter of Count Theobald IV. With the death of their father in 1152 Marie's brothers had become counts in their own right—Henry (I) of Troyes and Champagne, Theobald (V) of Blois and Chartres and Steven of Sancerre—and they were all nephews of Ida of Carinthia, countess of Nevers, an inveterate enemy of the abbot of Vézelay. All were trusted counsellors of the king as well, and two of them, Henry and Theobald, would later become his sons-in-law through their marriages to Marie and Alice, Louis's two daughters by Eleanor of Aquitaine (see W. L. Warren *Henry II* [Berkeley, 1973]: 45, 90 n, 109). In March Louis and the Queen had been divorced, and in May Eleanor had married Henry Plantagenet, count of Anjou, duke of Normandy, and now duke of Aquitaine as well. This news had created consternation at the French court, and Louis was busy assembling all of his vassals for an attack upon Plantagenet territories. Under the circumstances he needed all the baronial

prayed and rested there for a little, while all the populace still stood around and about them. When King Louis heard of the arrival of the Vézelay monks, he interrupted the consecration of the monastery of Saint-Denis, in which he was involved, and returned. So the brothers came to the royal palace. When the king went to meet them and stood on the palace steps, they all threw themselves at his feet weeping freely; for his part the king, also weeping and moved by piety, knelt, and rose only when they did. Then Gilo, prior of the band, spoke: "The cause of our arrival is known to you, my lord king, but sorrow and the throng of people around prevent us from explaining to you at present the full nature of our grievance. So if you will appoint a time and place, a few of us will come to you and make known in accurate detail what evil the count has done us; in the meantime we shall return to our lodgings, imploring as one your grace and mercy." And they all bowed, their heads touching the ground. The king replied: "Before you came, as soon as the news of this infamy had come to my ears, I sent my messengers to the count. What his reply is, or what he will do, I do not yet know. But this you may know for certain, that even if the count had as much land again as the king of England, besides his own, I should certainly not allow such an injury to be unavenged. For I am a pilgrim of my blessed lady Mary Magdalene,[1] and I shall never, as far as in me lies, fail her servants. So I ask that you will deign to stay in my house and I shall provide all that is necessary for your needs." The brothers expressed their humble thanks, but replied that all they wanted was his help in their dire necessity. Then seeing at the king's side their former host Simon *Infans* they thanked him in the king's sight for the service which he had rendered them; upon which the king showed Simon great favor. The Vézelay monks then left with the[ir?] people following, and all the brothers of the monastery of Saint-Germain-des-Prés came in procession as far as the old palace to meet them and received them with much weeping and sighing. And after going in with them by twos, as the custom is, and offering solemn prayer, they came to the abbot's house, where the tables were laid for them.

---

support he could get and he was in no position to risk antagonising so important a magnate as the count of Nevers even if he thought the abbot of Vézelay in the right, which is by no means certain." See, however, §72 below. The count, at the end of §56 above, is probably alleging a plausible pretext for his actions. The allegation that Vézelay lay within the king's *feodum* is interesting: see §62 at 299n.2 below, §68 at 303nn.3 & 4 and §69 at 304n.2. It is certainly ironic that the count of Nevers is forced in all these events to espouse the "revolt mentality" of the legendary Girart de Vienne/Roussillon—the very Gerard who founded the monastery of Vézelay with its "inborn liberty" in the first place—against the encroachment of royal power outside the traditional royal domain: "for the first time in almost 200 years the king of France extended his influence over the great provincial land-holdings, by interfering actively in the affairs of Flanders, Champagne-Brie and Brittany, and engaging in almost continuous strife with the British over Aquitaine . . ." (Calin [1962]: 129). Girard de Roussillon—himself a rebel against the crown—surfaced in the twelfth century, argues Calin, to supply some legitimation for baronial resistance to the crown, not (we may add) to support the liberties of his beleaguered monastery on the river Cure!

[1] An indication of how vital it was to have a powerful supernatural patron; it is the king's devotion to Mary Magdalene that persuades him to assist the monks.

58

The Abbot Sets out for Paris to See his Brethren [1668B/577. 2541]

1165

Now when Abbot William of Vézelay, who was at Villeselve, heard of the misfortunes of his house and of the arrival of his brothers, he was grieved, and all who were with him were troubled in spirit,[1] especially as they were so far away. So, rising on the same night in which the brothers left Moret, they rode all day, assailed by hunger and cold and snow, along circuitous and unfamiliar roads, before coming at length to Mello[2] in the second watch of the night, tired and sad. The next day they arrived in Paris and found their brothers still sitting at table; when they wished to rise the abbot ordered them to remain seated. The abbot, putting on a brave front, restrained his tears and manfully kept his sorrow within himself; but his companions were seized with such acuteness of grief, that they could hardly discern one person from another and could not bring themselves to reply to the greetings of their exiled brothers. In a wonderful way the exiled brothers, covered with the grime of travelling and hungry, comforted their brothers who had not participated to such an extent in their great trials, and exhorted them to trust in God's mercy and in the aid which the king had promised them.

59

He Pleads his Case Before the King   [1668C/577. 2558]

1165

When morning came,[3] they besought the Lord's aid, and Abbot William and Abbot Hugh [of Saint-Germain-de-Prés] went to the king's palace with Gilo and Geoffrey, Franco and Robert, Peter and Vincent, Hugh and Thibault [V, count of Blois] the king's kinsman, taking with them a few men as witness to what had been done. The king took his seat with his brothers, Henry archbishop of Rheims, Count Robert [of Dreux], and Peter de Courtenay and with other important courtiers.[4] Then Gilo rose and described in order the nature of the tyrant's invasion and of the expulsion of his brothers. Opposing him, John of Orleans replied that the abbot had usurped the count's rights, which he exercised in the town of Vézelay from the royal fisc,[5] and that the abbot had denied justice to the count for certain injuries which he had committed. "If," said the king, "he holds in fief from me[6] this right which he claims for himself, he should first have complained to me about the injury to my fief before he expelled the monks from their monastery." And John said:

---

[1] 1 Maccabees 4:27.

[2] The castle of the abbot's family.

[3] 7 December 1165.

[4] Robert of Dreux was the fifth son of Louis the Fat and the brother of Louis VII. Peter of Courtenay, also a descendant of Louis the Fat and a brother of Louis VII, became count of Nevers in 1184 by his marriage to Agnes of Nevers.

[5] *regio ex fisco.*

[6] *de feodo meo habet.*

"My lord count did not expel the monks, but they themselves left voluntarily, in contempt of my lord." Robert, surnamed the Fat, one of the Vézelay brothers, replied: "Does not he deprive my mouth effectively, who takes the food from my hand?" "That's true," replied the king. "So," continued Robert, "after the count invaded our monastery and sent into it his servants and delivered into their hands all our confiscated revenues, what was there to be gained by our staying there any longer?" "Nothing," replied the whole court. And the king said: "I have sent my messengers to the count, and would that he may do what is right! But if not, my power [*posse meum*] will not fail the church." The abbot and those who were with him thanked the king and went back to their lodgings. The abbot and his brothers were at Saint-Germain for three days, and then they returned to Moret, where they stayed for a month. And Hugh, archbishop of Sens, wrote to Abbot William of the monastery of Vézelay as follows:

60
[Hugh, Archbishop of Sens] Instructs the Abbot to Meet him at Sens to Treat of Peace with the Countess [1669B/578. 2588]

1165

Hugh, by the grace of God archbishop of Sens, to his very dear William, venerable abbot of Vézelay, greetings and love.

In furtherance of the business of the church of Vézelay and of yourself, we have sent to the countess of Nevers; and she being much desirous of peace, has given us security of one hundred pounds in pledges of gold and silver; and, if the complaints amount to more than this, she will provide me with a guarantee by good sureties and oath-takers to meet the excess. Therefore we order and advise you to come to Sens next Thursday,[1] and according to what you are able to prove in law, you will have restitution. But if you do not come on that day, the countess will consider herself insulted; and if she wishes to carry her complaint to the highest authority, we shall not be able to deny that we witnessed what she offers.

Farewell.

61

[The Abbot] Sets out for Sens Where he Disputes his Rights and the Losses Borne by Vézelay [1669C/578. 2601]

1165

To these words the abbot replied that the prescribed day was unsuitable and

---

[1] Thursday 16 December 1165. The royal "hearing" described in §59 had apparently been inconclusive; in §60 the archbishop of Sens, the appropriate archdiocesan for Vézelay, is still attempting a resolution. It is also clear that Abbot William of Vézelay still hopes the pope will emerge as the key arbiter in the matter (Huygens [1976:579. 2623]). Countess Ida has apparently had substantial "second thoughts"—cf. §56 292n.1 above.

he certainly could not meet then because he was so far from his monastery and because of the enmity of the countess and her son. However, if the countess herself would give safe-conduct to those of his men who would offer proof in law of the damages which he had sustained, he would gladly meet her on an appointed day which would suit them both. This was arranged and they both met together. But when the abbot demanded compensation for the damages which he had sustained and wished to prove his case lawfully, the countess denied the major part, blaming some of it on her son and saying that she ought not be held responsible for her son's crimes. The abbot replied to her that the malefactors were the countess's own men and the men of the provost of her lands, and therefore he demanded justly from her that which he had proved in law was taken by her men, to the value of 200 marks. Those who were of the countess's party were astonished, the archbishop and his clerks even more, and they asked the abbot to put a limit to the damages which he had proved, lest he exasperate the countess by such a heavy demand. To this the abbot replied: "I have already suffered her extreme exasperation undeservedly. Now how could she be even more exasperated? However, to recover her good will—not that it is really possible to change what is so firmly fixed—I shall renounce freely half of what I am able to prove, saving on the other points the execution of the pope's order [*mandati*]." "What order?" they asked. The abbot replied: "The order that she should satisfy me for the injuries which I have received, and give sureties for keeping the peace." This took place on the Saturday before Christmas day,[1] the day of the promotion to deacon of William bishop-elect of Chartres,[2] the brother of Count Henry [of Champagne], who had come there out of friendship to his brother. This William, extremely wearied with fasting, left in great indignation at the abbot; and the discussion was delayed until the following day. But although both sides made attempts to reach an agreement, negotiations were broken off with nothing achieved, for the countess did not wish either to compensate the abbot for the losses he had suffered or to give assurances for the maintenance of the peace, saying that she could not do what was asked of her without her son's consent. Therefore, the action was postponed until the third day of the feast of Circumcision.[3]

62
The Counts Thibault and Henry Offer Themselves as Mediators with the Count of Nevers [1670B/579. 2636]

1166

Now the king's messengers, who had returned from the count, delivered the news that they had got nowhere with him concerning the royal order [*mandato*], but that he had abundantly repaid them with threats and insults. The king

---

[1] 18 December 1165.

[2] William, bishop-elect of Chartres, is shown in 4 §38 to be a partisan of the count.

[3] 3 January 1166.

summoned his secretaries [*librariis*] immediately and ordered his whole army to be called up from everywhere, to meet him in arms on the twentieth day after Christmas. Count Thibault [of Blois] and Count Henry, after obtaining the king's permission with difficulty, met Count William, admonished him for the wickedness he had perpetrated and, having received from him a promise that he would obey the king's order, conducted him to Sens, where the king had come in early January to attend to other business. The abbot of Vézelay was also by chance present, to finalize his case with the countess before the bishops of Sens and Meaux. But as the countess refused either to return what was confiscated or to offer sureties for the keeping of the peace, this labor was rendered useless.

The next night Count Thibault sent a request to the abbot not to leave the next day before he spoke to him about the abbot's own business. When on the following day the abbot went to the royal court, Count Henry and Count Thibault met him and tried to persuade him to come to an agreement. The abbot replied to them: "I am in the hands of the pope and king, and without their permission I can do absolutely nothing." And so, going in to the king, they asked him about what the abbot had said. When the abbot was summoned before the king, he was interrogated by certain persons, not so much concerning his own peace as the tyrant's. But the abbot knew their cunning, and that they were trying in all possible ways to avert the king's favor from him, and so he deliberately placed the whole of the responsibility for making a final decision on the king, removing from himself both the praise [*gratiam*] and blame [*vituperium*] for the whole business.[1] So the king enquired of the count's proctors—for he did not speak with the count, nor did he want to see his face, as long as the quarrel was being heard—the king, I say, asked whether the count would make an end of this business according to what the king should decide. When this was refused, the king was very angry and said: "How is this? The abbot, who has suffered the injury and who is under no obligation to me at all, places himself totally at my disposal, but the count, who caused the injury and who is bound to me both by homage [*proprio homi- nio*] and because of the cause of this quarrel, refuses to obey my advice and that of my court. From now on let him take care that the abbot is not deceived in other matters[2] for I shall never be found lacking in his support."

63
The Count of Nevers Appears Before the King and
Promises to Make Good the Losses he had Inflicted

[1671A/580. 2673]

1166

Finally, after many verbal conflicts, the count was called into the king's

---

[1] Abbot Pons had not wanted to acknowledge the king's authority, because he thought it would be a limitation on the church's liberty, but by now his successor had no choice.

[2] *Iam de cetero caveat sibi abbas ne decipiatur.*

presence and promised with his hands between the king's,[1] that he would return to the abbot and his monks the church, its rents, its buildings and all the monastery's possessions in that condition in which they had been a week before the brothers' departure, without this action prejudicing either those quarrels which they already had with each other or the sentence of excommunication and interdict under which he was held. He also promised to restore all the church's belongings which were shown to have been in any way diminished or lost since three days before the brothers' departure, and to keep the peace from now on with the church and its possessions and the abbot and monks and their men, with this new condition, that if by chance any controversy arose between the count and the abbot or church, for a fortnight after the declaration of hostilities the burghers of Vézelay would have a truce, in which they would be able to move themselves and their goods to a safe place, while the church and all her possessions remained in peace. Concerning the restitution of the recent confiscations, to be judged according to the proof offered by the church's men, the count gave as his sureties Anselm de Trainel and his brother Garnier, Count [Renaud de Joigny], and Ignace, viscount of Joigny. Each of these four, responsible for a fourth part, swore in the hand of Count Thibault, that if the count refused after forty days to make good the legally established and proved losses, then within a fortnight of being summoned by the abbot they would deliver him up as a hostage[2] at Sens, until such time as they or the count made satisfaction to the abbot and the church.

64

The King Personally Restores the Abbot and Monks of Vézelay

[1671C/581. 2697]

1166

When these agreements had been reached the king, at the abbot's request, hastened to spend the feast of Epiphany[3] at Vézelay, and he led back the abbot to his place with great joy. Then the sons of Belial were thrown out of the monastery and the burghers' houses, and everyone was filled with joy and great gladness.[4] But those good-for-nothing, traitorous, pseudo-monks left the house at Asquins [*de domo Esconii*], and after laying waste to anything which fell into their hands, took to their heels.

After forty-five days had passed, the brothers returned from exile with tremendous joy and gladness. But one of the excommunicated men, named William Pidet, possessed by a devilish spirit, began to attack the monastery and make raids on its cattle. After he had been doing this for a long time, the church's men could no longer bear such damages, and so one day as he was

---

[1] *per manum suam in manu illius pollicendo.* See Bloch (1961: plates 2–4).

[2] *obsidatum tenerent.*

[3] 6 January 1166. Cox points out that the "exile" lasted 40 days, not 45 as the text below says. It is curious that Hugh should miss this obvious parallel with Christ's time "in the wilderness."

[4] Isaiah 35:10.

carrying off a huge plunder of some forty horses and donkeys, a great crowd of rustics followed him, both from the town of Vézelay and also from the little village of Chamoux. Now there were with him only six other thieves; four of these were taken and the others fled while William himself was surrounded. There was much snow on the ground, for it was the height of winter. After they had sought the wretch for a long time amid the bushes and thickets of the forest, at length someone saw him hidden from the knees up[1] and he was hit between the shoulders. They pulled him out and led him to a woodland lake, where they deprived him of his testicles and eyes; they let him go there, but as evening had now come, alas, the miserable man died. So he who used to attack the Church missed out on the last unction provided by the Church, and he who used to persecute his mother was slain by her faithful sons.

Subsequently, in the presence of the king's knights and the count's vassals [*clientes*], the abbot computed the total of the monastery's losses sustained by the church at the hands of the count's men from the brothers' departure to the present time; and the sum came to two hundred and forty pounds.

65
The Count Tries to Mollify the Abbot's Spirit [1672A/581. 2727]
1166

After this the count's messengers demanded from the abbot the cost of procuration on the feast of the blessed Mary Magdalene and made a few other absurd claims. The abbot replied to them: "When the count has made peace with me and is accepted back into communion with the Church, then I shall reply to him concerning this question." The archbishop of Lyon and the archbishop of Canterbury met at Crisenon, attempting to bring about, if they could, an agreement between the abbot and the count and countess. But their labor was in vain. For because the major part of all the church's burdens consisted in the immoderate demands on it for procuration, neither the abbot nor the church wished for a settlement which seemed to bring about a peace which was not real but feigned, unless the count either abandoned all his claims to procuration, or limited them to a prescribed amount of expense.

66
The Abbot Complains to the King About the Count
[1672B/582. 2740]
1166

When the middle of Lent was again drawing near,[2] William of Mello and his brother Renaud came to their paternal uncle, Abbot William of Vézelay, trying to bend his spirit towards a settlement. And at Escolives-Sainte-Camille, the abbot on one side, and on the other the count, met together; but vain

---

[1] *genutenus delitescere.*
[2] 3 April 1166.

were all the efforts made there.[1] So the abbot hastened to meet the king,
whom he found at Sens. He declared to him how the count had broken the
appointed forty days' truce. In fact it had been stated in the settlement made
at Sens that after the proof of his losses the abbot and the church would have
forty days' truce, with respect to all the accusations which the count had
against the abbot. And after that, if by chance the count did not wish to hold
off any longer, the abbot would again have a fortnight's truce from the day
when hostilities were declared. But the count, a week before the expiration of
the forty days' truce, broke faith with the abbot by not giving more than a
week's truce [after the declaration of hostilities], such that that week expired
at the same time as the forty days' period. When the king heard this, he could
scarcely contain himself and asked the abbot to return with him to Auxerre,
where the king reprimanded the count and ordered him to restore the
broken truce. The count was greatly saddened, so that he almost cried, but
was forced to obey, and granted a fortnight's truce starting from then. This
period was completed during the week before Palm Sunday.[2]

67
The Count of Champagne and Others Endeavor to
Arrange Peace, but Wrongly   [1672D/582. 2762]
1166

Then Henry, count of Champagne and Thibault, count of Blois and Anselm
of Trainel met with William, count of Nevers and William, abbot of Vézelay,
and discussed long and hard how to bring about a settlement between the
count of Nevers and the abbey of Vézelay. Now these two counts were blood
relations to the count of Nevers. What more shall I say? The abbot said that
in all his complaints he would abide by their advice and decision, except concerning the two occasions of procuration, by which the count would completely destroy the church. And so these illustrious men ruled that the abbot
should pay the count sixty pounds for each occasion when he owed procuration, except, however, that on that feast which the count rarely honored with
his presence the abbot and convent did not have to pay him anything at all.
That this settlement might be acceptable to the count, and might be confirmed as perpetually binding in law, it was stated that the abbot should give
the count seven hundred pounds. But the abbot offered only fifty pounds for
each occasion of hospitality and five hundred pounds for settlement. This was
notified to the count of Nevers. But, encouraged by his clerk Stephen and by
Stephen of Pierre-Perthuis, he utterly refused such a settlement, unless the
abbot gave him eighty pounds for each occasion of hospitality, and one thous-
and pounds for settlement. This statement seemed harsh in the eyes of the

---

[1] See Augustine *City of God* 9.8. Escolines St. Camille is located some ten kilometers
south of Auxerre. The Benedictine abbey of Crisenon (§65 above) is located some twenty-
five kilometers north of Vézelay, on the Yonne, about ten kilometers south of Escolines
as the crow flies.
[2] The week from 17 to 23 April 1166.

abbot, who was praised and supported by the count Henry, who said that he ought to give no more than he had offered. Thus, when evening had come, they parted from each other with nothing accomplished. At the abbot's request the king wrote thanking Count Henry and beseeching him to use all his power to bring about the settlement which he had set out. So Count Henry appointed for the abbot Monday in Palm Sunday week at Troyes and sent a message to the count of Nevers, asking him as his kinsman to deign to come to Troyes for the sake of a settlement between himself and the abbot. But the count wrote back that he ought rather come to Auxerre, if he had to go anywhere.[1] Henry, horrified at such an insult, sent on this reply to the king and the abbot. Therefore the abbot returned to the king whom he found at Orleans on Maundy Thursday. The abbot was invited by bishop Manasses to celebrate the service of the confection of the holy oil. After he had done so, he sent Vincent, the dean, to Vézelay with some of this chrism. When the abbot told the king Count William's reply to Count Henry, the king was absolutely thunderstruck and sent an order to Count William to come in person to Moret on the Wednesday after Easter and in the meantime to abstain from invasion of the monastery of Vézelay and to grant safe conduct to those coming from Vézelay to the meeting.

68

A Discussion in the Presence of the King   [1673C/583. 2804]

1166

The abbot spent Easter at Villemoutiers.[2] Four days later the king, the count, and the abbot, each with his retinue, met in the forest beyond Moret. The king asked the count to agree to a settlement according to Count Henry's advice. To this the count replied: "What I hold in the monastery of Vézelay I received from my ancestors, who received it as a fief from yours;[3] to treat or settle concerning this fief, rather than all my inheritance, seems to me not so much an act of peace as one of violence." To this the king replied: "If it is true that my ancestors granted it to yours as a fief, then that was done, doubtless, for reasons of protection, not destruction. But you, so far as we can gather, strain with all your power to destroy this monastery."[4] The count replied: "Saving the king's word, I am not destroying it." The king said to him: "As far as your actions indicate, its destruction is imminent. But let us forget all this and discuss a settlement, if the abbot agrees." The abbot replied: "The count says that the monastery of Vézelay was given by your ancestors to his. But look here, we hold in our hands the privileges of your ancestors, in which this monastery's liberty is commended and all rights of

---

[1] *At ille remandavit ei ipsum potius venire debere Altisiodorum, si forte opus haberet*; the *ipsum* here could refer to Count Henry or even to the abbot. It is, perhaps, a more obvious insult if *ipsum* is taken to refer to Count Henry who is then being asked to travel to meet the convenience of the count of Nevers.

[2] Villemoutiers was a dependent priory of Vézelay in the diocese of Sens.

[3] *susceperunt patres mei in foedum e patribus tuis.*

[4] See Frontinus *Strategematon* 2.1.7.

possession or customary rights of any outside powers are excluded. These privileges, both papal and royal, and the monastery of Vézelay itself, I commit into your hands. Compose and dispose according to the exercise of your justice."

69
The Count Refuses to Stand by the King's Decision
[1674B/584. 2827]

1166

So the king asked the count whether he would abide by the settlement proposed by Count Henry at Auxerre. The count replied: "I have not spoken a single word about a settlement with Count Henry." The king said: "I have said what I heard. But as for these matters, see what you can do for my sake." The count responded: "For your sake I will do what I can, but I will not come to a compromise over what is my right." The king was angry and replied: "The abbot, who is under no obligation to me in law, submits himself to me in the matter of his right[1] and relies totally on my judgment; and you who are tied to me by your direct homage[2] hold me, your lord, suspect and refuse to submit to my advice. Until now I have borne with your injustices in deference to your youth; until now I have taken on a great sin by tolerating your subversion of the sepulchre of the blessed Mary Magdalene. But from now on I shall not be found wanting in justice towards that monastery, if by chance the abbot raises complaints against you and seeks justice. In the meantime I forbid you henceforth by the royal authority to presume to disturb the monastery of Vézelay, its men or possessions; know that whatever evil you do to that monastery from now on redounds to the injury of my royal crown. But if you have anything against the abbot, behold I offer him to you for justice."[3] Then the abbot approached the king and asked for justice against the count. The king replied to him, "Because he [the count] came here to seek a compromise at my request, it does not befit the royal mercy to deliver him to justice at the moment. But wait until the count returns, and afterwards I shall appoint for you and him a day and place for discussion." And they met again the next day[4] in the house of the brothers of Vézelay which is on the river Loing at Moret.

70
The King Finally Insists on a Council at Moret   [1674D/585. 2854]

1166

With William, abbot of Vézelay were Hugh [abbot] of Saint-Germain-des-Prés, Stephen, abbot of St. Remi-en-Sens, Stephen, abbot of Saint-Père-de-Melun,

---

[1] *Abbas, qui nullo iure michi tenetur obnoxius, de iure proprio sese submittit.*
[2] *et tu, qui iure proprii hominii michi teneris.*
[3] *ecce ad iustitiam illum tibi exhibeo.*
[4] 28 April 1166.

[Garnier] abbot of Château-Landon, the jurist Mainerius, and Osmund, canon of Paris. Now certain people tried in all sorts of ways to turn the king's favor from the abbot or from the church of Vézelay; but all these attempts of Satan were in vain, and broken were the snares of secret cupidity because the abbot would in no way forsake the will and judgment of the king, while the count absolutely refused to stand by the king's judgment. Moreover, the count complained that the abbot was holding one of his men captive. When asked whom, he replied: "Andrew de l'Étang." The abbot said: "Andrew de l'Étang, who does not in any way belong to you, is mine from the sole of his foot to the crown of his head, for he is legally a serf of the monastery of Vézelay."[1] The count returned: "Andrew knows nothing of this condition of servitude unless it is forced on him." The abbot replied: "Look! On this matter also I stand by the judgement of the royal court."[2]

The courtiers and royal advisers said: "The custom of the royal court is such that if anyone is challenged about his servile status by another person, he is to be produced free from his possessor before us all. If he recognizes his possessor as his sole lord, the accuser, since the case is finished, will have no power over him. But if the serf says that he belongs to the accuser, then his body alone may be handed over to the accuser; but all his possessions, movable or immovable, remain with his possessor, saving his person alone." The abbot replied: "I praise this mode of judgment and this custom and will gladly follow them." Then the count, in his confusion desiring to turn the ignominy of his case against the abbot, presented a complaint concerning that traitor William [Pidet], who, losing his eyes and testicles, had perished by a just death: the count said that a monk who had been under his, the count's, own protection, had been slain by the abbot's orders. The whole court exclaimed against such a stupid and wicked accusation by the count; and the abbot said: "The accusation which you have levelled is utterly false, and I shall not trouble to reply to it." When the king learned of that pseudo-monk, he broke into loud laughter, and said to the count: "Is this what your [i.e., the Vézelay monks who supported the count against their abbot] monks are like?" And when he had heard of the manner of and the reason for that lost man's death, again laughing and reproaching he said: "O just and competent complaint of the count! O honorable accusation of a most noble prince! What does he want in this matter? A treacherous monk has delivered his body to the earth, his soul to the devil."

71
Meanwhile Hugh Letard Lays Waste to the Land of Vézelay
[1675C/586. 2894]

1166

While these things were going on at Moret, Hugh Letard, taking with him some of the count's servants, entered the land of the monastery of Vézelay,

---

[1] *meus est a planta pedis usque ad verticem sicut proprius servus monasterii Vizeliacensis.*
[2] On this case see Berlow (1980).

where he took a great deal of booty, including herds and flocks and various valuables. He even dragged the tenant-farmers' untanned hides from their ropes and made off with them, receiving more than two hundred pounds for the lot. Then he climbed the hill [of Vézelay] and cried through a herald in the market-place that if anyone of any condition brought anything to sell within the town of Vézelay or any part of its territory, he would suffer confiscation of his goods and injury to and captivity of his body. After Easter week had passed,[1] he stationed evil men and robbers, made most harsh by their own poverty, to watch every entrance, lest any men or women, children or old people should presume to descend to draw water or grind their wheat. Thus it came about that matrons and maids, trusting in reverence for their sex, went down the hill from time to time and were insulted and raped by these vilest of men and afflicted with many injuries. Therefore, forced by great necessity, the brothers themselves descended to draw water and to gather vegetables. But they too were assaulted, injured, and despoiled by these vagabonds and scoundrels who did not blush to attack those with poor clothes and a habit unsuitable for defense.

Stephen of Billy [-sur-Oisy], having received from the brothers five hundred *solidi* in cash and a large quantity of pepper and wax, left the town and went to the abbot, who was at that time staying at the monastery of Villemoutiers to avoid the traps set by the count. Since Stephen suspected the count's followers, he took his brother, a knight, and went by a detour to la Puisaye, trusting in a safe-conduct from William, provost of Druyes-les-Belles-Fontaines, who was married to his sister. But sometimes treachery abuses even the piety of blood relationships. For as soon as the knight had parted from his brother, William the provost sent William de Lainsecq, who followed the departing Stephen and took from him his money, his horses, and all that he carried. So Stephen went back and came to Ida, the count's mother, asking on the king's behalf for the restoration of his confiscated goods, for it all belonged to the monastery of Villemoutiers, which was under the king's lordship and protection. But she held the king's name in contempt and pretended that the monastery of Vézelay, which was in her protection and that of her son, had been plundered by the enemies of herself and her son. It was with difficulty, therefore, that she was persuaded by the prayers of Stephen's friends to order his horses and some of the wax to be returned to him. When this news came to the ears of the people of Vézelay, their hearts were full of consternation, bewailing the loss to their father rather than their own affliction. And the rumor spread that the count had ordered the senior and most powerful men of Vézelay to be seized and their goods to be destroyed or confiscated. These men were so terrified that they hid themselves within the monastery cloister. Here are some of their names: Beraldus the provost, Renaud de Saint-Christophe, Lambert of Maligny, Hugh Bread-kneader, Robert de Moutiers, John the Great and his nephew John de l'Hôpital, Peter Guibert, William Isembard, Durand the Leech, Walter the Hosier, Stephen Covemaalhe and his brother, Renaud *Runcinus*, John Gerard and his son Renaud, John the Red, Walter Bonardin, Robert Amalric, William

---

[1] 24 to 30 April 1166.

of Langres, Gerard *Dalmacii*, Durand de la Guiche, Lawrence *Minatgerius*, *Arbertus* Cardinal, Robert of St. Peter.

72

The Abbot Goes to the King at Beauvais to Complain of the Plunder Stolen by the Count's Servants [1676C/587. 2951]

1166

So Geoffrey the Englishman, who at that time held first place in the house of Vézelay after Gilo, wrote together with his brothers to the abbot, notifying him of the great affliction and grief which the town of Vézelay suffered from the siege of the count's followers. Thereupon the abbot came to Beauvais, where the king had, as it happened, arranged a meeting of a multitude of his bishops and magnates. When the king learned of the evils which Count William of Nevers had visited on the monastery of Vézelay, he appointed for him a day to treat with the abbot, in his presence, at Orleans on the Sunday before Pentecost,[1] ordering the count first to satisfy him [the king] concerning the contempt and transgression of his mandate in persecuting the monastery after his prohibition. When the day was announced to him, the count was very angry and retired with many threats. So the abbot went to [Hugh] duke of Burgundy, asking him if he would deign to give military aid to those who were besieged. At once the duke wrote to Guntard provost of Avallon, ordering him to conduct to Vézelay without fear all saleable goods from his lands, and even to defend them with arms if necessary. However, being but a boy in years and in mind, he was deceived by the count through the cunning of Anseric of Montréal, who was no less an enemy of the abbot and monastery than the count, and so Guntard lied in all that he promised, withheld the goods, and ordered any inhabitant of Vézelay found on his land to be held.

Now King Louis called his secretaries and wrote to all the prefects and princes of his kingdom, ordering them to collect an army of cavalry and foot-soldiers and to meet him at Sens on the Sunday before the feast of the blessed Mary Magdalene.[2] But the count, fearing the judgment of the royal court, excused himself from the day appointed for him. So the king then assigned him the first Sunday after Pentecost.[3] When he again excused himself, the king gave him the third Sunday after Pentecost. But the count excused himself yet a third time, sending William of Dompierre, who besought the king to hold just one more discussion, after which, when the allegations of both sides had been heard, he would in all things abide by the king's decision. And this saying seemed good in the eyes of the king, to whom peace was always pleasing and war onerous.

---

[1] 5 June 1166.

[2] 17 July (the feast of the Magdalene falling on 22 July).

[3] 19 June 1166. Hugh III of Burgundy ruled 1162–1193, but because of his age his mother, Marie de Champagne, acted as regent until 1165 (Cox). Bouchard (1987: 260).

73

The Genealogy of the Capetian Kings. Louis VII
Proceeds to Jerusalem   [1677B/588.2985]

987–1165

This King Louis is the son of Louis surnamed the Fat, son of Philip, son of
Henry, son of Robert, son of Hugh Capet, who was the first king after the
extinction of the lineage of Charles, which had held the throne for about 200
years. From the first year of Hugh until the first year of this Louis, who
reigned with his father for five years, about 140 years elapsed.[1] This is the
King Louis whose father Louis expanded his realm on all sides by joining his
son in marriage to the daughter of William [X], duke of Aquitaine and count
of Poitou, by whom he acquired all of Aquitaine, Gascony, the country of the
Basques, and Navarre as far as the Pyrenees and up to the Cross of Charles.
This is the King Louis who in the fifteenth year of his reign, when Eugenius
was presiding over the Roman See, went to Jerusalem with a great army
under a banner inscribed with the life-giving Cross, to fight the race inimical
to the Faith. But, by God's mysterious judgment, a great part of the army was
lost and he returned without triumph, and, following foolish advice, he
abandoned his wife with her lands, which had for some time been a part of
the realm, and afterwards married the daughter of the Spanish emperor.
When she died he took as a third wife Count Henry's sister, by whom he had
his first son, named Philip, in the thirty-third year of his reign, when Pope
Alexander was leaving France.[2]

---

[1] The first year of Hugh Capet's reign was 987; Louis VII began to reign on his own
in 1137 but had been associated in rule with his father since 1131.

[2] Louis separated from Eleanor of Aquitaine in 1152, married Constance of Castille in
1154, and then married Adele of Champagne in 1160. He took the cross at Vézelay on 31
March 1146, and terminated his campaign ingloriously at Easter 1149. Philip Augustus was
born in 1165. The chronicler seems to think this digression necessary because the king has
now emerged as the arbiter of the affairs of Vézelay rather than the pope. Hence,
perhaps, the count's shift of ground from the rights of advocacy/procuration to feudal
tenure as the basis of his attempt to maintain his position against the claims of the abbot
of Vézelay. That this shift was not expected by Hugh of Poitiers is indicated by—among
other things—the fact that the *Cartulary* has within it so few royal acts. See Introduction,
above 6n.2. Cox: "The 'Cross of Charles' mentioned here was located at the summit of the
Fort de Cize pass, between Saint-Jean-Pied-de-Port and Roncesvalles, by 1106 at the latest.
This was traditionally regarded as the gateway to Spain, and the cross had supposedly
been erected by Charlemagne himself on the very spot where his soldiers had begun to
build the road to Santiago. It therefore became customary for pilgrims passing that way
to kneel and pray, and to plant their own crosses nearby before continuing their journey.
See Barton Scholod, *Charlemagne in Spain: The Cultural Legacy of Roncesvalles* (Geneva,
1966: 79 n., 125–26). This rather ungenerous history of Louis VII's reign up to 1166 is
essentially correct. His participation in the second crusade occurred in 1147–49, and the
annulment of his marriage to Eleanor of Aquitaine became final in March 1152. In 1154
Louis married Constance, daughter of Alfonso VII of Castille, who died in 1160 after
giving birth to two daughters. Within a few months Louis married Adele of Champagne,
and the future King Philip Augustus was born on 21 August 1165. Thus, by marriage the
king had become a brother-in-law of Count Henry of Champagne, whose wife was the
sister of Ida, dowager-countess of Nevers. This may explain Louis' temporizing in the

74
The King, the Count, and the Abbot Meet at Moret
[1677D/589. 3008]

1166

The king, the count, and the abbot met at Moret. When opposing arguments had been advanced by both sides, the king desired that each of them should abide by the judgment of Henry, archbishop of Rheims and Henry, count of Champagne. The count agreed to do this, swearing faith in the hand of Peter [of Courtenay] the king's brother; and the abbot promised the same, but with the word of truth only.[1] When they asked for a day of final judgment—for the judges were not present—the king replied that he would assign them a suitable day about the feast of the blessed Denis.[2] In the meantime the abbot should return to his monastery, where he and his monks would enjoy longed-for peace and quiet, until the case should be concluded by these judges. The count confirmed with an oath that he would keep this peace. Thus each returned to his own people. Abbot William went to Troyes to see Count Henry and thence to Clairvaux, where he hoped to find Archbishop Henry, the king's brother. When he did not find him there, he returned and celebrated the feast of the blessed Mary Magdalene in his monastery.

Now King Louis moved his army against Count William of Chalon because of the evil massacre which his son William had made of the Cluniacs. For when he [William the younger] had occupied the castle of Lourdon, which lawfully belongs to the house of Cluny, the older men and the youths marched out from Cluny. But since they were a rash and unskilled throng, a skilled band of the count's soldiers met them at once and compelled them to fly, and almost all were slaughtered. So the king, advancing with his army, occupied the count's fortifications and defenses and the city of Chalon itself. All his [the count's] land as far as the river Saône he laid waste and delivered into the hands of Hugh, duke of Burgundy and William, count of Nevers, until the young man himself, who was the cause of all these ills, came with his mother to Vézelay before the king's face and, as far as he could, made satisfaction.[3] And because the count of Nevers was occupied with the whole

---

Nevers-Vézelay conflict—and our chronicler's obvious irritation with him."

[1] 2 Corinthians 6.7. Cox: "Pierre de Courtenay (1127–1183), the youngest of the sons of Louis VI and Adelaide de Savoie. He accompanied Louis VII on the Second Crusade, and he married Elisabeth, daughter and heiress of Raynald, baron of Courtenay, who died in 1160."

[2] The festival of St. Denis falls on 9 October.

[3] This expedition took place in spring of 1166. The count of Chalon had invaded Cluniac lands at the instigation of Frederick Barbarossa, and when the duke of Burgundy had been unable to restore order the king had been called in. Hugh III, duke of Burgundy, and William IV, count of Nevers had assisted the king. Cox cites the "vivid account of this episode" in J. Viard, ed., *Les Grandes Chroniques de France* (Paris, 1930: 6:79–81 [= *Historia gloriosa regis Ludovici*] by a monk of Saint-Germain-des-Prés. The slaughter mentioned "was apparently the work of Brabançon mercenaries who attacked the monks in procession, sacked the church, and killed 500 inhabitants of Cluny-ville. See Chagny (1938: 247–48), and Jean-Louis Bazin 'Les comtes héréditaires de Chalon-sur-Saône 880–

weight of this business, the king postponed the finalization of the controversy between him and the abbot until the feast of St. Martin.[1]

In the year of the Incarnate Word of God 1166, the 286th after the reception of the sacred body of the blessed lover of God, Mary Magdalene, the eleventh after the destruction of the odious commune of the burghers of Vézelay, on 10 November, William abbot of Vézelay and Count William of Nevers met before the king at Paris, and the count proposed. . . .[2]

[Folios 179–184 have cut vertically in half: *Chérest Étude II* 60, Huygens 1976: 185–86].

1237" (*Mémoires de la Société d'histoire et d'archéologie de Chalon-sur-Saône*, 2nd ser., IV, prem. partie, 1911: 56–79). According to these authors, the savage deeds were done on the orders of Count William I himself, not his son. The castle of Mont-Saint-Vincent, the count's most powerful stronghold after Chalon itself, was taken and burned to the ground, and the county of Chalon itself was confiscated and divided between the duke of Burgundy and the count of Nevers. Count William I fled and, according to Bazin, it is not known what became of him. The story recounted in monastic circles was that one night while dining in his place of refuge, he was called to the door by an unknown man on a horse who forced him to mount behind him and who then carried him off to an eternity of torment in the sulfur pits of Hell." The count thus becomes a kind of fusion between William of Malmesbury's witch of Berkeley and the later figures of Faust and Don Giovanni!

[1] 11 November 1166.

[2] Unfortunately the folios describing this crucial and successful meeting have been mutilated and cannot be deciphered. Huygens (1976: 185n.1) comments that "it all appears . . . almost impossible to decipher. We abandon the task to those more clairvoyant than we." It seems that after the points at dispute had been set forth the king pronounced his judgment. Procuration was a key point, with the abbot apparently agreeing to free himself of the obligation of providing it by paying a fee on each of the three occasions decided upon. The monks would not accept this concession and at last the count agreed to abandon his claims for hospitality. The meeting at Vézelay, which is being described when the manuscript is complete again, was arranged so that both parties could swear solemnly to the agreed treaty. Cox: ". . . the first three mutilated pages contain an account of the people at the meeting in Paris, where Count Henry of Champagne and Archbishop Henry of Reims, the king's brother-in-law and brother, respectively, acted as mediators. There was a rehearsal of many of the now familiar accusations on both sides, and the next four pages (Huygens [1976: 594–97]) describe the peace settlement item by item, after which the narrative resumes. At first it seems that all went well and ancient enmities were being laid to rest. The count's sister and younger brothers swore to uphold the treaty and amid universal joy, the count and the abbot embraced one another in the presence of the king (598). It is clear, however, that the count's mother, the 'pestiferous Ida,' was not yet ready to make peace and at one point the abbot declared that he had 'taken a wolf for a lamb' (Huygens [1976: 599.3307]). There was still some difficulty about procurations involving two persons named Raynald and Drogo (Huygens [1976: 600]) and Milon de Noyers, and the countess was refusing to confirm the settlement on oath (601). This time, however, the count stood by the treaty and apparently tried to reason with his mother (there is mention of 'grinding teeth,' 'groaning' and 'reddened cheeks,' Huygens lines 3374–3377, which suggest highly emotional scenes even in the presence of the king during the negotiations). But Count William, perhaps suitably impressed by the drastic punishment just meted out to his namesake the count of Chalon for having taken up arms against a celebrated monastic establishment, had clearly detached himself now from his mother's influence and had decided that it was time to really make peace with the monks of Vézelay. He made a public confession of his past faults and professed his intention of making amends, even to the point of undertaking the pilgrimage to Jerusalem (Huygens [1976: 602.3391–3414])."

75

The Count's Oath that He Will Keep Peace with Those of Vézelay
[1678D/603. 3415]

1166

Ignoring thus his mother's wicked words, the count rose and knelt before the holy gospels and the life-giving cross of Christ and the holy relics. When the abbot wished to dictate to him the form of the oath he cried: "Wait, allow me to say in my own words[1] what I feel in my heart and hold with faith; but if what I say is too much or too little, you may emend it!" Then he went on: "What is contained in the present charter [*cirographo*], as I understand in good faith and as you all know who are here, I shall hold and observe and shall cause my men to observe. So may God and these holy objects [*sancta ista*] aid me." And all exclaimed: "It is enough, it is enough. This is said well and clearly." Calling his brother Guy, the count ordered him to swear in the same manner, which he did, saying: "As my lord and brother the count has sworn in good faith, even so shall I hold and observe in good faith. So may God and these holy objects aid me." Then were called the provost of Auxerre, named John, and Columbus, provost of Tonnerre, and Miles provost of Mailly-le-Chateau, and Hugh Letard, provost of Châtel-Censoir, and others from the surrounding lands, who swore as had been laid down in the charter.

But Ida, the count's mother, seeking to escape, entered the oratory of the untouched virgin Mary, which was next to the chapter house, and summoned Miles and many others whom she hoped would obey her in her madness. After they had discussed all kinds of ways whereby the countess could avoid swearing the oath and could not find an honest way out, they called the count. When he came, his mother besought him not to compel her to swear. The count replied to her: "If you want me to incur the punishment for perjury, don't swear."[2] To which she said: "Willy-nilly, I agree on my word to whatever you of your own will have sworn." The count said to her: "If this is sufficient for the abbot, it is sufficient for me." And so she said: "Ask him, my son, to allow this [kind of] oath for your sake."[3] So the count went back and said to the abbot: "It is shameful for a woman to swear, especially my mother, who is noble in birth and power and also a widow; spare her, I pray, and do not compel her to swear; but accept her agreement on the strength of her word alone; I will give you an undertaking on her behalf that she will observe it." The abbot replied: "Do not dare to break this alliance of peace, for I know that your mother has been the initiator and cause of all your enmity; and certainly she makes many promises, but puts few of them into effect. But for love of you, if, as you have said, she has consented to keep the form of the settlement on her word alone, I shall permit any true knight to swear on her behalf with her standing before the relics." Thus it was done,

---

[1] *per me.*

[2] The count seems to be envisaging the possibility of his mother's acting against the church in a way that would go against what he had just sworn.

[3] "*Roga,*" *inquit, "fili, eum ut tibi det hoc iusiurandum.*"

with Baldwin swearing on her behalf. And there was great joy and exultation among all the people that day. Agreement and great friendship were concluded between the abbot and the count, and there was no distance between them, but one thought as the other. Then those who had worked for and encouraged all the hostility came to the abbot's feet and prayed and beseeched him to reconcile them to the count, to whom they were now odious. Then King Louis came to Vézelay,[1] and the abbot and his brothers thanked him for making peace. He was met there by the son of the count of Chalon, who, with the abbot's mediation, made peace with the king.[2]

To this meeting came also Stephen, abbot of Cluny, who because of his hatred of Abbot William of Vézelay disdained to enter the town of Vézelay but stayed at the manor called Neuffontaines and asked the king to meet him where he pleased. The king assigned him a place on the morrow at Saint-Père-sous-Vézelay, another manor of the monastery of Vézelay. When Abbot William of Vézelay heard of this, he sent Renaud [of Mello] the almoner and Godric prior of Chamoux to the abbot. After they had with difficulty been introduced to him, Stephen heard them out, and then, without sending answering greetings to William, replied that he would discuss with his brothers those matters which they had raised. With Stephen, abbot of Cluny, were Bernard, prior of St. Étienne de Nevers, Hugh of Souvigny, Thomas, Amblard, and many others, who all with one accord asked and recommended that he [Stephen] agree to the request of the abbot of Vézelay. For William had asked that the abbot of Cluny should come to Vézelay, where he would meet him with the duke of Burgundy, the count of Nevers, and all the company of great knights who had gathered there at that time; and with the streets adorned, the burning of much incense, and the ringing of all the bells, William would receive him in solemn procession, as if for a festival; and the abbot might occupy the chapter hall if he wished, he might sit at the refectory-bell if he liked, or he might even lodge in the abbot's chamber for as many days as he pleased. So the abbot of Cluny agreed to their advice and notified the abbot of Vézelay through Hugh and Amblard that he would satisfy his request. At once the abbot ordered the church and all the streets to be decorated, and through the crying of a herald he ordered all the people to decorate the fronts and porches of their homes fittingly and to proceed out with him respectfully to meet the abbot of Cluny.

In the meantime Thibault, prior of Cluny, later abbot of Molesme, arrived and he disparaged his brothers' advice. Coming with Pons, the prior of Paray-le-Monial, he tested Abbot William's intentions, inquiring with what honor he was intending to receive the abbot of Cluny. The abbot replied to him saying: "Taking with me the counts and magnates and knights, a multitude of whom you see are present, I shall meet my lord of Cluny in a solemn procession. When he has entered here, he may occupy the chapter and the refectory as he pleases, or live

---

[1] Between 11 November 1166 and the end of the year.

[2] See §74. Cox: "The part of his father's county that had been turned over to the count of Nevers after his defeat was returned to William II following his submission to the king at Vézelay, but the other half remained in the hands of the duke of Burgundy; apparently the king also kept the barony of Saint-Gengoux, which he had earlier appropriated for himself." Neuffontaines (see next paragraph) is some twelve kilometers as the crow flies south of Vézelay.

in my chambers as long as he wishes, and I will show him all honor, in grain, wine, meat, and fish." While Thibault muttered under his breath, Pons replied: "All this which you propose is certainly good, but insufficient for the person of the abbot of Cluny." Whereupon William asked: "What then do you think I should do further?" And Pons replied: "You know best what is fitting for him, especially in this monastery, which, besides the ordinary duties of hospitality, is held by him in great reverence."[1] "I know well," he said, "what is fitting for him, and therefore I shall show him all the honor which is fitting. But if by chance you intend more, then I wish you all to know this for sure, that I shall not concede him the seat which has been conferred on me."[2] But they said: "Don't tire yourself, for our lord abbot is unlikely to come here or receive your honoring of him [*obsequium*—but see Niermeyer 1976: 729–30]." To which the abbot said: "That is up to him; I have done my duty."

76
The Behavior of the Abbot of Cluny is Condemned by
the King and the Nobles   [1681A/ 605. 3518]

1166

The king and his lords heard this conversation, which displeased them much, and they said: "O how great is the arrogance of this man, who despises such honor when it is offered him and who expects the lord king and all of us to meet him." While they were saying this, Abbot William, who was before the king, was told that Abbot Stephen of Cluny had gone to the outside steps of the great church and was standing before the altar of the apostles Peter and Paul. Going down to him, the abbot led him into the upper house into the king's presence. Abbot Stephen remained there all day in vain without eating and when night's calm approached, he returned to the above-mentioned manor [Neuffontaines]. That day Abbot William was magnified in the sight of the king and the count of Nevers and all the magnates, for all disapproved of the superciliousness and arrogance of the Cluniacs. And Abbot William obtained the favor of the count of Nevers, and more and more as the days went by he gained the count's affection, so that the count trusted him in all his dealings and made known his secrets to him.

77
William of Nevers Proceeds to Jerusalem   [1681B/605. 3535]

1167

After these exchanges William [IV], count of Nevers, son of William [III] of Auxerre, son of William [II], who died a Carthusian, son of Renaud de Mailly,

---

[1] *quod preter communem hospitalitatem ampliori tenetur reverentia.*

[2] Continuing the long struggle against Cluniac dominance, Abbot William refuses to allow Abbot Stephen to occupy the abbatial chair, lest this be interpreted later as an acknowledgement of Vézelay's subordination to Cluny. Cox: "Theobald de Châtillon, who had been prior of Saint-Martin-des-Champs before becoming prior of Cluny, died on pilgrimage in 1171 AD. In houses belonging to the Cluniac order, the abbot of Cluny was entitled to assume full authority whenever he came on a visit."

son of William [I] of Nevers, son of Renaud, who was the son of Landric, first
of the line of the counts of Nevers, received the sign of the life-giving Cross
from the hands of Hugh, archbishop of Sens at La Charité, in order to go on
pilgrimage to Jerusalem.[1]

78

Heretics Known as *Deonarii* or Publicans Are Led to Judgment. The Main Points of Their Heresy [1681C/606. 3541]

1167

At that time certain heretics, called *Deonarii* or Publicans, were captured at
Vézelay.[2] When they were interrogated they tried to cover over by double
meanings and circumlocutions the most filthy sect of their heresy. So the
abbot ordered them to be separated and kept in confinement until their guilt
could be established by some bishops and other honest men who were going
to come. They were detained for some sixty or more days and often led
before the gathering to be questioned, now with threats, now with promises,
about the Catholic faith. At length, when this labor had been pursued in vain
for a long time, on the intervention of the archbishops of Lyon and Narbonne, and the bishop of Nevers, revered abbots and very many other
learned men, they were convicted of confessing with their mouth that the
divine was of one essence, while denying the efficacy of all the sacraments of
the Catholic church, namely the baptism of children, the eucharist, the sign
of the life-giving cross, the sprinkling of holy water, the building of churches,
expiation by tithes and offerings, marriage relationships, the institution of
monasticism, and all the offices of clerks and priests.

As Easter was approaching, two of them, hearing that it was soon to be
judged that they should endure extermination by fire, pretended that they
believed the teachings of the Catholic church and declared that they would
make satisfaction for peace with the Church by the trial of water. So during
the solemn Easter procession[3] they were led into the midst of a great crowd,
which occupied the whole cloister, including Guichard, archbishop of Lyons,
Bernard, bishop of Nevers, master Walter, bishop of Laon and William, abbot
of Vézelay. When they were interrogated about their faith point by point, they
said that they held the same beliefs as the Catholic church. When asked about
the execrable sacrament of their error,[4] they said that they knew nothing, ex-

---

[1] In 1167. The count did not return, but died of the plague in Acre on 24 October
1168. Cox: "According to Jean-Bernard Charrier, *et al.*, *Histoire de Nevers* (Editions
Horvath, Roanne, 1984: 1:65), he was only 22 years old at the time of his death."

[2] There is a translation of this chapter and a brief discussion in Wakefield and Evans
(1969: 247–49). For a discussion of the relations between heresy and the "communal
revolution" see above Aspects [B]. Cox: "Heretics were such a problem in the Nivernais
and Auxerrois by the 1180's that Bishop Hugh de Noyers of Auxerre (1183–1206) made
it a principal concern of his episcopate and was labelled 'the hammer of heretics' by his
admiring biographer. Bouchard (1979: 101–5)."

[3] 9 April 1167.

[4] *de execrabili sacramento erroris sui.* Cox: "interrogated concerning their detestable
sacrament of errors"; perhaps a mistake for *de execrabili sacramenti errore suo* (*sacramenti*
being objective genitive)?

cept the above-mentioned infidelity to the ecclesiastical sacraments. Asked whether they would prove by the ordeal of water that they really believed what they professed and that they knew nothing more of secret errors, they answered that they would do this willingly, without any adjudication. Then all the church exclaimed with one voice: "Thanks be to God." And the abbot in response asked all present: "What then, brothers, do you think should be done with those who still persevere in their obstinacy?" All replied: "Let them be burned, let them be burned."

The next day the two who seemed to have recanted were led forward and underwent trial by water. One of them by the judgment of all was saved by the water—although there were not a few who could form no certain opinion about it. But the other, when submerged in the water, was condemned by the mouths of nearly everyone. He was confined to prison, but since there were different views, even among the clergy, he was led again by his own request to the trial by water, and when he was submerged a second time, he was not received by the water even for an instant.[1] And so condemned twice, he was sentenced to the fire by all; but the abbot, having regard to his own presence,[2] ordered him to be publicly flogged and then banished. But the remaining seven were delivered to the flames and burnt in the valley of Asquins.

[End of MS; the last sentence, however, ends at the bottom left of the page with space for more words.][3]

---

[1] There is a similar case of heretics being tried by ordeal in the autobiography of Guibert of Nogent; see Benton (1970: 212–14) and Wakefield-Evans (1969: no. 9, 101–4) and, on the ordeal, Bartlett (1986). Abbot William sought advice about how to deal with the heretics from Herbert of Bosham, one of the party of Thomas à Becket. Herbert's reply is printed in *PL* 190.1462–63 and translated below as Appendix C. Indecisive as his advice is, the suggestion that the Vézelay abbot send the heretics to the king of France for judgment was portentous for the future.

[2] Cox: "The text here reads *sed deferens abbas presentiae suae, publice cesum eliminari precepit,* which could mean that the abbot, having regard for his own presence, ordered him publicly 'eliminated' by the sword (i.e., *caesum* meaning 'cut down' rather than 'beaten,' or even a mistake for *caesim,* 'with the edge of the sword'). The sentence would seem to make much more sense, however, if *suae* here is used for *eius* (a practice not uncommon even in CL), so that the lighter sentence (that is, in either case a fate better than being burned at the stake) is explained not by the abbot's presence but by the prisoner's bedraggled appearance (presumably soggy and dripping after his water ordeal), which moved the abbot to make an exception in his case. The choice of whipping and banishment rather than elimination by beheading is based upon the CL meaning of *eliminare,* 'to put outside the threshold' or 'expel,' which would seem to go more logically with a flogging than with decapitation." In fact, what the abbot is probably referring to is the prohibition whereby ecclesiastics may not inflict sentences of corporal punishment (cf. Appendix C below): in *his* presence, the sentence must be commuted. Less likely is the possibility that *deferens* means "dismissing him"; sending the condemned person away from his presence, the abbot commuted his sentence.

[3] The fact that the scribe had space to continue writing in MS. Auxerre 227, but did not do so, suggests that the surviving text is all that Hugh wrote. Had our manuscript been filled up entirely, the suspicion could have been aroused that the chronicle continued but our scribe had copied no more, or what he had copied had been lost.

Fig. 12. Modern view of countryside from the hill of Vézelay, to illustrate *Major Chronicle* 2 §17 (J. O. Ward). 'Gui de Bazoches, who joined the crusading armies at Vézelay in 1190, left a description of the town surrounded by verdant vineyards, delightful both in the charm of its site and in the abundance of the liquid "which gladdens the heart" (Berlow [1987] p.154 n.17).

Fig. 13. View of the hill of Vézelay from Asquins (J. O. Ward).
See *Major Chronicle* 4 § 55.

Appendix A

The Letter of William of Volpiano

Brother W[illiam], together with all his brethren, [wishes for] the gift of the highest happiness for his master O[dilo], who is sweeter than the honey from a honeycomb.[1]

Because we are all very keen to learn precisely how things are with you I am sending you this note as an indication of what has been happening to us. By divine grace and with the support of your merits I am very well in myself; however I am being worn down by certain external events and mishaps. You have already heard, I believe, that Count William[2] has put aside earthly concerns and has been buried at Dijon. About the death of Count Richard[3] I have had no message [missum] and have learnt nothing about it beyond what I have heard by way of gossip [a dicentibus].

Apart from these matters, I notify your paternity that lord Oddo,[4] without consultation with the bishop of Autun,[5] received the monastery of Vézelay, at the instigation of Count Landric[6] after the monks and abbot of that place had been ignominiously driven out. As a result, the bishop has been roused to such anger against you and us and our place[7] that he not only threatens to inflict on us those evils which he can do himself or through his men, such as taking away the monastery of Mesvres[8] or putting an interdict on all our altars that are in his episcopate; he even threatens to stir up hostility to us among as many bishops, clerics, and laymen, of whatever order or dignity, as he can.

---

[1] The writer of the letter is William of Volpiano, abbot of St. Benignus in Dijon (d. 1031), and an ex-monk of Cluny himself. He was an important church reformer in his own right. The letter must have been written in 1027 since Richard III, "duke" of Burgundy, who died in that year, is said to have just passed away. Odilo was abbot of Cluny 994–1049.

[2] Otto-William, count of Burgundy and Mâcon (981–1026). On this important figure see Bouchard (1987), 265–70.

[3] Richard III, "duke" of Normandy, who died in 1027.

[4] Nothing else is known of this person, who must have been the head of the Cluniacs who took over Vézelay. It can hardly be a reference to Odilo himself, who is generally described as having taken over Vézelay, because William would not need to notify him of what he had done himself!

[5] This was Helmoin, bishop from 1018 to 1055.

[6] This is Landric, count of Nevers from c. 991 to 1028. See Aspects [F] above.

[7] contra vos et nos locumque nostrum; in this translation the first person plural has usually been translated as "I," on the grounds that it is William addressing Odilo. Here, however, the first person plural has been used since the bishop's anger is directed apparently against all the Cluniacs, with whom William of Volpiano, as a former monk of Cluny and a reformer in his own right, identifies himself. Cowdrey (1970: 86) thinks that William had been asked to intervene in the quarrel and this would explain his disapproval of the ejection of the monks of Vézelay, which is combined with a real concern for the reputation of the Cluniacs.

[8] A Cluniac dependency which had been given to Odilo by the bishop of Autun.

He has also excommunicated the brothers of our congregation so that none of them can inhabit the aforesaid place, enter the church, or presume to celebrate any divine service in it. But they [the intruded Cluniacs], relying on the apostolic privileges by which their predecessors provided for the liberty of that place, considered his pronouncement to be worth nothing and did not bother to give up anything, despite the interdict. In fact, holding in contempt the letter that he had sent them on the matter, they cast it to the ground and trampled it underfoot. This not only aroused the bishop to greater anger, but all who heard of it, no matter how far away they were, gave vent to serious calumnies against us.

For everyone who hears of these events, not just our enemies but even those who before seemed to be our friends, charges the injustice of it to us, and we are accused of unheard of presumption and even, by the laymen, of terrible greed. They say that it is not possible to remove any abbot whatever from his honor for any reason at all without canonical examination and the judgment of the bishop to whose diocese it [the honor] is known to pertain. After I had heard these things and more of the like both from rivals and from colleagues and had been able to learn from the bishop that there was no possibility of his releasing the brothers from the chain of anathema by which he had bound them unless they were to leave that place and return with all their followers to you, I could find no plan more appropriate than that I should on your behalf command them to return to you as soon as possible, lest someone should die suddenly while still subject to the sentence of excommunication. I am not at all certain that Count Landric will permit this or that they themselves will be willing to do it. I have taken care to inform you of all this because I want to know by letter as soon as possible what your wish and your command are about this matter.

Farewell.

Appendix B

The 1137 Accord between the Abbot of Vézelay and the Burghers of the Town: Translation and Notes

[For the circumstances surrounding this document see above Aspects [B] I, Graham (1918: 55 ff.), Berlow (1971: 33, 170–87), Chérest (1863: 1, chap. 3–Huygens [1976: 38–59]), Bastard (1851: 347–520). For guidance on interpretation: Berlow (1980: 136 ff.) and (1971: chap. 4, 248 ff.) The document records a settlement following some form of confederation against the seigneurial power of Abbot Alberic of Vézelay. The best general introduction to the subject of the *Accord* is Dockès (1982). See also Geary (1986) and Barthelemy (1984).

Readers of the charter will note that considerable tensions and divisions must have been present within the citizen body at Vézelay. The inhabitants of the *poté* of Vézelay seem to have been divided roughly into three groups: *suburbani* or *rustici*, residents of the town itself with employment mainly in the fields, and town residents whose employment lay mainly in the walled city (money-changers, stall-keepers, retailers, administrators, monks and clergy, etc.). It would seem that the 1137 compromise was more favorable to the first two classes of citizen than the third, and it would also seem from the evidence that it was the third group, or sections within that group, who provided the major revolutionaries in 1152. The protagonists of the commune seem to have been drawn in the main from the class of money-changers, retailers, and lay abbatial administrators. The document offers an unusually close glimpse into the seigneurial affairs of the Vézelay district and its people.

This translation was made from the text found in Quantin 1.313–23. Guizot (1969) also contains a version of this *Accord* in French. We have had the benefit of an independent translation made by Rosalind Berlow together with her comments on the meaning of difficult passages, communicated to us by letter. If page references are not cited, "Berlow" in text and notes below refers to this material.

Other communal charters readily available in English translation are: *carta Franchesie Lorriaci* (charter of the commune of Lorris, in the French royal domain, c. 1108–1137): Lyon (1964: 57–61) or in Tierney (1970a: 155–56). See also Herlihy (1968: 180–84) for the charter of the town of St. Omer, 1127, in Flanders (to be read in conjunction with the chronicle of Galbert of Bruges, translated by J. B. Ross); the *institutio pacis* of the commune of Laon is translated below as Appendix F. See in general Petit-Dutaillis (1947, 1970: chap. 2, 37ff.).

In the present translation, expansions of the text, Latin equivalents and editorial comments for the sake of good sense are in square brackets; other notes and comments follow the text.

The paragraph numbers in the present translation are not in the Quantin text, but have been added for convenience of reference.]

Agreement Between the Abbot of Vézelay and the Inhabitants of the Town of Vézelay, 1137 AD

1. In the name of the Father, the Son and the Holy Ghost, to all his successors, duly elected, brother Alberic, abbot of Vézelay, gives perpetual greeting in Christ.

2. Since, with the passing of the years there also passes the memory of things done, we think it is necessary to fix permanently in this instrument of writing, and to commend to the memory of subsequent generations the course of certain discords and complaints [*discordiam quarundam querelarum*] that [developed] between ourselves and our burghers.... Their [successful] termination [will also be a matter for our record].

3. In the first place, it must be recorded that a day was set for the composition of the differences between ourselves and our burghers, and on that day, before a tribunal composed of lord Hugh, bishop of Auxerre, Hugh, abbot of Pontigny, Stephen, abbot of Reigny, Stephen, abbot of Trois-Fontaines, Geof-

frey prior of Clairvaux and . . . , we and our burghers set forth the grounds of our differences. On all these complaints we and our burghers, by common agreement in regard to [our expectation of a] praiseworthy judgment (*dictum et laudationem*) from [the above judges] and those whom they have summoned to their counsel, have adopted the position that whatever definitions they may make in regard to [our disputes], we are bound in justice to support forever. The grounds of complaint, on each side, were as follows:

4. [Quantin 315] We complained of our burghers that they did not render full payment to us of the tenth part of their wine and grain, [as they ought]. The tenth part of other items too, such as sheep, lambs, calves, pigs—these are also called "first fruits"—they either pay to us in part only, or else they do not pay them at all.

5. The burghers replied in regard to first fruits that we demanded of them more than a tenth part. They complain, for instance, that we demand one lamb in four [*de tribus agnis quartum*] . . . , and so (*sic*) concerning the other items.

6. We complained that the burghers were withholding from us the guest-accommodation which, by ancient custom, we were in the habit of requisitioning for the hosting of all those who normally gathered at Vézelay in Easter-time and at the feast of the blessed Mary Magdalene. . . . [We claim that the] church is charged with providing [for these people who visit it and that its means are the houses of the townsmen]. [These houses, however], against our prohibition, the burghers have been hiring out to pilgrims and merchants, with the result that we have had to hire other houses with our own money.

7. The burghers replied that they were obliged to provide accommodation only for the household of the count [of Nevers], and even this they owed every fourth year only. Such a privileged status, they argued, was conceded to them by Abbot Renaud, in the presence of William, the count of Nevers.

8. We, however, required their hospitality not only for the men of the count, but for all whom it was the church's duty to look after, and as often as turned out to be necessary. This appears clearly to have been the situation under our predecessors. We denied . . . their alleged concession from our predecessor Renaud.

9. We complained also that they did not pay the proper quota of their vines to us, neither the right quantity, nor quality, nor at the correct time, even though there was a clear agreement between us that the quota should be paid before the feast of St. Martin.

10. They alleged that we would not accept their quotas, demanding instead coin, . . . in excess of the market price of wine in the town; however, they did not deny that our predecessors had acted in this way.

11. We complained also that the marks with which the coin-changers were buying and selling coin—against ancient custom—were of differing weights. This caused loud complaint against us, because it opened the way to considerable fraud.

12. There was also a dispute concerning [the grass which] belonged to the abbot. For we argued that each man possessing one or more fields [*prata*] within the territory [= *in potestate*, "in the domain, or power of"] of the church of Vézelay should yield to us one bundle of grass [*trussiam de herba*] [for our horses] so long as the field or fields could produce it, scythed or

unscythed [*sive falcata esset, sive non*], whether I was present at Vézelay or not [Quantin 316]. The burghers said, however, that I ought have just the grass, and then only when I was actually at Vézelay.

13. There was also disagreement with regard to certain fields belonging by title to the endowments of the abbot and the brothers, which are called by another name *corvate* because they are held by burghers as well as rustics.

14. The burghers also complained that when their girls took husbands, the dean and the provost demanded money from them.

15. There was also a complaint on their part about fish from the waters of Masot ... [*de piscationibus aquarum de Masot ... de parginiaco*]. The burghers said that they had the right to fish in these waters wherever and whenever they wished. We denied this and said that it was not so in the days of our predecessors.

16. A complaint was made against the bushels of [=owed to] the [seigneurial] mill [*de bussellis molendinorum*]. The burghers claimed that under our abbacy these were far greater than was customary.

17. The burghers also complained that at vintage time, the dean [*decanus*] was in the habit of sending his servants into their vineyards to pick grapes [*racemos*], against their will or without their knowledge.

18. For the termination of these complaints, as was conceded and agreed to by both parties, the lord count of Nevers [drew up the judgments of the arbitrators] which have been set down in writing. [The signatories to the judgments were as follows:] Lord Stephen, abbot of Fontenay, Hubert, a cleric of Talaie, Matthew de Chatillon, Seguin the Fat, William of Fontenay, Adam de Noyers, Geoffrey d'Asnières, Robert de Chamoux, Odo de Montreuillon. The complaints of each party, after some discussion, were resolved as follows:

Concerning the tithe it was said that the burghers and country-dwellers should give the legitimate tenth according to the custom of the universal Church and surrounding parishes. Concerning hospitality it was said that the burghers ought to host as many guests of the abbot as he had occasion to entertain at his expense, since the church has possessed this right from the time of Lord Abbot Artaud, ... year by year (? *in annum*) as two adequate [*legitimi*] men, Barbelin the forester, and William du Pont and several others were prepared to swear. But since the town was now larger than it used to be, they added that those whose guest accommodation was used one Easter, should be spared the next. They spoke similarly of the arrangements that should prevail at the Feast of the blessed Mary Magdalene. They added that the dean, or marshal, ought not spare some on account of friendship, and burden others because of hatred.

19. Concerning the vineyard quota [*de censu vinearum*], which is also called *herban*, they decreed that the whole should be paid no later than the feast of St. Martin, which is in winter; that it should be paid in good wine, or else [in coin] [Quantin 317] according to the somewhat enhanced price at which it sold in the village [of Vézelay] itself. If [the *cens*—quota or tax] was not paid by the above-mentioned date, the abbot would be able to demand a late payment penalty.

20. It was decreed that as far as the mark was concerned, no one in Vézelay should buy or sell except according to the weight of Cologne. If anyone was apprehended using any other mark-weight, [he would be] fined according to the proper and just law.

21. It was decreed that the abbot's marshal should receive from each man belonging to the power of [the church of] Vézelay, and in possession of fields or field, one truss [of grass] for the provision of the abbot's horses, whether the abbot were in Vézelay or no, so long as grass could be found in the field. He should receive nothing from the hay [*de feno vero nihil accipiet*] [belonging to each tenant].

22. With regard to [the fields—*condominia*] which are called *corvate* [and] which were in the endowment of the abbot and the monks, it was decided that they should be relinquished altogether by anyone who holds them and returned again to the abbot's estate [*mensam*] unless [it can be proven that] they hold them legitimately by concession of the abbot and of the chapter, and this they ought to ... prove [clearly], and consider their claim [lapsed] until the proof should be successful.

23. Concerning girls of marriageable age, it was decreed that, without any monetary payment, they should be allowed to take husbands, but should make sure that the abbot or his officials—in particular, the dean, or provost—should know of the arrangements, lest men from another power or another lordship [come to control land in the power of Vézelay] by cunning or stealth, and thereby create a scandal.

24. Concerning the right to fish the waters between ... and Pierre-Perthuis. It was decreed that these waterways be common to both the burghers of Vézelay and the country-dwellers—except for the whirlpools—and in these fishing places they will fish with devices of all kinds except nets. If [they should catch] a salmon, they should return it to the officers of the abbot. Other fish that they take, they should first offer to the cellarer at the same price at which they would sell to others. Concerning the extent of water known as *Vergy* [*que de virginiaco dicitur*], which Abbot Artaud bought [and which the burghers were] claiming, it was decreed that no one should fish in it without the permission of the abbot, since Bardelin the forester was prepared to swear that he had not seen it used by any of the burghers or countrymen, either in the time of Abbot Artaud, or since.

25. With regard to the bushels of the seigneurial mill [*de bussellis molendinorum*], it was resolved that the measures [in force] ... in earlier times, or ... at least in the time of Abbot Alberic, [should prevail].

26. With regard to the vineyards, it was decreed that neither the dean, nor anyone else, should be able to enter into the vineyards of the burghers to collect grapes [*pro colligendis racemis*], without their knowledge and agreement.

27. This day [sufficed for] the aforesaid complaints. For [Quantin 318] the complaints that remained to be put forward and terminated, we decided upon and specified another day for our burghers. On this day the lord count of Nevers, again, and other persons came, at our prayer and summons, and their names are as follows: Lord [Hugh], bishop [of Auxerre]; Lords Hugh, abbot of Pontigny; Stephen, abbot of Reigny; Stephen of Trois-Fontaines; Gallo of Corbigny; Godfrey, prior of Clairvaux, and several others, in whose presence the complaints were [aired].

28. We complained that while we were in expectation of making peace and concord, the burghers made a confederation and conspiracy among themselves against us and our church, and [bound] our country-dwellers from several of our villages to themselves in the conspiracy. Many of our servants and

friends caught wind of the conspiracy from clear signs and very probable indications, and they reported it to us and offered themselves as evidence to prove it. Yet the burghers, as far as they could, denied the conspiracy.

29. The burghers complained that when they died without legitimate heirs or heiresses [*sine legitimis heredibus filiorum filiarumve*], we were in the habit of resuming their possessions, movables and immovables. They complained from this that we were unwilling to recognize their brothers or sisters, or any near relatives, as heirs of their goods. To which we replied that we did not wish to concede such a practice since our predecessors had not done so and since many lords, bishops, and abbots as well as laymen have the custom that when their men die, they resume their goods. It was not good advice for us to abandon [a custom] which prevailed among our predecessors right up to our own day, a custom which is common throughout the whole of our country.

30. The burghers complained also that they were not permitted to give any of their taxable lands or vineyards to sustain the sick, who are called lepers. To this we replied that such a practice had to be prohibited in order to prevent any opportunities for alienating the possessions of the church.

31. They complained that burial was forbidden their dead, and the due rites, until the relatives and friends of the dead had made satisfaction to us. We replied, however, that we not only did not do this, but also forbad anyone else to, even if it could be established that our ancestors had done so. However, we have found it [Quantin 319] agreeable to receive something from the goods of our men when they die just as we have been in the habit of receiving portions from them while they are alive. We did not think that in this we were outraging justice.

32. A complaint was also levelled by the burghers that we have been hiring out the stalls of the money-changers and merchants more dearly than our predecessors have done. To which we replied that our predecessors were in the habit of increasing the charge for the stalls, as well as the rent for houses and whatever else was for hire, in accordance with the improvement and growth of the town. We believe that we too ought to have this right, especially since we compel no one to hire our facilities, and even the burghers themselves have been accustomed to hire out their own houses ... at increased rates, without us making an objection.

33. The burghers complained that we did not allow them to place their money chests [*archas*] and benches [*scamna*] or the like, in the streets of the town without a payment. To which we replied that the streets are the property of the church, and we think that if we hire them out the way we hire other things out, we do no one an injury.

34. They likewise complained of the tallage [*tallia*] which by custom was due annually, after Christmas, from both burghers and country-dwellers alike. They said that four representatives of the burghers and country-dwellers, chosen by these people from their own midst, should be with the dean and provost when the aforesaid tallage was made up [decided upon, i.e., in amount and incidence], that their advice ought be taken into account and that the measure exacted from each ought to consider ... the ability of each burgher or country-dweller to pay, for some should pay more than others. They said that the four chosen would serve only for a year, another four being chosen for each new year. To this we replied that such a custom did

not prevail among our predecessors ... , that the dean and provost and other officials who exercise our powers [by delegation] ought to make up the aforesaid tallage according to what seemed best to them, using discretionary moderation in the case of individuals requiring it [*mensura tamen in omnibus a discretione servata*]. Some of our servants were prepared to swear that they had not seen the matter attended to otherwise, nor heard that it had ever been handled otherwise.

35. They complained also that a greater quota [*census*, "cens"] than was customary had been imposed upon their vineyards, to which we replied that we were in the habit of receiving not more than half a pint [*sextarius*] of wine from any day-work portion [*de uno jurnali*], according to time-honored custom. The increase we imposed because of the great expansion of vineyards in the region, ... but we have never demanded more than the half pint per day work portion, as is customary.

36. They likewise complained that our dean and provost, in accordance with their own whim, and without the [Quantin 320] knowledge of the burghers, were in the habit of placing guards on the burgher's vineyards. To this we replied that here as in other areas we wished to keep to time-honored custom ... to which we replied that....

37. [They complained that] their own pastures had been taken away from them and made subject to tax [*censualia*]. To which we replied that any land which can be proved ... to have been natural pasture from of old, yet is subject to the *cens*, will be withdrawn from the *cens* if those who currently hold it for a payment [*ad censum*] agree to abandon it.

38. Likewise they complained that we had placed a guard on [*in defensum posueramus*] forests which used to be held in common by the villagers. To this we replied that our forests had been made common for them in their necessity and they had almost entirely devastated them. We placed certain common groves under guard advisedly no more for our own good than for theirs, ... and we have left them enough to manage with.

39. Likewise they complained that we had done injury to our men of St. Peter [*hominibus nostris de Sancto Petro*] and of other villages of ours and ought to render justice to these villagers through the agency of the burghers [*et volebant ut per eos ipsis rectum faceremus*]. To this we replied that if the men of our villages have a complaint against us or our officials, we shall satisfy them ourselves, since the affairs of our country-dwellers have little to do with our burghers, nor do we wish to perform anything through our burghers which does not pertain to them.

40. We on our side complained that certain of our burghers had made weights and had hired them out [for use] in the village. [These weights exceeded] the ancient and just weights [used] in our sacristy, with which, by custom, was weighed whatever in the town had to be weighed. This novelty has taken root [*inolevit*] in our day.

41. And so, with both sides of the dispute presented, Lord Hugh, bishop of Auxerre, and the abbots Lord Hugh of Pontigny, Lord Stephen of Reigny, Lord Stephen of Trois-Fontaines, and Lord Godfrey Prior of Clairvaux, together with Lord William, count of Nevers, retired to adjudicate the complaints. For both we and our burghers had firmly agreed both on our own account and on the account of our successors, to hold firm whatever these

men decided in regard to the complaints. The count, assuredly, and those named as with him [= the other judges], together with others whom they had summoned, viz. Hubert de Talaie, Hugh Viscount of Clamecy, Hugh of Pierre-Perthuis and Rainald his brother, Geoffrey of Villars, Matthew of Chatillon, William of Chastellux [Quantin 321], Artaud of Chatillon, William Marshal, Odo of Montreuillon, Robert of Chamoux, Geoffrey of Asnières, reached an accord [*laudationem*] which in this manner they reported in our hearing and that of the burghers.

42. In regard to the conspiracy against the church and the abbot imputed to the burghers, it was decreed that they should choose seven from among themselves who would swear on behalf of themselves and the others that they neither made a confederation, trust, or pact [*confederationem, fidem, sacramentum*] against the church and abbot, nor had any knowledge of same. Those chosen to swear accordingly were: Aimo, son of Aimo, money-changer; David, money-changer; Pierre Létard; Gilbert Gasteau; Durand Glayeul; Durand Aubourg [*Alburgis*]; Fulbert, mercer.

43. It was decreed concerning those who died without legitimate male or female descendants that if they were freemen, their nearest free, legitimate kinsmen could be made their heirs, provided that they wished to live permanently at Vézelay and hold and keep the custom of the town. They should not, however, enter into possession of the goods or buildings of the deceased except by the hand of the abbot or his officials [i.e., by accepting the lordship of the abbot of Vézelay]. If they did not wish to abide by these conditions, they would be deprived of the inheritance, which would go instead to the church. It was decreed concerning things belonging to the men of the church, if they should die without legitimate sons or daughters, that they should remain in the possession and power of the abbot [*in manu et potestate abbatis*]. And if any man of the church [*homo ecclesie*] having sons or daughters comes to live separately from them during his own life, and retains for himself a portion of the inheritance, and then dies, what he appeared to possess on the day of his death shall remain in the rightful possession of the abbot and church.

44. It was likewise decreed that freemen can dispose of their goods, movable and immovable, as it suits them, to lepers, saving in everything the customs of the abbot and church. Lepers, however, cannot sell or pledge to men of another power any lands or buildings left to them. This clause arises from the fact that lepers and their church belong properly to the church of Vézelay. They can leave nothing at all, in fact, of their buildings, to other churches. Men of the church, indeed, without the consent of the abbot cannot leave land, vineyard, or any building to the aforesaid sick people [lepers], or any others, but they are not prevented from giving from their movable possessions as alms.

45. Likewise concerning the burial and last rites of the dead, it was decreed that these should be performed for them without monetary exaction.

46. Similarly concerning the stalls of the money-changers [Berlow: "tables of the money-dealers"] it was decreed that the abbot was quite free to increase the charge for them and to multiply them as [Quantin 322] he saw fit, since they were unequivocally the property of the church [*liberrima et propria ecclesie edificia*].

47. Similarly concerning the streets of the town it was decreed that no one

was allowed to place there money chests [*archas*, Berlow "booths"], benches and the like, without the permission of the abbot or his officials, since the streets belonged to the church.

48. Similarly concerning the guards placed on the vineyards, it was decreed that they should be chosen by the burghers, presented to the dean and the provost, made to swear fidelity to them, and then placed over the vineyards. For each guard, it was decreed that the dean receive 12 *denarii*. Likewise concerning the guards of the wine-presses [*torcularium*], it was decreed that, as was recognized by either party, the guards should exact one pint of wine from the filtering-bag for the abbot, and one *denarius* for themselves. If indeed they demand more, and a clamor should reach the ears of the abbot, the latter would do justice.

49. Likewise concerning pastures, it was decreed that the pastures which under oath and threat of excommunication could be shown to have been natural and common in former times, and which are now taxable [*in adcensum sunt*], should have their *cens* removed by the abbot and whoever holds them for payment [*ad censum*] should abandon them and they should revert to common usage.

50. Likewise concerning woods it was decreed that those woods could be placed under guard by the abbot [*abbatem posse in defensionem ponere*] which by common agreement had been forbidden to the locals [*in defensione*] from antiquity, before the burning of the town which happened in the time of Abbot Alberic; those which were then common, should remain so.

51. Likewise, concerning the men of St. Peter [St. Père-sous-Vézelay] and other villages of the abbot, it was decreed that the latter did the burghers no harm if he made no reply to them concerning the justice he would do concerning his country-dwellers, since the affairs of the abbot's countrydwellers [did not pertain] to the burghers ... [at this point, after a small break, appears a sentence which seems to deal with the sale of wine—*vini qua panni mensurant*—in the village].

52. Likewise concerning the making up of the tallage [*de facienda tallia*] on the burghers and country-dwellers, it was decreed that the abbot is empowered to make it up [*facere posse*] lawfully through the dean and provost and through his other officers, without the advice and presence of the burghers, since this was the custom in former times, nor could it be proved that any other method had ever been adopted. The tallage, it was decreed, would be levied against the burghers and country-dwellers who owned their own homes, and also against those who rented the homes of others—regardless of the ownership of the homes—when they have been in the town a year. The latter will also pay all other customary [tallages] of the town.

53. Likewise concerning the *cens* on vineyards [or vineyard quota], it was decreed that since both parties recognized that a half a pint of good wine should be paid [for each vineyard], per day work portion [*de jurnali vinee*], the abbot ought not to demand more than this. If any of the burghers, however, could prove that in former times his vineyard or vines were assessed at a lower rate by those whose duty it was, they should remain in the lower assessment; it shall remain so in the future, unless the vineyard is expanded, for the *cens* should be [Quantin 323] increased to cover what was planted after the original assessment was made.

54. Likewise, concerning the thirds, which are also called *champarts* [*campartes*], it was decreed that those who should pay them may not separate their harvests into three until they have summoned the officers whose duty it is to collect the thirds. But if the officers cannot manage to be present, after they have been notified, according to the custom, those who owe thirds should call someone from among their immediate neighbors [*de legitimis vicinis*], in whose presence as a witness they should legitimately make the division and carry the thirds into the granary.

55. Likewise, concerning the abbot's ban, it was decreed that the abbot could impose his ban once a year, for a full month of his choice, except for the eight days [Berlow: "the week"] before and after the three feasts of Easter, Pentecost, and of the Holy Mary Magdalene, as the burghers themselves bore witness [*quod et ipsi burgenses testificati sunt*]. If indeed the abbot could show through legitimate proof that he had a claim to a larger period in which to impose his ban he should be allowed only such extension of time as he could legitimately prove his claim to.

56. Likewise, concerning the weights and measures it was decreed that those who wished to possess them and to lend them without payment of a fee should have only weights in accordance with the antique and just weights of the sacristy. But if in any urgent situation it should be found necessary to hire them out [for payment], only the abbot can do so.

57. This accord [*laudatio*] was drawn up at Vézelay by the venerable persons hitherto named, ... and publicly read in the year of the incarnation of the Lord 1137 when Louis was king of the Franks.

[Copy drawn from a register belonging to M. Haran, mayor of Vézelay, containing the inventory of the entitlements [*titres*] of the abbey of Vézelay, drawn up in 1770, p. 183, after the original—Annuaire de l'Yonne, an 1845 p. 56—cf. Chérest 1.106, and Bastard 347.[2]]

Notes on the Vézelay Accord of 1137 AD

The notes are presented in accordance with the section numbers into which the *Accord* itself has been divided.

1. Quantin 314.

3. There is a gap in the text after Geoffrey, prior of Clairvaux.

4. "First Fruits": *primitiae*. Quantin 315.

5. *Decimae* (tenths) *et primitiae*: Chérest 1.93 describes these as, in effect, a land tax originating in a voluntary contribution payable by the faithful to the Church, to help with the expenses of worship: "alone at Vézelay they attained exorbitant proportions, absorbing one quarter of the produce." The tithe was a payment due the church, whereas the *cens* represented a payment to the feudal or seigneurial lord. The abbot of Vézelay, being both head of the church and seigneurial lord of the surrounding region, exacted both kinds of taxes (Chérest 1.93n.2). The charitable application of tithes in the early middle ages has been studied by Ullmann (1971: 1–39). On the absence of grain taxes and wine dues at Lorris see the Lorris *charter* §2; cf. also Bachrach (1988: 6ff.).

6. "requisitioning": *saisire.* "We claim that . . . pilgrims and merchants": the Latin, which is lacunose, reads: *Ecclesia de suo erat procurata . . . contra prohibitionem nostram, peregrinis locabant et mercatoribus; quapropter sepius cogebamur pecunia nostra abbas domos conducere. . . .* Berlow translates: "the church has sheltered its own. Against our prohibition they rented to pilgrims as well as merchants. Therefore we were often obliged to rent other houses with our money."

7. Rainald (Renaud, Raynald) of Semur was abbot of Vézelay 1106–1125 AD. See Chérest 1.285ff. (Huygens [1976: 144ff.]).

9. *Cens:* "quotas," a land-tax ("impot-foncier"); see *Cambridge Economic History of Europe* 1.435, and notes to §5 above; also Bachrach (1988: 5ff).

11. Chérest (1.75) stresses the importance of the money-changers [*nummularii*] at Véze-lay: "in the twelfth century, each province, each town, had its own coined money; . . . in the transactions between people of different territories, the mediation of a changer was almost always indispensable. But nowhere were their activities on such a scale as at Véze-lay, where they made speculative gains from the pilgrims as well as from the merchants." Money-changing was a great source of urban wealth at Vézelay: Chérest quotes the instance of Simon of Souvigny, who grew to great wealth as a *nummularius* in the space of ten years. On Simon see Berlow (1987: 153n.16). Later in this document some of the representatives of the burghers called upon to take an oath that no conspiracy had been entered into against the abbot were money-changers (§42 below). On the significance of the *monetarii* in the urban revolution of this period see Hibbert (1953), and Lopez (1953). See Berlow (1971: 299ff.).

12. What concession do the burghers ask for? That the abbot have the grass, but *not* trussed or delivered? Not scythed? Or were the abbot's horses simply to graze on the grass? Quantin 316.

13. This is Berlow's translation. The Latin reads: *fuit etiam querela de quibus condominiis ad mensas abbatis et fratrum proprie pertinentibus, que alio nomine corvate vocantur, quod ea tam burgenses quam rustici tenebant.* Berlow comments: "*Corvate* was also used for fields and still is on detailed maps. For instance the map of the region of the 'Ministère des travaux pub-lics et des transports' labels one area along the Cure north of Asquins simply as 'les Corvées.' The *mensa abbatis* was a fund, distinct from other endowments administered by the establishment." On the meaning of the word *corvée* see Bloch in *Cambridge Economic History of Europe* 1.288.

14. The provost, according to Vogade—editor of the Guizot translation (1969)—was the abbot's deputy, and the dean the provost's second.

15. On the ingrained respect for custom evident on every page of this document see Bloch (1961: 115 and chap. 8), and *Cambridge Economic History of Europe* 1.253.

16. During the course of the 1152–1155 revolution the abbot locked the burghers out of his ovens and mills, to their great confusion. It seems, from Hugh of Poitiers' descrip-tion (at the close of Book 3 of the *Major Chronicle* above) of the abbot's revenge on the rev-olutionaries that private wine-presses had been set up in the cellars of houses belonging to the burghers (cf. Graham [1918: 127]) doubtless to evade yet another seigneurial monopo-ly. On the seigneurial or "banal" rights of mill, oven, and wine-press, see Bloch *Cambridge Economic History of Europe* 1.262.

18. The marshal's duties concerned the care and maintenance of the abbot's stable: see below §21. On Robert of the Fields (*de Campis*) see above *Major Chronicle* 3: 221nn.2, 5 and Berlow (1987: 160n.105).

19. The Latin for the sentence beginning "that it should be paid in good wine . . ." is: *totus persolvatur, et de legitimo vino sive vini* (Quantin 317) *precium secundum quod carius vinum in villa vendetur.* Berlow translates "and with legitimate wine or the price of wine according to the most expensive wine sold in the town."

22. The translation—except for the last two lines (which are meaningless in the Latin)—is by Berlow. See the Lorris charter §15.

23. A sensitive issue: in a society where tenure was based upon custom, the marriage of two persons from different lordships meant the *practical* (though not, presumably, *theoretical*) union of their landed inheritances; where the wife brought land to a husband of another "poté" the land would, for all intents and purposes, be lost to the original lord and his tenants, unless due note was kept of the husband, so that dues and taxes based on the land could be exacted (tenure of the land was always customary, not absolute); even then time and descent might well blur the original ownership of the land. Presumably, lords tried to keep marriages within their own "poté." Berlow translates: "With regard to the marriage of girls, it was decided that they might accept husbands without an exaction of money, with, however, the knowledge of the abbot or his ministers, namely the *decanus* and the *prepositus* lest men of another domain or another lordship by fraud or stealth ... often cause scandals." Her comment is: "I think what the abbot is getting at is the publicity of marriage, which was a general concern of the church around this time. He seems to be doing everything in his power to extend his control over the subjects in the area rather than discouraging it." See Brand and Searle *et al.* (1983: 123ff.)–and Searle's original article (1979: 3–43). Brand *et al.* write (1983: 30) "marriage to someone outside the lordship was particularly dangerous for a lord ... the worst case was a female villein who married out and went to live (and work and breed) on her husband's holding..."; cf. too 123 on complications ensuing if the girl by "accidents of family history" were an heiress to the lands of a peasant family. For other problems see 139ff., and for specific discussion of the Vézelay Accord §23, see 154, citing Petot (1949: 201, 207). Searle cites a charter from the first quarter of the twelfth century, from the abbey of St. Père de Chartres, concerning an unlicensed marriage between a serf of the abbot and a man from another jurisdiction: what concerns the abbot is his potential loss of control over land (from his *potestas*) which the girl's father gave the couple as a dowry: "It was not the labor and the breeding capacity of Salomon's daughter that concerned the abbot. It was her father's attempt to endow her with land ultimately his lord's and to choose the lord's tenant without consultation" (155, and cf. 159). See Southern (1953: 102), Jordan (1986: 22ff.), Bloch (1961: 263), Haverkamp (1988: 205), below Appendix F §10, and Bachrach (1990: 94ff.).

24. Vergigny, Vargigny, *Varginiacum* to be distinguished from *Vergiacum, Vergeiacum, Virgiacum*, etc. (= Vergy): Huygens (1976: 679), Berlow (1971: 80–81, 110), *Major Chronicle* above 2 §5: 162n.4. See too, below 362.

29. The abbot's point is clear: customary tenants had no *right* to inherit land: the land belonged to the seigneurial lord, and might easily be resumed on the death of the tenant, especially if he died without clear heirs/heiresses. Lords were keen to prevent the breaking up of their tenant farms, either by partible inheritance, sale, or the endowment of daughters: see Duby (1968: 239–40), etc., and Bloch (1966: 71) (on the tendency for all tenures to become hereditary). See Haverkamp (1988: 205).

30. Cf. §44 and on lepers Moore (1987: 45ff.), etc.

34. On the *taille* or tallage (from a French word meaning to "cut," referring to the method of assessment of the tax, a lump sum being fixed upon, and then apportioned, or "cut up" into contributions by household or hearth), see Stephenson ([1954] 1967: 41–103). See also the Lorris charter §9.

35. *de uno jurnali*. Guizot translates "par journal." Latham (1965) cites 13c "measure of land, day-work" (see under *diurn-*). Niermeyer (1976: 345), under *diurnalis*, has "a land measure, the surface ploughed in one day." Bastard translates "par journal de terre" (1851: 348). Duby (1968: 117) says that in twelfth-century Lorraine the basis of rents was the *quartier* (originally, perhaps, quarter of a *mansus*)–about 15–16 day works (*journaux*), i.e., about 7–10 acres. Clearly the vineyards around Vézelay were also divided into day work portions, representing, perhaps, the area that could be picked in a day's work.

37. The Latin reads: ... *ad hoc respondimus ... pascua ablata sunt eis et censualia facta. Ad hoc respondimus quod illa pascua que possunt probari ... antiquitus naturalia pascue fuisse que adcensata sint, si ipsi qui ea ad censum tenent relinquerent et nos quoque censum eorum relinquemus.* ...

38. The "necessity" was the great fire in the town of Vézelay sometime between 1131 and 1138. (See Berlow [1971: 160ff.] for an earlier such fire.) The Latin for the last line is: *... tamen relictis adversum eos que sufficere possent.*

39. Chérest 1.111 and Bastard (1851: 351) take "St. Peter" to refer to the village of St. Père-sous-Vézelay, easily visible from the abbey of the Magdalene itself. Chérest writes: "without doubt the burghers hoped that an occasion in which they were authorized to examine the complaints of the suburban population would soon be followed by efficacious judicial guarantees for themselves." Bastard (1851: 351) notes that the 1137 document makes no mention of the means by which the burghers received justice: the only reference in this context is to the *rustici*, the men of the abbey who lived on its outlying properties. He says one could infer that if the burghers were seeking jurisdiction over the villagers of St. Père, they must have possessed jurisdiction over themselves, via elected magistrates. But the silence of the present document about any such magistrates suggests that the abbot possessed unmitigated justice in Vézelay. Contrast Lorris charter §31.

40. Bloch (1961: 215): "at the market of Auxerre the 'weight,' a monopoly of the count, was 'liege of the count' "—i.e., at his absolute disposal.

41. On pro-burgher elements in this panel, and on the overall inclination of the arbitrators, see Chérest 1.106–7. If *Gaufridum Clarevallensem* of §3 above and *Gaudefridus, prior Clarevallensis* are the same, then the translation of the proper names should be emended accordingly. Guizot translates "Godefroi abbé de Claireveaux" and "Godefroy prieur de Clairvaux," respectively. Quantin 321.

42. On the names in this section see above *Major Chronicle* 3: 220n.3, and Berlow (1987) who refers to "Durand the Innkeeper" and "Gilbert the Pastry-Chef."

43. "rightful possession (of the abbot and church)": the words used are *ius* and *potestas*; Berlow "in the jurisdiction and power." Was it customary for the enlarged family to remain together on the ancestral estates, at Vézelay? Chérest 1.91 comments on the distinction offered here between men (or serfs) of the church, and free men: "the latter class comprises in great part foreigners who had brought into the district an industry or useful profession which the abbey wished to retain by conceding them privileges more apparent than real. This group also included some locals who had acquired the same advantages. The mass of local inhabitants of Vézelay—once serfs of the monastery and still, on occasions referred to by this pejorative term—formed the first group. It is not that in the twelfth century any great divide separated the condition of the two classes. Except for some points of secondary importance they enjoyed the same civil rights and exercised them in the same manner. Indeed, representatives from both groups appear among the abbot's officials—Eudes, provost of Vézelay at the end of the eleventh century and father of Simon who murdered Abbot Artaud, was a *servus ecclesie*." There appear to have been no recognized distinctions in force among the *oppidani* or *burgenses* themselves. Free and unfree alike shared common goals. The few references to differences between the two groups in this charter are the only indications of differences between them that we possess (Chérest 1.111). See also Bloch in *Cambridge Economic History of Europe* 1.241ff. On §§43–44 contrast the Lorris charter §§17–18. For a different view see Berlow (1980: 137).

48. See note on §16 above. The Latin of the passage "the guards should exact one pint ..." is: *unum sextarium vini de sacco abbati custodes torcularium exigant et sibimet unum denarium.* Berlow translates "the guards of the wine press might demand one pint of ordinary wine for the abbot and one *denarius* for themselves."

49. See also §37. Presumably, the complaint is that "common," pasture or meadow, land had come on occasions to be turned into farms or farmland held in dependent tenure upon payment to the Church, like other arable land. The church owned the meadow land as much as it did any other land in its *potestas*, and may have sought to increase its revenues by reducing the amount of land held "common" as meadow, but the villagers had a clearly established customary right to such land: it ought to remain by custom without a tenant, at the disposal of the herds of the villagers. The remedy offered by the abbot is

that any such engrossed land will be returned to meadow, so long as the dependent tenant will agree to abandon it for meadow. It is also possible that the engrossment had been carried out by grasping villagers, without the knowledge of the church.

53. *Census de jurnali vinee*: Chérest (1.93) explains that this tax was analogous to the *champart* (§54 below): it concerned vineyards originally belonging to the monks and later alienated only at the price of a large share of the harvest (large abbeys frequently set aside certain estates, lands, vineyards, etc., for the particular sustenance of the convent, chapter, monks, as distinct from the abbot himself). The Latin of the last sentence is: *quia secundum incrementum earum* (Quantin 323) *quod post supradictum adcensationem factum est, augmentari debet et census*. Berlow translates: "And it should remain thus hereafter unless it is increased, because the census should also be increased according to their increments which have been made after the aforesaid assessment."

54. "Tierce ou Champart": a tax of one third of the harvest, determined while the crop is still *in situ*. The aim of this paragraph is to prevent fraud: "thirding" the crop only *after* a proportion has already been deducted from it by the tenant.

55. Vogade supposes that this paragraph refers to the "wine-ban" whereby for a certain period in each year only the lord was able to sell his wine, all private sale being banned. This took the form of a convenient monopoly allowing the lord to get rid of his surplus first, at favorable prices. On this and other "banalités" cf. Witt (1971: 975–76). Note also §10 of the charter of Lorris.

56. The significance of *prestare* and *locare* in this paragraph was pointed out to us by a colleague Dr. J. H. Pryor.

Appendix C

The Letter of Herbert of Bosham to the Abbot of Vézelay in Regard to the Heretics Known As the *Publicani*

[Herbert's[1] letter to William,[2] abbot of Vézelay, who had consulted him about certain heretics, commonly called *Dageneis* or *Deonae*, who had been seized in the town—see above *Major Chronicle* 4 §78.]

We received your letter of charity with joy. Now as to that matter about which you sought advice: would that there might be as much discernment [*discretionis*] as charity [in what I say] so that I might give my dearest brother valuable advice. Your pious gentleness has charged us [to say] what should be done about those heretics, called by you *Deonae*, who have been seized and

---

[1] Herbert of Bosham was in France as part of Thomas à Becket's party in exile. See Smalley (1973: 59–86). Commenting on this letter, Smalley says that Herbert "anticipated what would become standard practice in his advice" (69). There is only one MS of Herbert's letters (Cambridge, Corpus Christi College MS.123; see Duggan [1980: 201]). The text printed in *PL* 190.1462–63, from Giles, is probably corrupt in places. In addition, Herbert seems to feel obliged to present in his letter appropriately polemical and allegorical credentials; much of the obscurity of the letter derives from his affectation of the polemical discourse of the clergy against deviance. See Peters (1978: chap. 2), Ward (1988: 75ff.).

[2] William of Mello, abbot of Vézelay 1161–1171

openly convicted. We have consulted divine law about it but have not been able to find any punishment clearly recorded in written law for heretics of just this kind.

However, some progeny of the hateful power [i.e., the devil] have recently appeared and abuse Christ wherever they lurk[1] and infect whom they can with their hidden blemish [*labe occulta*]—for they are a pestilence walking in the darkness.[2] Truly, all the followers of this chieftain [*totum huius capitis corpus*] although their faces are diverse, do not differ in the effects they produce.[3] With the corrupting fire which follows close behind all of them they burn the harvests of strangers. Now since they are one in their vanity, their punishment will not be dissimilar. The inseparable members of a mob are all equally at fault and deserve equal punishment. Therefore justice demands that because the usual canonical punishment has been pronounced against some of them, a similar rigor of the law ought to be exercised against these ones too. About the punishment of heretics, Pope Liberius, speaking without making any distinctions [*indistincte*], says: "Those who, against the peace of the Church ... etc if they possess any dignity or the belt of knighthood [*militiae*], let it be taken from them; if they are private citizens [*privati*], let the nobles suffer the proscription of their possessions, and let the ignoble not only be flogged but be punished by perpetual exile."[4]

There are also many other legal chains by which mad beasts of this kind can be constrained so that their deceit, spurred on by loss of possessions or exile, is not published, to cause harm over land and sea. It is best to hold a deceitful serpent on a hook so that he can not escape. Those about whom you asked, devious mockers of the truth [*angulosi veritatis exsufflatores*], who

---

[1] The printed text reads *in angelis* ["among the angels"] but this seems unlikely. More likely is either *in Anglis* or *in angulis*; "among the English" would not be implausible for an Englishman [Herbert was born in Sussex], and this coheres with the reference in the next sentence to "the harvests of strangers" [i.e., the heretics are newcomers in each district]; William of Newburgh also reports on the appearance in England during the early 1160s of "certain erring folk of the sect commonly thought to be Publicans," and Wakefield and Evans (1969) print their translation of William's passage (no. 40, p. 245) next to the passage from the Vézelay *Chronicle* in which the reference to the *Publicani* [whose advent there prompted the original letter to which the present one is a reply] appears. One might not, however, expect an Englishman [Giles, whose edition of Herbert's letters is reprinted in the *PL* volume] to misread a reference to England. We have, therefore, read *in angulis* ["in the corners," or "wherever they lurk"] because it may have suggested to Herbert the phrase *angulosi exsufflatores* ["devious mockers"] that he uses later on. Moreover, it fits the general picture that Herbert tries to convey of the heretics as skulking in the shadows.

[2] *negotium enim in tenebris perambulans est*: see Psalm 82:5: *nescierunt, neque intellexerunt, in tenebris ambulant* ["they know not, neither will they understand: they walk in darkness"], and Psalm 91:5–6: ... *non timebis* ... *e negotio perambulante in tenebris* ["you will not be afraid ... for the pestilence that walketh in darkness"].

[3] *etsi diversae facies, in posterioribus tamen non discrepat*. A pun: *in posterioribus*—"in what comes after them," i.e., "their effects" or "their posteriors"; cf. also *Major Chronicle* above 4 at 288n.2. For the imagery of the serpent with its dangerous tail, see Revelations 9.

[4] This quotation was well known; it is found in the Pseudo-Isidore collection, in the collection of the eleventh-century canonist Cardinal Deusedit (book 3, chap. 45) and in Gratian 9.xxiv, *quaest*. 1, chap. 32 (*PL* 187.1280–81).

disturb the peace of the body of the Church with their hissing and stinging, expose any part of themselves to possible cuts or injury just to protect their head. Indeed they have already exposed themselves to the proscription of their possessions, not considering this a loss, but rather rejoicing—in the manner of the apostles, although not with apostolic joy—in this at least, that that part of their body that held their poisonous tongues was free from danger.

By what chains ought they be bound? How ought those serpents be crushed so that they do not infect the temperate air of our faith with their pestiferous breath? What law is available? They are destitute and can not be despoiled. Moreover the Church does not have a prison for exiles, since this whole world is a prison for the body of Christ, which is still in exile. Islands of exile are for Augustus, not for the one who has been crucified. Again, if we were to seek the judgement of the Old Law, justice would not be served [*jus questionem non haberet*], for its voice cries out for the sword. It is the same thing if one considers Roman law, which will not help, for it proposes the ultimate penalty.

But we who have cast out the old ways for the new that supersede them and for whom there is a new king and a new law, are prohibited from gathering the tares lest with them we should root out the wheat too.[1] So we will direct the stings of a new law against these recent serpents, since we who dispense the sacraments of the gentle and mild Lord of death are not allowed to be involved in a judgement of blood nor are ourselves permitted to inflict or order to be inflicted on any person at all the lopping off of their limbs, especially since in the new law of which we are the ministers, a new spiritual judgement has succeeded the old way of punishing the body. An exception is that a certain moderate bodily coercion has been entrusted to us, so moderate that it can not be called revenge for a crime but only the discipline of a master: that is the castigation of the body with lashes alone, which is quite different from [the infliction] of death or the lopping off of a limb.

Therefore, because there is no other way in which those [heretics about which you enquire] can be punished, probably all that is left is that they should be treated as though they were notorious as open murderers [*ut velut infames caedibus publicis deputentur*].[2] Since you claim that you have secular jurisdiction [*saecularem jurisdictionem*] in your town, I do not think that you will overturn the right order of the law [*juris ordinem convertere*] if you hand over the said people to your defender [*vestro defensori*][3]—I do not say that he

---

[1] See Matthew 13:29: "But he said, Nay: lest while ye gather up the tares ye root up also the wheat with them." The same allusion is made with the same purpose by Wazo, bishop of Liège, in a letter to Roger, bishop of Chalons-sur-Marne, about heretics with whom the latter was uncertain how to deal. Wazo's letter is translated in Moore (1975: 22–24).

[2] The *ut* clause could mean that the abbot ought to hand them over to be killed by the public authorities, but this would be inconsistent with the tenor of the rest of the letter.

[3] This is presumably a reference to the count of Nevers, who was acknowledged by the monks as their defender [*defensor*], although the abbot himself would not even admit this much. Apparently the abbot had explained to Herbert that he did have control of the secular affairs of the town, a claim which, as we know, he maintained persistently throughout the period of the *Major Chronicle*.

should inflict bodily harm on them but that he should have them heard before him and impose an end to the case that is consistent with his own human laws.

Best of all, it seems to me more judicious that they be conducted under appropriate guard to the most merciful and most Christian leader, the king of the Franks, especially if they have remained obdurate in their error. He who is by common law [*de communi jure*] the defender of all the churches of the kingdom ought to be by right their highest and chief guardian too—this, I believe, you do not deny. Lest I seem to assert what I am saying on my own [authority], let us hear what pope Pelagius wrote to the patrician Narses:[1] "Do not hesitate," he says "to repress men of this kind on your authority as ruler, because the Rules of the Fathers [*Regulae Patrum*] lay down especially that if any person holding ecclesiastical office has resisted anyone to whom he is subject or has gathered together a separate flock [*seorsum collegerit*] or has erected another altar or has perpetrated a schism, let him be excommunicated and damned. But if by chance he makes light of this and perseveres by maintaining his divisions and schisms, let him be subdued by the public power." These are the words of our father of holy memory, Pelagius.

Therefore if [such] ecclesiastics [*ecclesiasticae*] remain obdurate in their error they must be resolutely subdued and despoiled [of their goods] by the public power. May the angel of great counsel be with you so that you understand what is right and act in accordance with it.

Appendix D

The Little Book of Vézelay about the Relics and Translation of the Blessed Mary Magdalene

with a supplementary essay on "Cluny, Vézelay and the Magdalene Cult in the 11th and Early 12th Centuries," by E. L. Cox.

[Saxer, (1975) p.v writes: "when (in order to promote the cult of the Magdalene at Vézelay) the monks of Vézelay proceeded in 1265 and 1267 to the verification and transfer (to a new reliquary) of the relics of their patron saint (Mary Magdalene), they set up and prepared a certain number of official documents relating to these events. To these they added some pieces which had been in circulation in the West for two centuries already, on the subject of the translation of the (relics of) the Magdalene in Carolingian times. The putting together of these two classes of document represents the origin of what we call the *Vézelay Dossier* on the invention and translation of the relics of St. Mary Magdalene in 1265–67." King Louis IX of France, an ardent devotee of the cult of the Magdalene at Vézelay, was invited to the abbey in

---

[1] This letter is not found in Gratian, Deusedit, or Pseudo-Isidore. The pope's letter is printed in *PL* 69.595–96.

1267 to preside over the solemnities associated with the transfer of the relics of the saint from the copper box in which they had been found resting, to a new reliquary (Saxer 103, 206). Sections of the Dossier *not* translated below are: no. 3 (not published by Saxer in view of its length and his intention to publish it elsewhere), a homily on the Gospel text *Maria stabat ad monumentum*; no. 4 (Saxer 242–43), telling of a miracle wrought by the Magdalene; no. 5 (Saxer 244–52) detailing the service to commemorate the translation of the relics of Mary Magdalene which is celebrated on the 19th of March, and an antiphon on the psalms sung at Vespers on the vigil of the same commemoration; no. 6 (Saxer 253–54), being proof of the preceding details regarding Badilo, and of all other tellings of these events; no. 7 (Saxer 254–57), being papal letters/privileges supporting the foregoing narrative; nos. 8 and 9 (Saxer 258–68), being chronicle and other extracts supporting the narrative, together with episcopal, royal, and legatine letters relating to the ceremonies of 1267 and the antecedent circumstances of 1265 (Saxer 98). The passages translated below will be found on pp. 233–41 of Saxer and form §§1 [*Nativitas* ...] and 2 [*Incipit legenda* ...] of the *Dossier: Libellus Vizeliacensis de reliquiis et translatione Beate Marie Magdalene.*] See too below 367–68.

1.

The birth, origin and family of the glorious Mary Magdalene and her sister Martha and Lazarus

The most blessed Mary Magdalene was born to a family which was, judged by worldly pride, very famous, descending from a line of kings. Her father was called Syrus and her mother named Eucharia and her siblings were Lazarus and Martha. Rule of the greater part of Jerusalem, all of Bethany and the castle of Magdala, whence her surname Magdalene, is known to have pertained to her family.[1]

But as pleasure sometimes closely accompanies such affluence of possessions as she had, she made sure that she spent the years of her adolescence without being restrained by the curb of modesty. At length, however, defiled as she was with the stain of all her sins, she was inspired by the Holy Spirit to hasten to the house of Simon the leper to be bathed in the fountain of mercy, our Lord Jesus Christ, and to offer up the tears of her confession and the perfume of her holy devotion, as Luke the evangelist recounts.[2] And because of her great love she obtained remission of her many sins, as the Lord testifies.

Afterwards, because of the dedication of her devotion, she became such an intimate of Jesus Christ that when she was seated at his feet listening intently

---

[1] For an analysis of the myth that developed about the Magdalene see Saxer (1975) and Benedicta Ward, *Harlots of the Desert: A Study of Repentance in Early Monastic Sources*, (Kalamazoo: Cistercian Publications, 1987), 10–25. See Solt (1987: 175, 211n. 23). The principal relevant biblical passages upon which the medieval figure of Mary Magdalene was based are: Mat. 26:6–13, 27:56, 61, 28:1–10; Mark 14:3–9, 15:40, 47, 16:1–11; Luke 7:36–50, 8:2, 23:55–56, 24:1–11, 22; John 12:2–8, 19:25, 20:1, 11–18. See also *NCE*, s.v. "Mary Magdalene," and, for the twelfth century, Mycoff.

[2] Luke 7:37.

to his words, he deigned to be a gentle advocate for and sufficient defender of her against her sister, who was complaining that Mary did not assist her in serving him, and against Judas, who was muttering about the pouring of pure nard over his head.[1]

Indeed, she was so afire with the ardor of her love that she did not desert the Lord Jesus when he was in the hands of his persecutors and his disciples had withdrawn, but stayed faithfully with him up to his death on the cross and his deposition in his tomb.[2]

Because she persevered continually in her devotion and searched carefully for the Lord around his tomb, her love received a most joyful reward from him when she was the first mortal to see that very author of life rise from the dead and to announce to the apostles that he had overcome death and lived again.[3]

It is enough to have touched briefly on the events of her early life, by following the account of the evangelists.

Although most people will readily have on hand a fuller account, set out in a more leisurely style, of how that same blessed Mary Magdalene, with Saints Maximin, Lazarus, and Martha, as ordained by the divine clemency, crossed the sea and came into the region of Aix in the kingdom of Provence—it is set out in the life of that bishop[4] [Maximin]—I have labored to produce this account, brief as befits my insignificance, so that if nothing more substantial comes to their notice, those who are seeking an investigation of the truth may at least be pleased to learn this much.

2.

Here begins the legend of the translation of the glorious Mary Magdalene; that is, how her most sacred body was translated to the monastery of Vézelay in Burgundy, in the diocese of Autun by the blessed Badilo, in the time of Gerard of Roussillon, count of Provence and Burgundy. This translation is devoutly and solemnly celebrated every year on 19 March. The account [Historia].

Since it has pleased the divine mercy that the western shores should be illuminated by the presence of the body of the blessed Mary Magdalene, let me begin to set out, under the guidance of our Lord and Saviour, how the most holy remains [gleba] of that lover of God were translated by religious men from the territory of Aix in Provence to that place where today they are venerated by the pious devotion of the faithful.

Round about the 749th year after the passion or resurrection of the Lord, when Louis, the most pious of kings, and his son Charles were ruling, peace

---

[1] The medieval tradition conflated the various Mary's in the New Testament and created from them the Magdalene. For these two separate incidents see John 12:3 and Luke 10:40–42.

[2] Matthew 28:56–66.

[3] John 20:1–17.

[4] Nothing is known of this *Life*. Saxer (1975) regards it as an invention of the author: "un pur produit de son imagination" (19).

flourished and the church of Christ grew throughout the whole world, except for some attacks by Saracens, coming mainly from Spain.[1] At that time Gerard, the most outstanding of counts in nobility, arms, and the abundance of his wealth, and the nearest in blood to the aforesaid kings, possessed by hereditary right the greater part of Burgundy. His wife, Bertha by name, was not unequal to him in birth and was very distinguished in her way of life. Because they lacked offspring of either sex, they generously began to hand over their own possessions to those who were God-fearing and were paupers in His name. Hence with the highest devotion they handed over their entire patrimony and possessions for the construction of houses and churches for the omnipotent God, following the very sound advice that they should choose Christ as their heir in place of carnal offspring. Building therefore very many churches and monasteries on their substantial estates, where at the time there were none, they established a large number of servants of God in them, endowing them out of their own possessions so that they could live according to the Rule [*regulariter*] and without enduring penury.

At about the same time John,[2] the Roman pope, came into Gaul at the invitation of the king of the Franks and that same count Gerard. Among other distinguished deeds that he performed, [the pope], at the request of the count, consecrated, in honor of God and his mother Mary and the holy apostles Peter and Paul, the monasteries that Gerard had built. On his return to Rome the pope, out of his love for the aforesaid count, sent back to the places which he had consecrated the relics of many saints.

As time passed and the health of the kings of the Franks began to fail, barbarians, coming from lands across the seas, began to wreak terrible destruction throughout all the provinces of the Gauls, killing people, stealing their possessions, and burning their houses. Churches and monasteries were also consumed by fire and destroyed. Among these the monastery of Vézelay too, which, along with others of which we spoke before, had been built a little earlier by Count Gerard near the river Cure, was razed to the ground. As a result, to strengthen its defenses it was rebuilt by that same Gerard most conveniently on a small hill that arose nearby.[3] This concurred most honorably with the name of the place, for it is called *Vizeliacus*, as though from there those looking around can see the majestic horizons of heaven. Or perhaps *Vizeliacus* could be understood [as meaning] that the richest side of heaven may be seen from there.[4] When it was rebuilt in honor of Mary, the mother of God, and the holy apostles Peter and Paul, as it had been before, it shone out brightly with innumerable signs and miracles, the work of God.

At almost the same time it happened that the Saracens from Spain laid waste and almost destroyed Aquitaine and the greater part of Provence. They attacked and captured the metropolitan city of Aix, leading away a large

---

[1] The writer's knowledge of Carolingian history is very hazy. The attacks by the Saracens occurred rather earlier in the eighth century than he allows, whereas Louis the Pious and Charles the Bald ruled in the ninth century.

[2] John VIII (872–882), who crowned Charles the Bald as emperor.

[3] In fact, Gerard was dead by the time that the monastery was rebuilt.

[4] The rationale behind these suggested interpretations is not clear.

number of people as captives and burning the rest or putting them to the sword. They skinned alive very many men and women, as the Saracens are accustomed to do to people of our race, something I myself actually saw at a later time. After they had perpetrated this slaughter and destruction, which we believe occurred because of the sins of those people, they soon withdrew to their own land.

It was formerly held as well established by many people from far and wide that the blessed Mary Magdalene had been handed over by the holy bishop Maximin for burial in the territory of the city of Aix and that her most sacred bones were preserved there. Inspired by this story, both Count Gerard and Odo, abbot of the monastery of Vézelay, after careful thought sent one of the brothers, named Badilo, to the city of Aix, with a vow that if he could, with the Lord's help, find any relic of the body of the most sacred Mary Magdalene in those parts, he should return and bring it back to them. He undertook the journey at once with the support of an honest band of servants and arrived quickly and piously at the city of Aix.

When he entered it there appeared to him to be nothing there at all except images of terrible destruction and death. Seeing this savage punishment of Christian folk Badilo began out of piety to weep and sob bitterly. At length, mindful of the vow behind his journey he wandered curiously here and there throughout the different parts of that territory investigating whether he could find anyone who could lead him to find what he wanted.

He came to a place where there was a sepulcher erected with the greatest honor which, there could be no doubt, preserved a heavenly treasure. The carving of this sepulcher revealed her whose bodily remains were preserved within it. Covering its surface was a piece of work, rather like bas-relief, [showing] how Mary Magdalene, most dear to our Lord Jesus Christ, once washed his feet with her tears in the house of Simon and dried them with her hair, and how she anointed and most piously rubbed his most holy head with her hands. Similarly sculpted there too was an image of Mary when she questioned the Lord thinking that he was the gardener and saying "Sir, if you have borne him hence ... etc."[1] and then, wanting to touch his feet, she began to adore him. Then, on the righthand side, because she came to the Lord's tomb bearing spices she [was shown as] meriting the joy of a conversation with an angel; after that she [was shown] coming to the apostles and announcing to them what she had seen.

Badilo examined attentively all that he saw, rejoicing more than can be believed. He and his companions tore up any bushes, threw away from the area fragments of coal and ashes, and, as was only fitting, removed all the filth and made it very clean.

Then that man devoted to God began to think fearfully to himself that a location in that part of the country could not be suitable any longer in case, as is usually the situation with the inhabitants of those parts, envy began to attack or gnaw at them or the assaults of the Saracens pressed them. In fact, he was bitterly tormented about what was the most appropriate thing for him

---

[1] John 20:15.

to do since he had to return to his brothers who had sent him and he could find little opportunity to take those most sacred relics, which he desperately wanted to do. Caught in this mental dilemma, he committed himself steadfastly to the refuge of prayer, beseeching the help of almighty God and pleading with Mary, who had loved Jesus Christ and was most mercifully loved by him, that she should assist him as soon as she could to see what was the most suitable thing for him to do and the most advantageous for her. Then with fervent and constant prayers and fasting he began to wait for heavenly aid.

Finally divine inspiration came and, an opportunity presenting itself, one night the pious violator approached the tomb that was so well known to him, broke off part of its pediment and peered at what was contained therein. He saw a body still completely covered in skin, with its hands placed over its chest, and lying fully extended, as the custom is. A fragrance of such sweetness rushed out of there that no mortal could describe it. This alone was surely enough [evidence] for the just. For the body of her who was worthy to anoint with spices God in his bodily form ought to have been the most sweet smelling of all. The blessed bishop Maximin had understood this when he buried her because he embalmed her body with so many spices. Meanwhile, as the night passed, Badilo seemed to see a most beautiful woman, clothed in the whitest vestments and very carefully enveloped from the head down, whose voice announced the following: "Do not be afraid," she said, "since the same place has been predestined by God for us as for you."

As dawn broke he felt comforted by this vision and calling his servants to him indicated to them that they should be prepared that night to undertake the journey back to their home. When they heard this they began to rejoice throughout the town. As night approached he prepared his tools and when the first part of the night had passed he approached the tomb, extracted from it the body, which was, as I have said, still completely whole, and, wrapping it in the cleanest cloths, put it on his vehicle, with the other goods which he was endeavouring to carry. Then he set off on his return journey, most enthusiastic to get back to his own country.

As they passed through Salon-de-Provence, a castle in Provence, on their speedy return journey, a certain dead man whose kin and fellow-citizens were, as is the custom, watching over his funeral raised himself up from the bier in which he had been lying and, remaining in it, said in a loud voice: "Mary Magdalene is passing." Then, to the stupefaction of everyone, he said it again a second and a third time. Thereupon his fellow citizens began to investigate, scurrying hither and thither so that they might know whether what the revived dead man had said was true. Coming upon Badilo and his companions travelling so quickly they inquired of them with oaths and adjurations as to what they were carrying and so discovered the truth of the matter. Both parties glorified God, who worked miracles through his saints, and praised the blessed Mary Magdalene; then the citizens [of Salon-de-Provence] went back.

The others hastened on and came to the city of Nîmes. A very serious cause of fear for them was the size of the body as it lay stretched out; having been embalmed with herbs, as the custom is, it remained solid and so could not be hidden in any small or narrow place. And so taking counsel they jointly decided to turn aside that night to a certain church and to remain there for prayer. While there they separated the longer bones of the body and put them alongside the rest of the body so that they could fit it into a smaller place. Then they quickly recommenced the journey that they had begun.

They all remained healthy with their numbers intact to within a mile of the monastery of Vézelay, from which they had set out, to a place which is now called Coudray-Badilon. There the most holy body began to become so heavy that no matter how many more were added to their number they could not by any means carry it away. Marvelling at this, they sent someone to the monastery to announce to the abbot and the rest of the brothers their arrival and the hindrance to their progress which had suddenly arisen.

In their sudden joy, with censers of incense streaming [*vaporantibus*], candles lit and crosses preceding them, they [the brothers] went out clothed in snow-white vestments to meet those still waiting unwillingly in the aforesaid place. Arriving there they all prostrated themselves on the ground, praying to the omnipotence of the divine majesty and fervently beseeching Mary, who was so pleasing to our Lord Jesus Christ, to allow the remains of her body to be removed from that place to their monastery. As soon as they rose up from their prayers and tried to go on they were able to proceed with such speed and the weight seemed so insubstantial that it felt as if they were being carried rather than were carrying anything. Supremely exultant, with the ringing bells resounding, the singing of the monks echoing, and a multitude of candles burning, they brought the body into that church which had been consecrated from the first in honor of the mother of God and the holy apostles Peter and Paul. There on 19 March they set it down with fitting honor. Since then the blessed Mary Magdalene, beloved of God, has shone forth in that place through innumerable signs and miracles.

If anyone, whatever rank of person, has insolently and violently assailed any of the possessions that pertain to that place, it has been she who has exacted divine vengeance. There were some arrogant men who longed to usurp authority over that place, but the divine protector immediately restrained them.[1] For that place so abhors thefts or rank obscenities that, if they are perpetrated, they are immediately avenged by the clearest judgement of God.

Good health, whatever the illness, is soon obtained in that place by any man or woman. Moreover, anyone whose mind is burdened by the weight of sin or shame gains beneficial solace if they confess there to the wrongs that they have committed.

To sum up, Mary Magdalene—whose last name can be understood as [meaning] flower or illuminator—is a venerable model shining through the whole world and is mentioned most piously by the holy apostle. She is such that there is no one, even if he has a heart of stone, who is not immediately softened with remorse when he hears of her. Assuredly she delivers the reward of certain hope and perfect faith when the faithful ask her for mercy because she has the bold assurance of one who, when she approached the Lord Jesus, offered him the service of her most sincere humanity and so obtained remission of all her sins. For it ought to be believed unhesitatingly

---

[1] This could be a reference to the successful struggle of abbots Pons and William.

that she will obtain it [remission] without difficulty for those offenses about which she knows how to petition Christ. Divine help, proceeding from an invocation to the Magdalene, produces faith of this kind in urgent circumstances, with our Lord Jesus Christ granting it, who with the Father and the Holy Spirit lives and reigns as God for ever and ever. Amen.

Cluny, Vézelay, and the Magdalene Cult in the Eleventh and Early Twelfth Centuries

E. L. Cox

Among the saints whose cults began to flourish in the post-carolingian period, Mary Magdalene possessed several advantages. As someone who had known and followed Jesus in person, she could enjoy a prestige analogous to that enjoyed by the twelve apostles; indeed, in the Gnostic gospels that circulated among an intellectual underground in the second century, despite vigorous efforts by the church hierarchy to suppress them, Mary Magdalene is depicted as Jesus' closest confidant and most reliable interpreter, above all of the apostles, including Peter.[1] And even if none of those ideas had seeped into the eleventh century, Mary Magdalene's life story as it was understood in the West—the story of a repentant sinner who won the rewards of paradise from Jesus himself through her acts of devotion and hospitality—made her a symbol of hope and inspiration for virtually everyone in the Christian population. Her status as a woman may also have been an advantage at a time when women and female saints' cults were beginning to play a larger role in religious life generally. The growing interest of women in monasticism would lead Hugh of Cluny to found the abbey of Marcigny to accommodate those who were influenced by the Cluniac reform, and Robert d'Arbrissel to found Fontevrault by the end of the eleventh century. Saint Foy at Conques and Saint Geneviève in Paris were enjoying an increasing popularity at this time, as was the cult of the Virgin Mary, which experienced a period of unprecedented expansion during the eleventh and twelfth centuries.[2] Much emphasis was given in the popular literature to depicting the Virgin as a compassionate mother figure who, like Mary Magdalene, was always ready to lend assistance to all Christian folk, however sinful and humble their situation might be. Vézelay itself had originally been founded in honor of the Virgin Mary, so be-

---

[1] See Robert M. Grant, ed., *Gnosticism: A Source Book of Heretical Writings From the Early Christian Period* (New York, 1961); Majorie Malvern, *Venus in Sackcloth: The Magdalen's Origins and Metamorphoses* (Southern Illinois Univ., 1975: chaps. 2–4); James M. Robinson, ed., *The Nag Hammadi Library in English* (San Francisco, 1988: 523–27); and Elaine Pagels, *The Gnostic Gospels* (Penguin Books, 1979), index s.v. "Mary Magdalen."

[2] Marian prayers and sermons survive from Cluny as early as Abbot Odo's reign (926–42), but it was during the next two centuries that Marian literature became abundant at Cluny and elsewhere. Cf. *NCE* 9. The ascension of Mary and Martha was commemorated at Auxerre at least as early as the late sixth century. Saxer (1959: 35–38, 73).

lievers with a bent for female divinities had presumably already been attracted
to the sanctuary there even before the arrival of Mary Magdalene. The somewhat later belief that the Magdalene had made her way to France and had
ended her life there also enabled her to enjoy popularity as a Frankish saint
at a time when the vogue for Frankish saints was rapidly eclipsing the passion
for Roman saints.[1] As the cult of Mary Magdalene began to grow, particularly
in France and Germany, the task facing the monks at Vézelay was to convince
the world that they and they alone possessed her mortal remains. From the
outset this required them to explain how the saint had left Palestine and
come to rest in Burgundy. As early as the fourth century there was a cult honoring Mary and her sister Martha in Bethany, and in the sixth century Gregory of Tours reported that the tomb of Mary of Magdala was located near the
entrance to the grotto of the Seven Sleepers at Ephesus, where a Russian pilgrim named Daniel reported having visited it as late as 1106. At Vézelay there
was of course no knowledge of such claims at Ephesus, or anywhere else,
since the unknown author of the earliest record of the cult at Vézelay offered
as one of the reasons for believing in Vézelay's claims that, unlike the case of
many other saints, "no other place has ever pretended to have the body" of
Mary Magdalene.[2] In answering skeptics and scoffers, however, he relied
primarily upon divine intervention. Having reminded his readers that with
God all things are possible when he wishes to provide for the salvation of
mankind, he then went on to describe the fate of people who had denied that
the tomb at Vézelay really contained the body of the saint. Nearly all of them
had subsequently suffered punishment of various kinds, which induced them
to retract their denials and make amends by visiting her tomb and begging
her forgiveness. For the rest, there was a rapidly lengthening list of persons
attesting to miraculous interventions by Mary Magdalene in response to
prayers addressed to her at Vézelay.

A more historical explanation for Mary Magdalene's presence at Vézelay
was furnished by the legend of the "Holy Monk Badilon," reported by Baudry
of Cambrai at about the same time as the Vézelay author was reporting on
events at the tomb. In Baudry's version, the origin of which is unknown, the
remains of Mary Magdalene were brought directly from Jerusalem by a monk
named Badilon, who has been identified as the nephew of another monk
Badilon with whom he shared the monastic life at Autun. Badilon senior is
mentioned in two charters issued by Charles the Bald in 877, and in the *Life
of Saint Hugh, Monk of Autun*, as a monastic reformer who died in the odor of
sanctity at the abbey of Saint-Martin-d'Autun.[3] It is thought that Badilon the
nephew, after the sack of Saint-Martin in 879, rejoined his old comrades at
Vézelay, then went north to Hainault, where he became the abbot of a house
of canons-regular at Leuze and ended his life there amid overtones of holi-
ness similar to those which enveloped his venerable uncle at Autun. If Badilon junior has been correctly identified as a friend and companion of the
first abbot of Vézelay and a member of the group of reformers active in Bur-

[1] Geary (1978: 93), and see the *Libellus* translated immediately above.
[2] Saxer (1959: 31); Louis (1946: 162–63).
[3] Louis (1946: 164–65).

gundy in the late ninth century, then he would have been a logical choice for the founder of the Magdalene cult at Vézelay, especially if he had in fact made a pilgrimage to the Holy Land at some point during his career. Hugh the Poitevin gives 880 as the year in which Mary Magdalene's body was first brought to Vézelay, which would also place the event in the time of monk Badilon's career.[1] The Vézelay Anonymous and Baudry of Cambrai thus provide the earliest surviving accounts of the translation of Mary Magdalene from Palestine to Burgundy, but by Hugh the Poitevin's time they were to be modified in such a way as to give the monastic community at Vézelay and its founders a greater share of the credit, and the Magdalene a more "Frenchified" character. In a text dated in the late eleventh century, the monk Badilon is removed from the story in favor of a bishop of Autun and a knight Adelelmus, supposedly a brother of Vézelay's first abbot, Odo; and the provenance of the saint becomes Provence rather than Palestine. According to this new account,[2] in the reign of King Carloman (879–884), the bishop of Autun, Adalgarius (875–893), while visiting Abbot Odo (877–908) at Vézelay, began to speak movingly of the love of Mary Magdalene for Jesus Christ, and Adelelmus remarked that as a child he had seen her tomb at Arles. Abbot Odo, overcome with enthusiasm for Mary Magdalene, then fell to his knees and begged the bishop and his brother to see if they could mange to acquire some of her relics. An expedition to Arles was promptly organized with Adelelmus at its head, the object being to find the tomb and bring at least some of the precious remains back to Vézelay. On arrival the Burgundians found the city of Arles in ruins and abandoned by its inhabitants, but with the aid of prayers from Abbot Odo and Bishop Adalgarius they did succeed in locating the tomb of Mary Magdalene. After collecting her body they made their escape, despite pursuit by a ferocious horde of Saracens, thanks to a thick fog that miraculously enveloped them at the crucial moment; and they were thus able to deliver the saint's body—not just a few fragments thereof—whole and uncorrupt into the hands of the monks of Vézelay, who received it with immense rejoicing.[3] It has been plausibly argued that this late-eleventh-

---

[1] See the *Major Chronicle* above 4 §74.

[2] Louis (1946: 169–70). There is no documentary confirmation for the existence of an Adelelmus as there is for the other leading figures in the story.

[3] It is not at all clear why the monks at Vézelay decided to change their story from one of direct importation of the saint from Palestine to one in which she is brought from Provence. Louis (1946: 168–69) thought it was necessary in order to counter the claims on Mary Magdalene's burial place that were being advanced from the archbishop of Aix ca. 1070; but Saxer (1959: 95–108) has shown that the essential documents here are forgeries that must be placed more than a century later, between 1195 and 1205, much later than the Vézelay revised version. Geary (1978: 93) thinks it was the appeal of the "holy theft" tradition in monastic circles; but a holy theft could as well be undertaken from a site in the Near East as one in Provence, and in any case the transfer of Mary Magdalene from Provence to Vézelay is presented in the earliest versions as a rescue from a ruined shrine, not as a theft. Possibly it was rather the legend of Santiago de Compostela that influenced the monks at Vézelay, since it was during this same period that the story of how Saint James the Greater reached Spain also took its classic form, viz., by means of a miraculous boat that conveyed the saint's body from Palestine to Compostela. Like Saint James, who was supposedly the first apostle to reach Spain, Mary Magdalene was also to be credited

century version of Mary Magdalene's translation was intended both to reflect and to strengthen the cordial relations that existed during this period between the monastic community at Vézelay and their diocesan bishops at Autun. These relations quickly soured during the episcopate of Bishop Narigald [Norgaud] (1098–1112), however, and one result was yet another family of legends to account for Mary Magdalene's presence at Vézelay—what Louis calls the "Legend of Saint Badilon."[1] In this version the monk Badilon is restored to his position of honor in the story, replacing the non-historical knight Adelelmus; and the bishop of Autun is eliminated in favor of Count Gerard, Vézelay's founder. It is during a conversation between Abbot Odo and Count Gerard that news of the pillaging of Aix (which now replaces Arles in the story) and the destruction of the Magdalene's tomb is brought up. This news induces them to send one of their monks, the saintly Badilon, down to Aix in the hope that he will be able to rescue at least some of the saint's relics from ruin and disgrace.... By the early twelfth century Badilon's story[2] had become the official version of how Saint Mary Magdalene, friend and companion to Jesus among the hills of Judaea, had come to rest at Vézelay among the hills of French Burgundy.

The cult of Mary Magdalene was a great success, soon eclipsing the cults of the saints who had preceded her at Vézelay and even overshadowing devotion to the blessed Virgin Mary, which nevertheless always remained important. Once papal confirmation of Vézelay's claims had been obtained, the number of worshippers and supplicants coming to pay their respects at the abbey began to grow. With the increase in pilgrim traffic came both fame and fortune; the once-obscure monastery barely surviving in the backwoods of Burgundy now became so wealthy and populous that, as Hugh the Poitevin proudly declares, it was "notable and renowned to the ends of the earth."[3] As we have seen, there were many circumstances that help to explain the success of Abbot Geoffrey's Mary Magdalene initiative, but one circumstance in particular deserves emphasis at this point, namely, that during Geoffrey's reign Vézelay became affiliated with the Cluniac order, which, under the leadership of a remarkable series of saintly abbots, had become the predominant influence in the French church.[4] There can be little doubt that inclusion in the great network of Cluniac houses all over Europe that were promoting the idea of pilgrimages must have greatly publicized the cult of the Magdalene at Vézelay and influenced travelers to include it in their itineraries.

---

with an apostolate in Provence, which was made possible by a miraculous boat without oars or sails into which she and various others were cast adrift by wicked persecutors, but which conveyed them safely across the Mediterranean to southern France.

[1] Louis (1946: 172–73) See below Appendix G, above Aspect [F], and *Major Chronicle* 1, for the subsequent difficulties between Vézelay and Autun.

[2] Translated immediately above. This version of the translation is also given in Sigebert de Gembloux's *Chronicon*, written at his abbey in the diocese of Liège during the first decade of the twelfth century.

[3] See the *Major Chronicle* above 2 §2.

[4] In the bull of Pope Stephen IX in 1058, which was the first papal document to recognize the abbey as Mary Magdalene's burial place, possession of Vézelay is granted to the abbot of Cluny.

The abbey of Cluny was governed in the eleventh century by two outstanding personalities, Saint Odilo (994–1049) and Saint Hugh (1049–1109), under whom a Cluniac Order, properly speaking, came into existence and experienced an unprecedented period of expansion. Like the preceding abbots of Cluny, Odilo was called upon to carry out reforms in many monasteries both in France and in the empire, but instead of leaving them as wholly autonomous when he had completed his reorganization, he began the practice of subordinating some of them permanently to the authority of Cluny. Thus the idea of a centrally supervised international organization of monasteries gradually came into being, and by the end of Odilo's career the customs and regulations governing the relations between the mother house at Cluny and her far-flung daughters had been codified.[1] During the sixty-year reign of his successor the number of houses affiliated with Cluny greatly increased, as did the authority of the abbot of Cluny over them. Monasteries that chose to adopt the customs of Cluny on their own could remain fully independent if they wished, but all houses founded or reorganized by Cluny were obliged to enter the order and accept subordinate status. By the end of the eleventh century all such houses were to be ranked as priories, even former abbeys of very ancient foundation, except for a dozen or so which were allowed to retain abbatial rank out of consideration for a prestigious past. In the bull issued by Pope Gregory VII which confirmed these arrangements, Vézelay was named among the houses affiliated with Cluny that enjoyed this distinction.[2] It is not altogether clear what becoming a "possession" of Cluny meant for the abbey of Vézelay in the eleventh century. Unfortunately, almost nothing is known about the Abbot Boniface who succeeded Abbot Geoffrey between 1069 and 1075, nor about the Abbot Bernon who was the recipient of a bull dated 27 February 1076, in which Gregory VII confirmed Vézelay's historic privileges.[3] The Vézelay *Annals* record the re-foundation of the abbey of La Charité-sur-Loire by Cluny in 1069 and mention the death of its first abbot in 1088, which suggests that monks from Vézelay might have taken part in the establishment of the new house. Vézelay is not listed among the holdings of Cluny in the confirmation of its privileges granted by Pope Alexander II (1061–1073), but it does appear in that issued by Gregory VII on 9 December 1076 and again in the one granted by Urban II to Abbot Hugh in 16 March 1095. All this suggests that opposition to Cluniac tutelage had emerged at Vézelay prior to 1076 and that Abbot Hugh had had some difficulty in bringing the Vézelayans back under effective Cluniac supervision. Hugh's biographer (Abbot Renaud of Vézelay), indeed, cites among his more notable achievements his success in restoring the abbey there to its "original state of orderly rule"; and in 1103 Pope Paschal II named Vézelay specifically in the group of houses that Gregory VII had turned over to Cluny for reform.[4] Despite its new-found prestige as custodian of the tomb of Mary Mag-

---

[1] Evans (1931a: 18–20, 25–26).

[2] See Berlow (1971: 105). Gregory's bull is dated 9 December 1076.

[3] For this and what follows, see Berlow (1971: 104–6), but with the emended dating for the abbots given in Chérest (Huygens [1976: 142n.]).

[4] Quantin (1854/1860: 39–42).

dalene—or perhaps because of it—the abbey of Vézelay had thus evidently lapsed once more into a state of laxity and indiscipline. Details are lacking, but the papal bulls of 1095 and 1103 make it clear that the abbot of Cluny was to oversee all ordinations at the abbey and in its local churches, and that abbatial elections were to be carried out with the advice and consent of Cluny, acting in effect as the pope's lieutenant.[1] Perhaps the profound obscurity which envelops the abbots of Vézelay until the advent of Artaud in 1096 is an effect of the overshadowing personality of Saint Hugh of Cluny, for nothing is known about them except their names as listed in the *Annals*. But Vézelay obviously prospered greatly during these years, however irksome it may have been for the monks to find themselves supervised by outsiders, for the flow of visitors continued to increase both in number and in importance. The duke of Burgundy came with his whole court to worship at the shrine of the Magdalene in 1084, and according to William of Tyre, Pope Urban II originally planned to launch the first crusade from Vézelay.[2] Moreover, some effort was apparently being made at this time to augment the fame of the Magdalene's shrine at Vézelay by the addition of the relics of her brother and sister, Lazarus and Martha. In a letter written by Bishop Cono of Prenesta [Conon of Préneste] in February 1119 there is, for the first and only time, mention of "the bodies of saints Lazarus and his sister Martha" in the church of Vézelay, near the relics of saints Andéol and Pontian.[3] There is no further mention of Lazarus or Martha at Vézelay, nor of any cult in their honor there, but as early as 1078 the canons-regular at nearby Avallon had among their possessions a gold (or gold-sheathed) statuette of Lazarus which apparently contained relics of the saint. Soon after the transfer of the church of Avallon to Cluny in that year, and the substitution of monks for canons, the church of Saint Mary came to be known as "the church of Saint Mary and Saint Lazarus," and its principle relic was identified as Lazarus's head, which the monks claimed to have received as a gift from Duke Henry of Burgundy on 30 April 1000.[4] Since both Vézelay and Avallon were at that time members of the Cluniac order, and since there does not seem to have been any effort to establish a cult of Lazarus at Vézelay despite the apparent presence of his tomb there in 1119, it is reasonable to suppose that it was the monks of Vézelay who initiated the cult of Lazarus at Avallon, perhaps by supplying the saint's head themselves.

During this time the monks of Vézelay were also getting rich. Offerings left by visitors to the shrine of the Magdalene (which by the 1150s included a gold candelabrum donated by the empress Matilda, mother of Henry II of Eng-

---

[1] Berlow (1971: 60–61, 106–8).

[2] Louis (1946: 166); Berlow (1971: 119, 151). The duke in question was Odo I (1079–1102), who became duke of Burgundy when his older brother, Hugh, became a monk at Cluny.

[3] *Cartulary*, no.57 above.

[4] See Louis (1946: 177–79), who doubts that so important a relic as the saint's head could have been at Sainte-Marie-d'Avallon as early as 1000. He places the acquisition between 1078 and 1116.

land)[1] filled the abbey's treasure chests, and both the money and the fame made it easier to acquire property with which to enlarge the abbey's permanent endowment. For a picture of Vézelay's ecclesiastical holdings the crucial document is the confirmation issued by Pope Paschal II in 1103.[2] It reveals that from an endowment of perhaps a half-dozen village churches, all in the diocese of Autun and mostly in or near Vézelay itself by the end of the tenth century, the abbey had expanded its reach to include some thirty-eight churches in nine different dioceses by the end of the eleventh century. It is not always clear what possession of a given church as revenue-producing property entailed, but in addition to fees for the nomination of the pastor, there was normally an annual rent and perhaps a portion of the tithe. There might also be some income at least indirectly from judicial business or even commerce. At Bessy-sur-Cure, for example, which the monks acquired between 1103 and 1106, possession of the church included the cemetery, where residences and merchant stalls were located, and fees for the administration of justice as well as for commercial rentals were specifically mentioned.[3]

Appendix E

R. Latouche: *The Commune of Mans* (1070 AD)
Translated by Katie Ward from Latouche (1966b) 121–26

[Words in italics in the translation below are, generally, as found in Latouche's original. The key text repeatedly referred to by Latouche below is: *Actus pontificum Cenomannis in urbe degentium*, ed. Busson and Ledru (Le Mans, 1901). For background: Southern (1953: 81ff.); D. C. Douglas, *William the Conqueror: The Norman Impact upon England* (London, 1964), index, s.vv. "Maine," "le Mans"; B. S. Bachrach,"The Angevin Strategy of Castle-building in the Reign of Fulk Nerra 987–1040," *American Historical Review* 88 (1983): 533–60, "Geoffrey Greymantle, Count of the Angevins, 960–987: A Study in French Politics," *Studies in Medieval and Renaissance History* 7 [o.s., 17] (1985): 1–67, "The Angevin Economy, 960–1060, Ancient or Feudal?" ibid. 10 [20] (1988): 1–55.]

In 1906 a fine piece of work appeared dealing with the County of Anjou in the eleventh century. This was the doctoral thesis of Louis Halphen. Four years later the Bibliothèque des Hautes Études printed a smaller book on the county of the Maine in the eleventh and twelfth centuries, the author of which had greatly profited from the experience of his mentor. The history of the two neighboring provinces was the origin of our friendly relations. After forty years I find it pleasing to revive with melancholy this distant memory by

---

[1] See the *Major Chronicle* above 4 §38.
[2] Published in Quantin (1854/1860: 2:39–42); analyzed in Berlow (1971: 383–91).
[3] Berlow (1971: 115–16).

recalling the commune of Le Mans of 1070. The Petit-Dutaillis volume on
"The French Communes" [1947] has lent a kind of up-to-dateness to its study.
One of the interesting things about this volume is that the author has defined
"the commune" in its simplest terms: "A sworn conspiracy, nothing else."
Now the chronicler of the bishops of Le Mans, who is the only one ever to
have recounted the communal movement of 1070 at Le Mans, gives a description of it which coincides exactly with Petit-Dutaillis's definition: "and so they
made a conspiracy which they called a commune [*communionem*] and they
bound themselves equally with stringent oaths." This coincidence should be
highlighted, particularly as, in the general opinion of medievalists, the commune of Le Mans was the first example of a "manifestation communaliste."
It is even somewhat surprising that Petit-Dutaillis did not place more stress
than he did upon this curious insurrection. Indeed a fine example of "commune in its purest form" was to be found there, for Le Mans has never had
a communal charter.

What was the origin of the movement and why did it fail dismally? These
two questions should be asked. The political cause is known: the unpopularity
of Norman domination. The people of Le Mans, who had begun to revolt
right from the start of the year 1063 when William the Bastard had annexed
the county of Maine, took advantage of the duke's absence—busy on the other
side of the *Manche* with the conquest of England—to rise up against him. The
defection was more or less general, including both the nobles [*proceres*] and
the people; the clergy alone remained faithful to the duke. This unanimity
ceased when the matter of organizing the government of the city arose. The
marquis of Italy, Azzo, called upon by the people of Le Mans because he had
married the countess Gersent—daughter of their former count *Herbert Eveille-
Chien*—did not succeed in establishing his power over the district of Maine; he
spent all the money he had brought with him by giving liberally to the people
of Le Mans, and when his treasury was exhausted he returned home leaving
his wife and his son Hugh in the hands of a powerful lord, Geoffrey of *Mayenne*. But subsequently the situation got worse. A conspiracy was formed
because the new master of Le Mans was imposing crushing taxes on the
inhabitants of the city [*cives*]. The narrative of the bishop's clerk is clear: it
was the people who swore [an oath of loyalty to] the commune, and if they
managed to draw the nobles, Geoffrey of *Mayenne* included, into the commune, the latter party yielded not without some reluctance.

It is time to turn our attention to these humbler classes [*menu peuple—populus*] who, in 1070, succeeded for a time in imposing their demands on the
nobles and even, as we will see, on the clergymen. We know a little about the
people through an impressive document, the *Cartulary of St. Vincent of Mans*,
which, rich in information on the history of rural life in the Maine during the
eleventh and twelfth centuries, is hardly less so for that of urban life. It provides us with the names of numerous Mans artisans who, when an act was
drawn up at the abbey, came and functioned there as witnesses. The most diverse professions turn up in these documents. Food industries are represented by numerous bakers [*pistor*] and some millers, but also by butchers—
who are referred to by the scribes alternatively as *buccarius, macellarius, carni-
fex*—and some inn-keepers [*tabernarius*]. Let us leave aside cooks and cook-
hands who are no doubt only domestic servants of the abbey or the bishopric,

as are the stable-men, donkey-boys, cattle drovers, and swine-herdsmen. Clothing features prominently with cloth merchants and tailors [*sartor*]. Many artisans were involved with the tanning of hides: tanners [*taneator*], furriers [*pelletarius, pelliparius*], shoemakers [*corduonarius, corvesarius, sutor*], some saddlers too. Builders' laborers are even more numerous: masons [*cementarius*] and carpenters [*carpentarius*]. Among those involved in woodwork, the coopers [*les tonneliers–botarius*] should be set apart: most of them are also attested to by the multitude of families who even at the end of the nineteenth century carried the name of Bouttié. In addition, too, glaziers [*vitrarius*], marble-masons [*plantonarius*], and countless blacksmiths [*faber*] are mentioned. Goldsmiths [*aurifaber*] figure more rarely. One notes the mint-workers [*monetarius*] who manufactured the Mans *deniers*, fairly widely used during the Middle Ages. To this already extensive list should be added horse-cart drivers [*cadrigarius*], coal and salt merchants [*carbonarius, salinarius*], and wax chandlers [*cerarii*]—the wax industry has remained active right up till today. Adding up all the names collected in the *Cartulary of St. Vincent* alone over a period no longer than a century, the total arrived at exceeds two hundred. Those who have strolled through the streets of the old city, so evocative of the past, *la Grand rue, la rue de la Truie qui file, la rue Héraud*, etc. will have no trouble imagining the life led by this *populus* of artisans in the eleventh century, some of whom were huddled together inside the Roman city wall. This little swarming *populus* hardly managed to make a living from its daily work, as is indicated by some loans taken out from the Jews.

The people lived one on top of the other, always keeping a close eye on the neighbors whom they delighted in ridiculing with such uncharitable nick-names as "Poor Simpleton" [*Pauper Sensu*], "Hopeless Bungler" [*Faciens Stulticiam*], "Bear" [*Ursus*], "See-Saw" [*Verberat Nates*—"Rumpbanger"), "Tricouillard" [*Qui dicitur habere tres testiculos*—"Who-is-said-to-have-threeballs"). Sometimes the nick-name is less ungracious: a baker is called "Fine Day" [*Pulcher Dies*], a witness whose profession is not indicated, "Goldbeard" [*Barba Deaurata*], an inn-keeper, "Jug" [Pitcher]. Is it the vogue for crusading which accounts for the sobriquet "Mohammed" for a baker's hand [*subpistor*]?

This population of small-time artisans launched the communal revolution. This is perhaps surprising, but we know that at Le Mans public opinion was very much in a state of flux, and when provoked the people showed their feelings with virulence. The author of the *Actus* presents a curious example of this. Twenty-two years after the failed commune of 1092, Hoël, bishop of Le Mans, who was chosen by the duke of Normandy, placed an interdict on the diocese of Le Mans in protest against the usurpation of the county by the son of Azzo, the count Hugh. All the major religious ceremonies were suspended and this measure provoked the anger of the people of Le Mans against the adversaries of the bishop. "The innkeepers and landlords, the butchers and bakers" our chronicler writes, "and also some women who kept merchandise of lesser value, and still others for whom the affluence of the provincial folk normally procured sizeable profits, grumbled impatiently about the enemies of the bishop because thanks to them they were being cheated out of the fruits of their trade." It is clear that these small-time artisans and shopkeepers acted not out of reasons of piety, but because of financial losses, just as a syndicate of hoteliers or retailers would do today, and the conclusion of the story proves that their complaint was heard and that Count Hugh was alarmed by their recriminations. These changing tides of opinion, these agitations had reached an endemic state in the town of Le Mans by the end of the eleventh century, to such an extent that one can read (in a private act of the *Cartulary of St. Vincent*) a clause anticipating the likelihood of a riot or revolution exploding in the town.

There was further agitation at the start of the twelfth century, but this time public opinion turned against the clergymen. The occasion was the bishop Hildebert of Lavardin's rash move in authorizing Henry of Lausanne to come and preach at Le Mans. The heresiarch took advantage of the bishop's absence (the latter had left for Rome) to draw in the crowds and stir up antagonism against the clergy. Three clergymen [*Hugues d'Oisseau, Guillaume Boitvin, Pierre Alric*] were beaten mercilessly and dragged along in the mud by the people.[1]

These incidents are significant: they show the touchiness of a section of the population and explain the uprising of 1070. But this revolt was only a flash in the pan. The episcopal historian tells the story of the commune which we will summarize thus: both the nobility and the clergy won over to the side of the populace; some hasty executions; people's eyes gashed out, some people hanged; a mass uprising against one of the nobles of the region, the lord of *Sillé*, who was supposed to be hostile to the commune; an expedition in the style of a crusade, the clergy, with the bishop up front, having been mobilized willingly or by force along with crosses and banners; this expedition failing dismally however and turning into a hasty retreat after a rumor of treason was adroitly spread about by the enemies of the communards [*communiers*] in order to create a panic. Such was the extent of this chaotic movement in which not only the people of the town took part, but also numerous peasant men and women.

The events which followed are rather confused; but the outcome is well-known. After two years of agitation William the Conqueror arrived in *le Maine* with a powerful army, and presented himself at the gates of the city. The leaders of the nobility, alarmed at these threats, held an interview with him and surrendered. The humbler classes were no longer involved; but William promised the rebels immunity and undertook to conserve the old laws and customs of the town, and we will point out in passing that the text makes no reference to a communal charter and that there will in fact never be one.

What were the causes of the failure? First of all, the power of William the Conqueror who, by his presence alone, restored order to a town disrupted by various movements. But there is a deeper reason to explain why any attempt to establish a commune in Le Mans was irremediably doomed to failure. On examining the eleventh-century township, whom did we come across? Humble people, modest artisans whose kinsmen had formerly belonged to the *familia* of St. Vincent's Abbey and of other religious establishments, and who, as commerce revived, had set up in business on their own; but what we have not discovered—even as we advance into the twelfth and thirteenth centuries—is

---

[1] See Wakefield-Evans (1969: 107-15), Moore (1975: 33-38, 40).

a rich and powerful urban patriciate. There are no major, important professions, nor will there ever be. The weavers [*textores*], who figure, and very rarely, in the *Cartulary of St. Vincent*, are small-time artisans, completely isolated. As for merchants [*mercatores*], the few offered us in that same *Cartulary* come across as sorry cases, the merchant of Coulaine for example, who practiced his profession as shopkeeper in a village on the outskirts of Le Mans. Even in the thirteenth century, at a time when corporations were flourishing elsewhere, the only one which will be seen to donate a stained glass window to Le Mans cathedral, on the solemn occasion of the transferring of Saint Julien's relics—Saint Julien being the town's patron saint (1254)—is that of the vinegrowers.

The Le Mans proletariat was active; it manifested its dissatisfaction of its own volition and, with the co-operation of the peasantry, managed in 1070 to set up a "commune in its purest form," and even, through acts of violence, to draw a section of the clergy and the nobility reluctantly into the conspiracy; but it was incapable of getting past the stage which separates an insurrectional movement from its success. It lacked the means for carrying it off successfully.

Such events have repeated themselves throughout all periods of history, and even in our time it has been observed that legislatures which started off with the triumph of the leading parties have been dissolved in a cautiously conservative manner as a consequence of financiers and businessmen withdrawing their services altogether. The same goes for the Middle Ages. The communes did not last, and were consecrated by charters only in cases where the patriciate of landlords and rich merchants existed to take the government in hand and negotiate with the lord. If the revolution failed at Le Mans, it was because this important social element was lacking. Cutting the revolution short was a mere game for William the Conqueror. With the complicity of a nobility hostile to the agitation of the masses and of a clergy devoted to the Norman cause, the commune was brought to heel.

Is the case of Le Mans unique? It is thanks to the chatterings of a Le Mans priest that we know about the Le Mans saga. Similar movements might have been formed elsewhere and it would be interesting not only to discover them, but also to research the cause of their failure. The most likely explanation in most cases is the absence of a local patriciate and the miserable conditions of the humbler classes.

Appendix F

The Institution of Peace (*Institutio Pacis*) for the Commune of Laon, 1128 AD

[One of the earliest and most influential of the communal charters was the *institutio pacis* which Louis VI granted by letter to the inhabitants of the northern French town of Laon. The letter was issued at Compiègne in 1128 AD. The following approximate translation is made from M. de Vilevault, Maître des Requêtes, ed., *Ordonnances des Rois de France de la Troisième Race* (Ordonnances de Charles VI avec supplément pour les volumes précédens) vol. 11 (Paris, 1769) 185–87.

The original document comes from the Registre de Philippe-Auguste, Bibl. du Roi, no. 9852ª, fol. 49r col. 1. This letter was previously printed in D'Achery's *Spicilegium* (1723) under the title *Constitutio Ludovici VI, Regis Francorum, quae leges pacis ab ipso constitutas in civitate Laudunensi continet.*

The institution was revoked by *ordonnance* of king and council in 1331 (reign of Phillipe VI, Trésor des Chartes, Registre coté 67, pièce 629, vol. 2, pp. 77–80 n.(a) of the collection from which the above translation has been made). Actually, Philip le Bel (or *Augustus*) had abolished the commune of Laon over a century earlier "for its notorious, enormous and detestable excesses" and the *ordonnance* of 1331 outlines the royal structure of government that replaced the abolished communal one. The *ordonnance* provides that "jamais commune, corps, college, eschevinage, maire, jurer ou aucun autre estat ou signe a ce appartenant ne soient instituer, ou établi à Laon."

The document here translated supplements the Vézelay *Accord* of 1137 (Appendix B above) and makes available for students further material for the study of social unrest in the twelfth century. The Laon communal revolution is well known from the account in Guibert of Nogent's *Memoirs* (Benton [1970: 145ff.], Latin text in *PL* 156. 907ff. and Labande 269ff.). Discussion of the pattern and significance of this "revolution" is limited to summaries and brief mentions: Petit-Dutaillis (1947: 72–79); Martinet (1972: chap. 1); Hilton (1973: 81–82); Scholz (1971: 123–31); Kennelly (1963: 44); Vermeesch (1966: 108–13); Witt (1971: 984). Despite the slight nature of this attention to the Laon commune, close study of Guibert's text reveals much of the fragmented structure of northern French society and the tensions developing within it during the twelfth century. The Laon communal charter or institution of peace, while not easily interpreted, provides further insight into the processes at work in the society of the day.]

In the name of the Holy and Undivided Trinity, amen. We, Louis, by grace of God King of the Franks, wish it to be known to all the faithful, now and in the future, that we have instituted this Instrument of Peace with the assent and counsel of our nobles and of the citizens of Laon. It is applicable in all that territory from the river Ardon right up to the Bois [wood] de Haute–Futaie, in such way that within these boundaries will be contained the *villa* [village] *Luillaci* as far as the circuit of its vines and hilly portion is concerned [*quantum ambitus vinearum et montis tenet*].

1. No one may seize any freeman or serf [*liberum vel servum*] for any wrong [*forisfacto*] without a justice [*sine iusticia*]; if a justice is not present the person apprehended may be detained by the aggrieved person without injury until a justice should arrive, or else he may be led to the home of the justiciar [*justiciarii domum*] and, in accordance with the judgment, the aggrieved person may receive satisfaction concerning that wrong.

2. If anyone do any injury to any cleric, knight, merchant (native or foreign) and be from the same state [*civitas*], he shall within four days of receiving a summons come before the *maior* and *jurati* for justice and shall clear himself of the accusation, or, in accordance with the judgment, make amends.

If he does not wish to make amends, then, with all who are of his particular household [*de peculiali eius familia*]—except tenants[1] who will not be compelled to go with him if they do not wish—he shall be expelled from the state, and not permitted to return until he has made appropriate amends for the wrong [*quousque foris facturam digna satisfaccione emendaverit*]. If he should possess houses or vineyards within the circuit of the state [*ambitum civitatis*], the *maior* and *jurati* should seek justice of the malefactor from the lord [*dominus*] or lords—if there are several—in whose district [*districto*] his possessions are, or, if they are allods [*in allodio*], from the bishop. If, within fifteen days of having been summoned by bishop or lords he is unwilling to correct his blame [*culpam suam emendare*], and justice cannot be obtained through either the bishop or the lord in whose district his possessions are, the *jurati* shall have license to destroy all the substance of the malefactor. But if the malefactor is from another state [*civitas*] and the matter has been brought to the ear of the bishop, and within fifteen days of receiving an admonition from the bishop, he has not made amends for the wrong, the *maior* and *jurati* shall be empowered to seek payment [*vindictam*] from him howsoever they may.

3. If anyone within the boundaries of the instituted peace unknowingly hires [*conduxerit*] a malefactor ejected from the state [*civitas*], and can prove ignorance under oath[2] he should return the same malefactor without let or hindrance on this occasion alone [? *illa sola vice*]; if, however, he cannot do so, the malefactor should be retained until appropriate satisfaction for the wrong has been made.

4. If in a quarrel—as often happens—anyone should strike another with fist or palm, or insult him (*vel turpe improperium ei dixerit*), and be convicted by legitimate witness, he should make amends to the person whom he has offended in accordance with the law under which he lives, and should make satisfaction to the *maior* and *jurati* of the violated peace. If, however, the person offended disdains the amends made by the offender, he shall not be permitted to demand any further amends from the offender either within the boundaries of the peace or outside them, and if he should have beaten him, let him pay the medical expenses for healing the wound [that he has inflicted upon] the wounded [man].

5. If anyone should hold mortal hatred against another, he shall not be allowed to pursue him as he goes out of the state or to lay ambush for him on his return. But if he kills him as he enters or leaves, or maims him [*aut quodlibet ei membrum truncaverit*] or is charged with harassment or ambush, he shall clear himself by divine judgment.[3] But if he has beaten or wounded him outside the boundaries of the peace, and is there convicted of harassment and ambush in accordance with the lawful witness of men of the peace, he will be allowed to clear himself by oath. But if he be found liable [*quod si reus inventus fuerit*], he shall pay head for head, limb for limb, or, at the discretion

---

[1] *Mercenarii.*

[2] *Sacramento.* On the oath see H. C. Lea, *Superstition and Force* (1866: parts 1 and 2); republished with additional documents by E. Peters (1974) as *The Duel and the Oath.*

[3] On the ordeal see part 3 of Lea as cited above (republished E. Peters [1973] as *The Ordeal*) and Bartlett ([1986] 1988).

of *maior* and *jurati*, for head or the kind [*qualitate*] of limb he should pay appropriate compensation.

6. If anyone has a charge against someone on a capital offense [*de aliquo capitali*], he should first make clamor concerning the man before the justice [*ad iusticiam*] in whose district he shall have been found. If he cannot obtain his rights [*jus suum*] from the justice, he should make clamor concerning his man before that man's lord, if he was in the state, or before his official [*ministerialis*][1] if the lord himself was not in the state [*civitas*]. If he still cannot obtain justice he should come before the *jurati* of the peace, saying that he has not been able to obtain justice in the ways specified above. The *jurati* should then come before the lord if he is in the state, and, if not, before his *ministerialis*, and diligently request the lord or his *ministerialis* to do justice for the man clamoring about his aggressor, and, if they are unsuccessful, or do not make any attempt, they should investigate how the aggrieved person should not lose his rights [*jus*].

7. If a thief is apprehended he should be taken to the person in whose land [*terra*] he was captured for justice [*ut de eo justiciam faciat*], and if the lord of the land [*dominus terrae*] shall not do justice, the *jurati* should.

8. Those guilty of ancient wrongs committed before the destruction of the city or the institution of this peace,[2] are completely pardoned, with thirteen exceptions, and these are their names: Fulco son of *Bomardus*, Ralph [*Radulphus*] de Capricione, *Hamo* the man of Lebert [*Lebertus*], Payen [*Paganus*] Seill., *Rotbertus, Remigius Bñt., Mainardus Drag, Reimbaldus* of Soissons [*Suess*], Payen Hostelup, Anselm [*Ansellus*] Fourhands [*Quatuor-manus*], Ralph Wastins, John [*Johannes*] de Molrem [*de Molreni*], Anselm son-in-law of Lebert. Beyond these, if anyone ejected from the state for an ancient wrong should wish to return, he should be invested with all his goods [*de omnibus suis investiatur*], such as he can show a claim to and did not sell or place out as a security [*nec vendidisse vel in vadimonio posuisse poterit ostendere*].

9. We also decree that men subject to a poll-tax [*homines capite censi*] should pay to their lords only the poll-tax [*censum capitis sui tantum*], and if they have not paid it within a certain period of time, they should make amends according to the law under which they live, nor, unless spontaneously acceding to their lords' requests [? *nec nisi spontanei a Dominis requisiti*], should they assign them anything [else], though the lords shall be permitted to bring them to court for their wrongs, and to have from them whatever the judgment requires.

10. Men of the peace, with the households [*familiis*] of churches and nobles [*procerum*] who are of the peace excepted, may take wives of whatsoever kind they choose; concerning households of churches which are outside the bounds of the peace, however, or of nobles who are of the peace, permission to take a wife shall only be granted by the lord.

11. If any vile and dishonest person shall dishonor an upright man or woman with disgusting insults, any upright man of the peace is permitted, upon intervention, to rebuke him and to curb him for his importunity with

---

[1] On *ministeriales* see Bloch (1967: chap. 3) and Arnold (1986).

[2] Laon was sacked in the course of the communal revolution of 1112.

one, two, or three blows, and it shall not be counted a wrong [*sine forisfacto*]. However, if the upright man is charged [*criminatus*] with striking the offender because of an ancient hatred, he shall be permitted to clear himself on oath [*juramento*], affirming that he struck him out of no ancient hatred, but only for the keeping of peace and concord.

12. We entirely prohibit mortmain.[1]

13. If anyone of the peace, marrying a daughter or granddaughter [*neptem*] or female blood-relation [*cognatam*] give land or money to her, and she dies without heir, whatever of land or money given and still in existence [*comparentis*], should be left over, ought be given back to those who gave it, or their heirs. Similarly, if a man dies without heir, except for the dowry that he gave to his wife, all his possessions should return to his relatives: the wife will hold the dowry in her lifetime but when she herself dies, it will return to the relatives of her husband. If, however, neither man nor woman has heirs, but, having made much gain from trading in merchandise, they have become of ample substance [*sed de mercimoniis questum facientes substantia fuerint ampliati*], and do not have heirs, when one of them has died the whole of the substance shall pass to the other. If, moreover, they do not have relatives, they will give two parts of their substance for the sake of their souls, as alms, and the third part will be expended on the construction of the city walls.

14. Further [*preterea*], no alien from among those subject to a poll-tax owing to any church or knight of the state [*nullus extraneus de capite censis ecclesiarum vel militum civitatis*] shall be received into this institution of the peace unless his lord agrees. If, through ignorance, someone is received into the peace without the agreement of his lord, he will be permitted to retire, secure, with all his substance, wherever he wishes, within fifteen days, and it will not be counted a wrong [*sine forisfacto*].

15. Whoever is admitted into that peace shall, within the space of a year, either build a house for himself, or purchase vineyards, or will bring into the state a set quantity of his movable substance,[2] with which he can be subjected to justice if, by chance, any complaints are made against him.

16. If anyone denies that he has heard the judicial edict [*bannum*] of the state, he shall either establish his innocence before the échevins, or shall clear himself by his own hand under oath [? *per scabinos tantum comprobetur, aut propria manu juramento se purget*].

17. The customs [*consuetudines*], moreover, which the castellan[3] asserts that he possesses in the state, he may obtain without let or hindrance if he can legitimately establish [*disracionare*] in the bishop's court that his predecessors of old had them; and if he cannot establish a claim to them all, he shall obtain only those to which he can lay claim.

---

[1] Mortmain: "a term used for land held by an ecclesiastical or other corporation that cannot be alienated"; see Cross (1974: 943).

[2] *Tantum sue mobilis substantie in civitatem afferat per que justiciari possit.*

[3] On the castellan see e.g., the articles on Poitou inf. A. Cazel's edition of S. Painter's essays (*Feudalism and Liberty* [Baltimore, 1961]); R. Hajdu, "Castles, Castellans and the Structure of Politics in Poitou 1152-1271," *Journal of Medieval History* 4 (1978: 27-54); and Weiss (1974).

18. We renew, moreover, the customary tallages [*consuetudinarias tallias*]¹ in such way that each man owing them should pay four *denarii* for each property subject to tallage [? *ut unusquisque hominum ipsas tallias debentium singulis terminis quibus tallias debet quatuor denarios solvat*]. Beyond this, moreover, he should pay no other tallage unless by chance outside the boundaries of the peace he holds some land owing tallage and should consider it sufficiently desirable as to pay tallage for it [? *quam ita caram habeat ut pro ea talliam solvat*].

19. Men of the peace shall not be compelled to plead a suit [*causam placitare*] beyond the state [*civitas*]. But if we have a suit against any of them, they should do justice for us in the court of the *jurati*.² If, however, we have suit against them all, they should make justice for us through the judgment of the bishop's court.³

20. If any cleric within the boundaries of the peace commits some wrong, he should, if he is a canon, do justice before the dean, to whom clamor has been made; if not a canon he should be constrained to do justice through the bishop or archdeacon, or their officials [*ministeriales*].

21. If any noble of the region commits a wrong against the men of the peace, and, summoned, is unwilling to make justice to them, then, if his men shall be found within the boundaries of the peace, they and their substance shall be seized as compensation [*in emendacionem*] for the injury done, by the justice [*per iusticiam illam*] in whose district they shall be found. This shall be done so that the men of the peace shall obtain their rights [*jus*], and so that the justice himself [*ipsa justicia*] shall not likewise be deprived of his jurisdiction [*jure*]:

22. For these and other benefits which our royal benignity has seen fit to confer upon the aforesaid citizens, the men of this peace have had this agreement [*conventio*] from us, that excepting the royal court [*excepta curia coronata*], they shall be exempt from obligation of expedition or knight service [*sine expedicione vel equitatu*]⁴ but shall on three occasions each year prepare maintenance for us [*procuraciones*] if we choose to enter the state, and if we do not so choose, they shall pay us twenty pounds.

23. We moreover establish this whole constitution [*constitucionem*] saving our own rights [*iure*], the bishop's rights, ecclesiastical rights, and the rights of the nobles who, within the boundaries of the peace, have their own distinct and lawful jurisdictions [*jus/jura*].⁵ If any from our own jurisdiction or that of the bishop or churches or nobles [*proceres*] have distrained anything belonging to the state,⁶ by chance, it shall be permissible to make amends for what has been distrained within the fifteenth day [from the date of the

---

¹ See Stephenson ([1954] 1967: 41ff.).

² *judicio iuratorum nobis iusticiam exequentur.*

³ *iudicio episcopalis curie nobis justiciam prosequentur.*

⁴ The full Latin text at this point reads: *quod excepta curia coronata sive expedicione vel equitatu, tribus vicibus in anno singulas procuraciones.* Note the reference in the next sentence to *procuraciones*—the subject of so much tension between the Vézelay abbot and the count of Nevers.

⁵ *Districta/distincta sua et legitima iura habent.*

⁶ *Civitatis aliquid forte interceperint.*

seizure] and it shall not be counted a wrong [*sine forisfactura*].[1]

SO THAT THEREFORE THIS INSTITUTION OF PEACE MIGHT REMAIN FIRM AND UNSHAKEN FOR EVER ETC. WE HAVE INSTRUCTED THAT IT BE CONFIRMED [BY THE HAND OF ?] S. LOUIS, KING, S. PHILIP, HIS SON, ETC. DONE IN THE YEAR OF THE INCARNATION OF THE LORD MCXXVIII, the twentieth year of the reign of King Louis [1128 AD]. THE VERSION DRAWN UP [? *data compendii*] BY THE HAND OF SIMON, CHANCELLOR.

Appendix G

The Beginnings of the Abbey of Vézelay
(858–1037)

E. L. Cox

Much scholarly debate has taken place over the years concerning the origins of Vézelay, which seems to have existed as a Roman or Gallo-Roman villa in the third or fourth century, long before it existed as an abbey. The villa was located in the valley of the Cure, a tributary of the Yonne, on or near the site of the present-day village of Saint-Père-sous-Vézelay, and its owner was one Vercellus or Vitellius, from whose name that of Vézelay is thought to derive.[2] Nothing is known about the history of the villa during the next several centuries, but a seventh-century life of Saint Aunaire does mention the donation of a *Decimiacum cum Vidiliaco* to the abbey of Saint-Germain-d'Auxerre. If the donated territory here has been correctly identified as "Domecy with Vézelay," then this would be the earliest known documentary reference to the Vézelay on the Cure. In any case, the estate had apparently passed into the hands of the Carolingian family by the ninth century, because at some point between 819 and 827 Empress Judith induced her husband, Louis the Pious, to make a gift of it to Count Gerard and his wife Bertha.

The Count Gerard in question belonged to a powerful family of Frankish warlords who had originally come from the Rhineland and had intermarried with the Carolingians. His wife was the daughter of a count of Tours with important possessions in the counties of Sens and Auxerre, and her sister Aelis was married first to Count Conrad of Argovia and then, in 863, to Robert the Strong, count of Anjou and Blois.[3] Count Gerard was thus an important personage in the Frankish kingdom, and by 828 he had become count of Paris.

---

[1] The word for "wrong" throughout the document is *forisfactura*, a "doing outside" or "beyond," implying that wrongdoing puts the wrongdoer outside the law of peace.

[2] Cf. Pissier.

[3] Cf. Calmette & David (1951: 35–36). Robert the Strong, an ancestor of the Capetian royal dynasty, was entrusted by Charles the Bald with the defense of the West Frankish kingdom between the Seine and the Loire. He died in 866.

Subsequently, however, he was caught up in the wars between the sons of
Louis the Pious over the division of their father's inheritance. He supported
the efforts of the eldest son, Lothair, to establish his claim to the entire inheritance after Louis' death in 840 against the bitter opposition of Lothair's
brother Louis "the German" (840–876) and his half-brother, Charles the Bald,
king of the West Franks (840–877). When Lothair's army was crushed at the
battle of Fontenoy-en-Puisaye (some thirty miles north-west of Vézelay) in 841,
Gerard's position in Burgundy was seriously compromised. After the defeat
he seems to have withdrawn to the south with Lothair, who gave him the
counties of Lyon and Vienne, perhaps as compensation for his losses in
Burgundy. On the death of Lothair in 855, Count Gerard was named regent
for the latter's youngest son, Charles, who became king of Provence. Gerard
also gave his support to the eldest son, Lothair II (855–869), who had inherited his father's Rhineland dominions, and this support soon involved him
once more in hostilities against the West Frankish king, Charles the Bald. In
861 Charles invaded Burgundy as far south as Mâcon, and in 863, when
Charles of Provence died, he made an attempt to seize the whole kingdom of
Burgundy-Provence, which was defended by Count Gerard as "duke" or
"marquis" of Vienne. Charles's attempt was unsuccessful, but after the death
of Lothair II in 869 the West Frankish king was finally able to bring this
region under his dominion. One of the central episodes in the wars undertak-
en to that end was the defense of the city of Vienne, which was held against
the invaders first by Countess Bertha, then by Count Gerard himself. Although they were induced to surrender the city without a fight on 24 December 870, the fall of Vienne was later made into an epic siege by the authors of
poems in the cycle of *chansons de geste* celebrating the exploits of a "Count
Girart de Vienne" (also known as "Girart de Roussillon"), with Gerard and
Bertha cast as leaders of a heroic defense.[1]

Count Gerard's affiliations with the Lotharingian branch of the Carolingian
family naturally put his possessions in northwestern Burgundy very much at
risk. In an effort to prevent at least some of them from falling into the hands
of his enemy, Charles the Bald, Gerard and his wife apparently had the idea
of converting them into endowments for monastic foundations and giving
them to the papacy. Thus the abbeys of Vézelay and Pothières came into
being. There is no reason to doubt the sincerity of religious motives in
inspiring these actions, but the stipulations in the foundation charters that
named Count Gerard as patron and protector of the new houses and granted
him and his wife full use of the deeded properties during their lifetimes make
it clear that political motives were at least as important as religious ones.[2] Of
the four earliest documents concerning the abbey of Vézelay, which are preserved in twelfth-century copies, only one bears a date, 868, and it is clear
that this one, a confirmation of the foundations by Charles the Bald, is the
latest of the four. Two of the remaining three documents are letters between
Gerard and Pope Nicholas I (858–867), who accepted the count's offer to

---

[1] Louis (1946: 117–18).
[2] Berlow (1971: 52–64). For the documents referred to immediately below see above
Aspects [A] and *Cartulary* nos. 1–3.

donate the new houses to the see of Saint Peter; and the other, no doubt the earliest of the four documents, announces the establishment of the two communities at Vézelay and Pothières, and describes the properties with which they were to be endowed. It is impossible to assign an exact date to this charter, but a passage in Flodoard's *History of the Church of Reims* reveals that in 861 Count Gerard was worried that King Charles was planning to seize "the monasteries that Gerard had given to the blessed Apostle Peter," so the abbeys were clearly in existence by that date. Since relations between Gerard and King Charles were still relatively harmonious in 858/859, scholars have generally concurred in accepting these as the likeliest dates for the founding of an abbey at Vézelay.

The original abbey of Vézelay was thus established in the valley beside the Cure, and was to be a house of nuns. They were to follow the *Rule* of Saint Benedict, and in return for the payment of one pound of silver each year to the see of Saint Peter, the sisters were to enjoy the special protection of the pope, who was to be their comfort and their counsel, and who was to ratify the elections of abbesses who would be freely chosen by their own community. Indeed, Pope Nicholas, who was determined to strengthen the authority of the papacy against the decentralizing tendencies of regional churches, granted to the nuns of Vézelay a very unusual measure of independence from diocesan control. The bishop of the diocese in which Vézelay was located (Autun) was expressly prohibited from performing masses at the convent without being invited to do so by the abbess, and he could not make any appointments to positions there. He was not to disturb the peace and quiet of these "handmaidens of God" with any sort of public assembly, nor was he to "presume to exact either *paratas* or *mansionaticos*" from them.[1] Thus a half-century before the founding of the famous abbey of Cluny, the sisters at Vézelay were already endowed with the kind of spiritual immunity that is often thought to have originated with Cluny.[2]

In addition to their ample endowment in spiritual privileges, the nuns of Vézelay were amply endowed in temporal possessions as well. In the foundation charter Count Gerard bestowed upon them the *villas* of Vézelay, Dornecy, and *Cisternas*, together with Fontenay and *Molnitas*, and whatever he and his wife had acquired in the territory of Avallon and Tonnerre. *Cisternas* and *Molnitas* (possibly the forest of Maulay between Vézelay and Dornecy) have not been identified, but Berlow has calculated the extent of the endowment at something between a minimum of thirty-seven square kilometers and a maximum of seventy-five.[3] This was a generous bequest indeed, and in his confirmation of the foundation, Charles the Bald enhanced its value with a grant of temporal immunity. No royal judge or public functionary was to

---

[1] Berlow (1971: 58–59); Huygens (1976: 243–58) gives the Latin texts. Victor Saxer and Paul Fabre before him have attempted to argue that the privileges of Vézelay were never meant to exempt it from regular episcopal visits, but Berlow has, I think successfully, refuted their arguments. *Paratas* and *mansionaticos* were both payments owed in support of diocesan visitations.

[2] For a full discussion of this point, see Berlow (1976: 573–88).

[3] Berlow (1971: 68–70).

intrude upon the properties of the abbey or assess them for contributions of any kind for any reason; and whatever might have been owing from them to the royal treasury was graciously remitted to the abbey for the sustenance of the nuns and of the poor people of the region. To their original endowment, Count Gerard and his wife later added the *villa* of Fley in the vicinity of Avallon, which consisted of a manor house, a church dedicated to Saint Symphorien, "buildings, houses, arable land, vineyards, fields, meadows, pastures, woods, tithes, streams, fountains, fisheries, mills, fruit-bearing and non-fruit-bearing trees, and waters."[1]

With such auspicious beginnings it was to be expected that the new abbey would thrive, but this does not seem to have been the case. As early as 867 there is mention of a severe famine in the region; and the continuing warfare between Charles the Bald and the nuns' founders and protectors must have made their situation precarious in spite of all their royal and papal immunities. Moreover, not a single document has survived to indicate who the original sisters were or how many of them there were, nor is there any documentation at all that bears witness to the activities of a functioning community. There is no mention of any abbess of Vézelay, which has led to speculation that perhaps there never was one other than Countess Bertha or her daughter Eve, who are thought to have associated themselves with the community at some point. In any case, it is clear that Count Gerard continued to manage the abbey's external affiars even if he and his wife did not participate in its internal administration. Bertha died in 873 / 874 and Count Gerard on 4 March 877, and both were buried at Vézelay's twin foundation, the abbey of Pothières.[2] Thereafter there are no references at all to the nunnery beside the Cure, save that on 10 September 877 Charles the Bald confirmed the abbey's privileges, but in favor of an abbot Odo; and on 19 September 877 Pope John VIII, then on his way to France for the Council of Troyes (August–September 878), gave his approval for the conversion of the abbey into a house for men, *sub habitu monachorum*.[3]

The explanation offered by the pope for this substitution of monks for nuns was that frequent hostile incursions in the region had made it impossible for the community of women to survive. Local brigandage must also have been a problem for them if the mishaps of the pope himself are any indication. While travelling northward to Troyes, John VIII reported that while they were at Chalon the inhabitants stole horses from members of his entourage, and at the abbey of Flavigny the servants of a priest named Adwardus stole a silver basin belonging to Saint Peter.[4] Some scholars believe that the new monastic community was founded in addition to the nunnery, and by Count Gerard himself, as indeed, our chronicler, Hugh the Poitevin, believed.[5] But

---

[1] Ibid., 71.

[2] Louis (1946: 121–23).

[3] *Cartulary* no. 4, Huygens (1976: 259–61), which is dated 878. Louis (1946: 120n., 136n.) argues convincingly, however, that the correct date should be 877.

[4] Louis (1946: 137).

[5] Cf. *Major Chronicle* above 2 §2. Calmette & David (1951: 48–53) affirm that the nunnery and the new monastery co-existed for another ten years or so, as does Saxer

there is no evidence of either the count or his wife seeking privileges or confirmations for a second foundation, and the tenor of the papal letter strongly supports the picture of a failing nunnery condemned to extinction by the disappearance of its founder and protector.[1]

The confirmation of Vézelay's privileges by Charles the Bald in 877 still referred to the abbey in the valley beside the Cure, but it is clear that this location did not offer its inhabitants, male or female, sufficient protection from marauders. Accordingly, it was decided to transfer the abbey from its site in the valley to the top of the nearby hill, where it could be strongly fortified and where it still stands today. Just when the move took place is not known. It could have occurred almost immediately following the death of Count Gerard, or not until some ten years later, after subsequent events had demonstrated beyond all doubt that the valley site was not tenable. During the winter of 878–879 a bandit count of Autun called Bernard de Gothia was ravaging the region around Autun and is thought to have pillaged the abbey of Saint Martin.[2] Bernard was rebelling against the king of the Franks, Louis le Bègue, and was eventually expelled from the Autunois by Duke Boso, but the damage sustained by non-combatants in the region can easily be imagined. Moreover, northwestern France was increasingly subject to attack by Norse invaders during the 870s and 880s, and in the autumn of 885 a Norse army reputedly 40,000 strong and arriving in 700 vessels came up the Seine and lay siege to Paris. The inhabitants managed to hold out for the next ten months under the leadership of Bishop Gozelin and Count Odo, until the arrival of King Charles the Fat with reinforcements. The Parisians were thus rescued, but at the expense of Burgundy, which the Norsemen were authorized to pillage by way of compensation for giving up the siege of Paris. In the autumn of 886 they destroyed the abbey of Saint-Rémy-de-Vareilles near Sens and burned the abbey of Saint-Germain-d'Auxerre before moving on to seize the town and abbey of Flavigny, some forty miles east of Vézelay.[3] Scholars are generally agreed that if the Vézelay on the Cure was still in existence in 886, the Norse invaders must have accomplished its final destruction. The confirmation of the abbey's privileges issued by Odo of Paris, now king of the Franks (887–898), is the earliest documentary reference to the fortified Vézelay on the hill.[4]

The construction of a new abbey with fortifications may have solved the problem of self-defense which the fledgling community had faced, but it did not solve the problem of poverty. Of the landed endowment given to the abbey in the time of Count Gerard and his wife, only the villas of Vézelay, Dornecy, and Fley seem to have remained.[5] There are several references to

---

(1959: 51). See Leyser (1979: 64–65) on the substitution of monks for nuns.

[1] Berlow (1971: 78).

[2] Louis (1946: 137–38, 155).

[3] Louis (1946: 141–42).

[4] See Aspects [A] above.

[5] Berlow (1971: 66–68). This conclusion is also based upon a comparison between the list of properties given to the abbey by Count Gerard and the list of abbey properties given in the bull of confirmation issued by Pope Paschal II in 1103. For the latter, see

famine and depopulation in the region during the last decades of the ninth century, which must have made supporting the monastic community very difficult even if these reduced holdings did suffice in normal times. The *Annals* of the abbey of Saint-Bénigne-de-Dijon report extreme suffering for the year 895, and in the nearby territory of Vergigny a *mansus* that was given to the monks in 900 went by the eloquent name of *Longa Fames*, Long Hunger.[1] The first task of the new abbot Odo was therefore to try to enlarge his abbey's shrunken endowment and, no doubt, try to restore to productivity properties in the original endowment that had been destroyed. What success he may have had in restoring abbey properties is not known, but in addition to securing royal and papal confirmations of Vézelay's privileges, some progress was made in the matter of new acquisitions. Several *mansi* with vineyards, woods, waters, and a mill at Vergigny were donated to the abbey by local proprietors, and in the 890s the bishop of Autun sought to assist the impoverished monks by giving them the churches of Saint Germain at Fontenay and Saint Léger in the Morvan. Finally, in 903 Pope Sergius confirmed Vézelay's right to receive tithes while also approving the election of one *Aripertus* as abbot to succeed Abbot Odo.

The achievements of Vézelay's first abbot, however modest, were sufficient to enable the abbey to survive, but times remained very hard for many years to come. To the ever-present threat of famine was added the peril of fire. In one of his sermons Abbot Odo of Cluny (926–942) reveals that the monastery had burned down, the result of an accident caused when a monk who had gone to get some liturgical vestments out of a trunk apparently allowed a burning candle to ignite them.[2] In 939 and again in 941 there were reports of widespread destitution in Gaul, and although there is no specific reference to famine at Vézelay, it is likely that the community there was also affected. Moreover, by the end of the century the monks were again having trouble retaining control of what had been given to them. In 973 Pope Benedict VI confirmed to Vézelay the grant of the tithes of four churches and included a specific prohition against interference from the bishops of Autun, who were ordered not to disturb the abbey's possession of these churches nor to diminish or transfer to others the tithes that belonged to Vézelay.[3] Thus, despite the exemptions from episcopal jurisdiction which had been conceded to the abbey at the time of its founding, the bishops of Autun were apparently taking advantage of its weakened condition to establish their rights of diocesan supervision there.

Berlow, (1971: Appendix A, 383–91), which compares the properties of Vézelay between the time of the bull of Paschal II 1103 AD (Quantin [1854–60]: 2: 39–42) and that of Alexander III, 1170 AD (Chérest 3:169–75).

[1] For these and other details, see Berlow (1971: 80–83, 141).

[2] The Latin text is given in Louis (1946: 156n.).

[3] *Cartulary* no. 9 (Huygens [1976: 276–79]).

Appendix H

Vézelay: Apogee and Decline

E. L. Cox

As far as we know, Abbot William ended his days at Vézelay peacefully. In 1170 he obtained from Pope Alexander III a confirmation of his abbey's ecclesiastical possessions which reveals how far-flung Vézelay's "empire" was by that time, with holdings in sixteen dioceses, two of them in Italy.[1] William de Mello died in 1171 and was succeeded by Gerard d'Arcy, brother of Geoffrey, lord of Arcy-sur-Cure, located some dozen miles north of Vézelay on the road to Auxerre. The lords of Arcy were vassals of the counts of Nevers and had a far from perfect record of harmonious relations with the monks of the Magdalene; but electing a member of the family as abbot was doubtless one way of turning a dangerous enemy into a useful friend.[2] Nothing else is known of Gerard's background, but he seems to have been a skilled and successful ruler of the Vézelay lordship during his long tenure of twenty-seven years, perhaps because as a local man he was more familiar than his predecessors had been with the subtleties of local politics and did not have to brave local prejudices against "foreigners." In 1181 he obtained from Pope Lucius III a bull specifying that not only the churches in Vézelay, but also the churches in all the villages of the *pôté*, were to be considered exempt from episcopal jurisdiction. This privilege was immediately challenged by the new bishop of Autun (Henry de Bourgogne had also died in 1171), but it was resoundingly confirmed by Urban III (1185–1187) and, for the last time, by Innocent IV in 1245. The abbot of Vézelay had thus attained what was in effect episcopal rank, and like the abbots of Cluny before him, he was now given permission to make use of the outward trappings of that rank when officiating on ceremonial occasions—the right to wear the episcopal mitre, the ring, the sandals, and the gloves.[3]

As for secular foes and rivals, Abbot Gerard's reign was equally prosperous. To satisfy the townsmen a charter of liberties was granted which, although not strikingly generous, was sufficiently so for the period to have made it the model for several other charters to towns in Burgundy.[4] The hated practice of mortmain, which had been limited by the charter of 1137, was now abolished entirely for all free men in exchange for the annual *taille*, which was now set at a fixed sum. The abbot abandoned his right of pursuit against both

---

[1] See Berlow (1971: 214) and her Appendix A.

[2] Geoffrey d'Arcy had been among the worst of the warlords who were ravaging the abbey's properties during the conflicts of 1152–1155. See the *Major Chronicle* above (2 §§15, 21, and 3: 201n.2; Bouchard [1987: 431]).

[3] Chérest 2:18–21. Eventually the abbots were even authorized to confer minor orders on the clergy of their abbey. For similar privileges granted to Saint Hugh of Cluny, see Evans (1931a: 35).

[4] In fact, the Vézelay charter has disappeared and its contents can only be inferred through the imitations it inspired at Avallon (1200), Mont-Saint-Jean (1222), and Montréal (1228). Cf. Calmette & David (1951: 154–56); Chérest 2:363–71.

serfs and free men, and all were given the right to move away as well as to sell or bequeath both movable and immovable property to whomever they wished. In criminal cases arbitrary detention was renounced for anyone who possessed enough property to satisfy the amount of any fines that might be assessed against him, except for persons accused of heresy, adultery, homicide, or brigandage. These concessions were granted not only to the inhabitants of Vézelay proper, but to all the inhabitants "within the crosses" that marked the boundaries of the *pôté*. For the townsmen proper there were new regulations concerning the fees for merchants and bankers and those charged for the use of the abbey's wine press, as well as provisions for supplying grass from the town meadows for the abbot's horses. Finally, it was provided that disputes should be settled by a committee made up of representatives of both the abbey and the townsmen.

These arrangements would seem to have fostered the continued development of the Vézelay business community. Already in the time of Abbot Pontius [Pons] the case of William de Montréal had revealed how high even a serf could rise in the local financial world, and throughout the thirteenth century there are references to the activity of Vézelay bankers and moneychangers in and even beyond the confines of Burgundy. Viticulture also continued to be a major occupation and source of income for both the monks and the citizens. Guy de Bazoches, arriving in Vézelay in 1190 when the armies of the Third Crusade were assembling there under Richard Lionheart and Philip Augustus, exclaimed with delight over the verdant vineyards covering the slopes and the abundance of excellent wine. And by 1197, at the latest, not just the abbey complex, but the whole town of Vézelay was protected by new walls and fortifications.[1]

The counts of Nevers were always a danger for Vézelay, however, and Count Guy, after a good beginning, was soon causing trouble for the monks again. It is not clear whether the count himself or only his henchmen were actively harassing the abbey, but Guy was held responsible and was excommunicated by the bishops of Nevers and Autun in 1172–1173. "By divine mercy," in the words of Fromond, biographer of Bishop William of Auxerre, the count fell ill soon after, which put an end to his harassment of churches; and for a while it was thought that he would die. The monks of Vézelay must have thanked God for this relief, as did Fromond, who reports that when it looked as if Guy would succumb while excommunicate, the bishop of Auxerre finally took upon himself the count's sins against Vézelay and granted him absolution. This won William the gratitude of both Guy and his mother, and when he recovered from his illness, both made donations of money and serfs to the church of Auxerre. Then, in the spring of 1174, Guy was defeated in a battle against the duke of Burgundy, to whom he had refused to do homage, and he was thrown into prison at Beaune. He died not long after his release (in October 1175), at the age of twenty-five.[2]

Count Guy was succeeded by two children, William V and Agnes, but since

---

[1] Berlow (1971: 209, 276, 280–81, 302).

[2] De Lespinasse (1909–1914: 1:376–85). Bouchard (1987: 349) gives the date of Guy's death as 19 October 1176.

both were very young, Louis VII appointed the two dowager countesses, Matilda de Bourgogne and Ida of Carinthia, as regents even though Guy's younger brother, Raynald, count of Tonnerre, was apparently still alive. The family of the "pestiferous Ida" was now heading for extinction in the male line, however, and with a rapidity that would have delighted Hugh the Poitevin. Raynald died without heirs, Ida herself died in 1179, and Count William V in 1181, when he was still a child. The new king, Philip Augustus, therefore took both the counties of Nevers-Auxerre and the little heiress, Agnes de Nevers, into his own custody. In 1184 he married Agnes to his cousin Peter de Courtenay; and after she died in 1193, their only child, Matilda, was married to Hervé de Donzy. Hervé thus became the new count of Nevers (1199–1222), but his power was considerably decreased by the subtraction of the counties of Auxerre and Tonnerre, which remained in the possession of Peter de Courtenay (1199–1218). In 1187 while Peter was still count of Nevers, Abbot Gerard d'Arcy made yet another effort to settle once and for all the vexed problem of procurations. With Philip Augustus acting as mediator, the count and countess agreed that thereafter nothing in kind would be exacted from the monks at either Easter or on 22 July, in return for an annual payment of 1500 silver marks to the count's treasury. So substantial a sum certainly attests to the abbey's prosperity at this period in its history, and the arbitration was certainly a worthy attempt to remove this issue as a source of conflict between the monks and their formidable patrons. But the issue could not be settled permanently, as it turned out, because the counts of Nevers were always short of funds; and as long as Vézelay was a potential source of ready cash or free hospitality, they were determined to take advantage of the fact. In 1211 the matter was on appeal at the curia yet again, and Innocent III was denouncing Hervé de Donzy for his habit of arriving at the abbey with such a huge entourage that each visit cost the monks 1500 silver marks.[1]

Despite its endless tribulations at the hands of the counts of Nevers, Vézelay enjoyed its period of greatest prosperity and prestige in the twelfth and early thirteenth centuries; but influences were at work that would undermine both in the decades to come. One of those influences, paradoxically, was the continuing interest in Mary Magdalene and her family in the West, which led to further "discoveries" and increasingly serious rivals to the shrine at Vézelay. When Guy de Bazoches wrote to his nephew after visiting Vézelay in the summer of 1190, he repeated the story of how Count Gerard had arranged for the transfer of Mary Magdalene's last remains from the ruins of Aix-en-Provence to the safety of Vézelay. But when he and the other crusaders reached Marseille, they encountered the legend of the "boat people" from Palestine, including the claim that Lazarus had been among them and had become the first bishop of Marseille. Like the good Frenchman that he was, Guy still held to the story that Count Gerard had brought Lazarus's remains to Burgundy at the same time as those of Mary Magdalene, thus supporting the claims of the churches of both Vézelay and Autun, where a magnificent

---

[1] Louis (1946: 191); Berlow (1971: 221).

tomb for Lazarus had been created in the 1170s.[1] Richard of Devizes, however, who reached Marseille with the English crusader fleet without passing through Burgundy, accepted the claims of the church of Saint-Victor-de-Marseille that the authentic body of Lazarus was in its possession, having been officially re-interred there by Bishop Raymond II in 1122.[2] Then, in about 1187, the body of Saint Martha, which in 1119 had been reported entombed at Vézelay, was "discovered" in the church dedicated to her at Tarascon on the banks of the Rhône. The clergy there explained that in addition to converting the pagan population of the area following her arrival in Provence with the other boat people, Martha had miraculously tamed a river monster that had been terrorizing the region; and the legendary image of her conducting the newly docile "Tarasque" about on a leash took on the form that has persisted in the regional folklore to the present day.

This tendency for Martha and Lazarus to migrate southward from Burgundy to Provence was troubling enough for the monks of the Magdalene, but worse was to come. Not only were there persistent rumors, fostered by the monks of Saint-Victor-de-Marseille, that the real Mary Magdalene was still in Provence, but there was also competition coming from Italy. By the thirteenth century a church in Sinigaglia claimed to have Mary Magdalene, and in Rome Pope Honorius III (1216–1227) apparently presided over a re-burial there of what purported to be her body (although without the head), in seeming ignorance of the papacy's earlier recognition of Vézelay's claims.[3] In the course of the thirteenth century, however, the Provençal claims on Mary Magdalene strengthened and multiplied until they began to overshadow all others. Among those who changed their minds on the subject was Salimbene de Adam, the Franciscan friar, who was writing his memoirs in the 1280s. He recalled having once visited Vézelay, "a noble town in Burgundy, where the body of the Magdalene was then [1248] believed to be," but he subsequently lived for a time at Hyères in Provence, where he encountered the regional legends. He visited the church of Saint Martha at Tarascon, where he was given the saint's arm bone to kiss and was told that a visit to her tomb had cured King Clovis (d. 511) of a kidney ailment. Then, under the date of 1283, Salimbene reports the final discovery of the true body of Mary Magdalene (minus one leg) in "the castle of Saint Maximinus." Saint Maximin was identified as one of the seventy-two disciples of Jesus and as the tutor of Mary Magdalene, and Salimbene was fully prepared to accept the claim that the church which housed his last remains, some twenty-five miles east of Aix, also housed hers. "Now, all of the quarrels, abuses, and false representations concerning the body of Saint Mary Magdalene should cease. For the people of Senigallia [sic] said that they had the body; yet the citizens of Vézelay, a populous fortress in Burgundy, also claimed it and the legend connected with it. But it is clear that the body of a single woman cannot be in three separate places."[4]

[1] Louis (1946: 188–90).
[2] Saxer (1959: 208)
[3] Louis (1946: 192).
[4] J. L. Baird, G. Baglivi, J. R. Kane, eds., *The Chronicle of Salimbene de Adam* (Bingham-

Salimbene then went on to recount the legend of La Sainte-Baume, that Mary Magdalene had spent the last years of her life in a cave in the mountains of La Baume, some miles southeast of Aix-en-Provence. This was already a very old legend, and La Sainte-Baume was already a well-known pilgrimage site, where visitors were offered detailed descriptions of how Mary Magdalene had been nourished by angels during her daily levitations above the entrance to her grotto.[1] The legend of La Sainte-Baume was not incompatible with Vézelay's legends about the translation of her body to Burgundy, but of course the claim that she was buried in the church of Saint-Maximin was, and the monks of Vézelay were inspired to additional efforts in defense of their own claims. As early as 1221 they had obtained from the abbey of Leuze in the diocese of Cambrai some relics of the holy monk Badilon, together with documentation intended to lend authenticity to the story of his successful mission to Provence in search of Mary Magdalene's tomb. In 1236 Abbot Guichard sought to strengthen Vézelay's position further by soliciting the support of the royal family. A mass was established there on the anniversary of Louis VIII's death, and after Louis IX's recovery from a serious illness in 1244, he and the two queens, Blanche de Castile and Marguerite de Provence, came to Vézelay on pilgrimage. The king's name was added to the abbey's necrology, and it was agreed that every year one hundred poor people would be fed in his honor, as had been done annually on the anniversary of the abbey's founder, Count Gerard.[2]

The pilgrimage traffic continued to decline, however, and soon the abbey was falling badly into debt. Abbot John d'Auxerre decided that the reason why many people had begun to doubt the presence of the real Mary Magdalene at Vézelay was that they were never permitted to see for themselves the contents of her tomb. Accordingly, on the night of 4–5 October 1265, in the presence of bishops Guy of Auxerre and Peter of Caesarea and the entire community of monks, the coffin under the high altar was solemnly opened for inspection. This time no dense black fog enveloped the tomb, as had reportedly occurred when the same action was about to be taken some two hundred years earlier, and the coffin was found to contain a great many bones carefully wrapped in silk amid a vast abundance of female hair. With these things there was also a document issued by a "King Charles," which certified that these were indeed the earthly remains of Mary Magdalene, friend and companion of Jesus Christ. This happy verification of Vézelay's relics now required only confirmation and publicity, and again the monks turned to the royal family for assistance. Louis IX agreed to preside over the transfer of the relics to a new casket of solid silver, which occurred on 24 April 1267 in the presence of the king's brother Alfonse of Toulouse, his son-in-law Theobald of Champagne, king of Navarre, three royal princes, Duke Hugh IV of Burgundy, the cardinal-legate Simon de Brion, and a vast multitude of the faithful. Out of gratitude for their assistance, both the cardinal

---

ton, NY: Medieval & Renaissance Texts & Studies, 1986): 216, 294–95, 530–32.

[1] Jacobus de Voragine, *The Golden Legend*, Ryan & Ripperger, eds. (New York, 1941: 360–62).

[2] Louis (1946: 193).

and the king were given fragments of the saint for their private collections, an arm and part of the jaw with three teeth for Louis IX, a rib for Simon de Brion.[1]

All this should have furnished powerful reinforcement for the cult of the Magdalene at Vézelay, but unfortunately the monks of Saint-Maximin were now determined to establish beyond all doubt that they, and not the monks of Vézelay, possessed the real earthly remains of Mary Magdalene. They were well situated to do so since even the Vézelayans accepted the boat people legend that she had first reached the West by landing in Provence, although by the early thirteenth century Marseille's claim to have been the point of disembarcation was being disputed by villagers living in the estuary of the Rhône.[2] Saint-Maximin could also count upon the support of a royal family, in the person of Charles, prince of Salerno and count of Provence, the son of Louis IX's brother Charles d'Anjou, now king of Sicily. Accordingly, the brethren of Saint-Maximin now put forth an explanation for the presence of Mary Magdalene's remains in their crypt which cleverly accepted the Vézelay story of the role of Count Gerard and monk Badilon—just as the Vézelayans had accepted the legend of the miraculous rowboat that had brought the saint to France and the story of her apostolate in Provence before her retirement and death at La Sainte-Baume. Building upon the Sainte-Baume account of how the Magdalene had chosen to atone for the sinfulness of her early life by living there as a hermit in a cave, they explained that when she sensed that her death was approaching, she had come down from her retreat to receive the last rites from her old tutor, Saint Maximin, and to request burial in his church. This request was granted, but later, when news came of Saracen invaders ravaging the region, the monks, fearing for the safety of their precious relics, had removed them from the tomb prepared for them and had hidden them in an old Roman sarcophagus. What monk Badilon had found and transported back to Vézelay, therefore, was not the bones of Mary Magdalene, but a miscellany of old bones put into her tomb to deceive would-be thieves and Saracen marauders.

To prove the truth of their story a grand public event was staged on 9 December 1279 following the excavation of the crypt of the church at Saint-Maximin. There, in the presence of a distinguished assembly of witnesses including the prince of Salerno, they "discovered" in an ancient marble sarcophagus an old wooden casket, the remains of a human skeleton, and a parchment document which attested that these were indeed the true remains of Saint Mary Magdalene, which had been hidden there on 6 December 710, at the time of the Saracen invasions during the reign of "King Odoin of the Franks." Since by all accounts, including those of Vézelay, Monk Badilon and Count Gerard had lived at a much later date (Hugh the Poitevin dated Mary

---

[1] Louis (1946: 193–95); Pissier (1923: 43).

[2] Louis (1946: 192). Gervaise of Tilbury, in his *Otia Imperialia*, affirms that the boat from Palestine landed at the spot now known as Les Saintes-Maries-de-la-Mer, so named because in addition to Mary Magdalene and her siblings, the miraculous rowboat also contained Mary Jacoby and Mary Salome, together with several other persons not mentioned in the earlier versions of the story.

Magdalene's arrival at Vézelay in 880,[1] apparently unaware that Count Gerard had died in 877), this parchment seemed to prove Saint-Maximin's story that monk Badilon and the brethren of Vézelay had been completely mistaken concerning the success of their mission. To publicize the point a grand translation ceremony was held on 5 May 1280, in which the prince of Salerno presided with the assistance of the archbishops of Narbonne, Arles, and Aix. The head of the saint was placed in a gold reliquary, the rest of her in a silver casket, and both were solemnly installed in the crypt of the church of Saint-Maximin to the accompaniment of hymns of joy and thanksgiving. Pope Martin IV, the former cardinal-legate Simon de Brion, despite his partiality for the Angevin princes, did what he could for Vézelay by reiterating papal authentification of Vézelay's shrine and sending to the archbishop of Sens the rib of the Magdalene which he had been given at the translation ceremonies there in 1267. But it was a lost cause. Soon miracles similar to those recounted at Vézelay in the mid-eleventh century, in which those who believed in the authenticity of the relics were rewarded and unbelievers were punished, began to be reported in Provence.[2] Saint-Maximin's forged documents proved to be more persuasive than Vézelay's, and the pilgrimage traffic continued to decline. Finally, in 1295 Pope Boniface VIII reversed the verdicts of his predecessors and officially recognized the relics at Saint-Maximin as the true remains of Mary Magdalene. The church was turned over to the Dominican order, whose friars were charged with acting as custodians of the shrine, and the full weight of mendicant influence in the church shifted in favor of the Provençal legends and away from those of Burgundy and the Benedictines.

The loss of Mary Magdalene meant decline both for the town of Vézelay and for the abbey. Victor Saxer has argued that the monks of Vézelay were themselves responsible for the public's loss of faith in their relics, with all of the consequences that have been described. Following Chérest's lead, he claims that corruption and "incurie" [negligence] had overtaken the monastic community during the thirteenth century, and that these faults, rather than the claims of rival sites for the Magdalene cult, were principally to blame for Vézelay's decline as a pilgrimage center.[3] In support of this hypothesis, Saxer alleges that the abbots had adopted "la fâcheuse habitude" of residing outside the monastery; that an abbot of Flavigny who had been deposed for fraud and who had formerly been a monastic officer at Vézelay, was received back at the abbey, until expelled by the pope; and that Abbot Hugh, who had been a member of the monastic community since the age of eight and had succeeded Gerard d'Arcy in 1198, was himself deposed by Pope Innocent III in 1207 for an impressive variety of reprehensible actions: he had purchased his own election as abbot, he accepted candidates as monks and conceded

---

[1] See the *Major Chronicle* above 4 §74. Salimbene does not mention the parchment in his version of the discovery of the body at Saint-Maximin, but he does mention (530) an epitaph on the tomb that "one could hardly read . . . even with a magnifying glass because of the antiquity of the writing."

[2] For example, see Salimbene, 531–32.

[3] Saxer (1959: 185–88).

benefices only in exchange for cash payments, he had given one of the abbey's priories to his brother, a layman, and he had exhausted the abbey's financial resources by luxurious living and by bestowing large dowries upon his illegitimate son and daughter on the occasion of their marriages. In addition to these cases of corruption in high places, there was another case of the monks rebelling against their abbot. The rebellion had taken place in 1258, led by Roger de Pierre-Perthuis, and Abbot John d'Auxerre had been forced to call in the count of Nevers, Odo de Bourgogne, for help in suppressing the revolt and restoring his authority.[1] In 1259 Pope Alexander IV ordered one of his legates to undertake an investigation of conditions at Vézelay with a view to proposing remedial measures; and less than a month before the ceremonial verification of Mary Magdalene's relics at the abbey in October 1265, a letter from Pope Clement IV ordered Cardinal Simon de Brion to look into reports that Vézelay's temporal prosperity was "seriously undermined" and its spiritual regime "prodigiously corrupted."

These make an impressive array of unfavorable events and accusations, but are they in fact sufficient to sustain the argument that the failings of the monastic community were responsible for the decline in Vézelay's prosperity and in the importance of its shrine? One can hardly cite, as Saxer does in support of the accusation that the abbots of Vézelay had made a habit of living elsewhere than in their abbey, the fact that during the crises of the 1150s and 1160s when their lives were in danger, the abbots frequently took refuge elsewhere; yet that is the only evidence offered of this "fâcheuse habitude."[2] And since there is no indication that their absences in the twelfth century led to any decline in the pilgrim traffic to Vézelay—indeed, the pilgrim traffic flourished as never before during that period—it is difficult to see why the absence of an abbot in residence would have had that effect in the thirteenth century. Similar doubts also arise in connection with the charges of corruption at the abbey—that the monastery was badly in debt, that unsavory characters had been received into the monastic community, that discipline had relaxed to the point that the monks were publicly ill-famed and had even conspired to rebel against their abbot. Unfortunately, as the foregoing history of Vézelay makes abundantly clear, all of these things had also been true of the abbey at various periods during the eleventh and twelfth centuries, when the abbey's fame and prosperity were reaching their peak. Pilgrims, after all, did not come to Vézelay to see the abbot or the monks; they came to worship at the tomb of one of the best known companions and disciples of Jesus Christ.

Belief that the abbey of Vézelay did possess the body of Saint Mary Magdalene would therefore have been essential to the continuance of the pilgrim traffic, and Saxer furnishes ample evidence that that belief was being badly shaken during the course of the thirteenth century—although not belief in the efficacy of the saint herself.[3] While interest in the cult of Mary Magdalene seems to have slackened somewhat in England, it more than maintained itself in the kingdom of France, with many new sanctuaries dedicated to the saint,

---

[1] Chérest 2:131–33.

[2] Saxer (1959: 187n.).

[3] Ibid., 196–227.

notably in the valley of the Loire, in the Seine basin, and in Normandy. And in the territories to the south and east of France the cult flourished with an unprecedented vigor in the thirteenth century, revealing that Mary Magdalene had lost none of her popular appeal. This was especially true in the Dauphiné, in Provence, in Italy, and in the Germanies, where the spread of new foundations was particularly fostered by the creation, circa 1225, of a new order dedicated to the rehabilitation of fallen women and placed under the divine patronage of Mary Magdalene.[1] These developments meant prosperity for the Magdalene cult, but not necessarily for Vézelay, because many of the new shrines claimed to have authentic relics of the saint in their own possession, and some of them were relics of major importance and wholly incompatible with Vézelay's claim to possess the saint's body.

As we have seen, even before the supposed discovery of Mary Magdalene's skeleton at Saint-Maximin in 1279, the people of Sinigaglia had been claiming to have her body in their possession, and as early as Honorius III (1216–1227) the altar dedicated to Mary Magdalene in the canons' choir at the Lateran also reportedly contained her body, but without the head.[2] In 1205 Conrad de Krosik, bishop of Halberstadt (1201–1209), returned from Constantinople with a vast supply of relics for his church, which included part of the skull of Mary Magdalene (*de craneo Marie Magdalene*). And when Jean de Joinville returned from his crusade with Louis IX in 1254, he reported that the royal party, after disembarking at Hyères, made a visit to La Sainte-Baume and to "a city that is called Aix-en-Provence, where the body of the Magdalene is said to lie."[3] There were thus at least three locations in western Europe besides Vézelay that by the thirteenth century claimed to possess the body of Mary Magdalene even before the excavations had taken place at Saint-Maximin; and as more Europeans were travelling then, and more widely than ever before, such a situation could only have contributed to an increasing skepticism about all of their claims. In addition, since the clergy of every new church or chapel dedicated to Mary Magdalene was eager for it to have relics of the saint, bits and pieces of the Magdalene came to be more and more widely diffused throughout Christian Europe. Just which bits and pieces they were is not always revealed in the sources that document their existence, but in 1252 the Carthusian monastery at Montrieux in Provence made known that their collection included Mary Magdalene's "bones, hair, and staff" (*baculus*), and by 1259 the church of Wettingen in the diocese of Constance also possessed some of her hair. The monks of Vézelay paradoxically contributed to this dangerous diffusion of Magdalene relics by acts of generosity such as those which followed the ceremonial re-interment of their own relics in 1267, when

---

[1] Ibid., 223.

[2] Saxer (1959: 215). In 1297 the altar was re-consecrated on the orders of Pope Boniface VIII, at which time it was again said to contain the body of Mary Magdalene but "without the head and an arm" (*in quo altari recondidit corpus ipsius sanctae, sine capite et brachio*). It is difficult to see how the pope could have reconciled this information with his own official recognition of the authenticity of the body found at Saint-Maximin's two years earlier, but he apparently did.

[3] Jean de Joinville, *Histoire de Saint Louis*, Natalis de Wailly, ed. (Paris, 1874: chap. 134, 365).

they not only gave a jaw with three teeth to King Louis IX and a rib to Cardinal Simon de Brion, but also made a gift of Magdalene relics to a nunnery in Orleans which, in consequence, exchanged its dedication to Notre Dame for the patronage of Mary Magdalene. With so many relics of the saint available in local churches and chapels, it is small wonder that fewer and fewer pilgrims felt impelled to make the journey to Vézelay, especially since, by the monks' own admission, the verification of the contents of their own tomb in October 1265 had produced only a quantity of individually wrapped bones and a mass of hair, not a bona fide skeleton. Those who wished to address their prayers to the Magdalene in the presence of some substantial remnant of the saint could do so in a considerable number of locations other than Vézelay by the end of the thirteenth century.[1]

All this, of course, is not to say that the monastic community at Vézelay was entirely the innocent victim of circumstances in the matter of the abbey's decline. It is possible that monastic finances had not in fact been well managed, and that after so long a time during which the abbey's income had supported very large expenditures, its officers were slower than they should have been to realize the necessity of retrenchments as income began to fall off. The monastic community could theoretically have adopted a more frugal standard of living, but to do so would have required a drastically altered conception of a mission which had become rooted in centuries of tradition.[2] Charges of fiscal mismanagement were made against the thirteenth-century abbots then as they are now, but given the lack of financial records for the period, it is very difficult to evaluate such charges. According to the papal legates sent to investigate the scandalous regime of Abbot Hugh, deposed in 1207, the surplus of 30,000 *solidi* left by his predecessor had been turned into a deficit of more than 2,220 *livres*.[3] Succeeding abbots did struggle to restore the abbey to solvency, but their task was made doubly difficult by the refusal of the counts of Nevers to abide by earlier agreements limiting the abbey's monetary obligations towards them. When their exorbitant financial demands were refused, even in part, the counts, as in the past, did not scruple to send armed men out to pillage the abbey's properties, thus further reducing its sources of income. Abbot John d'Auxerre (1252–1274), whose turbulent reign witnessed an armed occupation of the abbey by the king's men as well as a rebellion by his own monks against his authority, was accused after his death of having left the monastery crushed by debt and depleted in resources, but it is by no means clear that the accusation was justified. During the reign of Abbot Guichard (1230–1245) Guy de Forez, count of Nevers, at war with the count of Champagne, extorted such enormous sums from the abbey and the townsmen of Vézelay that the burghers threatened to emigrate en masse into the territories of the king in a desperate search for protection.[4] It was doubt-

---

[1] For other examples of the dispersion of Magdalene relics, see Chérest 2:149.

[2] Southern (1970: 223–37) gives an excellent picture of the role which Benedictine abbeys like Vézelay had come to play in medieval society, and why drastic reform was "both socially and mentally an impossible feat ..." (235).

[3] Chérest 2:86–92 gives the text of the papal letter in translation.

[4] Ibid., 111–16.

less this same hope for royal protection that induced both Abbot Guichard and John d'Auxerre to try to associate the royal family more closely with the Mary Magdalene cult at Vézelay between 1236 and 1267, when it began to appear that Louis IX's youngest son, John "Tristan," would become the new count of Nevers, Auxerre, and Tonnerre.[1] Abbot John's major expenditures were those necessitated by his vigorous efforts to establish his own authority at Vézelay and to defend Vézelay's historic liberties against both baronial and royal encroachments, and he clearly believed that his revival of the Magdalene cult and the patronage of the royal family would in the end recompense his expenditures.

It may well be that the crises which the monks of the Magdalene had to face during the thirteenth century were the result less of incompetent leadership than of conditions that were adversely affecting monasteries almost everywhere at the time. Already in the twelfth century the cost of living was rising substantially while the sources of additional landed endowments in the vicinity of older Benedictine houses like Vézelay were drying up, as the countryside around the abbey became more densely populated and more firmly integrated into other lordships. Donations of widely scattered properties located at great distances from the mother house meant sending monks away from the abbey for long periods of time, which fostered a loosening of monastic discipline and a burden of administration that must often have absorbed much of the income.[2] In Vézelay's case, as we have seen, by 1170 the abbey's holdings were located in sixteen different dioceses, two of them in Italy; and it is perhaps to the point that Peter the Auvergnat, who had been sent down to administer abbey properties in the Auvergne after his expulsion from Saint-Michel-de-Tonnerre, was one of the leaders of the conspiracy against Abbot William in 1165.[3]

In addition to the increasing costs of maintaining a large monastic establishment with expensive obligations of hospitality, charity, and religious services, abbeys like Vézelay were also facing increasing competition from other religious orders. The rapid rise of the Cistercian order in Burgundy during the twelfth century as a result of a perceived laxity in the older houses, notably those associated with the Cluniac Order, was already drawing both patrons and donors away from monasteries like Vézelay that would earlier have been the principal beneficiaries of their generosity. During the thirteenth century the extraordinary success of the mendicant orders meant that another rival for the affections and benefactions of the faithful had arrived on the scene. Vézelay was among the very first of the established houses to be affected by the rising popularity of the Franciscans because as early as 1217 permission to establish a refuge there had been granted to brothers Pacificus and Louis, who had been deputed by Saint Francis to carry his message into the kingdom of France. The first Franciscans were housed in a small hermitage located on the north slope of the Vézelay hill, near where Abbot Pontius [Pons] had built the church of Sainte-Croix to commemorate the preaching

---

[1] Ibid., 118–19, 145–51.
[2] Cf. Southern (1970: 232–33).
[3] See the *Major Chronicle* 4 §38.

of the Second Crusade. Abbot Peter gave the friars permission to celebrate mass in Sainte-Croix, and for some years the two communities lived peaceably together. But the popularity of the friars, whose simple, frugal life was so strikingly different from the pomp and splendor with which the monks of the Magdalene felt duty-bound to honor their patroness, soon began to attract the devotion of people whose support would otherwise have gone to the abbey. The monks finally became so enflamed against their Franciscan rivals that they destroyed their hermitage and tried to drive them away from the town. The papacy intervened on behalf of the friars, however, conferring upon them legal possession not only of their hermitage, known as La Cordelle, but also of the church of Sainte-Croix, which had belonged to the monks. The Franciscans were thus in Vézelay to stay, and just as the Dominican friars at Saint-Maximin in Provence were to undermine the abbey's claims to Mary Magdalene, so the Franciscan friars at Vézelay were undermining the abbey's claims to the devotion of its own parishioners. As long as the cult of Mary Magdalene continued to bring crowds of visitors to the abbey, the effects of rising costs and rival religious groups could be offset. But, as we have seen, the determined efforts made during the thirteenth century by the monks of Vézelay to revive interest in their collection of Magdalene relics were not a success.

In addition to financial woes and flagging popularity, the monks of Vézelay were also faced with a growing threat to their political independence. The counts of Nevers, while contributing substantially to the abbey's fiscal problems by the measures which they took to solve their own problems at the abbey's expense, nevertheless had ceased to claim jurisdiction over the monastery and its subjects. But as the power of the kings of France began to expand in the counties of Nevers, Auxerre, and Tonnerre, in part as a result of the failure of male heirs in the comital line, royal officials gradually came to replace comital officials in an increasing number of offices and an increasing number of locations. Already in 1210 King Philip Augustus had succeeded in obtaining from the count of Nevers the castle of Voutenay-sur-Cure, which lay on the northern boundary of the abbey's *pôté*, only nine miles away from Vézelay itself. Then, in 1255, Abbot John d'Auxerre found himself summoned to appear before the Parlement of Paris to answer for acts of violence which had been committed by the abbey's men when the royal provost at Villeneuve-sur-Yonne tried to make an arrest at Asquins, next to Vézelay in the very heart of its supposedly independent lordship. In the course of that affair the royal bailli of Sens actually dispatched an expeditionary force that occupied the abbey for a brief period. Finally, in a dispute between the abbot and the dean of the abbey which broke out in 1273, the latter appealed to the king's bailli at Sens for help, and the case again was taken before the Parlement of Paris. In the end, the Parlement recognized that only the pope had the authority to adjudicate in such a dispute, but the monastic community was reminded once again of the presence of a powerful new neighbor in the vicinity who was only too willing to make the abbey's business its own.[1]

---

[1] Chérest 2:153–56.

That willingness was soon to find practical expression. In 1270 both Louis IX and John "Tristan," count of Nevers, died on crusade, and Yolande de Bourgogne, John's widow, married Robert de Bethune, eldest son of the count of Flanders. A decade later, when Countess Yolande died leaving a child as her heir, King Philip III, who had just annexed the county of Champagne to the royal domain, placed Vézelay under the direct protection of the crown. On whose initiative this was done is not known. This transfer of the Vézelay guardianship from the count of Nevers to the king of France was confirmed and repeated by Philip IV in 1293. In 1308, when Louis de Flandre, who had now come into his inheritance as count of Nevers, began to reclaim his dynastic rights and attack the abbey's properties, the monks appealed to the king for help, and the count was condemned to pay for the damage he had caused. There is every indication that Louis de Flandre was in no way disposed to accept the loss of the abbey of Vézelay to the king of France, but circumstances were soon to threaten him with the loss of his entire French inheritance. In the course of the wars between Philip IV and the Flemings, Louis and his father were both summoned to Paris to answer charges of treason. Count Robert was easily vindicated, but his son, fearing conviction on the charges, took flight. As a result, in 1310 the king and his great vassals declared the confiscation of Louis' counties of Rethel and Nevers; and in January 1312 at Montargis Philip IV further declared that even if Louis de Flandre should at some future time recover possession of his counties in France, the abbey of Vézelay, with all of its possessions and dependencies in the county of Nevers, would forever remain "in the wardship, suzerainty, and jurisdiction" of the king of France.[1]

In the 1130s Peter the Venerable had hailed the monastic community at Vézelay with the words of the Old Testament psalmist: "Behold a fertile mountain, a mountain filled with abundance, a mountain where the Lord is pleased to dwell."[2] Two hundred years later, the mountain was considerably less fertile, and its Lord was the king of France.

Fig. 14

Fig. 15

---

[1] Ibid., 175–76.

[2] Constable (1967: 2:193).

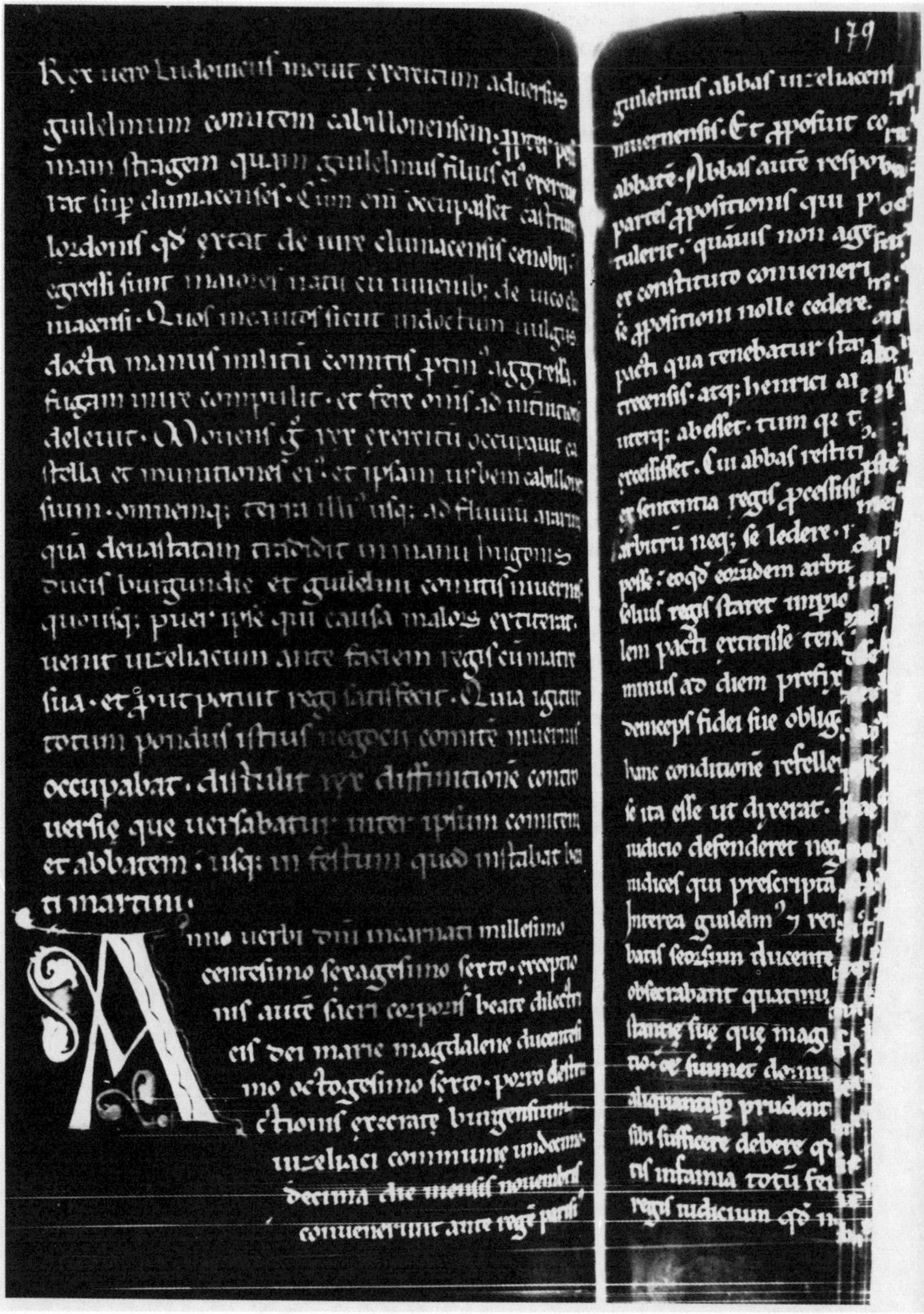

Fig. 16. Folios 178v–179r; cf. *Major Chronicle* 4 § 74.

General Bibliography and Abbreviations Used

Alessio (1982): Alessio, G. *Cronaca di Novalesa*. Torino, 1982.

Annales E.S.C.: *Annales: Économies, Sociétés, Civilizations*.

Arnold (1985): Arnold, B. *German Knighthood 1050–1300*. Oxford, 1985.

Arnold (1986): Arnold, B. "Servile Retainers or Noble Knights? The Medieval Ministeriales in Germany." *Reading Medieval Studies* 12 (1986): 73–84.

Arnold (1991): Arnold, B. *Princes and Territories in Medieval Germany*. Cambridge, 1991.

Aubert (1966): Aubert, M. *Romanesque Cathedrals and Abbeys of France*. Trans. C. Girdlestone. Liverpool, 1966.

Bachrach (1988): Bachrach, B. S. "The Angevin Economy, 960–1060: Ancient or Feudal?" *Studies in Medieval and Renaissance History* 10 (old series 20) (1988): 3–55.

Bachrach (1990): Bachrach, B. S. and D. Nicholas, eds. *Law, Custom and the Social Fabric in Medieval Europe* (Studies in Medieval Culture, 28). Kalamazoo, 1990.

Baker (1979): Baker, D. "Crossroads and Crises in the Religious Life of the Later 11th Century." *Studies in Church History* 16 (1979): 137–48.

Baldwin (1968): Baldwin, M. W. *Alexander III and the Twelfth Century*. London, 1968.

Barlow (1980): Barlow, F. "The Canonisation and Early Lives of Hugh I, Abbot of Cluny." *Analecta Bollandiana* 98, 3–4 (1980): 297–334.

Barlow (1986): Barlow, F. *Thomas Becket*. London, 1986.

Barraclough (1933): Barraclough, G. "The Making of a Bishop in the Middle Ages." *Catholic Historical Review* 19 (1933): 275ff.

Barraclough (1957): Barraclough, G. *The Origins of Modern Germany*. Oxford, 1957.

Barraclough (1968): Barraclough, G. *The Medieval Papacy*. London, 1968.

Barthelemy (1984): Barthelemy, D. *Les deux ages de la seigneurie banale: Pouvoir et société dans la terre des sires de Coucy, milieu XIe–milieu XIIIe siècle*. Paris, 1984.

Bartlett ([1986] 1988): Bartlett, R. *Trial by Fire and Water: The Medieval Judicial Ordeal*. Oxford, 1986; repr. 1988.

Bastard (1848): Bastard, L. de. "De la commune de Vézelay." In *BSSY* 2 (1848): 527–52.

Bastard (1851): Bastard, L. de. "Recherches sur l'insurrection communale de Vézelay au XIIe siècle." In *BEC* 2 (1851): 339–65.

Bautier (1970): Bautier, R. H. "L'Historiographie en France aux Xe et XIe siècles." In "La Storiografia altomedievale." *Settimane di Studio del Centro Italiano di Studi sull' Alto Medioevo* xvii. Spoleto, 1970.

BEC: *Bibliothèque de l'École des Chartes*.

Beckwith (1974): Beckwith, J. *Early Medieval Art*. London, 1974.

Benson and Constable (1982): Benson, R. L., and G. Constable, eds. *Renaissance and Renewal in the Twelfth Century*. Cambridge, MA, 1982.

Benton (1962): Benton, J. F. "Nicolas de Clairvaux à la recherche du vin d'Auxerre, d'après une lettre inédite du XII siècle." In *Annales de Bourgogne* 34 (1962): 252–55.

Benton (1970): Benton, J. F., ed. *Self and Society in Medieval France: The Memoirs of Abbot Guibert of Nogent (1064–c1125)*. Trans. C. C. Swinton Bland. New York, 1970.

Benton (1982): Benton, J. F. "Consciousness of Self and Perceptions of Individuality." In Benson and Constable (1982: 277–82).

Berlow (1971): Berlow, R. K. "Social and Economic Aspects of the Early History of Vézelay (Ninth to Twelfth Centuries)." Ph.D. diss., City Univ. of New York, 1971.

Berlow (1976): Berlow, R. K. "Spiritual Immunity at Vézelay, 9th to 12th Centuries." *Catholic Historical Review* 62 (1976): 573–88.

Berlow (1980): Berlow, R. K. "The Case of André du Marais." *American Journal of Legal History* 24 (1980): 133–44.

Berlow (1981): Berlow, R. K. "The Case of the Disappearing Abbot." *Studia Monastica* 23 (1981): 325–38.

Berlow (1987): Berlow, R. K. "The Rebels of Vézelay (1152–1155)." *Studies in Medieval and Renaissance History* 9 [OS 19] (1987): 137–63 (earlier versions of this paper were presented originally in 1975).

Bethel (1969): Bethel, D. "English Black Monks and Episcopal Elections in the 1120's." *English Historical Review* 84 (1969): 673–98.

Black (1984): Black, A. *Guilds and Civil Society in European Political Thought from the Twelfth Century to the Present*. Ithaca: Cornell Univ. Press, 1984.

Blake (1962): Blake, E. O., ed. *Liber Eliensis*. Camden Society Third Series, vol. 92. London, 1962.

Blake and Morris (1985): Blake, E. O., and C. Morris. "A Hermit Goes to War: Peter and the Origins of the First Crusade." *Studies in Church History* 22 (1985): 79–107.

Bloch (1961): Bloch, M. *Feudal Society*. Trans. L. A. Manyon. London, 1961.

Bloch (1964): Bloch, M. "From the Royal Court to the Court of Rome: The Suit of the Serfs of Rosny-sous-Bois." In Tierney (1970b: 127–34) and in Thrupp (1964: 3–10).

Bloch (1966): Bloch, M. *French Rural History*. Trans. J. Sondheimer. London, 1966.

Bloch (1967): Bloch, M. *Land and Work in Medieval Europe*. Trans. J. E. Anderson. London, 1967: "A Problem in Comparative History: The Administrative Classes in France and Germany," 82–123; "The Advent and Triumph of the Water Mill," 136–68.

Bloch (1975): Bloch, M. *Slavery and Serfdom in the Middle Ages: Selected Papers*. Trans. W. Beer. Berkeley, 1975.

Bober (1965): Bober, M. M. *Karl Marx's Interpretation of History: A Study of the Central Thesis of the Marx-Engels Doctrine of Social Evolution*. New York, 1965.

Boethius (1918): Boethius. *De Consolatione Philosophiae*. Trans. H. F. Stewart and E. K. Rand. Loeb Classical Library, 1918.

Borst (1953): Borst, A. *Die Katharer*. Stuttgart, 1953.

Bouchard (1977): Bouchard, Constance B. "The Geographical, Social and Ecclesiastical Origins of the Bishops of Auxerre and Sens in the Central Middle Ages." *Church History* 46 (1977): 277–95.

Bouchard (1979): Bouchard, Constance B. *Spirituality and Administration: The*

Role of the Bishop in Twelfth-Century Auxerre. Medieval Academy of America, 1979.

Bouchard (1987): Bouchard, Constance B. *Sword, Miter and Cloister: Nobility and the Church in Burgundy, 980–1198.* Ithaca: Cornell Univ. Press, 1987.

Bouchard D. (1977): Bouchard, D. F., ed. *Language, Counter-memory, Practice: Selected Essays and Interviews by Michel Foucault.* Ithaca: Cornell Univ. Press, 1977.

Boudrillat (1931): Boudrillat, A. "Avoué, Avouerie Ecclésiastique." In *Dictionnaire d'Histoire et de Géographie Ecclésiastiques* 5: Paris, 1931.

Bourquelot (1852): Bourquelot, F. "Observations sur l'établissement de la commune de Vézelay." In *BEC* 3 (1852): 447–63.

Boussard (1967): Boussard, J. "A Serf in Anjou at the End of the 11th Century." In Thrupp (1967: 124–26).

Brand (1983): Brand, P., E. Searle, et al. "Seigneurial Control of Women's Marriage: A Debate." *Past and Present* 99 (1983): 123ff.

Breisach (1983): Breisach, E. *Historiography: Ancient, Medieval and Modern.* Chicago, 1983.

Breisach (1985): Breisach, E., ed. *Classical Rhetoric and Medieval Historiography.* Studies in Medieval Culture 19. Kalamazoo, 1985.

Brett (1975): Brett, M. *The English Church Under Henry I.* Oxford, 1975.

Brooke (1970): Brooke, C. N. L. "The Missionary at Home: The Church in the Towns 1000–1250." *Studies in Church History* 6 (1970): 59–83.

Brooke (1976): see Chibnall (1976).

Brooke (1984): Brooke, C. N. L. and R. K. *Popular Religion in the Middle Ages, Western Europe 1000–1300.* London, 1984; repr. 1985.

Brooke (1985): Brooke, C. N. L. "Monk and Canon: Some Patterns in the Religious Life of the Twelfth Century." *Studies in Church History* 22 (1985): 109–29.

Brooke and Morey (1967): Brooke, C. N. L., and A. Morey., eds. *The Letters and Charters of Gilbert Foliot, Abbot of Gloucester 1139–48, Bishop of Hereford 1148–63 and London 1163–87.* Cambridge, 1967.

Bruel (1974): Bruel, A. *Recueil des Chartes de L'Abbaye de Cluny.* Paris, 1876–1903; repr. Frankfurt-am-Main, 1974.

Brundage (1967): Brundage, J. A. "The Crusader's Wife: A Canonistic Quandary." *Studia Gratiana* 12 (1967) [*Collect. Steph. Kuttner* 2:425–41]; "The Crusader's Wife Revisited." Ibid. 14 (1967) [*Collect. S. Kuttner* 4:241–52].

Brundage (1987): Brundage, J. A. *Law, Sex and Christian Society in Medieval Europe.* Chicago, 1987.

BSSY: Bulletin de la Société des Sciences Historiques et Naturelles de l'Yonne.

Butler ([1906] 1969): Butler, W. F. *The Lombard Communes: A History of the Republics of Northern Italy.* 1906; repr. New York, 1969.

Butler (1949): Butler, H. E., trans. *The Chronicle of Jocelin of Brakelond.* Edinburgh, 1949.

Calin (1962): Calin, W. *The Old French Epic of Revolt : Raoul de Cambrai, Renaud de Montauban, Gormond et Isembard.* Geneva, 1962.

Calmette and David (1951): Calmette, J., and H. David. *Les grandes heures de Vézelay.* Paris, 1951.

Cantor (1960–61): Cantor, N. "The Crisis of Western Monasticism 1050–

1130." *American Historical Review* 66 (1960–61): 47–67.

Carozzi (1979): Carozzi, C., ed. and trans. *Adalbéron de Laon. Poème au Roi Robert*. Paris, 1979.

Carter (1981): Carter, P. "The Historical Content of William of Malmesbury's Miracles of the Virgin." In Davis (1981).

Chagny (1938): Chagny, A. *Cluny et son Empire*. Paris/Lyon, 1938.

Chaume (1977): Chaume., M. *Les Origines du Duché de Bourgogne*. Dijon, 1925 (1st part), 1937 (2nd part); repr. Darmstadt, 1977.

Cheney (1973): Cheney, C. R. "Church Building in the Middle Ages." Reprinted in his *Medieval Texts and Studies*, 346–63. Oxford, 1973.

Chérest : Chérest, A. "Vézelay. Étude historique." *BSSY* 16 (1862): 209–525 and 22 (1868): 5–631. Reprinted in 3 vols. (Auxerre, 1868) as an "extrait" from *BSSY*; partially reprinted with annotations in Huygens (1976: 1–194).

Cheyettte (1968): Cheyette, F. L., ed. *Lordship and Community in Medieval Europe*. Holt, Rinehart and Winston, 1968.

Cheyette (1970): Cheyette, F. L. "Suum cuique tribuere." *French Historical Studies* 6 (1970): 275–86.

Chibnall (1956): Chibnall, M., trans. *John of Salisbury's Memoirs of the Papal Court*. London: Th. Nelson, 1956.

Chibnall (1976): Chibnall, M. "Charter and Chronicle: The Use of Archive Sources by Norman Historians." In *Church and Government in the Middle Ages: Essays Presented to C. R. Cheney on His 70th Birthday*. Ed. C. N. L. Brooke et al., 1–17. Cambridge, 1976.

Chibnall (1984): Chibnall, M. *The World of Orderic Vitalis*. Oxford, 1984.

CL: Classical Latin.

Clanchy (1979): Clanchy, M. T. *From Memory to Written Record: England 1066–1307*. London, 1979.

Cohen (1980): Cohen, E. "Roads and Pilgrimage: A Study in Economic Interaction." *Studi Medievali*, ser. 3, vol. 21 (1980): 321–41.

Cohn (1970): Cohn, N. *The Pursuit of the Millenium; Revolutionary Millenarians and Mystical Anarchists of the Middle Ages*. Paladin, 1970.

Conant (1966): Conant, K. J. *Carolingian and Romanesque Architecture 800–1200*. Pelican History of Art, 1966.

Constable (1967): Constable, G., ed. *The Letters of Peter the Venerable*. 2 vols. Cambridge, MA, 1967.

Constable (1975): Constable, G. "The Monastic Policy of Peter the Venerable." In Colloques internationaux du centre national de la recherche scientifique. *Pierre Abelard, Pierre le Vénérable: les courants philosophiques, littéraires et artistiques en occident au milieu du XII siècle*, 119–41. Paris, 1975.

Constable (1976): Constable, G. "Cluniac Administration and Administrators in the 12th Century." In Jordan (1976: 17ff.).

Constable and Benson (1982): Constable, G., and R. L. Benson. *Renaissance and Renewal in the Twelfth Century*. Cambridge, MA, 1982.

Cope (1986): Cope, Christopher. *Phoenix Frustrated: The Lost Kingdom of Burgundy*. London, 1986.

Coupe (1987): Coupe, M. D. "Peter the Hermit—A Reassessment." *Nottingham Medieval Studies* 31 (1987): 37–45.

Cowdrey (1970): Cowdrey, H. E. J. *The Cluniacs and the Gregorian Reform*. Oxford, 1970.

Cowdrey (1973): Cowdrey, H. E. J. "Cluny and the First Crusade." *Revue Bénédictine* 83 (1973): 285–311.

Cox (1990): Cox, Eugene. Typescript annotated translation of the *Major Chronicle* and *A History of the Abbey of Vézelay 858–1312* (1990). See Preface above.

Cross (1974): Cross, F. L., ed. *The Oxford Dictionary of the Christian Church.* 2d ed. London, 1974.

Crozet (1975): Crozet, R. "L'épiscopat de France et l'Ordre de Cîteaux au XIIe siècle." *Cahiers de Civilization Médiévale* 18 (1975): 263–68.

D'Achery (1659): D'Achery, L. *Veterum aliquot scriptorum, qui in Galliae Bibliothecis, maxime Benedictinorum latuerant, spicilegium.* Ed. in quarto vol. 3. Paris, 1659.

D'Achery (1723): D'Achery, L. *Spicilegium sive collectio veterum aliquot scriptorum qui in Galliae Bibliothecis delituerant....* Nova editio ... par L. F. J. de la Barre, ed. In fol., vol. 2. Paris, 1723.

Dalarun (1985): Dalarun. J. *L'impossible sainteté: La vie retrouvée de Robert d'Arbrissel (v. 1045–1116), fondateur de Fontevraud.* Paris, 1985.

Davies (1973): Davies, W. "Liber Landauensis: Its Construction and Credibility." *English Historical Review* 88 (1973): 335–51.

Davies (1988): Davies, W. "Forgery in the Cartulaire de Redon." In *Fälschungen im Mittelalter.* Hannover, 1988.

Davies and Fouracre (1986): Davies, W., and P. Fouracre., eds. *The Settlement of Disputes in Early Medieval Europe.* Cambridge, 1986.

Davis (1958): Davis, G. R. C. *Medieval Cartularies of Great Britain.* London, 1958.

Davis (1981): Davis, R. H. C., and J. M. Wallace-Hadrill. *The Writing of History in the Middle Ages: Essays Presented to R. W. Southern.* Oxford, 1981.

de Burgh (1953): de Burgh, W. G. *The Legacy of the Ancient World.* 2 vols. Penguin Books, 1953.

Delaruelle: See *L'Eremitismo.*

Delautre (1981): Delautre, H. "La Madeleine de Vézelay, architecture cosmique et symbolique de la lumière." *Bulletin de la Societé d'Avallon, Histoire, Sciences, Lettres et Arts* (119–21 for 1977–79) (1981): 24–36.

Demm (1972): Demm, E. "A Program for Revolution in a Medieval Monastery—Herbord's *Vita* of Bishop Otto of Bamberg." *Studia Monastica* 14 (1972): 49–74.

Dhondt (1952): Dhondt, J. "Petit-Dutaillis et les communes Françaises." *Annales ESC* 7 (1952): 378–84.

Dimier (1972): Dimier, A. "Violences, rixes et homicides chez les Cisterciens." *Revue des Sciences Religieuses* 46 (1972): 38–57.

Dobb ([1946] 1963): Dobb, M. *Studies in the Development of Capitalism.* London, 1946; repr. 1963.

Dockès (1982): Dockès, P. *Medieval Slavery and Liberation.* Trans. A. Goldhammer. Chicago, 1982.

Duby (1966): Duby, G. *The Making of the Christian West 980–1140.* Skira, 1966; republished with its companion volumes in one volume, without color plates as *The Age of the Cathedrals: Art and Society 980–1420.* Trans. E. Levieux and B. Thompson, London 1981; and again, in 1986, with all original color material, as part 1 of G. Duby, *History of Medieval Art 980–1440*, Skira/Weidenfeld and Nicolson, 1986.

Duby (1968): Duby, G. *Rural Economy and Country Life in the Medieval West.* Trans. C. Postan. London, 1968.

Duby (1974): Duby, G. *The Early Growth of the European Economy: Warriors and Peasants from the Seventh to the Twelfth Century.* Trans. H. B. Clarke. London, 1974.

Duby (1982a): Duby, G. *The Three Orders: Feudal Society Imagined.* Trans. A. Goldhammer. Chicago, 1982.

Duby (1982b): Duby, G. "The Culture of the Knightly Class: Audience and Patronage." In Benson and Constable (1982: 249–54).

Duby (1985): Duby G. *The Knight, the Lady and the Priest.* Trans. B. Bray. Peregrine Books, 1985.

Duby (1986): See Duby (1966) above.

Duggan (1963): Duggan, C. *Twelfth-Century Decretal Collections.* London, 1963.

Duggan (1980): Duggan, A. *Thomas Becket: A Textual History of His Letters.* Oxford, 1980.

École Pratique des Hautes Études. Centre de Recherches d'Histoire et de Philologie. *Sous la Règle de Saint Benoît: Structures monastiques et sociétés en France du Moyen Age à l'époque moderne.* Geneva, 1982.

Emery (1952): Emery, R. W. "The Use of the Surname in the Study of Medieval History." *Medievalia et Humanistica* 7 (1952): 45–50.

L'Eremitismo: *L'Eremitismo in Occidente nei Secoli XI e XII.* Pubblic. dell'Università Cattolica del Sacre Cuore, Settimane di Studio. Miscellanea del Centro di studi Medioevali 4 ser. 3, varia, 4. Milan, 1965.

Evans (1931): Evans, Austin P. "Social Aspects of Medieval Heresy." In *Persecution and Liberty: Essays in Honor of George Lincoln Burr.* New York, 1931.

Evans (1931a): Evans, J. *Monastic Life at Cluny 910–1157.* Oxford, 1931.

Evans (1966): Evans, J., ed. *The Flowering of the Middle Ages.* London, 1966.

Evans (1983): Evans, G. *The Mind of St. Bernard of Clairvaux.* Oxford, 1983.

Faillon ([1855] 1865): Faillon, M. *Monuments inédits sur l'apostolat de Sainte-Marie Madeleine en Provence.* Paris 1855; repr. 1865.

Favier (1963): Favier, J. *Un Conseiller de Philippe le Bel: Enguerran de Marigny.* Paris, 1963.

Finucane (1977): Finucane, R. C. *Miracles and Pilgrims: Popular Beliefs in Medieval England.* London, 1977.

Fisher (1979): Fisher, P., trans. *Saxo Grammaticus History of the Danes.* 2 vols. Brewer, 1979.

Flint (1975): Flint, V. I. J. "The *Elucidarius* of Honorius Augustodunensis and the Reform in Late Eleventh-Century England." *Revue Bénédictine* 85 (1975): 178–89; repr. Flint (1988).

Flint (1976): Flint, V. I. J. "The 'School of Laon': A Reconsideration." *Recherches de Théologie Ancienne et Médiévale* 43 (1976): 89–110, repr. Flint (1988).

Flint (1981): Flint, V. I. J. "World history in the Early Twelfth Century: The *Imago Mundi* of Honorius Augustodunensis." In Davis (1981); repr. Flint (1988).

Flint (1988): Flint, V. I. J. *Ideas in the Medieval West: Texts and Their Contents.* Collected Studies: London, 1988.

Flori (1975): Flori, J. "La notion de Chevalrie dans les Chansons de Geste de

XII siècle: Etude historique de vocabulaire." *Le Moyen Age* 81 (1975): 211ff. and 407ff.

Foucault (1977): Foucault, M. "What Is an Author?" In D. Bouchard (1977: 113ff.).

Fredborg (1988): Fredborg, K. M., ed. *The Latin Rhetorical Commentaries by Thierry of Chartres*. Toronto, 1988.

Fuhrmann (1986): Fuhrmann, H. *Germany in the High Middle Ages c1050–1200*. Trans. T. Reuter. Cambridge, 1986.

Galbert of Bruges: See Ross (1960).

Geary (1978): Geary, P. J. *Furta Sacra*. Princeton, 1978.

Geary (1979): Geary, P. J. "L'humiliation des saints." *Annales ESC* 34 (1979): 27–42. See also his "La coercion des saints dans le pratique religieuse médiévale." In *La Culture Populaire du Moyen âge. Études présentées au quatrième colloque de l'institute d'études médiévales de l'Université de Montréal*. Ed. P. Boglioni. Montréal, 1979.

Geary (1986): Geary, P. J. "Le Vivre en conflit dans une France sans etat: Typologie des mécanismes de règlement des conflits (1050–1200)." *Annales ESC* 41, no. 5 (Sept-Oct 1986): 1107–33.

Gibson (1981): Gibson, M. "History at Bec in the Twelfth Century." In Davis (1981).

Gierke (1958): Gierke, O. *Political Theories of the Middle Ages*. Trans. F. W. Maitland (1900; repr. Boston, 1958).

Giles (1847): Giles, J. A., ed. *Petri Blesensis ... opera omnia. ...* 1 *Epistulae*. Oxford, 1847.

Goffart (1966): Goffart, W. *The Le Mans Forgeries*. Cambridge, 1966.

Graham (1918): Graham, Rose. *An Abbot of Vézelay*. London, 1918.

Gransden (1980): Gransden, A. "Antiquarian Studies in Fifteenth-Century England." *The Antiquaries Journal* 60, part 1 (1980): 75–97.

Greenaway (1931): Greenaway, G. W. *Arnold of Brescia*. Cambridge, 1931.

Guenée (1980): Guenée, B. *Histoire et Culture Historique dans L'occident Médiéval*. Paris, 1980.

Guibert of Nogent: See Benton (1970) and Labande (1981).

Guilford (1920): Guilford, E. L. *Select Extracts Illustrating Sports and Pastimes in the Middle Ages*. London, 1920.

Guizot (1852): Guizot, F. *History of the Origin of Representative Government in Europe*. Trans. A. R. Scoble. London, 1852.

Guizot (1969): Guizot. F., trans. *Chronique de l'Abbaye de Vézelay (XIIe siècle): Histoire du monastère de la Madeleine par Hugues de Poitiers*. First appearing in *Collection des Mémoires relatifs à l'histoire de France*, (93)99–337. Paris, 1825. Reissued with annotations by F. Vogade. Vézelay, 1969. All references in the present volume are to the 1969 reissue.

Hallam (1983): Hallam, E. *Capetian France 987–1328*. London, 1983.

Halphen/Poupardin (1913): Halphen, L. and R. Poupardin, eds. *Chroniques des comtes d'Anjou et des seigneurs d'Amboise*. Paris, 1913.

Hamilton (1870): Hamilton, W. E. S. A., ed. *Willelmi Malmesbiriensis Monachi de Gestis Pontificum Anglorum Quinque*. London, Rolls Series, 1870.

Hampe (1973): Hampe, K. *Germany under the Salian and Hohenstaufen Emperors*. Trans. R. Bennett. Oxford, 1973.

Hanning (1966): Hanning, R. W. *The Vision of History in Early Britain: From*

Gildas to Geoffrey of Monmouth. New York, 1966.

Häring (1964): Häring, N. "Thierry of Chartres and Dominicus Gundissalinus." *Medieval Studies* 26 (1964): 271–86.

Häring (1966): Häring, N. "Notes on the Council and Consistory of Rheims (1148)." *Mediaeval Studies* 28 (1966): 39–59.

Haskins ([1927] 1970): Haskins, C. H. *The Renaissance of the Twelfth Century.* New York, 1970.

Haverkamp (1988): Haverkamp, A. *Medieval Germany 1056–1273.* Oxford, 1988.

Hay (1977): Hay, D. *Annalists and Historians: Western Historiography from the VIIIth to the XVIIIth Century.* London, 1977.

Head and Landes (1987): Head, T., and R. Landes, eds. *Essays on the Peace of God: The Church and the People in Eleventh-Century France.* Historical Reflections/Reflexions Historiques 14, no. 3 (1987): 381–549.

Hearne (1720): Hearne, T. ed. *Textus Roffensis.* Oxford, 1720.

Heinemeyer (1964): Heinemeyer, W. "Die Verhandlung an der Saône im Jahre 1162." *Deutsches Archiv f. Erforschung des MA* 20 (1964): 155–89.

Herlihy (1968): Herlihy, D. *Medieval Culture and Society.* New York, 1968.

Hibbert (1953): Hibbert, A. B. "The Origins of the Medieval Town Patriciate." *Past and Present* 3 (1953): 15–27; repr. in Tierney (1970b: 135ff.) and Tierney (1974: 154ff.).

Hilton (1973): Hilton, Rodney. *Bond Men Made Free: Medieval Peasant Movements and the English Rising of 1381.* London, 1973.

Hinschius (1963): Hinschius, Paulus. *Decretales pseudo-Isidorianae, Et Capitula Angilramni.* Repr. Aalen, 1963.

Holdsworth and Wiseman (1986): Holdsworth, C., and T. P. Wiseman, eds. *The Inheritance of Historiography 350–900.* Exeter, 1986.

Howe (1988): Howe, J. "The Nobility's Reform of the Medieval Church." *American Historical Review* 93 (1988): 317–39.

Hunt (1967): Hunt, N. *Cluny under Saint Hugh, 1049–1109.* London, 1967.

Hunt (1971): Hunt, N., ed. *Cluniac Monasticism in the Central Middle Ages.* Hamden, CN, 1971.

Huygens (1976): Huygens, R. B. C. *Monumenta Vizeliacensia: Textes relatifs à l'histoire de l'abbaye de Vézelay.* Corpus Christianorum, Continuatio Medievalis 42. Brepols, Turnhout, 1976.

Huygens (1980): Huygens, R. B. C. *Vizeliacensia II: Textes relatifs àl'histoire de l'abbaye de Vézelay.* Corpus Christianorum, Continuatio Medievalis 42 Suppl. 1980.

Jaeger (1985): Jaeger, C. S. *The Origins of Courtliness: Civilizing Trends and the Formation of Courtly Ideals 939–1210.* Philadelphia, 1985.

James (1953): James, B. S., trans. *The Letters of St. Bernard of Clairvaux.* London, 1953.

James (1986): James, J. *The Travellers Key to Medieval France: A Guide to the Sacred Architecture of Medieval France.* New York, 1986.

John of Salisbury: See Chibnall (1956).

Johnson (1963): Johnson, Douglas. *Guizot: Aspects of French History 1787–1874.* London, 1963.

Johnson (1989): Johnson, S. "A Re-assessment of the Origins of Medieval Heresy in Western Europe, with Particular Reference to the Role of Towns and Urban Change." M.A. thesis, Sydney Univ., 1989.

Jones (1943): Jones, C. W. *Bedae Opera de Temporibus*. Cambridge, MA, 1943.

Jordan (1976): Jordan, W. C., B. McNab, and T. Ruiz, eds. *Order and Innovation in the Middle Ages: Essays in Honor of J. R. Strayer*. Princeton, 1976.

Jordan (1986): Jordan, W. C. *From Servitude to Freedom: Manumission in the Séonnais in the Thirteenth Century*. Philadelphia, 1986.

Joris (1988): Joris, A. "Espagne et Lotharingie vers l'an mil. Aux origines des franchises urbaines?" *Le Moyen Age* 94 (1988): 5-19.

Kaiser (1981): Kaiser, Reinhold. *Bischofsherrschaft zwischen Königtum und Fürstenmacht: Studien zur bischöflichen Stadtherrschaft im west fränkisch-französischen Reich im frühen und hohen Mittelalter*. Pariser Historische Studien. Bd 17. Bonn, 1981.

Kantorowicz (1957): Kantorowicz, E. H. *The King's Two Bodies: A Study in Medieval Political Theology*. Princeton, 1957.

Katzenellenbogen (1944): Katzenellenbogen, A. "The Central Tympanum at Vézelay, its Encyclopedic Meaning and its Relation to the First Crusade." *Art Bulletin* 26 (1944): 141-51.

Kedar (1973): Kedar, B. Z. "Toponymic Surnames as Evidence of Origin: Some Medieval Views." *Viator* 4 (1973): 123-29.

Keller (1970): Keller, H. "Die Soziale und Politische Verfassung Mailands in den Anfangen des Komunalen Lebens; zu einem neuen Buch ..." *Historische Zeitschrift* 211 (1970): 34-64.

Kelly (1986): Kelly, J. N. D. *The Oxford Dictionary of Popes*. Oxford, 1986.

Kennelly (1963): Kennelly, D. "Medieval Towns and the Peace of God." *Medievalia et Humanistica* 15 (1963): 35-53.

Klibansky (1961): Klibansky, R. "Peter Abailard and Bernard of Clairvaux: A Letter by Abailard." *Mediaeval and Renaissance Studies* 5 (1961): 1-27.

Knowles ([1949] 1962): Knowles, D. *The Monastic Order in England*. Cambridge, 1949; repr. 1962.

Knowles (1963): Knowles, D. *The Historian and Character*. London, 1963.

Knowles (1969): Knowles, D. *Christian Monasticism*. London, 1969.

Labande (1981): Labande, E. R., intr., ed., trans., *Guibert de Nogent, Autobiographie* (Les Belles Lettres). Paris, 1981.

Lacaze (1971): Lacaze, Y. "Le Rôle des Traditions dans la Genèse d'un Sentiment Nationale au XVe Siècle: La Bourgogne de Philippe Le Bon." *BEC* (1971): 303-85.

Lackner (1972): Lackner, Bede. *The Eleventh Century Background of Cîteaux*. Washington D. C., 1972.

Lacroix (1874): Lacroix, P., *Military and Religious Life in the Middle Ages and Renaissance*. London, 1874.

Ladurie: See Le Roy Ladurie.

Langmuir (1970): Langmuir, Gavin I. "Community and Legal Change in Capetian France." *French Historical Studies* 6 (1970): 275-86.

Latham (1965): Latham, R. E. *Revised Medieval Latin Word-list from British and Irish Sources*. London, 1965.

Latouche (1966a): Latouche, R. *The Birth of the Western Economy: Economic Aspects of the Dark Ages*. Trans. E. M. Wilkinson. New York, 1966.

Latouche (1966b): Latouche, R. *Études Médiévales: La France de l'Ouest des Pyrénées aux Alpes*. Paris, 1966.

Lea (1892): Lea, H. C. *Superstition and Force: Essays on the Wager of Law, the Wager of Battle, the Ordeal, Torture.* 4th ed. Philadelphia, 1892.

Leach (1985): Leach, E., S. Mukherjee, and J. Ward. *Feudalism: Comparative Studies.* Sydney, 1985.

Lebreton (1955): Lebreton, M. M. "Les sermons de Julien moine de Vézelay." *Studia Anselmiana* 37 (1955): 118–32.

Leclercq (1949): Leclercq, J., ed. and trans. *Yves de Chartres–Correspondance* 1 Paris, 1949.

Leclercq (1961): Leclercq, J. *The Love of Learning and the Desire for God: A Study of Monastic Culture.* New York, 1961.

Leclercq (1962, 1966, 1969): Leclercq, J. *Recueil d'Études sur Saint Bernard et ses écrits.* 3 vols. Rome 1962, 1966, 1969.

Leclercq (1970): Leclercq, J. "Monastic Historiography from Leo IX to Callistus II." *Studia Monastica* 12 (1970): 57–86.

Leclercq (1971): Leclercq, J. "The Monastic Crisis of the 11th and 12th Centuries." In Hunt (1971).

L'Eretismo: See above under "E."

Le Roy Ladurie (1979): Le Roy Ladurie. *Carnival in Romans.* Trans. M. Feeney. New York, 1979.

Le Roy Ladurie (1980): *Montaillou, The World Famous Portrait of Life in a Medieval Village.* Trans. B. Bray. Penguin Books, 1980.

Lespinasse (1909–14): Lespinasse, R. de. *Le Nivernais et les comtes de Nevers* 1–3. Paris, 1909–1914.

Lewis (1987): Lewis, Suzanne. *The Art of Matthew Paris in the Chronica Majora.* Scholar Press, 1987.

Lewis & Short: Lewis, C. T., and C. Short. *A Latin Dictionary.* Oxford, 1879; repr. 1933.

Leyser (1979): Leyser, K. J., *Rule and Conflict in an Early Medieval Society.* London, 1979.

Leyser (1984): Leyser, H. *Hermits and the New Monasticism: A Study of Religious Communities in Western Europe 1000–1150.* London, 1984.

Little (1971): Little. L. K. "Pride Goes Before Avarice: Social Change and the Vices in Latin Christendom." *American Historical Review* 76 (1971): 16–49.

Little (1978): Little, L. K. *Religious Poverty and the Profit Economy in Medieval Europe.* Ithaca, 1978.

Lombard-Jourdan (1972): Lombard-Jourdan, A. "Oppidum et banlieu: Sur l'origine et les dimensions du territoire urbain." *Annales ESC* 27 (1972): 373–95.

Lopez (1953): Lopez, R. S. "An Aristocracy of Money in the Early Middle Ages." *Speculum* 28 (1953): 1–43.

Lopez ([1959] 1965): Lopez, R. S. *The Tenth Century: How Dark the Dark Ages?* Holt, Rinehart and Winston, 1959; repr. 1965.

Lot (1903): Lot, F. "La Chanson de Landri." *Romania* 32 (1903): 1–17.

Lot and Fawtier (1962): Lot, F., and R. Fawtier. *Histoire des Institutions Francaises au Moyen Age* 3. Paris, 1962.

Louis (1946): Louis, R. *De l'histoire à legende, I Giraut, Comte de Vienne (... 819–877) et ses fondations monastiques.* Auxerre, 1946.

Loyn and Percival (1975): Loyn, H. R., and J. Percival. *The Reign of Charlemagne: Documents on Carolingian Government and Administration.* London, 1975.

Luchaire (1883): Luchaire, A. *Histoire des institutions monarchiques de la France sous les premiers Capétiens*. 2 vols. Paris, 1883.

Luchaire (1885): Luchaire, A. *Études sur les actes de Louis VII*. Paris, 1885.

Luchaire (1890): Luchaire, A. *Les communes françaises à l'époque des Capétiens directs*. Paris, 1890. Revised edition ed. L. Halphen (1911).

Lynch (1975): Lynch, Jos. "Monastic Recruitment in the 11th and 12th Centuries." *American Benedictine Review* 26 (1975): 425–47.

Lynch (1976): Lynch, Jos. *Simoniacal Entry into Religious Life from 1000 to 1260*. Columbus, 1976.

Lyon (1964): Lyon, B., ed. *The High Middle Ages 1000–1300*. New York, 1964.

Mackinney (1930): Mackinney, L. C. "The People and Public Opinion in the Eleventh-Century Peace Movement." *Speculum* 5 (1930): 181–206.

Mackrell (1973): Mackrell, J. Q. C. *The Attack on "Feudalism" in Eighteenth-Century France*. London, 1973.

Magasin St. Bernard: See Vogade-Pouyaud.

Markus (1970): Markus, R. A. *Saeculum: History and Society in the Theology of St. Augustine*. Cambridge, 1970.

Martinet (1972): Martinet, S. *Montloon*. Laon, 1972.

Marx (1975): Marx, Karl. *Pre-Capitalist Economic Formations*. Trans. J. Cohen, ed. E. J. Hobsbawm. New York, 1965.

Mayer (1972): Mayer, H. E. *The Crusades*. Trans. J. Gillingham. Oxford, 1972.

McGregor and Wright (1977): F. McGregor, and N. Wright, eds. *European History and Its Historians*. Adelaide, 1977.

MGH: *Monumenta Germaniae Historica*.

Michelin Guide: *Michelin Tourist Guide Burgundy*. Clermont-Ferrand, 1988.

Mierow (1953): Mierow, C. C., trans. Otto of Freising, *The Deeds of Frederick Barbarossa*. New York, 1953; repr. 1966.

Miller, Prosser and Benson (1973): Miller, J. M., M. H. Prosser, and T. W. Benson, eds. *Readings in Medieval Rhetoric*. Indiana Univ. Press, 1973.

Mirot (1945): Mirot, L. "Les origines des premiers comtes héréditaires de Nevers." *Annales de Bourgogne* 17 (1945): 7–15.

Molinier (1887): Molinier, A. *Vie de Louis le Gros par Suger, suivie de l'histoire du Roi Louis VII*. Paris, 1887.

Moore (1975): Moore, R. I., ed. *The Birth of Popular Heresy*. London, 1975.

Moore (1980): Moore, R. I. "Family, Community and Cult on the Eve of the Gregorian Reform." *Transactions of the Royal Historical Society* ser. 5, vol. 30 (1980): 49–69.

Moore (1986): Moore, R. I. "New Sects and Secret Meetings: Association and Authority in the Eleventh and Twelfth Centuries." *Studies in Church History* 23 (1986): 47–68.

Moore (1987): Moore, R. I. *The Formation of a Persecuting Society: Power and Deviance in Medieval Europe 950–1250*. Oxford, 1987.

Morey and Brooke (1965): Morey, A., and C. N. L. Brooke. *Gilbert Foliot and His Letters*. Cambridge, 1965.

Morgan (1982): Morgan, D. O., ed. *Medieval Historical Writing in the Christian and Islamic Worlds*. London, 1982.

Morrison (1969): Morrison, K. F. *Tradition and Authority in the Western Church 300–1140*. Princeton, 1969.

Mortensen (1987): Mortensen, L. B. "Saxo Grammaticus' View of the Origin of the Danes and His Historiographical Models." *Cahiers de l'Institut du Moyen Age Grec et Latin* 55 (1987): 169–83.

MPG: Migne, J. P. L. *Patrologiae cursus completus, Series Graeca.*

Mukherjee and Ward (1989): Mukherjee, S., and J. Ward, eds. *Revolution as History.* Sydney, 1989.

Mundy (1985): Mundy, J. H. *The Repression of Catharism at Toulouse: The Royal Diploma of 1279.* Toronto, 1985.

Munz (1969): Munz, P. *Frederick Barbarossa.* London, 1969.

Murphy (1974): Murphy, J. J. *Rhetoric in the Middle Ages: A History of Rhetorical Theory from St. Augustine to the Renaissance.* Berkeley, 1974.

Murray (1978): Murray, A. "Money and Robbers 900–1100." *Journal of Medieval History* 4 (1978): 55–94.

Mycoff (1988): Mycoff, D. A. "The Legend of Mary Magdalene in a Twelfth-Century Cistercian Context." *Cistercian Studies* 23 (1988): 310–18.

Mycoff (1989): Mycoff, D. A. *The Life of Saint Mary Magdalen and of Her Sister Saint Martha: A Medieval Biography* [attributed to Rabanus Maurus]. Cistercian Studies #108. Kalamazoo, 1989.

NCE: *New Catholic Encyclopedia.* Cf. such articles as "Vézelay," "Ordination," "Excommunication"; others are cited in the course of the present volume.

Nederman (1989): Nederman, C. "The Changing Face of Tyranny: The Reign of King Stephen in John of Salisbury's Political Thought." *Nottingham Medieval Studies* 33 (1989): 1–20.

Nelson (1972): Nelson, Janet L. "Society, Theodicy and the Origins of Medieval Heresy: Towards a Reassessment of the Medieval Evidence." *Studies in Church History* 9 (1972): 65–77.

Nelson (1980): Nelson, Janet L. "Survey Article: Religion in 'Histoire Totale': Some Recent Work on Medieval Heresy and Popular Religion." *Religion* 10 (1980): 60–85.

Nichols (1983): Nichols, S. G. *Romanesque Signs: Early Medieval Narrative and Iconography.* New Haven, 1983.

Niermeyer (1976): Niermeyer, J. F. *Mediae Latinitatis Lexicon Minus.* 2 vols. Leiden, 1976.

Obelkevich (1979): Obelkevich, J., ed. *Religion and the People 800–1700.* Chapel Hill, 1979.

Oexle (1979): Oexle, O. G. "Die mittelalterlichen Gilden: ihre Selbstdeutung und ihr Beitrag zur Formung sozialer Strukturen." In *Soziale Ordnungen im Selbstverständnis des Mittelalters, Miscellanea Mediaevalia veröff. des Thomas-Inst. der Univ. Köln* 12/1. Ed. A. Zimmerman, 230–26. Berlin, NY, 1979.

Ouellette (1982): Ouellette, Helen T., ed. *William of Malmesbury's Polyhistor.* Binghamton, NY, 1982.

Oursel (1982): Oursel, R. *Routes Romanes.* Saint-Léger-Vauban: Zodiaque, 1982.

Pacaut (1953): Pacaut, M. "Louis VII et Alexandre III (1159–1180)." *Revue d'Histoire de l'Église de France* 39 (1953): 5–45.

Pacaut (1955): Pacaut, M. "Les légats d'Alexandre III (1159–1181)." *Revue d'Histoire Ecclésiastique* 50 (1955): 821–38.

Pacaut (1957): Pacaut, M. *Louis VII et les Elections Episcopales dans le Royaume de France.* Paris, 1957.

Pacaut (1964): Pacaut, M. *Louis VII et Son Royaume.* Paris, 1964.

Pacaut (1970): Pacaut, M. *Frederick Barbarossa.* London, 1970.

Painter (1961): Painter, S. *Feudalism and Liberty*, ed. F. A. Cazel. Baltimore, 1961.

Peters (1973): Peters, E. *The Ordeal*. Philadelphia, 1973.

Peters (1974): Peters, E. *The Duel and the Oath*. Philadelphia, 1974.

Peters (1978): Peters, E. *The Magician, the Witch and the Law*. Philadelphia, 1978.

Peters (1980): Peters, E. *Heresy and Authority in Medieval Europe*. Philadelphia, 1980.

Peters (1988): Peters, E. *Inquisition*. London, 1988.

Petit-Dutaillis ([1947] 1970): Petit-Dutaillis, Ch. *Les communes françaises. Caractères et évolution des origines au XVIIIe siècle*. Paris, 1947; repr. 1970; English translation: North Holland, Amsterdam 1978 under title of *French Communes in the Middle Ages*. All references are to the French edition.

Petit-Dutaillis (1964): Petit-Dutaillis, Ch. *The Feudal Monarchy in France and England from the 10th to the 13th Century*. Trans. E. D. Hunt. New York, 1964.

Petot (1949): Petot, P. "License de mariage et formariage des serfs dans les coutoumiers français au moyen âge." *Annales d'histoire de droit* 2 (1949): 199–208.

Phipps (1985): Phipps, Colin "Romuald—Model Hermit: Eremetical Theory in Saint Peter Damian's *Vita Beati Romualdi*, Chapters 16–27." *Studies in Church History* 22 (1985): 65–77.

Pissier (1902/1903): Pissier, A. "Notice historique sur Saint-Père-sous-Vézelay." In *BSSY* 56 (1902): 133–76 and 275–368; and 57 (1903): 11–91.

Pissier (1923): Pissier, A. *Le Culte de Sainte Marie Madeleine à Vézelay (Saint-Père-sous-Vézelay)*.

PL = J. P. Migne, ed. *Patrologiae cursus completus, Series Latina*.

Poole (1926): Poole, R. L. *Chronicles and Annals: A Brief Outline of their Origin and Growth*. Oxford, 1926.

Poole (1934): Poole, R. L. "The Beginning of the Year in the Middle Ages." In his *Studies in Chronology and History*, 1–27. Oxford, 1934.

Postgate (1950): Postgate, J. P. *Select Elegies of Propertius*. London, 1950.

Potthast ([1896] 1957): Potthast, A. *Wegweiser durch die Geschichtswerke des Europäischen Mittelalters bis 1500* 1. Graz, 1896; repr. 1957.

Pounds (1974): Pounds, N. G. *An Economic History of Medieval Europe*. London, 1974.

Pullan (1966): Pullan, B. *Sources for the History of Medieval Europe from the Mid-8th to the Mid-13th Century*. Oxford, 1966.

Quantin (1854/1860): Quantin, M. *Cartulaire général de l'Yonne*. 2 vols. Auxerre, 1854 and 1860.

Ray (1974): Ray, R. D. "Medieval Historiography Through the Twelfth Century: Problems and Progress of Research." *Viator* 5 (1974): 35–59.

Recueil: *Recueil des Historiens de France*. 24 vols. Paris, 1737–1904.

Reynolds (1984): Reynolds, S. *Kingdoms and Communities in Western Europe 900–1300*. Oxford, 1984.

RHC: *Recueil des Historiens des Croisades, Historiens Occidentaux*. 5 vols. Paris, 1844–1895.

Robertson (1881): Robertson, J. C. *Materials for the History of Thomas Becket, Archbishop of Canterbury*. 7 vols. London, Rolls Series, 1881.

Rosenwein (1971): Rosenwein, B. "Feudal War and Monastic Peace: Cluniac Liturgy as Ritual Aggression." *Viator* 2 (1971): 129–57.

Rosenwein (1982): Rosenwein, B. *Rhinoceros Bound: Cluny in the Tenth Century.* Philadelphia, 1982.

Rosenwein and Little (1974): Rosenwein, B., and L. K. Little. "Social Meaning in the Monastic and Mendicant Spiritualities." *Past and Present* 63 (1974): 4–32.

Ross (1960): Ross, J. B., trans. *The Murder of Charles the Good, Count of Flanders, by Galbert of Bruges.* New York, 1960.

Rouse (1967): Rouse, R. H., and Mary A. "John of Salisbury and the Doctrine of Tyrannicide." *Speculum* 42 (1967): 693–709.

Rouse (1979): Rouse, R. H., and Mary A. *Preachers, Florilegia and Sermons: Studies on the Manipulus Florum of Thomas of Ireland.* Toronto, 1979.

Runciman (1952): Runciman, S. *A History of the Crusades.* Harmondsworth, 1952.

Russell (1965): Russell, J. B. *Dissent and Reform in the Early Middle Ages.* Univ. of California Press, 1965.

Salet and Adhémar (1948): Salet, F., and J. Adhémar. *La Madeleine de Vézelay* [+ *Étude iconographique par Jean Adhémar*]. Melun, 1948.

Salvini (1969): Salvini, R. *Medieval Sculpture.* New York, 1969.

Sassier (1980): Sassier, Y. *Recherches sur le pouvoir comtal en Auxerrois du Xe au début du XIIIe siècle.* Paris-Auxerre, 1980.

Sassier (1986): Sassier, Y. "L'Expansion Clunisienne En Nivernois et Auxerrois." *Memoires de la Société pour l'histoire du droit et des institutions des anciens pays bourguignons comtois et romands* (1986): 57–75.

Saulnier and Stratford (1984): Saulnier, L., and N. Stratford. *La Sculpture Oubliée de Vézelay: Catalogue du Musée Lapidaire.* Geneva and Paris, 1984.

Saxer (1955): Saxer, V. "L'origine des reliques de sainte Marie Madeleine à Vézelay dans la tradition historique du moyen âge." *Revue des sciences religieuses* 29 (1955): 1–18.

Saxer (1956): Saxer, V. "Le statut juridique de Vézelay des origines à la fin de XIIe siècle. Contribution à l'histoire des privilèges monastiques d'immunité et d'exemption." *Revue de Droit canonique* 6 (1956): 225–62.

Saxer (1959): Saxer, V. *Le culte de Marie Madeleine en Occident des origines à la fin du moyen âge.* Auxerre-Paris, 1959.

Saxer (1975): Saxer, V. *Le Dossier Vézelien de Marie Madeleine. Invention et translation des reliques en 1265–1267. Contribution à l'histoire du culte de la sainte à Vézelay à l'apogée du moyen âge.* Subsidia hagiographica 57. Brussels, 1975.

Schmitt (1984): Schmitt, J. C. "Temps, Folklore et Politique au XIIe siècle: a propos de deux recits de Walter Map *De nugis curialium* I 9 et IV 13 (= I 11)." In *Le Temps Chrétien de la fin de l'Antiquité au Moyen Age IIIe–XIIIe siècle* (Colloques Internationaux du Centre National de la Recherche Scientifique no. 604), 489–515. Paris, 1984.

Scholz (1971): Scholz, Bernhard W. "Why Men Rebel." *History Today* 21 (1971): 123–31.

Scott (1972): Scott, J. "Intellectual Life in the Monastery of Christchurch, Canterbury 1070–1205." B.A. thesis, Sydney Univ., 1972.

Scott (1981): Scott, J. *The Early History of Glastonbury.* Woodbridge, Suffolk, 1981.

Scott (1988): Scott, J., R. Thomson, and J. Ward. *Hugh of Poitiers, the Vézelay Chronicle and Other Documents from MS. Auxerre 227 and Elsewhere, Translated into English with Notes, Introduction and Accompanying Material.* Sydney: Medieval Texts in Translation no. 3, Sydney Univ. Printing Service, 1988. This publication represents the unimproved, and shorter, "first edition" of the present volume.

Searle (1979): Searle, E. "Seigneurial Control of Women's Marriage: The Antecedents and Functions of Merchet in England." *Past and Present* 82 (1979): 3–43.

Seidel (1981): Seidel, Linda. *Songs of Glory: The Romanesque Façades of Aquitaine.* Chicago, 1981.

Shriver (1974): Shriver, G. H., ed. *Contemporary Reflections on the Medieval Christian Tradition.* Durham, N. C., 1974.

Siberry (1990): Siberry, E. "The Crusading Counts of Nevers." *Nottingham Medieval Studies* 34 (1990): 64–70.

Skinner (1984): Skinner, Mary "Benedictine Life for Women in Central France, 850–1100: A Feminist Revival." In J. A. Nichols and L. T. Shank, eds. *Medieval Religious Women*, vol. 1: *Distant Echoes*. Kalamazoo, 1984.

Smalley (1970): Smalley, B. *The Study of the Bible in the Middle Ages.* Notre Dame, 1970.

Smalley (1973): Smalley, B. *The Becket Conflict and the Schools.* Oxford, 1973.

Smalley (1974): Smalley, B. *Historians of the Middle Ages.* London, 1974.

Solt (1987): Solt, C. W. "Romanesque French Reliquaries." *Studies in Medieval and Renaissance History* 9 [Old Series 19] (1987): 167–236.

Somerville (1977): Somerville, R. *Pope Alexander III and the Council of Tours (1163): A Study of Ecclesiastical Politics in the Twelfth Century.* Univ. of California Press, 1977.

Southern (1953): Southern, R. W. *The Making of the Middle Ages.* London, 1953.

Southern (1970): Southern, R. W. *Western Society and the Church in the Middle Ages.* Harmondsworth, 1970.

Speaight (1990): Speaight, R. *The Companion Guide to Burgundy.* Rev. and expanded by F. Pagan. London, 1990.

Stenton (1913): Stenton, F. *The Early History of the Abbey of Abingdon.* Oxford, 1913.

Stephenson ([1954] 1967): Stephenson, C. "The Origin and Nature of the *Taille.*" In B. D. Lyon, ed. *Medieval Institutions, Selected Essays.* Ithaca, 1954; repr. 1967.

Stevenson (1858): Stevenson, J., ed. *Chronicon Monasterii de Abingdon.* London, Rolls Series, 1858.

Stock (1983): Stock, B. *The Implications of Literacy: Written Language and Models of Interpretation in the 11th and 12th Centuries.* Princeton, 1983.

Stroll (1987): Stroll, M. *The Jewish Pope: Ideology and Politics in the Papal Schism of 1130.* Leiden, 1987.

Stubbs (1887–1889): Stubbs, W., ed. *Willelmi Malmesbiriensis Monachi de Gestis Regum Anglorum Libri Quinque.* 2 vols. London, Rolls Series, 1887–1889.

Sumption (1975): Sumption, J. *Pilgrimage: An Image of Medieval Religion.* London, 1975.

Taylor (1961): Taylor, J., trans. *The Didascalicon of Hugh of St. Victor: A Medieval Guide to the Arts.* New York, 1961.

Taylor (1980): Taylor, M. "The Pentecost at Vézelay." *Gesta* 19 (1980): 9–15.
Tellenbach (1966): Tellenbach, Gerd. *Church, State and Christian Society at the Time of the Investiture Contest.* Trans. R. F. Bennett. Oxford, 1966.
Thierry (1851): Thierry, Augustin. *Lettres sur L'Histoire de France.* Paris, 1851.
Thomson (1973): Thomson, R. M., ed. *Tractatus Garsiae.* Leiden, 1973.
Thomson (1974): Thomson, R. M., ed. and trans. *The Chronicle of the Election of Hugh, Abbot of Bury St. Edmunds and Later Bishop of Ely.* Oxford, 1974.
Thomson (1975): Thomson, R. M. "An English Eye-witness of the Peace of Venice 1177." *Speculum* 50 (1975): 21–32.
Thomson (1978): Thomson, R. M. "The Origins of Latin Satire in Twelfth Century Europe." *Mittellateinisches Jahrbuch* 13 (1978): 78–83.
Thomson (1987): Thomson, R. M. *William of Malmesbury.* Woodbridge, Suffolk, 1987.
Thrupp (1964): Thrupp, S. L., ed. *Change in Medieval Society.* New York, 1964.
Thrupp (1967): Thrupp, S. L., ed. *Early Medieval Society.* New York, 1967.
Tierney (1970a): Tierney, B., ed. *The Middle Ages 1: Sources of Medieval History.* New York, 1970, 1973, 1978, 1983.
Tierney (1970b): Tierney, B., ed. *The Middle Ages 2: Readings in Medieval History.* New York, 1970, 1974.
Tierney (1974): See Tierney (1970b).
Turner (1969): Turner, V. *The Ritual Process: Structure and Anti-structure.* Chicago, 1969.
Ullmann (1961): Ullmann, W. *Principles of Government and Politics in the Middle Ages.* London, 1961.
Ullmann (1969): Ullmann, W. *The Carolingian Renaissance and the Idea of Kingship.* London, 1969.
Ullmann (1971): Ullmann, W. "Public Welfare and Social Legislation in the Early Medieval Councils." *Studies in Church History* 7 (1971): 1–39.
Ullmann (1972): Ullmann, W. *A Short History of the Papacy in the Middle Ages.* London, 1972.
Ullmann (1975): Ullmann, W. *Law and Politics in the Middle Ages.* London, 1975.
Van Engen (1983): Van Engen, J. *Rupert of Deutz.* London, 1983.
Van Engen (1986): Van Engen, J. "The 'Crisis of Cenobitism' Reconsidered: Benedictine Monasticism in the Years 1050–1150." *Speculum* 61 (1986): 269–304.
Vaughan (1986): Vaughan, R., ed. and trans. *Chronicles of Matthew Paris: Monastic Life in the Thirteenth Century.* New York, 1986.
Verhulst (1989): Verhulst, A. "The Origins of Towns in the Low Countries and the Pirenne Thesis." *Past and Present* 122 (1989): 3–35.
Vermeesch (1966): Vermeesch, A. *Essai sur les Origines et la signification de la commune dans le Nord de la France.* Heule, 1966.
Vielliard ([1938] 1978): Viellard, Jeanne, ed. and trans. *Le Guide du Pèlerin de Saint-Jacques de Compostelle, texte latin du XIIe siècle.* Macon, 1938; repr. 1978.
Vogade-Pouyaud: Pouyaud, R., and F. Vogade. *Vézelay and Surroundings.* Magasin St. Bernard, Vézelay, n.d.
Vogade (1987): Vogade, F. *Vézelay: Histoire, Iconographie, Symbolisme.* Bellegarde, 1987.
Vorreux (1972): Vorreux, D., ed. and trans. *Julien de Vézelay. Sermons.* Sources Chrétiennes no. 192. Paris, 1972.

Wahrmund ([1916] 1962): Wahrmund, L., ed. *Der Ordo Judiciarius des Aegidius de Fuscarariis*. 1916; repr. Scientia Verlag Aalen, 1962.

Wakefield and Evans (1969): Wakefield, W. L., and A. P. Evans. *Heresies of the High Middle Ages*. New York, 1969.

Walther (1963-70): Walther, H. *Lateinische Sprichwörter und Sentenzen des Mittelalters in Alphabetischer Anordnung*. Göttingen, 1963-1970.

Ward (1975): Ward, J. O. "Twelfth-Century Social Unrest: The Vézelay Charter of 1137, a Case of Unsuccessful Arbitration." *Studium* (Sydney) 7 (1975).

Ward (1977a): Ward, J. O. *The Middle Ages*. Holt, Rinehart and Winston, 1977.

Ward (1977b): Ward, J. O. *The Conflict of Faith and Fact*. Holt, Rinehart and Winston, 1977.

Ward (1977c): Ward, J. O. *Towns and Revolution in the Middle Ages*. Holt, Rinehart and Winston, 1977.

Ward (1977d): Ward, J. O. "Classical Rhetoric and the Writing of History in Medieval and Renaissance Culture." In McGregor and Wright (1977: 1-10).

Ward (1977e): Ward, J. O. "The Laon Institutio Pacis of 1128 AD, Translation and Commentary." *Studium* (Sydney) 8 (1977).

Ward (1979): Ward, J. O. "Gothic Architecture, Universities and the Decline of the Humanities in Twelfth-Century Europe." In L. C. Frappell, ed., *Principalities, Powers and Estates: Studies in Medieval and Early Modern Government and Society*. Adelaide, 1979.

Ward (1981): Ward, J. O. "Women, Witchcraft and Social Patterning in the Later Roman Lawcodes." *Prudentia* 13:2 (1981): 99-118.

Ward (1982): Ward, B. *Miracles and the Medieval Mind: Theory, Record and Event*. Philadelphia, 1982.

Ward (1985): Ward, J. O. "Some Principles of Rhetorical Historiography in the Twelfth Century." In Breisach (1985: 103-65).

Ward (1985b): Ward, J. O. "Feudalism: Interpretative Category or Framework of Life in the Medieval West?" in Leach (1985: 40-67).

Ward (1988): Ward, J. O. "Magic and Rhetoric from Antiquity to the Renaissance: Some Ruminations." *Rhetorica* 6 (1988): 57-118.

Ward (1989): See Mukherjee and Ward (1989).

Ward (1990): Ward, J. O. "Rhetoric, Truth, Literacy and the Renaissance of the Twelfth Century." In R. L. Enos, ed., *Oral and Written Communication: Historical Approaches* 4 (1990).

Weinstein (1982): Weinstein, D., and R. Bell. *Saints and Society: Two Worlds of Western Christendom 1000-1700*. Chicago: Univ. of Chicago Press, 1982.

Weintraub ([1966] 1969): Weintraub, G. *Visions of Culture: Voltaire, Guizot, Burkhardt. Lamprecht, Huizinga, Ortega y Gasset*. Chicago: Univ. of Chicago Press, 1966; repr. 1969.

Weiss (1974): Weiss, M. "The Castellan: The Early Career of Hubert de Burgh." *Viator* 5 (1974): 235-52.

Williams (1952): Williams, W. *St. Bernard of Clairvaux*. Manchester, 1952.

Wilks (1971): Wilks, M. J. "*Ecclesiastica* and *Regalia*: Papal Investiture Policy from the Council of Guastalla to the First Lateran Council." *Studies in Church History* 7 (1971): 69-85.

Wilson (1983): Wilson, S. *Saints and Their Cults: Studies in Religious Sociology, Folklore and History*. Cambridge, 1983.

Witt (1971): Witt, R. G. "The Landlord and the Economic Revival of the Middle Ages in Northern Europe 1000–1250." *American Historical Review* 76 (1971): 965–88.

Yunck (1963): Yunck, J. A. *The Lineage of Lady Meed: The Development of Medieval Venality Satire.* Univ. of Notre Dame Press, 1963.

Zacour (1969). Zacour, N. *An Introduction to Medieval Institutions.* New York, 1969.

Zarnecki (1972): Zarnecki, G. *The Monastic Achievement.* London, 1972.

Ziolkowski (1985): Ziolkowski, J. *Alan of Lille's Grammar of Sex: The Meaning of Grammar to a Twelfth-Century Intellectual.* Cambridge, MA, 1985.

Fig. 17. All that is left today of the Upper Church of St. Peter (J. O. Ward).

Topical Index

The following Topical Index, when combined with the Questions for Analysis, will guide the reader quickly to the ways in which the present volume can open up important perspectives on key issues and themes in central medieval western society and culture. The index is selective rather than exhaustive. Some proper names are included (see also the entry "proper names"), but for more comprehensive coverage here the reader is advised to consult Huygens (1976: 632ff.). The correct place in the present volume can be readily located by reference to the Huygens page and line number given after each of the major "chapters" into which the *Major Chronicle* is divided in the present translation, or by reference to the charter number in the *Cartulary*, etc. The word "passim" below indicates that the reader can expect to locate many occasional references relevant to this entry that are not reported in the present index. Further information on some themes can also be acquired by consulting the Index of Latin Terms and Phrases below.

Advocacy and rights of justice 6, 8, 14, 23–26, 66–67, 133, 158, 160: *See also* Justice, rights of

Agricultural activities: *See* Economic activity

Allod: *See* Feudalism

Annals 87–91: *See also* Historiography

Art and architecture, building 1, 48–51, 78, 132n.3, 214n.7, 256

Banal dues and rights: *See* Serfdom

Bernard of Clairvaux 73, 85, 110, 160

Bishops, powers, ambitions, duties of 5, 16, 20–22, 65–66, 69–70, 78, 85, 92–94, 112–13, 115–16, 119–27, 131–50, 176–79, 196–97, 219–20, 255, 263–64, 267, 283, 297–98, 303: *See also* Vézelay: later history of; and letters addressed to bishops in the *Cartulary* 97–129

Blood-letting 95

Bosham, Herbert of, letter by 331–33

Caesar 291

Capetian monarchy 308: *See also* Crown

Castration 301

Chansons de geste 3–4, 78, 295: *See also* Vézelay: origins of; and the *Brief History of the First Counts of Nevers* 92–96

Charters: *See* Communal revolution; Documents; and see the *Cartulary* 97–129

Church and state, political theory 291

Cluny, Cluniacs 11, 16–20, 67, 69, 71, 75–84, 125, 188–89, 191–95, 198, 228–29, 230, 232–35, 254, 309, 312–13, 317–18, 341–47

Commercial activities: *See* Economic activity

Communal revolution, communal charters, class divisions, conspiracy, confederation 4, 7, 9, 11, 29–42, 67, 89, 121–22, 128, 168–69, 172–73, 181–92, 195–218, 310, 318–31, 347–57, 363–64

Counts, power, preoccupations, status, lifestyle of 5–6, 8–9, 11, 23–26, 36–38, 66–71, 84–85, 92–96, 110–13, 116, 117, 121–28, 157–218, 230–31, 237, 246–318: *See also* Vézelay: later history of

Crime, punishment (hanging, etc.) 162–63, 216–18, 267, 310, 352–57, 364: *See also* Disputes, resolution of; Justice, rights of

Crown, power, ambitions, status, role and duties of 10–11, 30, 68–71, 76–77, 92–93, 111–12, 117, 125, 127–28, 160, 179, 198–218, 240–45, 247, 250–51, 256, 261–62, 281–82, 293–313, 334–35: *See also* Vézelay: origins of; Vézelay: later history of; and the documents issued by or to the crown in the *Cartulary* 97–129. For the role of the crown in the resolution of the Vézelay disputes, *see* Disputes, resolution of

Crusades 137, 140, 160, 309

Diplomacy: *See* Disputes

Disputes, resolution of, diplomacy, negotiations 65–71, 110–13, 117, 119–29, 134–50, 159–64, 167, 169, 171–220, 240–45, 247–313: *See also* Excommunication, interdict

Documents, role of, writing, literacy 10–11, 32, 34–35, 63–65, 79, 104, 115,

Index of Latin Terms and Phrases

The following index includes such important or technical or interesting Latin vocabulary
as is cited or provided in the present volume. Words and phrases are given in the form
in which they occur in the texts translated in this volume and are followed by page references to the present volume. Non-essential words in the phrases cited are placed in
brackets.

Questions For Analysis

The following questions, selected from many that could be framed, are intended to guide readers to the significant issues raised by the material to be found in the present volume. All would be eminently suitable for student or class assignment.

1. How and why was the Vézelay dispute ultimately terminated?

2. What reasons can be adduced to explain the ultimate success of the crown in terminating the Vézelay dispute?

3. What role did the pope play in resolving the issues at stake between counts of Nevers and abbots of Vézelay?

4. Was the people's intervention or the crown's intervention ultimately decisive in resolving the Vézelay disputes? Why?

5. Why do you think the dukes of Burgundy played so small a role in the Vézelay disputes? (See Arnold 1991, chap. 5.)

6. From the evidence of the present volume, how important do you think relics were in the mind and mentality of (a) the aristocracy of the day and (b) the people?

7. Who or what was really responsible for the outbreak of the disputes at Vézelay chronicled in the present volume?

8. Do you feel count or abbot had the most right on his side in the Vézelay disputes?

9. Did the count lead the townsmen or vice versa, and why?

10. What matters of dispute embittered the relations between Cluny and Vézelay during the eleventh and twelfth centuries?

11. Were the Vézelay disputes basically about serfdom?

12. What were the counts' real motives in pursuing their goals against the abbey of Vézelay?

13. Why was the abbey of Vézelay so controversial a place in the twelfth century?

14. To what extent was Hugh the Poitevin an impartial witness to the events he was chronicling?

15. Do you think the individual items contained within the *Cartulary* in the present volume were in any way "forged" or "tampered with"? Why?

16. How effectively do you think Count Gerard and Countess Bertha provided for the future of their monastic foundations?

17. Why do you think the townsmen and the abbots of Vézelay did not accuse each other of heresy?

18. How far were the issues at stake at Bruges, as chronicled by Galbert of Bruges, at Laon, as chronicled by Guibert of Nogent, and at Vézelay as chronicled by Hugh the Poitevin similar, and why?

19. Do you think the abbots and monks at Vézelay advanced or hindered their case by their constant reference to charters and documents and privileges from the past?

20. How far and why were there serious divisions within the population at Vézelay in regard to the controversial issues canvassed by Hugh the Poitevin in his chronicle?

21. What rights did the bishops have on their side in the disputes chronicled in the present volume?

22. What role do you think literacy played in the affairs of the abbey of Vézelay in the twelfth century?

23. Does the twelfth-century history of Vézelay support the notion of a vital social and spiritual role played by the monasticism of the day?

24. Compare Vézelay as an intellectual and spiritual center with a contemporary cathedral center.

25. How far were the disputes in which the Vézelay abbey became involved in the twelfth century peculiarly characteristic of the time?

26. Was the monastic "walk-out" described in Book 4 of the *Major Chronicle* an effective tactic in the circumstances? What alternatives lay before the monks?

27. How, in your view, might the troubles of the Vézelay abbey in the twelfth century have been avoided?

28. Whose interests, in your view, prevailed in the 1137 *Accord*? Why?

29. Discuss communal charters as a source for social history in the twelfth century.

30. Discuss the role of the crown in resolving the disputes at Vézelay and Laon during the twelfth century.

31. What differences to the course and outcome of the revolutions in question derive from the fact that the central figure at Laon was a bishop, while the central figure at Vézelay was an abbot?

32. You are a cardinal sent by the pope to the Nevers/Vézelay region with the brief to resolve the disputes, and not to return without a successful outcome. Write a report that you might have been called upon to deliver to the pope upon your return to Rome.

33. One of the heretics recorded in the last chapter of the *Major Chronicle* is taken to the abbatial prison for an indefinite period. He describes to a sympathetic compatriot his experiences in a letter that he is allowed to write from the prison. Write the letter.

34. You are a papal judge-delegate charged with evaluating for the pope, from the testimonies of the witnesses, the case of the bishop of Autun against the abbot of Vézelay as recorded in Book 1 of the *Major Chronicle*. Write your report to the pope.

35. You are a delegate from a late-twentieth-century Equal Opportunity unit and you construct a report for a Commission subcommittee charged with drawing up a balance sheet for twelfth-century Burgundy. The commission must submit its findings to a minister who is constructing a case that the late twentieth century must, in its equal opportunity legislation, compensate for the wrongs of the past (compare the task Augustine set Orosius).

36. How typical was the role played by Countess Ida, in regard to the place and position of aristocratic women in the twelfth century?

37. To what extent do you think the Investiture Controversy played a key role in the minds of those who supported the case of the abbots of Vézelay in the twelfth century?

38. Why did the French crown support the case of the abbot of Vézelay and not that of either the bishops or the counts of the region?

39. Do you think the history of Vézelay in the twelfth century warrants the attention it has received since the time of Thierry and Guizot? Why/why not?

40. "Although, in the short term, the abbots of Vézelay won their battles with counts and bishops, in the long term, time was running out for the power and autonomy of the abbey of Vézelay." Discuss.

41. What obstacles did the burghers of Vézelay face in achieving their goals and how predictable or inevitable was their failure?

42. What was the value of monasticism to society in the eyes of its supporters in the twelfth century?

43. How far were papal pleas the key factor in inducing Louis VII to intercede on Vézelay's behalf in the disputes that troubled the monastery during his reign?

44. Assess the importance of pilgrimage and/or feast-days/fairs in the life of the twelfth-century French aristocracy from the material presented in this volume.